Hands On HTML

Send Us Your Comments:

To comment on this book or any other PRIMA TECH title, visit Prima's reader response page on the Web at **www.primapublishing.com/comments.**

How to Order:

For information on quantity discounts, contact the publisher: Prima Publishing, P.O. Box 1260BK, Rocklin, CA 95677-1260; (916) 632-4400. On letterhead, include information concerning the intended use of the books and the number of books you wish to purchase. For individual orders, turn to the back of this book for more information, or visit the PRIMA TECH Web site at **www.prima-tech.com.**

Hands On HTML

Greg Robertson
with Simply Written, Inc.
and Tim Altom

A DIVISION OF PRIMA PUBLISHING

A Division of Prima Publishing

ISBN: 0-7615-1885-1
Library of Congress Catalog Card Number: 98-67707
Printed in the United States of America

99 00 01 02 03 II 10 9 8 7 6 5 4 3 2 1

Publisher:
Stacy L. Hiquet

Associate Publisher:
Nancy Stevenson

Managing Editor:
Dan J. Foster

Sr. Acquisitions Editor
Deborah F. Abshier

Senior Editor
Kelli R. Crump

Project Editors:
Chris Haidri
Kevin Harreld

Technical Reviewer:
Emily Kim

Copy Editor:
Robert Campbell

Interior Layout:
Marian Hartsough Associates

Illustrations:
Bill Grimes

Cover Design:
Prima Design Team

Indexer:
Katherine Stimson

To my wife, May-Lee,
for more than 16 years of genuine wedded bliss,
and to our children, Eric and Maya,
of whom we are infinitely proud.
I love you all more than I know how to express.

—GR

To Jerilynne, Alex, Crystal, and Matt.

—TA

Acknowledgments

First and foremost, I want to thank my wife and children for putting up with the odd (and long!) hours, the stress, and the time commitment involved while I worked on this book. Without your love and encouragement, the result would have been far less than it is.

Next, I want to thank all the great people at Prima Publishing for giving me this opportunity. Debbie Abshier and Dan Foster get my gratitude for their patience and cooperation. Kevin Harreld and Chris Haidri shepherded the book through the development and editorial process with skill and extreme attention to detail. Bob Campbell fixed my grammatical "oversights." Dave Plotkin was indispensable in putting together the CD that accompanies this book. And of course, I cannot forget Emily Kim, whose development and technical review of the manuscript forced me to make the book much, much better than it was originally.

I also want to thank the folks who gave me permission to photograph their guitars for use in this book's projects. Rose Van Der Haven permitted me to use a photograph of her acoustic guitar. Preston Perkins, owner of Sawmill Music Center in Dublin, Ohio, allowed me to photograph any guitar in the shop. Next time you're in the Columbus area, make sure you stop by his store. Steve Sutherland, owner of Musicians' Exchange in Hilliard, Ohio, likewise gave me free run of his vintage and used guitars. Visit him on the Web at **http://www.guitars-amps.com**. Blues guitarist Tony Houston took the trouble to bring over his Fender Jazzmaster so that I could photograph it and its unique finish, so I want to thank him, too.

Finally, thanks go to the individuals and companies who gave us permission to include some of their software or URLs for their Web sites in the book and on the CD.

Thanks to you all.

—Greg Robertson

I'd like to thank the editorial crew at Prima. Every writer needs a good editor, and in my case more than one. Thanks to you all.

Thanks go out to the memory of the late science writer Isaac Asimov, whose books convinced me in my childhood that I had to write about technology.

—Tim Altom

About the Authors

Greg Robertson's undergraduate and graduate degrees in German and Biblical Studies have done him little good as a freelance writer and editor of computer books. Still, he managed to contribute to *The Essential Netscape Communicator Book* (Prima Publishing), and he has edited more computer books than he cares (or is able) to remember, dating back to 1988. His other writing interests include humor and religion.

Tim Altom has a degree in English/journalism from Indiana University. He has been an electronics technician, writer, and programmer on hardware from mainframes to machine tools. He is vice president of Simply Written Inc., an Indianapolis-based technical writing firm. He is a member of the Society for Technical Communication (STC), and has been both president of the Hoosier Chapter of STC and manager of the Society's Certification Issues Committee. Tim has authored several articles for STC's professional journals, including pieces on dyslexia and the history of why everyone uses big words in writing. He is an Adobe Certified Expert in Acrobat, as well as co-creator of the Clustar Method™, a task-based documentation methodology. This is his third book.

Contents at a Glance

Introduction xix

Chapter 1 Understanding HTML and Design Basics 1

Hand On Project 1
The Basic Web Site 17

Project Overview 18

Chapter 2 What Is the Basic Web Site? 19

Chapter 3 Designing the Basic Web Site. 31

Chapter 4 Beginning to Build the Basic Web Site 63

Chapter 5 Finishing Up the Basic Web Site 131

Project 1 Summary 189

Hands On Project 2
The Intermediate Web Site 191

Project Overview 192

Chapter 6 What Is the Intermediate Web Site? 193

Chapter 7 Designing the Intermediate Web Site. 207

Chapter 8 Beginning to Build the Intermediate Web Site 249

Chapter 9 Finishing Up the Intermediate Web Site 285

Project 2 Summary 329

Hands On Project 3 The Advanced Web Site 331

Project Overview 332

Chapter 10 What Is the Advanced Web Site? 333

Chapter 11 Designing the Advanced Web Site 341

Chapter 12 Beginning to Build the Advanced Web Site 373

Chapter 13 Finishing Up the Advanced Web Site 405

Project 3 Summary 421

Chapter 14 Uploading and Promoting Your Web Site 423

Appendix A Quick Reference Guide to HTML 4.0 465

Appendix B Overview of Some Popular HTML Editors 493

Appendix C What's On the CD-ROM? 505

Glossary 521

Index 529

Contents

Introduction xix

Chapter 1 Understanding HTML and Design Basics . . . 1

Software to Use to Create Your Web Site 1
- HTML Editors 2
- Windows Notepad 2
- Graphics Programs 3

What Is HTML? 4
What Is Dynamic HTML? 5
The Ins and Outs of Tags 7
Understanding URLs 8
Frame Layout Help. 9
Scripting Software 12
Considering Browser Compatibility. 12
Rules and Advice for Writing HTML 14
Summary 16

HAND ON PROJECT 1
THE BASIC WEB SITE 17

Project Overview 18

Chapter 2 What Is the Basic Web Site? 19

Defining a Basic Web Site. 20
Setting Your Goals for the Site 20
- Determining Your Audience 22
- What Type of Information Do You Want to Present? 24
- Finding the Information to Include. 24

Summary 28

Chapter 3 Designing the Basic Web Site 31

Deciding What to Put on Your Web Site 32
Using Graphics: The Art of Using Art 32
Determining the Purpose of Graphics in Your Web Site 33
Sizing Up Your Alternatives: GIF versus JPEG 35
Using Animated GIFs 37
Web Site Builder as Graphic Artist: Sketching Out Your Site . . 38
Considerations in Designing Your Web Site 40
Laying Out the Project 1 Web Site 42
Designing the Welcome Page 46
Designing the Individual Guitar Pages 57
Summary 62

Chapter 4 Beginning to Build the Basic Web Site 63

Laying the Groundwork for Text 64
Declaring the HTML Version 65
Creating the Basic Structure of Your Document 69
Beginning the Body of Your Web Site 76
Choosing a Color for Project 1 76
Using a Background Image 78
Designating Link Colors 81
Working with Text 83
Creating Paragraphs 83
Inserting Line Breaks 85
Aligning Text 86
Formatting Text 89
Dividing Up Your Text 103
Coloring with RGB 111
Creating Lists 114
Types of Lists 114
Creating an Unordered List 114
Creating an Ordered List 123
Combining Ordered and Unordered Lists 126
Creating Definition Lists 127
Summary 130

Chapter 5 Finishing Up the Basic Web Site 131

Creating Additional Pages for Your Web Site 132
Adding the Second Page of the Web Site 132
Adding the Third Page of the Web Site 136
Adding the Fourth Page of the Web Site 138
Linking to Other Locations. 141
Creating Links within Your Web Site. 141
Linking to Another Web Site 153
Communicating with Visitors to Your Site. 155
Adding Graphics. 157
Tips for Creating Graphics 158
Inserting Banners on the Web Pages 161
Using the ALT Attribute with Graphics 164
Adding More Graphics 165
Adding Photographs to Your Web Site. 169
Flowing Text around Graphics. 171
Testing the Basic Web Site. 180
Viewing the Site through Your Browser 181
Using the W3C Validation Service 182
Validating with CSE. 182
Checking Links 184
Comparing Browsers 186
Summary 187

Project 1 Summary 189

HANDS ON PROJECT 2
THE INTERMEDIATE WEB SITE 191

Project Overview 192

Chapter 6 What Is the Intermediate Web Site? 193

Setting Your Goals for the Site. 193
How the Intermediate Site Differs from the Basic Site 194
What Additional Information Do You Want to Present? 194
What Type of Information Will the User Provide You? 195
Getting to Know Tables 195

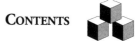

Learning about Frames 196
Introducing Image Maps 197
Accepting User Feedback with Forms 199
Spicing Up Your Web Site 201
    Using Sound 201
    Using Video 202
    Using Animation 204
Summary 205

Chapter 7 Designing the Intermediate Web Site . . . 207

Laying Out the Pages 208
    The Home Page 211
    The Guitar of the Month Page 211
    The Current Specials Page 213
    The Current Inventory Page 213
    The Services Page 214
    The Articles Page 215
    The Contact Page 215
Creating Tables 217
    Defining a Simple Table 217
    Fine-Tuning a Table 224
    Giving a Table Some Flair 228
Using Frames 230
    Creating Frames 231
    Creating the Contents of the Frames 238
    Creating the links.html Page 238
    Linking Pages 244
Summary 248

Chapter 8 Beginning to Build the Intermediate Web Site 249

Creating More Effective Tables 249
    Defining a More Complex Table 250
    Creating the Opening Page 256
    Using Other Table-Formatting Options 260

Making Further Use of Frames 261
Adding More HTML for Links 262
Loading More Pages for the Web Site 263
Providing Alternate Content 264
Creating Client-Side Image Maps 268
An Overview of the GIF-Creation Process 268
Creating the Top Frame's Contents 269
Creating the Guitar of the Month Page 278
Summary 284

Chapter 9 Finishing Up the Intermediate Web Site 285

Creating Forms 286
Determining the Purpose of Your Forms 286
Starting a Form 289
Creating the Contact Page 289
Processing Forms 300
Hear Ye! Hear Ye! 301
Considering a Few Technical Concerns 302
To Stream or Not to Stream? 304
Adding a Sound Clip to the Web Site 306
Seen Any Good Videos Lately? 309
Downloadable Files versus Streaming Video 309
An Overview of the Video Creation Process 312
Adding GIF Animation to the Web Site 317
Testing the Intermediate Web Site 322
Viewing the Site through Your Browser 323
Using the W3C Validation Service 323
Validating with CSE HTML Validator 324
Comparing Browsers 325
Avoiding Problems 326
Summary 327

Project 2 Summary 329

HANDS ON PROJECT 3
THE ADVANCED WEB SITE 331

Project Overview 332

Chapter 10 What Is the Advanced Web Site? 333

Setting the Tone for the Site 334
The Opening Page 334
The Book Page 336
The Guitar Brand Page 338
Summary 340

Chapter 11 Designing the Advanced Web Site. 341

Look and Feel. 341
Operations 342
 How Close to the Bleeding Edge? 342
 Browser Compatibility 342
Designing the Pages 343
 Designing the Opening Page. 344
 Designing the Book Page 357
 Designing the Guitar Brand Page 363
Designing the Style Sheet 365
 Headings 366
 Body Text 368
 Links 368
 Tables 369
 What Does Cascading Mean? 370
Defining the Construction Tasks 371
 The Opening Page 371
 The Book Page. 371
 The Guitar Brand Page. 371
 The CSS 372
Summary 372

Chapter 12 Beginning to Build the Advanced Web Site 373

Testing 374
Finishing the Opening Page 375
Adding the Scripts for the Book Page. 376
    Writing the Scripts 377
    Additional JavaScript Resources. 402
Summary 403

Chapter 13 Finishing Up the Advanced Web Site 405

Using the Java Applet on the Guitar Brand Page 405
    Using an Applet 406
    Java and JavaScript 410
Writing and Using the CSS 410
    Linking the Style Sheet. 411
    Defining Fonts and Text 412
    Defining Links 418
    Defining Tables 419
Summary 420

Project 3 Summary 421

Chapter 14 Uploading and Promoting Your Web Site 423

Putting Your Site on the Web 423
    Information for America Online Subscribers 424
    Information for CompuServe Subscribers 427
    Information for Subscribers to Internet Service Providers 429
    Information for Users of Corporate or University Networks or Intranets. 432
Publicizing Your Web Site. 432
    Web Promotion Services. 434
    Adding Your Web Site to Search Engines. 434
    Adding Your Web Site to Web Directories 447
    Other Means of Making Your Site Known. 460
Summary 464

Appendix A Quick Reference Guide to HTML 4.0 465

Appendix B Overview of Some Popular HTML Editors 493

1-4-All 493
Adobe PageMill 495
Agile HTML Editor 496
Arachnophilia. 497
CoffeeCup HTML Editor++ Pro. 498
CoffeeCup HTML Express 500
Dreamweaver 500
FrontPage 98 502
HomeSite. 502
HotDog Professional. 504

Appendix C What's On the CD-ROM? 505

Glossary 521

Index 529

Introduction

Anyone interested in learning HTML these days need not look far to find a book on the subject. Any bookstore has at least one shelf dedicated to computing on the World Wide Web, and most have more than one book teaching readers how to use HTML. Given that, why the need for this book? Most of the books that are available teach HTML piecemeal, without really showing how all the elements behind the scenes of a Web site work together. Other books are really no more than references. This book takes a different approach.

Goals of This Book

Many people create Web sites today by means of HTML editors. There is certainly nothing wrong with that approach, but what those people typically learn is the use of their particular HTML editor, not the essential details of HTML. We believe that the best means of creating a Web site is to deal with the HTML directly. This "hand-coding" is the best way to really learn HTML—and therefore is the approach of this book.

We are not suggesting that Web site builders must always create Web sites by hand. Indeed, HTML editors become better with each upgrade. Still, those editors may not be able to write clean code, free of superfluous tags or attributes. HTML editors can do a great job of creating a Web site's foundation, but if you really know HTML, you can dig into the code itself and fine-tune it. Such fine-tuning may mean searching for and removing superfluous tags and attributes, or working with graphics in a manner slightly more efficient than what an HTML editor comes up with. Fine-tuning also can mean doing things with your Web page that your HTML editor cannot do at all. By really learning HTML, you become equipped to troubleshoot and sharpen the sites that you build, and you enjoy a level of flexibility and dexterity in terms of your Web development efforts that's available only to those who have had experience working directly with HTML.

How to Use This Book

Hands On HTML falls naturally into four sections. The opening section consists of a single chapter that discusses the fundamentals of HTML. The chapter is geared toward people who don't know anything about HTML or those who have dealt with HTML but would like a refresher. Included in the chapter are the basic concepts of HTML, such as tags and attributes, and a brief mention of Dynamic HTML.

That first chapter also deals with other software tools that you may want or need to use. These programs include HTML editors, Windows Notepad, graphics programs, sources to help you create frames for your site, and software that can write scripts for you.

Another topic covered in that chapter is making your Web site compatible with various browsers. Most people are aware of Microsoft Internet Explorer and Netscape Navigator, but do not realize that many other browsers are used in varying degrees by people all around the world. Microsoft and Netscape, in other words, are not the only game in town when it comes to browsers. Browser compatibility is an important topic, because all browsers don't treat HTML in the same way, and they don't all recognize the same tags and attributes. Moreover, multiple versions of each browser are in use today, and they have different levels of compatibility with the current version of the HTML standard. All these issues merit consideration when building Web sites.

The final topic in the first chapter concerns *rules* for writing HTML, as well as *advice* for writing good HTML. This information can help you get the HTML right the first time, saving you time later by helping you to avoid common problems.

The remainder of the first section consists of building your first actual Web site. The next two sections of the book also each consist of a fully functional Web site that you create from the ground up (there will be some shortcuts you can take, but for the most part you should expect to get your hands dirty writing lots of actual HTML throughout the three example projects in this book). All the supporting material you need to create the example sites—such as textual content for the sites, graphics that fit the theme of the sites, and audio/video files or other special files that help you to create sophisticated, truly useful sites—can be found on the CD that accompanies this book. The chapters within each project include both general and step-by-step instructions for creating the sites, as well as explanations of how all the key tags and attributes work at every stage of your Web site construction.

You begin with a straightforward personal Web site in Project 1. In the process of creating this site, you learn many of the basic tags and their attributes. All the essentials of a Web site are presented: hyperlinks, graphics, lists, headings, color choices, inserting a Mailto link to gather feedback from site visitors, and other common techniques. This basic Web site gives you all you really need to create an effective, attractive Web site for yourself.

When you work on the intermediate Web site in Project 2, things become more complex. The complexity, however, yields many more possibilities for the Web site. This second project is geared toward a business, rather than personal, site, but anyone can use the techniques presented in this project. The skills you'll practice include using tables to display data as well as to format text and graphics, creating image maps, and using frames, forms, animation, audio, and video. Not all of these techniques are necessary for every Web site, but they certainly can enliven a Web site and add some professional pizzazz to it.

Project 3 delves into a couple of the latest buzzwords in the world of HTML: Dynamic HTML and Cascading Style Sheets. Many extremely effective Web sites make excellent use of these advanced techniques. Using these capabilities of HTML 4.0 can result in attractive, sometimes almost mesmerizing, effects that contribute to the overall impact of a Web site. These advanced techniques require scripting, so that is also discussed as you create the third project.

Following the last project is a chapter that tells you how to get your newly created, beautiful Web sites up and flourishing on the Web. There are specific instructions for users of CompuServe and America Online, as well as those who connect to the Web via an Internet service provider. Perhaps even more important, the chapter tells you how to promote your site in many different ways after you have it operational online. After all, there's no point in creating a Web site if no one drops by to look at it. You want to let as many people know about your site as possible.

The fourth section of the book contains several additional elements. Appendix A lists the HTML 4.0 tags and their most commonly used attributes, briefly explaining what they do, and also telling you which tags are on the way to obsolescence. Appendix B is a brief comparison of the features of several popular HTML editors. Some readers might want to use HTML authoring tools and editors to create a site quickly, and then use their knowledge of hand-coding HTML (freshly gleaned from the projects in this book) to refine and polish the site. By getting a feel for some of the popular HTML editors, you can decide which ones might have features or capabilities you want. Finally, the glossary contains a list of terms related to HTML, just in case you forget what something is and want to look it up quickly.

Conventions Used in This Book

This book uses a few conventions in an effort to present information consistently. Review the following conventions before starting to read the book:

Text you type. Any text that you're supposed to type appears in **bold** to help distinguish it from regular text. For example:

> Begin the document body by typing `<BODY BGCOLOR="#009999">` on the first blank line.

Placeholders. Anything that serves as a placeholder (something for which you must substitute an actual value when writing your HTML pages) appears in *italic*, as in the following example:

> The tag you should use is <H*n*>, where *n* is a numeral indicating the desired heading level for the greeting.

Selection keys. There aren't many Windows-related activities discussed in this book, but on those occasions when you're instructed to select a menu option or other onscreen item that does have an underlined letter for use in a Ctrl+key or Alt+key combination, the selection key is underlined in this book, as shown in this example:

> Select File, Open from the main menu.

Filenames, paths, onscreen text, and HTML values. A number of special items throughout the book may appear in a `special typeface` to help you distinguish them from regular text:

> By including the `right` value for the `ALIGN` attribute, you guarantee that the image map graphic (`image04.gif`) will appear flush against the right margin when the page is rendered in a browser.

Examples of HTML structure. Sometimes you'll see examples of the general format of some aspect of HTML, like an outline of the tags that form a certain portion of an HTML page. These general examples have the following appearance:

```
<!DOCTYPE>
<HTML>
<HEAD>
      <TITLE>Your title here</TITLE>
      <META>
      <META>
      ...
</HEAD>
<BODY>
Your site's information goes here
...
...
</BODY>
</HTML>
```

You do *not* type these lines of HTML. They are only general examples to show you the appropriate syntax or structure for a given task that's being discussed.

Special Elements

Definitions of important words and concepts appear in the margins.

You will see occasional special elements that stand out from the text. These items are designed to highlight information or to supplement what the text says. These special elements take the following forms:

A *tip* informs you of a better way to accomplish something or gives you a bit of insider information to help you get the most out of your Web site design efforts.

A *note* is extra information that you may or may not be interested in reading. It often is *nonessential* information as far as accomplishing a given task is concerned, but it usually expands on the current topic in a way that might enrich your learning experience.

A *caution* is something you definitely need to read, because it alerts you to potential pitfalls or warns you when a particular operation is risky and might cause you to lose some of your work or experience other problems.

EXERCISE

Exercises give you the opportunity to use a particular skill introduced in the regular text. Each exercise is identified by a special bar running alongside all the instructions and discussion that pertain to the exercise.

ANALYSIS

After many of the exercises, an *analysis* section walks you through the HTML line by line and explains the statements (and the reasoning behind them) in greater detail. After reading the analysis, you'll have an understanding of the specific logic of the HTML and you'll know the exact purpose of the tags and attributes that were used at that location.

This icon points out references to items that you can find on the CD accompanying the book.

This icon points out an URL or other reference to a Web site, newsgroup, or other online resource that contains information pertinent to the current discussion in the chapter text.

The Necessary Software

All you need to carry out this book's projects is a simple text editor and the sample files on the accompanying CD. The book's three example projects are designed to be completed using Windows Notepad, but you can use a simple text editor other than Notepad if you prefer. You do not need a dedicated HTML editor to create these projects. The only requirement is that the text editor you use must create simple text files without applying any formatting.

If you want to build more complex sites on your own, either after finishing this book or concurrent with working through this book, you may need or want some other types of software. To create graphics, for example, consider getting a graphics program such as Paint Shop Pro or Photoshop or any of the others that are available. Likewise, creating animations or adding audio or video to your Web site requires specialized software, such as GIF Animator, Animation Shop, RealAudio, RealVideo, or Shockwave. In addition, if you decide to write scripts, you may need JavaScript, VBScript, Perl, or another programming language. You also may decide to get software that writes scripts for you or that helps with creating frames for your Web sites.

CHAPTER 1

Understanding HTML and Design Basics

As far as programming efforts go, writing Hypertext Markup Language (HTML) documents is probably about as easy as it gets. Anyone reading this book who already has experience writing code in a programming language should have little trouble becoming accustomed to HTML—and then mastering it. The goal of this book is to teach you HTML via the creation of three progressively more complex sites that are immediately usable.

Software to Use to Create Your Web Site

Contrary to what you may have been led to believe, you do not *need* to use an HTML editor to create a Web page. Many such editors are available, but this book celebrates the fact that you need nothing more than Windows Notepad to create the HTML. Using Notepad may take longer than using an HTML editor to achieve the desired result, but you really *learn* how HTML works. If you ever need to troubleshoot HTML, this knowledge will stand you in good stead. Knowing HTML also means that you can tweak the results you get from your HTML editor. Besides, there's nothing better than the sheer satisfaction you get from doing something "the hard way." For anyone who is interested, however, Appendix B compares features of some of the most popular HTML editors, as well as those included on the CD that accompanies this book.

HTML Editors

Computer store shelves overflow with boxes containing commercial software to make creating Web sites easy and—dare I say it?—fun. Many of these programs are very popular with users who want to create their own (or even someone else's) Web site. FrontPage 98, Adobe PageMill, HoTMetaL, ColdFusion, and many other commercial software products are available for anyone who desires to go that route to create a Web site. By and large, commercial HTML editors do a fine job. Their popularity is evidence of their ease of use and capabilities. Shareware, such as HotDog Pro, also is available to help would-be HTML authors accomplish their goals.

Of course, commercial software and shareware serve a definite purpose. For many people, it's a quick way to create a Web site without having knowledge of HTML—and that's all they want to do. They don't want to know how HTML works. After using these software packages for a while, however, some people may begin to wonder how to accomplish a specific effect they've seen that their software can't create. Most of these people decide to learn HTML. They learn enough that they can go in and revamp or fine-tune the code to make their Web site do exactly what they want it to do.

Windows Notepad

In reality, however, Windows Notepad is all you need in order to produce HTML that does the job. In fact, you probably can learn to do a better job with Notepad than you can with one of the dedicated HTML editors.

By working directly with the HTML, you really learn what the tags and attributes are doing. You also can troubleshoot if a problem arises. And you can rework the document as later versions of HTML arrive on the scene. Only time will tell what new HTML standards will bring, but this book will get you up to speed with the latest version. Then all you have to do is keep up with each version of HTML as it comes along. Your Web site can always be up to date—and state of the art—if you put the effort into it.

Graphics Programs

As accomplished as HTML 4.0 is, it can't do everything by itself. Graphics software is a necessity if you want to include photographs or other graphics on your Web site. This section discusses the most common type of ancillary program: graphics software.

Graphics programs are about as old as personal computing itself and make up a very popular category of software. In the old days, you were limited to bitmap images created in Microsoft Paint or some such program. Since then, however, the computer graphics world has exploded in technological advancements. Now you can scan any photograph or drawing that will fit on the bed of your scanner and use it on your Web site (after obtaining permission from the copyright holder, of course). Also, you can take photographs with a digital camera that doesn't even contain any film, place the images directly into your computer, and then use them in your HTML documents.

Even more interesting is the fact that you no longer have to be satisfied with the photograph you took with your camera. Many graphics software products enable you to digitally enhance, add to, subtract from, and rearrange the elements in a photograph.

The Web is limited in the types of graphics files it can use. The primary usable file types are GIF and JPEG. (The latest is PNG, but it is still rare on the Web.) The most commonly used types of graphics software for the Web are paint and photo-editing programs.

The number of graphics software options available to you is huge. A discussion of all of them would be enough to fill a separate book, so you need to investigate the type of software you want, comparing the various packages that are available in order to find the one that most closely fits your requirements. To facilitate your decision, read software reviews in computer magazines and online. Ask acquaintances or professional computer graphic artists about the software you are considering, to find out what they use or like. Try the shareware that's out there. See if demos are available online for the commercial software that interests you. It may take a little time, but you can find just the right software for your needs.

Some graphics programs are included on the CD accompanying this book. You can play around with those to see what types of features you prefer!

What Is HTML?

The **World Wide Web,** *or* **Web,** *is the graphical component of the Internet.*

The computer world is full of acronyms—some pronounceable, some not. The acronym for the primary World Wide Web language is HTML (*Hypertext Markup Language*). Many other programming elements—such as Java applets and ActiveX controls—also are part of the Web, but without HTML the Web wouldn't be such an exciting place for so many people to spend so much time. The creation of the Web and widespread implementation of HTML have resulted in a worldwide explosion of everyday people logging onto the Internet. The Internet is no longer confined primarily to scientists and computer geeks.

Hypertext Markup Language, *or* **HTML,** *is the programming (or formatting) language that makes the Web possible.*

HTML code is essentially a set of instructions given to a Web browser for the formatting and layout of a Web page. HTML doesn't actually tell a computer how the Web page will look to a visitor. Rather, you use HTML to compose the page, to specify all the elements that appear on the page—the text, graphics, horizontal rules, headings, and so on. In addition, you use HTML to tell a computer what color to use where, and to indicate the relative size of text (headings versus regular text, for example). Although that description may sound like you use fairly complete instructions that leave little room for error or differences, in reality, the final appearance of a Web page is left to the visitor's browser. The size of text in a heading may vary from browser to browser, for example,

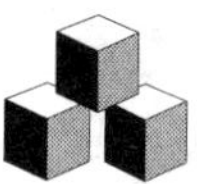

as may the font the browser uses for the heading. Moreover, not all monitors reproduce colors the same way; in other words, red on one monitor may be darker or lighter on a different monitor. Additionally, some monitors may only be able to reproduce a few colors for simple graphics, whereas other monitors can reproduce colors for detailed photographs with thousands of colors. In essence, HTML provides browsers with guidelines, but the browsers create the final product, and the look of the page on individual computers depends on each user's unique computer setup.

This chapter doesn't attempt to explain all of the HTML tags and attributes. That reference information is contained in Appendix A. What this entire book does is teach you how to use HTML as you work through the three projects. In the course of doing the projects, you use many of the HTML tags and a number of their attributes. The goal is to help you feel comfortable with HTML by the end of the book, so that you can feel free to experiment with any tags and attributes you haven't yet tried. No doubt you will continue to work with your Web site—or even build other Web sites. This book lays a solid foundation for you.

HTML enables you to do many things besides create (and color) text: You can insert graphics and sounds, insert simple animation, use a graphic in the background, create hyperlinks, and do many other things. Anyone who has spent time surfing the Web has experienced HTML's capabilities. Those same people, however, also have experienced HTML's shortcomings. That is where the exciting world of dynamic HTML (DHTML) comes into play.

What Is Dynamic HTML?

The word *dynamic* implies movement and change. One of the major shortcomings of HTML has been its static nature. Often, Web developers use other programming languages (such as Perl, ColdFusion, JavaScript, Java, and ActiveX controls) in conjunction with HTML to provide dynamic information to the Web, because HTML alone can provide only static information. Furthermore, the capability to click on links to go to other pages also helps to give the impression that HTML can create dynamic Web pages. The capability to click on a hot link to go to another page may seem almost magical to the new Web user going online for the first time. (Well, *I* always thought it was pretty cool.) That same user, however, soon becomes jaded by the sameness of Web sites. Ho-hum.

Enter *Dynamic HTML (DHTML).* DHTML uses layering and exact positioning of elements (among other things) in conjunction with *cascading style sheets (CSSs),* to create new effects that don't require return trips to the Web server. Here's an example of using the CSS capability: A person who creates a Web site can attach a style sheet to it so that the elements appear as he or she wants (for example, with particular font styles, colors, and spacing). A person viewing the site, however, may have his or her *own* style sheet in order to compensate for either technological shortcomings or human handicaps. These two style sheets can *cascade,* so that the viewer's style sheet supersedes the author's original one, enabling the viewer to get the most out of the site.

By using cascading style sheets and DHTML together, Web authors can add a new level of interactivity and interest to their Web sites. Talk about magical! You can make text float across the page, can make text colors change according to the movement of the mouse, can make a table of contents expand automatically, can . . . well, you get the idea. In addition, if a visitor to your Web site is using a browser that doesn't support DHTML, such as Internet Explorer 3.0 or Netscape Navigator 3.0, he or she will never know the difference. That's because well-written DHTML calmly reverts to compatibility with earlier browser versions. Your Web site visitors need never know that you've used Dynamic HTML to create your site. Up-to-date visitors, however, will recognize that something different and interesting is going on at your site. And that may prove to be the incentive for them to come back time and again.

Both Microsoft and Netscape have implementations of DHTML. Unfortunately, they are not compatible with each other. Netscape can use Microsoft's implementation, but Microsoft cannot use Netscape's, because Netscape makes use of nonstandard approaches to DHTML. This book primarily deals with the Microsoft implementation of DHTML, because of its more widespread compatibility. After all, you want your Web site to be available to as many people as possible.

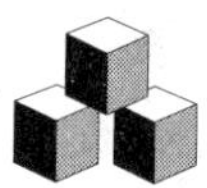

The Ins and Outs of Tags

Essentially, HTML consists of tags and their attributes and values. The *tags* give browsers the information they need to display the Web page. Many tags also take *attributes,* and the available attributes vary according to the tag. Most tags have more than one possible attribute. You assign a *value* to an attribute. An example of all three is the following:

```
<BODY TEXT="blue">
```

The tag is `<BODY>`, the attribute is `TEXT`, and the attribute's value is `"blue"`.

Note

Whenever you use an attribute, you must use a value with it to specify what characteristic you want the attribute to have.

When you use attributes with a tag, all the attributes fit between the two brackets (< and >) of the start tag. Most tags have two variations, one that you use to indicate where the tag begins (the *start tag*), and another to indicate where that particular tag ends (the *end tag*). The tag that you place at the beginning of your HTML code for a Web page, for example, is the following:

```
<HTML>
```

At the very end of your HTML code, you place this end tag:

```
</HTML>
```

As you can see, the only difference between these start and end tags is the placement of a slash before the letters `HTML` in the end tag.

***A container tag** has both start and end tags. Everything between the start and end tags is affected by that particular container tag.*

HTML tags come in two basic varieties:

- Container tag
- Empty tag

The preceding `<HTML>` tag is an example of a container tag.

An example of an empty tag is as follows:

```
<META NAME="author" CONTENT="Greg Robertson">
```

The <P> tag, which indicates a paragraph of text, is an example of a variation on the container tag. <P> does have an optional end tag, </P>, but some HTML authors omit this end tag. Even though leaving out the </P> may not hurt anything, you should use this closing tag—it's good practice.

An empty tag is one that doesn't have an end tag.

In this example, the tag is <META>, which contains so-called "meta-information." Meta-information doesn't show up in a visitor's browser, but can still be significant. Here, the NAME and CONTENT attributes work together to indicate that the author of the Web page is Greg Robertson. Chapter 4 goes into more detail on the <META> tag.

Understanding URLs

A *Uniform Resource Locator* (*URL*) is simply an address on the Internet. When you enter an URL, you are telling your browser exactly where to go to find the page you want, just the way putting an address on a letter tells postal employees exactly where your letter should go.

Most people pronounce URL as "earl" instead of saying the individual letters "U-R-L."

URLs take the following general form:

http://www.yourcompany.com/inventory/newguitars.html

In this fictional URL, `http` is short for *hypertext transfer protocol (HTTP)*, which is the most common beginning for Internet addresses these days. Unless you start one otherwise, browsers assume that each URL you enter begins with `http`.

Another possible beginning is `ftp`, which stands for *file transfer protocol (FTP)*. You can use FTP, for example, to upload files to a Web server, such as when you finish your site and place it on the Web.

The slashes separate the parts of the address—notice that two slashes are required after `http` (or `ftp`, or whatever begins a given address), while subsequent slashes occur singly.

The **www** in this URL stands for *World Wide Web.* The **yourcompany.com** in this example is the domain name, and references the particular server on the Web where the file you're looking for is located. The **inventory** portion of the address is a folder (directory) on that server, and **newguitars.html** is an exact page within that folder.

Other variations are possible, and addresses can go several levels deeper, but this example suffices to show the basic format of an URL.

Frame Layout Help

Frames, which play an important role in Project 2 of this book, can be difficult to design and implement. The biggest problem is that not all browsers are capable of handling frames, so you must make allowance for visitors to your site who don't have frame capability. In the second place, poor design or coding can result in malfunctions or, at the least, annoying performance. Many Web developers advise avoiding using frames.

By *not* using frames, you also are avoiding a common difficulty visitors have when they add your site to their list of favorites. They can add your site—that's not a problem—but they cannot bookmark *a certain page* within your site. No matter where they are in your site, the bookmark will be to the first page of your site. Visitors then must navigate to where they want to be—if they even remember how to get there. Navigating one or two links into a site isn't bad, but if it requires more than that, visitors may decide it's not worth it.

In my experience, one of the most annoying aspects of visiting a frames-enabled site is when the frame extends beyond the width of the screen and I cannot resize the frames without losing something in one of them (such as navigation buttons). The result of this situation is that I sometimes must scroll from left to right—and then from right to left—in order to read a frame's contents. Having to repeat that scrolling every couple of seconds becomes extraordinarily annoying.

One other issue to consider is managing the frames. You must make sure that hyperlinks call up the correct page—as you must do with *all* hyperlinks—but you also must make sure that the page loads into the correct frame. It isn't very helpful to have a hyperlinked page load into, say, the frame that contains your navigation buttons.

Frames are not all negative, however. One advantage to using frames is the sheer amount of information you can fit onto the screen at one time. You can put your company logo in one frame, for example, while a second frame contains navigation buttons or a menu for your site. You can keep those two frames present at all times, and use a third frame to display various pages when the visitor clicks links in the navigation frame.

Using one of the frames as a holder for a menu also helps keep the overall Web site file size down. That's because the menu needn't be included in its entirety on every page of the Web site if you keep it loaded in a separate frame.

Another definite advantage of frames is the capability to easily display more than one page at a time.

The bottom line is that there's no need to shy away from frames and the functionality they can add to a Web site, and a careful implementation of frames will minimize or completely avoid the disadvantages mentioned above. Project 2 in this book is going to give you experience working with frames so that you'll have a good idea of how and when you might want to incorporate frames in your own future HTML code.

Here's an alternative that might be helpful once you're comfortable with how frames work. In some cases, you may decide you don't want to write the HTML to implement frames yourself but you still want to use frames. In that event, you can find assistance at the following URL:

http://www.isomedia.com/homes/kosta/wdc/templates.htm

The author of these templates offers them to you free of charge as long as you meet both of the following requirements:

- You do not use them for commercial purposes.
- You e-mail him the URL of your site so that he can link to it.

He encourages HTML authors to use these templates, and to modify them to fit specific needs. If appropriate for the situation, of course, you can simply use these templates as is.

Tip

In reality, countless examples of Web sites with frames are available for your examination. Every frames-enabled site you run across on the Web is there for you to study: Just use your browser's source-viewing command to view the HTML for the Web page. When the HTML source code appears in Notepad, use the File, Save command to save it to one of your disk drives. Then you can study the site to your heart's content.

Caution

Do *not* take any graphics from Web sites and use them on your own site, unless you first receive permission from the owner of the original site. You can easily wind up in violation of someone's copyright, which can quickly become a costly mistake.

Be careful, too, about downloading HTML for a site you like and then incorporating it wholesale into your own site. Many companies spend big money designing and building a Web site that they believe uniquely conveys their identity. Your taking that HTML and converting it to your own use may raise legal issues in their minds. Such scenarios are reminiscent of the "look and feel" lawsuits that permeated the software industry a few years ago.

Note

Please, don't just copy code from a Web site and use it, even though that may be common practice. Perhaps the vast majority of Web developers don't care if you use their code in your site, but it is always appropriate to e-mail the site's Webmaster and ask permission to use the HTML. Even if the Webmaster grants you permission and asks for nothing in return, I think it's good form to place a comment tag where you insert the borrowed code and credit the person who has allowed you to use it.

Scripting Software

Not all HTML authors are also programmers. Probably most of them are not. So many advanced techniques and functions require using JavaScript or VBScript, however, that it's difficult to avoid writing at least some scripts. If you are one of the many HTML authors who don't want to learn how to write scripts, help for you is only a few mouse clicks away.

***Scripting** refers to writing small **programs** (scripts) to get your Web site to perform certain functions.*

JavaScript in particular is useful for Web developers. A number of programs are available to do the nitty-gritty scripting for you. Also, many people (and companies) already have written JavaScript code that you can insert into your HTML to perform certain functions, such as to validate the data visitors input into your forms. In addition, many HTML editors can help with writing JavaScript for your Web site.

Some of the script-related software you may want to consider are Java Script It, NetObjects ScriptBuilder, Netscape Visual JavaScript, Anthill Scripter, and Form Validation Tools from Artswork. Also, Website Abstraction offers ten JavaScripts that are free for noncommercial use. Spend a little time on the World Wide Web, and undoubtedly you will find many other tools that are helpful for implementing JavaScript or VBScript in your Web site.

Considering Browser Compatibility

One of the biggest issues facing anyone who designs and builds Web sites is compatibility among browsers. The two major browsers in use today are Microsoft Internet Explorer (IE) and Netscape Navigator, each of which is in its 4.0 incarnation. Unfortunately, not all Web users have the latest versions, although more are upgrading every day. Some people are still using the 3.0 versions of those browsers—or even earlier ones than that. IE and Navigator aren't the only games in town, either. Other browsers are available and in use around the world, such as NCSA Mosaic and Lynx.

To make things even trickier, some browsers support frames, and others do not. All those different browsers and different versions of browsers mean that building a Web site that can work perfectly with *all* of them is virtually impossible. That means making decisions up front about what browsers you want your site to support, and then designing and building the site to accomplish that goal.

A prime consideration in designing your site for browser compatibility is the audience you expect to have. It's one thing if you own a company that specializes in disaster recovery for corporate computer systems. It's quite another situation when you want to use your site to showcase your collection of pocket watches. In the former case, businesses of all sorts will want to know what you can do for them, and there is a good chance that their browsers will be up to date. After all, if they are concerned enough to consider their need for disaster recovery, they are likely to be up to date in their computer equipment. Everyday Web users with an interest in pocket watches, however, may or may not have the latest in browsers. Undoubtedly, the degree of certainty that they have the latest browser is far lower than in the first example. Simply put, you need to know your audience and plan your browser compatibility based on the most likely scenario.

Note

The projects in this book are geared toward as wide an audience as possible. In addition, the second project is designed to work with browsers that don't have frames capability as well as those that do. As you develop future Web sites, however, whenever it becomes necessary to choose browsers to support (because not all browsers are compatible with a given feature), IE and Navigator should get the nod. Always remember that users of old browsers will not be able to experience the wonders of Dynamic HTML, cascading style sheets, and certain other advanced Web site features you learn about later in this book.

Rules and Advice for Writing HTML

HTML, which some people consider more a "formatting" language than a programming language, requires you to follow certain rules. Rules may vary somewhat from one programming language to another, but those for HTML are few. They probably won't surprise experienced programmers:

1. Use the less-than and greater-than signs (< and >) as the outer part of the tag, as in `<BODY>`.
2. If the tag you are using requires an end tag, don't forget to put it in. The end tag is the same as the start tag, except that it includes a slash immediately to the right of the < symbol, as in `</BODY>`.
3. Although no longer required, you should begin your HTML file with the `<HTML>` tag and end with the `</HTML>` tag. Everything else goes between those two tags.
4. When designating attributes, you use the equal sign (=), as in `TEXT=`. Do not put a space on either side of the equal sign when including attributes.
5. In the attribute designation, place quotation marks on both sides of the value, as in `TEXT="#871E11"`. Many times, you may be able to write HTML without the quotation marks, but it's better to include them. That way, you avoid problems with any browsers that may have trouble interpreting what you mean. Besides, the quotation marks make it easier to find any attributes you want to change when you're modifying your HTML files.
6. Use the pound sign (#) when indicating colors by means of their hexadecimal codes, as in the following:

   ```
   <BODY TEXT="#871E11">
   ```

   For a full discussion of hexadecimal codes, see Chapter 4, "Beginning to Build the Basic Web Site."

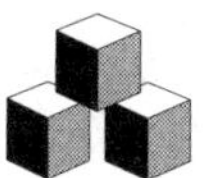

7. You often will need to nest tags, so make sure that you keep track of the end tags in order not to forget any of them.
8. When nesting tags, it is *very* important to keep track of start and end tags so that you don't overlap them. In other words, if you want to underline a sentence in bold type, you put one set of tags around the sentence, and then put the other set of tags around the first set, as follows:

   ```
   <U><B>This sentence appears underlined and in bold type.</B></U>
   ```

   Note that in the preceding example, both bold tags fall within the underline tags. The *wrong* way—overlapping the tags—looks like this:

   ```
   <U><B>This sentence may or may not appear underlined and in bold type.
   In fact, depending on how any given browser deals with such incorrectly
   placed tags, your file may not appear at all!</U></B>
   ```

9. Use all uppercase letters for tags and attributes, such as `<BODY>` and `TEXT`. You *can* use lowercase letters, but that makes the tags and attributes more difficult to identify when you want to make changes to the HTML.
10. Strive for readability in your code. Use tabs and returns to make your code more readable. Press Enter after each line of HTML code, because that vastly improves the ease with which you can read and follow the HTML. You don't necessarily *need* multiple blank lines between lines of HTML, but it doesn't hurt, either. In addition, it's a good idea to indent code to show the relationships among the lines of code. In other words, be logical about how your code looks, and think in terms of revisiting that HTML sometime in the future when you are modifying your site. Make it as easy on yourself as you can. Following is an example of how you might want to indent your HTML to indicate which tags are subordinate to other tags. In this case, as you learn in the first

project, the indents tell you that one entire list is subordinate to a single item in another list:

```
<UL>
<LI>
<LI>
   <UL>
   <LI>
   <LI>
   <LI>
   </UL>
<LI>
<LI>
</UL>
```

11. Check your work as you go, so that you don't put in hours of effort only to find that the Web page doesn't perform as you expected. An early mistake can have far-reaching effects on your expended effort as well as on your final product.

Summary

This chapter has attempted to provide an ever-so-brief introduction to HTML. Much more could be said, of course, but that information comes in the remaining chapters of this book. This chapter has laid out the basic rules of writing HTML; particular aspects of its syntax are covered throughout the rest of the book as the need arises.

This chapter also has touched on issues such as other software that can help you build your Web site, including graphics programs, programs to help you work with frames, and software to help you with scripts for your site. Finally, the chapter has given some attention to the issue of browser compatibility and Web site design.

As far as programming languages are concerned, HTML is relatively straightforward. Of course, the more complex the task at hand, the more complex the HTML likely will be. Still, you may be surprised by the kinds of exciting things you can accomplish with HTML and DHTML. Completing the three projects in this book will show you how much you can accomplish with such a simple language.

HANDS ON PROJECT 1

THE BASIC WEB SITE

- Learning techniques for Web site design
- Organizing your content effectively
- Laying out all the pages in your site
- Mastering the most common HTML tags
- Making provisions for visitors with different browsers
- Adjusting fonts and backgrounds
- Working with graphics

Project Overview

This project creates a simple personal Web site. Make no mistake, however: "simple" doesn't mean that it involves few tags or is plain in appearance. By the time you finish the project, you will have an excellent grounding in basic HTML tags and how to use attributes with them, and will know some guidelines for designing a Web site.

You begin by gathering information. What information do you want to include in the Web site, for example? You must know exactly what you want to accomplish with your Web site. After determining goals, you go about the task of gathering the information that you want to place on the Web site.

A vitally important step comes next: designing the Web site. After determining what you want your site to include, you set about deciding where and how to present the information to your site's visitors. You sketch how you want the site to look—this step involves considering both text and graphics.

After settling on a design, it's time to figure out how to write the HTML to make your design a reality. That step takes up the bulk of the time for this project. You enter and format your text, provide graphics to break up the text, and add color to make things sparkle. Then it's time to test your creation.

CHAPTER 2

What Is the Basic Web Site?

This chapter deals with several preliminary issues, and after you understand and make decisions regarding those issues, you will be better equipped to build a Web site that does what you want it to do. Failure to consider these issues is sure to limit your site's effectiveness in terms of what you want to accomplish with it.

One purpose of this chapter is to discuss what "basic Web site" means in the context of this book. In addition, you learn about setting goals for your site, including deciding on the type of information your site will present and where you get that information. Finally, the chapter presents several points for you to bear in mind as you create the content for your Web site.

Defining a Basic Web Site

For purposes of this book, a basic Web site is one that meets the following criteria:

- It does not use frames, forms, tables, style sheets, or Dynamic HTML.
- It is intended to be compatible with HTML versions as far back as possible, but especially with versions 3.2 and 4.0.
- A basic Web site can contain links to other pages within the Web site or to other Web sites.

The preceding definition of a basic Web site is my own, so it is probably not defined elsewhere. As you can see, those criteria make up a limiting set of standards as far as HTML 4.0's capabilities are concerned. Although you cannot abide by these criteria and develop an earth-shattering, HTML 4.0-compatible Web site, you still can create an attractive and informative Web site. A basic Web site is an excellent place to begin studying HTML, because such simple requirements do a couple of things:

- They are a means of learning the basics of writing HTML without having to worry about the mechanics of advanced topics, such as style sheets and Dynamic HTML. There's plenty of time for that later.
- These criteria free you to concentrate on the *content* of the Web site.

The results of both points will prove to be beneficial. In the first place, the mechanics of basic HTML will be second nature after some practice. Then it's easier to concentrate on the more advanced techniques. In the second place, by concentrating on your site's content, you can create a Web site with truly useful and informative information—the kind of site that people surfing the Web want.

Setting Your Goals for the Site

The limitations of a basic Web site, as defined for this book, make this type of site an excellent candidate for a personal Web site. The lack of

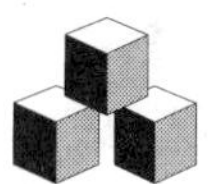

scripts and forms, for example, limits this site's usefulness as a place to carry on business activities. In addition, personal Web sites don't *need* all the fancy gizmos and capabilities offered by forms, tables, style sheets, animation, and DHTML—although you certainly can implement those things later.

For this book, I didn't want to create a dummy Web site filled with "Greek text"—that is, meaningless combinations of letters that only *look* like words. Neither did I want to create a Web site with lots of "placeholder" text: `This is a level-one heading`, `Insert your first graphic here`, and similar things. As a result, in Project 1 you'll be building a real Web site for guitar lovers and collectors. Figure 2.1 offers a glimpse of what a portion of the finished Web site will look like to visitors.

I realize that not everyone reading this book is interested in guitars. If you prefer to create your own version of the site—rather than type the text I ask you to use—you are free to do so. Of course, that means you must supply appropriate graphics and text to replace those on the CD that accompanies this book. In other words, you'll take the skeleton of the pages built throughout this project and put in your own text and

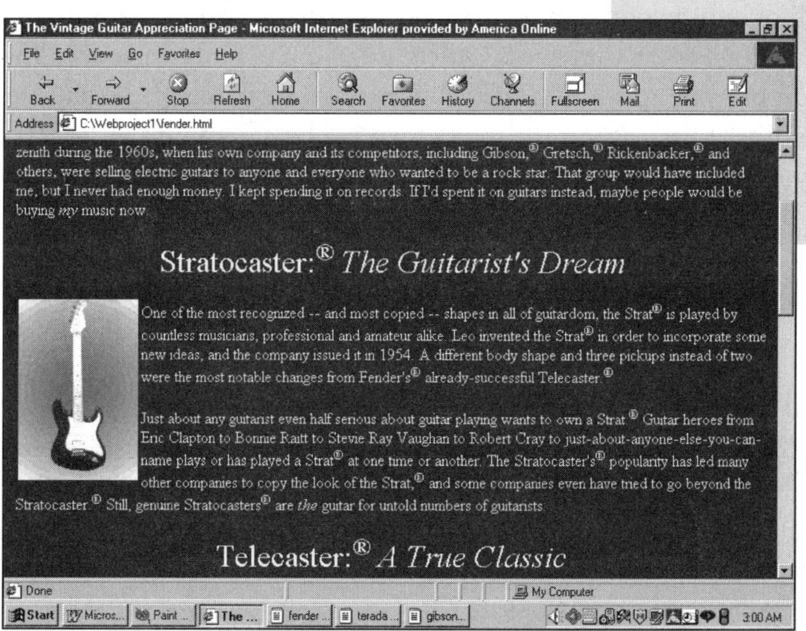

Figure 2.1 The guitar appreciation Web site will be up and running once you've completed Project 1.

graphics to replace mine. Proceed in whatever fashion you prefer, but I *strongly* suggest that you build the sites in the book to gain experience before going on to create your own.

Determining Your Audience

The goals you have in mind for a site you're about to create should revolve around your purpose for the site and the audience of Web users you expect to be interested in the information you present. For this project, the result is a personal Web site that deals with a hobby.

Other than friends and family, the most likely audience for a personal Web site consists of people who have interests like those of the site's owner. That's because personal Web sites generally aren't linked to business sites or to other sites which vast numbers of people frequent. Personal Web sites may be linked to each other, of course, especially among people who know each other—friends and family members, for example. Other than by such links, though, how is someone going to find your Web site?

Search engines, that's how. At one time or another, everyone who fires up an Internet-connected computer gets on the World Wide Web in search of information. Many people are looking for companies offering products or services they need. Others are trying to find reference information of some sort. Still others just want to surf around, perhaps to find out whether anyone else shares their hobby of, hmmm . . . collecting guitars.

It's important to realize when you are creating a personal Web site that people most likely are going to find you via search engines, and most likely are going to find you because you share an interest in something.

I considered a number of possible topics for Project 1. Besides wanting to make it something I'm interested in, I needed to make it a topic that could be carried through into the second and third projects. After much thought, I decided to build a Web site that reflects my hobby of guitar playing. (I don't play guitar particularly well, by the way, but I *do* know something about them and enjoy sharing that information with others.)

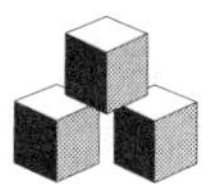

The second project brings the guitar theme into a business context, and the third project extends the theme to an even more sophisticated setting, a guitar museum.

Whether constructing a simple, straightforward personal Web site or a full-fledged corporate site, you need to consider other aspects of your audience—your visitors' browser capabilities and preferences, as well as physical impairments that some visitors may have, such as poor vision or even total blindness. Obviously, these concerns go beyond mere compatibility with earlier versions of browsers.

The key word to bear in mind when thinking of your potential audience is *accessibility.* Everyone is familiar with wheelchair-accessible buildings, for example. Web site designers do well to keep accessibility in mind when designing a site. A person with impaired vision can enjoy surfing the Web and benefit from it as much as anyone else.

Additionally, some people out there, either by choice or by happenstance, use browsers that don't display graphics, such as Lynx. Other users may have the latest version of Netscape Navigator or Internet Explorer—but have the graphics feature turned off in order to speed up their viewing of the content of a Web page. Some of the same Web-designing techniques that apply to making a site accessible to vision-impaired Web users also apply to those people who have graphics turned off or whose browsers are incompatible with graphics.

Taken together, those groups of Web users—all of them potential visitors to your site, whatever type of site you have—make up a significant percentage of the total. No one who takes care to build a Web site wants to exclude so many people from it.

Note

Wherever possible, this book's projects use techniques designed to enable vision-impaired people and users of non-graphical browsers to take full advantage of what the Web sites have to offer.

The audience envisioned for the Project 1 Web site is wide-ranging. Although you're building a hobby-based site, it's important to remember that millions of people play guitar, and tens of thousands of them (at least!) collect guitars as well. That means your potential audience is extremely large.

What Type of Information Do You Want to Present?

The presentation of this personal Web site's content will be straightforward. Straightforward presentation, of course, does not mean that the material itself must be simple. After all, if your interest happens to be quantum physics instead, the material most likely is not simple—but its presentation can be.

On the other hand, your interests might involve football, basketball, and showing off pictures of your family. Those topics are far simpler to explain and should make sense to far more people than quantum physics, but that type of content is no easier or more difficult to put on a Web site than quantum physics theories.

Of course, the kind of information you want to present depends totally on you. The goal of this project is to show you how to make that information—any sort of information—available to everyone with Internet access.

Finding the Information to Include

In the real world of building Web sites, you must find or create the information you want to present to your site's visitors. The purpose of this section is to discuss various possible sources for the text and graphics you place on your Web site.

Writing Your Own Material

Because this first project is a personal Web site—not a business site—the text I am putting on it is my own writing, based on my knowledge and imagination, and reflecting my interest. Other elements included on the site, such as graphics and photographs, also are my own. When you create a Web site for yourself, the same is likely to be true of you and your site.

With that assumption, here are some things to bear in mind as you write the words that you want to put on the Web:

1. Most people don't expect a personal Web site to be a work of literature, but don't let that stop you from producing a site that *is* a work of literature! I'm not trying to turn you into another Charles Dickens. All I'm asking is that you give attention to your writing. Your visitors will certainly appreciate it—and maybe even be impressed.

Tip

You might want to get a copy of *The Elements of Style,* by William Strunk, Jr. and E.B. White. It's a tiny paperback full of excellent advice about how to write well.

If you're uncomfortable with grammar—most people are—and you have a sense of humor, try *The Deluxe Transitive Vampire* (subtitled *The Ultimate Handbook of Grammar for the Innocent, the Eager, and the Doomed*), by Karen Elizabeth Gordon. If punctuation is your weak area, take a look at Gordon's companion volume, *The New Well-Tempered Sentence: A Punctuation Handbook for the Innocent, the Eager, and the Doomed.* Another option, which covers both punctuation and grammar, is *Grammatically Correct,* by Anne Stilman. Of course, many other excellent books on grammar and punctuation are available. Find ones that you like and will use.

2. After you have written the text for your Web site and are satisfied with it, ask someone else to read it. Ideally, that person should read your writing with two purposes in mind: 1) to check grammar and punctuation, and 2) to check style. By *style* I mean things like the following:
   - Is it interesting?
   - Is it clear?
   - Does it convey the point(s) you want to get across?

- Are there any gaps in information you may have overlooked? (Outsiders—people who are not close to the subject—often can spot lapses in logic, missing steps, or other types of gaps that the author doesn't see.)

The need for proofreading may be less applicable to a personal Web site than to a business site, depending on the type of material you've placed on it. Nevertheless, it certainly doesn't hurt!

3. An easily overlooked point is the international nature of a Web site's audience. Businesses in particular need to remember that what is considered proper varies from culture to culture throughout the world. In the United States, for example, it's not unusual for people who have just met to start calling each other by first name almost immediately. In most other cultures, however, you can be someone's neighbor for 20 years and still address him as "Mr. So-and-so" or "Mrs. Such-and-such." Suppose that your business site enables visitors to send e-mail with questions or requests for information. If you're culturally aware, you won't respond to a German businessman—especially someone you've never met—by replying "Dear Jürgen." Formality is almost always safer than informality in this sort of situation.

Even if you don't want to put as much effort into your text as I recommend, at the very least you should make sure that all words are spelled and capitalized correctly. Your visitors will appreciate it.

Including Secondary Sources

Writing your own text for a Web site may be only part of the process. To one degree or another, you may also want or need to include material written by others.

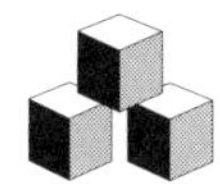

If you think back to those schooldays in your dim past, you may recall teachers talking about the difference between primary sources and secondary sources. My distinction between primary and secondary sources may not be exactly the same as what you learned in school; in the context of this book, the distinction to draw between types of source material for your Web site relates mostly to legal issues.

Strictly speaking, the words you write or graphics you create for your Web site make up the only primary source material on your site. Others who knowingly contribute their own writing or graphics to your Web site are supplying their own primary source material, but it is still secondary material to you. The significant word in the latter case is *knowingly.*

As defined here, secondary source material consists of writing (or anything else, such as graphics) which you include on your Web site that didn't originate with you. In other words, if you find an interesting article on Niels Bohr and type it (or scan it) into your Web site's section on quantum physics, it's a secondary source.

And it's illegal to use it on your site—*unless you have permission.*

United States copyright law states that the person who creates a work in fixed form owns the copyright. The work does *not* have to be registered with the Copyright Office—although many people still do that in order to have a record of a definite date for their creation. Even when no copyright notice appears on a work, the copyright still belongs to the person who created it. Of course, people can and sometimes do make contractual agreements allowing their copyrighted material to be used by other people or companies.

Since the most recent copyright law's passage in 1976, the copyright on anything you create is in place for your lifetime plus 50 years. Of course, if you sell the copyright, then someone else owns it. For anything created before 1976, the copyright (including renewals of copyright) is in effect for at most 75 years from the date of publication.

The point is this: If you find a document or graphic somewhere—in a book or magazine, on the Web, anywhere—then someone owns the copyright (with a couple of exceptions, discussed in the following tip). If you want to use that document or graphic—or even just a portion thereof—on your Web site, then you must obtain permission from the copyright owner. You might not have any trouble at all obtaining such permission, although things tend to get sticky quickly if you ever want to use borrowed material in a way that might earn money.

Copyright is not an issue with works that now are in the *public domain*. Basically, that means two groups of works: works that are really old (say, pre-1900), and works whose creators specifically put them into the public domain. Bear in mind, however, that if you find a new edition of Edgar Allen Poe's "The Raven" and you want to scan and use one of the illustrations—an illustration created specifically for that edition—you must obtain permission. Even though the *text* of "The Raven" is old, someone likely still owns a copyright on the illustration you want to use.

Bear in mind that documents are not the only works covered under copyright law. Photographs, illustrations, songs (you may want to include audio on your site), videos, and movies—all these things and a handful of others fall under copyright law. The best advice is not to use anything on your Web site that you don't create personally, unless you get permission first. Get that permission in written form and keep it on file, just in case someone claims someday that you're using the work illegally.

Summary

This chapter has covered several aspects of a basic Web site, some of which are often overlooked. The central point of this chapter is that a Web site, even a simple personal site, requires consideration of your audience and the presentation of well-planned content. Launching a jumble of words and photographs onto the World Wide Web is not going to

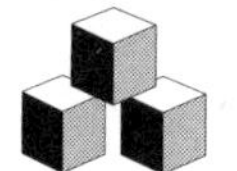

make your site popular. Interesting, useful information presented in an attractive, well-designed, and—as much as possible—compact site very well might become popular. At least it stands a chance, because people do pass the word about great Web sites they've visited.

This chapter also has recommended that you put real effort into the writing that you place on the site. Many people are put off by misspellings and poor punctuation. Those kinds of mistakes often make visitors wonder about the reliability of the material presented. *After all,* a visitor may think, *if this guy isn't careful enough to check his spelling, how can I be sure that the information he presents here is accurate?*

Finally, the often-neglected issue of copyright is quite important. You cannot legally reuse other people's text or incorporate someone else's images without obtaining permission from the copyright owner. If you do, you may be startled one day to find yourself being sued for copyright infringement. Consider yourself to have gotten fair warning!

Designing the Basic Web Site

When you decide to create a Web site, you don't just toss together all the HTML you know and then throw the result up on the Web. Instead, you take the time to plan your Web site.

Planning a site *does* involve deciding what information you want to include—as discussed in Chapter 2—but that's only the beginning. You no doubt have seen some sites on the Web that appear to have been put up with no thought given to anything *other than* the content. The lack of site planning is evident.

The purpose of this chapter is to discuss the planning of a basic Web site in the course of actually completing the planning of the Project 1 Web site. Much of the design approach used in the chapter is applicable to all Web sites, not just those considered "basic" in the sense used in this book.

Deciding What to Put on Your Web Site

You learned in Chapter 2 that the Project 1 Web site is about guitars. I could place all kinds of information on the site, of course: links to companies, listings of every guitar ever made in the United States, biographies of my favorite guitarists, plans for anyone who wants to build his or her own guitar, or a treatise on why I enjoy playing guitar.

Theoretically, I'm not at all limited in the information that can be included on the Web site. Practically, however, I *am* limited. Not only am I not competent in certain guitar areas (such as building them), but I am not interested in typing the hundreds of pages that would be necessary to create a complete and exhaustive guitar Web site. Of necessity, I must choose what I want to include.

Likewise, you need to consider carefully what you want to place on any given Web site. Don't try to create a *complete* Web site about any particular topic—not all at once, anyway. Of course, if your site remains online for a long time, you can add pages to it as you have the energy or the need. Over time, maybe you *will* create a complete Web site about your topic of interest.

Almost regardless of your site's topic, you are likely to want to include graphics of some sort: photographs, computer-drawn graphics, scanned images, or other types of graphic art. That's one of the considerations you must take into account in designing your site, as the next section explains.

Using Graphics: The Art of Using Art

One of the Web's biggest drawing cards is its capability to display far more than black text on a gray background, although those kinds of documents are still quite common. The capability to jazz up a Web site with graphics is a tempting one—and most people fall prey to the temptation.

Determining the Purpose of Graphics in Your Web Site

Most people have experienced at least one negative aspect of the Web: a Web site that takes F—O—R—E—V—E—R to download. Various factors play a role in these interminable downloads, but quite often the culprit is a large number of graphics or graphics that are large in file size.

Unfortunately, far too many Web site creators use graphics simply because they *can.* And it is not unusual to find personal Web sites that basically consist of graphics, a token amount of text, and a bunch of links to other sites.

When planning your site, you must determine several things about graphics:

1. Are graphics in some form (photographs, images from a drawing program, and so on) *necessary* for your site? If your business is selling vintage and collectible violins through your Web site, visitors will want to see what you're selling. In fact, they probably will want several views of each item so that they can see details. In a case like that, you *must* use graphics on your Web site.
2. Are graphics not necessary but really more a supplement to the text on your site? Suppose that your site offers the scientific community the results of experiments carried on at your company. You *may* need to use graphics, perhaps to show charts that graph numerical results. On the other hand, some results can be explained in text form and don't require graphics.
3. Are graphics completely unnecessary for understanding your Web site? If you write humorous reflections on your daily life and post them to your Web site, you don't *need* graphics at all.
4. Again, who is your audience? If you expect your audience to be mostly corporate employees with high-speed Internet connections, you probably don't need to be too concerned with the size of your graphics; those corporate connections should be fast enough. If you anticipate, however, that your primary audience will consist of people sitting at home and connecting via their telephone line and a 14.4 Kbps modem, then you need

to be *extremely* concerned about how many graphics you use and how big they are.

What is the purpose of the site you want to put on the Web? Give consideration to the preceding questions before deciding to drop in graphics hither and yon simply because you've got plenty of server space available to you. Make those graphics earn their keep.

Caution

Not only do graphics take time to download, but they also use up disk space on the server that hosts your Web site.

Before you decide that I'm nothing but a killjoy where graphics are concerned, let me say a bit more about the topic. When I say that some sites don't need graphics at all, it's true: They don't *need* them. But at the same time, a personal Web site without any graphics isn't much fun at all. By all means, use graphics on your personal Web site or on any other kind of Web site, but do so in moderation. And keep their sizes (in bytes) as small as possible. Chapter 5 deals more with graphics and how to optimize them for Web sites.

Tip

Here's a general guideline for using graphics on your Web site: Each page of your Web site should have a maximum of 50K in graphics. Less than that is even better. The problem is that many (or even most) people surf the Web by connecting via modem, which is far from the fastest method of downloading Web sites. That's why limiting graphics sizes is important.

Let the purpose of the graphics on your site determine how many you use. A violin seller needs to have images available to potential buyers—especially detailed photos that can show identifying marks, defects, workmanship, and so on.

In other words, numerous photos and other graphics are justifiable under the right circumstances. And it's when you do need—or want—to include numerous graphics that you must be concerned about the issue of graphics types and sizes, as well as alternatives to graphics for the sake of visitors with nongraphical browsers.

Sizing Up Your Alternatives: GIF versus JPEG

Dozens of graphics file formats are available today, and many graphics programs can handle a large number of them. When it comes to graphics on the Web, however, two formats dominate: GIF (Graphics Interchange Format) and JPEG (Joint Photographics Expert Group). Both GIF and JPEG are in widespread use on the Web, but each has its own purpose.

Note

A new format, PNG, is available for use on the Web; it has limited, but growing, support. Expect to see its use increase in the future.

Generally, GIF is the format of choice for Web graphics that have few colors. The GIF format also is good for photographs containing few colors, because you can create a smaller GIF file than you can a JPEG file when few colors are involved.

The JPEG format is best when you are interested in displaying photographs or other graphics with many colors and color gradients. You use graphics software to work with both kinds of files. If you want to manipulate photographs—to change their colors or cut out extraneous backgrounds, for example—one of the many photograph-manipulation programs is made to order. If you want to create GIF files, you can try any number of paint programs.

Note

This book cannot discuss the pros and cons of all available graphics packages. Before deciding on one, you should ask others what they like to use, try out demos (including those on this book's CD), download shareware and freeware, and read reviews. Unless you have experience with this type of software, allow yourself sufficient time to learn how to use it.

If you don't want to create your own images, you can buy CDs full of all sorts of images that you can use. One type of images is *clip art,* which is a collection of simple drawings that illustrate all sorts of items and situations, such as the sun and moon, sports equipment, holiday objects, or two people talking to each other. Another source of images is a *photo CD,* which is a CD that contains photographs you can use in your Web site or for other applications. Of course, legal use presumes that you have bought the clip art or photo CD and are abiding by any legal stipulations set forth by the manufacturer or distributor.

The subject of graphics is quite relevant to the Web site in this first project. This Web site has one primary drawback: Guitar lovers and vintage guitar collectors like to examine photographs of guitars. Sometimes they want to see photos simply because they appreciate the beauty of the instruments. At other times they want to see what distinguishes one guitar from another one that seems to be the same. Because of the nature of the Project 1 Web site, then, I'll be including graphics. Those graphics mostly will take the form of JPEGs, but some GIFs will be included as well. The problem is that photographs (JPEGs) take time to download.

If you find yourself in a similar situation—that is, needing to use a lot of graphics on a Web site you're designing in the future—don't despair. Help is available in the form of specialized graphics software. This type of software can *optimize* your graphics for use on the Web. Some examples of this software are DeBabelizer, ImageReady, Ulead SmartSaver, and Macromedia Fireworks. By no means are these the only programs, however; they are only a representative sample.

Image optimization involves reducing file size while maintaining as high an image quality as possible. You can use most of the specialized graphics packages to do one or more other things, as well, such as optimize GIF animations, preview optimized images, edit images, create image maps, or other tasks. The prices vary widely, so carefully consider your needs and the software's capabilities before making a decision. Also, try before you buy whenever possible.

There's one bit of good news related to larger images—browsers can reuse images that are already downloaded. If your company has a logo that you want to include on each page of your Web site, for example, that's not a problem. Once the logo is downloaded for the first page, it is available for all subsequent pages. That's because, unless the user has done some unusual modification of their browser settings, the downloaded image is held in the cache of the viewer's computer, and the browser simply pulls it from the cache again every time it's needed.

Using Animated GIFs

Animated GIFs—those little cartoon-like images that move on a Web page—can be cute additions to a Web page. They also can become really annoying in record time.

If you want to create an animated GIF image for your Web page, you can do so with a number of programs. GIF animations work like television cartoons. First, you have to create individual frames, each of which is different from the preceding one. Maybe you made a flipbook when you were a child, one of those small booklets or pads of paper with a picture on each page. If you looked at the pages as you flipped through them quickly, the picture seemed to change and move. It was a do-it-yourself cartoon.

You use the same technique to create the illusion of movement in an animated GIF. As with everything else in a Web site, though, you need to decide what you want to achieve with the animation.

Find it Online

Following are a couple of Web sites for you to visit when you want to download shareware of any kind, including graphics and GIF animation programs. Don't forget, however, to pay the creator of each particular software product that you decide to use.

http://www.tucows.com/
http://www.shareware.com/

As you plan your animation, bear in mind that each frame of your animation is a separate GIF. Each GIF must be downloaded to your visitor's computer, and each new GIF adds time to the process. Too much time, and your visitor may decide to leave early.

One way to shorten the download time with a GIF animation is to reuse parts of the animation frames. Check the documentation for your GIF animator—sometimes you can greatly control the file size of an animated GIF by reusing elements of frames.

If you don't want to create your own animation, you may be in luck anyway. You can download and buy already-created GIFs to drop into your Web site. Search the Web, and you'll find all kinds of commercial software as well as shareware that may provide you with just the animation you need. Project 2 covers animation in more detail.

Use the minimum number of frames necessary to accomplish the goal you have set for the animation.

Animated GIFs boil down to this: You *may* be better off not using them, because after the novelty wears off—which happens very quickly—they can be extremely annoying. A way to counteract this annoyance factor is to limit the number of times the animation plays. Animations that play only one or two times are tolerable, but you still must be careful about the size of the file. If you decide to use an animated GIF, plan it out and use as few frames as possible in order to save download time. In addition, make sure that you use a program that optimizes the animated GIF for you.

Web Site Builder as Graphic Artist: Sketching Out Your Site

Most people want to create an attractive site when they put a Web site online. After all, people from all over the world may see it, and everyone wants to make a good first impression. For most people, probably the most difficult aspect of putting up a Web site—whether just a single page or a full-fledged corporate site—is deciding on the site's layout. Even after you know what kind of material you want to include and whether or not you want to use graphics, you still have to decide on the arrangement of those elements on the page.

Tip

Don't be afraid to get layout and design ideas from Web sites you visit. When you view a site, you know immediately whether you find it aesthetically pleasing or gaudy and ugly. And after navigating around the site for a few minutes, you can tell whether you like the way the site is put together, the way it *works*.

Caution

Having made the statement in the preceding tip, however, it's important also to note that you should not actually take graphics from another site and plunk them into your own site. This warning is especially relevant if you're trying to recreate the look of the original Web site that used those graphics. Feel free to view the HTML to see how the Web designer accomplished the layout; just don't try to duplicate the appearance of that Web site. Create your own, distinctive graphics, and vary the design to suit your site and its contents.

The aesthetics of a Web site are very important, because appearance is the first thing a visitor notices. If a Web surfer lands on your site and sees that it's ugly or gaudy, he or she may not stick around long enough to look at the site's contents. Your brilliantly written, perfectly spelled, correctly punctuated, and extraordinarily informative site may scare off most visitors if your design consists of a red background with bright yellow text and nothing more. They don't get much uglier than that!

The physical placement of your Web site's elements, as well as the color scheme you choose, is integral to the aesthetic appeal of your site. It's true that not everyone has the same taste, and there's nothing you can do about that. It is also true that certain rules of design that yield pleasing results in books and magazines are just as applicable to Web sites. Magazine art directors spend a great deal of time coming up with the right look for their readers, and book publishers employ art directors who do the same thing for book covers and the layout of text on their books' pages.

Considerations in Designing Your Web Site

Rules are everywhere, whether they are the rules of the road or rules of good Web site design. Many of the site design rules, perhaps even most of them, are probably things you have never consciously considered. Still, if you look at a magazine or view a Web site that doesn't follow the generally accepted rules, you will very likely notice that something doesn't look right. You may not be able to pinpoint the problem, but you'll notice it.

Some of the page design rules to which you should give your attention are the following:

1. Keep an eye on the white space. *White space* is the empty space between paragraphs and graphics. Make sure that you have enough of it! On the other hand, don't go *overboard* with white space, because then your site takes on the appearance of having minimal content. Some sites consist of little more than links to other sites, and they often have this overabundance of white space (or essentially consist of logo graphics that serve as links to those sites).

   If your Web site looks as if it came right out of your physician's library of reference books on internal medicine, then you need to lighten it up. In other words, if your site is solid text, you need to soften its appearance. White space and graphics are tailor-made for that purpose. Readers quickly become fatigued by a wall of text—and probably bored as well. They aren't likely to stick around for long. Of course, a possible exception to this rule is the realm of scientific or scholarly papers that visitors read in the course of doing research. For run-of-the-mill Web surfers who are just passing through, however, text alone will rarely make them stay—especially if it's an unattractive solid block of text.

2. Balance out the page. It's better not to have all the page's graphics clumped together in one corner and nothing but text everywhere else, for example. Instead, intermingle the text and graphics into

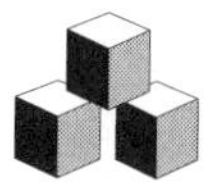

Use headings to break up your text into sections. This technique helps to tear down that daunting wall of text. You also can create a table of contents at the top of the page and use the elements of the table of contents as hyperlinks to the headings within the text. That gives visitors the opportunity to go straight to the section of text that interests them.

an eye-pleasing arrangement. Be careful not to insert graphics randomly, though, because then your page looks haphazard. Establish a recognizable pattern in the placement of text and graphics.

3. Use a variety of font sizes—within reason. You can accomplish this result in a couple of ways: You can use the heading levels, as appropriate, along with the normal, default font size, or you can specify font size as needed (although the latter technique is only applicable to HTML 3.2 and later). Chapter 4 covers the proper use of heading and font tags.
4. Be careful about using multiple fonts. Your best bet is to limit yourself to two, or maybe three, fonts on your Web site.
5. Don't be afraid to use bold, italic, underlining, capitalization, and other character formatting—but don't *overuse* them, either. Apply such formatting when it adds to the page's appearance (such as to vary the text's sameness) and readability or understandability (to distinguish a word being defined from its definition, for example). If you overuse character formatting, your page may look like a ransom note culled from the text in assorted tabloids and teen magazines. You may want to ask someone else's opinion before settling on a final look for your Web site.
6. Good writing in all the languages with which I am familiar includes the concept of paragraphs. Here's a hint: If you write a paragraph that takes up the entire screen and then some, it's too long. Break it into one or more paragraphs. This point is closely related to the issue of white space.

7. Don't use newspaper-style columns on your page. They may look professional, but you need to remember your audience. A number of your visitors, notably those with impaired vision, may use devices to read your page to them. These devices don't follow columns. Rather, they read straight across the page. Your columns will create confusion, not favorable impressions.

Having said all that, it is worthwhile to bear in mind that not everyone will agree on what makes a Web site attractive. Web sites are like art in at least one sense. Picasso may be considered a genius who created masterpieces, but I'll take a Rembrandt over a Picasso any day of the week. In other words, it's a matter of taste. You know an attractive site when you see one—after all, beauty *is* in the eye of the beholder.

Still, it is wise to stay away from overused techniques. What once was innovative and exciting now falls into the realm of cliché, precisely *because* so many people have used it since it was known as "innovative" and "exciting." On the other hand, when you're building a personal Web site, as in this first project, you have the freedom to do what you like; that's why it's called a *personal* Web site. You aren't likely to be able to do that in a corporate Web site.

If someone complains about the look of your Web site, remember that there's no accounting for someone else's taste. If your *boss* complains about a corporate Web site you're putting together, however, that's a different story!

Laying Out the Project 1 Web Site

Now is the time to get down to the business of sketching out the Web site you want to build. The place to begin is with a flowchart of the pages in your Web site. If your site consists of just one page—no links to other pages in your own site—you probably don't need to carry out this first step. Otherwise, you should create this sketch in order to clarify the relationship between pages. You need to make sure to include all the links

Despite a Web site's similarity to magazines and books in terms of design considerations, you must also remember the tremendous differences between them. A Web site should not be a static, linear, top-to-bottom document. Rather, it should be dynamic, offering hyperlinks to locations throughout the document as well as to other sites. Create multiple pages for your Web site. Place hyperlinks to various places within the site, not just from the first page to the next, and then to the next, and so on. Allow visitors to skip around in ways that will create a satisfying experience for each unique visitor.

between pages, and a graphic layout of page relationships is the best way to do it.

Look at the content of your Web site. Does it lend itself to a certain number of pages? If your material naturally falls into two or three categories, for example, then two or three pages may very well fit your requirements. The site created in this project is about my personal interest in guitars, which is one category. Within that category, however, I plan to have three subcategories. In addition, I like the idea of a "Welcome" page containing links to the other three pages. A Welcome page is a good way to introduce visitors to the contents of your site. For this project, then, I think four pages are in order. Figure 3.1 shows a sketch of the page relationships for the Project 1 Web site.

This initial flowchart gives a broad overview of the way the site's pages fit together. Note the arrows pointing from one page to another in this figure. Those arrows represent the links between pages, and links are what make HTML so useful and powerful. As you can see, the Welcome page contains links to each of the other three pages. From the Guitars 1 page, a viewer can return to the Welcome page or go to the Guitars 2 or Guitars 3 page. Likewise, a viewer can go from the Welcome page to the Guitars 2 or Guitars 3 page and then return to the Welcome page or proceed to either of the other specific guitar pages. In short, a viewer can get from any one page to any other page in this site with just one click.

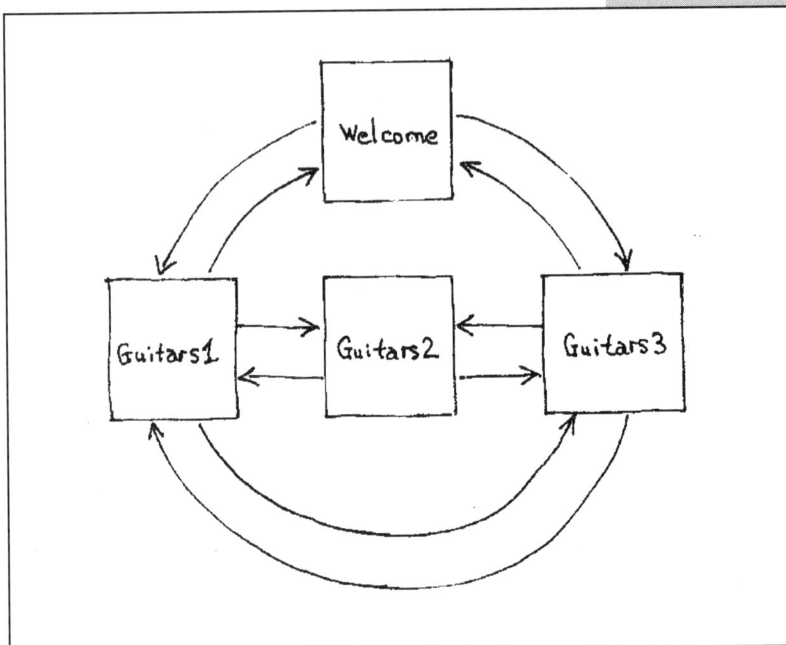

Figure 3.1 Four pages should be enough for the site you're creating in Project 1.

Note

Don't try to put too much information on any one page of your Web site. If a viewer has to click in the scroll box half a dozen times or more to go from the top to the bottom of one page, you've probably got too much material there. Break up one long page into two or more shorter pages. Again, a *possible* exception here is scientific or scholarly papers, but even those usually lend themselves to being broken into smaller parts, perhaps at major headings, for example.

You can use the table of contents tip mentioned earlier to help if you must leave the text in one long document. Use the document's headings to create a table of contents at the top of the page, create hyperlinks to each heading, and then, at the end of each section, insert another hyperlink back to the table of contents. Keeping the document on one page can help when viewers want to print the whole document, because they don't have to go from page to page and print each one individually.

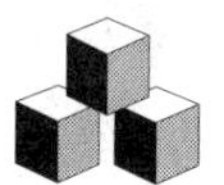

Note

If you are creating a Web site of your own, rather than duplicating the one in this book, think about the number of pages you will need. If it's more than one, make sure that you draw your own flowchart. Yours may be more complex than the one shown in Figure 3.1; the more complex it is, the more important the flowchart is.

The Project 1 site is straightforward. Other sites, however, can become quite complex, depending on the purpose of the site and how extensive it is. That's the reason it is so important to have a schematic of the site's layout, even for a simple Web site like this one.

What the sketch in Figure 3.1 does *not* show is the actual content of the individual pages. That is the next step in the design process. The second step's sketches are where you indicate the contents of a page, their layout, the exact links you want to include, and so on.

Following are some points to keep in mind as you design your Web site:

- Don't take HTML directly from other Web sites. You can see how other sites have solved layout problems, for example, but don't copy another site's design, because copyright may become an issue. Nor should you take graphics from other sites, unless you have written permission. Instead, use your own creativity to design and build your site. As you build the Project 1 site (or your own version of it), keep in mind that it is a simple personal Web site, not a Web site for a multibillion-dollar corporation. Most of the fancy effects you see on corporate Web sites are beyond the scope of this project. To refresh your memory, refer to the criteria for Project 1 that were presented in Chapter 2.
- Try not to get one design stuck in your mind so that you're unable to see other possibilities. You can place graphics and text on pages in more ways than anyone can count—but some arrangements are more attractive than others. Let me remind you again, however, that Web beauty is in the eye of the Web builder.

- Don't be satisfied with your first effort. Draw several alternatives, even radically different alternatives. Use your imagination, and try to picture your site in living color.

I have decided to split this Project's Web site into four pages, the first of which is basically a screen to welcome visitors. From there, visitors can navigate to the particular sections that interest them.

Designing the Welcome Page

Now that you know the number of pages this project uses, it's time to get some practice laying out the individual pages. To begin, I'll tell you the elements that need to go on the Welcome page of this Web site, in no particular order, and you can design your own version of the page. Don't forget to be logical, of course! The word "Welcome," for example, probably wouldn't make sense at the bottom of the page.

I'll prompt you to consider various design elements as you work through the page. I'll simultaneously walk you through the design I decided to use. Although the project in this book follows my design, you may decide that you like your own better. Great! After creating the project in the book and learning the basics of HTML, you may want to go back and build your version of it in order to get even more hands-on practice.

A* banner *is a graphic at the top of a Web page that may consist of text (such as a company name), art (such as a logo), or some combination of text and art.

The elements of the Welcome page are as follows:

- A one-line subtitle: "I hope you enjoy your foray into one of my favorite topics"
- A paragraph of introductory text
- Two photographs
- A large graphic of four guitars
- Two banners: "Welcome" and "The Vintage Guitar Appreciation Page"
- Two informational articles, one of which includes a list of definitions: "Tips for Buying Used or Vintage Guitars" and "The Buyer's Guide to Grading Guitars"
- Copyright and contact information

- A series of links to the Web site's other pages, in the form of a combined numbered/bulleted list

Note

Banners on commercial sites often contain a company name and/or logo, and sometimes a slogan or sales pitch of some sort. Banners can be very colorful and artistic, or can be plain and simple. They also can make use of animation or other fancy effects. The banners you'll place on the Web site for Project 1 will be simple text banners.

Tip

At the "sketching out" stage, rules regarding fonts aren't normally applicable. Those kinds of rules come into play when you start building your Web site. You can safely ignore the font-related design guidelines as you work through the following exercise.

EXERCISE

Here are specific steps you should work through to pin down the design of your first page:

1. Sketch your vision of the top of your Web site's Welcome page. Does it have a banner? Is it strictly text? Does it combine text and graphics? Which of the preceding elements do you think should come first, and how do you lay them out?

   What I decided to do was go for a symmetrical look. I'm putting into practice one of the rules listed earlier—namely, balancing out the page. The top of the Welcome page as I envision it uses the "Welcome" banner centered at the very top of the page. Centering it starts the page off with a balanced appearance. Below that banner I placed the second banner, which reads "The Vintage Guitar Appreciation Page."

   The two banners together convey the primary message of the opening page. They welcome viewers and immediately inform them of the site's topic.

2. Now what do you want to do? How does your white space look? Too much of it? Too little? Is your page balanced?

   I decided that I also wanted some decoration for the top of the page, because the two banners alone left too much blank space on the sides. This concern came from the rule regarding white space (#1). Instead of being concerned about not enough white space, however, I was concerned about the opposite: *too much* white space. For that reason, I decided to use two identical photographs. These photographs maintain the theme of the site, guitars, because they are photographs of a beautifully inlaid acoustic guitar peghead.

   Figure 3.2 shows my sketch of the Welcome page as it stands at this point.

3. What element do you want to place on your page next? How do you want it aligned: left, right, or centered?

   The next element I wanted to put on the page was the subtitle ("I hope you enjoy . . . "). I think of it as a part of the welcome message that leads into the page. Having inserted the subtitle, I decided it was time to get into more substantial text. For that reason, I didn't want to jump right into either one of the articles. Nor did I insert the links yet. Instead, I thought that text explaining the purpose of the site was in order. Therefore, I placed the introductory paragraph after the subtitle, and centered it horizontally on the page. The paragraph is *justified text*—that is, it has even left and right margins. As you can see in Figure 3.3, I was still trying to adhere to the balanced page and white space rules of design.

Figure 3.2
Here is my sketch of the top of the Welcome page.

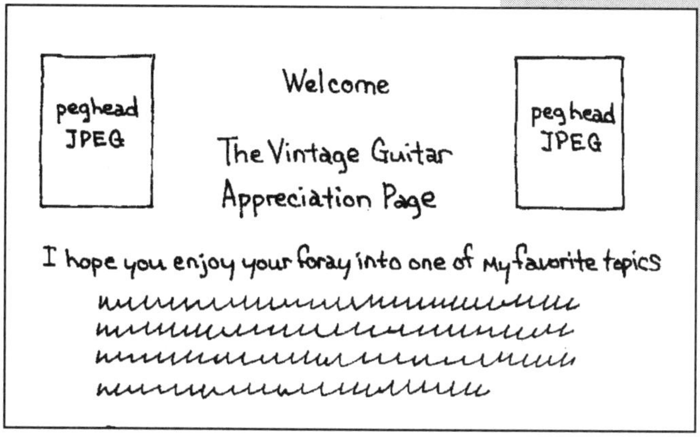

Figure 3.3 The Welcome page now includes a subtitle and an introductory paragraph.

4. Take a minute now to review your own sketch. Your design probably is different from mine, which is fine. The question is, are you remembering to adhere to the rules listed earlier? How does it look to you so far?

   At this point, it's a good idea to list the remaining elements that go on the Welcome page, as far as my own design is concerned. You should do the same for your design, to make sure that you don't leave anything out. The remaining elements are the following:

   - A large graphic of four guitars
   - Two informational articles
   - Copyright and contact information
   - A series of links to the site's other pages, in the form of a combined numbered/bulleted list

> **Note**
>
> **If you have surfed the Web much, you know that the copyright and contact information typically is placed at the bottom of the page.**

5. Look at the elements you still need to insert into your own design. Logically, which one should come next? Using the design rules as a guide, what kind of alignment does that element call for in your design?

In my own design, I decide to place the list of links next. These links are to the other pages of the Web site, so their placement after the paragraph introducing the Web site seems to be a logical next step. The problem is that the list is narrow in width. If I leave the list aligned on the left side of the page, which is the default alignment, then a very large blank space—white space—takes up the remaining space over to the right margin. Talk about out of balance! The opposite alignment, placing the list along the right margin, yields a similar problematic result—too much white space on the left. Centering the text balances the page, but this time leaves too much white space on each side of the list.

My decision is to place the list along the left margin. To fill up the white space on the right, I insert the large graphic of four guitars. Figure 3.4 shows the current state of the Web page as I have designed it.

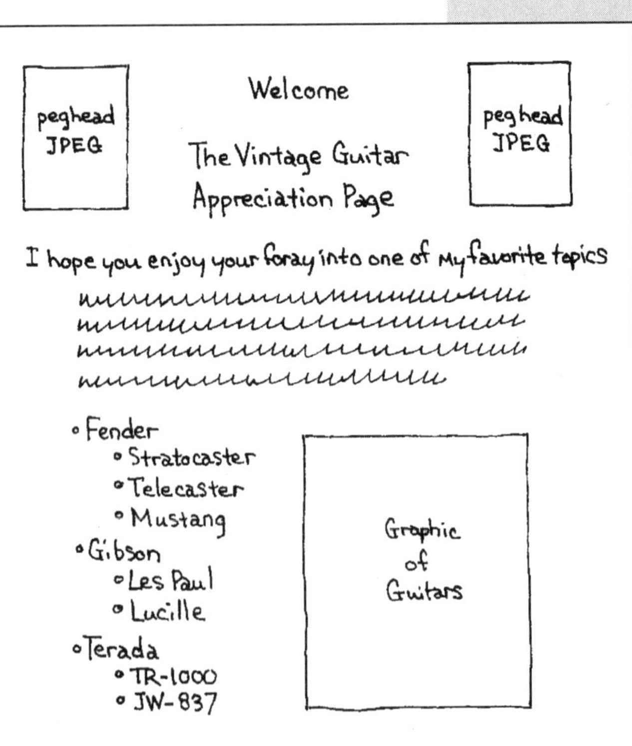

Figure 3.4 The large graphic fills up white space next to the bulleted list.

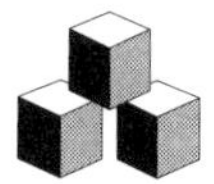

6. At most, you should have only a couple of elements left now. As you place them on the page in your sketch, review the page's appearance one more time. Do you have any alternatives in placement, or do the elements require you to place them in a particular location to maintain an attractive layout?

   Next I inserted the two articles. I don't think they necessarily have to be in any particular order. Finally, I finished the Welcome page by placing the copyright and contact information at the bottom, which is where such information typically appears in Web sites. Note that, throughout the design of this page, I did *not* use newspaper-style columns (rule #7). Instead, I stayed with paragraphs that went from margin to margin. Figure 3.5 shows

Figure 3.5 This is the final layout of the Welcome page for Project 1.

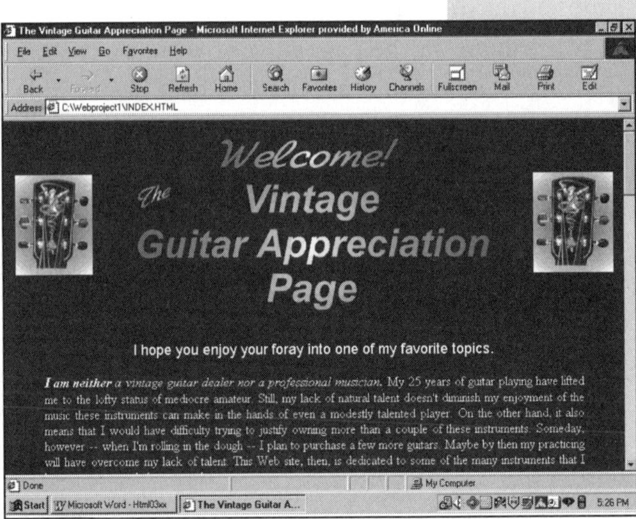

Figure 3.6 Shown here in a browser is the actual Welcome page from the Project 1 Web site.

my final layout of the page, and Figure 3.6 shows the actual Web site which reflects that layout.

ANALYSIS

So, how did *your* design turn out? Are you satisfied with it? Do you like yours better than mine, perhaps? Did you frequently check the list of design rules to make sure that you weren't ignoring them?

The design I finally chose required a significant amount of trial and error on my part. I discussed *my* thinking in each step as you worked through the exercise. That is not to say, of course, that my way is the only way to do it. Again, I encourage you to try building your design after you have built my design in Project 1. Building your design is an excellent way to practice what you're learning in Project 1, as well as to see how your design looks in real life.

That takes care of my Welcome page design, but I didn't arrive at this design the first time out. In order to show you the process, I'll briefly explain what I tried before settling on a design for this project.

Figure 3.7 shows the rough layout I first tried for this Welcome page.

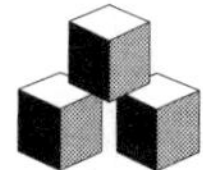

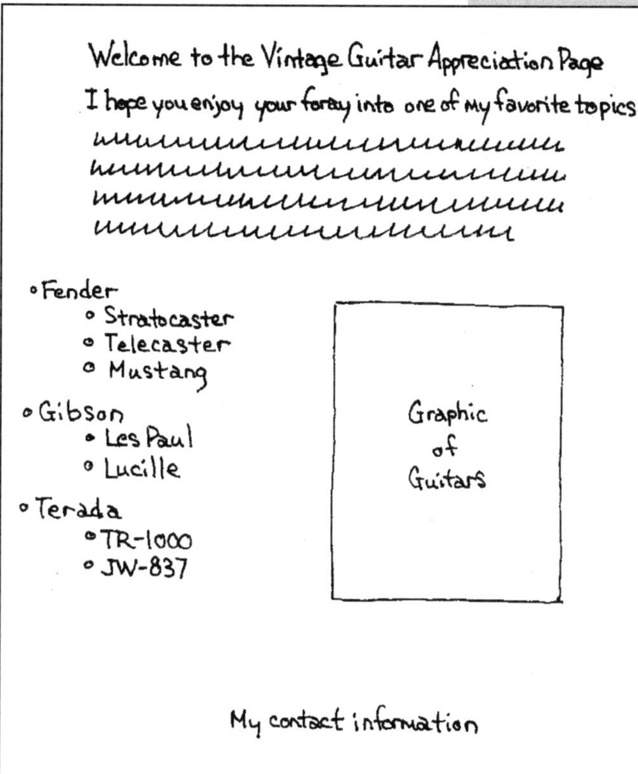

Figure 3.7 Here is the first design for the Welcome page.

At the top of the page is a centered heading that says "Welcome to the Vintage Guitar Appreciation Page." Beneath that is a centered heading that says, "I hope you enjoy your foray into one of my favorite topics." After that comes a paragraph of text.

Below the text paragraph and to the left are links to other parts of this Web site. To the right of the links is the four-guitar graphic. The page ends with the copyright and contact information.

When I created this page, I thought it looked all right, but I wasn't really satisfied with it. I decided that it needed some more color at or near the top, perhaps in the form of graphics of some kind. I decided to try another approach to the page. That attempt is shown in Figure 3.8.

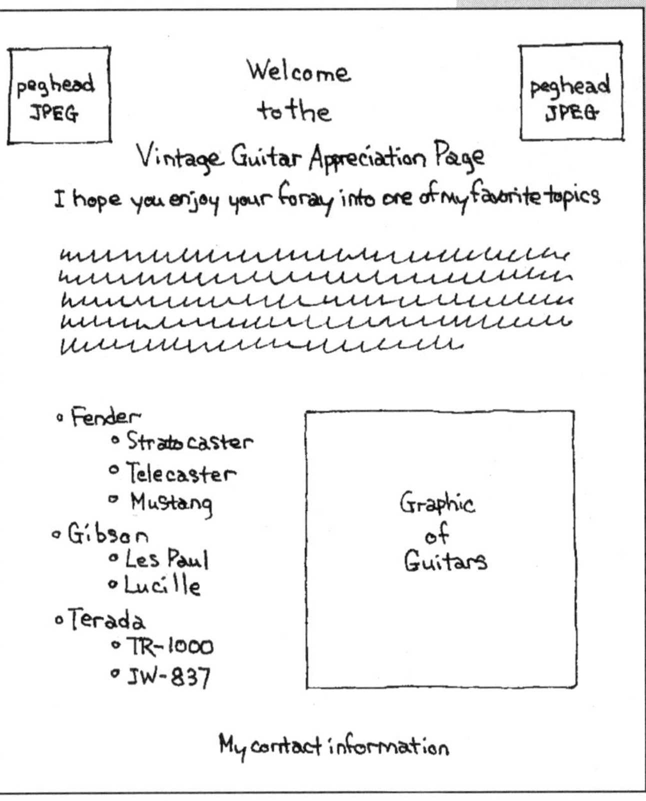

Figure 3.8 This was my second attempt at designing the Welcome page.

At the top of the page is a banner that reads "Welcome" and beneath that the words "to the" appear on another, smaller banner. On either side of those banners is a GIF of a guitar's inlaid peghead. Going down the page, you can see my tentative wording for the next banner, "Vintage Guitar Appreciation Page." The remainder of the page is the same as the preceding design.

Figure 3.9 shows yet another variation. After finishing the sketch shown in Figure 3.8, I decided that I didn't like the look of the two words "to the" between the two graphics. Instead, I decided just to put three identical JPEGs of the peghead across the top. I compensated for the loss of the words "to the" by adding "The" to the title, so that it's "The Vintage Guitar Appreciation Page."

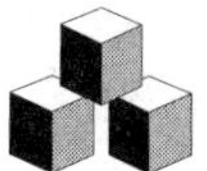

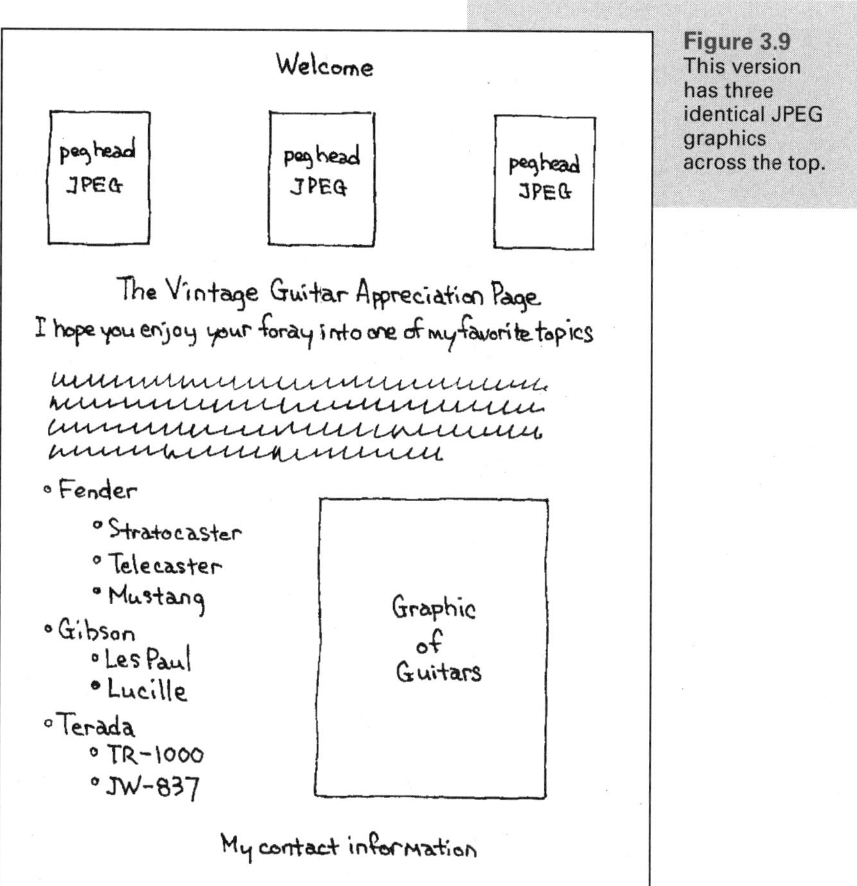

Figure 3.9 This version has three identical JPEG graphics across the top.

After giving it some more thought, I decided to use two peghead graphics instead of three, and to move the Welcome graphic down so that it resides between the two peghead graphics. I also decided to place the other banner ("The Vintage Guitar Appreciation Page") immediately below the Welcome banner—both are centered. Below the rearranged graphics that you can see at the top of Figure 3.10, the page is the same as the one shown in Figure 3.9.

I gave the page even *more* thought, and decided to add some more text to this page, below the bulleted list of links and the graphic that I originally had intended to place at the bottom of the page. The first section

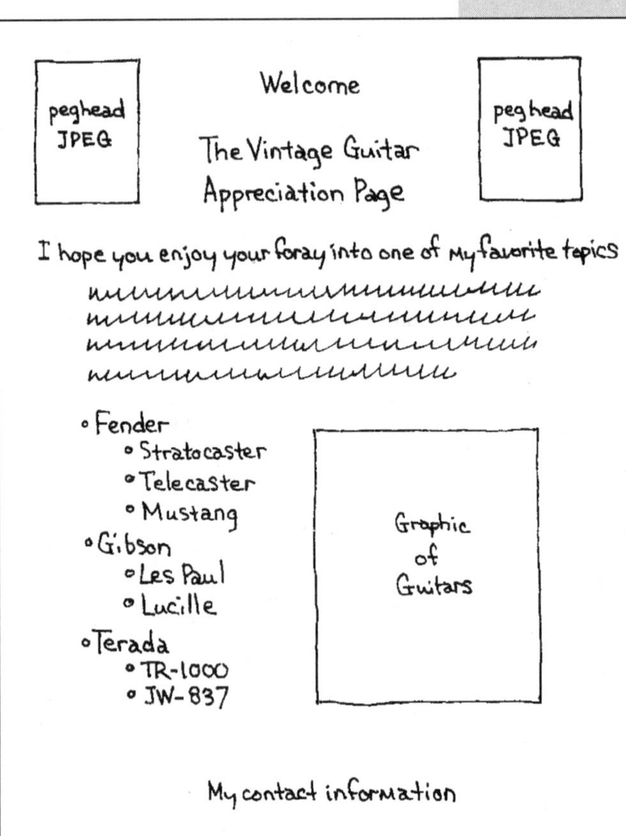

Figure 3.10 With this version I had finalized everything at the top of the page, but something was still missing at the bottom.

of added text is a list of tips for people who are interested in buying or collecting guitars. The second section of added text discusses judging the quality of used guitars. Including those two sections resulted in the final design that you saw earlier in the chapter (refer to Figure 3.5).

As you can see, completing the nitty-gritty details of my design took some effort and experimentation. As you begin designing Web sites on your own, don't be surprised when you find yourself constantly tweaking things and trying various approaches before you finally make up your mind.

Designing the Individual Guitar Pages

Three pages remain in this Web site, so it's time to continue designing. Begin laying out the remaining pages by starting with the Fender page.

The Fender page contains the following elements:

- One large graphic of four guitars
- One banner: "Fender"
- Three headings, each naming a specific guitar model
- One introductory paragraph
- Two paragraphs of text about each guitar model
- A list of links to locations within the Web site as well as to company Web sites
- Three photographs (one of each guitar model)

Again, feel free to design the page however you want, using the preceding elements on the page in any arrangement that suits your taste. Don't forget to refresh your memory of the design rules, however, and refer to them whenever necessary.

EXERCISE

1. Where do you want to begin this page? Which of the preceding elements is a logical element to place at the top of the page? How do you align it?

   As you might have surmised from my design of the Welcome page, I want to start the top of the Fender page with the banner. In this case, the banner reads "Fender." That simple banner immediately establishes the topic for this page of the Web site.

2. Do you want to place any other elements next to the one you've already decided should go at the top, in order to balance out the top or to fill in too much white space?

   This time, however, I don't want to place any graphics on either side of the banner. The reason is that the Fender banner doesn't take much vertical space, which means that the empty white space on each side of it isn't particularly large, unlike the white space on the Welcome page (before the two identical peghead graphics were added).

3. Take stock of the remaining elements. Which one looks good as the next element?

   The next item on the page, I decide, should be the introductory paragraph. As with the Welcome page, I want to start off the Fender page with some text introducing viewers to the subject of the page.

   This page is about three different models of guitar made by Fender. For that reason, most of the remaining elements of the page are in threes: three photographs, three headings, and three sets of two-paragraph guitar descriptions. The bulk of this page will be taken up by the guitar descriptions.

4. Check the balance between text and graphics on your page. Are all the graphics clustered together in one spot? Do you have enough white space? What comes next?

   At this point, I am left with the guitar descriptions to put in my design. I decide to start with the Stratocaster, although your design may be different. I've chosen the Stratocaster because it's the best known of Fender's guitars. I insert the Stratocaster heading centered between the two margins. Immediately below it and to the left I insert the photograph of the Stratocaster.

   Rather than leave the photograph alone and aligned to the left under the heading, I think it makes more sense to include the descriptive text next to the photograph. Not placing the text next to the photograph would leave the page with an unbalanced appearance. To the right of the photograph would be a vast horizontal expanse of white space—something I don't want. Figure 3.11 shows a sketch of the top of the Fender page.

5. What's next for your layout? If you are now placing the guitars on the page, where do you want to place the photograph of the second guitar? Or maybe you're working with the links. Where would they look best?

   While designing this page, I've decided that the page would be out of balance if I put all the photographs on the left side of the page. Instead, I decide to create a sort of flowing, back-and-forth effect. The centered heading for each guitar forms a visual "bridge" between the photos.

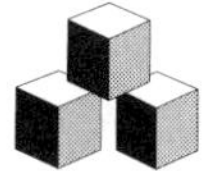

Figure 3.11 The layout of the top of the Fender page.

Now I'm ready to place the description of the second guitar, the Telecaster, on the page. This time, however, I want to vary the placement of elements a bit. The Telecaster heading, like the Stratocaster heading, is centered horizontally. The difference in layout comes in the location of the photograph: flush right instead of flush left. The accompanying text fills in the white space to the left of the photograph.

6. Are you placing the third guitar description now, as I am? Where do you want to place the photograph? Check your current layout against the rules of design. Do you need to make any changes?

   I set up the Mustang description just like the Stratocaster description. I put the photograph on the left and the accompanying text on the right. The centered heading above the photographs, in my opinion, indeed creates a bridge between them. Still, the page is not quite finished.

7. What elements do you have left to place on the page? Are you sure you haven't left out something that would make more sense higher up on the page?

   For me, the vertical list of links comes next. It's common to find links along the top or side of a Web page, but I place them at the bottom of the guitar pages in this Web site because putting them at the top or on the side essentially requires the use of frames. As a basic Web site, this project has no frames, so that pretty much

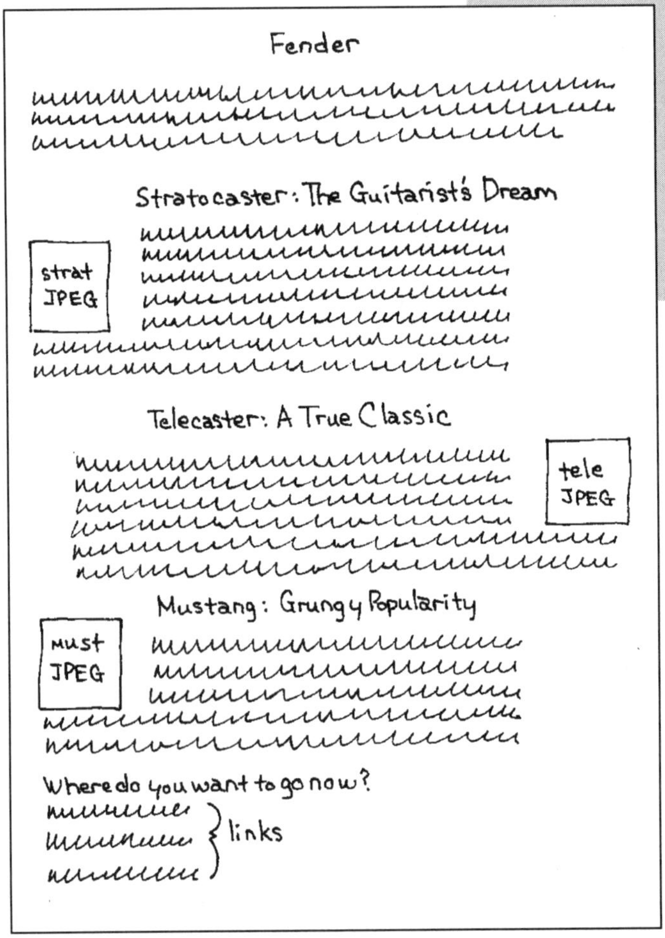

Figure 3.12 The design of the Fender page at this point includes all three guitar descriptions, plus links to the other pages on the site.

assigns them to the bottom of the page. Figure 3.12 shows the Fender page as it currently stands.

The same problem arises here, however, that arose in the Welcome page—the existence of a large amount of white space beside the list of links. I use the same solution here that I used in the Welcome page: the same large graphic of four guitars. Not only does the graphic fill that white space, but it also provides some continuity between the two pages of the Web site.

8. Review the sketch of your design idea with the design rules in mind. Did you manage to avoid having too much (or too little)

white space? Where did you place the photographs? All along the left or right? Or down the middle of the page? Did you left-align the headings? Whatever you did, you may decide that your design is better than mine. Take a moment to sketch out a third design, neither mine nor your first one, but one that's entirely different. Maybe you'll find something that's even better in your eyes.

The Gibson and Terada pages are laid out exactly the same as the Fender page. The only difference is that each of those contains only two guitar descriptions, not three. Because of their mostly-identical design, I will not describe their layout here.

At this point, you might want to pull up and review the gibson.html and terada.html pages that were included on the CD accompanying this book, just to see how these pages look with two guitar descriptions instead of three, and with descriptions of different lengths than those on the Fender page.

ANALYSIS

As I did for the Welcome page earlier in this chapter, I've explained my thinking while walking through the design process for the first guitar page. If your design varies from my mine, as it probably does, that's not a problem. For this and any other Web site you design, just be sure to check your work against the design rules. Following those rules goes a long way toward helping you design an attractive site.

Don't make each page of your Web site completely different in design from all the others on your site. Your visitors may think they have followed a link to some other Web site. That's the reason for the same design for each of the three manufacturer-specific pages. In addition, as you'll learn while building the project, each page has the same background, which further solidifies the impression of their common origin. This similarity in design lets viewers know—maybe even subconsciously—that they are still visiting the same Web site and haven't been shipped off elsewhere.

The preceding sections illustrate the process of sketching out a Web site. Of course, the given example is only one of countless ways this (or any other) Web site can be designed. You may not care for the design just described. For that matter, if I put it on the Web, *I* may not care for it in three months. What this example does is show one way to deal with the placement of images and text in relation to each other.

The design you come up with for your Web site is not permanent, for you can change it anytime you want. For a simple personal Web site like the one in this first project, making changes is a simple matter. This project doesn't employ tables, forms, style sheets, and other advanced techniques, so changes aren't very involved. As you work on your design, remember to try various approaches until you find the one you like best.

Summary

This chapter has covered many aspects of Web sites, some of which are often overlooked. The central point of this chapter is that a Web site, even a simple one, requires planning. After you have decided what you want to place on your Web site, it's time to decide how you want it to look. This chapter has dealt with the process of designing the site by sketching out various possibilities.

Sketching out your site's design involves where you place graphics, as well as what kind of graphics they are, GIFs or JPEGs. You have learned to be judicious in the use of graphics on your Web site. They take time to download, and they also use up space on your site's host server. You don't have to leave graphics out altogether, but their use requires planning to achieve maximum effect with minimum download time.

How you distribute the graphics within and around the text is one of the determining factors involved in your site's aesthetic appeal. Other very important factors are the amount of white space, fonts and font sizes, character formatting (italic, bold, and so on), the length of paragraphs, and avoiding newspaper-style columns.

This chapter discussed the layout used for Project 1. An unlimited number of layouts could be possible, but the instructions provided in the following chapters for building Project 1 will lead to the particular layout that has been described in this chapter.

Beginning to Build the Basic Web Site

The preceding chapters laid the groundwork for this chapter by discussing a number of points, including the type of Web site this first project is (a personal Web site), how to decide what to place on a Web site, how to present the desired information most effectively via good writing, how to design an attractive Web site, and numerous other points. Beginning with this chapter, you learn the details of how to use the majority of HTML tags, as well as many of their attributes and values.

This chapter explores a variety of text formatting techniques, as well as ways to introduce colors into the Web site and divide up your text so that navigating the site is an aesthetically pleasing experience for visitors. This chapter also gives you a chance to work with different types of lists, which are among the most common organizational tools for the contents of Web pages.

Laying the Groundwork for Text

The first step in beginning an HTML document is to open the text editor you plan to use. Recall that the projects in this book are not based on using HTML-generating editors such as FrontPage and HoTMetaL. You will actually be writing the HTML on your own in any simple text editor. If, at some point, you decide to use an HTML editor, you can refer to Appendix B for a brief overview of a number of HTML editors.

EXERCISE

1. Create a folder in which to place your HTML document. Name the folder `Webproject1`. As you create (or import) the various HTML files, place them all in the `Webproject1` folder. That makes everything easier.
2. Within the `Webproject1` folder, create a subfolder named `Images`. As you create your GIF and JPEG graphics, place them in this `Images` folder. Keeping HTML documents separate from graphics files helps maintain order and simplifies finding and working with files.

If you want to use Notepad as the text editor, just click the Start button on the Windows desktop and then choose Programs, Accessories, Notepad.

Most programs can work with numerous file formats, but default to their native file format in the Open dialog box. Microsoft Word, for example, defaults to a list of the `.doc` files, WordPerfect to a list of the `.wpd` files, and so on. To make sure that you are seeing all the files that contain HTML, select All Files (or HTML Files, if that's an option) in whatever text editor you use. Otherwise, you might not see the names of any `.html` files you've created.

Before starting to build your Project 1 HTML document, take a look at the following example of the order in which you use the fundamental tags in an HTML file:

```
<!DOCTYPE>
<HTML>
<HEAD>
    <TITLE>Your title here</TITLE>
    <META>
    <META>
</HEAD>
<BODY>
Your site's information goes here
</BODY>
</HTML>
```

That's the general structure of an HTML document, and it's really quite straightforward. The `<!DOCTYPE>` tag comes first, and then everything else is nested between the `<HTML>` and `</HTML>` tags. Also, information at the top of the document, such as the `<TITLE>` and `<META>` tags, should be nested within the `<HEAD>` and `</HEAD>` tags. Everything else should be nested between the `<BODY>` and `</BODY>` tags. Keep this structure in mind as you create Web sites.

Declaring the HTML Version

A document type declaration (DTD) is a means of directly indicating in your document what version and type of HTML you used.

You use the `<!DOCTYPE>` tag to indicate HTML version compatibility. This information is important because the version number is used to validate the tags in the HTML document. You can indicate the desired level of compatibility by making the following the *very first* tag in your HTML document:

```
<!DOCTYPE HTML PUBLIC "-//W3C//DTD HTML 4.0 Transitional//EN"
    "http://www.w3.org/TR/REC-html40/loose.dtd">
```

These are the parts of this tag:

`<!DOCTYPE>` is the tag itself.

`HTML` indicates to the browser what type of document this is—that is, an HTML document, not a word processor document or any other type.

`PUBLIC` is an identifier (the default one) used in conjunction with the URL to enable the user's browser to download the document type declaration and its entity sets (the available characters for the indicated version of HTML), if needed.

`HTML 4.0 Transitional` is the version of HTML in use (explained in more detail later in this section).

`EN` indicates that the document is in English.

The URL that finishes the tag indicates where specifications for this version of HTML are located.

The **World Wide Web Consortium,** *or* **W3C,** *is the organization that sets official HTML standards.*

New tags and attributes are proposed on an ongoing basis to the W3C, and the W3C then decides which ones to accept for the next official version of HTML. Many of the new tags and attributes come from extensions to HTML that Microsoft or Netscape has incorporated into their own product first.

Find it Online

You can find the World Wide Web Consortium at the following address:

http://www.w3.org/

The *document type,* discussed in more detail in later paragraphs, refers to the version and type of HTML used in the site. Version refers to HTML 3.2, 4.0, and so on, whereas type refers to whether it's a strict, loose, or frameset usage of that HTML version.

As part of the HTML 4.0 specification, the W3C says that HTML authors should indicate the version of HTML used when creating the page. The W3C recognizes three document type declarations of HTML 4.0:

http://www.w3.org/TR/REC-html40/strict.dtd

A **deprecated** *HTML element is on its way to obsolescence because a new element has replaced it. You can still use it, but it's not preferred.*

- HTML 4.0 Strict: As its name implies, HTML 4.0 Strict's interpretation of HTML code applies to only those elements and attributes that are in the current standard. In other words, this DTD doesn't include elements that have been deprecated or that

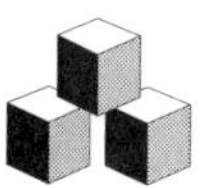

are unique to frameset HTML. For Web authors, the problem with this DTD is that many people have browsers that use proprietary tags. These people do not receive the benefit of the new standard; if you use HTML 4.0 Strict, it's certain that at least some users will have problems of some sort with your site. If the W3C had its way, though, everyone would use HTML 4.0 Strict.

http://www.w3.org/TR/REC-html40/loose.dtd

- HTML 4.0 Transitional: The W3C realizes that a vast number of browsers in use do not support HTML 4.0, which means that HTML authors cannot use the Strict DTD to its fullest capability if they want to reach the widest possible audience. In other words, whereas the latest browser versions are backward-compliant—that is, they can work with older versions of HTML—the Web site creator must be concerned with people who use older browser versions that can't handle HTML 4.0. That being the case, the W3C recognizes a second DTD. You use the Transitional DTD when you want the HTML document to be usable by browsers that are not compliant with HTML 4.0 standards. The Transitional designation indicates that the document contains elements from the HTML 4.0 Strict DTD, as well as deprecated elements (and attributes, of course) from earlier versions of HTML.

http://www.w3.org/TR/REC-html40/frameset.dtd

- HTML 4.0 Frameset: The Frameset DTD is for use on sites that use frames. In the simplest practical terms, the Frameset DTD is the same as the Transitional DTD, except that the `<FRAMESET>` tag replaces the `<BODY>` tag.

HTML 4.0 is the latest version of HTML, and if you want *anyone* to be able to view your site, your HTML should conform to HTML 4.0 Transitional.

You should be aware that Netscape and Microsoft sometimes create their own HTML tags for use with their own browsers (Navigator and IE, respectively). Those additional tags, which are not part of HTML 4.0, don't necessarily work in other browsers. Some Navigator and IE tags *will* make it into future versions of HTML, but they aren't there yet. If you use these tags, you run the risk that some browsers will not understand all aspects of your HTML document.

If you write an HTML document that uses only HTML 4.0 elements and attributes—in other words, HTML 4.0 Strict—you use the following declaration at the top of your HTML document:

```
<!DOCTYPE HTML PUBLIC "-//W3C//DTD HTML 4.0//EN"
"http://www.w3.org/TR/REC-html40/strict.dtd">
```

Note that the only differences between this DTD and the one given at the beginning of this section are the additional word `Transitional` in the first example and the substitution of `strict.dtd` in the URL in the second example for `loose.dtd` from the first example.

Note

The first page of a Web site usually is named `index.html`, `index.htm`, or `default.htm`, so that's the convention followed in this book's projects. By default, Web servers look for and serve up those pages in whatever specific folder is requested by an URL in a browser. Other files in a Web site usually have names that describe their contents, which makes it easier for the site creators to keep track of what's in each document. When you save any HTML file for your Web site, save it with the `.html` extension.

Returning to your text editor, begin creating the first Web page for Project 1 by typing the following as the DTD for the document:

```
<!DOCTYPE HTML PUBLIC "-//W3C//DTD HTML 4.0 Transitional//EN"
"http://www.w3.org/TR/REC-html40/loose.dtd">
```

Save the document with the name **index.html**.

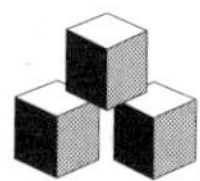

Web browsers don't care whether you put extra returns between the lines of HTML, indent the lines of HTML, or use uppercase letters when typing the tags and attributes. Doing those things does not affect the presentation of your page. Note, however, that those techniques greatly enhance the readability of your HTML.

I suggest you use an extra return between sections, such as between the <HEAD> section and the <BODY> section. In addition, indent lines of HTML to help yourself or someone else easily see relationships between lines. When you indent, you can use either the spacebar or the Tab key.

Additionally, the convention for typing tags and attributes is as follows: Use all uppercase letters when typing the tags and attributes, but lowercase when typing values for the attributes. This makes it easier to spot the tags and attributes.

Creating the Basic Structure of Your Document

After the <!DOCTYPE> tag, the first line you should put in an HTML document is the <HTML> tag. This tag tells a browser that it is dealing with an HTML document, and then the browser can open up your Web page in all its glory. In HTML 4.0, this tag (as well as the <HEAD> and <BODY> tags) is assumed (and therefore not required), but still should be included as a matter of good coding practice.

Before you can begin typing your content, you must type the most fundamental tag of all HTML documents. In your `index.html` document, type the following two lines below your <!DOCTYPE> tag:

```
<HTML>
</HTML>
```

Just so that you don't forget to finish what you started, always start an HTML document by typing *both* of these tags first. Then make sure that you place everything else between them.

Next, type the following two tags after the <HTML> tag:

```
<HEAD>
</HEAD>
```

Save the `index.html` file. Within the <HEAD> tag, you can indicate several pieces of information, as discussed in the following section.

Giving Your Document a Title

One of the most important things you can do within the <HEAD> tag is give your page a title. Giving your page a title is important for a few reasons. First, the <TITLE> tag is a required HTML tag. Second, most browsers display your page's title in the title bar so visitors can quickly see where they are. Third, and most important, search engines frequently give precedence to a site or page whose title also contains search keywords (explained more when the <META> tag is discussed in the next section). Accordingly, a carefully crafted <TITLE> tag can help you rank higher in search engine results. In addition, a search engine may display your title when it shows the results of a search. That helps potential viewers decide immediately whether your site is one they want to visit.

You nest the title within the <HEAD> section. Create a title for this first project by creating a new line after the <!DOCTYPE> tag, indenting, and then typing the following:

```
<TITLE>The Vintage Guitar Appreciation Page</TITLE>
```

Make the title as descriptive of the site's contents as you can.

Including Meta-Information

The <META> tag is a particularly useful element to nest within the <HEAD> section, because search engines look for the <META> tag to find out what your Web page contains. You use the NAME and CONTENT attributes with the <META> tag to put in keywords that describe your site's contents. This

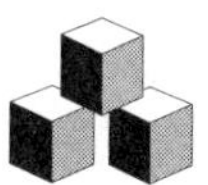

first project is about vintage guitars, so add the following <META> tag to your index.html file immediately after the </TITLE> end tag and before the </HEAD> end tag:

```
<META NAME="keywords" CONTENT="guitar, vintage guitar, guitar collecting,
Fender, Gibson, Terada, Stratocaster, Telecaster, Mustang, Les Paul, Lucille,
TR-1000, JW-837, Leo Fender, Orville Gibson">
```

When entering keywords for your site, consider both what the site contains and what terms other Web users might use to conduct their searches.

ANALYSIS

The site in Project 1 is about guitars, so I *could* simply use "guitars" as the keyword. Someone searching for information, however, may be searching for information about particular brands of guitars, so I added to the keyword list the names of the three guitar manufacturers that I'm including in this site. Other searchers may be looking for information about certain guitars, so I also added the names of the guitar models included in the site.

In trying to think like someone who might be conducting an Internet search for the kind of information I'm including in the site, I also considered guitar collectors. Therefore, I included "guitar collecting" and "vintage guitar" in the list of keywords. Finally, I included the names of the founders of two of the guitar manufacturers covered in the site.

These keywords, taken together, should enable the anticipated audience to find this Web site.

You can use the <META> tag in another way as well: to describe the contents of your Web site. Type the following as a second <META> tag, below the one you just typed and above the </HEAD> end tag:

```
<META NAME="description" CONTENT="A little vintage guitar history, some tips
on buying vintage guitars, and a few words about some of my favorite gui-
tars.">
```

ANALYSIS

Here I wanted to include a description of exactly what's in the Web site. I have no intention of creating an exhaustive history of any particular guitar or manufacturer. Rather, my idea is simply to give a few brief notes on the history of particular guitars. Most of them are old ("old" usually equals "collectible" in the guitar business), so I included the word "vintage" in the description as well. Another part of the site involves telling readers what they should know (or where to get the right information) before taking the plunge and buying used or vintage guitars.

As stated in an earlier chapter, many thousands of people collect (or want to collect) guitars, so I made mention here of the tips I'll be including on the Web site. Finally, I included the fact that at least a portion of the site is about my favorite guitars. Notice that in this description I used a couple of the keywords again ("vintage guitar" and "guitar").

As you can see, a `<META>` tag consists of three parts: the tag itself, the `NAME` attribute, and the `CONTENT` attribute. A search engine works by indexing a site, based on things such as the keywords, the title, the description, and so on. When someone performs a search, the search engine checks its index to locate all the relevant Web sites, so it's important that you make full use of the `<META>` tag. Usually, a search engine displays both the title of your document and the URL in the search results.

Besides listing your site's keywords and a description, you can use the `<META>` tag for other purposes, such as the following:

- Make another document load automatically after a preset amount of time.
- List the author of the document, or any other information you want, such as the date of creation.

Writing Notes

Programmers frequently write notes to themselves (or to future programmers) to explain what a given section of code does or, perhaps, how it works. These comments don't affect the operation of the program at all.

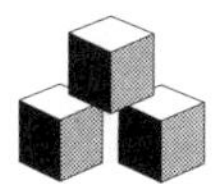

As a Web site builder, you have the same technique available to you. You may want to note that a certain section of HTML was written by someone else, for example, or that the JavaScript immediately following the comment causes a menu to expand. The tag used for commenting, <!– –>, surrounds the comment. This tag has no effect on the operation of the HTML, and neither the tag nor its contents will show up in the viewer's browser.

EXERCISE

Add a comment tag to the HTML by following these steps:

1. In your text editor, open the `index.html` document.
2. Place the insertion point at the far-right end of the <HTML> tag, and then press Enter.
3. On the new blank line, type the following HTML:

   ```
   <!– This Web site was created by hand by Greg Robertson –>
   ```

4. Save the document.

ANALYSIS

The comment tag is not required, but it can be very helpful. Every programmer should use comments in HTML code to document the work. Certain kinds of information can be very helpful when troubleshooting or revising code.

As you can see in Step 3, comments within your HTML take the following form:

```
<!– Descriptive text for the comment goes here –>
```

As you write HTML, remember to insert comments to help clarify what's going on. In the exercise above, the comment merely stated who created the Web site and that it was done by hand rather than with Web page software.

At this point, the <HEAD> tag is finished, and the `index.html` document should look like the following (although yours may be indented differently):

```
<!DOCTYPE HTML PUBLIC "-//W3C//DTD HTML 4.0 Transitional//EN"
"http://www.w3.org/TR/REC-html40/loose.dtd">
<HTML>
<!– This Web site was created by hand by Greg Robertson –>
```

```
<HEAD>
<TITLE>The Vintage Guitar Appreciation Page</TITLE>
<META NAME="keywords" CONTENT="guitar, vintage guitar, guitar collecting,
Fender, Gibson, Terada, Stratocaster, Telecaster, Mustang, Les Paul, Lucille,
TR-1000, JW-837, Leo Fender, Orville Gibson">
<META NAME="description" CONTENT="A little vintage guitar history, some tips
on buying vintage guitars, and a few words about some of my favorite gui-
tars.">
</HEAD>

</HTML>
```

To see how your Web page looks, you can open the `index.html` file in your browser. Follow the appropriate instructions below.

For Internet Explorer 3.0 and 4.0, follow these steps:

1. Start IE (if it isn't already open).
2. If you are just starting the browser, IE may ask for your password. Providing your password will cause you to log onto the Internet, so you may want to click on the Work Offline button. This opens your browser but doesn't log you onto the Internet.

   In IE 3.0, the Connection dialog box may open. If so, click on the Cancel button. In IE 3.0, another dialog box alerts you that it cannot find the file. Click on the OK button. This action brings up the browser, but no Web page.
3. Choose File, Open, Browse.
4. Navigate to the folder that contains `index.html`.
5. Double-click the `index.html` file.
6. Click on the OK button, and the Web page opens.

For Netscape Navigator 4.0 (part of Netscape Communicator), follow these steps:

1. Start Navigator 4.0.
2. If the Connection dialog box opens, click on the Cancel button.
3. Another dialog box alerts you that it cannot find the server. Click on the OK button. This action brings up the browser, but no Web page.
4. Choose File, Open Page, Choose File.

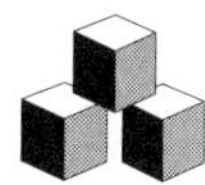

5. Navigate to the folder that contains `index.html`.
6. Double-click the `index.html` file.
7. Click on the Open button, and the Web page opens.

For Netscape Navigator 3.0, follow these steps:

1. Start Navigator 3.0.
2. If the Connection dialog box opens, click on the Cancel button.
3. Another dialog box alerts you that it cannot find the server. Click on the OK button. This action brings up the browser, but no Web page.
4. Choose File, Open File in Browser.
5. Navigate to the folder that contains `index.html`.
6. Double-click the `index.html` file, and the Web page opens.

Figure 4.1 shows you what this personal Web site looks like onscreen so far—unimpressive! All that's visible at this point is the title of the home page in the Web browser's title bar.

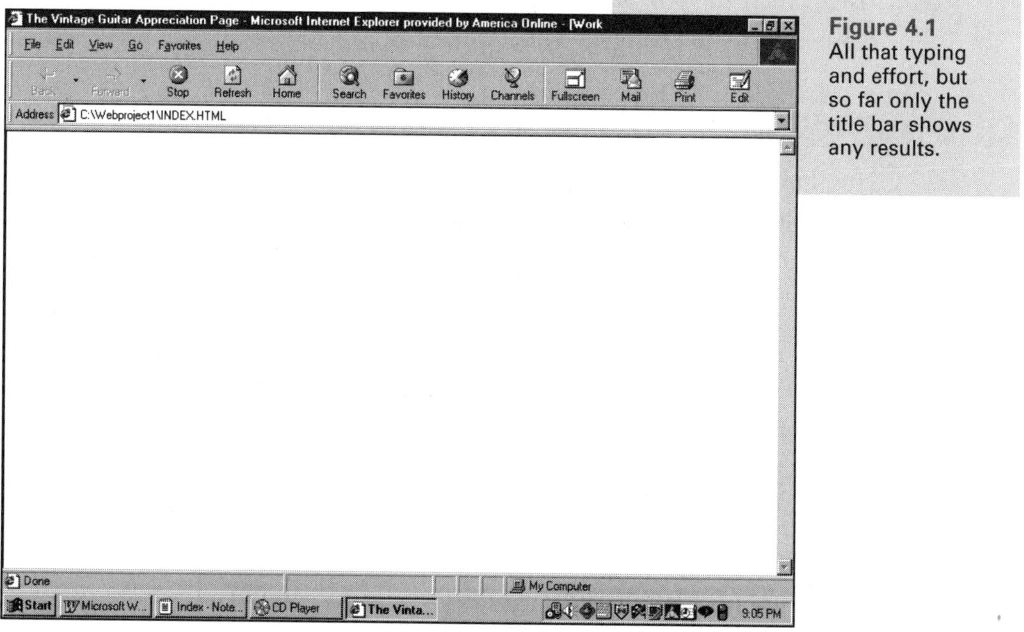

Figure 4.1
All that typing and effort, but so far only the title bar shows any results.

Beginning the Body of Your Web Site

The <BODY> tag is the heart of an HTML document, because its contents are what make a Web page useful. You place all the contents of your Web page between the <BODY> and </BODY> tags.

In the index.html document, type the following two tags below the </HEAD> tag and above the </HTML> tag:

```
<BODY>
</BODY>
```

By typing the end tag at the same time as the start tag, you avoid forgetting to do it later. In addition, it is easier to avoid the problem of overlapping tags if you are automatically nesting them. Just remember to place the remaining tags of your document body between the <BODY> and </BODY> tags. Save the index.html document.

The <BODY> tag has a number of attributes: BGCOLOR, BACKGROUND, TEXT, LINK, ALINK, and VLINK. The following sections discuss each of them.

As you saw in Figure 4.1, the current state of the index.html document isn't much to look at. Using the <BODY> tag's attributes, you can make some dramatic changes to the appearance of the document.

Choosing a Color for Project 1

In choosing a color scheme for this project, I decided I wanted to use a dark background in conjunction with light text. After experimenting with a number of background colors, I decided simply to go with black. In my opinion, black has a classic look. In addition, most colors can go with black—although not necessarily with each other. In short, it should not be too difficult to find colors that look good against a black background.

Assigning the background color for this project is easy. All you have to do is add the BGCOLOR attribute to the <BODY> tag and give it a value. Of course, the default color of text, black, doesn't show up on a black background, so it's necessary to create text that is in a contrasting color. You use the TEXT attribute for that purpose. (At this point, however, no text exists on the Web site.)

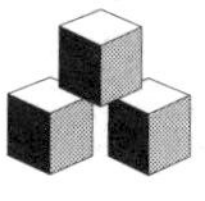

EXERCISE

1. Switch to the `index.html` file in your text editor.
2. Place the insertion point *within* the `<BODY>` tag, between the `Y` and the `>`.
3. Change the `<BODY>` tag to the following:

```
<BODY BGCOLOR="black" TEXT="white">
```

4. Save the `index.html` document.
5. Switch to your browser and refresh the screen. Figure 4.2 shows the new look of the Web page.

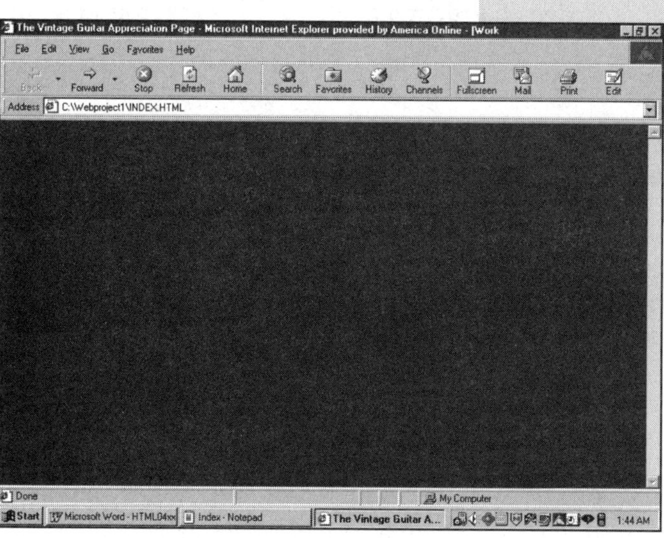

Figure 4.2 A black background drastically changes the look of the Web site.

ANALYSIS

In Step 3, you altered the `<BODY>` tag, because that's where you set colors for a couple of page elements, the background color and the text color. The `BGCOLOR` attribute is short for "background color," and `"black"` is the value you gave to this attribute. In Step 3, you also set a new text color to overcome the problem caused by the default text color being black. You gave the value `"white"` to the `TEXT` attribute. You alternatively can assign colors by using hexadecimal values, as discussed in the section "Coloring with RGB" later in this chapter.

If you don't like my choice of colors, of course, you're welcome to play around with the color values. The GIF graphics for this project are "transparent," so they can work with any color of background.

Using a Background Image

Another possibility for adding color is to use a background image of some sort. Such an image may have a textured look, such as sandstone or marble, or it may be more of a geometric design, such as a stripe of one color along one edge and the remainder of the background a different color.

If you decide to go with a multiple-color type of background design—or any other design that includes a background that is partially dark—be careful. I don't know how many times I've seen backgrounds in which part of the black text is lying on top of a black or dark blue design element in the background. When that happens, the text in that area is unreadable.

***Tiling** is the repetition of a background image until it fills the whole screen.*

Background images are not difficult to come by. You can find free backgrounds on the Web, for example, or you can buy commercial or shareware products that include backgrounds. If you are of a creative bent, you can use a graphics program to create your *own* background.

A background image usually is fairly small. When the browser loads it, it tiles the image. A potential problem that is easy to overlook at first, especially when you create your own background image, is that of creating an image that doesn't tile very well.

Some people try to avoid tiling problems by using a very large background image. Suppose that you have a background with a wide black stripe running down the left edge of the screen, but you've been careful to make sure that your dark text is to the right of the stripe. Everything looks great on your monitor. You have to remember, however, that a

Caution

When creating a background image, you need to make sure that adjacent images blend into each other well. If your image has diagonal stripes, for example, but they don't line up with each other correctly, the stripes in one image won't line up with the stripes in the surrounding images. When that happens, it's easy to see each individual tiled image. If the image is light enough, the result may not be ugly, but certainly it will be distracting. If, however, you create an image that looks like a close-up of sandstone, it probably will be satisfactory, because its pattern is random and people's eyes won't notice discrepancies where tiles meet.

higher resolution monitor that displays more pixels in a horizontal direction may tile even a larger image. The result is that someone with a large monitor still might end up with black text on top of your black stripe. In addition to this potential problem, a large image also is a larger file, and takes longer to download.

ON THE

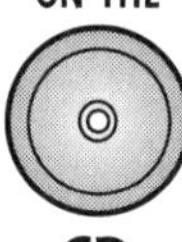

CD

I have included a background image for you to use if you want to experiment. You can find it on the CD that accompanies this book, as `Webproject1/Images/sunback.gif`. The final version of this Web page does not use it, however, because I think a solid black background looks better than a background image once the graphics are applied later in the project.

EXERCISE

The tag for using a background image is simple. Follow these steps to try it out:

1. Switch to your browser and open the `index.html` file.
2. In the `<BODY>` tag, delete the `BGCOLOR="black"` portion.
3. In place of the deleted attribute, type the following attribute:

```
BACKGROUND="Images/sunback.gif"
```

The preceding assumes that you have kept the desired background image in the `Images` subfolder within the `Webproject1` folder, and that your HTML document is in the `Webproject1` folder.

4. Save the `index.html` file.
5. Switch to your browser and refresh the screen. Figure 4.3 shows what you should see.

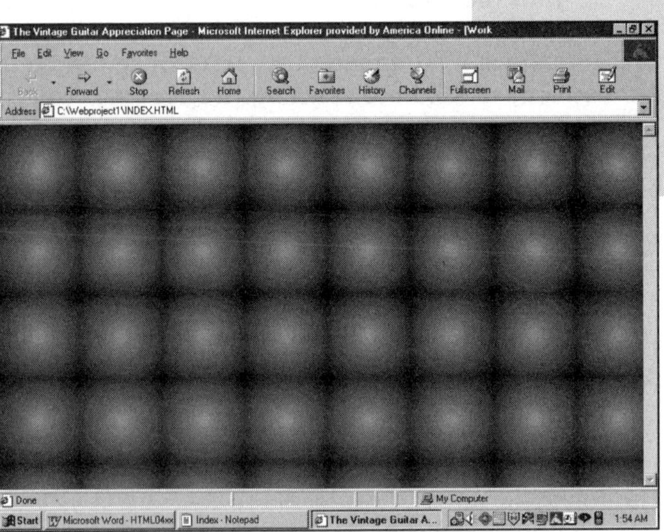

Figure 4.3 A tiled background appears instead of a solid color.

ANALYSIS

In Step 2, you deleted the `BGCOLOR` attribute. In Step 3, you replaced the solid background color with a tiled image. You used the `BACKGROUND` attribute and designated the GIF file you wanted as the background image. The trick is what is placed between the quotation marks to specify the value of the attribute. Assuming you kept the same files in the same folders when you placed them on your computer, here is the way the folder structure is set up:

```
\Webproject1\Images
```

The HTML files are in the `Webproject1` folder, and all the images are in the `Images` subfolder.

When you use a background image (or any graphic, for that matter), you have to tell the browser where to find the image. Here, the HTML files and the `Images` subfolder were both within the `Webproject1` folder. Because they had the `Webproject1` folder in common, you didn't need to list that folder in the path to the image file. Instead, you used a

partial path. You simply started the path with the name of the subfolder that contains the images (`Images`) and then inserted a slash, followed by the name of the image file (`sunback.gif`):

```
Images/sunback.gif
```

When you have finished experimenting with the background image, please return to `index.html` and change `BACKGROUND="sunback.gif"` to `BGCOLOR="black"`. That sets up the Web site for the remainder of the building tasks you'll be undertaking.

Designating Link Colors

One other set of attributes for the `<BODY>` tag is relevant to beginning the body of the Project 1 Web site. You use these attributes to set the colors of text links. Links have three possible states: the unactivated link, the already-visited link, and the activated link. An unactivated link is one that leads to an item you have not yet visited (these links usually are blue). An already-visited link is one that you have clicked on. An activated link is one that you have clicked on, but you haven't released the mouse button yet.

You assign colors in HTML by one of two methods. The easy—but far more limited—method uses plain English. HTML understands sixteen color words:

black	blue	green	red
gray	navy	olive	purple
silver	teal	lime	fuchsia
white	aqua	yellow	maroon

The fact that HTML recognizes these sixteen colors doesn't mean that all of them are appropriate as background colors, or that they look good together! Some of the gaudiest possible color combinations can be created using that list. Use your common sense and aesthetic sensibility when choosing combinations to use on your Web site.

The second method of assigning colors in HTML uses hexadecimal (hex) codes; this method is vastly more flexible, but takes more effort to understand. An explanation of hex color codes appears later in this chapter.

EXERCISE

Unactivated hyperlinks typically are blue on the Web by default, but you can choose whatever color you want. Follow these steps to create a set of colors for the links in Project 1:

1. Start your text editor, and open `index.html`.
2. Place the insertion point just before the closing bracket in this `<BODY>` tag that appears near the top of the file:

```
<BODY BGCOLOR="black" TEXT="white">
```

3. To this `<BODY>` tag add some other attributes so that the tag looks like the following:

```
<BODY BGCOLOR="black" TEXT="white" LINK="yellow" VLINK="red"
ALINK="lime">
```

4. Save the `index.html` file.

> **Note**
>
> **The colors you applied in the preceding steps will have no effect on the page in your browser yet. That's because you still don't have any text or links. You're still laying the groundwork for text.**

 ANALYSIS

When choosing settings for the hyperlink colors, consider the background color. In the case of the Project 1 Web site, the black background eliminates dark colors from consideration, because there would not be enough contrast to make the links easy to read. In Step 3, you set the three link colors. The color for the unactivated links (`LINK`) is yellow, which provides good contrast with the black background and goes with the yellow-orange-red color scheme. The color for visited links (`VLINK`) is red. The contrast with the black isn't quite as good as yellow, but red is visible and also goes with the color scheme of the Web site.

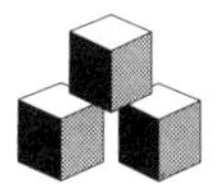

Finally, the color of active links (ALINK) is lime. This color does *not* fit the color scheme, but *does* provide good contrast. I'm not particularly concerned about it not matching the color scheme, because this color is visible only as long as the mouse button is pressed. After the viewer releases the mouse button, the link becomes red.

Working with Text

The phrase "working with text" refers generally to a number of things, such as creating paragraphs, inserting headings, and formatting particular text in special ways (aligning, italicizing, boldfacing, underlining, and so on). How you arrange text and graphics on the page is also of concern in this section.

Creating Paragraphs

One of the first things to remember when beginning your site's text is that you always start a paragraph of text with the paragraph tag, `<P>`. The second thing to remember is that although you don't *have* to use the end tag `</P>`, good coding practice dictates that you do; using both of the tags ensures that your paragraph is rendered correctly in all browsers.

EXERCISE

1. In the `index.html` file you already have created, type the following HTML just below the `<BODY>` tag:

```
<P>I am neither a vintage guitar dealer nor a professional musician.
My 25 years of guitar playing have lifted me to the lofty status of
mediocre amateur. Still, my lack of natural talent doesn't diminish
my enjoyment of the music these instruments can make in the hands of
even a modestly talented player. On the other hand, it also means
that I would have difficulty trying to justify owning more than a
couple of these instruments. Someday, however – when I'm rolling in
the dough – I plan to purchase a few more guitars. Maybe by then my
practicing will have overcome my lack of talent. This Web site,
then, is dedicated to some of the many instruments that I hope to
own – and play – one day.</P>
```

2. Save the `index.html` document.

You easily can switch among open programs in Windows by pressing Alt+Tab. When I tell you to press Alt+Tab, as I do in the next step, all you do is press and hold down the Alt key on your keyboard and then press the Tab key as many times as necessary to locate the desired program. After you locate the program, release the Alt key, and the program will open.

3. Switch to your Web browser by pressing Alt+Tab until the browser appears onscreen.
4. Click on your browser's Refresh button. (This button sometimes has the name Reload.) You can find this button or menu command as follows:
   - For Internet Explorer versions 3 and 4, you can use the Refresh button on the toolbar, or you can choose Refresh from the View menu. You also can press the F5 key or Ctrl+R.
   - For Netscape Navigator versions 3 and 4, you can click on the Reload button or choose Reload from the View menu. You also can press Ctrl+R.
   - If you use Opera version 2, you can click on the Reload button or choose Reload from the Navigation menu. You also can press the F5 key.
   - If you use a browser not listed here, you still shouldn't have much trouble locating the correct button or menu command. Look for Reload or Refresh, and if you see both, use Reload.

   Figure 4.4 shows the results in Internet Explorer 4.0.

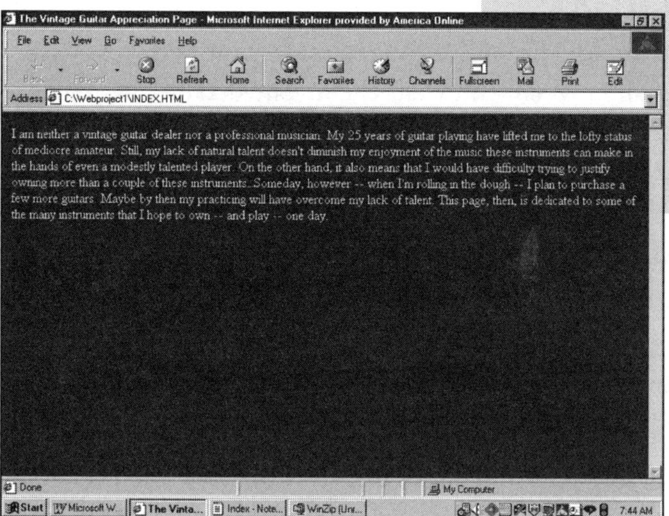

Figure 4.4 Finally! Something worth seeing appears in your Web browser.

ANALYSIS

This exercise illustrated all the basics involved in viewing your HTML in a browser. The primary action took place in Step 1, where you added the first `<P>` tag and then gave the Web page some content. (Note the `</P>` tag at the end of the paragraph of body text.) In Step 2, you saved the document, and in the next step, you pressed Alt+Tab to switch between open programs. In Step 4, you reloaded (or refreshed) your browser screen to update it with the changes you made to the HTML document, `index.html`.

Inserting Line Breaks

You probably will find it helpful, or even necessary, to break a line of text now and then. If you simply press Enter where you want the line break to occur, a line break appears in your HTML file, but nothing will appear different in the browser. That's because the browser does not recognize blank space between lines in HTML. If you use the `<P>` tag for the next line, you start a new paragraph, and you *do* end up with a blank line between them in your browser. If you don't want a blank space between lines—when typing song lyrics or a poem, for example, in which lines are usually short—then you need a different tag, the `<BR>` tag.

Aligning Text

You can use the <ALIGN> tag to make your body text paragraphs or headings align where you want them. The default alignment is the left margin, but it's simple enough to center the text or align it to the right margin.

Justifying Text

***Justified** text is text that extends from margin to margin on every line.*

With justified text, neither the left nor the right side of the paragraph is ragged; each side is nice and even. The extra space on a line is divided between the words, so that (usually) no big gaps are apparent. Justified text normally has a very neat appearance.

Justifying text sometimes can help improve the overall appearance of a document. Unfortunately, you cannot accomplish that goal for all browsers. In fact, only the latest versions of Navigator and IE support it. Version 3 of each does not. If a visitor to your site uses a browser that doesn't support justified text, he or she simply sees a normal, left-justified paragraph.

Note

Rather than repeat entire paragraphs when I'm telling you where to do something in the HTML document, I'll sometimes abbreviate the text by using an ellipsis (. . .).

EXERCISE

1. Switch to your text editor and open the `index.html` document.
2. Place the insertion point after the `P` in the `<P>` tag at the beginning of the paragraph that says:

   ```
   <P>I am neither a vintage guitar dealer . . . </P>
   ```

3. Press the spacebar once, and then type the following:

   ```
   ALIGN="justify"
   ```

4. Save the file.
5. Press Alt+Tab to switch to your browser again. Refresh the page, and you should see a screen that looks similar to Figure 4.5.

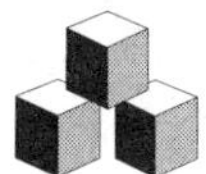

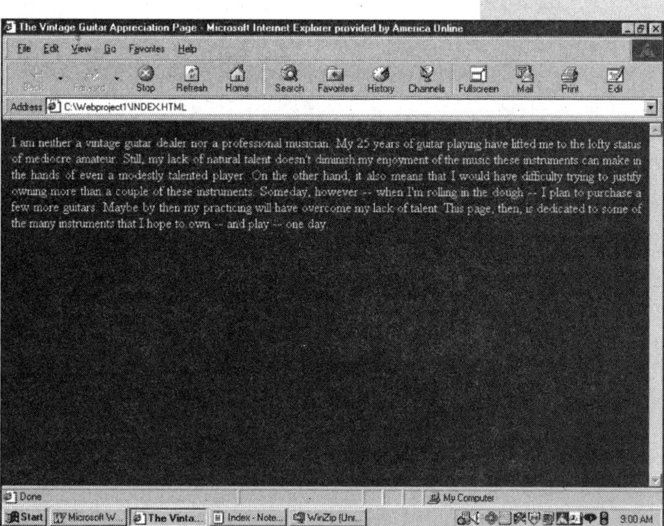

Figure 4.5 The first paragraph of text is now justified.

Note

The `justify` attribute value affects only one paragraph. If you want to justify the next paragraph of your page, insert `ALIGN="justify"` in the next `<P>` tag.

Of course, `justify` isn't the only value available for the `ALIGN` attribute. You can use the `left`, `right`, and `center` values in exactly the same way. Left alignment is the default, aligning the paragraph to the left margin and yielding a ragged right side. Right alignment aligns the paragraph to the right margin and results in a ragged left side of the paragraph. Center alignment centers each individual line of a paragraph, giving your paragraph ragged left *and* right edges.

Indenting Both Sides of a Paragraph

One more thing you can do with the paragraph of justified text is set it off from the rest of the text that you add to the page. I think this is a good idea for this paragraph, because it's the introduction to the Web site, and I want to make it a little different. One way of doing that is to indent the paragraph on both sides. That way, it stands out from the rest of the page. The solution is to use another paragraph formatting tag. That tag, `<BLOCKQUOTE>`, actually is intended to set off long quotations, just as you have seen in books, but I'm using it here to emphasize the first paragraph on the page.

EXERCISE

1. Switch back to your text editor and, if it's not already open, open the `index.html` file.
2. Place the insertion point in front of the `<P>` tag.
3. Press Enter to create a blank line above the existing paragraph of text. With the insertion point on that blank line, type the following tag:

   ```
   <BLOCKQUOTE>
   ```

4. Now place the insertion point after the `</P>` tag, and press Enter to create a blank line.
5. Type the following end tag:

   ```
   </BLOCKQUOTE>
   ```

6. Save the `index.html` document.
7. Switch to your browser, and then refresh the screen. Figure 4.6 shows the new appearance of the paragraph.

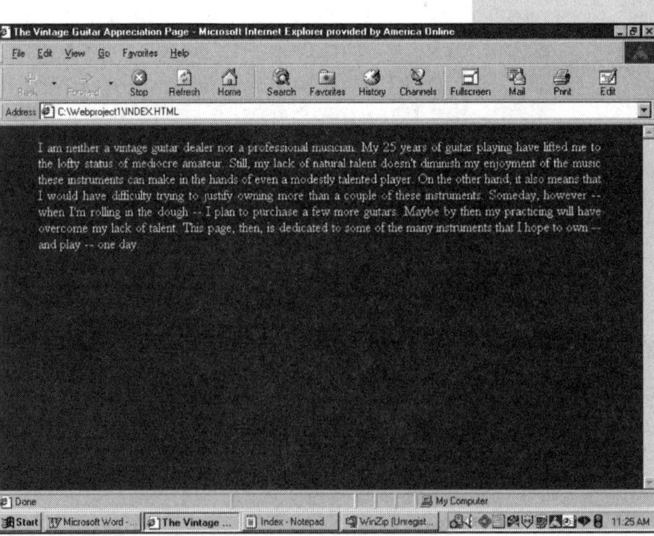

Figure 4.6 The justified and indented paragraph will look noticeably different from normal text.

ANALYSIS

By adding the <BLOCKQUOTE> tag before the <P> tag and the </BLOCKQUOTE> tag after the </P> tag, in Steps 3 and 5 respectively, you nested the two sets of tags. The tags therefore affect the paragraph, and I think the result looks more attractive than the original attempt. The indents on both sides of the paragraph leave more space between the paragraph and the margins. All in all, it's a big improvement.

Formatting Text

HTML enables you to do a number of things with the text of your Web site. You can change the size of the font used as normal text, add emphasis of various kinds, change the font size of individual words, and use a monospace font where necessary, among other things.

Changing Font Size

Font sizes are designated relative to each other, and range from 1 (smallest) to 7 (largest). The standard font size in HTML is 3, so if you don't do anything to change this, all your normal paragraph text is at size 3.

Headings, which are not governed by the <FONT> tag and its SIZE attribute, vary in size according to the heading level you use (this will be explained in detail later).

EXERCISE

This is a fine time to experiment with the <FONT> tag and its SIZE attribute. You should create a new HTML file for this specific purpose. That way, you'll avoid accidentally modifying the Project 1 HTML file that you are creating. In your text editor, open a new file and type the following HTML:

```
<P><FONT SIZE="1">This text is size 1.</FONT></P>
<P><FONT SIZE="2">This text is size 2.</FONT></P>
<P><FONT SIZE="3">This text is size 3.</FONT></P>
<P><FONT SIZE="4">This text is size 4.</FONT></P>
<P><FONT SIZE="5">This text is size 5.</FONT></P>
<P><FONT SIZE="6">This text is size 6.</FONT></P>
<P><FONT SIZE="7">This text is size 7.</FONT></P>
```

Save the file as `testing.html`. Use this document to play around to your satisfaction. Figure 4.7 illustrates the available font sizes displayed in IE.

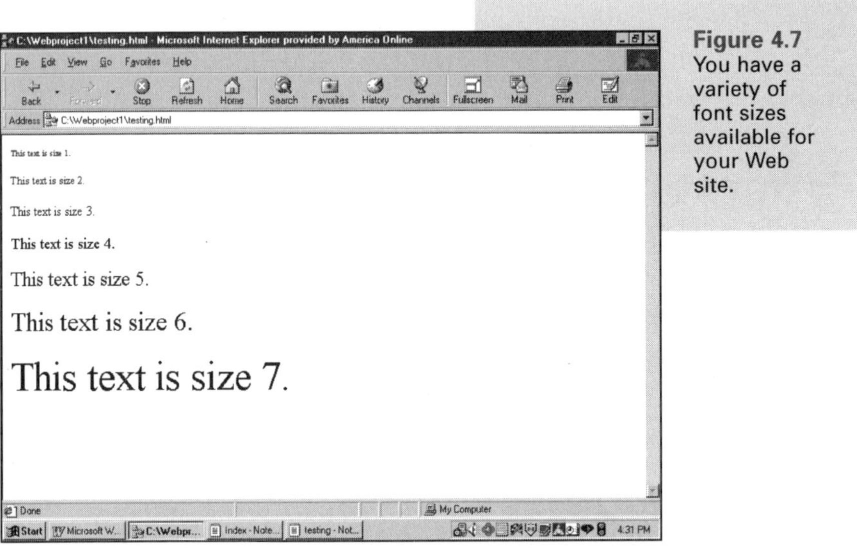

Figure 4.7 You have a variety of font sizes available for your Web site.

The Project 1 Web site uses the standard font size of 3, but as Figure 4.7 shows, you can experiment to find exactly the font size you need. You can apply the `<FONT>` tag to entire paragraphs, sentences, individual words, or even one letter.

You don't have to specify font sizes by number. Instead, you can use *relative font sizes.* With relative font sizes, you indicate that you want to make a given selection of text larger or smaller by using a + (plus) or – (minus) sign along with a number that tells *how much* smaller or larger you want it to be.

Here's an example. If your Web site uses the default font size of 3 for normal text, you can enlarge text to size 4 by indicating the relative size of the text. In your text editor, open the `testing.html` file, and then type the following between the `This text is size 4` and `This text is size 5` lines:

```
<P><FONT SIZE="+1">With the default font size of 3, the value
of "+1" is the same as size 4.</FONT></P>
```

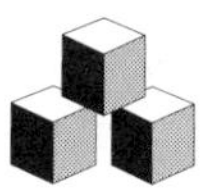

Figure 4.8 shows that both methods result practically in the same size font.

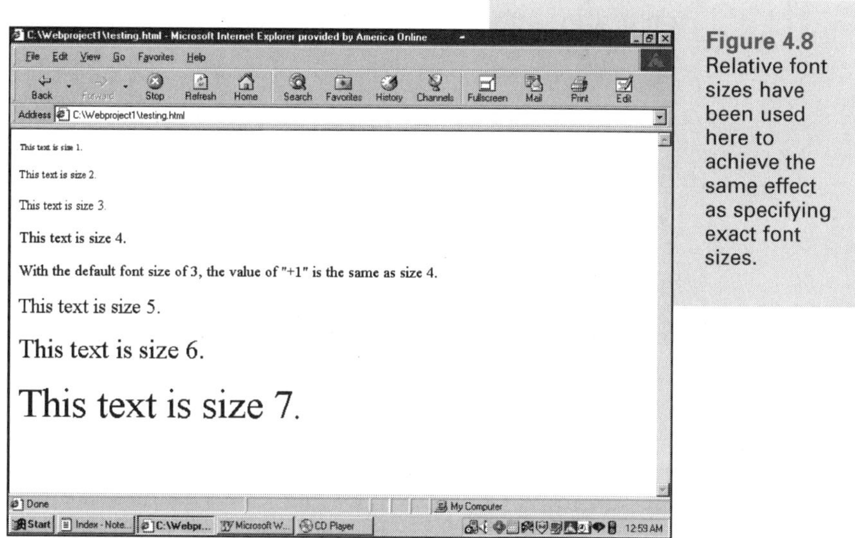

Figure 4.8
Relative font sizes have been used here to achieve the same effect as specifying exact font sizes.

ANALYSIS

Look at the value you used for the `SIZE` attribute. Rather than specifying the size as 4, the value `+1` was used to indicate that the size should be one larger than the base font size (in this example, the base font size was 3).

Using relative font sizes can be especially helpful when you have established a base font size other than 3. You then don't need to worry about specific sizes—only about whether you want given text to be larger or smaller than the Web site's base font size. The next section discusses setting a site's base font size.

Establishing a Base Font

If you want to use something other than the standard size of 3 for the large majority of text in a Web page, you can set a particular font size as the base font for that page. You use the `<BASEFONT>` tag for this purpose, but if a particular browser doesn't recognize it, the tag has no effect. The `<BASEFONT>` tag does not have an end tag.

You must place the <BASEFONT> tag in the HTML somewhere *before* any text appears onscreen. In practice, you should nest the <BASEFONT> tag within the <HEAD> section, or at the top of the <BODY> section, before any tags that put text onscreen.

To change the base font size, all you need to do is use the <BASEFONT> tag as follows, inserting the base font size you want (from 1 to 7):

```
<BASEFONT SIZE="4">
```

This example raises the base font size from 3 to 4.

The Project 1 Web site stays with the standard size 3 font, so you don't need to type the <BASEFONT> tag in the HTML for this project. Of course, you can experiment with it (or any other tags) if you want, but please do so in a different file.

If you want to make your Web site legible to people who can see but need larger size print—similar to a large-print edition of a book or magazine—try changing the base font size to something larger than the standard size of 3.

Caution

The larger the base font you establish, the fewer larger font sizes you'll have available for use in that page.

Coloring Text and Specifying a Typeface

You can do more with the <FONT> tag than just change the size of text. The <FONT> tag's attributes are also good for adding color to your Web site and for giving you some control over the appearance of the text in your Web site.

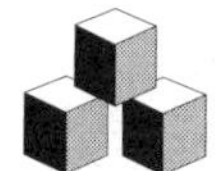

EXERCISE

Add a little more to the Welcome page of the Project 1 Web site by following these steps:

1. In your text editor, open the `index.html` document.
2. Place the insertion point before the `<BLOCKQUOTE>` tag, and then press Enter.
3. Type the following on the new blank line:

```
<P><FONT COLOR="yellow" SIZE="+1" FACE="arial">I hope you enjoy your
foray into one of my favorite topics.</FONT></P>
```

4. Now place the insertion point just above the `</BODY>` tag near the end of the document, and then press Enter.
5. Type the following tag on the new blank line:

```
<P><FONT SIZE="-1">Copyright 1999 by Greg Robertson</FONT></P>
```

6. Save the `index.html` file.
7. Switch to your browser and refresh the screen. Figure 4.9 shows the new appearance of the Welcome page.

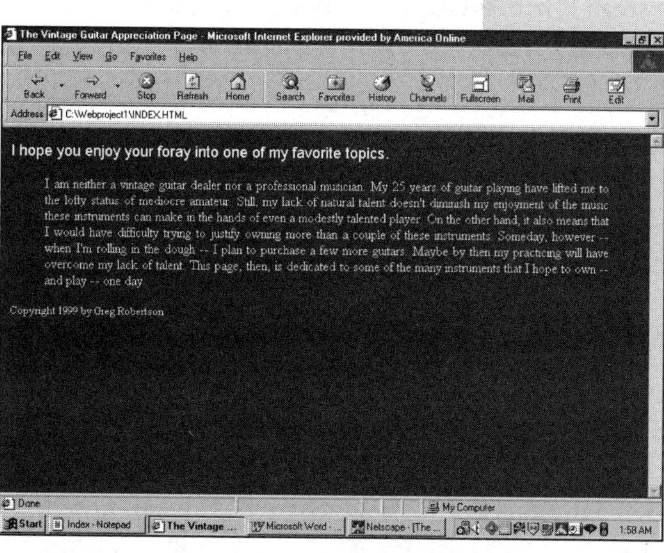

Figure 4.9 Several attributes have been used with the `<FONT>` tag to create the look of these lines.

ANALYSIS

In Step 3, you created a part of the welcome message for the Welcome page. Note the use of three attributes of the `<FONT>` tag: `COLOR`, `SIZE`, and `FACE`. The chapter already has explained how to use the `SIZE` attribute. This time the value is a relative value (`+1`) rather than an absolute value.

Using the `COLOR` attribute, you can assign any color you want to the text within the `<FONT>` container tag. In this case, you used one of the color words that HTML understands, `yellow`, which fits the color scheme of the Web site.

Another new `<FONT>` attribute you entered in Step 3 is `FACE`, which relates to serif and sans-serif fonts. If you take any book and glance through it, you'll probably find that the text is in a serif font. Other elements, however, such as headings within chapters, may very well be in a sans-serif font. A *serif* is a short line that extends from the strokes used to make the shape of the letter. For example, look at the following letter, which is in a serif font:

Y

The small line that crosses the bottom of the Y, as well as the ones that cross the upper arms of the Y, are serifs.

A sans serif ("without serif") font is one that doesn't have serifs on the letters. The following letter is in a sans-serif font:

Y

A sans-serif font is easier to read from a distance or in a larger font size. Smaller text, especially when it consists of several lines or more (as in a paragraph), is much easier to read in a serif font.

Using the `FACE` attribute gives you some degree of control over the appearance of your text in any given browser. Within the two basic types, serif and sans-serif, are dozens of designs, each with its own unique appearance. The sans-serif type, for example, includes popular typefaces such as Helvetica and Arial, as well as less-used typefaces such as Century Gothic. In the HTML you entered in Step 3, you specified the Arial typeface. Any browser that supports Arial will display this line

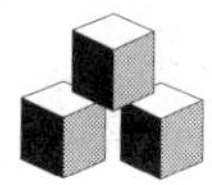

of text in that typeface. If a given browser does not have built-in support for Arial, then it will substitute the closest typeface it does support.

If you want to be sure that your text, or some portion of your text, is in a sans-serif typeface, use the `FACE` attribute. You can specify *exactly* the typeface you want (such as Century Gothic), or you can generalize and simply specify a sans-serif typeface. You also can list several typeface options, in order of your preference. For example, you can use `FACE` as follows:

```
FACE="Century Gothic, Arial, sans-serif"
```

When a browser reads this `FACE` attribute, it considers the typefaces in order, and displays the text in the first typeface it finds that it supports. The browser will display Century Gothic text if it supports it. If it doesn't support that typeface, it will go to the next one, Arial, and display the text in that typeface. If it doesn't offer support for either of the two specified typefaces, it will display the text in its default sans-serif typeface.

The best reason to put multiple typefaces in the `FACE` attribute is to make sure that as many browsers as possible will find at least one typeface supported. You never should, however, rely on a certain typeface to make your Web site design work.

There's one more thing in this exercise worth mentioning. In Step 5, you used a relative font size to reduce the size of the copyright statement. Using the value `-1` for the `SIZE` attribute is common practice for reducing the size of the copyright statement on a Web site.

At this point, the lines of text you just added are left-aligned. You learn how to adjust the alignment later in the chapter.

Enlarging Text

Another technique is available for limited changing of text size. Besides specifying a font size or using relative font sizing, you can use the `<BIG>` tag to increase the size of text by 1. In other words, if your site uses the standard font size of 3, and you apply the `<BIG>` tag to a word, that word is sized at 4.

EXERCISE

1. Switch to your text editor and open the index.html document, if it's not already open.
2. Go to the paragraph which begins "I am neither" and place the insertion point immediately after the <P ALIGN="justify"> tag.
3. Type the following start tag:

```
<BIG>
```

4. After the word "I," insert the following end tag:

```
</BIG>
```

5. Save the document.
6. Switch to your browser. *Before* you refresh the screen, take a look at the word "I" in that paragraph. As you click the Refresh (or Reload) button, keep an eye on that word and verify that it becomes larger.

Don't go overboard using the <BIG> tag. Realize that if you use this tag on one word in the middle of a paragraph, the leading between lines changes. The result is that the paragraph doesn't have the same amount of space between all the lines in the paragraph. The larger the size of the base font you're using, the more noticeable the difference in leading—and the uglier the result. Unless you're using the <BIG> tag for entire paragraphs, I recommend that you use it sparingly, if at all, anywhere other than at the beginning of a paragraph.

Leading ***(pronounced "ledding") is the amount of space between lines of text within a paragraph.***

Shrinking Text

You likewise have another alternative when you want to reduce the size of some text. This task is just as simple as enlarging text, because all you need is the <SMALL> tag. The <SMALL> tag works the same way that the <BIG> tag works.

EXERCISE

1. In your text editor, open the `index.html` document.
2. Place the insertion point after the `</P>` tag in the copyright notice near the bottom of the file, and press Enter to create a blank line.
3. On the blank line, type the following HTML:

```
<P><SMALL><FONT COLOR="yellow" FACE="arial">If you have enjoyed your
visit, please let others know about this Web site!</FONT></SMALL></P>
```

4. Save the `index.html` document.
5. Switch to your browser and refresh the screen. Figure 4.10 shows the screen.

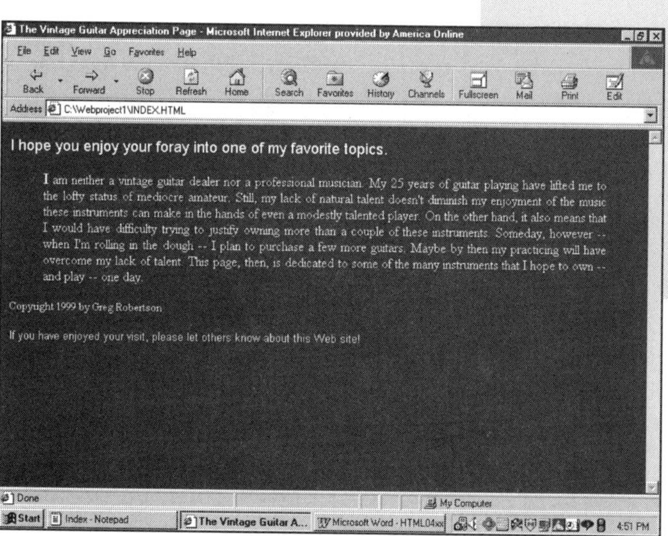

Figure 4.10 Using the <SMALL> tag makes the text one size smaller than the Web site's standard size.

ANALYSIS

When you typed the HTML in Step 3, you nested the `<SMALL>` and `</SMALL>` tags within the `<P>` and `</P>` tags. Looking more closely, you'll notice that `<FONT>` and `</FONT>` tags are nested within the `<SMALL>` container. In addition, the `<FONT>` tag includes the `COLOR` and `FACE` attributes, which have the same values (`"yellow"` and `"arial"`) used in the line of text added at the top of the document. The repeated use of these values helps create consistency in the Web site.

Emphasizing Words

Just as books often use bold or italic to make certain words or phrases stand out, you can do the same with your Web site. In each case, both start and end tags are required.

PHYSICAL VERSUS LOGICAL FORMATTING

Logical formatting *refers to using the* <EM> *and* <STRONG> *tags.*

The original idea behind HTML was to allow individual browsers to determine the specifics of the HTML formatting. That's why two of the text-formatting tags seem rather nonspecific in their meanings. These two logical formatting tags are `<EM>` and `<STRONG>`.

The `<EM>` tag tells the browser to place an emphasis on the text, and the `<STRONG>` tag tells the browser to place a strong emphasis on the text. It is left to the browser to determine exactly how to present emphasized or strongly emphasized text. Generally, `<EM>` is rendered as italicized text, and `<STRONG>` is rendered as bold text.

In* physical formatting, *you tell a browser exactly what to do with text (such as italicize it or put it in boldface).

The physical formatting tags are `<I>` (to produce italicized text) and `<B>` (to produce boldface text). Whether you use physical formatting tags or logical formatting tags doesn't matter much; based on the default settings of the major browsers, the results should be the same.

CREATING ITALIC TEXT

You may want to italicize a word or phrase in your Web site for any of a number of reasons. Perhaps you want to define a term, for example, or merely emphasize the word.

EXERCISE ▼

1. In your text editor, open the `index.html` file.
2. Place the insertion point between the `<P ALIGN="justify">` and `<BIG>` tags in the first paragraph of body text.
3. Type this start tag:

```
<EM>
```

4. Go to the end of the sentence—immediately after the period—and type this end tag:

```
</EM>
```

5. Move the insertion point to the copyright line (near the bottom of the file) and change this line by adding the `<EM>` and `</EM>` tags, as follows:

```
<P><EM>Copyright 1999</EM> by Greg Robertson</P>
```

6. Save the `index.html` document.
7. Switch to your browser and refresh the screen. Figure 4.11 shows the newly emphasized text in IE.

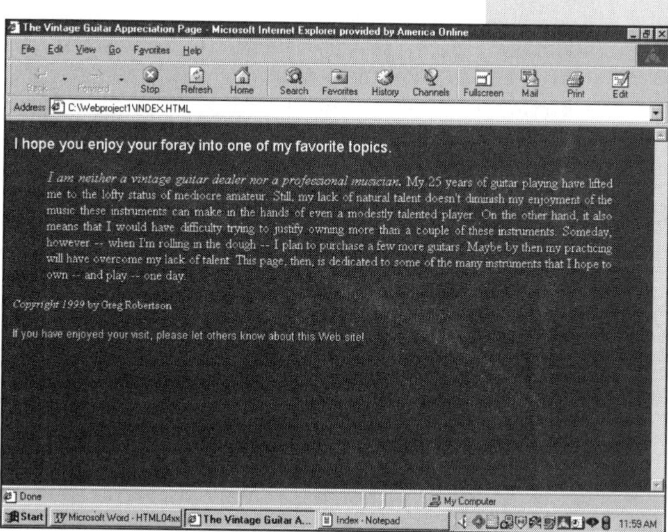

Figure 4.11 The <EM> and </EM> tags create italicized text on the Web page.

ANALYSIS

You italicized the first sentence of the opening paragraph in Steps 3 and 4. Then you did the same thing to `Copyright 1999` by placing the `<EM>` and `</EM>` tags around those words in Step 5. You could have achieved the same effect through physical formatting by using the `<I>` and `</I>` tags.

CREATING BOLD TEXT

Boldface is another means of emphasizing text, but most people use it less frequently within paragraphs of text than they use italic. You are more likely to use (and find) boldface text in headings.

EXERCISE

Suppose that you want to strongly emphasize a couple of points on your Web site. Maybe boldfacing that text will do the trick.

1. Open the `index.html` file in your text editor.
2. In the first paragraph of body text, add the `<STRONG>` and `</STRONG>` tags so that the sentence looks like this:

```
<P ALIGN="justify"><EM><STRONG><BIG>I</BIG> am neither</STRONG> a vin-
tage guitar dealer nor a professional musician.</EM>
```

3. Scroll to the end of the document, find the following line, and add the `<STRONG>` and `</STRONG>` tags as follows:

```
<P><SMALL><FONT COLOR="yellow" FACE="arial"><STRONG>If you have enjoyed
your visit, please let others know about this Web
site!</STRONG></FONT></SMALL></P>
```

4. Save the `index.html` file.
5. Switch to your browser and refresh the screen. Figure 4.12 shows how the request below the copyright line appears now.

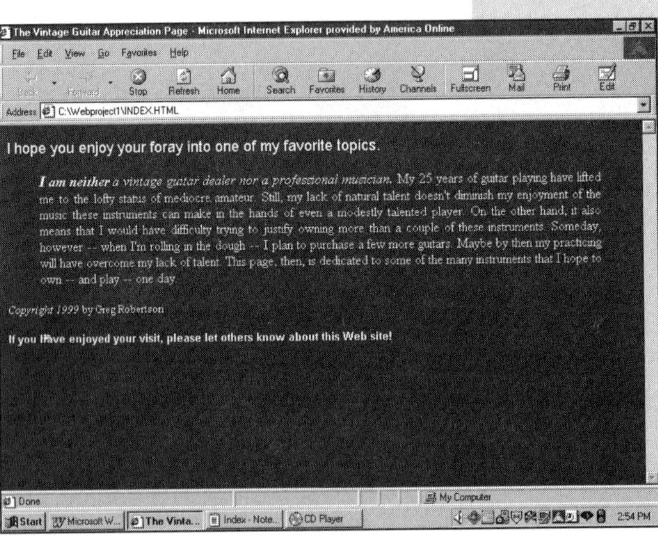

Figure 4.12 Boldfacing the first few words and the request at the bottom of the page draws the viewer's attention.

ANALYSIS

Using the <STRONG> and </STRONG> tags boldfaces the text contained between them. In this case, you added boldface to the first three words of the already-italicized first sentence, as well as to the request at the bottom of the Web page. You could have achieved the same effect through physical formatting by using the <B> and </B> tags.

OTHER TEXT-FORMATTING TAGS

Other text-formatting tags are available, but <EM> (or <I>) and <STRONG> (or <B>) are the ones you are most likely to need. If you want to underline text, you use the <U> and </U> tags.

You might want to create *strikethrough* text, which has a horizontal line through it like this:

~~This is strikethrough text.~~

You have several choices. You can use a deprecated element such as <S> or <STRIKE>, or can use the HTML 4.0 tag <DEL>. As of this writing, IE 4.0 supports <DEL>, but Navigator 4.06 does not. You may want to use the <S> or <STRIKE> tag for a while, until both major browsers support <DEL>.

Tip

Be careful about using underlining in your Web site. Usually, hyperlinks are underlined (as well as in a different color), and someone may automatically assume that your underlined text is another hyperlink.

You also can create superscript text (with the <SUP> tag) and subscript text (with the <SUB> tag). The most common use of the superscript tag is for footnotes or mathematical equations. Unless you are putting academic or scientific papers on the Web, you are not likely to need this tag too often. As with the other text-formatting tags, <SUP> and <SUB> require end tags.

Caution

Browsers based on versions of HTML prior to 3.2 do not recognize the <SUP> tag.

Adding superscripts or subscripts changes the leading between lines. To overcome that problem, you can use the `<FONT>` tag with the `SIZE` attribute to reduce the superscript or subscript to a size that doesn't affect the leading. In the case of the standard size 3 text, try using a font size of 2 for the superscript or subscript. Nest the `<SUP>` and `<FONT>` tags as follows:

```
<SUP><FONT SIZE="2">1</FONT></SUP>
```

You may prefer to use relative font sizes instead. Here, that would be `<FONT SIZE="-1">` instead of `<FONT SIZE="2">`.

A *proportionally spaced* font is one in which the letters take up varying amounts of horizontal space, depending on the width of the letter. A lowercase `i`, for example, is narrower than an uppercase `W`. An example of a proportionally spaced font is Times New Roman.

A *fixed-width,* or *monospace,* font is one in which each letter takes up the same amount of horizontal space as every other letter. An example of a fixed-width font is Courier.

The text on Web sites usually is proportionally spaced. Proportionally spaced fonts are easy to read, and they have a professional appearance. If you want to create fixed-width text, you have several tags available to you: `<TT>`, `<SAMP>`, and `<CODE>`. These are pretty much the same, so you might as well follow the traditional approach and use the `<TT>` (teletype) tag. The main purpose of these tags is to create text that is set off from surrounding text by its appearance. Monospaced text within proportionally spaced text usually is pretty easy to spot.

Note

A visitor's browser is the determining factor in the exact font the visitor sees. Each browser comes with default settings, and while most people don't change those defaults, some do. Even when you try to force a visitor's browser to use the font settings you prefer, he or she might have set up the browser to override your settings.

Dividing Up Your Text

Virtually no book or magazine article you are likely to read is solid text. Instead, graphic artists and art directors spend a great deal of time and effort trying to make the things they publish attractive. Headings are one way to break up text. Books have chapter headings, for example, and magazine articles often have section headings. The following section shows you how to add headings to your Web site.

Making Headings

A ***heading*** *is a title for a section of your Web site.*

Headings make excellent dividers for your text. They add white space and break up the wall of nearly solid text that you might otherwise have on your site. They provide viewers with additional information by forecasting the topic of the text following the heading. Headings even can add color to your site when used in conjunction with the `<FONT>` tag.

Headings come in six sizes, and you designate a heading level by using the `<H`*n*`>` tag, where *n* is a number from 1 through 6. The largest heading is `<H1>` and the smallest is `<H6>`. Remember, however, that the viewer's browser determines the font, the font style (regular, italic, and so on), and the font size of headings—in other words, each browser may render the heading slightly differently. When you designate one of these headings in your Web page, you are indicating that you want to use a given heading in preference to the others, and you know that it will be relatively larger or smaller than the others. If you have several levels of headings (that is, headings with subheadings), just make sure that the subheadings are smaller than the headings to which they are subordinate. You don't *have* to start with a level-1 heading, but that's common practice.

▼ EXERCISE

To add headings to the index.html document, follow these steps:

1. In your text editor, open the index.html document.
2. Place the insertion point immediately below the `</BLOCKQUOTE>` tag. Type the following lines of HTML:

```
<H1 ALIGN="center"><FONT COLOR="yellow">Tips for Buying Used or Vintage
Guitars</FONT></H1>

<H1 ALIGN="center"><FONT COLOR="yellow">The Buyer's Guide to Grading
Guitars</FONT></H1>
```

3. Save the `index.html` document.
4. Switch to your browser and refresh the screen. You should see something similar to what's shown in Figure 4.13.

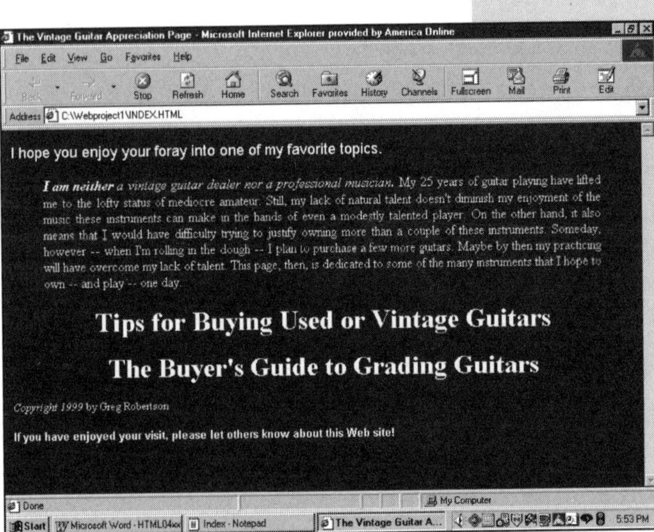

Figure 4.13 Level-1 headings are large in Internet Explorer 4.0.

ANALYSIS

In these steps you added two headings (the titles of two articles that you'll add later in this chapter). The use of the `<H1>` tag made them level-1 headings. In IE and Navigator, those headings are in a serif font. You used the `<FONT>` tag and its `COLOR` attribute to specify that the headings should appear in yellow.

New in these two lines of HTML is the `ALIGN` attribute within the `<H1>` heading. You can use three values with this attribute: `left`, `right`, and `center`. The default alignment for a heading is `left`. Many Web designers use `center` for headings to keep pages in balance.

Creating Divisions

The original use of the `<DIV>` tag was to align elements within a division (a portion of a document). These elements could include things such as graphics, text, and lists. For example, you might have a graphic and two paragraphs of text that you want aligned to the right. By nesting them all between <DIV> and </DIV> tags, you can use one ALIGN attribute to align everything within the division to the right. Outside of the <DIV> tag, everything is left-aligned by default.

EXERCISE

Create a division in the index.html document by following these steps:

1. In your text editor, open the index.html document.
2. Place the insertion point to the left of the copyright line, and press Enter.
3. On the new line, type the following start tag:

```
<DIV ALIGN="center">
```

4. Place the insertion point immediately after the </P> tag in the "If you have enjoyed . . . " line, and press Enter.
5. On the new line, type the following end tag:

```
</DIV>
```

6. Save the document.
7. Switch to your browser and refresh the screen. Figure 4.14 shows the new state of the Web site.

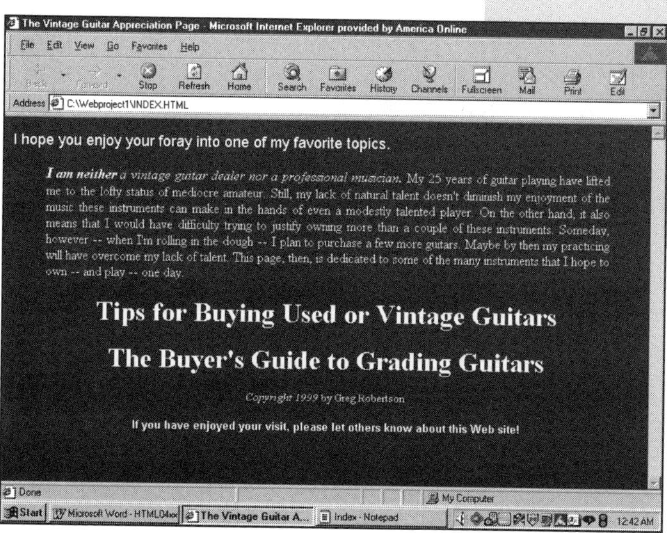

Figure 4.14 It's easy to create a division using the <DIV> container tag.

ANALYSIS

In Step 4, you began creating the division by inserting the start tag. You used `ALIGN="center"` to establish the alignment for everything within the division. At this point, the centered text consists of the copyright line and the line urging visitors to spread the word about the site.

Some older browsers may not recognize the `<DIV>` tag. For these browsers, an alternative is available to you. In reality, it's not so much an alternative as it is a complementary tag.

EXERCISE

To take care of older as well as newer browsers, you can use the `<DIV>` tag in conjunction with the `<CENTER>` tag. Complete the following steps:

1. In your text editor, open the `index.html` document.
2. Place the insertion point to the right of `<DIV ALIGN="center">`, and press Enter.
3. On the new line, type this start tag:

```
</CENTER>
```

4. Place the insertion point to the right of the `</DIV>` tag, and press Enter.
5. On the new line, type this end tag:

```
</CENTER>
```

6. Place the insertion point to the left of the "I hope you enjoy..." line near the top of the document, and press Enter.
7. On the blank line created in Step 6, type the following HTML (press Enter after typing the first line):

```
<DIV ALIGN="center">
<CENTER>
```

8. Place the insertion point to the right of the "I hope you enjoy..." line, and press Enter.
9. On the blank line created in Step 8, type the following HTML (press Enter after typing the first line):

```
</CENTER>
</DIV ALIGN="center">
```

10. Save the `index.html` document.

ANALYSIS

Adding the <CENTER> and </CENTER> tags achieves the same result as using the <DIV> tag with the ALIGN="center" attribute. The primary reason to add the <CENTER> container tag is to cover browsers that do not recognize the <DIV> tag. Be aware, however, that the W3C has deprecated the <CENTER> tag. Using it in combination with the <DIV> tag is just a little extra measure of assurance that the page will appear to all viewers the way you want it to.

In Steps 6 through 9, you used both <CENTER> and <DIV> to center the line at the top of the Web site which says, "I hope you enjoy your foray into one of my favorite topics."

Using Horizontal Rules

A horizontal rule is a straight line that runs across the Web page.

Another means of separating text into sections is to use horizontal rules. Horizontal rules, of course, do not contain any text, but they can be an eye-pleasing means of creating divisions within the text. A standard horizontal rule runs from margin to margin, is usually gray in color, and has a slight shading to it (at least in the two major browsers).

EXERCISE

To create a horizontal rule, follow these steps:

1. In your text editor, open the index.html document.
2. Place the insertion point to the left of the <DIV> tag near the end of the document, and then press Enter.
3. Add the following HTML on the blank line created in Step 2:

```
<HR SIZE="1" WIDTH="80%" ALIGN="center" NOSHADE COLOR="yellow">
```

4. Save the index.html document.
5. Switch to your browser, refresh the page, and view the result. Figure 4.15 shows the horizontal rule across the bottom of the Web page.

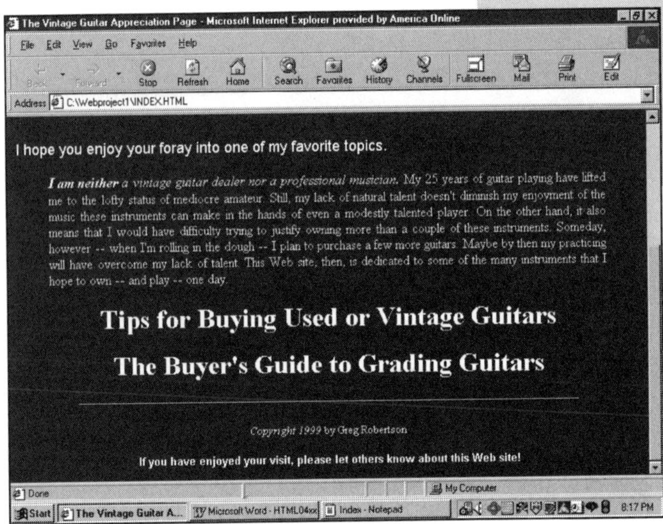

Figure 4.15 A horizontal rule separates parts of a Web page.

ANALYSIS

In this exercise, you added a horizontal rule with various attributes. In Step 3, you gave the horizontal rule a different size (height) than the standard of 2; this one has a size of 1 pixel. As you can see, all you need to do to change the height of a horizontal rule is to add the `SIZE` attribute and specify the height (in pixels). Although you really can't tell in such a short one, a horizontal rule actually looks like a hollow rectangle in some browsers, with a top border that is darker than the other three. The larger the size you use, the more easily you can see the rectangle effect. This is especially evident in Navigator. IE, however, shows the top and left borders, but not the bottom and right borders.

The horizontal rule you created in Step 3 is one without shading, because you used the `NOSHADE` attribute. Because of the small size of this horizontal rule, however, it's difficult to see any difference between one with shading and one without shading. A shaded horizontal rule is one that has a three-dimensional appearance; by removing the shading, you essentially "fill in the box" to take away the three-dimensional effect. The `NOSHADE` attribute removes shading from the horizontal rule, which means that the horizontal rule looks like a line, regardless of browser.

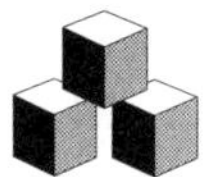

Different browsers display an unshaded rule in different ways, so don't let the attractiveness of your design depend *entirely* on the look of an unshaded rule in a particular browser.

In Step 3, you also used the `WIDTH` attribute to make a horizontal rule that doesn't run all the way from margin to margin. When you want to change the length of a horizontal rule, think in terms of the *full length* of a basic horizontal rule. The percentage value you give to the `WIDTH` attribute is the percentage of the full window width you want the horizontal rule to occupy. In this case, the horizontal rule takes up 80 percent of the full window width. By default, the browser positioned the horizontal rule in the center of the window.

Note

Not all browsers support the `WIDTH` attribute. If someone views your Web site using a browser that doesn't, he or she will see a full-length rule instead.

The `ALIGN="center"` attribute for the `<HR>` tag in Step 3 isn't really necessary, but it serves to show you how to use the `ALIGN` attribute with horizontal rules. The example page design calls for a centered horizontal rule, but your page design may call for aligning a horizontal rule to the left or right margin instead.

Finally, you used the `COLOR` attribute with the value `yellow` when creating this horizontal rule. Yellow is used, of course, to fit the Web site's color scheme. When you assign a color to a horizontal rule, the smaller the height of the rule, the lighter its color appears to be.

Note

The `COLOR` attribute assigns a single color to the horizontal rule. The multicolored horizontal rules often seen on Web pages are actually graphics. Graphics are covered later in this project.

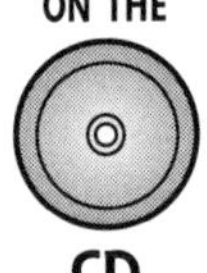

At this stage, the `index.html` document is as follows (this can be found on the CD accompanying this book as the file `Project1Index01.html`):

```
<!DOCTYPE HTML PUBLIC "-//W3/DTD HTML 4.0 Transitional//EN"
"http://www.w3.org/TR/REC-html40/loose.dtd">
<HTML>
<!— This Web site was created by hand by Greg Robertson —>
<HEAD>
<TITLE>The Vintage Guitar Appreciation Page</TITLE>
<META NAME="keywords" CONTENT="guitar, vintage guitar, guitar collecting,
Fender, Gibson, Terada, Stratocaster, Telecaster, Mustang, Les Paul, Lucille,
TR-1000, JW-837, Leo Fender, Orville Gibson">
<META NAME="description" CONTENT="A little vintage guitar history, some tips
on buying vintage guitars, and a few words about some of my favorite
guitars.">
</HEAD>
<BODY BGCOLOR="black" TEXT="white" LINK="yellow" VLINK="red" ALINK="lime">
    <DIV ALIGN="center">
            <CENTER>
<P><FONT COLOR="yellow" SIZE="+1" FACE="arial">I hope you enjoy your foray
into one of my favorite topics.</FONT></P>
    </CENTER>
    </DIV>
<BLOCKQUOTE>
<P ALIGN="justify"><EM><STRONG><BIG>I</BIG> am neither</STRONG> a vintage
guitar dealer nor a professional musician.</EM> My 25 years of guitar playing
have lifted me to the lofty status of mediocre amateur. Still, my lack of
natural talent doesn't diminish my enjoyment of the music these instruments
can make in the hands of even a modestly talented player. On the other hand,
it also means that I would have difficulty trying to justify owning more
than a couple of these instruments. Someday, however — when I'm rolling in
the dough — I plan to purchase a few more guitars. Maybe by then my
practicing will have overcome my lack of talent. This Web site, then, is
dedicated to some of the many instruments that I hope to own — and play —
one day.</P>
</BLOCKQUOTE>
<H1 ALIGN="center"><FONT COLOR="yellow">Tips for Buying Used or Vintage
Guitars</FONT></H1>
<H1 ALIGN="center"><FONT COLOR="yellow">The Buyer's Guide to Grading
Guitars</FONT></H1>
<HR SIZE="1" WIDTH="80%" ALIGN="center" NOSHADE COLOR="yellow">
<DIV ALIGN="center">
<P><FONT SIZE="-1"><EM>Copyright 1999</EM> by Greg Robertson</FONT></P>
<P><SMALL><FONT COLOR="yellow" FACE="arial"><STRONG>If you have enjoyed your
visit, please let others know about this Web
site!</STRONG></FONT></SMALL></P>
</DIV>
</BODY>
</HTML>
```

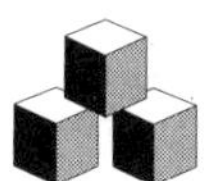

Coloring with RGB

When dealing with color on a Web site, don't forget that you want contrasting colors (that is, light and dark) for text and background. As you've seen in the Project 1 Web site so far, you can color both text and the background. You shouldn't simply choose individual colors you like, however. I may like red and pink as colors, for example, but a red background with pink text isn't going to look good—nor is it going to be readable. Remember, too, that part of your audience may have problems with color blindness or some other vision problem that requires a good light-and-dark color combination. It's easy to specify colors to use on your Web page. *Which* colors you use is the trick.

You have two methods available to specify a color in HTML. You can use one of sixteen words that HTML understands (listed earlier in this chapter in the section "Designating Link Colors"), or you can designate the color by its hexadecimal code.

A* hexadecimal (hex) code *is a value in the base-16 mathematical system.

The second method is far more comprehensive and flexible. When you open a graphics program such as Paint Shop Pro and indicate that you want to create an image that can contain up to 16.7 million colors, bear in mind that every one of those colors has its own, unique hexadecimal (*hex*) code. Your eyes cannot even distinguish between a great many of those colors, because they are too close to each other.

In regular life, we use the base-10 system, in which the possible values for each number *place* (ones, tens, hundreds, and so on) run from 0 through 9. In the base-2 (*binary*) system, which is fundamental to computers, the only possible values for each place are 0 and 1 (off and on). The hex codes in the base-16 system look odd because they combine numerals with letters (for example, 6A is a hex number that equals 106 in base-10). The 16 characters required for representing hex values are the letters A through F as well as the usual 10 numerals. Hex codes, thus, consist of combinations of the following characters:

0 1 2 3 4 5 6 7 8 9 A B C D E F

You create colors by assigning hexadecimal values to the RGB components of the color. RGB is short for "red green blue," and each one has

255 possible values. Each of the three RGB components has two characters, so each hexadecimal value representing a color consists of six characters. The six characters are actually considered in pairs: the first pair for red, the second pair for green, and the third pair for blue. The character values run from 0 through F, with values closer to 0 being darker and values closer to F being lighter.

Tip

If your hex color code is `000000`, you see black, which is the *absence* of color. If your code is `FFFFFF`, you see white, which is the presence of all colors. If that seems like an odd way to think about it, remember that if you are in total darkness, you can see no color at all. On the other hand, if you think of a rainbow or a prism diffracting light, you end up with the color spectrum, that is, light is broken up into its constituent parts. Put them back together, and you have all colors in colorless light.

EXERCISE

Experiment with background colors a little bit as follows:

1. In your text editor, open the `index.html` document.
2. Near the top of the document, locate the `<BODY>` tag. Change the `BGCOLOR="black"` attribute to the following:

```
BGCOLOR="#440000"
```

3. Save the document.
4. Switch to your browser and refresh the screen.

ANALYSIS

In Step 2, you changed the background color from black to a hex value of `440000`. Remember that the first two digits are the value of the red component in the color you're specifying, and that the closer to 0 each of the two digits is, the darker the color is. On my monitor, the hex value of `440000` is so dark as to be black.

Now try lightening it up. Repeat the exercise, but this time use a hex value of `bb0000`. The result in my browser is a much lighter and brighter red that looks (to my eyes) like a brick red. Experiment with other values for the red component to see how the background changes.

You may want to try various values for the green and blue components. If you try `004400` and then `00bb00` as the green values, for example, you experience the same transition—the former yields a color that might as well be black, and the latter gives a lighter green color.

Before continuing with this chapter, change the value for the `BGCOLOR` attribute back to `"black"` instead of a hex code.

If you try these color combinations and find something that's *almost* what you wanted, but not quite, you can alter it a little bit at a time until you find what you want. You can experiment and change the hex characters incrementally. Change the first number of the pair for a more significant change, and the second number for a less significant change.

In theory, you have a virtually unlimited number of colors from which to choose. In practice, though, you should limit your choices to far fewer. That's because not every monitor is capable of displaying all those colors. Many people, for example, have monitors that are limited to 256 colors.

Once again, the controlling factor is your audience. If you expect the vast majority of your audience to have the hardware to display 16.7 million colors, then you don't need to feel limited to 256 colors. If you know for a fact that a large proportion of your audience will not have that capability—or even if you just aren't sure—don't waste time coming up with hundreds of custom colors for use on your Web site.

Note

You may want to limit your color choices to even fewer than 256. The so-called "browser-safe" color palette consists of 216 colors that are common to both PCs and Macs. By using these colors, you can ensure that your Web site will look the same on any of the most common computers. You can find this palette in many locations on the Web. You don't *have* to use these colors, but if you don't, you run the risk that the beautiful, color-coordinated Web site you've created on your PC will be ugly and gaudy on a Mac, or vice versa. To create browser-safe colors, use combinations of 00, 33, 66, 99, CC, and FF for the RGB values. The Web site at the following URL contains an excellent hex color chart and an explanation of hex colors, among other things:

http://www.phoenix.net/~jacobson/rgb.html

Creating Lists

It's a rare Web site that doesn't contain one or more lists. Such a list may be nothing more than an inventory of the places a couple of retirees visited on their last vacation. Certainly lists can be very helpful when you want to present information concisely and in an easy-to-grasp format.

Types of Lists

An **ordered list** *is one in which the items are numbered or otherwise explicitly sequenced.*

Lists come in two varieties: ordered and unordered (bulleted). Normally, an ordered list uses item numbering of some sort because the elements within the list need to be presented in a certain order. For example, if you are laying out the order-fulfillment process within your company, from order to delivery of the product, you want to show exactly what happens at what stage. That's the only way to ensure that employees know what to do when.

An **unordered list** *or* **bulleted list** *does not have numbers; rather, the items use bullets of some kind.*

In an unordered list, on the other hand, it doesn't matter which item comes first. If you create a site that lists every guitar in your collection, for example, their order is irrelevant.

Creating an Unordered List

Both kinds of lists, unordered and ordered, have a common element: `<LI>`. This tag, which doesn't require an end tag, goes before each item in the list, whether it's an unordered or ordered list. The `<LI>` tag denotes each item within the list.

To designate a list of the unordered variety, you use the `<UL>` tag.

For legal reasons, the Web sites in this book contain trademark and registered trademark symbols for the various products referenced on the sites. If you mention product names in your Web site, I urge you to include such symbols and service marks, also.

EXERCISE

Create an unordered list by following these steps:

1. In your text editor, open the `index.html` file.

If you want to keep a version of the HTML file from earlier in this chapter while continuing to work on the file, just save the `index.html` file with a different name. With the `index.html` file open in Notepad (or whatever text editor you're using), choose File, Save As. In the File Name area of the Save As dialog box, type another name for `index.html`. Call it index_1.html or some other name that will help you remember what it is. Close the renamed file, and reopen `index.html`. To reopen `index.html`, choose File, Open in your browser, and then navigate to `index.html`.

2. Place the insertion point after the `</BLOCKQUOTE>` tag near the end of the document.
3. Type the following tags, pressing Enter after each one:

```
<UL>
<LI>FENDER<SUP>&reg;</SUP>
<LI>GIBSON<SUP>&reg;</SUP>
<LI>TERADA
</UL>
```

4. Save the document.
5. Switch to your browser and refresh the screen. Figure 4.16 shows the results.

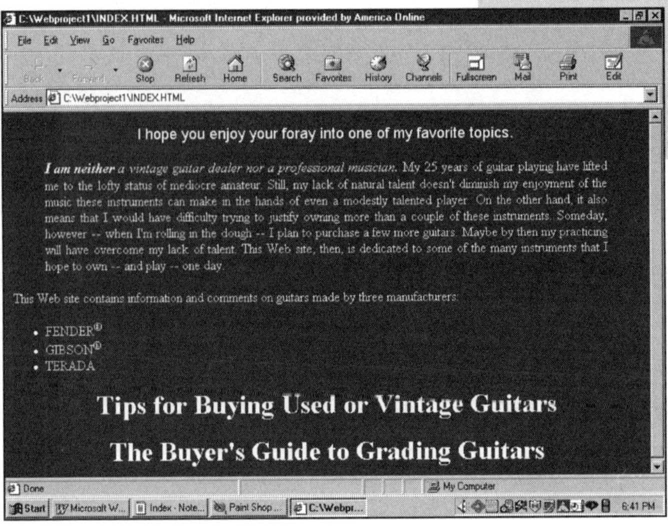

Figure 4.16 You've now got a nice, neat bulleted list.

ANALYSIS

In Step 3, the `<UL>` tag you typed indicates that an unordered list is to follow, and the `<LI>` tags denote the bulleted list items. As you can see, you merely type the list items next to the `<LI>` tags. The `<SUP>®</SUP>` after the `FENDER` and `GIBSON` company names creates a superscripted registered trademark symbol: ®. Keyboards don't have the registered trademark symbol on them, but you can create this symbol as well as many other special characters by means of defined HTML codes. In fact, you must use defined HTML codes even for some characters that *do* occur on keyboards, such as the ampersand (&) and quotation mark (").

The problem is that HTML uses certain characters to interpret HTML documents. These four characters are the ampersand (&), the less than and greater than symbols (< >)—also called *angle brackets*—and the quotation mark ("). For these characters, as well as others, you can ensure that the character you want to appear does appear, by using the correct HTML code for it. As you may have deduced from the preceding example, `®`, the code begins with an ampersand (&) and ends with a semicolon (;). Each special character code takes that format; what you place in the middle determines the character that's produced onscreen. To create the registered trademark symbol, you place `reg` between the ampersand and semicolon.

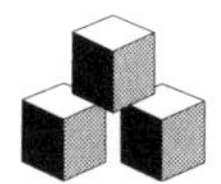

Note

In addition, placing the code for the trademark symbol between the ^{and} tags makes the symbol a superscript. Unfortunately, as mentioned earlier in the chapter, superscripts affect the leading, so the resulting paragraph might not look as good as it would have without a superscript.

Some of the more commonly needed characters and their codes follow:

& (ampersand)	&
< (less than)	<
> (greater than)	>
" (quotation mark)	"
™ (trademark)	™
® (registered trademark)	®
© (copyright)	©

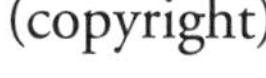

If you need to know the code for another character, you can find it online at the W3C Web site:

http://www.w3.org/MarkUp/HTMLPlus/htmlplus_13.html

In Step 3, you also typed the </UL> tag to end the list. It's all quite simple and effective.

If you employ bulleted or numbered lists in your Web site, make it clear to your viewers what each list is by writing at least a sentence to appear beforehand and introduce the list.

The problem with the list as it appears right now is that it is isolated. It comes out of nowhere, and nothing indicates what the list means.

EXERCISE

To clarify the list's purpose, do the following:

1. Switch back to your text editor, and place the insertion point immediately after the </BLOCKQUOTE> tag (but not on the same line as the <UL> tag), and press Enter twice to create two new, blank lines.
2. Type the following on the second new, blank line:

```
<P>This Web site contains information and comments on guitars made by
three manufacturers:</P>
```

3. Save the document.
4. Switch to your browser and refresh the screen to see the results.

ANALYSIS

Note that this list contains only three items—and all are made by one manufacturer. The Web site I have designed, however, contains information on seven guitars, made by three manufacturers. Therefore, you need to add some more bulleted items to the preceding ones.

EXERCISE

Follow these steps to complete the bulleted list:

1. Place the insertion point at the far-right end of the FENDER item, and then press Enter.
2. Add the following lines, pressing Enter after each one:

```
<LI>Stratocaster<SUP>&reg;</SUP>
<LI>Telecaster<SUP>&reg;</SUP>
<LI>Mustang<SUP>&reg;</SUP>
```

3. Place the insertion point to the right of the GIBSON entry, and then press Enter.
4. Add the following lines, pressing Enter after each one:

```
<LI>Les Paul<SUP>&reg;</SUP>
<LI>Lucille<SUP>&trade;</SUP>
```

5. Place the insertion point to the right of the TERADA entry, and then press Enter.

6. Add the following lines, pressing Enter after each one:

```
<LI>TR-1000
<LI>JW-837
```

7. Save the file.
8. Switch to your browser and refresh the screen. Figure 4.17 shows the list with the additional items.

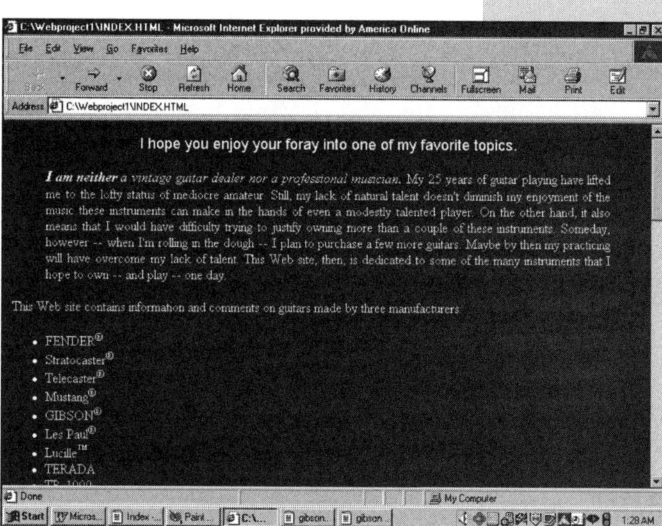

Figure 4.17 All the manufacturer and guitar entries are here—but the list is still not right.

ANALYSIS

In Step 2, you added the names of the three Fender guitars discussed in the Web site. Similarly, in Steps 4 and 6, you added the names of the two Gibson guitars and two Terada guitars. The bulleted list now contains the names of three manufacturers and seven guitars. The problem is that these items are all in one large list; the only distinction between manufacturer and model is the use of all uppercase letters for the manufacturers' names. More changes must be made to the list.

Although the list contains all the manufacturers and guitars discussed in the Web site, further improvements are necessary.

1. Switch to your text editor and open the `index.html` file.
2. Place the insertion point to the right of the `<LI>FENDER` tag, and then press Enter.
3. On the new, blank line, type the following tag:

   ```
   <UL>
   ```

4. Place the insertion point to the right of the last Fender guitar line (`<LI>Mustang`), and then press Enter.
5. On the new, blank line, type the following tag:

   ```
   </UL>
   ```

6. Repeat Steps 2 through 5 for the `GIBSON` portion of the list, and repeat them again for the `TERADA` portion of the list.
7. Save the document.
8. Switch to your browser and refresh the screen. Figure 4.18 shows the revised, more informative list of guitars.

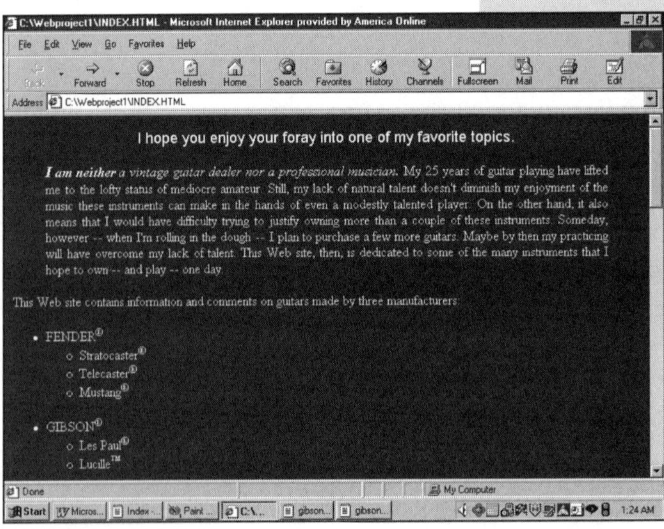

Figure 4.18 The latest version of the bulleted list visibly separates manufacturers and their products.

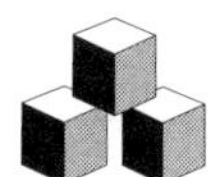

ANALYSIS

By inserting the <UL> and </UL> tags in Steps 3 and 5, you created nested lists out of the guitars made by Fender. When you repeated Steps 2 through 5, you created nested lists for the Gibson and Terada guitars. In other words, in this series of steps you turned one bulleted list into three lists, each headed by a company name and containing a bulleted list of guitars built by that particular company. The original list of guitar manufacturers now has three nested, bulleted lists of guitars, making it easier for visitors to figure out.

EXERCISE

Now make just a few simple changes to the bulleted list by following these steps:

1. Switch back to your text editor, and place the insertion point between `L` and `>` in the first <UL> tag.
2. Expand that tag to say the following:

```
<UL TYPE="disc">
```

3. Place the insertion point in the second <UL> tag, which is just above the `<LI>Stratocaster` tag, and change that tag to the following:

```
<UL TYPE="circle">
```

4. Repeat Step 3 for the <UL> tags just above `<LI>Les Paul` and `<LI>TR-1000`.
5. Save the `index.html` document.
6. Switch to your browser and refresh the screen.

ANALYSIS

This exercise showed you how to control the type of bullet that appears next to an item in a bulleted list. Three types are possible: `disc`, `circle`, and `square`. If you compare the results of this exercise (after adding the `TYPE` attribute) with the bulleted list that was shown in Figure 4.18, you should see the same thing. The default type is `disc`, and a nested list below a bulleted item has a default bullet type of `circle`. If you have yet another nested list below a nested list (that is, a third level of lists), the default bullet type for the third level is `square`. To avoid any surprises from one browser to another, though, the best approach is to specify the type of bullet you want to appear in each list.

Here is an excellent place to show how helpful indenting lines of HTML can be. Without indents, the HTML for the bulleted list created in the preceding exercises looks like the following:

```
<UL TYPE="disc">
<LI>FENDER<SUP>&reg;</SUP>
<UL TYPE="circle">
<LI>Stratocaster<SUP>&reg;</SUP>
<LI>Telecaster<SUP>&reg;</SUP>
<LI>Mustang<SUP>&reg;</SUP>
</UL>
<LI>GIBSON<SUP>&reg;</SUP>
<UL TYPE="circle">
<LI>Les Paul<SUP>&reg;</SUP>
<LI>Lucille<SUP>&trade;</SUP>
</UL>
<LI>TERADA
<UL TYPE="circle">
<LI>TR-1000
<LI>JW-837
</UL>
</UL>
```

You can look at this code and figure out what's going on, but it will probably take you longer than is necessary. Indenting the code as follows greatly clarifies things:

```
<UL TYPE="disc">
<LI>FENDER<SUP>&reg;</SUP>
    <UL TYPE="circle">
    <LI>Stratocaster<SUP>&reg;</SUP>
    <LI>Telecaster<SUP>&reg;</SUP>
    <LI>Mustang<SUP>&reg;</SUP>
    </UL>
<LI>GIBSON<SUP>&reg;</SUP>
    <UL TYPE="circle">
    <LI>Les Paul<SUP>&reg;</SUP>
    <LI>Lucille<SUP>&trade;</SUP>
    </UL>
<LI>TERADA
    <UL TYPE="circle">
    <LI>TR-1000
    <LI>JW-837
    </UL>
</UL>
```

The list begins and ends with <UL> and </UL> tags, and that list consists of three items (designated by <LI> tags): FENDER, GIBSON, and TERADA. Under each of those is another list using nested tags (another set of <UL> and </UL> tags, as well as the <LI> tags for the items within the nested list).

Creating an Ordered List

Creating an ordered list is the same as creating an unordered list, except for the tag you place at the top of the list. Consider using an ordered list when order counts, such as in the following situations:

- Telling Web visitors the order in which to perform steps to order a product from you
- Indicating the rank order of anything

EXERCISE

Add an ordered list to the Web site by following these steps:

1. In your text editor, open the index.html file.
2. Place the insertion point at the far-right end of the HTML for the first article title:

```
<H1 ALIGN="center"><FONT COLOR="yellow">Tips for Buying Used or Vintage
Guitars</FONT></H1>
```

3. Press Enter.

The HTML used in Step 4 is available on the CD that accompanies this book, in the file Project1TIPS.html.

4. Type the following HTML, pressing Enter after each paragraph:

```
<P>Before buying a used guitar, especially for a significant sum of
money, you should take a number of steps:</P>
<OL TYPE="1">
<LI>Know the subject! With hundreds of manufacturers all around the
world, this step a monumental task. Your best course of action may be
to concentrate on a few manufacturers or types of guitars. For example,
concern yourself primarily with Martin<SUP>&reg;</SUP> guitars, or
```

```
Gibson<SUP>&reg;</SUP> acoustics, or Fender<SUP>&reg;</SUP> electrics,
or classical guitars.<BR><BR>

<LI>If you're interested in the collectibility of the guitar, you need
to know how the guitar was equipped when it came from the factory.
Since manufacturers make changes in the same model from year to year,
you should have at least one reference that you can check for accurate
information. One of the best is <EM>Gruhn's Guide to Vintage
Guitars,</EM> which lists details regarding all kinds of guitars,
although it does not cover every guitar made by every manufacturer.
Books about individual guitar companies are also available, and they
provide company histories and have lots of pictures. Some of the best
of these books concern manufacturers such as Epiphone,<SUP>&reg;</SUP>
Martin,<SUP>&reg;</SUP> Gibson,<SUP>&reg;</SUP> Ovation,<SUP>&reg;</SUP>
and Guild<SUP>&reg;</SUP>.<BR><BR>

<LI>If you're buying the guitar in person, look it over very carefully.
Some problems and defects are easy to spot, such as cracks, missing
tuners, necks pulling away from the body, and so on. Other problems and
defects require closer examination. Such problems include warping of
the neck, bracing problems within the body, bad fretwork, and so
on.<BR><BR>

<LI>Be familiar with the going price for the guitar you've got in mind.
This can be tough to gauge, because prices vary due to a number of
factors. If a famous, popular guitarist plays a certain guitar, fans of
that guitarist may very well push up the price simply because they are
trying to emulate him or her by buying the same guitar. It's a case of
supply and demand. Prices also vary from year to year, and even from
region to region. Reference books that are well worth owning are
<EM>Blue Book of Acoustic Guitars</EM> (revised yearly), <EM>Blue Book
of Electric Guitars</EM> (revised yearly), and <EM>The Official Vintage
Guitar Price Guide.</EM> In addition, some monthly publications also
deal with vintage guitars. Look especially at <EM>Vintage Guitar
Magazine</EM> and <EM>Twentieth-Century Guitar.</EM> These magazines
carry advertisements from dozens of vintage guitar dealers from all
around the United States, Europe, and even Japan. That information can
help you gauge at least the price range for a certain type of guitar.
Of course, condition and originality are the primary determining
factors for most collectible guitars.<BR><BR>

<LI>Be aware that if you buy and sell guitars very much, sooner or
later you are going to lose money on a deal. The more you know,
however, the less you'll lose. So be informed!

</OL>
```

5. Save the document.
6. Switch to your browser and refresh the screen. Figure 4.19 shows how the first few steps appear.

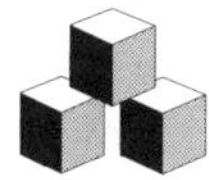

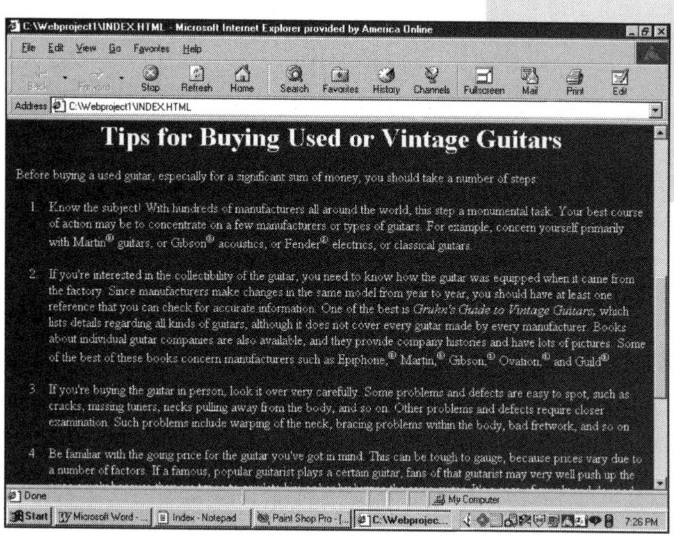

Figure 4.19 The new numbered list is displayed here in IE.

ANALYSIS

Step 4 is where all the action takes place in this process. The text you added in this exercise corresponds to an article title that you entered earlier in the chapter. The first line of HTML in this exercise begins with the `<P>` tag, because that paragraph introduces the numbered list that follows. Next comes the `<OL TYPE="1">` tag, which indicates an ordered list follows. This tag does more than that, however. The `TYPE` attribute used with the `<OL>` tag determines the type of numbering or sequencing used in the ordered list. The possible values for the `TYPE` attribute when used with the `<OL>` tag are:

- `1` (numerical order—1, 2, 3, and so on)
- `a` (lowercase characters in alphabetical order—a, b, c, and so on)
- `A` (uppercase characters in alphabetical order—A, B, C, and so on)
- `i` (lowercase Roman numerals—i, ii, iii, and so on)
- `I` (uppercase Roman numerals—I, II, III, and so on)

You also have the option of starting your list with a character other than the usual starting numeral or character, such as `D`, `ii`, or `V`. To achieve this effect, you add the `START` attribute to the `<OL>` tag, as in:

```
<OL START="D">
```

Note that the <LI> tag on the next line, which is the same tag used for the elements of an unordered list, results this time in a number rather than a bullet next to the item. The <OL> tag, of course, is responsible for the numbering.

Each list item ends with

; these dual tags add a blank line between the list items. At the end of the list is the </OL> end tag. Note that emphasis tags also occur within the text of a couple of the list items.

Combining Ordered and Unordered Lists

In case you were wondering, it is possible to combine unordered and ordered lists. Mixing lists may not be something you'll need to do often, but it certainly opens up new possibilities for formatting your Web site's contents.

EXERCISE

To experiment with mixing the two types of lists, follow these steps:

1. In your text editor, open the index.html file.
2. Locate the <UL TYPE="disc"> tag at the top of the bulleted list, and change it to the following:

```
<OL TYPE="1">
```

3. Locate the </UL> tag at the very bottom of the bulleted list, and change it to the following:

```
</OL>
```

4. Locate each of the </UL> tags that ends a nested list. One is under the Mustang entry, one under the Lucille entry, and one under the JW-837 entry. To the right of each </UL> tag, add the following tag:

```
<BR>
```

5. Save the document.
6. Switch to your browser and refresh the screen. You should see a screen that looks like the one shown in Figure 4.20.

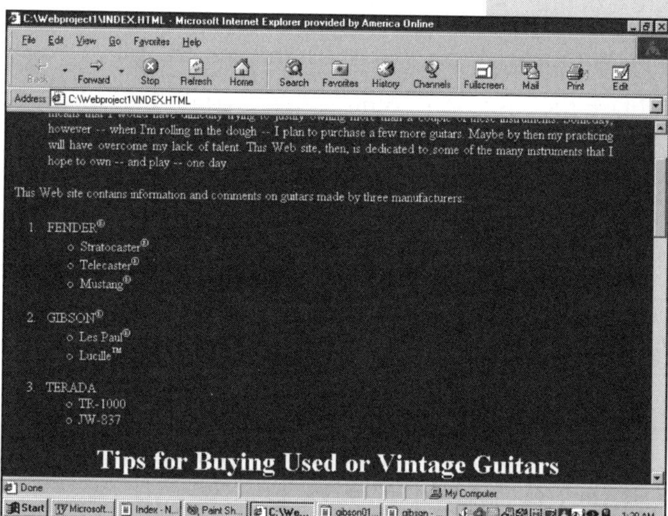

Figure 4.20 This is the mixed ordered and unordered list.

ANALYSIS

The basic idea in this exercise was to change the existing multi-level bulleted list into a combination of ordered and unordered lists. The change was easy to make in this instance, because the only tags that needed to change were the ones starting and stopping the main bulleted list. In Step 2, you changed the unordered list to an ordered list with a `TYPE` of `1`. In Step 3, you changed the end `</UL>` tag to the end tag for an ordered list.

In Step 4, you added `<BR>` tags to create blank lines after the `FENDER`, `GIBSON`, and `TERADA` lists. This extra spacing helps to separate the three sections of the list.

Creating Definition Lists

Another set of tags that you may find useful is intended for a list of definitions. Perhaps your Web site contains a glossary. If so, using these tags may be a perfect way to format the items in that glossary.

EXERCISE

Create a definition list by following these steps:

1. In your text editor, open the `index.html` file.
2. Place the insertion point at the far-right end of the following HTML (which specifies the second article title):

```
<H1 ALIGN="center"><FONT COLOR="yellow">The Buyer's Guide to Grading
Guitars</FONT></H1>
```

3. Press Enter.
4. Add the following HTML (available on the CD that accompanies this book as the file `Project1Guide.html`), pressing Enter after the paragraph end tag:

```
<P>This guide is for anyone who has an interest in guitars, whether for
playing, for collecting, or for both. When you read advertisements for
used or vintage guitars, you'll see a number of terms and abbreviations
that are meaningful to the knowledgeable buyer. Several of those
abbreviations describe the guitar's condition. Unfortunately, not all
sellers use the same terminology (or even the same number of terms),
and therefore universal agreement on these terms doesn't exist. In
addition, judging the condition of a guitar is quite subjective. Still,
to provide some guidance, here are some terms you are likely to see
frequently. You also may see descriptions that add a + or - to one of
these terms, indicating that the condition is somewhere between two
ratings. The description "Good +" means, for example, that the guitar
is somewhere between good condition and very good condition. If you buy
a guitar via the Internet or mail order, and you haven't actually seen
or played the instrument, make sure that you buy from a reputable
dealer whom you trust.</P>
```

5. Beginning on the blank line that you created by pressing Enter at the end of Step 4, add the following tags (press Enter after each line):

```
<DL>
<DT><STRONG><FONT COLOR="yellow">New</STRONG>
<DD>Brand new. These guitars come with a manufacturer's warranty and
everything.
<DT><STRONG><FONT COLOR="yellow">Mint</FONT></STRONG>
<DD>Perfect. A guitar in mint condition looks like it just came out of
the box: no scratches, no wear.
<DT><STRONG><FONT COLOR="yellow">Near Mint</FONT></STRONG>
<DD>The guitar looks almost new. Same as <STRONG>NM</STRONG>.
```

```
<DT><STRONG><FONT COLOR="yellow">Excellent</FONT></STRONG>
<DD>A guitar in excellent condition may have a few <EM>minor</EM> signs
of handling or use, such as minor scratches that don't penetrate the
finish. Same as <EM>EX, EC, EXC.</EM>
<DT><STRONG><FONT COLOR="yellow">Very Good</FONT></STRONG>
<DD>A very "clean" guitar; that is, it shows some signs of use, such as
a minor scratch or ding, but otherwise it is in great shape. Same as
<STRONG>VG, VGC.</STRONG>
<DT><STRONG><FONT COLOR="yellow">Good</FONT></STRONG>
<DD>This guitar is also clean, but has more scratches and "bumps and
bruises" than a very good guitar.
<DT><STRONG><FONT COLOR="yellow">Fair</FONT></STRONG>
<DD>A fair guitar is quite playable, but has a significant number of
dings, scratches, and wear.
<DT><STRONG><FONT COLOR="yellow">Poor</FONT></STRONG>
<DD> A poor guitar shows a great deal of wear and has suffered an
abundance of scratches and bumps; it's playable, but maybe not as
playable as you'd like, and it certainly isn't attractive.
</DL>
```

6. Save `index.html`.
7. Switch to your browser and refresh the screen. Figure 4.21 shows the portion of the screen that contains the definition list.

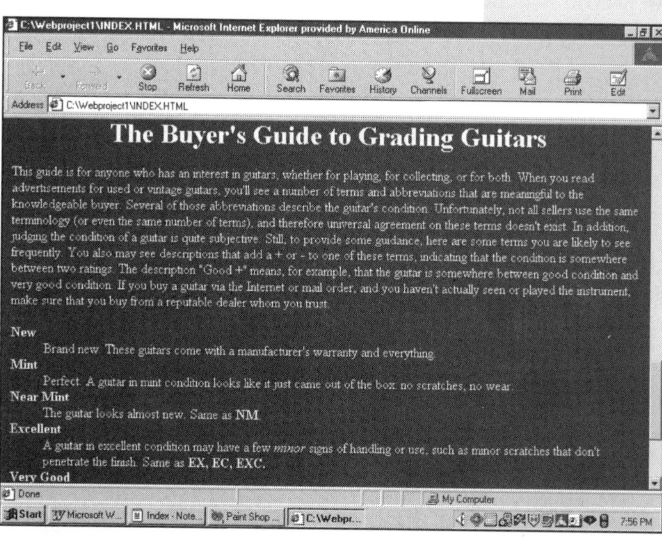

Figure 4.21 The finished list of definitions is shown here.

ANALYSIS

In Step 4, you typed the introductory paragraph for the "Buyer's Guide to Grading Guitars" article. Step 5 is where you created the remaining text of the article. This article takes the form of a list of definitions, so you preceded the first definition with the <DL> tag, which indicates the beginning of a definition list. The next tag is <DT>, which is the tag for a definition term (New is the first term). Along with the <DT> tag you typed two tags and an attribute: the <STRONG> tag to make the term bold, and the <FONT> tag with the COLOR attribute to make the term yellow for added emphasis as well as to fit the Web site's color scheme. The final component of a definition list entry is the definition itself, which is denoted by the <DD> tag. The rest of the definition entries follow the same pattern as the first entry.

The only end tag required for a definition list is the </DL> tag, which ends the list. The <DT> and <DD> tags for the individual entries don't have end tags.

Summary

In the course of beginning to build the Project 1 Web site, you've learned about tags required for each Web page, and tags used to store various vital pieces of information about a Web site. Among those tags are <!DOCTYPE>, <HTML>, <HEAD>, and <META>.

In addition, this chapter has covered many of the basic formatting tags used in HTML, including <BODY>, <P>, <BR>, <FONT>, and the tags for emphasis and relative sizing. You've also learned how to create and modify horizontal rules using the <HR> tag, and how to adjust the background of a Web site. Several important attributes have been discussed, most notably NAME, ALIGN, and SIZE.

One very common element of Web sites is the list. Lists come in unordered (bulleted) and ordered (numbered) varieties, as well as combinations of the two. This chapter has shown you how to create several types of lists.

In the process of learning to use all the above-named tags and attributes, you have built most of the first page for the Project 1 Web site. In Chapter 5, you will finish creating this Web site by adding more pages, and by working with links and graphics.

Finishing Up the Basic Web Site

In Chapter 4, you built the foundation of the basic Web site for Project 1, and formatted the information on the Welcome page in a variety of ways to make it appealing and easy to follow. If that sort of page were all the Web offered, however, few people would be out there surfing around. The features that make the Web so wildly popular are its capability to display graphics and the ease with which a user can move from site to site by clicking on a link. This chapter walks you through the details of doing a number of other things with the Project 1 Web site, including creating links within the site, linking the site to other sites, implementing a mechanism to get feedback from your visitors, and adding graphics.

This chapter also provides some basic testing strategies you can use once you've finished building the site, to make sure that your HTML efforts are ready for the Web.

Creating Additional Pages for Your Web Site

In order to complete the remainder of this project, you need to add more pages to your Web site. You have a couple of options here. The first, and probably easiest, option is simply to copy the files you need from the CD that accompanies this book. The other option is to type the necessary text yourself. It's your choice, but typing the text will give you a better feel for how the HTML works because you are more likely to pay attention to the tags and their attributes.

Adding the Second Page of the Web Site

The first page of the Project 1 Web site, which you worked on throughout Chapter 4, is the Welcome page (`index.html`). Now you'll create the second page of this Web site, the Fender page.

ON THE CD

The HTML in this section is available on the CD that accompanies this book, as the file `fender01.html`.

EXERCISE

Follow these steps to create the Fender page yourself:

1. If the `index.html` file is still open, close it.
2. Open a new file in your text editor.
3. Type the following HTML:

```
<!DOCTYPE HTML PUBLIC "-//W3/DTD HTML 4.0 Transitional//EN"
"http://www.w3.org/TR/REC-html40/loose.dtd">
<HTML>
   <HEAD>
      <TITLE>The Vintage Guitar Appreciation Page</TITLE>
      <META NAME="keywords" CONTENT="guitar, vintage guitar, guitar
      collecting, Fender, Gibson, Terada, Stratocaster, Telecaster,
      Mustang, Les Paul, Lucille, TR-1000, JW-837, Leo Fender, Orville
      Gibson">
   <META NAME="description" CONTENT="A little guitar history, some tips
   on buying vintage guitars, and a few words about some of my favorite
   guitars.">
   </HEAD>
```

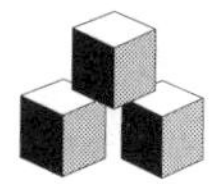


```
<BODY BGCOLOR="black" TEXT="white" LINK="yellow" VLINK="red"
ALINK="lime">

<P><FONT SIZE="4">Once upon a time, </FONT>Leo Fender built an
object that looked like a guitar neck with a slightly wider chunk of
wood stuck on the end opposite the tuning pegs – and music hasn't
been the same since. No, he wasn't the inventor of the
electric guitar, but he certainly stirred up public interest in
them. Many people think the revolution he kicked into gear in
the 1940s reached its zenith during the 1960s, when his own company
and its competitors, including Gibson,<SUP>&reg;</SUP>
Gretsch,<SUP>&reg;</SUP> Rickenbacker,<SUP>&reg;</SUP> and others,
were selling electric guitars to anyone and everyone who wanted to
be a rock star. That group would have included me, but I never had
enough money. I kept spending it on records. If I'd spent it on
guitars instead, maybe people would be buying <EM>my</EM> music
now.</P>

<DIV ALIGN="center">

<CENTER>

<P><FONT SIZE="6" COLOR="yellow">Stratocaster:<SUP>&reg;</SUP>
<EM>The Guitarist's Dream</EM></FONT></P>

</CENTER>

</DIV>

<P>One of the most recognized – and most copied – shapes in
all of guitardom, the Strat is played by countless musicians,
professional and amateur alike. Leo invented the Strat in order to
incorporate some new ideas, and the company issued it in 1954. A
different body shape and three pickups instead of two were the most
notable changes from Fender's already-successful
Telecaster.<SUP>&reg;</SUP></P>

<P>Just about any guitarist even half serious about guitar playing
wants to own a Strat. Guitar heroes from Eric Clapton to Bonnie
Raitt to Stevie Ray Vaughan to Robert Cray to just-about-anyone-
else-you-can-name plays or has played a Strat<SUP>&reg;</SUP> at
one time or another. The Stratocaster's<SUP>&reg;</SUP> popularity
has led many other companies to copy the look of the Strat,
<SUP>&reg;</SUP> and some companies even have tried to go beyond
the Stratocaster.<SUP>&reg;</SUP> Still, genuine Stratocasters
<SUP>&reg;</SUP> are <EM>the</EM> guitar for untold numbers of
guitarists.</P>

<DIV ALIGN="center">

<CENTER>

<P><FONT SIZE="6" COLOR="yellow">Telecaster:<SUP>&reg;</SUP> <EM>A
True Classic</EM></FONT></P>

</CENTER>

</DIV>
```

```
<P>One of Fender's<SUP>&reg;</SUP> slightly less popular models –
which means it is only <EM>enormously</EM> popular – is the
Telecaster.<SUP>&reg;</SUP> Originally known as the Broadcaster,
Fender<SUP>&reg;</SUP> had to drop that name because
Gretsch<SUP>&reg;</SUP>already had trademarked the name
"Broadkaster"<SUP>&reg;</SUP> for a set of drums. In between, some
of these soon-to-be-Telecasters went out as so-called "Nocasters":
The name "Fender"<SUP>&reg;</SUP> remained on the headstock, but the
rest of the decal was cut off; hence, the decal had no "caster" on
it at all.</P>

<P>Through the years, the Telecaster<SUP>&reg;</SUP> has been a big
seller for Fender,<SUP>&reg;</SUP> and it is probably the company's
best-known and most recognized six-string guitar after the
Stratocaster.<SUP>&reg;</SUP> Despite the popularity of
Strats,<SUP>&reg;</SUP> however, I have always preferred the look
and sound of Telecasters.<SUP>&reg;</SUP> Country musicians
especially seem to take full advantage of the twangy possibilities
of the Telecaster.<SUP>&reg;</SUP> The Telecaster<SUP>&reg;</SUP> is
one of those guitars that I <EM>really</EM> wish I owned. When I was
a teenager, one of my friends bought one and I got to play it a bit,
but I think he sold it some years later. He probably wishes he still
had it. Most guitarists, when they look back, regret having sold
certain instruments. I regret not ever buying one in the first
place.</P>

<DIV ALIGN="center">

<CENTER>

<P><FONT SIZE="6" COLOR="yellow">Mustang:<SUP>&reg;</SUP> <EM>Grungy
Popularity</EM></FONT></P>

</CENTER>

</DIV>

<P>The Fender<SUP>&reg;</SUP> Mustang<SUP>&reg;</SUP> always has been
more of a beginner's guitar than one intended for professional use.
It is interesting to note, therefore, that the
Mustang's<SUP>&reg;</SUP> renewed popularity in recent years has
been due to its status as a favorite of a 90s rock guitar star: Kurt
Cobain. Cobain didn't necessarily use stock versions of the guitar
– he frequently had them modified – but Mustangs<SUP>&reg;</SUP>
were some of his favorites.</P>

<P>The Mustang<SUP>&reg;</SUP> shown here is approximately 30 years
old (the neck is dated 1968). My ownership of it began in 1979, when
I bought it at a pawn shop in Wichita, Kansas. A friend of mine, who
knew (and still knows) a tremendous amount about guitars, looked it
over and suggested I buy it. He said it was a good deal. I paid $200
for the guitar and a Fender<SUP>&reg;</SUP> Princeton<SUP>&reg;</SUP>
amplifier that was made about the same time. I have not modified the
guitar in any way, and I never even have had to replace a tube in
```

```
    the amplifier. All I've done is change the guitar strings
    occasionally. I've been happy with it.</P>
    </BODY>
</HTML>
```

4. Save the file with the name `fender01.html`.
5. Switch to your browser and open the `fender01.html` page. Figure 5.1 shows the top of this page.

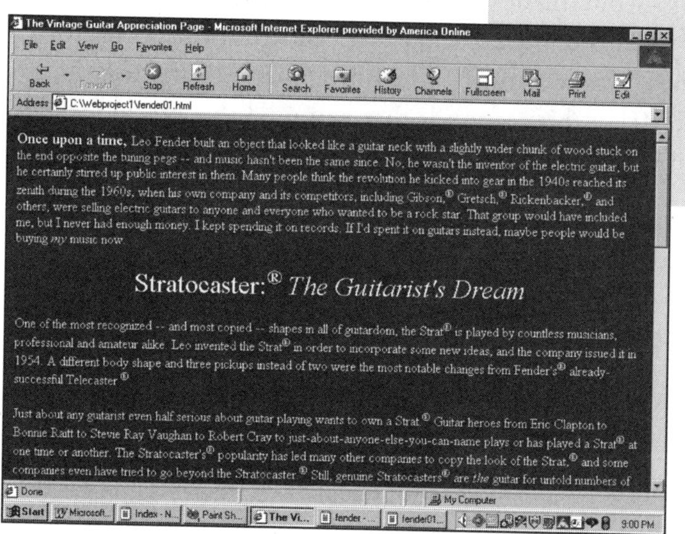

Figure 5.1 The browser here shows the beginning of the Fender page.

ANALYSIS

In Step 2, you opened a new file for this new page of the Web site. A new page avoids the problem of making the entire Web site one long page. You may have noticed that the first several tags are the same as those for the `index.html` page. I decided to keep all that information the same, because this page will contain links to all the other pages. I figured that someone searching for information on, say, Gibson guitars, could use the link to get to that page of the site. In Step 3, you typed the HTML for the Fender page. After the tags that contain important information but don't appear onscreen—such as the `<!DOCTYPE>`, `<META>`, and `<HTML>` tags—came a paragraph of introduction to the page, which was followed by a section about Fender Stratocasters.

In the first phrase of the introductory paragraph, you increased slightly the size of the font (from the standard 3 to 4) in order to make it stand out a bit.

In keeping with practice established earlier in the project, you used *two* tags to center the Stratocaster heading: the deprecated `<CENTER>` tag and the now-preferred `<DIV ALIGN="center">` tag. The Stratocaster heading, in fact, isn't a heading at all. It is actually a size-6 font. When I tried using a level-1 heading, IE kept the formatting (regular and italic text)—but made the whole line bold. I wanted plenty of contrast between the black background and the words onscreen, but the bold yellow was too much. The only other noteworthy point regarding the HTML in this section is that you used the logical formatting tags `<EM>` and `</EM>` instead of the physical formatting tags `<I>` and `</I>`.

The remaining items on this page were set up the same as the Stratocaster section.

Adding the Third Page of the Web Site

Now create the third page of the Project 1 Web site, the Gibson page. Again, it probably is best if you type it all yourself to notice the details.

ON THE CD

The HTML in this section is available on the CD that accompanies this book, as the file `gibson01.html`.

EXERCISE

Follow these steps to create the Gibson page yourself:

1. In your text editor, close the `fender01.html` file if it's still open.
2. Open a new file in your text editor.
3. Type the following HTML:

```
<!DOCTYPE HTML PUBLIC "-//W3/DTD HTML 4.0 Transitional//EN"
"http://www.w3.org/TR/REC-html40/loose.dtd">
   <HTML>
      <HEAD>
         <TITLE>The Vintage Guitar Appreciation Page</TITLE>
         <META NAME="keywords" CONTENT="guitar, vintage guitar, guitar
         collecting, Fender, Gibson, Terada, Stratocaster, Telecaster,
```

```
    Mustang, Les Paul, Lucille, TR-1000, JW-837, Leo Fender,
    Orville Gibson">
    <META NAME="description" CONTENT="A little guitar history, some
    tips on buying vintage guitars, and a few words about some of
    my favorite guitars.">
  </HEAD>
<BODY BGCOLOR="black" TEXT="white" LINK="yellow" VLINK="red"
ALINK="lime">
  <P><FONT SIZE="4">Orville Gibson was in his fifties</FONT> by the
  time Leo Fender was born, having established his mandolin and
  guitar company in Kalamazoo, Michigan, some seven years earlier.
  As far as the early years are concerned, the company Gibson built
  is especially famous for its early mandolins and archtop guitars,
  both of which are highly prized by collectors. Later years have
  seen the introduction of many, many other models. Some of those
  models are the J-200 and the ES-175, the Flying
  V<SUP>&trade;</SUP> and the Explorer,<SUP>&trade;</SUP> the SG
  and, of course, the . . .</P>
<DIV ALIGN="center">
<CENTER>
  <P><FONT SIZE="6" COLOR="yellow">Les Paul:<SUP>&reg;</SUP> <EM>The
  Stuff of Legend</EM></FONT></P>
</CENTER>
</DIV>
<P> For countless guitarists, the Les Paul<SUP>&reg;</SUP> is their
version of the Holy Grail. The shape of the Les Paul<SUP>&reg;</SUP>
is instantly recognizable among guitarists. The asymmetrical body,
with one cutaway on the lower side of the neck, enables guitarists
to play notes on the upper reaches of the neck (a staple of many
screaming lead guitar solos). Gibson<SUP>&reg;</SUP> also makes a
double cutaway version of the Les Paul, <SUP>&reg;</SUP> but the
single cutaway is the shape everyone associates with a guitar of
this name.</P>
<P>Les Paul was more than the person whose name
Gibson<SUP>&reg;</SUP> put on these guitars. He was an accomplished
and popular guitarist, as well as an inventor. Around 1940, he
created The Log, which was essentially a guitar neck attached to a
block of wood, and with two sides taken from another guitar. Les
Paul devised a pickup system that he attached to The Log. Thus was
born his version of an electric guitar. The Gibson<SUP>&reg;</SUP>
company was not impressed . . . at least, not until Leo Fender
started gaining the upper hand in the electric guitar market by mass
producing <EM>his</EM> line of guitars. The rest is history. I once
played a 1957 Les Paul<SUP>&reg;</SUP> GoldTop, but I've never owned
a Les Paul<SUP>&reg;</SUP> with <EM>any</EM> color of top. I can
dream, though, can't I?</P>
```

```
<DIV ALIGN="center">
<CENTER>
   <P><FONT SIZE="6" COLOR="yellow">Lucille:<SUP>&trade;</SUP>
   <EM>Black and Blues All Over</EM></FONT></P>
</CENTER>
</DIV>
     <P>B.B. King is one of the most famous blues guitarists of all
     time. And his guitar bears one of the most unusual names in
     the world of guitars: Lucille.<SUP>&trade;</SUP> In reality,
     King has had a number of guitars over the years, and he has
     referred to them all as Lucille. Gibson didn't assign his
     original Lucille that name, of course; he just began calling
     "her" Lucille.<SUP>&trade;</SUP></P>
     <P>King has preferred to play Gibsons for decades. In 1982,
     the long, informal association of B.B. King with Gibson finally
     resulted in a formal relationship. As a result, Gibson
     introduced the Lucille<SUP>&trade;</SUP> model. The
     Lucille<SUP>&trade;</SUP> model is actually a variation of the
     famous Gibson ES-335. The semi-hollow body and the neck are
     laminated maple, and the fingerboard is ebony. The guitar comes
     with two humbucking pickups and numerous tone, volume, and
     other controls. One of Lucille's<SUP>&trade;</SUP> more unusual
     characteristics (for a semi-hollow body guitar) is the lack of
     soundholes. The example shown in the picture here happens to
     have a number of autographs on it. Among those who signed the
     guitar are B.B. King (of course!), Buddy Guy, Lonnie Brooks,
     and Sam Moore.</P>
   </BODY>
</HTML>
```

4. Save the `gibson01.html` file.
5. Switch to your browser and open `gibson01.html`.

The Gibson page is set up the same as the Fender page you worked on earlier in the chapter. Remember that the goal is to keep the same color scheme and design throughout the Web site in order to present visitors with a consistent appearance.

Adding the Fourth Page of the Web Site

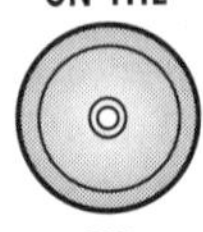

Now create the fourth page of the Project 1 Web site.

The HTML in this section is available on the CD that accompanies this book, as the file `terada01.html`.

EXERCISE

Follow these steps to create the Terada page yourself:

1. In your text editor, close the `gibson01.html` file if it's still open.
2. Open a new file in your text editor.
3. Type the following HTML:

```
<!DOCTYPE HTML PUBLIC "-//W3/DTD HTML 4.0 Transitional//EN"
"http://www.w3.org/TR/REC-html40/loose.dtd">
<HTML>
 <HEAD>
   <TITLE>The Vintage Guitar Appreciation Page</TITLE>
   <META NAME="keywords" CONTENT="guitar, vintage guitar, guitar
   collecting, Fender, Gibson, Terada, Stratocaster, Telecaster,
   Mustang, Les Paul, Lucille, TR-1000, JW-837, Leo Fender, Orville
   Gibson">
     <META NAME="description" CONTENT="A little guitar history, some
     tips on buying vintage guitars, and a few words about some of
     my favorite guitars.">
 </HEAD>
 <BODY BGCOLOR="black" TEXT="white" LINK="yellow" VLINK="red"
 ALINK="lime">
   <P><FONT SIZE="4">No doubt you're saying</FONT> to yourself right
   now, "Terada? Never heard of it." It wouldn't surprise me if you
   are. I'll admit that I'm including this guitar in such select
   company because of sentimental reasons. My first guitar was a
   Terada acoustic. Terada is a Japanese guitar manufacturer that
   generally seems to be little known outside Japan. The company
   began in 1912 as a manufacturer of toy violins, and started
   making stringed instruments seriously in the mid-1950s. By the
   1970s, Terada was producing more than 10,000 guitars per month in
   its three factories around Nagoya, Japan — guitars intended for
   both overseas and domestic markets. Currently, Terada builds only
   about one-eighth the number of guitars it made back in the 1970s.
   Terada has manufactured instruments for American companies in the
   past, and the company is still in business in Japan. I have seen
   gear lists for Japanese rock bands that included Terada guitars.
   So far, however, I have found only two other people who own
   Terada guitars. I located one of them via the Internet, and she
   gave me the e-mail address of the second person. I've never met
   either one of them.</P>
 <DIV ALIGN="center">
 <CENTER>
   <P><FONT SIZE="6" COLOR="yellow">TR-1000: <EM>My First
   Guitar</EM></FONT></P>
 </CENTER>
```

```
</DIV>
   <P>I had never seen Terada guitars before I bought this one in
   1974, and I have never seen one since - not in person, anyway. I
   think I paid about $120 for this guitar, but I don't know what it
   would cost to find an equivalent one today. I think this guitar
   sounds nice, although I'll admit that I've never performed a
   side-by-side comparison with other guitars. I've the spent the
   past 24+ years playing it from time to time, but never playing it
   for a long enough period of time to become especially good at it.
   That's why I refer to myself as a mediocre amateur. Music genes
   are not abundant in my DNA.</P>
   <P>The TR-1000 is about a 00 size guitar, so it's smaller than
   the dreadnought guitars that so many people have. According to
   information I received from the manufacturer (thanks to Rose), my
   guitar was built in 1973. This guitar has a laminated spruce top,
   and laminated rosewood back and sides, with a mahogany neck. The
   fingerboard also is rosewood. My TR-1000 is highly unlikely to
   make anyone's list of great guitars, but I like it. Besides,
   after I buy a better guitar - what do you think, a Taylor or a
   Martin? - I think I'll set up my Terada for playing slide.</P>
<DIV ALIGN="center">
<CENTER>
   <P><FONT SIZE="6" COLOR="yellow">JW-837: <EM>C&amp;W
   Lives!</EM></FONT></P>
</CENTER>
</DIV>
   <P>This Terada is a JW-837 Super Jumbo guitar, and it is owned by
   my friend Rose. I "met" Rose one day when I was searching for the
   word "Terada" on the Web, looking for information about the
   company and its products. Rose, who lives in Hilversum, Holland,
   really likes this guitar. Her teacher told her that it sounded
   almost exactly like his old Gibson<SUP>&reg;</SUP> J-200. Indeed,
   it is a copy of that guitar, and this variation has a sunburst
   finish and a country-and-western motif on the pickguard. This JW-
   837 also has a laminated spruce top, but the back is three-piece
   laminated maple with wood mosaic inlays. The sides are laminated
   maple, and the neck is mahogany. The fingerboard is rosewood.</P>
 </BODY>
</HTML>
```

4. Save the document file as `terada01.html`.
5. Switch to your browser and open `terada01.html`. This page should have the same look as `fender01.html` and `gibson01.html`, but with different text.

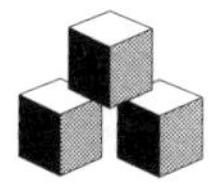

ANALYSIS

Only two things are different about this page compared with the other two manufacturer pages. One of the differences is the content. The other difference appears in the HTML in Step 3, where you have the following:

```
<P><FONT SIZE="6" COLOR="yellow">JW-837: <EM>C&amp;W
Lives!</EM></FONT></P>
```

Notice the `C&W` part. In a browser, this code appears as `C&W`. Recall from earlier in the project that certain characters, including the ampersand, require special character codes in HTML. In this case, you need to use `C&W` to produce `C&W` in a browser.

All three pages are set up the same way, so all three pages have the same appearance. The entire Web site has a consistent color scheme and design: black for the background, white for the text, and yellow for headings and important text.

Now that the text for all the Web site's pages is in place, it's time to go to work on the most useful of a Web site's capabilities: links.

Linking to Other Locations

***A hyperlink** is a means of immediately and easily going from one location to another.*

This section deals with the heart of the Web: linking from one page to another. The capability of jumping from location to location is one of the prime reasons that the Web is so useful.

The destination of a hyperlink can be another Web site on the other side of the world, or merely a specific location within your own Web site. You click on a word or graphic that has a link embedded in the HTML, and the browser takes you to the corresponding URL.

Creating Links within Your Web Site

Probably the most frequently used—and most useful—type of hyperlink takes visitors from wherever they are in a Web site to another location within that same Web site. Such a link may be to a certain page of the Web site, for example, or to just about anything else within your Web site. The uses of these internal links are limited only by your imagination.

Linking to Another Page on Your Web Site

Sometimes you'll want a hyperlink to take the user to a particular page, but not necessarily to a specific location on that page. Doing this is a breeze.

EXERCISE

One of the first hyperlinking tasks in the Project 1 Web site is to give visitors a means of getting to particular topics in which they are interested. The Welcome page has a ready-made place to insert those hyperlinks. Follow these steps to create some hyperlinks:

1. In your text editor, open the `index.html` file.
2. Scroll down to the combined unordered-ordered list that appears about one-third of the way through the file.
3. Change the `<LI>FENDER` line to the following:

```
<LI><A HREF="fender.html">FENDER<SUP>&reg;</SUP></A>
```

4. Move down to the `<LI>GIBSON` line, and change it to the following:

```
<LI><A HREF="gibson.html">GIBSON<SUP>&reg;</SUP></A>
```

5. Move down to the `<LI>TERADA` line, and change it to the following:

```
<LI><A HREF="terada.html">TERADA</A>
```

6. Save the document.
7. Switch to your browser and refresh the screen. Figure 5.2 shows the new links in the ordered list. Look for the underlined (and differently colored) text.

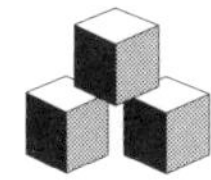

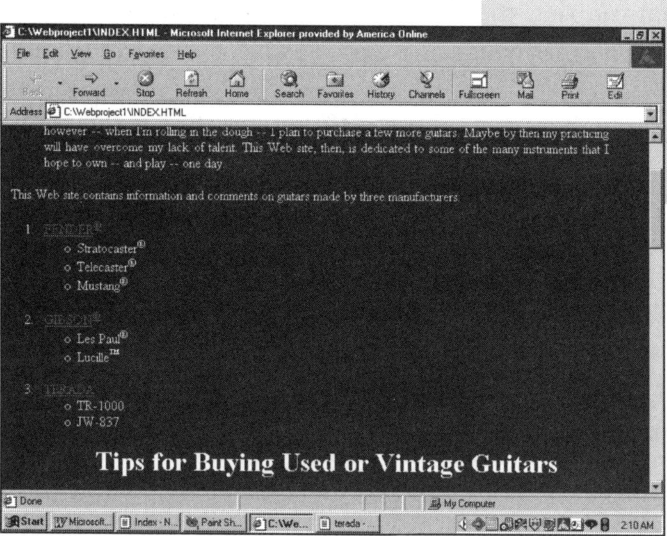

Figure 5.2 You've turned ordered list items into hyperlinks.

ANALYSIS

A link to a location on your Web site consists of just a few parts. The `<A>` tag is the *anchor* tag, and it requires an end tag, `</A>`. `HREF` is short for *hypertext reference,* and is one of the attributes for the `<A>` tag. The value you assign to the `HREF` attribute in an internal link is the name of the file to which you are linking. In the case of Step 3, the link is to the Fender page on the Web site. In Step 4, the link is to the Gibson page, and in Step 5, it is to the Terada page.

If you're building the Web site as you work through the book, you don't actually have finished versions of the Fender, Gibson, and Terada pages yet. At this point, you have `fender01.html`, `gibson01.html`, and `terada01.html` files. When everything is completed, however, you will save them as `fender.html`, `gibson.html`, and `terada.html`. That's why you're not including `01` in the filenames for the hypertext references.

The whole tag—in Step 3, for example, `<A HREF="fender.html">`—is the *link target.* After the word `FENDER` comes the anchor end tag, `</A>`. The word `FENDER` itself is the *link text.* This is the part of the text that, when you view the page in the browser, is underlined and in a different color. In other words, the word FENDER is now the actual link that a visitor can click. After the pages are finished, if you click on one of the hyperlinks you've just created, then you'll end up—if everything has gone according to plan—at the top of the page for the link you've clicked. Voilà!

You may have noticed that the numbers next to the manufacturers' names are not part of the hyperlinks. You can make them part of the links, if you want, by simply including the <LI> tag in the link text. In that case, the correct tag linking to the Fender page would be the following:

```
<A HREF="fender.html"><LI>FENDER</A>
```

In creating these internal links, you used *relative URLs* as opposed to *absolute URLs*. An absolute URL is the full address of the file to which you are linking. When you are linking to a different Web site, for example, you have to give that site's (and the exact page's) full address, as in the following example:

```
http://www.yourguitarcompany.com/inventory/newstock.html
```

If you are linking to part of your own Web site, however, the page *from* which you are linking and the page *to* which you are linking usually have part of their addresses in common. If someone at Your Guitar Company is creating a link from the `/inventory/newstock` folder to `/inventory/sales.html`, for example, she needs to use only `"sales.html"` in the link target, because `http://www.yourguitarcompany.com/inventory` is common to both the source and destination of the link.

If that employee is creating a link from the `/inventory/newstock` folder to the `/inventory/sales/june` folder, the relative URL is a bit longer. In this case, the path for the link target would be `"sales/june"` and the page name also would be needed in order to link to a specific page.

It's best to always use absolute URLs in external links and relative URLs in internal links.

Note

You can use the <A> tag in conjunction with a number of different elements, including the following: <P>, <LI>, <DT>, <DD>, <PRE>, <ADDRESS>, and headings (<H1>, <H2>, and so on).

Linking to a Specific Location on a Page

Suppose that you want to help visitors find a specific section of your Web site. You don't need to link them to a page and then make them scroll down the page until they find the section of interest. Instead, you can take them directly to the section they want.

EXERCISE

Try creating links to specific locations on the Web site you have created in Project 1. Follow these steps:

1. In your text editor, open the `index.html` file.
2. In the bulleted list, find the entry for Stratocaster. Change that entry to the following:

```
<LI><A HREF="fender.html#Stratocaster">Stratocaster<SUP>&reg;</SUP></A>
```

3. Go down to the entry for Telecaster, and change it to the following:

```
<LI><A HREF="fender.html#Telecaster">Telecaster<SUP>&reg;</SUP></A>
```

4. Go down to the Mustang entry, and change it to this:

```
<LI><A HREF="fender.html#Mustang">Mustang<SUP>&reg;</SUP></A>
```

5. Just so you don't lose anything, save your work at this point.
6. Continue to the Les Paul entry, and change it to the following:

```
<LI><A HREF="gibson.html#Les Paul">Les Paul<SUP>&reg;</SUP></A>
```

7. Change the Lucille entry to this:

```
<LI><A HREF="gibson.html#Lucille">Lucille<SUP>&trade;</SUP></A>
```

8. In the Terada section, change the TR-1000 entry to this:

```
<LI><A HREF="terada.html#TR-1000">TR-1000</A>
```

9. Change the JW-837 entry to this:

```
<LI><A HREF="terada.html#JW-837">JW-837</A>
```

10. Save the `index.html` file.
11. Switch to your browser and open `index.html`. Figure 5.3 shows the results of your effort on these links.

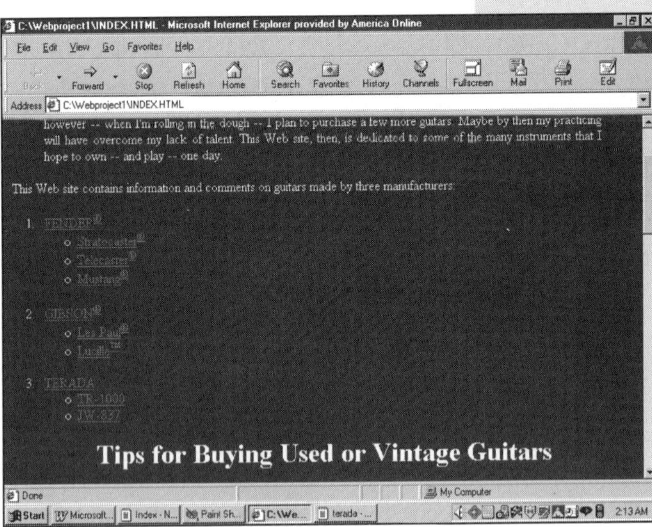

Figure 5.3 The entire list now is a set of links to various locations on the Web site.

ANALYSIS

A *target name,* or *fragment identifier,* is indicated by the `#` in an anchor tag. The browser needs this identifier to know where to send a visitor who clicks on that link.

This 11-step exercise actually is only half the process of establishing links to particular locations on the Web site. First, of course, comes the anchor tag, `<A>`, which you inserted in this exercise. Along with that tag is the familiar `HREF` attribute. The trick is in the value assigned to the `HREF` attribute. The first part of this value is the path to the file to which you are linking. In this case, since this file is in the same folder (`Webproject1`) as your Welcome page file, all you needed was the filename. Immediately after the filename, however, you typed a pound sign (`#`) to tell the browser

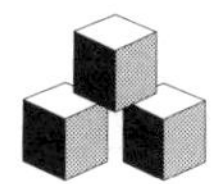

you were linking to a `NAME` attribute of the anchor tag. After the pound sign comes the name of the location to which you are linking. This name can be whatever you want, but make sure that it's understandable.

EXERCISE

Continue the creation of internal hyperlinks by following the steps in the next exercise. When you finish, you will have created hyperlinks to several specific locations within the Web site.

These are the steps for putting the hyperlinks fully in place:

1. In your text editor, open the `fender01.html` file.
2. Locate the following HTML (a little more than one-third of the way into the document):

```
<P><FONT SIZE="6" COLOR="yellow">Stratocaster:<SUP>&reg;</SUP> <EM>The
Guitarist's Dream</EM></FONT></P>
```

3. Change it to the following:

```
<P><FONT SIZE="6" COLOR="yellow"><A NAME="Stratocaster">Stratocaster:
<SUP>&reg;</SUP> <EM>The Guitarist's Dream</EM></A></FONT></P>
```

4. Now find this tag:

```
<P><FONT SIZE="6" COLOR="yellow">Telecaster:<SUP>&reg;</SUP> <EM>A True
Classic</EM></FONT></P>
```

5. Change it to this:

```
<P><FONT SIZE="6" COLOR="yellow"><A NAME="Telecaster">Telecaster:
<SUP>&reg;</SUP> <EM>A True Classic</EM></A></FONT></P>
```

6. Continuing down the file, find this Mustang HTML:

```
<P><FONT SIZE="6" COLOR="yellow">Mustang:<SUP>&reg;</SUP> <EM>Grungy
Popularity</EM></FONT></P>
```

7. Change it to the following:

```
<P><FONT SIZE="6" COLOR="yellow"><A NAME="Mustang">Mustang:
<SUP>&reg;</SUP> <EM>Grungy Popularity</EM></A></FONT></P>
```

8. Save the `fender01.html` file.

ANALYSIS

In changing the `fender01.html` file, you supplied the second half of the hyperlinks you started in the preceding series of steps. You again used the `<A>` tag, but this time, you used the `NAME` attribute in the place where you used the `HREF` attribute in the first part of the process. The value placed within quotation marks consists solely of a name, which is the name assigned to the destination when you started this linking process in the preceding series of steps. In other words, you used the `NAME` attribute to identify a given section of the document as the destination for a link. You finish off the link by nesting the `</A>` end tag in the correct location, after the text you're using as the link, and before the `</FONT>` tag.

To finish all the internal links, make the following changes in the indicated files:

1. In your text editor, open the `gibson01.html` file.
2. Find this HTML:

```
<P><FONT SIZE="6" COLOR="yellow">Les Paul:<SUP>&reg;</SUP> <EM>The
Stuff of Legend</EM></FONT></P>
```

3. Change it to the following:

```
<P><FONT SIZE="6" COLOR="yellow"><A NAME="Les Paul">Les
Paul:<SUP>&reg;</SUP> <EM>The Stuff of Legend</EM></A></FONT></P>
```

4. Now find this HTML:

```
<P><FONT SIZE="6" COLOR="yellow">Lucille:<SUP>&trade;</SUP> <EM>Black
and Blues All Over</EM></FONT></P>
```

5. Change it to the following:

```
<P><FONT SIZE="6" COLOR="yellow"><A NAME="Lucille">Lucille:
<SUP>&trade;</SUP> <EM>Black and Blues All Over</EM></A></FONT></P>
```

6. Save the `gibson01.html` file.
7. Open the `terada01.html` file in your text editor.
8. Find this HTML:

```
<P><FONT SIZE="6" COLOR="yellow">TR-1000: <EM>My First
Guitar</EM></FONT></P>
```

9. Change it to the following:

```
<P><FONT SIZE="6" COLOR="yellow"><A NAME="TR-1000">TR-1000: <EM>My
First Guitar</EM></A></FONT></P>
```

10. Now find this HTML:

```
<P><FONT SIZE="6" COLOR="yellow">JW-837: <EM>C&amp;W
Lives!</EM></FONT></P>
```

11. Change it to the following:

```
<P><FONT SIZE="6" COLOR="yellow"><A NAME="JW-837">JW-837: <EM>
C&amp;W Lives!</EM></A></FONT></P>
```

12. Save the `terada01.html` file.

Adding Navigational Links

The problem with using a browser's Back button is that you can go only to a place where you've been before—including every stop along the way. Far better are links that jump over intervening locations and go directly to the beginning, for example, or to other destinations that the Web site visitor may want to access.

To add a "Home" link—a link to the first page of the Web site—follow these steps:

1. In your text editor, open the `fender01.html` file.
2. Place the insertion point at the end of the HTML, just above the `</BODY>` tag.
3. Press Enter, and type the following HTML on a blank line above the `</BODY>` tag:

```
<P><FONT SIZE="+1" COLOR="yellow" FACE="arial">Where do you want to go
now?</FONT></P>
```

4. Press Enter, and then type the following HTML:

```
<P>Please take me back to the <A HREF="index.html">beginning</A> of
this Web site.</P>
```

5. Press Enter again, and type this:

```
<P>I'd really rather look at your comments on <A
HREF="gibson.html">Gibson<SUP>&reg;</SUP></A> guitars.</P>
```

6. Press Enter again, and type this:

```
<P>What's this about <A HREF="terada.html">Terada</A> guitars?</P>
```

7. Press Enter again, and type this:

```
<P>Read some <A HREF="index.html#Buying">tips for guitar
buyers</A>.</P>
```

8. Press Enter again, and type this:

```
<P>Read some comments on <A HREF="index.html#Grading">how to grade gui-
tars</A>.</P>
```

9. Save the `fender01.html` file.
10. In your text editor, open the `index.html` file.
11. A little less than halfway through the document, find the following HTML:

```
<H1 ALIGN="center"><FONT COLOR="yellow">Tips for Buying Used or Vintage
Guitars</FONT></H1>
```

12. Change that line to the following:

```
<H1 ALIGN="center"><FONT COLOR="yellow"><A NAME="Buying">Tips for Buy-
ing Used or Vintage Guitars</A></FONT></H1>
```

13. Look for the beginning of the section after that, which is currently this:

```
<H1 ALIGN="center"><FONT COLOR="yellow">The Buyer's Guide to Grading
Guitars</FONT></H1>
```

14. Change that line to the following:

```
<H1 ALIGN="center"><FONT COLOR="yellow"><A NAME="Grading">The Buyer's
Guide to Grading Guitars</A></FONT></H1>
```

15. Save the `index.html` file.
16. Switch to your browser and open `fender01.html`. Figure 5.4 shows what you should see now on the Fender page.

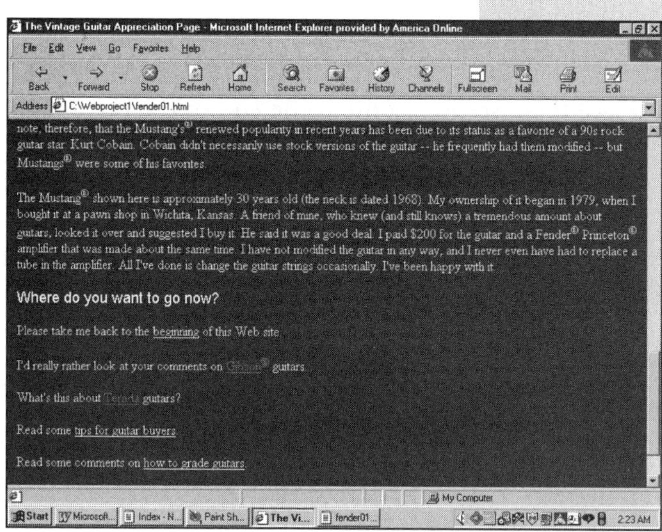

Figure 5.4 Navigational links now appear at the bottom of the Fender page.

ANALYSIS

Navigational links can appear anywhere on a Web page. Sometimes they are at the top, sometimes at the bottom, and sometimes along the side. They may even appear in more than one of those places on the same page.

In Step 3, you created a yellow sentence in Arial font in a slightly larger font size, which serves to introduce the list of links. In Steps 4 through 8, you added five navigational links. These links are in sentence form rather than just words (such as "Home," "Gibson," or "Terada"), although using words would have been a valid approach also. I think that sentences make the links clearer, at least in these instances.

The first added link takes users back to your Welcome page (the home page). The next two added links take users to your Gibson and Terada pages, respectively. The final two added links take users directly to two articles on the first page of the Web site, one to "Tips for Buying Used or Vintage Guitars" and one to "The Buyer's Guide to Grading Guitars." Steps 11 through 14 were necessary so that those links would work.

Now you need to add the equivalent links to the Gibson and Terada pages.

To complete the other navigational links, follow these steps:

1. In your text editor, open the `gibson01.html` file.
2. Place the insertion point at the end of the text for that page, just to the right of `Sam Moore.</P>`.

In Steps 3 and 7, you add almost the same introductory heading that preceded the links on the Fender page.

3. Press Enter to create a blank line, and then type the following HTML (press Enter again before each new line):

```
<P><FONT SIZE="+1" COLOR="yellow" FACE="arial">Where do you want to
go now?</FONT></P>
<P>Please take me back to the <A HREF="index.html">beginning</A> of
this Web site.</P>
<P>I want to read your comments on <A
HREF="fender.html">Fender<SUP>&reg;</SUP></A> guitars.</P>
<P>What's this about <A HREF="terada.html">Terada</A> guitars?</P>
<P>Read some <A HREF="index.html#Buying">tips for guitar
buyers</A>.</P>
<P>Read some comments on <A HREF="index.html#Grading">how to grade
guitars</A>.</P>
```

4. Save the `gibson01.html` document.
5. To add the links to the Terada page, open the `terada01.html` file in your text editor.
6. Place the insertion point at the end of the text for that page, just to the right of `fingerboard is rosewood.</P>`.
7. Press Enter to create a blank line, and then type the following HTML (press Enter again before each new line):

```
<P><FONT SIZE="+1" COLOR="yellow" FACE="arial">Where do you want to
go now?</FONT></P>
<P>Please take me back to the <A HREF="index.html">beginning</A> of
this Web site.</P>
<P>I want to read your comments on <A
HREF="fender.html">Fender<SUP>&reg;</SUP></A> guitars.</P>
```

```
<P>What do you have to say about <A
HREF="gibson.html">Gibson<SUP>&reg;</SUP></A> guitars?</P>
<P>Read some <A HREF="index.html#Buying">tips for guitar
buyers</A>.</P>
<P>Read some comments on <A HREF="index.html#Grading">how to grade
guitars</A>.</P>
```

8. Save the `terada01.html` file.

Remember that at this point the links you've created don't work, because the filenames have not been finalized. In the next part of the chapter, you'll change those names, and then the links should work.

Linking to Another Web Site

A very common type of hyperlink in Web sites is the type that links visitors to other Web sites. You can link your own site to friends' Web sites, hobby-related sites, business sites—anything. It's not at all difficult to do.

Follow these steps to create a couple of links to other Web sites:

1. In your text editor, open the `fender01.html` file.
2. Place the insertion point after the `</P>` tag at the end of the last paragraph of text on the page (which ends with `how to grade guitars</A>.</P>`), and then press Enter to create a blank line.
3. Type the following HTML, pressing Enter after each line:

```
<P>Visit the Web site of <A HREF="http://www.fender.com">Fender Musical
Instruments</A>.</P>
<P>Visit the Web site of <A HREF="http://www.gibson.com">Gibson Musical
Instruments</A>.</P>
```

4. Choose File, Save As, and then save the `fender01.html` document *with a new name:* **fender.html**.
5. Switch to your browser and open the new `fender.html` Web page.

   You should have links to the Fender and Gibson corporate Web sites as the last of the links at the end of the Web page (see Figure 5.5).

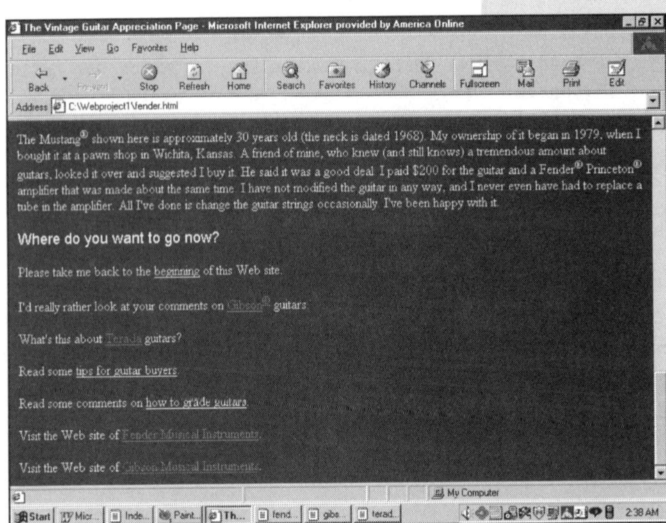

Figure 5.5 A couple of links to other Web sites are now present on the Project 1 Web site.

6. Repeat Steps 1 through 5 for the `gibson01.html` and `terada01.html` pages. In Step 4, save these files as **gibson.html** and **terada.html**, respectively.

ANALYSIS

Each time you completed Step 3, you inserted two new hyperlinks. These were *external* links—links to different Web sites. In this case, the URLs for the external links were `"http://www.fender.com"` and `"http://www.gibson.com"` (places where visitors can find more information about particular guitar brands).

In Step 4, you made another significant change—you finalized the filename for each guitar page by saving the file without `01` in the filename.

Note

Just to make sure that everything came out all right, open `index.html` in your browser. Try clicking on the links, from the Welcome page as well as from the other pages. If the links don't work at all or don't take you where they should, go back and take a close look at the HTML involved at both ends of the links. Be on the lookout for missing tags, such as `<A>` and `</A>`, as well as mistakes with the necessary attributes (`HREF` and `NAME`) or quotation marks.

Communicating with Visitors to Your Site

Just about every Web site has a link to the site's Webmaster or the owner of the site. These links are easy to create, and you should include one on your Web site in order to get helpful feedback from visitors. Someone viewing your site may be the first person to inform you of broken links, for example. On a more positive note, some may simply want to let you know how much fun your site is.

EXERCISE

Follow these steps to open a channel of communication between you and your visitors:

1. In your text editor, open the `index.html` file.
2. Place the insertion point at the far-right end of the following HTML, which is at the end of the file, and then press Enter:

```
<P><SMALL><FONT COLOR="yellow" FACE="arial"><STRONG>If you have enjoyed
your visit, please let others know about this Web
site!</STRONG></FONT></SMALL></P>
```

3. Pressing Enter after each line, type the following:

```
<ADDRESS>

<P><FONT SIZE="-1">If you want to pass on any suggestions,
words of praise, or — if you must — complaints, please send
e-mail to <A HREF="mailto:webmaster@myguitarcollection.com">
webmaster@myguitarcollection.com</A>.</FONT></P>

</ADDRESS>
```

4. Save the `index.html` file. Figure 5.6 shows the appearance of the new link at the bottom of the Welcome page.

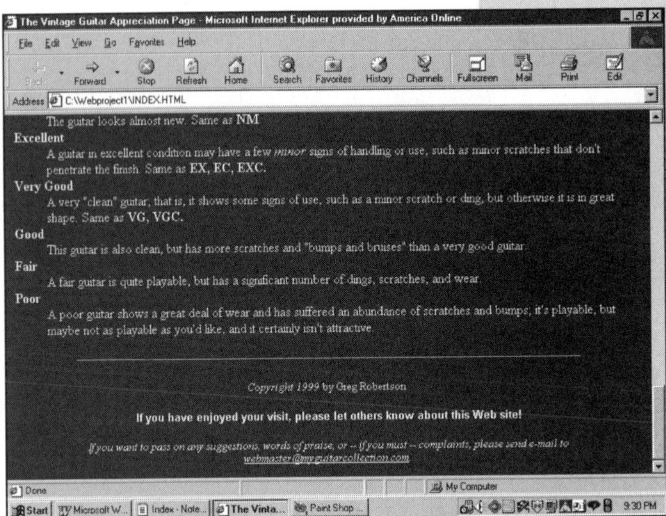

Figure 5.6 The Mailto link is an easy way to enable visitors to communicate with you.

ANALYSIS

The HTML you added in Step 3 uses the `<ADDRESS>` tag. You don't *have* to use it, but it is part of the HTML 4.0 standard, so it doesn't hurt. The text contained within an `<ADDRESS>` tag is italicized by default. Normally, you use the `<ADDRESS>` tag to hold not only your e-mail address, but also your mailing address and telephone number. You can include other information, if you want, such as the date you last updated the site. I didn't include that kind of information here, but you're welcome to do so in your own Web site, of course.

This HTML also uses the regular `<A>` tag and `HREF` attribute, but note the value of the `HREF` attribute. This is a *Mailto link*, which you use to designate an e-mail address for you or the Webmaster. When a user with a browser capable of handling Mailto links clicks on this hyperlink, a form pops up so that the viewer can send e-mail to the address you've specified. Many viewers, however, have browsers that cannot use Mailto links. For these people, you need to include text that spells out an e-mail address for them. That's why the link text is the e-mail address (webmaster@myguitarcollection.com). With the e-mail address as the link text, everyone can see your correct e-mail address and type it into their own e-mail software if necessary. That way, everyone can

communicate with you if they choose to do so. (You're not *limited* to using an e-mail address as the link text, but it makes sense if you definitely want others to be able to contact you or your Webmaster.)

You now have created all four pages of the Web site. Continue to the next section, where you'll incorporate graphics throughout the site.

Adding Graphics

Ah, graphics—one of the pillars upon which the popularity of the Web is based. Graphics most commonly take two forms on the Web. For photographs, the most popular format is JPEG. For graphics created in other programs, such as Paint Shop Pro or Adobe Illustrator, the most commonly used format is GIF. A third format, PNG (Portable Network Graphics), is available but not yet in common use. I suspect it will become much more popular as support for it grows.

Refer to Chapter 3, "Designing the Basic Web Site," for a quick summary of the main issues that surround graphics on the Web.

An* inline graphic *is one that's placed directly in the flow of the document.

For an inline graphic, you indicate in the HTML where the graphic goes, what its filename is, and where the browser can load it from. The process of inserting graphics is itself not difficult. The challenge is producing graphics that are not too large, yet are clear and serve your purpose.

This book doesn't attempt to explain how to create graphics files (JPEG or GIF); the assumption here is that you will supply the graphics for your own Web site. The example graphics used in the Web sites built during this books' three projects, of course, are included on the CD that accompanies this book. In addition, the following section provides some tips for creating your own graphics.

Tips for Creating Graphics

Following are some points to keep in mind as you create graphics for use on your Web site. Remember that your overall aim is to minimize download time for all graphics, a task that is easier said than done.

- Use GIF images when only a few colors are involved.
- Don't create graphics that are larger than you need; decide what size you want them to be, and then create them at that size.
- When dealing with photographs, either those that you have scanned or those that are part of a software package, make sure that you keep the original intact. To work with a photo, open the image, and then use Save As to save it under a different file name.
- The trick when working with photographs is to leave the photograph uncompressed until you have modified it to the way you want it to be. A TIFF file is one such uncompressed image type. Another example is Paint Shop Pro's own PSP file type. In both cases, you don't compress the image when you save it as that type, whereas saving it as a JPEG file does compress it. In short, don't save an image as a JPEG file until you know you're ready to save the final version of the image.
- For photographs, you usually should use JPEG images as the file type that you want to appear on your Web site. The exception is when only a few colors are present and there aren't any color gradations to worry about. In that case, it may work to create a GIF file out of it. Generally speaking, however, when you have many colors, or when you have gradual color changes within the image, a JPEG file works best. If you really aren't sure, try creating one of each, and then compare the quality and file size of the two images.
- Your goal should be to maximize quality and minimize file size. Unfortunately, you cannot achieve ideal results simply by following a 1-2-3 series of steps; experimentation is necessary.

When creating a JPEG file, you must wait until you have the image the size you want before saving it as a JPEG file. That's because every time you save a file in JPEG format, the image is compressed again. Every compression results in loss of quality. Saving an image as a JPEG file three or four times may result in a good file size, but the quality is likely to be horrible—or at least unacceptable.

- The amount of compression you apply to an image when saving it as a JPEG depends on you. The graphics software should enable you to set the amount of compression from 1 percent to 99 percent. The least amount of compression (1 percent) results in the best image quality but the largest file size. The most compression (99 percent) is just the opposite: the worst quality but the smallest file size. Somewhere in between is the optimum combination of compression and file size.

Tip

As you try to find the best compression rate, always work from the uncompressed image, and just keep saving your experiments with different names, such as `image1.jpg`, `image2.jpg`, `image3.jpg`, and so on. Compare them side by side onscreen to check quality, and then look at the file size. You might want to change compression in 10-percent increments at first. After you find the acceptable range of image quality, such as 20-percent compression to 40-percent compression, work in 5-percent increments to find the best combination of quality and file size. Remember, however, to work from the uncompressed image again, and to use Save As so as not to change the uncompressed image. When creating a JPEG, begin by trying 30 percent compression. You may find that this will give you acceptable results, both in terms of image quality and file size. In short, experiment.

- In the case of JPEGs, use your software to crop out any unnecessary parts of the image *before* saving it as a JPEG.

Don't load a large graphic and then use it at a reduced size. That's possible, but you waste loading time. You're better off loading a graphic at the size you want, or at least not loading one bigger than the largest size of that graphic you'll need. Remember that the larger a graphic is, the longer it takes for viewers to download—and the longer the viewers must wait.

If you use a great many graphics, or if you want to build Web sites for others, you may want to consider buying Debabelizer by Equilibrium. You use Debabelizer to optimize photographs for use on the Web; i.e., Debabelizer makes photos take up as little disk space as possible while still maintaining quality. Originally a Mac product, it is now also available for PCs. This program is more expensive than other similar programs, but may well be worth it to you, especially if you plan to use it a lot. It's your call.

A **pixel** *is, basically, a dot of light. Screen resolution and some other things are measured in pixels.*

In reference to monitors, you often hear *screen resolution* given as a measurement of the form 1024×768 or 800×600. Those numbers refer to the number of pixels across the screen (say, 1024) and the number of pixels down the screen (say, 768). The more pixels you have, the better the resolution, and the better the image quality. If an artist draws your face, using only 100 dots to do so, and then draws it again, this time using 1000 dots, which one will look better? The latter will, because more dots can achieve a "higher resolution."

GIFs and JPEGs are image types that consist of pixels. Many graphics programs, however, create images that are *vector-based.* Vector-based images don't contain *any* pixels. Instead, they contain commands that use mathematical formulas to draw shapes. These commands indicate where to draw the shape, as well as how thick lines should be, the colors to use, any patterns involved, and so on. You can convert vector images to bitmaps, but not vice versa.

Inserting Banners on the Web Pages

Graphics on a Web site have two basic purposes: to serve as illustrations (logos, decorations, or photographs, for example) or to act as hyperlinks. Some graphics serve both purposes simultaneously. This section of the chapter concentrates on the use of graphics as illustrations.

Switch to (or open) your browser and take a look at the Web site as it stands currently. It's all well and good—as far as it goes. What this Web site needs now is some graphical appeal!

A* banner *is a graphic (not inline) that receives some sort of featured placement on a Web site.

Banners typically run along the top of a Web page, although you can place them in other locations. Common uses for banners include company logos, designs that jazz up a Web page, welcome messages, and advertisements.

EXERCISE

Follow these steps to insert a banner graphic:

1. In your text editor, open the `index.html` file.
2. Press Enter to create a blank line after the following tag, which is near the top of the document:

```
<BODY BGCOLOR="black" TEXT="white" LINK="yellow" VLINK="red"
ALINK="lime">
```

3. Type the following HTML, pressing Enter after each paragraph:

```
<DIV ALIGN="center">

<CENTER>

<IMG ALIGN="center" SRC="images/welcome.gif" WIDTH="400" HEIGHT="50"
ALT="Welcome banner">

<IMG ALIGN="left" SRC="images/peghead1a.jpg" WIDTH="100" HEIGHT="122"
ALT="Photo of guitar peghead">

<IMG ALIGN="right" SRC="images/peghead1a.jpg" WIDTH="100" HEIGHT="122"
ALT="Photo of guitar peghead">

<IMG SRC="images/TheAppPage9.gif" WIDTH="510" HEIGHT="180" ALT="The
Vintage Guitar Appreciation Page banner">

</CENTER>

</DIV>
```

4. Save the `index.html` document.
5. Switch to your browser and refresh the screen. Figure 5.7 shows the new look of the Web page.

Figure 5.7 The graphics use the same attractive color scheme and font.

In Step 3, you did a number of things. First, by inserting the combination of `<DIV ALIGN="center">` and `<CENTER>` tags at the top of the `<BODY>` section, you ensured that the HTML you typed would be centered at the top of the `<BODY>` section.

Let's review a couple of points about using graphics. First, you use the `<IMG>` tag to tell a browser where the graphic goes. You must use the required `SRC` attribute (source) with the `<IMG>` tag, because the value for `SRC` tells the browser where to locate the graphic file that you want to insert. In this case—assuming you've placed all the book's graphics files in the same subfolder (`images`)—all you need to do is give the name of the subfolder and then a slash, followed by the name of the particular graphic file. You place this source information (that is, the path to the file) within quotation marks.

`SRC` isn't the only attribute present. Each `<IMG>` tag also has the `ALIGN` attribute. Note the order: `ALIGN="center"; ALIGN="left"; ALIGN="right"`. This order yields a symmetrical appearance. You can switch left and right alignment without changing the appearance, as long as the center alignment comes first. If you change the order to left/right/center, the two peghead graphics move to the top of the page, so that they are on the same level as the "Welcome" graphic. If you change the order to left/center/right, however, the appearance changes so that it is no longer symmetrical; it's more of a stairstep effect, with the graphics going "downhill." I prefer the first look: "Welcome" at the top of the page, with the two peghead graphics lower and even with each other on either side of it.

Note

One of the possibilities when aligning graphics is aligning them vertically *within a line of text.* As you have seen already, you can determine horizontal alignment by using the values `left`, `right`, and `center`, as appropriate. You merely place the `ALIGN` attribute after the `SRC` attribute of your graphic and then indicate how you want the graphic aligned.

Likewise, you can align graphics vertically within and in relation to a line of text, using the values `top`, `middle`, and `bottom`. I suggest, however, that any graphics you place in a line of text should be quite small—not much larger than the text, if at all. The problem is that any text above or below the line containing the graphic does not wrap around the graphic; you just end up with a lot of blank space around the graphic where other lines of text should be. Except in rare situations, a graphic in a line of text ruins the leading.

The fourth graphic, "The Vintage Guitar Appreciation Page," is directly below the "Welcome" graphic. It is centered horizontally between the two peghead graphics.

Another thing to note about the graphics is that each one has `WIDTH` and `HEIGHT` attributes. Browsers that understand those attributes reserve the given dimensions for the graphic. As a result, the browser doesn't have to wait until the entire graphic is downloaded before formatting other items on the page. Boxes appear onscreen because the browser knows the size and placement of the graphic before it is fully loaded.

One other item you added in this exercise was the very useful `ALT` attribute, which will be discussed in the next section.

The graphics added at the top of the Web page create a great deal of visual interest. The color adds the pizzazz that the page needed, and the font used gives a sense of movement. In addition, the graphics serve to welcome visitors to the site and inform them of the site's content.

One way to add some variety to the fonts you use—and to guarantee that you get the look you want—is to use graphics in place of actual text. GIFs are ideal for this purpose, especially as a banner on your page. That way, instead of relying on someone else's browser to have the font you want, you can create a GIF graphic that is actually text in the desired font. Keep in mind, however, that this technique is significantly more involved than just typing the words in Notepad, applying an HTML attribute, and saving the change. In addition, search engines won't find the words within GIFs when indexing your site. Using too many of these GIF headings also slows down your Web site when it is downloading. Be judicious in your use of GIFs as headings.

Using the ALT Attribute with Graphics

Many Web users have browsers that can't handle graphics. Some other users have turned off their browsers' graphics capabilities to speed things up. In addition, visually impaired users or others who use technology to read Web pages to them would appreciate knowing what a given graphic is.

To help these groups of users, you can use the `ALT` attribute, which functions as a source of information. As you may have noted in the preceding exercise, you use this attribute as follows:

```
<IMG SRC="images/welcome.gif" ALT="Welcome banner">
```

In the preceding exercise, of course, other attributes were also present in the `<IMG>` tags.

In the interest of accessibility, always include the ALT attribute with all graphics in your Web site.

When you use the ALT attribute, clearly identify the graphic. If, as in the preceding example, the graphic is a GIF of the word "Welcome," you might use the ALT attribute as indicated in the example above.

Don't use the ALT attribute as shown in the following example, because it tells the visitor nothing:

```
<IMG SRC="images/welcome.gif" ALT="graphic">
```

Whereas `ALT="graphic"` says nothing useful, a simple description of the nature of the graphic— `"Welcome banner"` —tells users of nongraphical or graphics-disabled browsers everything they need to know about a graphic that they can't see.

Note

The ALT attribute has another very helpful use. If a viewer has set up his or her browser to ignore graphics, but sees a particularly intriguing ALT description of a graphic, he or she can force the browser to load just that image by right-clicking the image's reserved area, and then clicking on the shortcut menu option to show the graphic. Use the ALT attribute to full advantage so that viewers will always know exactly what graphics are on your site, whether or not they ever want to view them!

Adding More Graphics

By putting a banner at the top of each of the additional Web pages you created earlier in this chapter, it is possible to accomplish two things. First, you identify the subject of the page. Second, you add some graphical interest to the page.

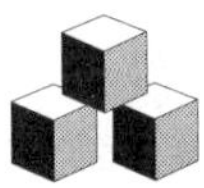

EXERCISE

To place a banner at the top of the second page of your Web site—the Fender page—follow these steps:

1. In your text editor, open the `fender.html` file.
2. Near the top of the document, place the insertion point at the far-right end of the following tag:

```
<BODY BGCOLOR="black" TEXT="white" LINK="yellow" VLINK="red"
ALINK="lime">
```

3. Press Enter to create a blank line, and then type the following lines of HTML, pressing Enter after each line:

```
<DIV ALIGN="center">
<CENTER>
  <IMG SRC="images/fender.gif" WIDTH="300" HEIGHT="60" ALT="Fender
  name">
</CENTER>
</DIV>
```

4. Save the `fender.html` document.
5. Switch to your browser and refresh the screen. Figure 5.8 shows what you should see.

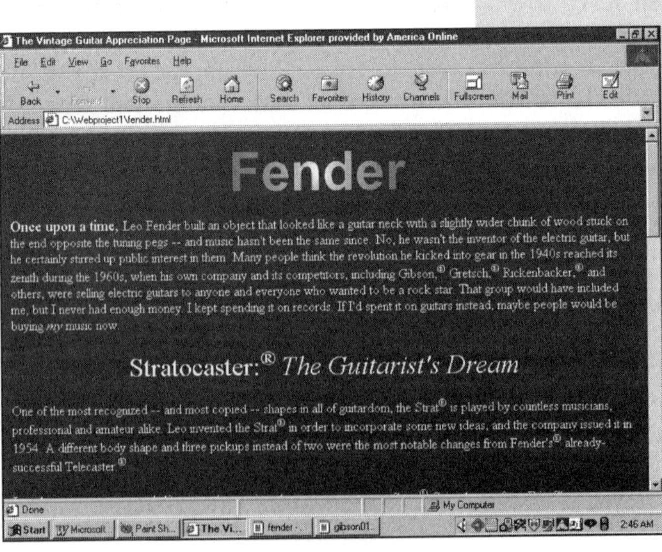

Figure 5.8
A colorful banner now sits atop the Fender page.

ANALYSIS

You did all the work in Step 3, and it was quite easy. First, you used the now-familiar combination of `<DIV ALIGN="center">` and `<CENTER>` to ensure that the logo is centered at the top of the page. By placing the HTML immediately after the `<BODY>` tag, you know that this graphic will be the first item to appear on the page. After the `<CENTER>` tag you used the `<IMG>` tag, including the `SRC`, `WIDTH`, `HEIGHT`, and `ALT` attributes.

On your computer, you may have noticed the colors used in the `fender.gif` graphic. Like the graphics on the first page of the Web site, this graphic uses the red-and-yellow sunburst effect. This common color scheme helps to establish a "look and feel" for the Web site: black background, red-and-yellow sunburst GIFs, and yellow headings.

Follow similar steps to add a logo to the third page:

1. In your text editor, open the `gibson.html` file.
2. Near the top of the document, place the insertion point at the far-right end of the following tag:

```
<BODY BGCOLOR="black" TEXT="white" LINK="yellow" VLINK="red"
ALINK="lime">
```

3. Press Enter to create a blank line, and then type the following lines of HTML, pressing Enter after each line:

```
<DIV ALIGN="center">
<CENTER>
  <IMG SRC="images/gibson.gif" WIDTH="300" HEIGHT="60" ALT="Gibson
  name">
</CENTER>
</DIV>
```

4. Save the `gibson.html` document.
5. Switch to your browser and refresh the screen. Figure 5.9 shows how the top of the Gibson page appears.

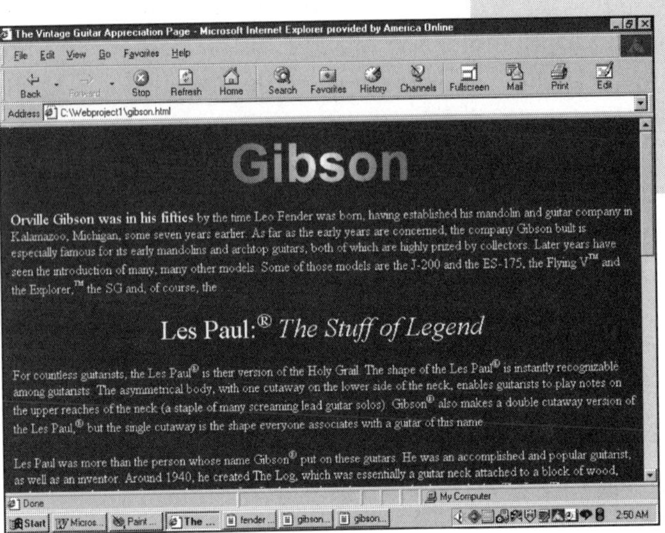

Figure 5.9 The Gibson page now has a graphic to lead things off.

Finally, add a logo to the top of the Terada page. Use the following steps, which are like the preceding ones, to do so:

1. In your text editor, open the `terada.html` file.
2. Near the top of the document, place the insertion point at the far-right end of the following tag:

```
<BODY BGCOLOR="black" TEXT="white" LINK="yellow" VLINK="red"
ALINK="lime">
```

3. Press Enter to create a blank line, and then type the following lines of HTML, pressing Enter after each line:

```
<DIV ALIGN="center">
<CENTER>
<IMG SRC="images/terada.gif" WIDTH="300" HEIGHT="60" ALT="Terada name">
</CENTER>
</DIV>
```

4. Save the `terada.html` document.
5. Switch to your browser and refresh the screen. Figure 5.10 shows how the top of the Terada page appears.

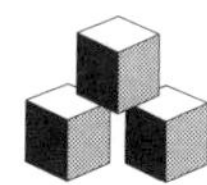

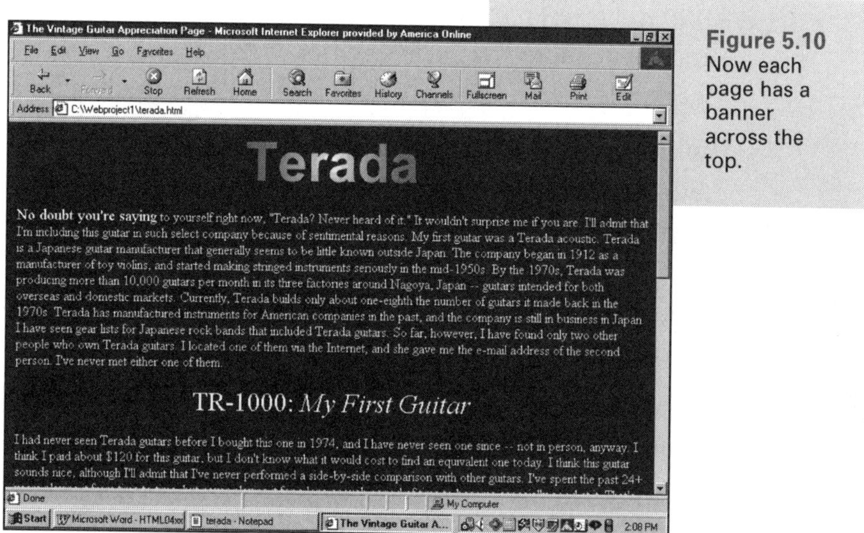

Figure 5.10 Now each page has a banner across the top.

Adding Photographs to Your Web Site

The other kind of graphics used on Web sites, which opens up the Web to all kinds of possibilities, is photographs. On the personal level, for example, you can send photos to friends or family members anywhere in the world. (Of course, the recipient also must have a Web connection.) On the business level, you can use your Web site to display your products to potential customers—and then provide an order form right there online.

If you want to learn more about Web graphics, you can find out just about anything you need to know—from the very basics to advanced techniques—by checking out the following Web site:

http://www.builder.com/Graphics/Spotlight/?st.cn.Web.today.bl

Doing the JPEG Balancing Act

When dealing with GIF files such as the ones discussed earlier in this chapter, the situation is straightforward. A GIF graphic has a certain file size, depending on its image size, the number of colors, and so on. With

JPEGs, however, the compression factor is the most important consideration. The more you compress a photograph, the fewer colors it has; the fewer colors it has, the less realistic it is—but the smaller its file size is.

When you create a JPEG, you have the opportunity to decide how much compression occurs. The less compression you apply, the better the image's quality. The problem is that an uncompressed JPEG file can run into tens of thousands of colors (or even more)—and several megabytes in file size. Most people are not going to wait around for a 2MB photograph to download to their computer.

Every time you save a JPEG file, the file is compressed further—and the image looks worse than it did before. If you compress the JPEG file at 40 percent the first time, and then open and resave the file, you are compressing the JPEG file at 40 percent *again*. The only way around that difficulty is to turn off compression before you save the JPEG file again.

Before saving a photo as a JPEG file, make it the size you want, using an uncompressed file type. Also make any alterations to it that you want, such as cutting out extraneous background. Only when you have exactly what you want should you save it as a JPEG file.

The trick to JPEGs is finding the right amount of compression. Allow yourself time to experiment with various compression settings. You might want to take the same, uncompressed photograph, and save it at compression rates from 10 to 50 percent, for example, in 10-percent increments. Then compare the quality of the result with the size (in KB) of the JPEG file. Find the JPEG with quality acceptable for your purposes but that is significantly reduced in file size.

The JPEG graphics for the projects in this book were saved at 30-percent compression.

Using Thumbnail Images

A **thumbnail** *is a small version of a graphic that loads quickly and takes up very little room.*

One popular use for images is to use them as "thumbnails," a name descriptive of their approximate size. These small images give viewers an idea of what the full-size graphics look like, and clicking on a particular thumbnail usually takes viewers to the full-size version of that image. Suppose that you have a large collection of 25 guitars that you want to show off on your Web site. Rather than force every visitor to download 25 full-size photographs, you can have 25 thumbnails download first. Because of their small physical file size, they download very quickly.

When you display the thumbnails onscreen, they can be coded with HTML to contain links to the full-size photographs. In a real sense, then, thumbnails can form an index of your graphics. Suppose that the thumbnail version of your Strat is named `stratthumb.jpg`, and the full-size version of the same photo is named `strat.jpg`. If you want to use the thumbnail of the photo as a link to the full-size image, the general form of the HTML is as follows:

```
<A HREF="strat.jpg"><IMG SRC="stratthumb.jpg" HEIGHT="55" WIDTH="55"></A>
```

Of course, this HTML may be nested within other elements, just as any `<A>` container tag may be. Clicking on the thumbnail will bring up the full-size photograph, and the user won't have to download any full-size photos that he or she doesn't want to see, thus potentially saving a great deal of downloading time, while still making all the full-size photos conveniently available to any viewer who does want to see one or more of them.

Flowing Text around Graphics

The vast majority of Web sites are neither all graphics nor all text, and the site you are building in Project 1 has both textual and graphical elements in it. The goal is to create an attractive site that makes use of both elements. The topic of this section is working with graphics and text so that they flow together.

EXERCISE

The pages of the Project 1 Web site are adequate—and certainly more visually appealing since inserting some graphics—but adding some JPEG images should make the site even more interesting. With that in mind, follow these steps to learn how to gain a little bit more control over images in your Web pages:

1. In your text editor, open the `fender.html` file.
2. Place the insertion point at the far-right end of the `</DIV>` tag after the following HTML:

```
<P><FONT SIZE="6" COLOR="yellow"> <A NAME="Stratocaster"> Stratocaster:
<EM>The Guitarist's Dream</EM></A></FONT></P>
```

3. Press Enter twice. On the second blank line you've created, type the following HTML:

```
<IMG ALIGN="left" WIDTH="120" HEIGHT="178" HSPACE="20"
SRC="images/strat3vert.jpg" ALT="A black Fender Stratocaster">
```

4. Save the `fender.html` document.
5. Switch to your browser and open `fender.html`. Figure 5.11 shows the result of this operation.

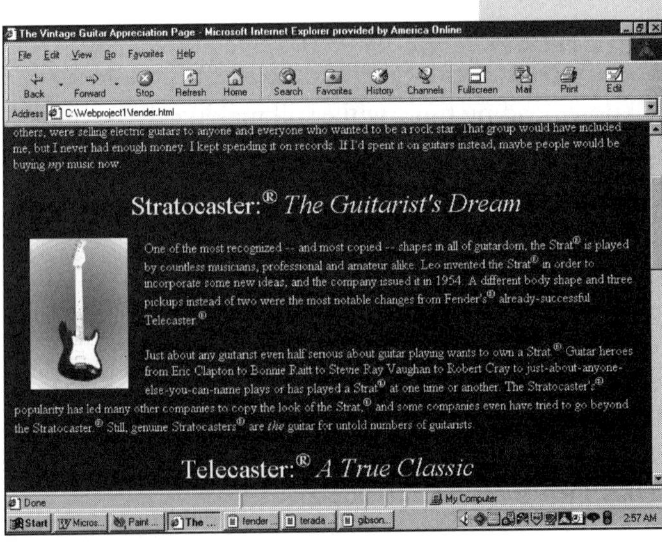

Figure 5.11
A beautiful Fender Stratocaster poses proudly on the Web page.

ANALYSIS

In Step 3, you typed HTML that did several things to establish the location and alignment of the image. First, it aligned the image to the left (although left is the default alignment, so `ALIGN="left"` wasn't strictly necessary). Next came the `WIDTH` and `HEIGHT` attributes, specifying the precise size of the image (120×178). The original photograph is from a 35mm camera. In 35mm film, the image on the negative has a ratio of 2:3. I wanted to make the width of the image on the Web page 120 pixels wide. After I scanned the photograph, I resized the image in Paint Shop Pro to make it 120 pixels wide. When I did so, Paint Shop Pro automatically resized the height, which came out 178 pixels.

The `HSPACE` attribute inserts a designated amount of horizontal space around the graphic, separating it from the text. In this case, the value `20` establishes a sort of "buffer zone" of 20 pixels between the photo and the text, as well as between the photo and the left margin. I chose 20 because I thought the results looked better than with 15 or 25. To see the difference between the 20-pixel space and no space, refer to Figure 5.12, which shows the Web page without the `HSPACE="20"` attribute.

Finally, you provided the name and location of the source file, as well as the `ALT` attribute to describe the picture to viewers who aren't seeing the actual graphic.

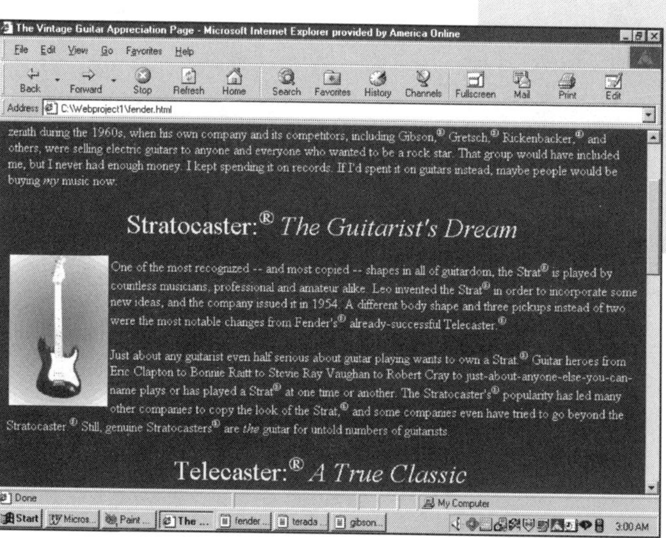

Figure 5.12 Without the `HSPACE="20"` attribute, the text and graphic are too close together.

EXERCISE

This time, place a graphic on the *right* side of the text by following these steps:

1. Switch back to `fender.html` in your text editor.
2. Place the insertion point at the far-right end of the `</DIV>` tag after the following line of HTML:

```
<P><FONT SIZE="6" COLOR="yellow"><A NAME="Telecaster">Telecaster: <EM>A
True Classic</EM></A></FONT></P>
```

3. Press Enter twice. On the second blank line you've created, type the following HTML:

```
<IMG ALIGN="right" WIDTH="120" HEIGHT="178" HSPACE="20"
SRC="images/tele1vert.jpg" ALT="A black Fender Telecaster">
```

4. Save the `fender.html` document.
5. Switch to your browser and refresh the screen. Your screen should look like the one shown in Figure 5.13.

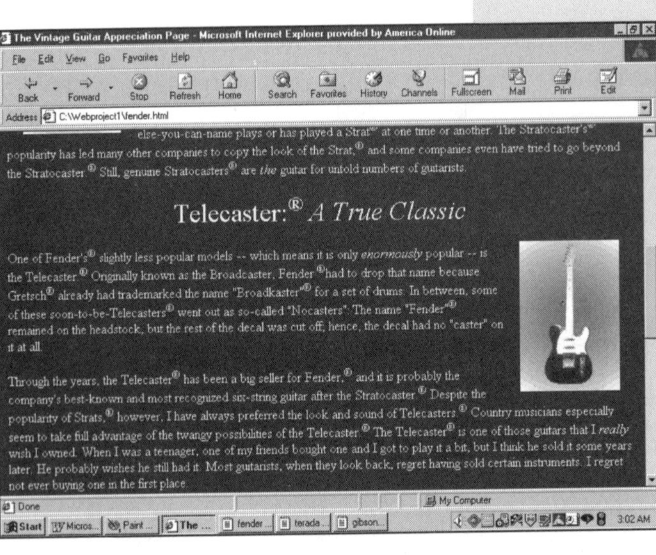

Figure 5.13
You also can right-align graphics so that text flows around them.

Tip

It also is possible to flow text between two graphics. This technique is similar to what you did on the Welcome page, where two identical graphics appear on either side of a third graphic. The HTML takes the following form:

```
<IMG ALIGN="right" WIDTH="120" HEIGHT="178" HSPACE="20"
SRC="images/strat3vert.jpg" ALT="A black Fender
Stratocaster">
<IMG ALIGN="left" WIDTH="120" HEIGHT="178" HSPACE="20"
SRC="images/strat3vert.jpg" ALT="A black Fender
Stratocaster">
```

As you can see, the only difference between the two `<IMG>` tags is that one is aligned to the left, and one to the right. The text that follows, which begins with a `<P>` tag, appears between the two graphics on the Web page. This is a neat little trick. Figure 5.14 shows what you get when you use this technique.

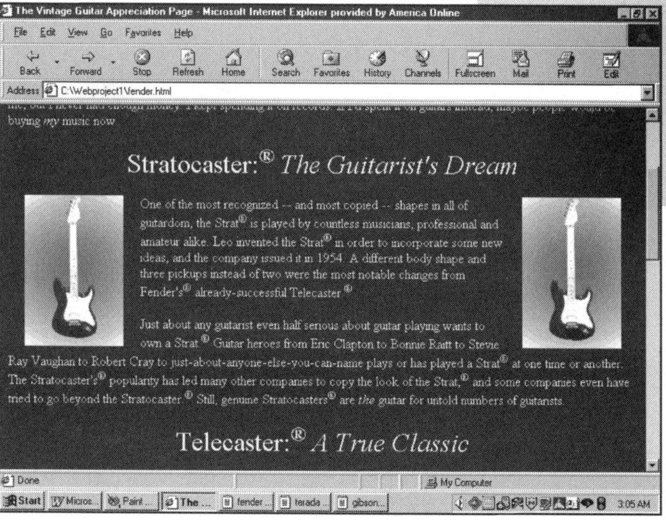

Figure 5.14 Text flows neatly between two graphics here.

Sometimes, you may want to insert a figure and have one paragraph of text wrap next to it—but not the following paragraph. To achieve this look, all you have to do is insert the `<BR>` tag in place of the `</P>` tag at the end of the text paragraph that appears next to the graphic, and include the `CLEAR` attribute with it. The value you assign to `CLEAR` depends on where the graphic is located. By using `CLEAR`, you designate that nothing else can appear onscreen until the margin you specify is clear. The possible values are `left`, `right`, and `all`, with `all` meaning that nothing else can appear until *both* margins are clear.

For Figure 5.13, for example, where the graphic was aligned on the right side of the page, you would add `<BR CLEAR="right">`. Conversely, if the graphic were on the left, you would use `<BR CLEAR="left">`.

Personally, I don't care for the appearance of the Web page formatted in this way. Just so you'll know, Figure 5.15 shows what it looks like.

You may want to try using the preceding technique to create captions for graphics on your Web site.

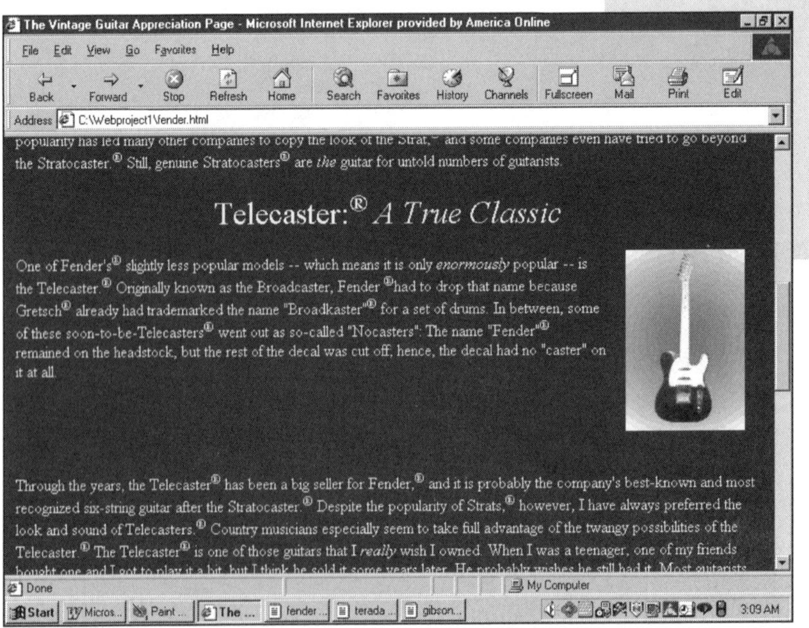

Figure 5.15 Use the CLEAR attribute with the <BR> tag to keep multiple paragraphs from wrapping around a graphic.

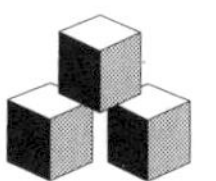

EXERCISE

Finish adding JPEGs to the Web pages by following these steps:

1. In the `fender.html` file, place the insertion point at the far-right end of the `</DIV>` tag after the following HTML:

```
<P><FONT SIZE="6" COLOR="yellow"><A NAME="Mustang">Mustang: <EM>Grungy
Popularity</EM></A></FONT></P>
```

2. Press Enter twice. On the second blank line you've created, type the following HTML:

```
<IMG ALIGN="left" WIDTH="120" HEIGHT="178" HSPACE="20"
SRC="images/must2vert.jpg" ALT="A blue Fender Mustang">
```

3. Save the `fender.html` file.
4. Switch to your browser and open `fender.html` to make sure that you now have a picture of a blue guitar left-aligned next to the first paragraph about Mustang guitars.
5. Open the `gibson.html` document in your text editor.
6. Place the insertion point at the far-right end of the `</DIV>` tag after the following HTML:

```
<P><FONT SIZE="6" COLOR="yellow"><A NAME="Les Paul">Les Paul: <EM>The
Stuff of Legend</EM></A></FONT></P>
```

7. Press Enter twice, and then type the following HTML on the second blank line you've created:

```
<IMG ALIGN="left" WIDTH="120" HEIGHT="178" HSPACE="20"
SRC="images/les2vert.jpg" ALT="A natural-finish Gibson Les Paul">
```

8. Next, place the insertion point at the far-right end of the `</DIV>` tag after the following HTML:

```
<P><FONT SIZE="6" COLOR="yellow"><A NAME="Lucille">Lucille:<SUP>
&trade;</SUP> <EM>Black and Blues All Over</EM></A></FONT></P>
```

9. Press Enter twice, and then type this HTML on the second blank line:

```
<IMG ALIGN="right" WIDTH="120" HEIGHT="178" HSPACE="20"
SRC="images/lucille2vert.jpg" ALT="A black Gibson Lucille model with
multiple autographs">
```

10. Save the `gibson.html` file.
11. Switch to your browser and open `gibson.html`.

    You should see a natural-finish guitar left-aligned next to the paragraph about Les Paul guitars, and a right-aligned autographed black guitar next to the paragraph about the Lucille guitar model.
12. Switch to your text editor and open the `terada.html` file.
13. Place the insertion point at the far-right end of the `</DIV>` tag after the following HTML:

```
<P><FONT SIZE="6" COLOR="yellow"><A NAME="TR-1000">TR-1000: <EM>My
First Guitar</EM></A></FONT></P>
```

14. Press Enter twice, and then type the following HTML on the second blank line:

```
<IMG ALIGN="left" WIDTH="120" HEIGHT="178" HSPACE="20"
SRC="images/tr10003vert.jpg" ALT="A Terada TR-1000 acoustic guitar">
```

15. Place the insertion point at the far-right end of the `</DIV>` tag after the following HTML:

```
<P><FONT SIZE="6" COLOR="yellow"><A NAME="JW-837">JW-837: <EM>C&amp;W
Lives!</EM></A></FONT></P>
```

16. Press Enter twice, and then type the following HTML on the second blank line:

```
<IMG ALIGN="right" WIDTH="120" HEIGHT="178" HSPACE="20"
SRC="images/jw837vert.jpg" ALT="A Terada JW-837 jumbo acoustic guitar">
```

17. Save the `terada.html` file.
18. Switch to your browser and open `terada.html`.

    You should see a typical acoustic guitar aligned to the left margin, next to the paragraph that discusses the TR-1000. If you scroll down, you should see a sunburst acoustic guitar right-aligned next to the discussion of the JW-837.

ANALYSIS

Nothing new happened in these steps. What you did was repeat the process of adding graphics, but this time you added them to all the manufacturer pages. The alignment of graphics on each page began on the left, with the next graphic aligned on the opposite side. The third graphic for the Fender page, therefore, was left-aligned.

EXERCISE

The one graphic remaining to insert belongs on the Welcome page.

1. In your text editor, open the `index.html` file.
2. Locate the following HTML, about one-third of the way into the document, and position the insertion point after it:

   ```
   <P>This Web site contains information and comments on guitars made by
   three manufacturers:</P>
   ```

3. Press Enter twice, and then type the following HTML on the second blank line:

   ```
   <IMG SRC="images/4guitars10.jpg" ALIGN="right" WIDTH="400" HEIGHT="250"
   HSPACE="25" ALT="A picture of four horizontal guitars"><BR
   CLEAR="left">
   ```

4. Save the `index.html` document.
5. Switch to your browser and open `index.html`. Figure 5.16 shows what you should see onscreen.

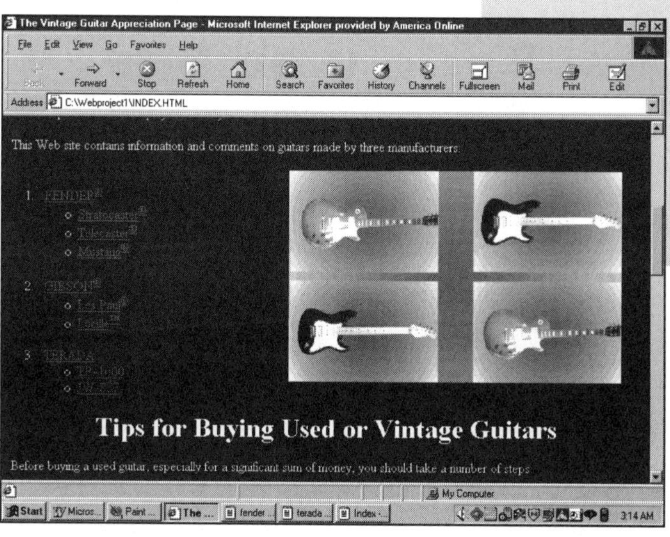

Figure 5.16 The new graphic fills in some empty space and adds some visual interest to the page.

ANALYSIS

The HTML you added to the document in Step 3 did a number of things, all geared toward adding one graphic to the Web page. The purpose of the graphic is twofold: to fill up a large blank space next to the bulleted list of guitar manufacturers and their products, and to add some visual interest to the page.

Several attributes contribute to the placement and appearance of the graphic. The graphic is right-aligned, and the `WIDTH` and `HEIGHT` attributes tell the browser the dimensions of the graphic to be downloaded. In addition, the `HSPACE` attribute provides a 25-pixel blank area around the graphic, effectively moving the graphic in slightly from the right margin. The `ALT` attribute is self-explanatory. Finally, the `<BR>` tag and `CLEAR` attribute make sure that the following heading doesn't appear until the left margin is clear. If you were to change the `CLEAR` attribute to `CLEAR="right"`, you would find that the graphic would appear by itself next to the right margin. The list of links, however, would appear below and to the left of the graphic. In effect, you would not fix the problem of a large blank space, but would create *two* large blank spaces.

Besides just filling up space, the background of this graphic continues the color scheme used throughout the Web site. In addition, the orientation of the guitars themselves lends a sense of motion to the page.

That completes the creation of this project's Web pages.

Testing the Basic Web Site

Now that you've finished creating the Project 1 Web site, just one task remains: testing it. You never know when you may have overlooked an end tag somewhere, for example. If you have been checking your work as you go, however, you probably have noticed when things didn't look the way you expected them to. And you most likely tried to figure out the problem immediately.

Other kinds of mistakes are subtler. In fact, many such mistakes may not even be evident when you check your work in a browser.

Viewing the Site through Your Browser

Of course, you've been checking the site in a browser throughout the building process. You know what the Web site looks like in your own browser. The technique of checking your work as you go is an excellent one. Unfortunately, even if your Web site looks great in the browser you use on a daily basis, you cannot guarantee the same results for all browsers.

You might as well give up on the idea of creating an interesting, state-of-the-art, visually attractive, and useful Web site that works equally well with *all* versions of *all* browsers. Chances are virtually nonexistent that you can pull it off. You may be able to create one that will work with all browsers, but you would be so limited by the available tags and attributes that you probably could not have a visually interesting one at the same time. The limited number of tags and attributes also would likely limit the usefulness of the site.

Still, if you make your Web site work with version 3.0 (or later) of Netscape Navigator and Microsoft Internet Explorer (IE), you can feel fairly confident of the widespread acceptability of your Web site. The caveat here is that you not use tags that work *only* with Navigator or IE. In other words, steer clear of Netscape-created tags that work with Navigator and nothing else. The same goes for Microsoft-created tags that work only with IE.

Having said that, it's also important to mention that many of these proprietary tags might end up being part of a future HTML standard. The widespread use of Navigator and IE makes the manufacturers of those products the industry leaders, and other browser manufacturers are likely to follow their lead. Moreover, Web builders become accustomed to using favorite tags and attributes, and may raise a ruckus if those are dropped or not included in a future HTML standard.

Using the W3C Validation Service

Even if your site works in Navigator 3.0 and IE 3.0, you certainly want to make it more widely available if possible. Checking the correctness of your HTML is a good first step. As mentioned in a previous chapter, the HTML standards organization (the World Wide Web Consortium, or W3C) has its own Web site:

http://validator.w3.org/

From there, you can access the W3C validation service. This might be a good place to start. According to the W3C Web site, its validation service uses several programs to do the work of checking your HTML documents.

Unfortunately, the W3C validation service can work only with documents that are already on a Web server somewhere. That's a problem, because at this point, your Web site exists only on the computer sitting on your desk. Of course, if you already happen to have a Web site online that you want to check, then by all means, try out the W3C validation service.

Validating with CSE

For purposes of validating your HTML from the computer on your desk, you have few options. The best seems to be CSE. This software (named after the computer science course where it originated) is actually shareware. During the evaluation period, you're entitled to 50 free document evaluations.

http://www.htmlvalidator.com/

It makes sense to start with the first page of your site. For Project 1, I began with the `index.html` document. CSE worked very quickly when I checked this document. When finished (in just over one second for 111 lines of HTML!), the program informed me that it detected no errors and had no warnings. That was good news. The software printed out the HTML, with each line numbered on the left, and with comments inserted and clearly marked.

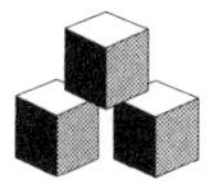

CSE distinguishes between messages and comments. *Messages* involve things like informing the user of deprecated elements, and the only two messages returned after the examination of `index.html` concerned deprecated elements (the `<CENTER>` tag and the `<FONT>` tag). The messages merely let me know that those elements may very well become obsolete in the future. Project 1 already deals with the possibility of the `<CENTER>` tag becoming obsolete by including the `<DIV ALIGN="center">` tag in conjunction with the `<CENTER>` tag. CSE suggests using style sheets in place of the `<FONT>` tag, but style sheets aren't covered until Project 3 of this book, so for this first project that message can just be ignored.

The two comments at the end were about CSE itself. Neither comment was relevant to checking the HTML.

If you plan to buy an HTML editor at some point, you may want to give serious consideration to HomeSite by Allaire or TextPad by Helios Software. Each of these products includes CSE. (Don't forget that Appendix B offers an overview of several of the most popular HTML editors!) If you're happy with another HTML editor you already have, or if you want to stick with Notepad and merely desire an HTML checker, then by all means look closely at CSE.

Next, I used CSE to check the `fender.html` document. Again, the software reported no errors or warnings. The only two messages were about the `<CENTER>` and `<FONT>` tags (the same messages reported for the Welcome page). The software again provided the same two comments about the CSE program.

When I checked the `gibson.html` document, I received the exact same report I had received for `fender.html`: no errors or warnings, and the same messages regarding the `<CENTER>` and `<FONT>` tags. Things looked very good so far.

If you use the copy-and-paste (or cut-and-paste) technique to copy sections of HTML from one document to another—as I did with the HTML at the top of each file—a mistake in the original can easily be passed on to several locations. Make sure that you fix any such mistakes in every HTML document where they've been pasted.

Finally, I checked the `terada.html` document, and as expected, received the same report as for the other guitar pages. All in all, CSE did an excellent job examining the HTML documents, and it's clear that for more complicated Web sites, running this type of validation software would be much more critical and beneficial than it was for this basic Web site.

Checking Links

A ***broken link*** *is one that no longer accesses the intended destination.*

Another important category of checking involves making sure that the links you have in your HTML are valid. Web sites with broken links—which often occur when a page to which you have linked is no longer at the URL your HTML specifies—can be very frustrating to users, so it's important to periodically check to make sure that everything is working as it should.

Always **make sure that your site's internal links work correctly. Beginning on the first page, check each link, working from one page to another and back again, until you know that they all work as they should.**

If you aren't using software to check the external links, you should check those manually, too. If they're all working when you build the site, great! Just make sure that you check them all periodically, perhaps once a week or so.

EXERCISE

Check the links in the Project 1 Web site by following these steps:

1. In your browser of choice, open the Welcome page.
2. Scroll down to the links that are in the combined numbered/bulleted list, and click on the first link, FENDER.
3. If the Fender page opens up, click on your browser's Back button to return to the Welcome page.
4. Click on the Stratocaster link. If the Stratocaster heading of the Fender page appears at the top of your browser, then that link is working.
5. Click on the browser's Back button to return to the Welcome page.
6. Continue clicking on the other links on the Welcome page, making sure that they all work as they should.
7. After checking all those links, click again on the FENDER link.
8. Scroll down to the links at the bottom of the Fender page.
9. Click on each link to make sure that it works, clicking the Back button each time to return to the Fender page. Remember that you must be online to check the two external links.
10. Finish checking your site's links by going to the Gibson and Terada pages in turn and clicking on each of the links they contain, just as you've done for the Fender page.

ANALYSIS

This method of manually checking links in a systematic fashion is the surest way to verify that your Web site is working as it should. If everything goes according to plan, all the links should check out. If any link doesn't work, check the corresponding HTML again. Be on the lookout especially for missing or incorrect <A> tags and HREF attributes.

Comparing Browsers

The only way to be absolutely sure that your Web site works as it should is to check it out in multiple browsers. Ideally, you would be able to test your Web site in *every* browser. The world isn't ideal, however, so the vast majority of Web builders are forced to limit the number of browsers they can check.

In working with this Web site, I had access to several popular browsers, and tested the Web site in each of them:

- America Online 4.0
- Internet Explorer 4.72
- Internet Explorer 3.02
- Netscape Communicator 4.01
- Netscape Navigator Gold 3.01

Many other browsers are available, of course, but I didn't have current versions of them on hand while developing this project. You can download most browsers from the Web, either for unlimited free use or at least for an evaluation period.

When you think you have your Web page tested and ready to go, you may want to download other browsers just to double-check compatibility. An alternative to loading new browsers on your own system is to carry a disk containing all your Web site files—using the same folder/subfolder structure as on the computer with which you created it—and test your site on the computers of friends who have browsers that you don't have.

While creating Project 1, I checked it in IE 4.72, often checking its appearance in other browsers as well. I used IE 4.72 as the standard by which I gauged the other browsers' presentation of the Web site. As you develop your own HTML pages, it's a perfectly valid approach for you to simply use your own browser of choice as the standard by which to measure the capabilities of all other browsers to display your Web pages.

Note

In comparing various browsers with whatever browser you use as your "standard," be aware that most browsers enable their users to set preferences for a number of characteristics. Some browsers allow more settings than others. Changes a user makes to these settings may change the way the user's browser displays various elements of your Web site.

As you compare your original work's appearance in your standard browser with its appearance in other browsers, you may notice small differences in line breaks. One browser, for example, may have the word `in` at the end of a line, whereas another browser may display the same `in` as the first word of the next line. Unless a browser uses a different font or size of font for its standard display, these differences will be minimal, although they may be noticeable to you when you closely compare browsers.

Summary

In this chapter, you have created the remaining pages needed for the Project 1 Web site. After learning the ins and outs of hyperlinks, you've made your Web site more useful by creating links to other Web sites, links to other pages on your own Web site, and even links to specific locations within a Web page.

This chapter has also focused on adding graphics to your Web site, not only discussing how to create graphics but also making suggestions about how to balance the file size of graphics with the requirements of fast downloading on the Web through file compression decisions, thumbnails, and so on. You learned that graphics on the Web usually take the form of GIF and JPEG files. The former are suitable for nonphotographic images, while the latter are best for working with photographs.

This chapter discussed an excellent way of checking your HTML after you write it—running the HTML through CSE *before* placing the pages on the Web. Other software tools can check your Web site's links, but they require your site to be online. After checking the HTML with

CSE, you should check each page by opening it in several browsers, paying particular attention to Navigator and Internet Explorer. Although differences in exact presentation of the Web site might exist from one browser to another, they usually are insignificant. In short, you can feel better once you've verified that the Web site works in almost exactly the same way for nearly all users.

The skills you've learned in this chapter are useful for putting the finishing touches on any basic Web site. In completing Project 1, you have practiced all the fundamentals of working with HTML, and have created a fully functional Web site! Have fun with it.

Project 1 Summary

The basic Web site you created in Project 1 is a fully functional one that you can use as a foundation for creating your own site on the World Wide Web. In creating this Web site, you learned the fundamentals of using HTML tags, attributes, and values, and used many of the most common ones to create this site.

You learned how to use a text editor to input and format text with HTML. Planning your site—which includes knowing how many pages you need, linking the pages, and balancing text and graphics—is a primary strategy for creating a useful and attractive site. The layout of text and graphics, the color of text and backgrounds, and white space are important elements in Web page design. In addition, you learned that concentrating on good writing, spelling, and punctuation can improve significantly the reception your Web site gets.

You now have a good idea of when to use GIF graphics and when to use JPEG graphics, both of which can add a great deal of visual interest to your Web page. You also understand the need to balance graphic size with quality, especially when using JPEG graphics.

You know how to create hyperlinks, which are among the most useful and important aspects of Web sites. You can link specific locations within your own Web site, for example, or link to other people's (or companies') Web sites. In addition, you used a hyperlink to enable visitors to send you e-mail.

Finally, you learned about testing your HTML to make sure that it works correctly. Most HTML validators require the HTML to be available on the Web, but you *can* use the CSE validator on your local computer. You also can use Web-based link checkers to make sure that your site's hyperlinks are operational.

HANDS ON PROJECT 2

THE INTERMEDIATE WEB SITE

- Creating a more complex site that utilizes some existing material, plus a number of new elements
- Packaging data, graphics, and other Web content in tables
- Using forms to gather input easily from your site's visitors
- Improving navigability by using frames
- Creating and implementing image maps
- Determining the sound and video requirements for your site
- Developing animation for the Web

Project Overview

In Project 2, the hobby-related guitar Web site from Project 1 becomes a Web-based business. Moving beyond the simple personal site concept, this project adds much more pizzazz and functionality to produce an intermediate-level site. To accomplish this goal, you learn many new techniques which are significantly advanced beyond those you used in the basic Web site.

In the course of building this Web site, you learn about many features that you probably have seen or used—even if unknowingly—if you have spent any time visiting Web sites. You learn to create an image map, which many sites use for navigation as well as for decoration. You also learn how to create tables, not only as a means of presenting information, but also as a way to place graphics on the page.

You learn how to create frames so that some items (like a logo or a table of contents) can remain on-screen at all times. Not all browsers can handle frames, however, so you discover how to present the same information so that it works simultaneously for those browsers as well.

A business on the World Wide Web is of little use if the business owner has no way to receive communication from customers—especially for taking orders or requests for information. Therefore, this project also includes instructions on how to create forms for the site.

Finally, this project involves some high-impact features—GIF animation, sound, and video—that have great potential as enhancements to your Web site.

What Is the Intermediate Web Site?

This second project is geared more toward owners of Web-based businesses, which make up a quickly growing segment of the World Wide Web, than it is toward personal Web site creators. Of course, anyone may find parts of this project useful, including for a personal Web site. The only part of this project that some personal Web site builders *may* not want to incorporate is the forms section, but plenty of people do find forms useful for their personal Web sites.

The scenario for this project is transforming a hobby (guitar collecting) into a business (buying and selling guitars).

Setting Your Goals for the Site

As with any other Web-site project, the first order of business is to decide on your goals for the site. My goals for this site fall into two basic categories. First, I need to be able to present the information about various guitars in an orderly fashion, as well as highlight one of the guitars. Second, I need a means of communicating with guitar buyers and sellers. Besides those two requirements, I want to jazz things up a bit to make the site interesting.

How the Intermediate Site Differs from the Basic Site

The most immediate difference between this site and the one built in Project 1 is the business orientation of this site. Most business sites, by nature, are more complex than a personal Web site. That's because of the need to present information about services or products for sale, and also because of the need to take orders from customers, either online or by phone.

As with the Project 1 Web site, the Project 2 Web site consists of several pages. This second site, however, makes use of numerous features not used in the first site. Among these features are image maps, tables, forms, and frames. In addition, Project 2 will add some zing to the visitor's Web site experience by incorporating sound, video, and animation. All these techniques are significant advances beyond what was done in the basic Web site.

This project does not use Dynamic HTML or cascading style sheets. Those state-of-the-art techniques are reserved for Project 3. Remember, Web builders were able to build excellent Web sites before DHTML and CSS became possible, and there's no reason that you can't do the same. The goal of this project is to help you build a business-oriented Web site that uses these more advanced techniques.

What Additional Information Do You Want to Present?

The primary additional information to be presented in this Web site is information about the guitars for sale through the Web site. Tables are the best way to give extensive information in a small amount of space while simultaneously enabling viewers to compare information. If I have five Stratocasters for sale, for example, I can use a table to highlight dif-

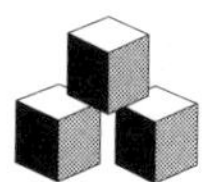

ferences (or common features) among them. Anyone interested in buying a Strat can quickly look at the vital statistics and determine which one, if any, is what he or she is looking for. (You would be amazed at the variety of Strats that are available!)

I also want to be able to highlight one guitar at a time in a sort of "guitar of the month" fashion, as well as list guitars that currently are available at a reduced price.

What Type of Information Will the User Provide You?

A visitor to this Web site may want to supply various sorts of information. He or she may want to be placed on the company's mailing list, for example, or may want to ask questions about a specific guitar that's for sale. At least one form will be required to receive information from visitors to the Web site.

Getting to Know Tables

An HTML* table *consists of rows and columns, and a* cell *is the intersection of a row and column.

In everyday noncomputer life, people commonly use tables in the form of telephone or address books. This type of table is nothing more than the presentation of information in rows and columns. Likewise, Web surfers are familiar with the use of tables onscreen—whether they know it or not. Many tables on Web sites take the traditional, familiar form of rows and columns. Others are totally hidden, at least as far as their appearance is concerned—rather than containing text, these tables may contain graphics that butt up against each other, giving them the appearance of one large graphic. In some other cases, tables contain a combination of text and graphics. For all intents and purposes, a table cell can contain almost anything: a data element, a heading, or some other portion of a Web page's content, such as a paragraph or an image.

In view of the nature of this second Web project—a Web-based business that buys and sells guitars—the usefulness of traditional tables to present information about guitars for sale is obvious. As you learn in this project, however, tables are very important elements in Web sites for other reasons. One of the big reasons for using tables is to position text and graphics on the page in ways that you can't by using the `ALIGN` attribute. Tables are versatile HTML elements—perhaps even a Web site builder's best friend, in some cases.

Learning about Frames

Another commonly used technique on Web sites—but one that is by no means universal—is frames. When you visit a Web site whose pages are divided into sections—and one or more sections remain unchanged while another section changes when you click on a link—you are seeing frames in action. In a site that uses frames, the borders between the frames may or may not be visible.

Frames can be very useful for presenting information, but they also can be problematic. Potential problems come in a couple of types. One type usually results from bad HTML coding. When a user clicks on a link in a site with bad coding, the expected Web page fails to appear in the correct frame. Instead, the wrong content appears, or the correct content appears but in the wrong frame. What the user expects is not what he or she gets.

Another type of problem arises when people try to view a Web site that uses frames with a browser that is not capable of handling frames. Unless the Web site creator makes allowance for that possibility on a Web site that uses frames, these users will have trouble with the site. To prevent trouble, the HTML author must provide alternate content for browsers that are not frames-enabled.

Because of the likelihood that many users will not have a frames-enabled browser, many Web site builders avoid creating a site that uses frames. Other builders don't want to deal with the extra effort involved in writing and updating the HTML code for a site that uses frames. Maintaining a site that uses frames can tax already-overburdened Webmasters.

That said, however, it's also fair to say that you can do much with frames that you cannot do without them. Using frames, for example, enables you to keep a navigation menu or table of contents onscreen at all times, without the browser having to reload the HTML for the table of contents or navigation menu as part of each new page. Also, frames enable you to present separate-but-related information in multiple frames at once, so tasks such as offering visitors comparisons between items can be carried out in a slick fashion. Frames can be extremely handy.

Introducing Image Maps

As you learned in the first project, graphics can add a great deal to a Web site. Not only can they create visual interest in an individual Web page, but they also can help you maintain a common color scheme or carry out a theme throughout a Web site. The same is true of both graphics you create and photographs you incorporate in a Web site. And, with a little help from you and some specialized graphics software, images of both types can do far more for your Web site—they can serve as image maps.

***A graphic that a user can click on to take particular actions is called an* image map *or* clickable image map.**

As you probably already realize, an image on a Web site can be anything that your imagination and creativity can conceive and then execute (or have someone else create). Any image you want to use can be turned into an image map. An image map contains links to other parts of a Web site or even to entirely different Web sites.

Image maps are graphics that do more than just "prettify" a Web site. An image map has one or more *hot regions* on it that, when clicked, function as links. Clicking on a hot region may bring up another Web page, for example, or may cause a graphic to appear seemingly out of nowhere. Image maps can be useful for navigating around your Web site or even tapping into resources outside your site.

The meaning of an image map, however, must be made clear to the targeted users of your Web site. One common type of image map is a literal map. A Web site providing weather condition information, for example, might display a map of Europe. Click on the city of Antwerp, and the site displays the weather for that location. Click on Barcelona, and the site tells you about the weather there.

Image maps, however, need not be literal maps. Instead, you can display an image map as a decorative graphic (see Figure 6.1) but simultaneously

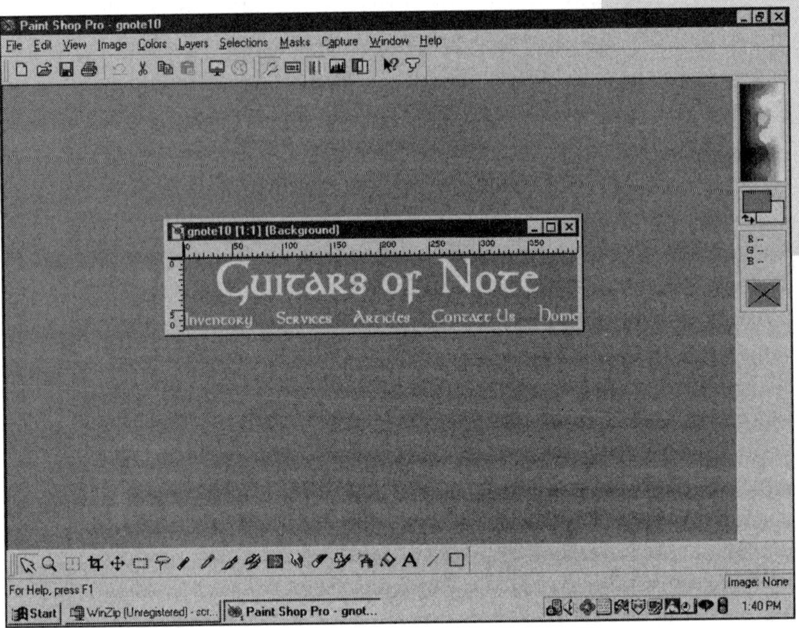

Figure 6.1 An image map can be both decorative and functional. The one being created here has a heading and five links.

have it do duty providing links to various places in your Web site. When a user clicks on a particular place in the graphic, he or she jumps to another desired location in the site. Image maps can make it fun and easy to navigate Web sites.

Image maps come in two varieties: *server-side image maps* and *client-side image maps.* The logic or computational power behind server-side image maps resides on the computer that is supplying the Web site's images and other content. The result is that the server machine must do all of the work, no matter whether 20 users or 20,000 users are using the image map.

In contrast, each user's computer carries out most of the work behind client-side image maps—and that's a big advantage. With client-side image maps, the computer processing power is distributed; rather than the server taking on the entire processing load, each user's computer carries its own load. With 20 users accessing the site, this is minimally helpful to the server, but with 20,000 users, this is of tremendous benefit.

Another advantage of client-side image maps is that the server on which you deploy your Web site doesn't need to support any special processing capabilities related to image maps. Client-side image maps are the best solution most of the time, and they're the kind of image map you learn how to create in this chapter.

Client-side image maps do have a disadvantage. Not all browsers support them. Most browsers do, but for others it's a problem. The ultimate solution once you attain proficiency with image maps is to use both kinds of image maps together.

Another way for you to enable visitors to navigate through your Web site is to include individual point-and-click images on some of your Web pages. These images can be in any of three image formats: GIF, JPG, and PNG. A graphic used in this manner may be a simple illustration created in a graphics program, or an elaborate decorative graphic that includes words as part of the graphic. The words incorporated into the graphic can inform the visitor of the particular content that she will see after clicking on that graphic.

Accepting User Feedback with Forms

If, while surfing the Web, you've ever ordered something, requested a company catalog, or filled out a survey, you've used a form of some sort. Forms are everywhere.

Forms of various types are extremely common on business Web sites. They enable companies to find new customers, to discover what customers or potential customers want, to take orders from customers, and so on. Communication via forms is critical to the success of a Web-based business. In fact, business sites without some sort of form are not terribly useful, except as a means of showing visitors what the company sells. Of course, without a means of taking orders or communicating with customers, even those sites are of little practical use.

Forms provide a way for visitors to interact with you—or at least with your site—rather than simply read the pages you have posted there. You can do all sorts of things with forms. Your forms can contain controls—such as buttons, check boxes, and text fields—that you can use to activate scripts, select data alternatives, or edit and display text. Typically, Web builders use forms to collect information from users, which a script or program on a Web server then processes. The Web server generates a custom response, based on input from the user, that is submitted back to the form. Some types of forms may not even require a human being on the receiving end to do anything.

Note

This book does not attempt to cover the ins and outs of forms processing on Web servers, because of the complexity of the topic. This book will teach you to use HTML to produce functional forms, but you may want to consult your ISP for details about the forms processing that's available on their servers, and consult other technical resources if you need to learn more about how servers handle forms.

You can use as many forms on your Web site as you think appropriate. Note, however, that too many forms *may* give some users the impression that you are too inquisitive. Few people mind giving their mailing address in order to receive a company catalog. Fewer people, however, are willing to put their e-mail address or telephone number on a form, fearing that it will be released to other companies and they will be subject to unwanted e-mail or annoying phone calls.

Nevertheless, well-designed forms can yield useful information about potential customers, as well as help maintain good relations with current customers. Use forms wisely.

Spicing Up Your Web Site

Despite the many great Web sites that were created in the early years of HTML—when tags and attributes were relatively limited—you can do so much more with HTML 4.0 that you owe it to yourself to take reasonable advantage of some of the pizzazz now possible. You may want to consider using animation, for example, or the latest in audio or video Web technology. The choice is yours.

Using Sound

Not many things on the Web are more startling than surfing to someone's site and suddenly hearing a greeting from the site's owner. Conversely, one of the most vexing aspects of the Web is deciding you want to hear a sound file the site offers, clicking on the link, and then waiting several minutes before you hear anything. And when you *do* hear something, the sound might be so muddled as to be unintelligible.

Ah, the potential and the pitfalls of sound on the Web!

Audio—especially repetitive music—can be annoying, so always give visitors the opportunity to turn it off. Better yet, don't make it play automatically. Instead, have visitors activate the music if they want to hear it.

Using sound on a Web site offers countless opportunities for Web site builders and owners. Rock bands—or bands of any musical persuasion, for that matter—can offer visitors little snippets of their songs as a means of enticing them to buy their latest CD. Radio stations can broadcast their programs live on the Web via their sites. News networks can allow Web site viewers to hear the important parts of a breaking news story. And Web site owners can simply say "Welcome to my Web site" or anything else they want visitors to hear.

Achieving the desired results by including sound on a Web site is not a simple proposition. For many people, adding sound requires extra hardware (a microphone, at the very least). For most people, adding sound also requires new software for recording and processing sound (which the Web builder must learn to use).

In addition, even with the hardware and software on hand, as well as an understanding of how to use them, other hurdles must be crossed. The best quality sound—like the best quality graphics—requires greatly increased download times. In fact, download times for top-quality sound can be massive, depending on the length of the audio you want to add. Of course, you can get around this difficulty by lowering the quality of sound. The problem, of course, is that the quality of sound degrades quickly. Muffled or muddled music on a Web site will not sell many CDs. Neither will the long download times required for excellent quality sound. Somewhere in between is the best compromise.

If you want to broadcast *live* audio, you've got to consider the cost as well as whether your ISP has that capability in the first place. Streaming audio may work for most Web builders who just want to provide a way for visitors to be able to hear a few sound clips at their own discretion. In *streaming audio*, users don't have to wait for the entire audio file to download. Rather, the file is downloaded in pieces and the user begins to hear audio right away. It's a bit more complicated than that; later in the project you'll learn more details.

Overall, having sound on your Web site is worth considering, especially if you think it will add quality to your site.

Using Video

If you thought adding sound to your Web site presented challenges, wait until you start looking into video! Video can make any Web site more exciting, and you may have viewed video on Web sites before. Unfortunately, most people don't have the computer muscle power to get the most out of video on a Web site. The issues involved with video are much like those with audio: the files are large, most users don't want to

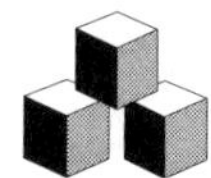

wait for long files to download, and streaming may or may not be the answer.

This time, however, the potential problems aren't entirely on the user's side. That's because the hardware and software required to create streaming video for the Web generally are not cheap. For top-quality, streaming Web video, you can expect to pay significant amounts of money. Even if you hire a professional to create the video for you, that's only part of the cost. You also must find an ISP with the correct server technology and pay the requisite monthly or annual fees (which can be significant). If you can afford the costs related to streaming video, though, it certainly can add considerable zing to your site.

Your site, however, may not require streaming video. Perhaps you just want to provide a very short video greeting visitors to your site. Maybe you have interviewed a celebrity and you want to play a clip of that, because it is the highlight of your career so far. If your site tells readers how to do something that is hard to understand without seeing it take place, you may want to play a clip that demonstrates part of the technique.

As in the case of audio, however, you must balance the quality of your video with the download time. Most important here is keeping in mind the audience you are intending to reach. If they tend to have state-of-the-art computers and high-speed Internet connections, then you probably can safely use higher quality video. If they have average computers and connect to the Internet via normal telephone lines, then you probably need to keep the video quality lower in order to minimize download time.

Caution

If you want, you can provide links to both higher and lower quality versions of the same video clips. Of course, this means extra work for you, because you have to create both files, but it helps viewers a great deal by giving them the opportunity to choose which version they prefer to download.

Using Animation

As you have surfed the Web, you probably have run across Web sites that use animation as a means of enlivening the site. These animations are not as complex as the animations you might see onscreen when you go catch the latest (computer-generated!) Disney animated feature at the theater. Rather, a Web site animation usually is created from GIF files and consists of just a few individual frames. Animations also can be a series of frames that are not intended to create the impression of movement but rather are a sequence of images that change automatically. The visual interest an animation creates is the primary reason to consider using one in your Web site. The work in achieving that visual interest is the primary reason to consider *not* using animation in your Web site.

An animation* frame *is one of a series of images that, viewed sequentially at a fast enough rate, create the impression of movement or change.

There are two big problems with animation. First, if an animation is not done well, it can greatly increase download time for a Web page, which is not good if you want to attract and keep visitors. Second, an animation can become annoying very quickly. Fortunately, both problems have relatively simple solutions.

The solution to long download times is to optimize your animation. Various animation creation programs can handle this task for you. You create the frames of the animation, and then you let the software optimize it. Optimization refers to creating the best quality animation in the smallest file size possible.

The annoyance factor also has a solution. For most people, two or three repetitions of an animation are more than enough. If the animation plays over and over again until visitors leave that page of your Web site, they'll be ready to get out of there as fast as possible. This is not the type of reaction you want. The key to solving this problem is simply limiting how many times the animation runs. For almost any animation, once is plenty.

Creating animation involves using software created for that purpose. Such software is available commercially or as shareware. Unlike much full-fledged graphics software, animation software is available at very reasonable prices. This makes animation an easy-to-achieve effect for anyone's Web site.

Summary

In this brief chapter, you've received an introduction to the topics that you're going to work with throughout Project 2. You've learned about many new techniques you can use in any Web site, greatly expanding the kinds of effects you can achieve as well as the usefulness of the site. The elements that you'll get to practice in this project include tables, frames, image maps, forms, audio, video, and animation.

Of course, you still need to do the usual things related to planning a Web site—decide what kind of information to present, how best to present it, what specific information you'll ask your visitors to provide, and so on. You've begun the process in this chapter, and you'll solidify the design for the Project 2 Web site in Chapter 7.

Designing the Intermediate Web Site

As usual, the first task in building the Web site is to design it. As in Project 1, this design must include the number of pages required as well as the layout of each individual page. The Project 2 Web site will be more complex than the Project 1 site. Taking the design one step at a time, though, and looking logically at the number of discrete pages needed, should lead to a functional design that you can build with minimal aggravation in the following chapters.

Figure 7.1 shows the opening page of the Project 2 Web site.

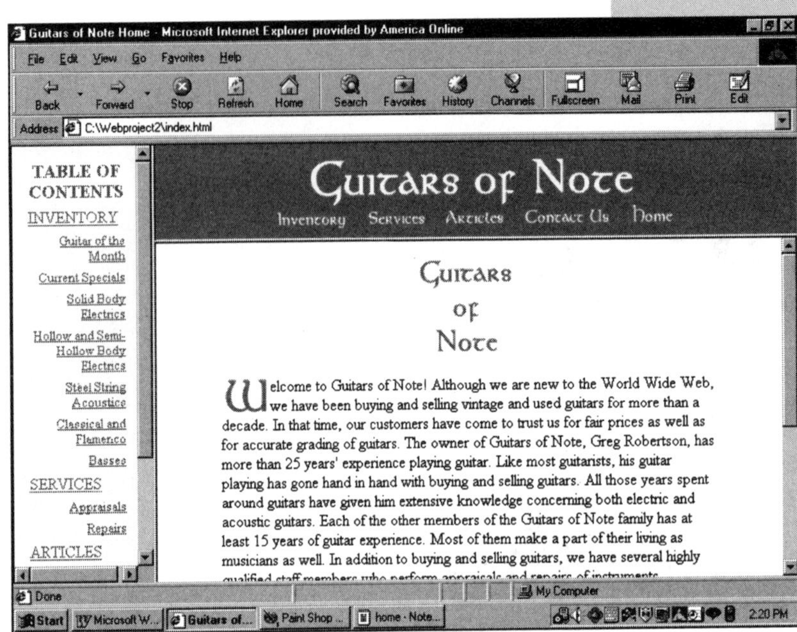

Figure 7.1 The Project 2 Web site is going to look like this.

Laying Out the Pages

***Frames** in a Web site are individual windows that can appear onscreen simultaneously and can contain separate information.*

This site uses frames as part of its design. Sites that use frames typically have either two or three frames (many more are possible, but not practical). For this project, three frames are in order. Figure 7.2 shows the frame layout I have in mind, but no specifics about the frames' contents.

As I envision it, the top frame remains constant, showing the name of the business (Guitars of Note). The purpose of this static frame, of

For viewers to get the most out of a Web site that uses frames, they must have a frames-capable browser. Many businesses do not use frames in their Web sites so as to avoid complications. Instead, they use tables to lay out their sites' contents. If you build a business Web site, you also may want to consider that simpler approach, at least until you can be fairly certain that most of your potential customers have frames-capable browsers.

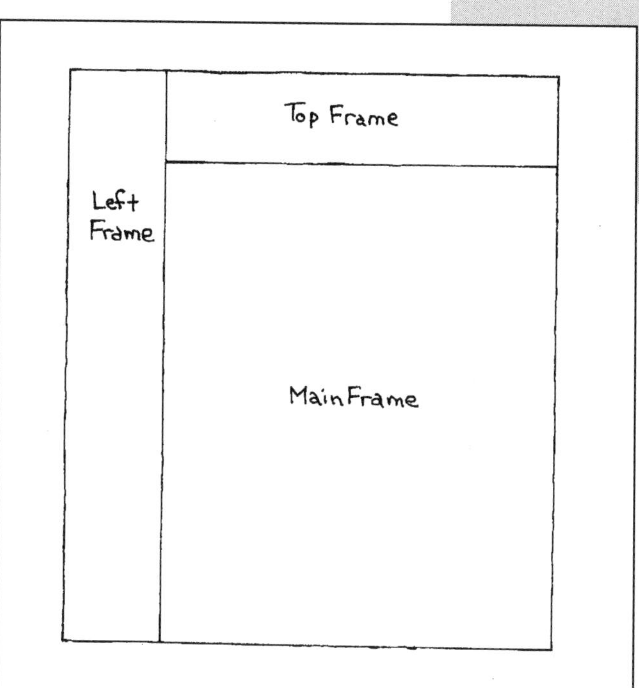

Figure 7.2 This is a rough layout of the frames for the Project 2 Web site.

course, is to keep the name of the company visible at all times, as well as to keep the primary links available to users. These links are available through a row of buttons beneath the company name.

> **Caution**
>
> **Don't forget that some users do not have graphics capability. That means you should supply text versions of any graphic buttons, as well as ALT text for any images.**

In the left frame, I want to place the same links that appear in the top frame, but also include other links. These other links are actually links to specific portions of the Web site. This frame, too, remains the same regardless of where a visitor is in the site. Another difference between these links and the ones in the top frame is that the links in the left frame are standard text links (not graphics), such as those you created in the Project 1 Web site.

The right frame, or main frame, is where all the pages of the Web site appear. It's the largest frame, and the one that displays the content a user wants to see. When a user clicks on the Services link to read about the services offered by Guitars of Note, for example, that information appears in the main frame.

Figure 7.3 shows the layout of the frames again, but this time, the figure also shows the general contents of the top and left frames.

As you can see, many more links are present in the left frame than are in the top frame. These additional links usually go to specific spots within the Web site's pages, rather than to the top of a page. All the links are intended to help users get to specific locations very quickly.

Note

One good reason to use frames is that you can keep all main links in front of the user at all times. That way, you don't need to place links on every page that you create.

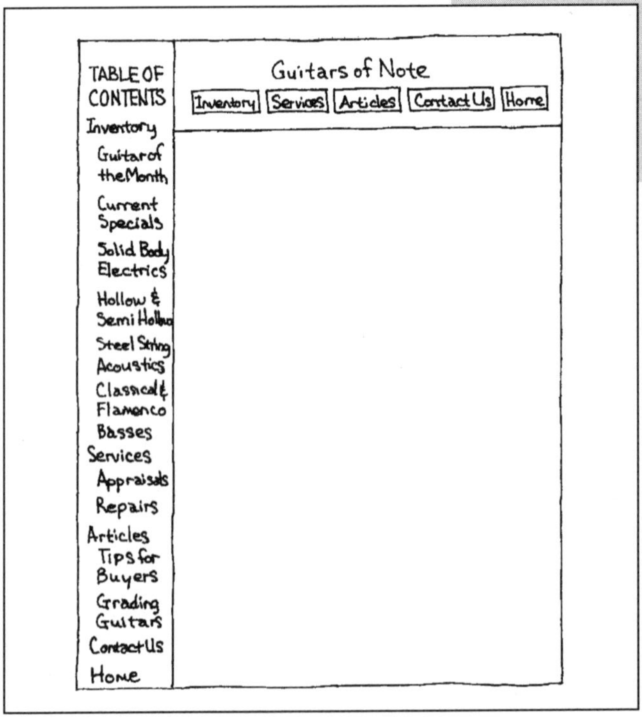

Figure 7.3
The top frame has buttons that match the primary links in the left frame.

Judging by the number of links in the left frame, you may have surmised that this Web site includes many pages. If so, you are correct. The Project 1 Web site involved only a few pages of HTML, but the Project 2 Web site involves several pages.

When putting links on your Web site, limit the number of top-level links on the main page to no more than six or eight. This limitation helps keeps the page from being too crowded.

The Home Page

The page listed as the last link, `Home`, is much like the Welcome page of the Project 1 Web site. This time, however, the text on the page discusses the business. Figure 7.4 shows the layout of the Home page.

The Guitar of the Month Page

I want a portion of the Web site to be a feature page where I can select an in-stock guitar and highlight it for the month. Figure 7.5 shows the

Figure 7.4
This page is a straightforward description of the business and the Web site.

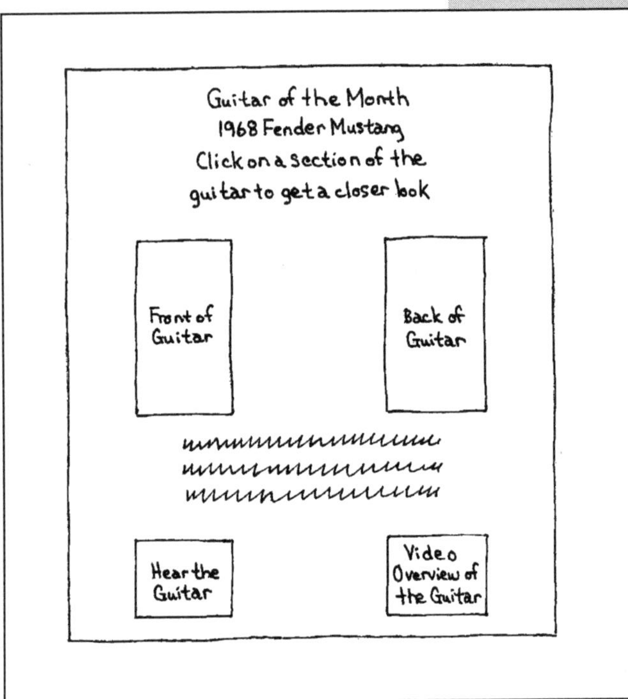

Figure 7.5 The Guitar of the Month page uses image maps as well as audio and video clips.

planned layout of the Guitar of the Month page, which has several new elements. The graphic on the left will show the front of the guitar, and the graphic on the right will show the back of the guitar. The two graphics, however, are actually image maps. By creating hot regions on the graphics, I enable a visitor to click on a portion of the large graphic to bring up a detail photo. If, for example, someone wants to get a close look at the tuners, he or she can click on the peghead in the picture of the front of the guitar. That click displays the desired detail view. This functionality enables potential buyers to see the guitar up close before deciding whether or not they are interested in buying it.

Another new technique you see here is the use of sound on the Web site. If someone wants to hear what the guitar sounds like, they can click on the link below the paragraph describing the guitar to play a sound clip.

Another link on the Guitar of the Month page allows visitors to play a video clip about the featured guitar.

The Current Specials Page

The Current Specials link takes the user to a page that lists specifics of a few guitars that are on sale at the moment. The instruments on this page have been sitting around too long, so if the price is lowered a bit, someone may decide that one of them is too tempting of a deal to pass up.

Figure 7.6 shows the layout of this page. The new technique in use here is the table. In this case, a table is a straightforward table of data (make, model, and so on).

The Current Inventory Page

The Current Inventory page contains a great deal of information. In fact, this page contains the bulk of information a potential customer might seek. This page consists of five separate tables, each of which lists various pieces of information about a certain general type of guitar. The general types are: Solid Body Electrics, Hollow and Semi-Hollow Body Electrics, Steel String Acoustics, Classical and Flamenco, and Basses.

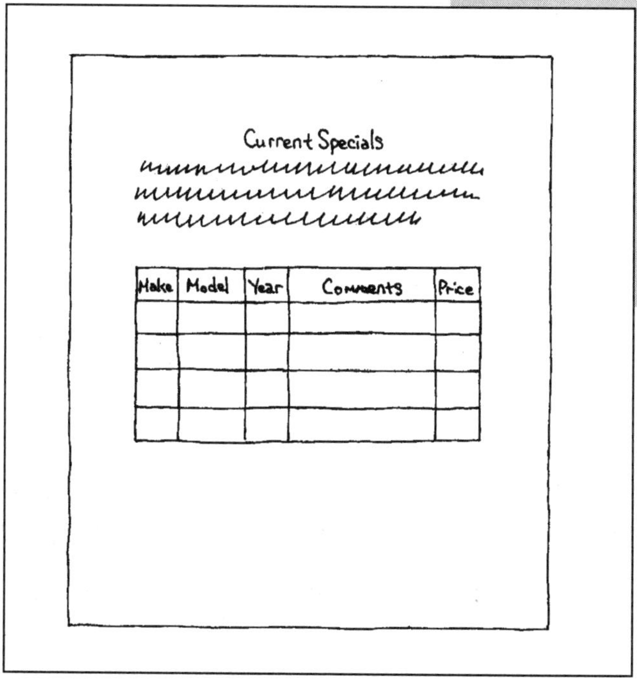

Figure 7.6
The Current Specials page makes use of HTML table tags to offer several pieces of information about each guitar that's on sale.

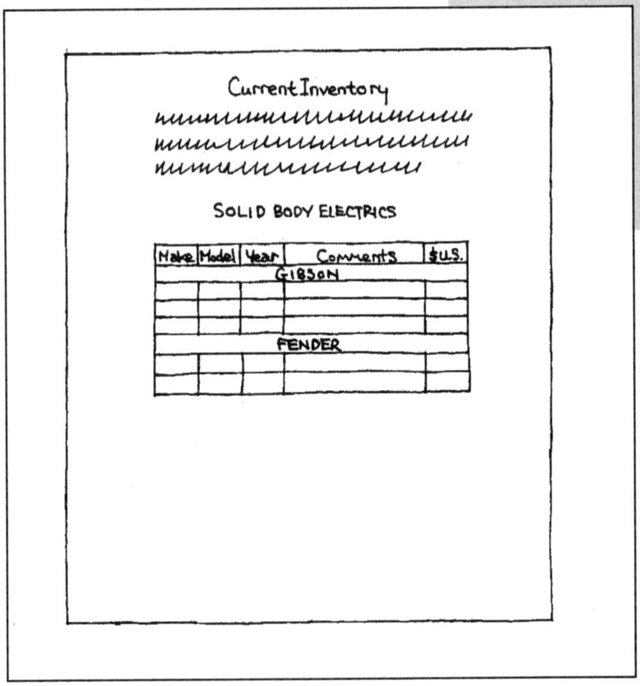

Figure 7.7
The Current Inventory page contains most of the information about the guitars for sale.

Each table has its own link (the name of the general guitar type) in the table of contents in the left frame. Figure 7.7 shows the Current Inventory page's layout with Solid Body Electrics selected.

The Services Page

Next comes the Services page. This page is straightforward text that discusses the services offered by Guitars of Note. One service is evaluating old instruments and the other is repairing guitars of any age. Figure 7.8 shows the layout of this page.

Two of the links you saw in the table of contents in the left frame—Appraisals and Repairs—are links to the individual sections within the Services page, rather than to the top of the page.

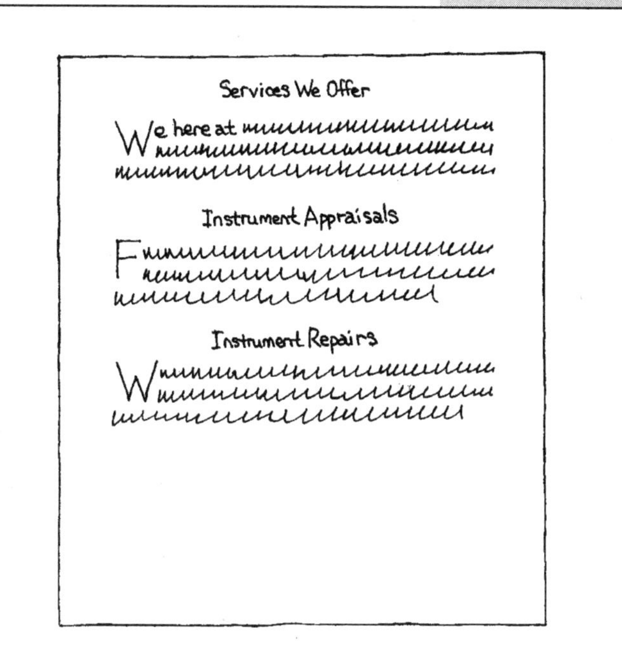

Figure 7.8
The Services page is all text.

The Articles Page

The Articles link in the table of contents in the left frame takes readers to a page that contains slightly modified versions of two sections that also were on the Project 1 Web site. One is a list of tips about buying old guitars, and the other is information about grading guitars. Figure 7.9 shows the layout of this all-text page.

The Contact Page

Visitors reach the Contact page in this Web site by clicking on the Contact Us link. This link leads to a form for interested visitors to fill out. Anyone who wants to be placed on the Guitars of Note mailing list or who wants to submit questions or comments can use this form for either purpose. This is a good place for visitors to offer general comments about the site or to give the company suggestions. Figure 7.10 shows the layout of this page.

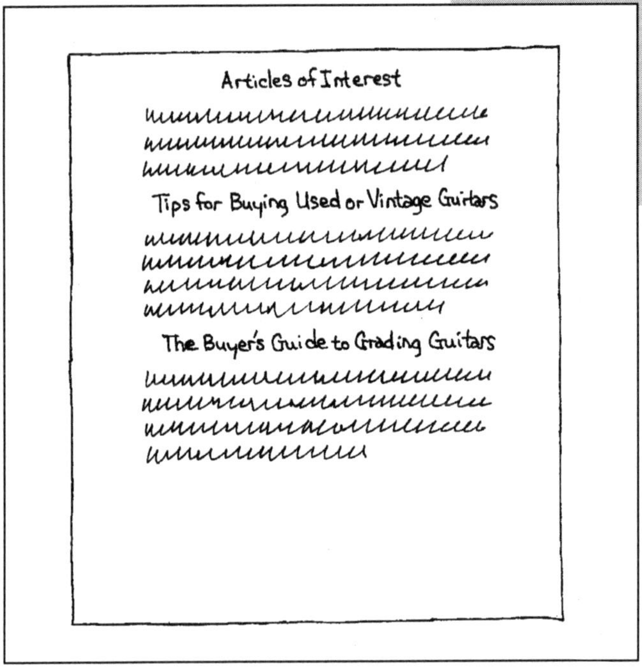

Figure 7.9
The Articles page reuses some text that was on the Project 1 Web site.

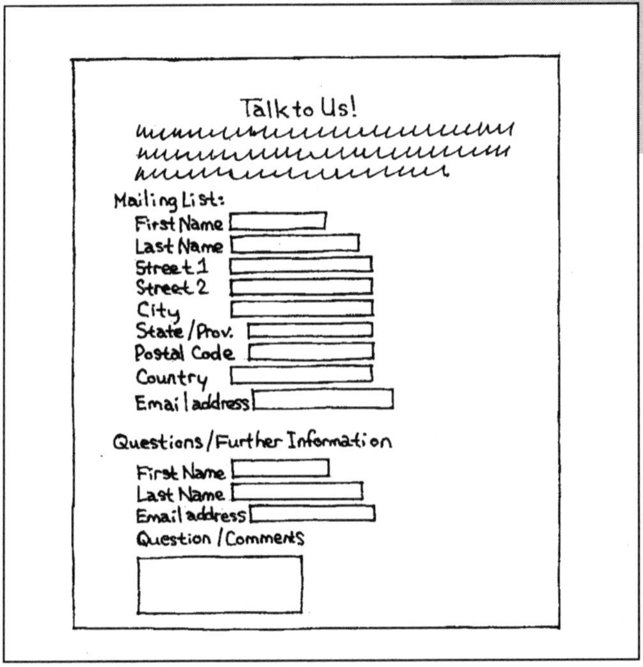

Figure 7.10
A form provides a certain level of interactivity to this Web site.

That completes the survey of this Web site's individual pages. You may have noted a lack of graphics on many of the pages. One reason is that graphics aren't needed on each page as decoration, because the top frame is present at all times, and it is decorative. The second reason is that the content of each page doesn't necessarily lend itself to graphics. The third reason, and the primary one, is to save download time. In place of graphics that appear automatically, visitors on this Web site have the option of downloading photos that they want to see. In addition, they have more interesting options available, like playing audio and video clips.

Creating Tables

A couple of pages on this Web site will contain data to quickly inform visitors of the specifics of various guitar models. Rather than have them read through paragraphs of text, I want visitors to be able to compare guitars quickly. Tables are an excellent way to display columnar fields of data, so that is the solution to this need. Tables also are indispensable for creating page layouts, as you learn elsewhere in this project.

Defining a Simple Table

You use the `<TABLE>` container tag to define a table. Several other tags, of course, are necessary to create the complete table. Figure 7.11 shows an example table from the Project 2 Web site.

The general structure for using table tags is as follows:

```
<TABLE>
  <TR>
    <TH></TH>
    <TH></TH>
  </TR>
  <TR>
    <TD></TD>
    <TD></TD>
  </TR>
</TABLE>
```

Refer to this general structure as well as to Figure 7.11 throughout the following discussion.

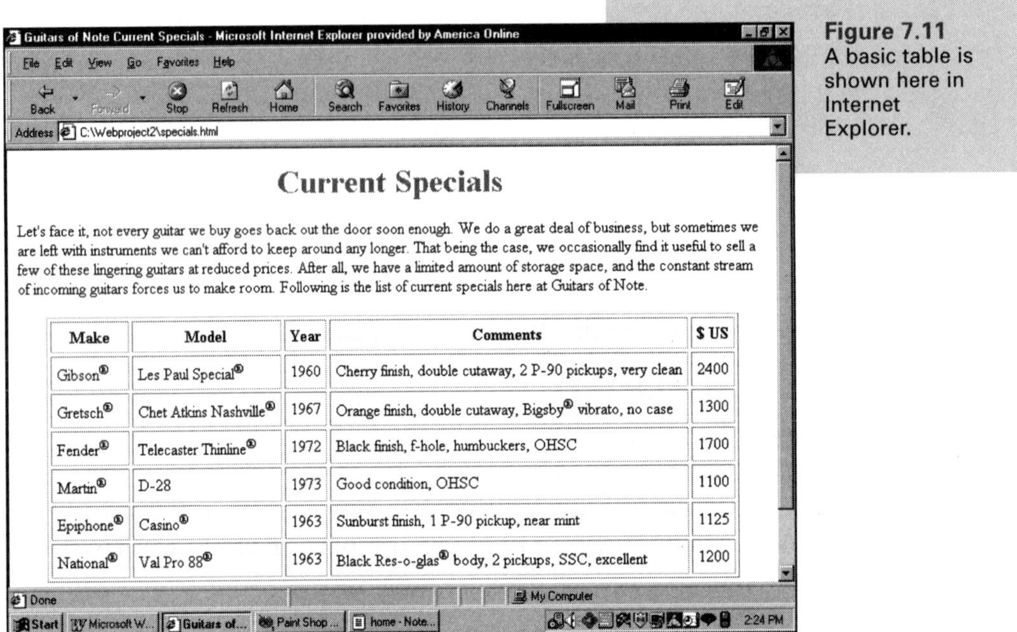

Current Specials

Let's face it, not every guitar we buy goes back out the door soon enough. We do a great deal of business, but sometimes we are left with instruments we can't afford to keep around any longer. That being the case, we occasionally find it useful to sell a few of these lingering guitars at reduced prices. After all, we have a limited amount of storage space, and the constant stream of incoming guitars forces us to make room. Following is the list of current specials here at Guitars of Note.

Make	Model	Year	Comments	$ US
Gibson®	Les Paul Special®	1960	Cherry finish, double cutaway, 2 P-90 pickups, very clean	2400
Gretsch®	Chet Atkins Nashville®	1967	Orange finish, double cutaway, Bigsby® vibrato, no case	1300
Fender®	Telecaster Thinline®	1972	Black finish, f-hole, humbuckers, OHSC	1700
Martin®	D-28	1973	Good condition, OHSC	1100
Epiphone®	Casino®	1963	Sunburst finish, 1 P-90 pickup, near mint	1125
National®	Val Pro 88®	1963	Black Res-o-glas® body, 2 pickups, SSC, excellent	1200

Figure 7.11
A basic table is shown here in Internet Explorer.

A row is a set of horizontally grouped cells.

A column is a set of vertically grouped cells.

As you can see, you begin a table with the `<TABLE>` tag and end it with the `</TABLE>` tag. Next, you define the top row of the table with the `<TR>` and `</TR>` tags. Nested within those two tags are tags that define the header cells of the table, assuming you want to have a heading at the top of each table column. In the general structure shown above, two such header cells are indicated by `<TH>` and `</TH>` tags. On the table shown in Figure 7.11, you see five column headings: `Make`, `Model`, `Year`, `Comments`, and `$ US`. In the HTML for this page, each of these header cells is defined by a `<TH>` and `</TH>` tag pair, so the HTML has to contain five of these tag pairs.

Following the row of header cells comes the second row of cells, again defined by the `<TR>` and `</TR>` tags. This time, however, the cells are data cells, not header cells, so each cell is defined by a `<TD>` and `</TD>` tag pair. The same is true of all the remaining rows in the table shown in Figure 7.11—a `<TD>` and `</TD>` tag pair defines each data cell within each of the remaining six rows, and each row is housed within a `<TR>` and `</TR>` tag pair.

Refer to Appendix A for the attributes of the <TR> tag or of any other tag involved in building tables.

A* header cell *contains a heading at the top of a column.
A* data cell *is any other cell which contains some of the table's contents.

After you define the number of rows in a table—by inserting that many <TR> tags—you define the table's cells. You can define two kinds of cells using HTML: header cells and data cells.

As mentioned earlier, the top cell of a column commonly holds a heading for that column. You also might want to use the leftmost cell of each row as a horizontal "heading" that indicates the kind of data displayed by the row.

The tags you use to define header cells are <TH> and </TH>. By default, the contents of a table header cell are automatically centered within the cell and appear in boldface type.

If you want your header cell to be at the left end of a row instead of the top of a column, your HTML for that row takes a format like the following:

```
<TR>
    <TH></TH>
    <TD></TD>
    <TD></TD>
    <TD></TD>
</TR>
```

The table row defined here spans four columns, with the left-most column containing the header cell.

Usually, most of a table consists of data cells. You use the <TD> and </TD> tag pair to define each data cell. By default, text in data cells is left-aligned. You can format text in a data cell by including the appropriate formatting tags, such as <STRONG> and </STRONG> (or <B> and </B>) for bold text or <EM> and </EM> (or <I> and </I>) for italic text. Simply nest these formatting tags between the <TD> and </TD> tags.

Caution

Make sure that you create all the HTML documents for this second project in their own folder, separate from the first project's files. Name the folder `Webproject2` or something else that you'll remember. If you save your new `index.html` document for Project 2 in the same folder that holds the `index.html` document for Project 1, you'll overwrite the Project 1 Welcome page.

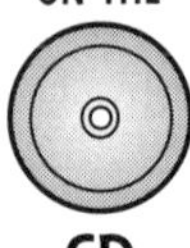

ON THE CD

Although you should actually type the HTML in the following exercises, you can find the final version of the document on the CD that accompanies this book, as `specials.html`.

EXERCISE

Now it's time to build one of the tables this site requires. Follow these steps:

1. Open a new file in Notepad (or whatever text editor you are using).
2. Type the following HTML to begin the page:

```
<!DOCTYPE HTML PUBLIC"-//W3/DTD HTML 4.0 Frameset//EN"
"http://www.w3.org/TR/REC-html40/frameset.dtd">
<HTML>
   <HEAD>
   <TITLE>Guitars of Note Current Specials</TITLE>
   <META NAME="keywords" CONTENT="guitar, vintage guitar, guitar
   collecting, solid body, semi-hollow body, hollow body, classical,
   flamenco, steel string, bass, Fender, Gibson, Gretsch, Rickenbacker,
   Martin, National, Epiphone, Guild, Ibanez, Hagstrom, Ovation, Jose
   Oribe, Pimentel, Raimundo, Ramirez, Armstrong, Telecaster, Mustang,
   Les Paul, Jaguar, Country Gentleman, S100 Polara, Val Pro, Artist,
   White Falcon, Anniversary, Hummingbird, Chet Atkins, Nashville,
   Songbird, Precision, Musicmaster, Plexiglas, Thinline, Casino, E360TD
   Riviera, J-160E, J-200, ES-335, ES-150, ES-175, D-28, D-35, 1168-5P,
   EB2, 4001, VI">
   <META NAME="description" CONTENT="Guitars for sale, specializing in
   vintage collectibles.">
   </HEAD>
```

3. Before going any further, save the document as `specials.html`.

4. Now begin the body of the document by typing the following introductory paragraph:

```
<BODY>
   <H1 ALIGN="center"><FONT COLOR="red">Current Specials</FONT></H1>
   <P>Let's face it, not every guitar we buy goes back out the door
   soon enough. We do a great deal of business, but sometimes we are
   left with instruments we can't afford to keep around any longer.
   That being the case, we occasionally find it useful to sell a few of
   these lingering guitars at reduced prices. After all, we have a
   limited amount of storage space, and the constant stream of incoming
   guitars forces us to make room. Following is the list of current
   specials here at Guitars of Note.</P>
```

5. Create the first part of the table itself by typing the following HTML:

```
<TABLE>
<TR>
   <TH>Make</TH>
   <TH>Model</TH>
   <TH>Year</TH>
   <TH>Comments</TH>
   <TH>$ US</TH>
</TR>
</TABLE>
</BODY>
</HTML>
```

   Figure 7.12 shows the `specials.html` page as it appears now. So far, it doesn't look much like a table, because it has only column headings.

6. Place the insertion point in front of the `</TABLE>` tag, and press Enter twice.

7. Beginning on the second blank line just created, type the following HTML:

```
<TR>
   <TD>Gibson</TD>
   <TD>Les Paul Special</TD>
   <TD>1960</TD>
```

```
        <TD>Cherry finish, double cutaway, 2 P-90 pickups, very clean</TD>
        <TD>2400</TD>
    </TR>
    <TR>
        <TD>Gretsch</TD>
        <TD>Chet Atkins Nashville</TD>
        <TD>1967</TD>
        <TD>Orange finish, double cutaway, Bigsby vibrato, no case</TD>
        <TD>1300</TD>
    </TR>
    <TR>
        <TD>Fender</TD>
        <TD>Telecaster Thinline</TD>
        <TD>1972</TD>
        <TD>Black finish, f-hole, humbuckers, OHSC</TD>
        <TD>1700</TD>
    </TR>
    <TR>
        <TD>Martin</TD>
        <TD>D-28</TD>
        <TD>1973</TD>
        <TD>Good condition, OHSC</TD>
        <TD>1100</TD>
    </TR>
    <TR>
        <TD>Epiphone</TD>
        <TD>Casino</TD>
        <TD>1963</TD>
        <TD>Sunburst finish, 1 P-90 pickup, near mint</TD>
        <TD>1125</TD>
    </TR>
    <TR>
        <TD>National</TD>
        <TD>Val Pro 88</TD>
        <TD>1963</TD>
        <TD>Black Res-o-glas body, 2 pickups, SSC, excellent</TD>
        <TD>1200</TD>
    </TR>
```

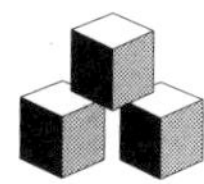

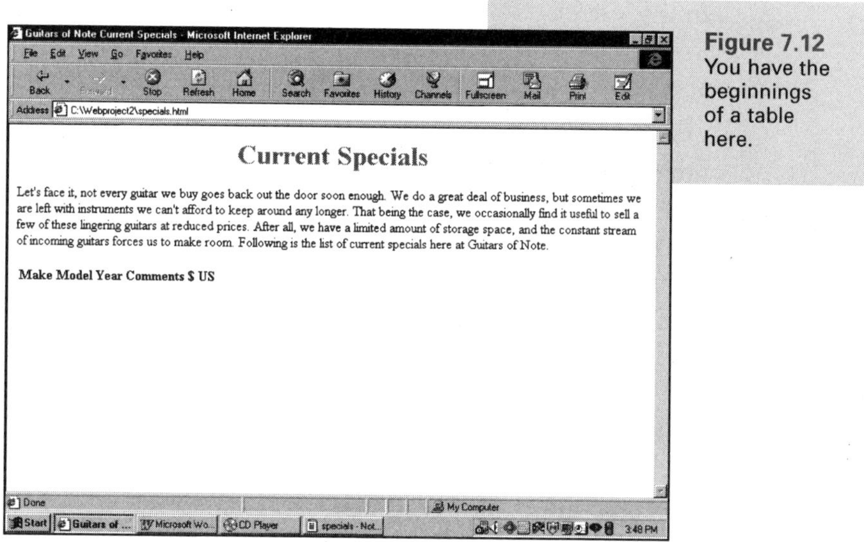

Figure 7.12 You have the beginnings of a table here.

8. Save the `specials.html` document.
9. Switch to your browser and open `specials.html`.

Figure 7.13 shows the `specials.html` page with text in the table's cells, as it appears in IE 4.

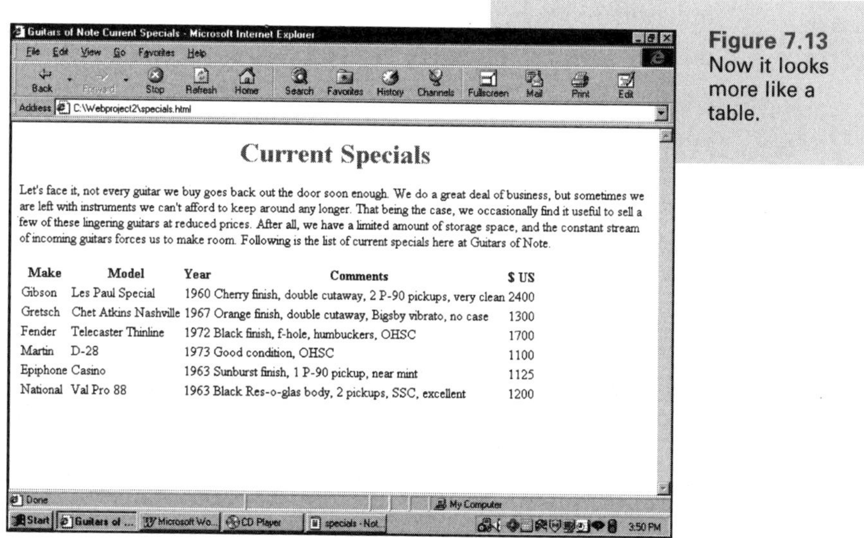

Make	Model	Year	Comments	$ US
Gibson	Les Paul Special	1960	Cherry finish, double cutaway, 2 P-90 pickups, very clean	2400
Gretsch	Chet Atkins Nashville	1967	Orange finish, double cutaway, Bigsby vibrato, no case	1300
Fender	Telecaster Thinline	1972	Black finish, f-hole, humbuckers, OHSC	1700
Martin	D-28	1973	Good condition, OHSC	1100
Epiphone	Casino	1963	Sunburst finish, 1 P-90 pickup, near mint	1125
National	Val Pro 88	1963	Black Res-o-glas body, 2 pickups, SSC, excellent	1200

Figure 7.13 Now it looks more like a table.

ANALYSIS

In this exercise, you created a basic table. In the first step, you created a new document in your text editor, and in the second step, you entered all the page's "behind-the-scenes" information: HTML version, page title, page description, keywords, and so on. Step 3 is where you saved the document for the first time. The text you typed in Step 4 introduces visitors to the upcoming table. So far, you're familiar with all these HTML tags from Project 1.

Step 5 begins the table-creation process. You first inserted the `<TABLE>` tag to indicate the beginning of a table. The next tag, `<TR>`, designates the start of the first row. Each of the next five lines of HTML has a `<TH>` container that creates one table header cell, with the header cell's contents between the start and end tags. You ended the row of column headings with a `</TR>` end tag.

Additional white space within your HTML will not mess up your table, so don't be shy about using extra returns and tabs to keep your HTML code readable. I prefer placing each tag on its own line for purposes of readability.

In Step 7, you added the remaining table cells and their contents. The only difference here from the cell headings created in Step 5 is that you use `<TD>` container tags (think "table *data*") instead of `<TH>` container tags.

Fine-Tuning a Table

EXERCISE ▼

Figure 7.13 showed the orderliness of a table. Unfortunately, however, the columns aren't all separated adequately, and the table isn't particularly attractive.

Modify the table a bit by following these steps:

1. Make sure the `specials.html` document is open in your text editor.
2. Place the insertion point in the `<TABLE>` tag at the top of the table.

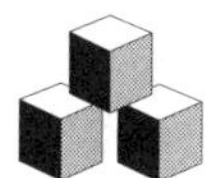

3. Change this tag to the following:

```
<TABLE BORDER="1">
```

4. Save the document.
5. Switch to your browser and refresh the screen.

Figure 7.14 shows the look of the table with the new one-pixel border.

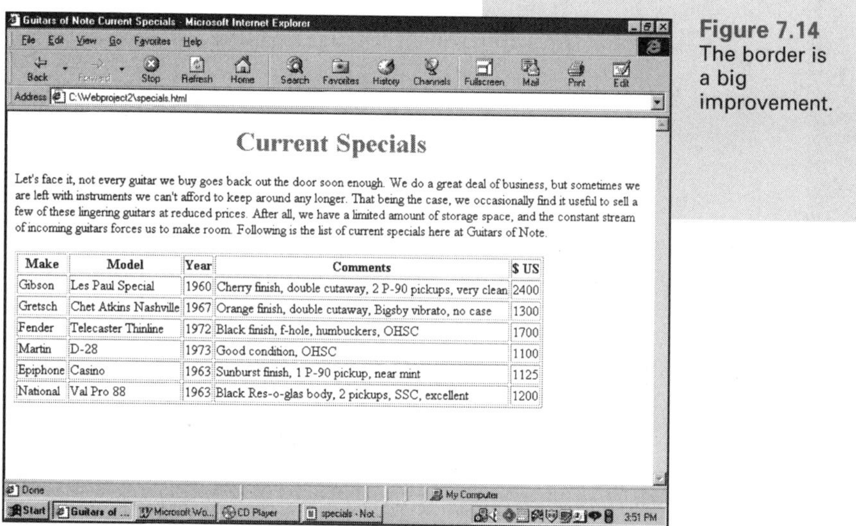

Make	Model	Year	Comments	$ US
Gibson	Les Paul Special	1960	Cherry finish, double cutaway, 2 P-90 pickups, very clean	2400
Gretsch	Chet Atkins Nashville	1967	Orange finish, double cutaway, Bigsby vibrato, no case	1300
Fender	Telecaster Thinline	1972	Black finish, f-hole, humbuckers, OHSC	1700
Martin	D-28	1973	Good condition, OHSC	1100
Epiphone	Casino	1963	Sunburst finish, 1 P-90 pickup, near mint	1125
National	Val Pro 88	1963	Black Res-o-glas body, 2 pickups, SSC, excellent	1200

Figure 7.14
The border is a big improvement.

ANALYSIS

The one change you made, in Step 3, was to add a border around the table. By adding that border, you also added borders between cells. At least now the table looks like a table—it's easy to distinguish columns and cells from each other. The value of the `BORDER` attribute—in this case, `1`—specifies the width of the line that forms the border.

Although much improved in appearance, this table still needs work. The problem is that the cell contents simply are too close to the cell borders. You can add two attributes to the `<TABLE>` tag to change the appearance of the cell contents in relation to the borders: `CELLPADDING` and `CELLSPACING`.

EXERCISE

Make more improvements to the table by following these steps:

1. Switch back to `specials.html` in your text editor.
2. Place the insertion point before the table's start tag.
3. Press Enter, and then type the following (starting on the new blank line you've created):

```
<DIV ALIGN="center">
<CENTER>
```

4. Place the insertion point in the table's start tag.
5. Change that tag to the following:

```
<TABLE BORDER="1" CELLPADDING="5">
```

6. Place the insertion point after the table's end tag.
7. Press Enter, and then type the following tags:

```
</CENTER>
</DIV>
```

8. Save the `specials.html` document.
9. Switch to your browser and refresh the screen.

Figure 7.15 shows the revised table.

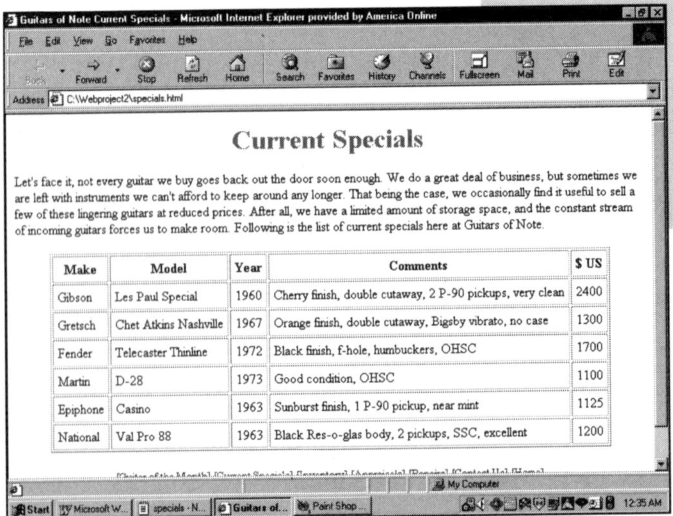

Make	Model	Year	Comments	$ US
Gibson	Les Paul Special	1960	Cherry finish, double cutaway, 2 P-90 pickups, very clean	2400
Gretsch	Chet Atkins Nashville	1967	Orange finish, double cutaway, Bigsby vibrato, no case	1300
Fender	Telecaster Thinline	1972	Black finish, f-hole, humbuckers, OHSC	1700
Martin	D-28	1973	Good condition, OHSC	1100
Epiphone	Casino	1963	Sunburst finish, 1 P-90 pickup, near mint	1125
National	Val Pro 88	1963	Black Res-o-glas body, 2 pickups, SSC, excellent	1200

Figure 7.15 Using the `CELLPADDING` attribute, you've improved the table's readability.

ANALYSIS

You centered the table in this series of steps by inserting the `<CENTER>` and `</CENTER>` tags in Steps 3 and 7, respectively. Because that tag is deprecated, however, you also added the `<DIV ALIGN="center">` and `</DIV>` tags (as discussed in Project 1, this ensures that you cover the majority of browsers).

In Step 5, you added space between the cell contents and the cell borders by "padding" the cell. The `CELLPADDING` attribute's assigned value of `5` places five pixels of space between the cell's text and its borders, not just before and after the contents, but also above and below the contents.

Now you'll continue modifying the table's appearance by doing a little more work with it.

EXERCISE

Follow these steps to adjust the cell spacing:

1. Make sure `specials.html` is open in your text editor.
2. Locate the following tag:

   ```
   <TABLE BORDER="1" CELLPADDING="5">
   ```

3. After `CELLPADDING="5"` but before the right angle bracket that ends the tag, add a space and then type the following:

   ```
   CELLSPACING="3"
   ```

4. Save the `specials.html` document.
5. Switch to your browser and refresh the screen.

Figure 7.16 shows the newly modified table.

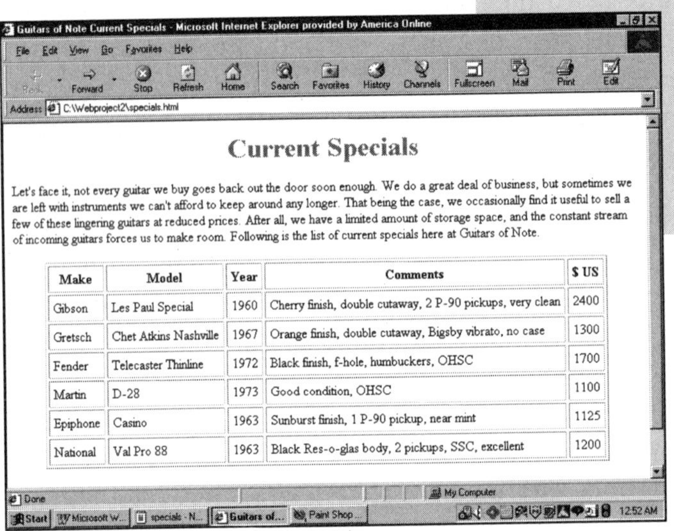

Figure 7.16 Adding the CELLSPACING attribute has yielded more space between cells.

ANALYSIS

The only change to the table in this exercise took place in Step 3, where you added the `CELLSPACING` attribute with a value of `3`. This attribute is different from the `CELLPADDING` attribute in that `CELLSPACING` adds space between the cells themselves, without adding space between the cell contents and the cell borders. In other words, `CELLSPACING` adds width to the border around each cell. If you compare Figure 7.15 with Figure 7.16, you'll see that the latter has more space between cells, but the same amount of padding within each cell. A larger value of `CELLSPACING` gives more noticeable results.

Giving a Table Some Flair

Although perfectly readable and aesthetically pleasant enough, the table in Figure 7.16 is drab. One way to enliven the table is to add some color to it.

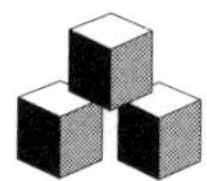

EXERCISE

Add color to the table by following these steps:

1. Open `specials.html` in your text editor.
2. Locate the HTML for the row of column headings.
3. Change the `<TR>` tag for that row to the following:

```
<TR BGCOLOR="yellow">
```

4. Change each of the `<TR>` tags for the body of the table to the following:

```
<TR BGCOLOR="#ccffff">
```

5. Save `specials.html`.
6. Switch to your browser and refresh the screen.

Figure 7.17 shows the new version of the table.

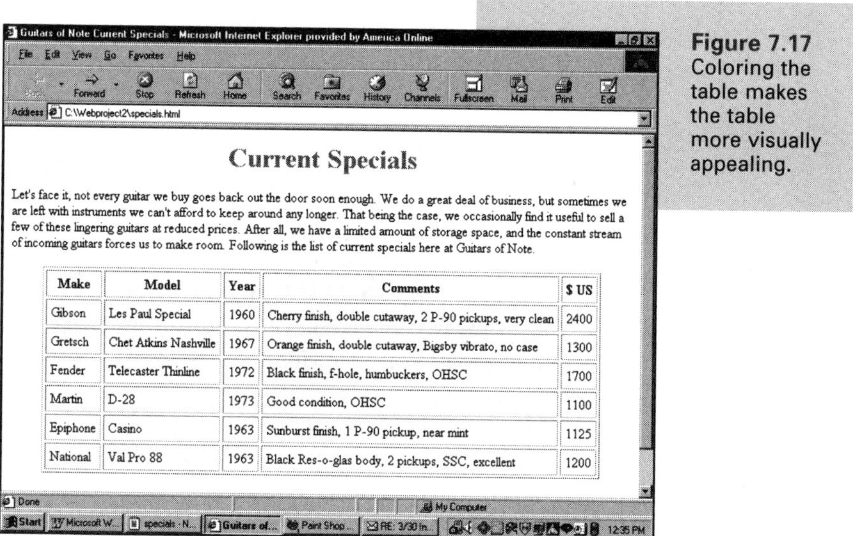

Current Specials

Let's face it, not every guitar we buy goes back out the door soon enough. We do a great deal of business, but sometimes we are left with instruments we can't afford to keep around any longer. That being the case, we occasionally find it useful to sell a few of these lingering guitars at reduced prices. After all, we have a limited amount of storage space, and the constant stream of incoming guitars forces us to make room. Following is the list of current specials here at Guitars of Note.

Make	Model	Year	Comments	$ US
Gibson	Les Paul Special	1960	Cherry finish, double cutaway, 2 P-90 pickups, very clean	2400
Gretsch	Chet Atkins Nashville	1967	Orange finish, double cutaway, Bigsby vibrato, no case	1300
Fender	Telecaster Thinline	1972	Black finish, f-hole, humbuckers, OHSC	1700
Martin	D-28	1973	Good condition, OHSC	1100
Epiphone	Casino	1963	Sunburst finish, 1 P-90 pickup, near mint	1125
National	Val Pro 88	1963	Black Res-o-glas body, 2 pickups, SSC, excellent	1200

Figure 7.17 Coloring the table makes the table more visually appealing.

As you can see, adding color to table cell backgrounds is analogous to coloring the background of a Web site. All you have to do is insert the `BGCOLOR` attribute and the desired value in the `<TR>` tag for any row you want to color. That's what you did in Steps 3 and 4. The row of column headings now has a yellow background, and the rows in the table body have a light blue-green background.

You can color individual cells rather than an entire row. All you have to do is add the `BGCOLOR` attribute to the cell you want to color. If you want to make a cell background red, for example, the tag for that cell takes the following form:

```
<TD BGCOLOR="red">Gibson</TD>
```

If you want to color the border around the table and between the cells, you can do that as well. To make the borders in a table blue, for example, add the `BGCOLOR` attribute to the `<TABLE>` tag as follows:

```
<TABLE BGCOLOR="blue">
```

You may be wondering about possible conflicts among these various attributes. The order of precedence is as follows: cell, row, table. That is, coloring a cell background takes precedence over coloring a row or coloring the entire table. Similarly, coloring a row takes precedence over coloring the entire table—but not over coloring an individual cell.

Using Frames

***Tiled** refers to windows arranged so that they all appear onscreen simultaneously (with none of them hidden behind another).*

Creating frames is a way to divide a Web browser's window into *tiled* areas. Each frame in the browser's window contains a Web page. Frames are quite common on the Internet. In fact, some of the best sites on the Web today use frames. On the other hand, using frames doesn't guarantee your Web site's quality, and some truly bad sites use frames also. Figure 7.18 shows the three frames you create in Project 2.

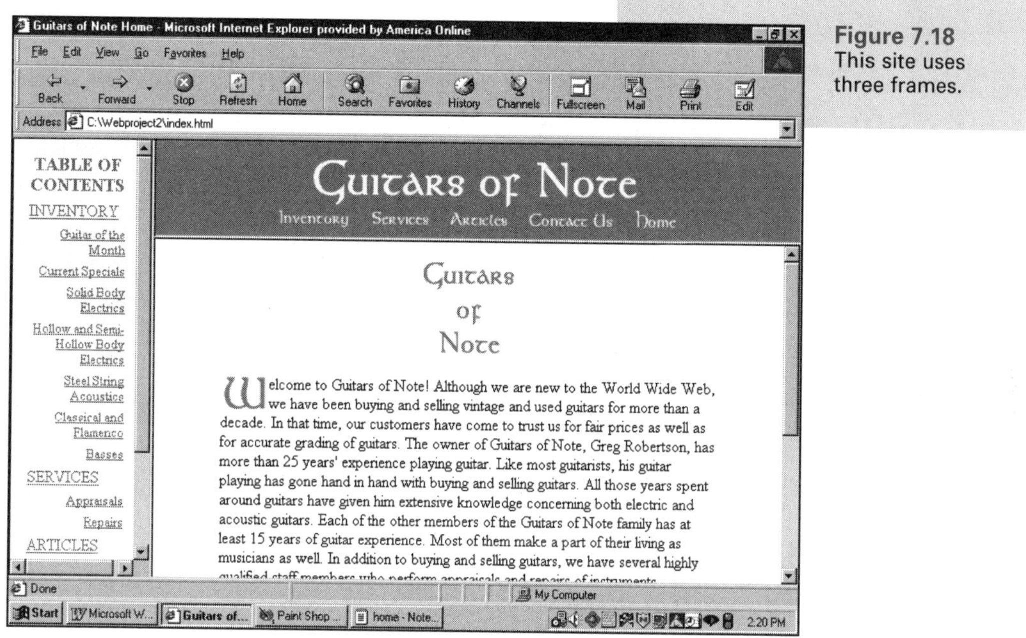

Figure 7.18 This site uses three frames.

Unfortunately, using frames has inherent drawbacks. One such drawback is the difficulty of creating frames by hand. This difficulty isn't due to the tags you need to learn, however, because you need to know only a few tags. The difficulty arises when managing a large number of Web pages through frames. Coding by hand can become confusing, if not overwhelming. Nevertheless, it's possible. In keeping with the philosophy of this book, however—that it's a good idea to know the technology behind your Web site—you learn how to create frames by hand here, even if you end up using Web-building tools to create them in the future.

Creating Frames

***A frame** is a window inside the browser window.*

The first thing to do when creating a frame-based Web site is to lay out how you want the browser window divided into frames. Refer to Figure 7.2 to see how the browser window is laid out for this project. You create frames by using the `<FRAMESET>` container tag.

No <BODY> and </BODY> tags are used in code that defines frames. The <FRAMESET> and </FRAMESET> tags form a special kind of body of code and *will not work* if surrounded by <BODY> and </BODY> tags.

EXERCISE

Begin working with frames by following these steps:

1. In your text editor, open a new document in the `Webproject2` folder.
2. Type the following HTML to begin adding the frames for the Web site:

```
<!DOCTYPE HTML PUBLIC"-//W3/DTD HTML 4.0 Frameset//EN"
"http://www.w3.org/TR/REC-html40/frameset.dtd">
<HTML>
<HEAD>
   <TITLE>Guitars of Note Home</TITLE>
   <META NAME="keywords" CONTENT="guitar, vintage guitar, guitar
   collecting, solid body, semi-hollow body, hollow body, classical,
   flamenco, steel string, bass, Fender, Gibson, Gretsch, Rickenbacker,
   Martin, National, Epiphone, Guild, Ibanez, Hagstrom, Ovation, Jose
   Oribe, Pimentel, Raimundo, Ramirez, Armstrong, Telecaster, Mustang,
   Les Paul, Jaguar, Country Gentleman, S100 Polara, Val Pro, Artist,
   White Falcon, Anniversary, Hummingbird, Chet Atkins, Nashville,
   Songbird, Precision, Musicmaster, Plexiglas, Thinline, Casino, E360TD
   Riviera, J-160E, J-200, ES-335, ES-150, ES-175, D-28, D-35, 1168-5P,
   EB2, 4001, VI">
   <META NAME="description" CONTENT="Guitars for sale, specializing in
   vintage collectibles.">
</HEAD>
```

3. Save this new document as `index.html`.
4. Type the following HTML to continue the process:

```
<FRAMESET COLS="18%,82%">
   <FRAME>
</FRAMESET>
</HTML>
```

5. Save the `index.html` document.
6. Switch to your browser and open `index.html`.

Figure 7.19 shows the result.

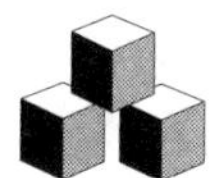

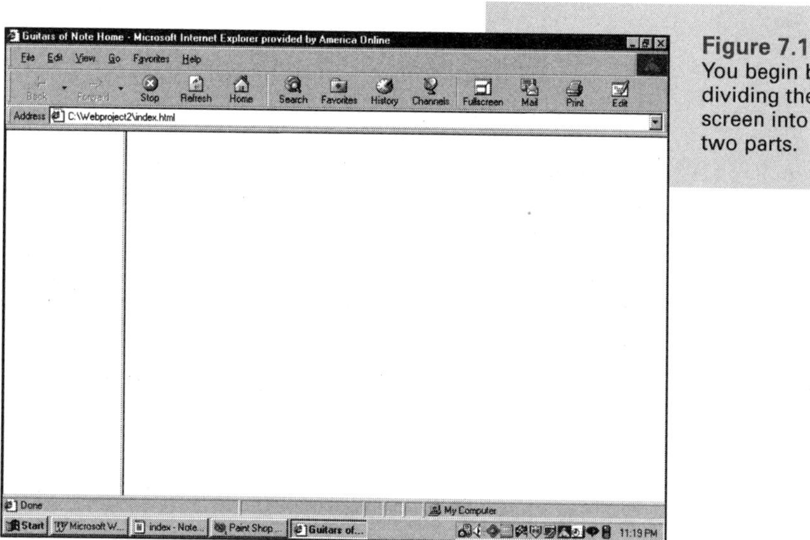

Figure 7.19 You begin by dividing the screen into two parts.

ANALYSIS

In Step 1 of this exercise, you opened a new document, making sure that you created it in the folder for the Project 2 Web site. In Step 2, you added the usual "hidden" information vital to the proper functioning of the Web site.

In Step 4, you began creating the frames for the Web site. You started with a <FRAMESET> tag containing the COLS attribute to establish columns on the page. The COLS attribute takes a list of values for the size of each column you want, surrounded by double quotation marks ("). Here the COLS attribute has two values, 18% and 82%. Refer again to Figure 7.19, where you see one narrow column on the far-left side of the browser window; this column takes up 18 percent of the full screen width. The second column takes up 82 percent of the screen width. So far, so good.

The <FRAME> tag is necessary for the <FRAMESET> tag to accomplish anything. If this frameset had just the two vertical columns shown in Figure 7.19, you would have typed two <FRAME> tags instead of one. In this case, however, only one <FRAME> tag is necessary, because the frame on the right is to be divided further. You also use the <FRAME> tag for those other two parts.

You ended the creation of the vertically divided frameset by inserting the required `</FRAMESET>` tag. Then you used the `</HTML>` tag to end the HTML document.

The frames for the Web site are not finished yet, so continue to build them by working through the next exercise.

EXERCISE

Complete the frameset for the Project 2 Web site by following these steps:

1. In your text editor, open `index.html`.
2. Place the insertion point after the `<FRAME>` tag, press Enter, and type the following HTML:

```
<FRAMESET ROWS="22%,78%">
  <FRAME>
  <FRAME>
</FRAMESET>
```

3. Save the `index.html` document.
4. Switch to your browser and refresh the screen.

Figure 7.20 shows the new arrangement of frames.

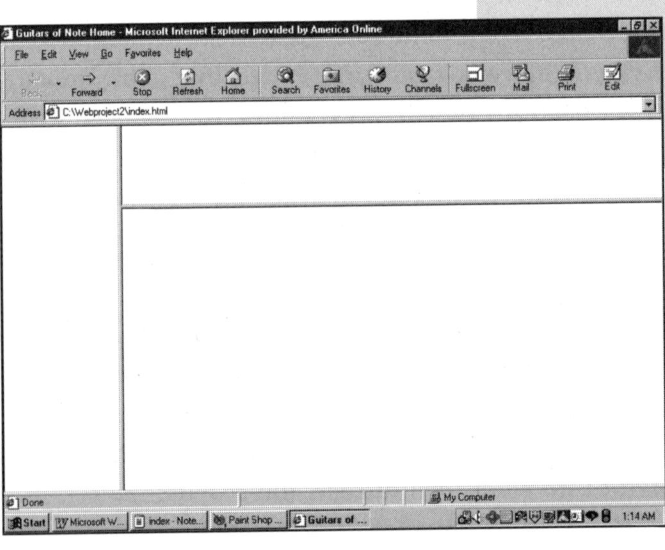

Figure 7.20 At this point, all the frames are present.

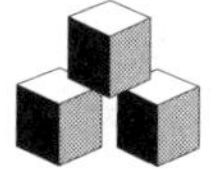

ANALYSIS

In the exercise preceding this one, you placed the first <FRAME> tag after the first <FRAMESET> tag, designating where the first frame is located. You also typed a </FRAMESET> tag in the first series of steps, which completed one entire frameset. In the second step of *this* exercise, you placed a second <FRAMESET> tag after the first <FRAME> tag, so it's nested within the first <FRAMESET> tag pair.

The first <FRAMESET> tag pair divides the screen into two vertical frames, using the COLS attribute. The second <FRAMESET> tag, however, has a ROWS attribute. The ROWS attribute takes a list of values that specify the size of each row you want. You can specify these values in pixels, percentages of browser window area, or the relative amount of available space. In this case, the ROWS attribute has values of 22% and 78%. By nesting the second <FRAMESET> tag within the first <FRAMESET> tag and placing it after the first <FRAME> tag, you divided the second column into two rows.

By using the COLS and ROWS attributes together, therefore, you divided the browser window into both horizontal and vertical frames.

You're not quite finished with the frames yet, but you're getting there. Continue with the next exercise.

EXERCISE

Follow these steps to modify the frames a bit more:

1. Open index.html document in your text editor.
2. Change the <FRAMESET COLS="18%,82%"> tag to the following:

```
<FRAMESET COLS="18%,82%" FRAMESPACING="0">
```

3. Change the <FRAMESET ROWS="22%,78%"> tag to the following:

```
<FRAMESET ROWS="22%,78%" FRAMESPACING="0">
```

4. Save the index.html document.
5. Switch to your browser and refresh the screen.

Figure 7.21 shows the new look of the Web site.

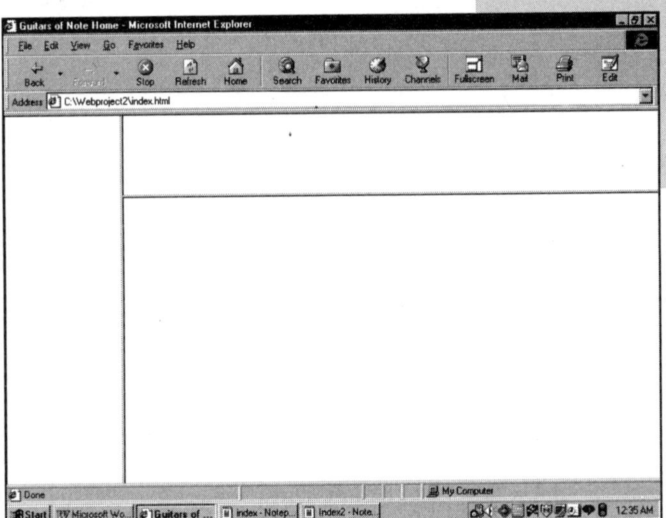

Figure 7.21 At this point, all the frames are in their final form.

ANALYSIS

You added the same attribute to both `<FRAMESET>` tags in Steps 2 and 3. The `FRAMESPACING` attribute determines the amount of space between frames. The value in this instance is `0`, which eliminates extra space between borders. If you change the `FRAMESPACING` value to something larger, the result is basically a gray area between borders, the width of which is determined by the value you've assigned. If you compare Figure 7.20 with Figure 7.21, you should be able to see a difference in the width of the space between frame borders. The final version, shown in Figure 7.21—which uses the `FRAMESPACING="0"` attribute—has narrower borders.

After the second `<FRAMESET>` tag come two `<FRAME>` tags, which you used because you are dividing this second `<FRAMESET>` into two horizontal frames.

Tip

FRAMEBORDER is another attribute you can use with the **<FRAMESET>** tag. The **FRAMEBORDER** attribute isn't used in **index.html** because your needs are served by the default value of **1**, which creates a one-pixel wide border. If you ever don't want a border around your frames, make sure your **<FRAMESET>** tag includes the **FRAMEBORDER** attribute with a value of **0**.

Note

When creating frames, be careful about where you insert the **<FRAMESET>** and **<FRAME>** tags. In Project 2, for example, if you used the first **<FRAMESET>** tag to divide the window into two columns and then ***immediately*** inserted the second **<FRAMESET>** tag to divide the column into two rows, the result would have been that the first (narrow) column got divided into rows, not the second (wide) column. By inserting the **<FRAME>** tag ***between*** the two **<FRAMESET>** tags, you divided the second (wide) column into rows, not the first column.

For now, one other piece of business involving frames is necessary. In order to make use of your new frames, you need a way to distinguish them from each other. You do so by giving them names.

To name your frames, follow these steps:

1. Open `index.html` in your text editor.
2. Change the first `<FRAME>` tag so that it reads as follows:

   ```
   <FRAME NAME="left">
   ```

3. Move the insertion point down a couple of lines to the next `<FRAME>` tag and change it to the following:

   ```
   <FRAME NAME="top">
   ```

4. Move the insertion point down to the third `<FRAME>` tag and change it to the following:

```
<FRAME NAME="content">
```

5. Save the `index.html` document.

ANALYSIS

The names you assigned the three frames in this exercise are basically descriptive. In Step 2, for example, you named the first frame `left` because that's where it is located when you look at this site in a browser. Likewise, the second frame is named `top`. The third frame's name, `content`, comes from the fact that this frame is where the content of the Web site will appear when visitors are viewing your site. The reason you need to name frames at all is that you must target particular frames when you are loading content into those frames from hyperlinks. You use the frame names to designate where the content should be loaded.

Creating the Contents of the Frames

Now that you have the frames, you need to know how to fill them with information. You create frame content by creating HTML pages. In other words, you create HTML documents and then place directions in the HTML to tell the documents where to appear in the frames. Actually, you already have created one of the pages that will go in the Web site, `specials.html`.

Creating the `links.html` Page

Before continuing the discussion of frames, creating another page of the Web site is in order. This page becomes a part of the Web site's permanent frame content. Figure 7.22 shows the final version of the site. The page you create in this section is in the left frame.

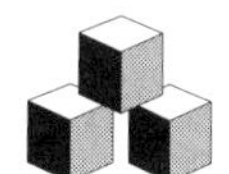

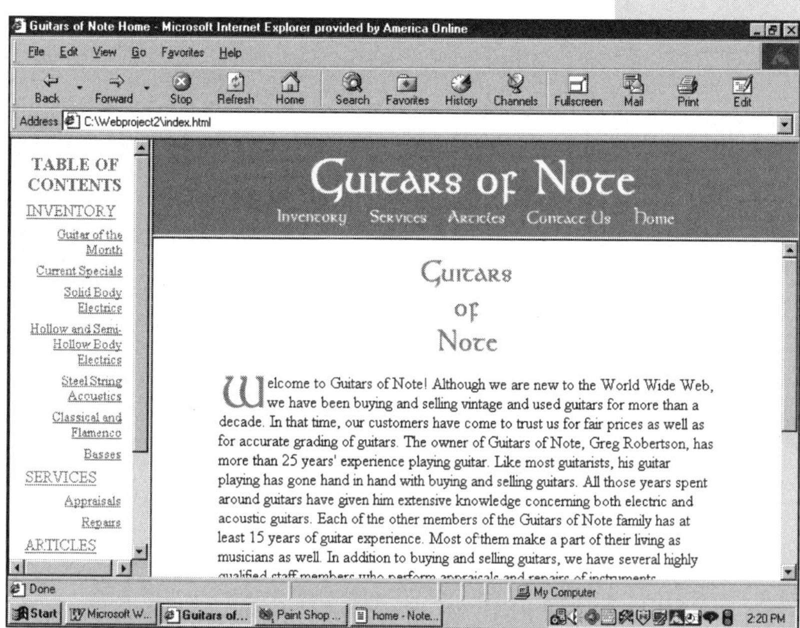

Figure 7.22 You are about to create the contents of the left frame.

Create a new page for the Guitars of Note Web site by following these steps:

1. In your text editor, open a new page.
2. As usual, start the page by adding the following HTML:

```
<!DOCTYPE HTML PUBLIC"-//W3/DTD HTML 4.0 Frameset//EN"
"http://www.w3.org/TR/REC-html40/frameset.dtd">
<HTML>
<HEAD>
   <TITLE>Guitars of Note Home</TITLE>
   <META NAME="keywords" CONTENT="guitar, vintage guitar, guitar
   collecting, solid body, semi-hollow body, hollow body, classical,
   flamenco, steel string, bass, Fender, Gibson, Gretsch, Rickenbacker,
   Martin, National, Epiphone, Guild, Ibanez, Hagstrom, Ovation, Jose
   Oribe, Pimentel, Raimundo, Ramirez, Armstrong, Telecaster, Mustang,
   Les Paul, Jaguar, Country Gentleman, S100 Polara, Val Pro, Artist,
   White Falcon, Anniversary, Hummingbird, Chet Atkins, Nashville,
   Songbird, Precision, Musicmaster, Plexiglas, Thinline, Casino, E360TD
   Riviera, J-160E, J-200, ES-335, ES-150, ES-175, D-28, D-35, 1168-5P,
   EB2, 4001, VI">
```

```
    <META NAME="description" CONTENT="Guitars for sale, specializing in
    vintage collectibles.">
  </HEAD>
```

3. Save the document as `links.html`.
4. Now create the visible contents of the page by typing the following HTML:

```
<BODY BGCOLOR="#ccffff">
<DIV ALIGN="center">
<CENTER>
<TABLE WIDTH="110" BORDER="0" CELLPADDING="0" CELLSPACING="0">
   <TR>
      <TH ALIGN="center" BGCOLOR="white"><FONT SIZE="+1"
      COLOR="red">TABLE OF CONTENTS</FONT></TH>
   </TR>
</TABLE>
```

5. Type the following HTML to continue creating the page:

```
<TABLE WIDTH="110" BORDER="0" CELLPADDING="0" CELLSPACING="6">
   <TR>
      <TD ALIGN="left"><A HREF="inventory.html"
      TARGET="content">INVENTORY</A></TD>
   </TR>
   <TR>
      <TD ALIGN="right"><A HREF="month.html" TARGET="content"><FONT
      SIZE="-1">Guitar of the Month</FONT></A></TD>
   </TR>
   <TR>
      <TD ALIGN="right"><A HREF="specials.html" TARGET="content"><FONT
      SIZE="-1">Current Specials</FONT></A></TD>
   </TR>
   <TR>
      <TD ALIGN="right"><A HREF="inventory.html#Solid" TARGET=
      "content"><FONT SIZE="-1">Solid Body Electrics</FONT></A></TD>
   </TR>
   <TR>
      <TD ALIGN="right"><A HREF="inventory.html#Hollow" TARGET=
      "content"><FONT SIZE="-1">Hollow and Semi-Hollow Body
      Electrics</FONT></A></TD>
   </TR>
```

```
<TR>
   <TD ALIGN="right"><A HREF="inventory.html#Steel" TARGET=
   "content"><FONT SIZE="-1">Steel String Acoustics</FONT></A></TD>
</TR>
<TR>
   <TD ALIGN="right"><A HREF="inventory.html#Classical" TARGET=
   "content"><FONT SIZE="-1">Classical and Flamenco</FONT></A></TD>
</TR>
<TR>
   <TD ALIGN="right"><A HREF="inventory.html#Basses" TARGET=
   "content"><FONT SIZE="-1">Basses</FONT></A></TD>
</TR>
<TR>
   <TD ALIGN="left"><A HREF="services.html" TARGET="content">
   SERVICES</A></TD>
</TR>
<TR>
   <TD ALIGN="right"><A HREF="services.html#Appraisals" TARGET=
   "content"><FONT SIZE="-1">Appraisals</FONT></A></TD>
</TR>
<TR>
   <TD ALIGN="right"><A HREF="services.html#Repairs" TARGET=
   "content"><FONT SIZE="-1">Repairs</FONT></A></TD>
</TR>
<TR>
   <TD ALIGN="left"><A HREF="articles.html" TARGET=
   "content">ARTICLES</A></TD>
</TR>
<TR>
   <TD ALIGN="right"><A HREF="articles.html#Buying" TARGET=
   "content"><FONT SIZE="-1">Tips for Buyers</FONT></A></TD>
</TR>
<TR>
   <TD ALIGN="right"><A HREF="articles.html#Grading" TARGET=
   "content"><FONT SIZE="-1">Grading Guitars</FONT></A></TD>
</TR>
<TR>
   <TD ALIGN="left"><A HREF="contact.html">CONTACT US</A></TD>
</TR>
<TR>
```

```
        <TD ALIGN="left"><A HREF="home.html" TARGET=
        "content">HOME</A></TD>
      </TR>
    </TABLE>
    </CENTER>
    </DIV>
    </BODY>
    </HTML>
```

6. Save the `links.html` document.
7. Switch to your browser and open `links.html`.

Figure 7.23 shows what the `links.html` document looks like.

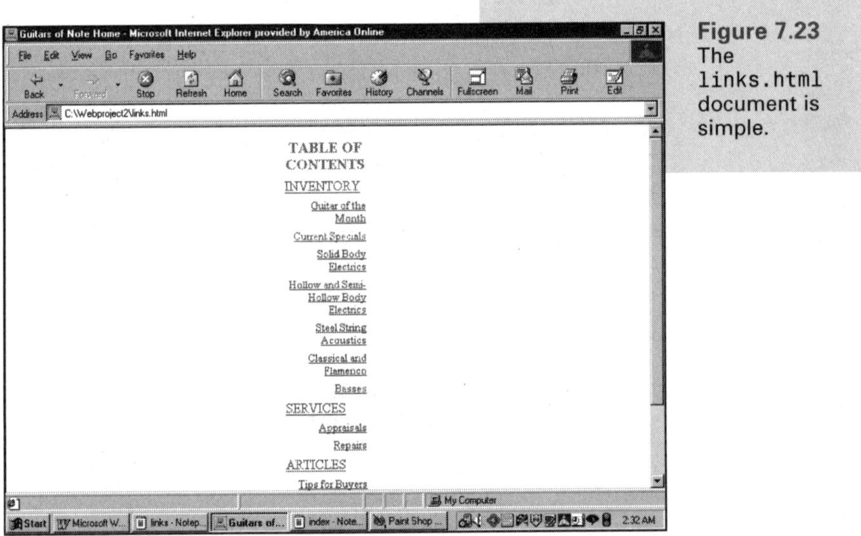

Figure 7.23 The `links.html` document is simple.

After creating the standard Web-page HTML (in Step 2), you established the color of the page's background, as well as a one-column table, in Step 4. This table actually is the heading for the `links.html` page. You might wonder why you shouldn't use a heading (`<H1>`, for example) or a table caption. The problem is that the words `TABLE OF CONTENTS` are not centered when you use one of these methods. The space between words makes them off-center. By centering the table and putting the

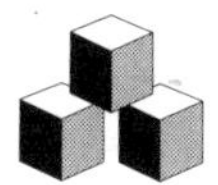

words TABLE OF CONTENTS in a table cell, however, the words are centered within the column automatically (and therefore on the page, which has only one column).

In the same step, you also increased the font size from the standard size, gave the cell a white background, and colored the words red. These settings are intended to make the heading stand out.

Also in Step 4, you entered the <CENTER> and </DIV ALIGN="center"> tags to ensure the centering of this and the following table. Note also the use of the WIDTH attribute in the <TABLE> tag. The value of 110 pixels makes sure that the table fits within the width of the left frame. Finally, you used a value of 0 for BORDER, CELLPADDING, and CELLSPACING.

In Step 5, you created another one-column table. This table contains all the links that appear in the left frame. Five of the cells contain left-aligned primary links: INVENTORY, SERVICES, ARTICLES, CONTACT US, and HOME. The BORDER and CELLPADDING attributes for these primary links have values of 0. The CELLSPACING attribute of each, however, has a value of 6. This value leaves space between rows of the table, making the table easier to read.

The reason for the links.html document's existence is that it contains links to other places within the Web site. The word INVENTORY is a link to the inventory.html page, which explains the presence of the anchor tag (<A HREF>). The same is true of all the other cells' contents.

After the INVENTORY link is a series of seven cells, each of which contains a link. The contents of each cell are aligned to the right this time, and the cell is made into a link by means of the <A HREF> tag. You have not created all these documents yet, but will do so later in the project. You made the font smaller for these by using the <FONT SIZE="-1"> tag, which reduces the font size by 1 in relation to the standard size. This reduced size helps distinguish the more-specific, secondary links from the larger, primary links. In all, the page has the five primary links named earlier and 11 secondary links to more specific locations.

Linking Pages

Now that you have created the frames and have pages to put in two of them, you can move on to linking the pages. Creating these links gives the frames content.

EXERCISE

Begin filling the frames of the Web site by following these steps:

1. In your text editor, open the `index.html` file.
2. Change the `<FRAME NAME="left">` tag to the following:

```
<FRAME NAME="left" SRC="links.html" SCROLLING="auto">
```

3. Save the `index.html` document.
4. Switch to your browser and open `index.html`.

Figure 7.24 shows this page as it now appears in IE.

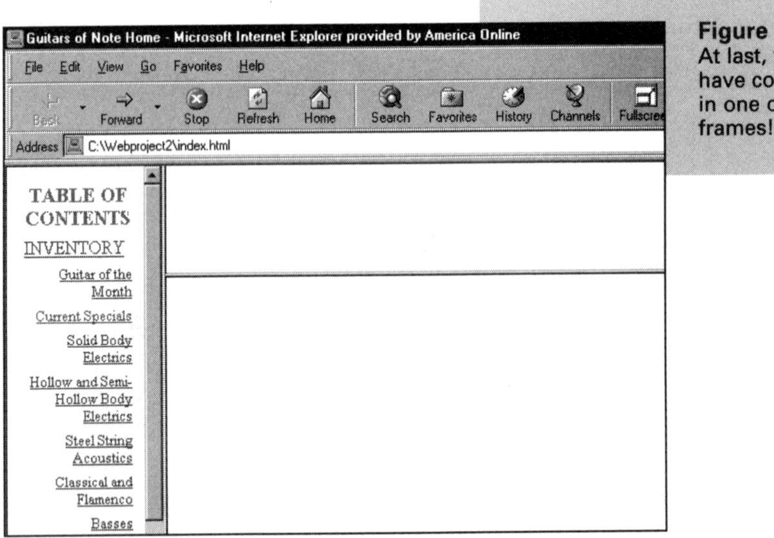

Figure 7.24
At last, you have content in one of the frames!

ANALYSIS

In this short exercise, you added two very important attributes. The first, `SRC="links.html"`, works like the `SRC` attribute you use whenever you place graphics in a Web page: `SRC` tells the browser where to find the file to place in the designated spot. In the case of frames, however, the source is an HTML file. For the left frame, you specified that the source was the `links.html` file just created.

Now refer to the preceding exercise. Note that the `TARGET` attribute is present in each of the links, with a value of `"content"`. Each link's anchor tag and its value is important, because it directs the link to display the given page in the content frame of the browser window. Without this target, the contents of the link page would appear in a new browser window in the middle of the screen, defeating the purpose of the frames.

The second attribute that you added in Step 2, `SCROLLING="auto"`, is a very important attribute for use in frames. You use this attribute to control what happens when a frame is loaded; it has three possible values: `yes`, `no`, and `auto`. If you know for sure that the frame is too small to fit all the content from the loaded page, you set the value to `yes`. This value makes a scroll bar (or two) appear within the frame, ensuring that viewers can see all the information contained in the page. The `no` value, of course, prevents any scroll bars from appearing within the frame. You might want to use this value when you know everything fits within the frame and there is no need for scrolling. The default value for `SCROLLING` is `auto` and means that the browser determines the need for one or more scroll bars based on the actual content of the frame. Using `auto` eliminates the need to figure out or control the size of all your Web pages that will appear in this frame.

Now that `links.html` is loaded into the left frame, enough of the frameset is finished to let you test at least a portion of your Web site.

EXERCISE

To make sure that your efforts are paying off, follow these steps:

1. Open `index.html` in your browser.
2. When the page opens, the `links.html` page should appear in the left frame. If it does, click on the `Current Specials` link.

Figure 7.25 shows what you should see.

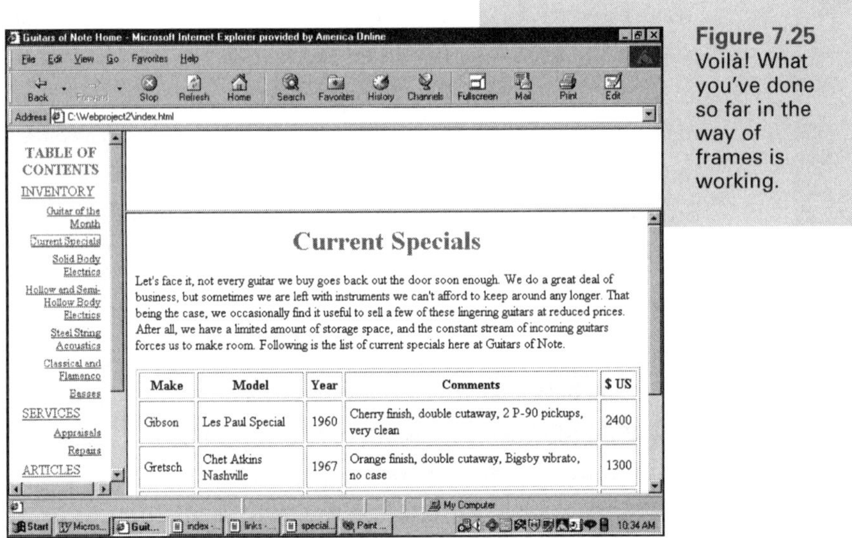

Figure 7.25 Voilà! What you've done so far in the way of frames is working.

ANALYSIS

It works! If you don't see the main frame filled with the Current Specials information, then go back and check your HTML on the `links.html` document. You may have mistyped or omitted something.

Note that the browser has inserted a scroll bar because the `specials.html` page is too large to fit inside the content frame. If you compare the Current Specials table in Figure 7.25 with the one shown in Figure 7.17, you'll notice that, whereas everything within the table cells in Figure 7.17 fits on a single line, those same cells are taller in Figure 7.25, fitting two lines in each cell. The browser displayed the table this way automatically to compensate for the narrower width of the content frame.

Now, it's time to finish preparing `index.html` for action.

EXERCISE

Add more content instructions for the frames by following these steps:

1. Open `index.html` in your text editor.
2. Locate the second `<FRAME>` tag, which is the first of the two within the second `<FRAMESET>` tag, and change it to the following:

```
<FRAME NAME="top" SRC="gnote2.html" SCROLLING="no">
```

3. Move the insertion point to the last `<FRAME>` tag and change it to the following:

```
<FRAME NAME="content" SRC="home.html" SCROLLING="auto">
```

4. Save the `index.html` document.
5. Switch to your browser and open `index.html`.

ANALYSIS

It didn't work, did it? First, you received a warning saying that the browser couldn't find the specified file. In fact, the browser couldn't find *two* files—`gnote2.html` and `home.html`—but it canceled navigation after not finding the first one. You added those `SRC` attributes in Steps 2 and 3, but neither document exists yet. After you create the `gnote2.html` and `home.html` documents, everything should work without any problem. Even after they *do* exist, however, you would get the same warning if one or both of them was not located in the correct folder on your computer. In essence, this warning means that a file isn't where the HTML said it would be.

After you clicked the OK button to acknowledge the warning, you should have seen a screen resembling the one shown in Figure 7.26.

Besides indicating the source for the top and content frames, you also designated the associated `SCROLLING` attributes. For the `gnote2.html` page, `SCROLLING` is set to `no`. As you'll discover later in the project, `gnote2.html` is a graphic, so scrolling is unnecessary.

The content (main) frame's source is `home.html`, another file you haven't created yet. The `home.html` page will appear by default whenever someone accesses the Web site. For that page you set `SCROLLING` to `auto`.

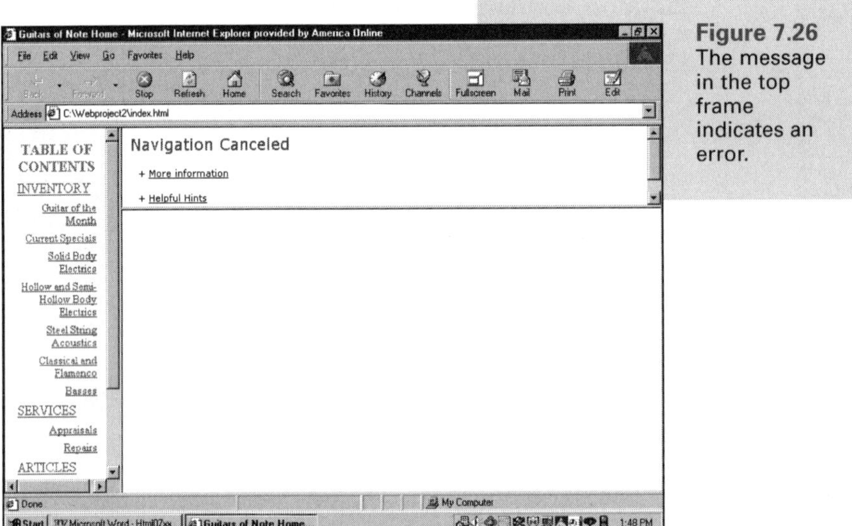

Figure 7.26 The message in the top frame indicates an error.

Summary

Before beginning this second project, it was necessary to determine the type of site it would be: a business-oriented site. That determination also involved setting goals for the site. In addition, laying out the design of the site came before writing any of the HTML.

You've taken two huge leaps in your understanding and application of HTML 4.0 in this chapter. First, you've learned how to present information in tables. Tables are an essential element in sites all over the World Wide Web. You've encountered many new tags and attributes while creating the tables in this project.

Second, you've learned how to create a site that uses frames, among the more difficult tasks in HTML. Frames are very common on the Web, but aren't necessarily easy to do well. This chapter has introduced the tags used to create frames. Although you can use software to help you create a frame-based site, there's nothing like the sense of accomplishment you get from doing it by hand.

Beginning to Build the Intermediate Web Site

In Chapter 7, you created the foundation of a Web site that uses frames, as well as a couple of components that fit into those frames. In this chapter, you create additional pages of the Web site. In the course of building the pages, you learn increasingly sophisticated ways to work with tables and frames, and you get some experience working with image maps to offer visitors more convenient and attractive ways to navigate through the content on your Web site.

Creating More Effective Tables

Tables can do more than hold plain data. You can insert graphics into cells, for example, which helps greatly with placing images on the page exactly where you want them. Another thing you can do to improve your tables is to make cells span multiple columns or rows. In the following sections, you make use of these table capabilities as you build more of the Project 2 Web site.

Defining a More Complex Table

You can create more complex tables than the one on the specials.html page you created in Chapter 7. In fact, you may find it *necessary* to create more complex tables from time to time, just to present information in the clearest, most logical way.

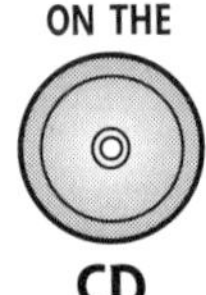

To get the most out of this book, you should type the HTML yourself throughout the projects. For your reference, though, a complete version of the file you create in the following exercise is available on the CD that accompanies this book, as inventory1.html.

The simple table created for the specials.html document is inadequate for the type of table contents you need elsewhere on the Web site. Follow these steps to build the page for your full inventory:

1. In your text editor, open a new document.
2. Insert the following HTML at the top of the document:

```
<!DOCTYPE HTML PUBLIC"-//W3/DTD HTML 4.0 Frameset//EN"
"http://www.w3.org/TR/REC-html40/frameset.dtd">
<HTML>
   <HEAD>
   <TITLE>Guitars of Note Current Inventory</TITLE>
   <META NAME="keywords" CONTENT="guitar, vintage guitar, guitar
   collecting, solid body, semi-hollow body, hollow body, classical,
   flamenco, steel string, bass, Fender, Gibson, Gretsch, Rickenbacker,
   Martin, National, Epiphone, Guild, Ibanez, Hagstrom, Ovation, Jose
   Oribe, Pimentel, Raimundo, Ramirez, Armstrong, Telecaster, Mustang,
   Les Paul, Jaguar, Country Gentleman, S100 Polara, Val Pro, Artist,
   White Falcon, Anniversary, Hummingbird, Chet Atkins, Nashville,
   Songbird, Precision, Musicmaster, Plexiglas, Thinline, Casino, E360TD
   Riviera, J-160E, J-200, ES-335, ES-150, ES-175, D-28, D-35, 1168-5P,
   EB2, 4001, VI">
   <META NAME="description" CONTENT="Guitars for sale, specializing in
   vintage collectibles.">
   </HEAD>
```

3. Save the document as inventory1.html.

4. Now begin the body of the document by typing the following heading and introductory paragraph:

```
<BODY>
   <DIV ALIGN="center">
   <CENTER>
   <H1><FONT COLOR="red">Current Inventory</FONT></H1>
   <P><FONT SIZE="+1" COLOR="blue"><EM><STRONG>Updated daily!</STRONG>
   </EM></FONT></P>
   </CENTER></DIV>
<P>The following tables list our current inventory of guitars in
several categories: Solid Body Electrics, Hollow and Semi-Hollow Body
Electrics, Steel String Acoustics, Classical and Flamenco, and Basses.
We invite you to browse through the list of instruments to look for
something specific, or simply to see what is there. You never know what
you'll find. You may find just the deal you've been looking for -- or
even just the deal you <EM>haven't</EM> been looking for!</P>
```

5. Save the `inventory1.html` document.

ANALYSIS

In this exercise you set the stage for the `inventory.html` page. Note the consistent use of red, `<H1>` headings on this page as well as on the `specials.html` page. In addition, this page uses text at a +1 font size directly under the main heading, to emphasize that the page is updated every day. The blue color makes it stand out from the paragraph of text that is beneath it. The `<CENTER>` and `<DIV ALIGN="center">` tags ensure the centering of the heading and the line of text beneath it.

EXERCISE

Now begin creating the tables for this page by following these steps:

1. In your text editor, open the `inventory1.html` document.
2. Add the first table to the page by typing the following HTML:

```
<DIV ALIGN="center">
<CENTER>
<H2><FONT COLOR="#009999">SOLID BODY ELECTRICS</FONT></H2>
<TABLE BORDER="1" CELLPADDING="5" CELLSPACING="3" WIDTH="85%">
   <TR BGCOLOR="yellow">
   <TH>Make</TH>
   <TH>Model</TH>
   <TH>Year</TH>
```

```
<TH>Comments</TH>
   <TH WIDTH="8%">$ US</TH>
</TR>
<TR>
   <TH COLSPAN="5" BGCOLOR="#009999"><FONT COLOR="white"
   SIZE="4"><STRONG>GIBSON</STRONG></FONT></TH>
</TR>
<TR BGCOLOR="#ccffff">
   <TH ROWSPAN="3">Gibson</TH>
   <TD>Les Paul Studio</TD>
   <TD>1982</TD>
   <TD>Black finish, gold-plated hardware, excellent, OHSC</TD>
   <TD ALIGN="right">825</TD>
</TR>
<TR BGCOLOR="#ccffff">
   <TD>Les Paul Standard</TD>
   <TD>1990</TD>
   <TD>Black finish, gold-plated hardware, humbuckers,
   near mint, OHSC</TD>
   <TD ALIGN="right">1400</TD>
</TR>
<TR BGCOLOR="#ccffff">
   <TD>Les Paul Custom</TD>
   <TD>1958</TD>
   <TD>Sunburst finish, Bigsby vibrato, patent-applied-for
   pickups, excellent, OHSC</TD>
   <TD ALIGN="right">9250</TD>
</TR>
<TR>
   <TH COLSPAN="5" BGCOLOR="#009999"><FONT COLOR="white"
   SIZE="4"><STRONG>FENDER</STRONG></FONT></TH>
</TR>
<TR BGCOLOR="#ccffff">
   <TH ROWSPAN="2">Fender</TH>
   <TD>Jaguar</TD>
   <TD>1967</TD>
   <TD>Sunburst finish, rosewood fingerboard, dot inlay, OHSC</TD>
```

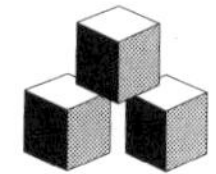


```
      <TD ALIGN="right">1300</TD>
    </TR>
    <TR BGCOLOR="#ccffff">
      <TD>Telecaster</TD>
      <TD>1955</TD>
      <TD>Blonde finish, maple neck, white pickguard, OHSC (tweed)</TD>
      <TD ALIGN="right">8250</TD>
    </TR>
    <TR>
      <TH COLSPAN="5" BGCOLOR="#009999"><FONT COLOR="white"
      SIZE="4"><STRONG>MISCELLANEOUS</STRONG></FONT></TH>
    </TR>
    <TR BGCOLOR="#ccffff">
      <TH>Guild</TH>
      <TD>S100 Polara</TD>
      <TD>1971</TD>
      <TD>Black, vibrato, excellent condition, OHSC</TD>
      <TD ALIGN="right">900</TD>
    </TR>
    <TR BGCOLOR="#ccffff">
      <TH>Ibanez</TH>
      <TD>Artist</TD>
      <TD>1982</TD>
      <TD>Sunburst, gold hardware, rosewood fingerboard,
      good condition, OHSC</TD>
    <TD ALIGN="right">500</TD>
    </TR>
</TABLE>
<BR>
</CENTER>
</DIV>
```

3. Save the `inventory1.html` document.
4. Switch to your browser and refresh the screen. Figure 8.1 shows the first table of the `inventory1.html` page displayed in Internet Explorer 4.

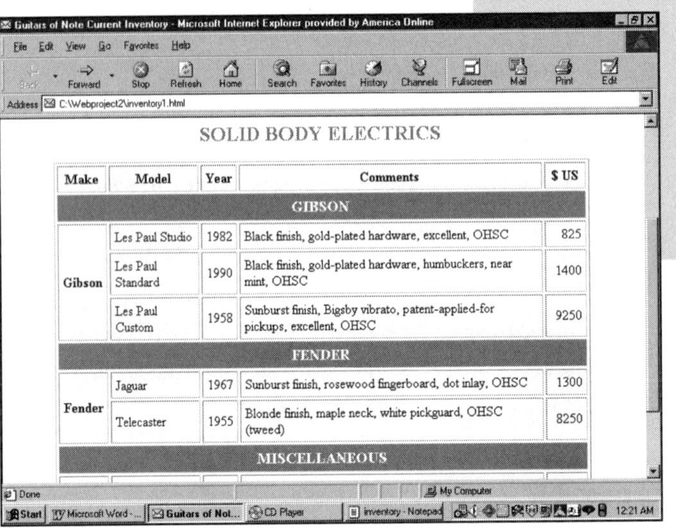

Figure 8.1 Structurally, this table is more sophisticated than the table in `specials.html`.

ANALYSIS

You did many important things in this exercise—all in Step 2! You started with the now-familiar centering tags, followed by the `<H2>` heading to use larger text (and any other formatting a given browser uses for `<H2>` headings). You also made the heading an attractive, dark green color.

The table itself begins with the next line of HTML. You used the `<TABLE>` tag and several of its attributes (`BORDER`, `CELLPADDING`, and `CELLSPACING`) to create the border of the table and the spacing between cells.

You also used the `WIDTH` attribute in this line to prevent the table from taking up the full width of the page. Actually, two value options are available. You can decide what percentage of the page width you want your table to occupy, as in `<TABLE WIDTH="85%">`. Or you can set an absolute value in terms of pixels, as in `<TABLE WIDTH="500">`. For this page, your `WIDTH` attribute sets the table's width at 85 percent of the full screen width.

Next is the first row of the table, where you added the `BGCOLOR` attribute to the `<TR>` tag. Then follow the five headings for the row's columns. Notice the use of the `WIDTH` attribute in the last column. When you create a table, the cells take on whatever size is necessary to fill the page

horizontally and to fit in the information you put in the cells. In the case of this table, for example, the widest column is the Comments column, because it contains the most text. If you want to control the width of your columns, however, you can do so by inserting the WIDTH attribute in the top row of the column (or columns) you want to control. In other words, setting the width in the top row of a column automatically makes all the subsequent cells in that column the same width.

In the case of this table, the price column ($ US) needed to be wider to allow room for five- and six-figure prices. Some vintage guitars are *really* expensive!

The next row you created had one new attribute: COLSPAN. You use the COLSPAN attribute when you want a cell to span more than one column. You want to use this particular row as a sort of subheading within the table, so you want it to span all five columns. The value of 5 for the COLSPAN attribute tells a browser that this row spans the first column and the following four columns (a total of five).

Note

If you wanted a cell to span only the third and fourth columns of a row, you would add the following attribute to the third cell's tag:

```
COLSPAN="2"
```

Because that one cell spans *two* columns, you would enter <TD> tags for only four columns overall, not five. If you left in five <TD> tags, the third cell would still span the third and fourth columns, but then a fifth cell would be added to the far-right end of the row—and would stick out beyond the right border of the table.

The other things that occurred in this row are all familiar to you. You added a background color (the same as the caption color), increased the size of the text in the cell (from 3 to 4), colored the text white, and made the cell's text (GIBSON) bold by using the <STRONG> tag pair. All these attributes and values, along with the COLSPAN attribute, created a subheading within the table.

Yet another new attribute is in the first row header cell. The `ROWSPAN` attribute works the same way as the `COLSPAN` attribute, but spans the table vertically rather than horizontally. As with the `COLSPAN` attribute, you must leave out the spanned cells to avoid extending this column down past the bottom of the other columns.

The next row of the table is a basic table row with just two changes. First, you gave the row a light-green background color that goes well with the color of the subheading above it. Second, you added the `ALIGN` attribute to the last cell, giving it a value of `right`. This column contains the price of each guitar listed. Because the cell's contents are left-aligned automatically, the prices do not line up. By inserting `ALIGN="right"` you ensured that the price is aligned on the right side of the cell. You did the same in all other price cells in the rest of the table, giving this column an orderly appearance.

The remainder of the table is in two sections, one for Fender guitars and one for Miscellaneous guitars. Each of these sections is formatted the way the Gibson section is formatted, so the details are not analyzed here.

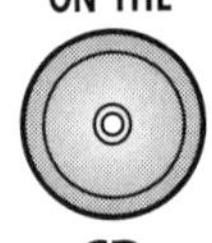

This page of the Web site, `inventory1.html`, contains several more tables, all of which are formatted in the same way as the Solid Body Electrics table was formatted above. If you want to insert the remainder of the HTML for the page, you can copy it from the CD that accompanies this book. The name of the document containing all the tables is `inventory2.html`. The final version of the document you need for this project, however, will not be named `inventory2.html`; `inventory2.html` is just an intermediate document.

Creating the Opening Page

When visitors first land at the Guitars of Note Web site, they don't want to be dumped into the middle of something and not know what's going on. Visitors need an opening page that orients them to the site. The Home page serves that function quite well.

EXERCISE

To create the Home page of the Guitars of Note Web site, follow these steps:

1. In your text editor, open a new document.
2. Begin creating the document by typing the following HTML:

```
<!DOCTYPE HTML PUBLIC"-//W3/DTD HTML 4.0 Frameset//EN"
"http://www.w3.org/TR/REC-html40/frameset.dtd">
<HTML>
  <HEAD>
  <TITLE>Guitars of Note Home</TITLE>
  <META NAME="keywords" CONTENT="guitar, vintage guitar, guitar
  collecting, solid body, semi-hollow body, hollow body, classical,
  flamenco, steel string, bass, Fender, Gibson, Gretsch, Rickenbacker,
  Martin, National, Epiphone, Guild, Ibanez, Hagstrom, Ovation, Jose
  Oribe, Pimentel, Raimundo, Ramirez, Armstrong, Telecaster, Mustang,
  Les Paul, Jaguar, Country Gentleman, S100 Polara, Val Pro, Artist,
  White Falcon, Anniversary, Hummingbird, Chet Atkins, Nashville,
  Songbird, Precision, Musicmaster, Plexiglas, Thinline, Casino, E360TD
  Riviera, J-160E, J-200, ES-335, ES-150, ES-175, D-28, D-35, 1168-5P,
  EB2, 4001, VI">
  <META NAME="description" CONTENT="Guitars for sale, specializing in
  vintage collectibles.">
  </HEAD>
  <BODY>
```

3. Save the document as `home.html`.
4. Begin the text for the opening page by typing this HTML:

```
<DIV ALIGN="center">
<CENTER>
<TABLE WIDTH="500" BORDER="0" CELLPADDING="0" CELLSPACING="0">
  <TR>
    <TD><IMG SRC="images/w9.gif" ALIGN="left" WIDTH="43" HEIGHT="35"
    ALT="drop-cap W"> elcome to Guitars of Note! Although we are new
    to the World Wide Web, we have been buying and selling vintage
    and used guitars for more than a decade. In that time, our
    customers have come to trust us for fair prices as well as for
    accurate grading of guitars. The owner of Guitars of Note, Greg
    Robertson, has more than 25 years' experience playing guitar.
```

```
        Like most guitarists, his guitar playing has gone hand in hand
        with buying and selling guitars. All those years spent around
        guitars have given him extensive knowledge concerning both
        electric and acoustic guitars. Each of the other members of the
        Guitars of Note family has at least 15 years of guitar
        experience. Most of them make a part of their living as musicians
        as well. In addition to buying and selling guitars, we have
        several highly qualified staff members who perform appraisals and
        repairs of instruments.</TD>
    </TR>
</TABLE>
<BR>
```

5. Finish the text for the page by creating another table:

```
<TABLE WIDTH="500" BORDER="0" CELLPADDING="0" CELLSPACING="0">
    <TR>
        <TD><IMG SRC="images/n9.gif" ALIGN="left" WIDTH="35" HEIGHT="35"
        ALT="drop-cap N"> ow that you know what we do here at Guitars of
        Note, we hope that you will take your time. Browse through our
        site, take a look at the guitars we have available, and read the
        articles we have posted. Whatever you do, don't leave until
        you've checked out our Guitar of the Month, as well as our
        special deals. Even if we don't have anything you want right now,
        check back often. We take in guitars every day - and we sell
        them every day, too - so our inventory changes constantly. We
        may not have what you want today, but tomorrow we may have that
        dream guitar you've been searching for since 1988!</TD>
    </TR>
</TABLE>
</CENTER>
</DIV>
</BODY>
</HTML>
```

6. Save the `home.html` document.
7. Switch to your browser and open `home.html`. Figure 8.2 shows what you should see.

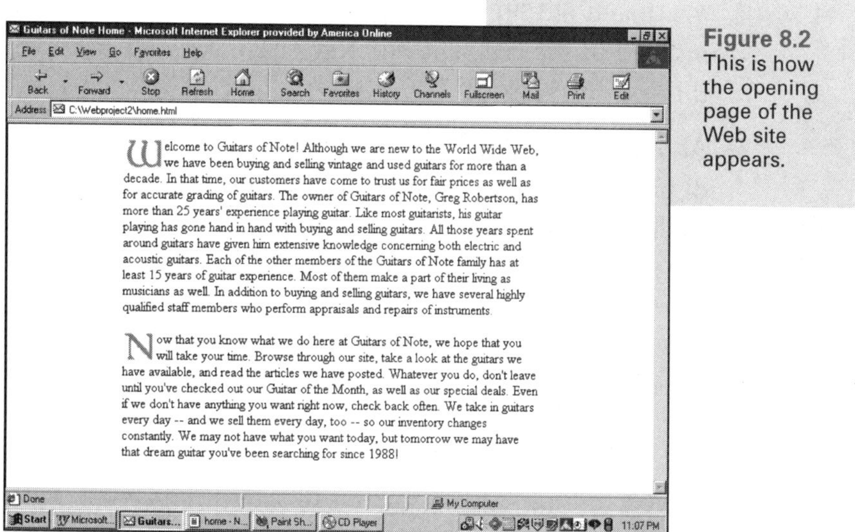

Figure 8.2 This is how the opening page of the Web site appears.

This page of the site, like all the others, begins with the particulars of the HTML version, keywords, and so on. In the `<BODY>` of the page, the first thing you do is center the element that follows. Next comes the HTML that indicates you are creating a table. That may have come as a surprise to you, because when you look at the result in your browser, it's all plain text—with a couple of exceptions. The drop-cap `W` that begins the first paragraph and the drop-cap `N` that begins the second one are actually graphics. In order to make these graphics work with the text, it is necessary to create a table and then insert each graphic into a table cell. If you look at the `<TABLE>` tag, you'll see that the width of the table is established as 500 pixels. That same tag also indicates that there should be no borders, no space between the cells, and no padding between the cell contents and the edge of the cell. These settings minimize distances between the graphic and the text.

The first `<TR>` tag creates the first—and only!—row of the table. This row consists of just one cell. That cell contains the graphic, and has attributes that designate the source of the graphic (`w9.gif`), its alignment within the cell (left), its width (43 pixels), and its height (35 pixels). The

WIDTH and HEIGHT figures are based on the size of the drop cap to be inserted in the cell. The ALT text tells users who can't see graphics that this is a drop-cap W.

Also included in the first cell is the entire text of the first paragraph for display on the page. Remember that browsers adjust the cell height to fit in everything placed in the cell. In this case, that's a graphic and a lot of text. You may recall from Project 1 that by aligning a graphic to the left (or right), you can make text flow around it. The same principle is at work here: The text wraps around the left-aligned graphic. The difference is that this wrapping takes place within a table cell.

In order to see what you're doing when working with columns and graphics in a table, try coloring the backgrounds of the cells in different colors. Use pink for a graphic's cell, for example, and lavender for the text cell. (If the graphic fills the entire cell, of course, you don't need a background color for the graphic's cell.) That way, you can see what's happening with the cells. You also can try using the BORDER="1" setting to see cell borders, but using a border can affect how much text fits on a line. You probably will need to fine-tune the code after removing the border.

The second paragraph of the home.html page is set up exactly like the first paragraph, so there's no need to detail it here. The only difference is the size of the graphic (35 pixels by 35 pixels, because the N is not as wide as the W).

Using Other Table-Formatting Options

The preceding exercises do not exhaust the table-formatting possibilities. For example, you can align cell contents to the left or right, as well as center them. By default, the contents of header cells (<TH>) are centered, whereas the contents of data cells (<TD>) are left-aligned.

Note

If you want to use percentage values, you can enter a value of 100 (the total width of the page) or less, but don't forget that you also must take into account any borders the table has. Borders take up some percentage of the page width.

If you want your entire table to be one color, you can do that, too. Just insert the `BGCOLOR` attribute in the `<TABLE>` tag, and set the color to whatever you desire. If you use the attribute in this way, you color not only the cells but also any space between cells (that is, if you are using the `CELLSPACING` attribute with any value other than `0`). If you want to place borders in your table, you can color them by adding the `BORDERCOLOR` attribute to the `<TABLE>` tag (of course, you must have a `BORDER` value larger than `0`). You can even use combinations of these coloring techniques. For example, you can use the tag `<TABLE BGCOLOR="blue" BORDERCOLOR="red" BORDER="1" CELLSPACING="3">` to come up with an interesting effect. In this case, the spaces between borders would be blue, and they would be outlined by a one-pixel-wide red border. Add to that any other colors you designate for individual cells, and you could have quite a colorful table!

Note

Various browsers may not handle background colors in the `<TABLE>` tag in the same way. You may be better off coloring cells individually if you want to be sure of the table's appearance.

Making Further Use of Frames

So far, you've created a few pages or parts of pages for use with the frames in this second project. To continue building this Web site, work through the following sections to create more pages.

Adding More HTML for Links

You're going to begin by adding more link-related HTML to a page that you already have created. That way, you'll have it ready to go as you continue creating this site.

Earlier exercises did not produce all the HTML needed for the following exercise, but the entire HTML needed here is on the CD in the `inventory2.html` file. If you haven't copied that file to your hard disk yet, do so now, and work with that file in the upcoming steps.

EXERCISE

Follow these steps to begin creating links in one of the pages:

1. In your text editor, open the inventory2.html document.
2. Locate this HTML code:

```
<H2><FONT COLOR="#009999">SOLID BODY ELECTRICS</FONT></H2>
```

   Change it to this:

```
<H2><FONT COLOR="#009999"><A NAME="Solid">SOLID BODY ELECTRICS
</A></FONT></H2>
```

3. Change the <H2><FONT COLOR="#009999">HOLLOW AND SEMI-HOLLOW BODY ELECTRICS</FONT></H2> code to the following:

```
<H2><FONT COLOR="#009999"><A NAME="Hollow">HOLLOW AND SEMI-HOLLOW
BODY ELECTRICS</A></FONT></H2>
```

4. Going on, change the <H2><FONT COLOR="#009999">STEEL STRING ACOUSTICS</FONT></H2> code to this:

```
<H2><FONT COLOR="#009999"><A NAME="Steel">STEEL STRING ACOUSTICS
</A></FONT></H2>
```

5. Locate the <H2><FONT COLOR="#009999">CLASSICAL AND FLAMENCO</FONT></H2> code and change it to this:

```
<H2><FONT COLOR="#009999"><A NAME="Classical">CLASSICAL AND FLAMENCO
</A></FONT></H2>
```

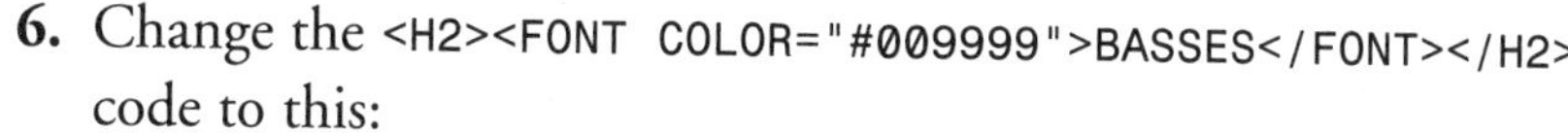

6. Change the `<H2><FONT COLOR="#009999">BASSES</FONT></H2>` code to this:

```
<H2><FONT COLOR="#009999"><A NAME="Basses">BASSES</A></FONT></H2>
```

7. Save the `inventory2.html` document.

ANALYSIS

In Steps 2 through 6, you used the `<A>` tag to name the portion of the table that lists the various types of guitars: solid body electrics, hollow and semi-hollow body electrics, steel string acoustics, classical and flamenco, and basses. As you may recall, the `links.html` page created earlier has links to each type of guitar for sale via the Web site, so each portion of the table listing different types of guitars gets its own `NAME` attribute, which you supplied here.

Loading More Pages for the Web Site

Two more pages are available to you to begin to fill out the Web site. Neither page, however, contains any new tags or attributes, so it's really not necessary to create them yourself. Instead, you can just copy them from the CD that accompanies this book.

The first of these two pages is `articles.html`. In essence, this page consists of part of the text from the first project's Welcome page. To be specific, this copied HTML consists of the articles "Tips for Buying Used or Vintage Guitars" and "The Buyer's Guide to Grading Guitars," in slightly modified form and with an introductory paragraph and page heading. The `links.html` page contains links to this page and to the two article titles.

The other page to add is `services.html`. This page essentially takes the format of the `home.html` page. The page has a heading, an introductory paragraph, and two subheadings. The subheadings indicate the topic of the paragraphs that follow, and those paragraphs describe the services offered by Guitars of Note. Again, the `links.html` document has links to the page as well as to the two subheadings.

To continue with the Project 2 Web site, copy `articles.html` and `services.html` from the CD to the local folder in which you've been building the second project.

If you try to load the Web site as it exists now, you will receive an error message, because you have not created the top frame. The left and content frames, however, should load with the `links.html` and `home.html` pages, as shown in Figure 8.3.

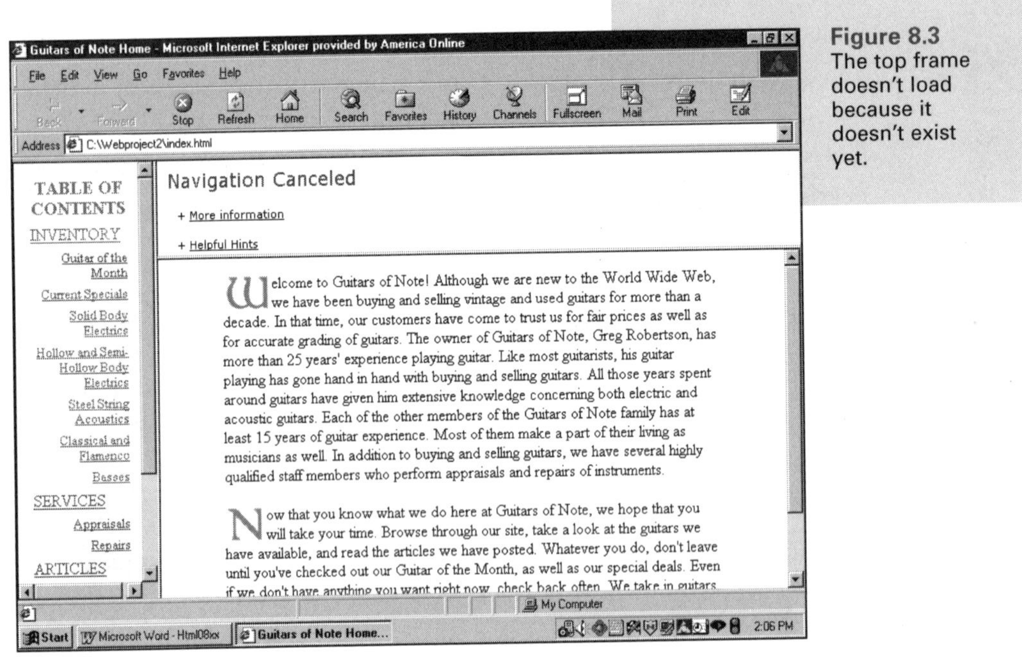

Figure 8.3
The top frame doesn't load because it doesn't exist yet.

Providing Alternate Content

So far, the second Web site project is shaping up pretty well—for people who have browsers capable of processing frames. Some browsers, however, are unable to process frames. In order for those users to be able to view your site, you need to provide the information in an alternate format.

You can provide an alternate layout for these browsers by using the `<NOFRAMES>` and `</NOFRAMES>` tag pair, which has no attributes. You simply place the start and end tags in your HTML document with the alternate reference between them.

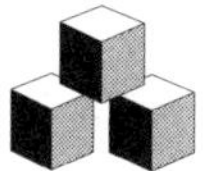

EXERCISE

Follow these steps to create alternate content intended for a browser that cannot process frames:

1. In your text editor, open the `index.html` document.
2. Place the insertion point immediately after the last `</FRAMESET>` tag.
3. Press Enter twice, and then type the following new HTML:

```
<BODY>
<NOFRAMES>
Thank you for visiting the Guitars of Note Web site! Although this Web
site was designed for viewing with a frames-capable browser, you still
can get the full benefit of this site's contents by clicking here to
view the <A HREF="home.html">non-frames version</A> of the site.
Enjoy your visit, and please come back!
</NOFRAMES>
</BODY>
```

4. Save the `index.html` document.

ANALYSIS

The `<NOFRAMES>` tag you entered in Step 3 is for the benefit of anyone using a browser that cannot handle frames. Such browsers ignore all the `<FRAMESET>` tags and their contents. (A browser that can process frames, on the other hand, ignores the `<NOFRAMES>` tag and its contents.) By ignoring the `<FRAMESET>` tags and their contents, a browser that cannot process frames continues through the HTML until it finds something it *can* understand: the `<BODY>` tag. (Remember, a frames-capable browser ignores `<BODY>` tags.)

When a non-frames-capable browser reaches the `<BODY>` tag you typed in Step 4, it processes the HTML as it would any other document. In this case, it displays the `<NOFRAMES>` text you entered in that same step. These few lines of text include a link to `home.html`—the opening page that a frames-capable browser displays in the content frame.

You finished the alternate content text by providing the `</NOFRAMES>` and `</BODY>` end tags.

EXERCISE

If you *really* want to go all-out, you can leave the HTML pages for frames-capable browsers alone, and then create additional versions of each of the Project 2 pages (except `links.html` and `gnote2.html`) for use by browsers that cannot handle frames. That isn't absolutely necessary, however.

The most common alternative to creating new versions of the HTML pages is to add links to the pages. That is the approach the following exercise takes.

Add links to the Web site's pages by following these steps:

1. In your text editor, open the `home.html` document.
2. Place the insertion point at the bottom of the document, after the last `</DIV>` tag.
3. Press Enter, and then type the following HTML:

```
<BR>
<P ALIGN="center">
<A HREF="month.html"><FONT SIZE="-1">[Guitar of the Month]</FONT></A>
<A HREF="specials.html"><FONT SIZE="-1">[Current Specials]</FONT></A>
<A HREF="inventory.html"><FONT SIZE="-1">[Inventory]</FONT></A>
<A HREF="services.html#Appraisals"><FONT SIZE="-1">[Appraisals]
</FONT></A>
<A HREF="services.html#Repairs"><FONT SIZE="-1">[Repairs]</FONT></A>
<A HREF="contact.html"><FONT SIZE="-1">[Contact Us]</FONT></A>
<A HREF="home.html"><FONT SIZE="-1">[Home]</FONT></A><BR>
<A HREF="articles.html#Buying"><FONT SIZE="-1">[Tips for Buying Used or
Vintage Guitars]</FONT></A>
<A HREF="articles.html#Grading"><FONT SIZE="-1">[A Buyer's Guide to
Grading Guitars]</FONT></A>
</P>
```

4. Save the `home.html` document.
5. Switch to your browser and open `home.html`. Figure 8.4 shows approximately how this page will look to someone who has a browser that doesn't support frames.

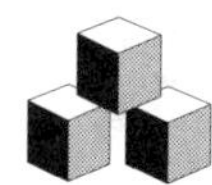

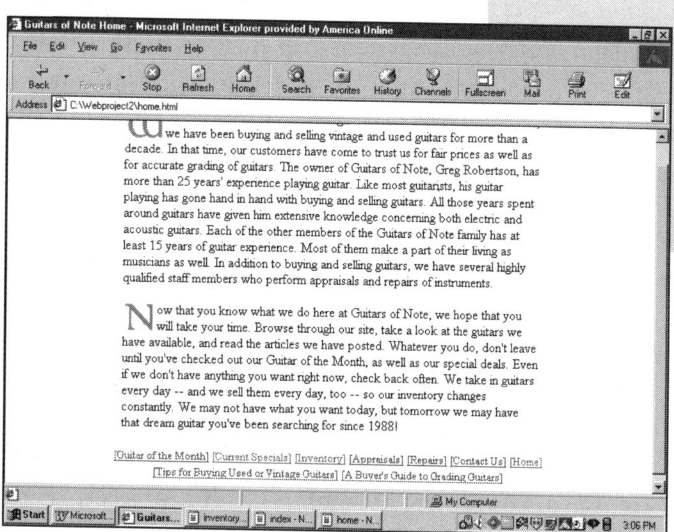

Figure 8.4 Links have been added for users whose browsers can't process frames.

ANALYSIS

The links you added here are straightforward. You began with a `<BR>` tag to add a little space between the preceding paragraphs and the links. Next, you created a paragraph and centered it with the `<P ALIGN="center">` tag. The following nine lines of HTML are the links. These do not exactly match the links in the left frame (`links.html`). Instead, they are the most important ones. Some are the primary links from the left frame (`Inventory`, `Contact Us`, and `Home`), and the others are the more specific links from the left frame (`Guitar of the Month`, `Current Specials`, `Appraisals`, `Repairs`, `Tips for Buying Used or Vintage Guitars`, and `A Buyer's Guide to Grading Guitars`). To help differentiate one link from another, each link is surrounded by square brackets ([and]). Note that the `Home` link also has a `<BR>` tag after it to create a line break. Otherwise, the list of links would go across the browser window from margin to margin, and the last link would be split into two parts, a look that is unattractive.

You *could* leave it at this: links on the `home.html` page only. The problem is that a user would have to keep clicking on the browser's Back button to return to `home.html` in order to click on another link. It is preferable, therefore, that you copy the preceding HTML and add it at the appropriate place on each of the other HTML pages in the Web site.

Creating Client-Side Image Maps

A **hot region** *or* **hot spot** *is an area within an image map on which a user clicks to activate a link.*

You create client-side image maps by using HTML tags and attributes specially designed for the task. The process really isn't difficult, but you cannot do it with only a text editor. In order to precisely map out the hot regions of the image map, you need to use a program that enables you to use a coordinate system. For this project, a good choice is MapEdit, which is easy to use and does the job.

If you want to download MapEdit (or any of a number of other image mapping tools), you'll enjoy a trip to the following URL:

http://www.tucows.com/

An Overview of the GIF-Creation Process

Although this book's scope prevents specific instructions in how to create graphics using graphics software, it's possible at least to give you an overview of the process as it works in general.

The graphic to be created is intended to appear in the top frame of the Project 2 Web site. In addition, this graphic will remain there all the time, no matter what frame someone may be viewing. The purpose of the graphic is threefold:

- To keep the name of the company onscreen at all times
- To provide links to the major sections of the Web site
- To add a little decoration

Next, it's necessary to figure out the size of the graphic. The size of the top frame is 82 percent of the screen's width. The height of that frame is 22 percent of the screen's height. To maintain an uncluttered, easy-to-read appearance, the words in the graphic should not run from one end of the frame to the other. To err on the conservative side when creating the graphic, a size of 400 pixels wide by 70 pixels high should do the trick.

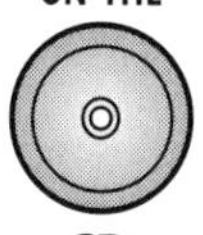

You can find the graphic created for this project on the CD, as `gnote10.gif`.

The background color of the graphic is the same dark green (`#009999`) used for various elements of other pages on the Web site. In this case, however, the background color was set to Transparent in the graphics program. Theoretically, then, any background color should show through the green background of the graphic. In practice, the appearance may not be perfect. If you stick with the particular shade of green chosen (`#009999`), however, there should be no problem. Among the matching green elements in this project are the drop caps in a couple of the HTML documents and the background color of some rows in the tables of instrument information. In other words, this color is common throughout the Web site. Similarly, the yellow text color in the `gnote10.gif` graphic also is present in some of the row backgrounds in the tables of instrument information.

The font used for the words on the graphic—UmberSSK—is decorative in a medieval sort of way. The larger font for the row of button names under the company name is necessary, because if the words were much smaller their yellow color would begin to blend in with the green background, and the words might be difficult to read. Figure 8.5 shows what the graphic looks like in Paint Shop Pro.

Creating the Top Frame's Contents

After creating the graphic, the next step is to make it usable in the Web site. You need to remember, however, that a frame doesn't display straight graphics; it displays an HTML document.

As always, you're strongly urged to type the following HTML because you can learn better that way, but the finished page is available on the CD, as `gnote2.html`.

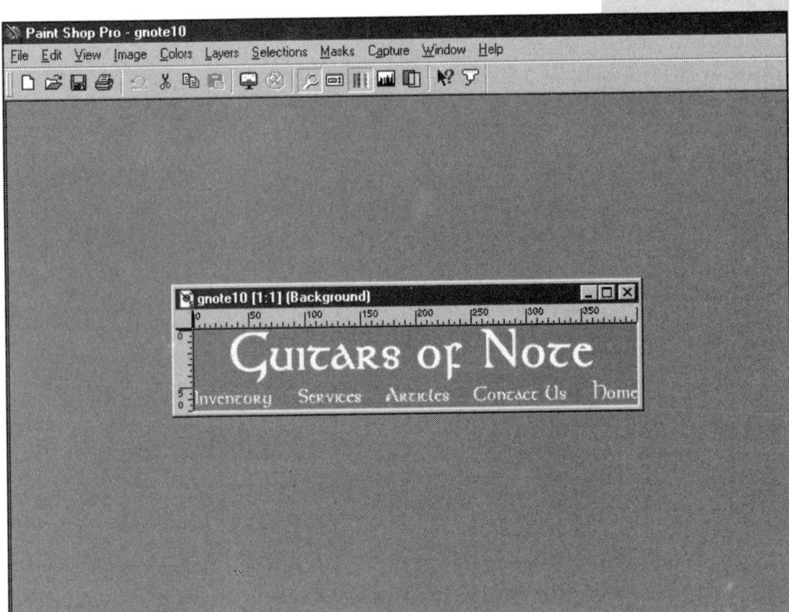

Figure 8.5 This is the finished `gnote10.gif` graphic in Paint Shop Pro.

EXERCISE

Make the company name graphic usable by following these steps:

1. In your text editor, open a new document.
2. Begin with the following greatly reduced amount of HTML:

```
<!DOCTYPE HTML PUBLIC"-//W3/DTD HTML 4.0 Frameset//EN"
"http://www.w3.org/TR/REC-html40/frameset.dtd">
<HTML>
<HEAD>
   <TITLE>Guitars of Note logo</TITLE>
</HEAD>
<BODY BGCOLOR="#009999">
<DIV ALIGN="center">
<CENTER>
<IMG SRC="images/gnote10.gif" WIDTH="400" HEIGHT="70" BORDER="0"
ALT="Button navigation bar" USEMAP="#gnote">
</CENTER>
</DIV>
</BODY>
</HTML>
```

3. Save the document as gnote2.html.
4. Switch to your browser and open gnote2.html. Figure 8.6 shows what you should see.

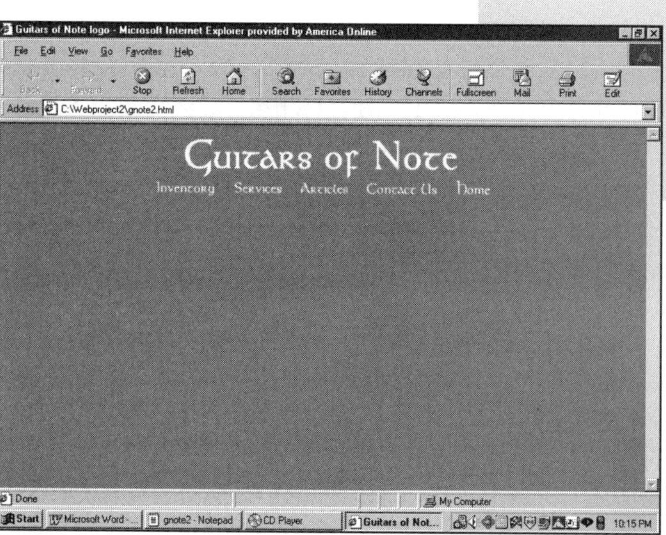

Figure 8.6
You're halfway there with the top frame's contents.

The first part of the HTML you entered in Step 2, you no doubt noticed, doesn't contain all the <META> tag information you've been entering in other pages. Since this page is only a graphic, it really wasn't necessary to put in <META> tags. Probably the most valuable bit of information is the name of the company in the title.

You also created a background color for the page: #009999. Again, this is the dark green that has been used frequently throughout the Web site, including as the transparent background for the gnote10.gif graphic. This should make the graphic and the page background seamless where they overlap, giving the effect of one graphic in the browser.

To control where the image will appear, you used the <DIV ALIGN="center"> and <CENTER> combination.

The <IMG> tag contains several bits of important information, including the source of the image file, the width and height of the image, and the ALT text for the image. In addition, this tag contains the BORDER="0" attribute. Without the value of `0`, a blue border would appear around the graphic. The reason for the blue border is that this graphic is to become a link, and the blue border is comparable to the default blue underline that identifies regular text links.

Now that the image is ready, you need to turn it into an image map. The purpose of an image map, you'll recall, is to use a graphic as a means of linking to other places. For this technique to work, you must define discrete hot regions on the graphic, and then assign each hot region the target information for one link. The most difficult part of this process is carefully defining the hot regions—unless you have an image map program to help you.

Note

If you have an image map program other than MapEdit, feel free to use it, although the steps here won't necessarily apply.

EXERCISE

Follow these steps to create an image map out of the `gnote2.html` document:

1. Start the MapEdit program.
2. Navigate to the `gnote2.html` document, and then click Open.
3. A window appears that lists the path to the image file it found in the `gnote2.html` document. Highlight `images\gnote10.gif` in the window.
4. Click OK. A small window opens that shows the graphic and also has a menu bar and toolbar across the top.
5. Click on the square on the toolbar, and then place the mouse pointer above and to the left of the word `Inventory`.
6. Drag the mouse pointer to the opposite corner of the word. As you do, a rectangle forms. When you have the rectangle where you want it, click the mouse button again. The rectangle then stays where you put it, and the Object URL dialog box appears (see Figure 8.7).

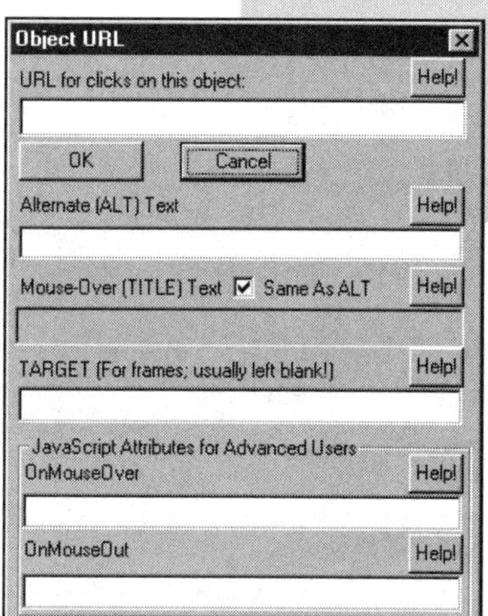

Figure 8.7
The next step is to fill in the needed information.

If you make a mistake while dragging the rectangle, press Esc and then start over again.

7. In the top text box (URL for clicks on this object), type the name of the HTML file that you want to open when a user clicks on the Inventory hot region, which is **inventory.html** in this case.
8. In the next text box (Alternate [ALT] Text), type the alternate text that you want to appear when a mouse pointer lands on the hot region. Here, you type the following:

   Link to Inventory page
9. For the purposes of this Web site—because the site doesn't use Javascript—the only other text box to fill in is the TARGET text box. Here, you type **content** to indicate the name of the frame where the Inventory page should appear.
10. After filling in all the necessary text boxes, click OK. The small MapEdit window reappears. In IE, the hot regions are outlined on the graphic, as shown in Figure 8.8.
11. Now click on the Test tool on the toolbar. It's the tool showing an arrow pointing to the top-left corner.

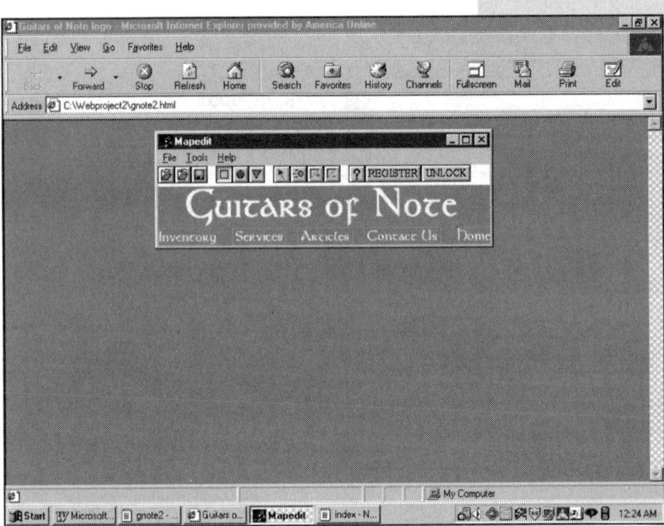

Figure 8.8 Internet Explorer shows you exactly where the hot regions are—whether you like it or not.

12. Click on the Inventory link. The rectangular link changes colors (reverse video), and the Object URL dialog box appears again (see Figure 8.9). You can edit the link's properties at this point if something is wrong.

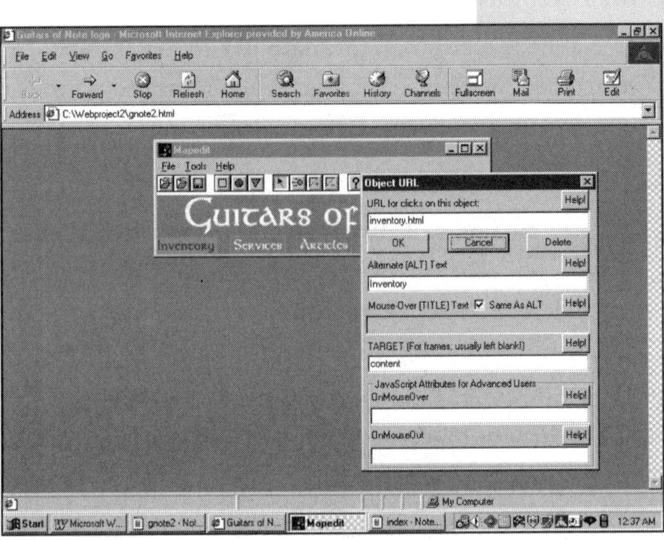

Figure 8.9 You still can edit the particular details of your link if you need to do so.

13. Repeat Steps 5 through 12 for each of the other four hot regions you're creating.

If you prefer, you can create all the rectangles and then go back and test them all at once. That approach is faster for most people.

ANALYSIS

When you use MapEdit or a program like it, the process of creating image maps becomes infinitely simpler and quicker. When you opened `gnote2.html` in Step 2, MapEdit checked to see what graphics files were present in the document, and then listed them. In this case, only one graphic file was present, so you selected that GIF file to work with.

The great part about using this type of software is that it does all the hard work of determining coordinates for you. That's what happens when you draw the rectangles. MapEdit keeps track of the starting point's coordinates and the ending point's coordinates. These two pairs of coordinates are all you need to define a rectangular hot region.

You're not limited to using rectangles as the hot regions on your image maps. Circles and polygons are also possible, whether you code the coordinates by hand or use an image mapping program. To create a polygon in MapEdit, you click at each vertex of the desired polygon. When you've finished the polygon, you right-click to close the polygon and open the Object URL dialog box.

Another excellent aspect of using MapEdit is that after you've filled out the Object URL dialog box for each of the hot regions, the program takes care of almost everything else. Not only does it know the coordinates, but it also inserts that information into the HTML document. In addition, MapEdit inserts the `USEMAP` attribute into the `<IMG>` tag, creates the `<MAP>` tag and names it (if you haven't done so ahead of time),

and creates all the <AREA> tags and their associated attributes. The image map created in the preceding exercises, for example, resulted in the following HTML inserted into the gnote2.html document:

```
<map name="gnote">
<area shape="rect" alt="Link to Inventory page" coords="0,49,73,69"
 href="inventory.html" title="Link to Inventory page" target="content">
<area shape="rect" alt="Link to Services page" coords="89,49,154,69"
 href="services.html" title="Link to Services page" target="content">
<area shape="rect" alt="Link to Articles page" coords="168,49,233,69"
 href="articles.html" title="Link to Articles page" target="content">
<area shape="rect" alt="Link to Contact page" coords="247,49,340,69"
 href="contact.html" title="Link to Contact page" target="content">
<area shape="rect" alt="Link to Home page" coords="354,48,399,69"
 href="home.html" title="Link to Home page" target="content">
<area shape="default" nohref>
</map>
```

To match the conventions used in the other HTML documents in this project, these lines need some editing. You need to put the tags and attributes in uppercase, insert the </CENTER> and </DIV> tags after the </MAP> tag, and ensure that </BODY> and </HTML> round out the document. In addition, the last <AREA> tag should have an ALT attribute, so add **ALT="gnote10.gif graphic"**. Nevertheless, MapEdit has done the vast majority of the nitty-gritty work. Not only does MapEdit save time, but it also helps prevent errors because the code it produces can be trusted to be valid.

Note

If you haven't already inserted the USEMAP attribute in the <IMG> tag, MapEdit does it for you, and names the map after the image's filename. In the preceding example, I had already included USEMAP="#gnote", so MapEdit used that name.

Note

The use of a pound sign (#) without a path indicates that the map information is in the same page as the USEMAP attribute. If you prefer, however, you can place that information elsewhere, and then make sure that the value for USEMAP includes the necessary path.

Placing your image map specifications in one file is particularly useful if you use one or more standard image maps for navigation throughout your Web site. Not only is this compact and efficient, but it's also easier to maintain than having specifications sprinkled across several different HTML files.

The `USEMAP` attribute in the `<IMG>` tag tells the browser that the map to use is named `gnote`. The following line is `<MAP NAME="gnote">`, which indicates the start of the `gnote` map. Each of the following lines consists of an `<AREA>` tag and various attributes. The first attribute is `SHAPE`, whose value is `rect` (for rectangle). Other possible values are `circle` and `poly`. Next comes the `ALT` attribute, where your alternate text goes. The value of the `COORDS` attribute consists of the rectangle's coordinates. The `HREF` attribute indicates which HTML document opens when a user clicks on the hot region. The `TITLE` attribute contains the same text as the `ALT` attribute. Finally, the `TARGET` attribute indicates the frame in which the given HTML document will open. MapEdit also inserted `</MAP>` to end the definition of the map.

Next comes the `<IMG>` tag, whose source is the `gnote10.gif` graphic, located in the `\images` folder. The `ALT` text indicates that this graphic is the button navigation bar, and the `WIDTH` and `HEIGHT` attributes indicate the size of the graphic. The `BORDER="0"` attribute ensures that no border appears around the graphic itself, because that would set the graphic off from the background. The background and the graphic have the same color so that they don't appear to be two distinct things.

Figure 8.10 shows what you see when you've placed the mouse pointer on one of the links and clicked (but not yet released the mouse button).

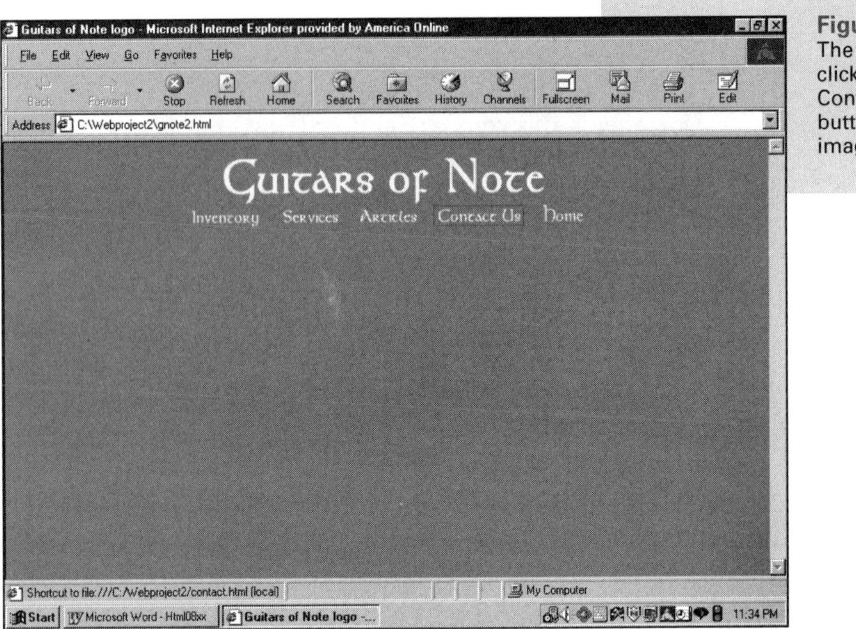

Figure 8.10 The user is clicking on the Contact Us button on the image map.

Creating the Guitar of the Month Page

Now that you have some experience with creating an image map, it's time to create another page of the Web site. This page, the Guitar of the Month page, is slightly different in its use of hot regions. Rather than jumping to a different page, clicking on a hot region on the Guitar of the Month page brings up an image. The HTML technique for the image map is the same, however.

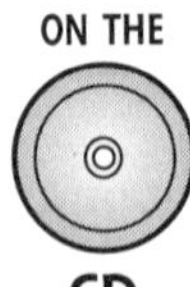

As always, if you insist on not typing the HTML yourself—although you really should—you can find the final version of this page on the CD that accompanies this book. The name of the file is `month.html`.

EXERCISE

Create this new Web page by following these steps:

1. In your text editor, open a new file.
2. Begin the page by typing the following HTML:

```
<!DOCTYPE HTML PUBLIC"-//W3/DTD HTML 4.0 Frameset//EN"
"http://www.w3.org/TR/REC-html40/frameset.dtd">
<HTML>
<HEAD>
   <TITLE>Guitars of Note "Guitar of the Month"</TITLE>
   <META NAME="keywords" CONTENT="guitar, vintage guitar, guitar
   collecting, solid body, semi-hollow body, hollow body, classical,
   flamenco, steel string, bass, Fender, Gibson, Gretsch, Rickenbacker,
   Martin, National, Epiphone, Guild, Ibanez, Hagstrom, Ovation, Jose
   Oribe, Pimentel, Raimundo, Ramirez, Armstrong, Telecaster, Mustang,
   Les Paul, Jaguar, Country Gentleman, S100 Polara, Val Pro, Artist,
   White Falcon, Anniversary, Hummingbird, Chet Atkins, Nashville,
   Songbird, Precision, Musicmaster, Plexiglas, Thinline, Casino, E360TD
   Riviera, J-160E, J-200, ES-335, ES-150, ES-175, D-28, D-35, 1168-5P,
   EB2, 4001, VI">
   <META NAME="description" CONTENT="Guitars for sale, specializing in
   vintage collectibles.">
</HEAD>
<BODY>
```

3. Save the document as `month.html`.
4. Continue by entering the following HTML:

```
<DIV ALIGN="center">
<CENTER>
   <H1><FONT COLOR="red">Guitar of the Month</FONT></H1>
   <H2><FONT COLOR="blue"><EM>1968 Fender Mustang</EM></FONT></H2>
</CENTER>
</DIV>
<P>This month's guitar is a really nice one: an all-original Fender
Mustang. If you check the serial number on the neck plate and then
cross-reference it with a database, you may think the guitar dates to
about 1965. In reality, however, the guitar dates to 1968, because that
is the date on the neck (which you can see only by removing the neck
from the body). The asymmetrical double cutaway body is made of ash,
and it has a bolt-on maple neck. The rosewood fingerboard has pearl dot
inlay, and the pickguard is pearloid. The color is light blue (with a
slight green tinge), and there is very little finish checking. The neck
has 22 frets, and it has Kluson Deluxe tuners (one of which is slightly
bent). The guitar has two single-coil pickups, and each has a three-
```

```
position switch. The guitar comes with a Fender vibrato and a removable
arm, as well as volume and tone controls. The paint is chipped off down
to the wood in a few small spots, but they are nothing serious.
Otherwise, the guitar shows little wear. And best of all, this Mustang
is easy to play and sounds great!</P>
```

5. Begin the next section of the page by typing the following:

```
<DIV ALIGN="center">
<CENTER>
   <H3><FONT COLOR="#009999">Click on a section of the guitar to get a
   closer look!</FONT></H3>
<TABLE BORDER="0">
   <TR>
      <TD><FONT SIZE="+2" COLOR="blue">Front of Guitar</FONT></TD>
      <TD WIDTH="75"></TD>
      <TD><FONT SIZE="+2" COLOR="blue">Back of Guitar</FONT></TD>
   </TR>
   <TR>
      <TD><IMG SRC="images/front398.jpg" BORDER="0" USEMAP="#front"
      WIDTH="146" HEIGHT="216" ALT="Front of Fender Mustang"></TD>
      <TD WIDTH="75"></TD>
      <TD><IMG SRC="images/back398.jpg" BORDER="0" USEMAP="#back"
      WIDTH="146" HEIGHT="216" ALT="Back of Fender Mustang"></TD>
   </TR>
</TABLE>
<BR>
```

6. Next, add the second table on this page:

```
<TABLE>
   <TR>
      <TD><FONT SIZE="+2" COLOR="blue">Detail of Front</FONT></TD>
      <TD WIDTH="75"></TD>
      <TD><FONT SIZE="+2" COLOR="blue">Detail of Back</FONT>
   </TR>
   <TR>
      <TD><IMG SRC="images/fbody472.jpg" BORDER="0"
      USEMAP="#fbody"></TD>
      <TD WIDTH="75"></TD>
      <TD><IMG SRC="images/bbody472.jpg" BORDER="0"
      USEMAP="#bbody"></TD>
   </TR>
```

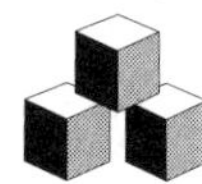


```
</TABLE>
</CENTER>
</DIV>
```

7. Finally, add the last section of the page:

```
<MAP NAME="front">
<AREA SHAPE="rect" COORDS="55,23,90,63" HREF="images/fhead472.jpg"
TARGET="content" ALT="Front of headstock">
<AREA SHAPE="rect" COORDS="55,66,85,130" HREF="images/fboard472.jpg"
TARGET="content" ALT="Fretboard">
<AREA SHAPE="rect" COORDS="35,135,110,210" HREF="images/fbody472.jpg"
TARGET="content" ALT="Front of body">
</MAP>
<MAP NAME="back">
<AREA SHAPE="rect" COORDS="53,25,83,63" HREF="images/bhead472.jpg"
TARGET="content" ALT="Back of headstock">
<AREA SHAPE="rect" COORDS="60,70,80,125" HREF="images/neck472.jpg"
TARGET="content" ALT="Back of neck">
<AREA SHAPE="rect" COORDS="35,130,105,210" HREF="images/bbody472.jpg"
TARGET="content" ALT="Back of body">
</MAP>
<MAP NAME="fbody">
<AREA SHAPE="rect" COORDS="52,116,155,188" HREF="images/guard472.jpg"
TARGET="content" ALT="Pickguard">
<AREA SHAPE="rect" COORDS="64,197,118,240" HREF="images/vibro472.jpg"
TARGET="content" ALT="Fretboard">
<AREA SHAPE="rect" COORDS="120,200,160,252" HREF="images/knobs472.jpg"
TARGET="content" ALT="Front of body">
</MAP>
<MAP NAME="bbody">
<AREA SHAPE="rect" COORDS="75,90,115,135" HREF="images/plate472.jpg"
TARGET="content" ALT="Neck plate">
</MAP>
</BODY>
</HTML>
```

8. Save the `month.html` document.
9. In your browser, open `index.html`.
10. Click on one of the Guitar of the Month links. Figure 8.11 shows what you should see.

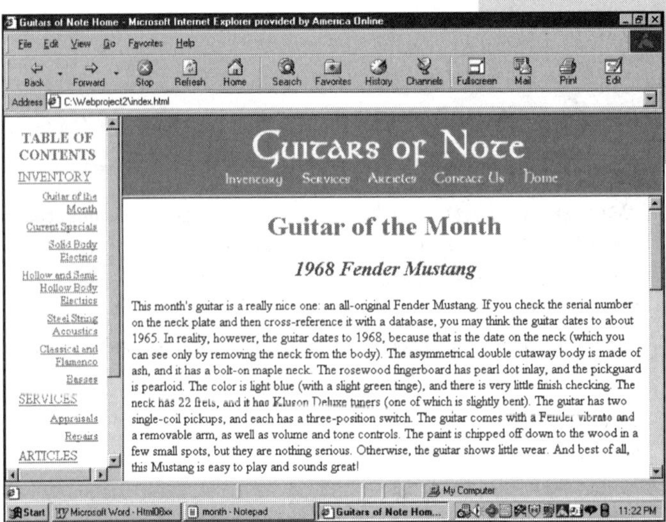

Figure 8.11 This is the top of the Guitar of the Month page.

ANALYSIS

You started this page by adding the usual preliminary HTML tags in Step 2. In Step 4, you entered and centered two headings. The red level-1 heading gives a title to the page (Guitar of the Month). The blue level-2 heading tells viewers what the Guitar of the Month is (1968 Fender Mustang). Next comes a paragraph that discusses various aspects of the guitar.

The centered level-3 heading that follows the paragraph of information instructs users to click on a part of the guitar's image to see a close-up of that part of the guitar (Step 5). The next page element is a table with a `BORDER` value of `0`. The first row of this table contains three cells. The first cell has a heading (`Front of Guitar`) and the third cell has a heading (`Back of Guitar`). In between is a blank cell whose width is set at 75 pixels. Normally, you don't want to place blank cells in a table. Because of the need to separate the columns here, though, a blank cell seemed like a simple solution. Without a blank cell, the graphics would appear side by side with virtually no space between them. (The `CELLSPACING` attribute could separate the cells horizontally—but also would separate the graphics from the cells above them so that they no longer seemed connected to each other.)

The blue text within the cell has a font size of +2. Basically, this short sentence fragment functions as a caption for what appears below it.

The second row of the table contains an image map in the first and third cells. As in the first row, the middle cell is blank, with a width of 75 pixels. The first image map uses the `"#front"` map. The image map in the third column uses the `"#back"` map. In both of these graphics, the `BORDER` value is `0` to prevent the blue outline (link indication) around the graphic.

The bottom pair of photographs and their headings make up a second table that's set up the same way as the first table.

Each of the four photographs is an image map. The top-left and top-right photos each have three hot regions. The bottom-left photo has three hot regions, and the bottom-right photo has one hot region. The purpose of these hot regions is to enable the viewer to click on a particular part of the guitar and see a close-up of that part. It's all geared toward the interests of people who buy vintage guitars, who are extremely interested in the condition of a given guitar.

The use of hot regions in these photos is different than the use of hot regions in the `gnote2.html` document. Instead of clicking on a hot region and being transported to a different page or document, clicking on a hot region in this page results in the appearance of another photograph in the content frame. Clicking the browser's Back button thereafter returns the user to the Guitar of the Month page.

This series of four image maps in conjunction with the associated close-up photos is intended to enable viewers to get a good look at the Guitar of the Month from all angles. Not having to download all the photos from the server at once means that initial download time is greatly minimized for users. A visitor can download any or all the detail photos when he or she desires. In addition, the largest of these JPEGs is only about 21K, and several are less than 10K in size, so download time for any individual photo should be fairly short.

Summary

In this chapter, you created additional pages to fill all the frames in the Web site. This chapter explained how to create more interesting tables for use throughout your Web site, as well as how to create image maps to give visitors fast and fun ways to move around among the site's contents.

The process of creating an image map is simple: create the image in a graphics program, and then use a specialized image map program to define the hot regions in the image. Most dedicated image map software builds out the necessary HTML for you, so you just need to plug the resulting HTML for the image maps into your Web pages in appropriate locations.

In the next chapter, you'll further enhance the intermediate Web site by allowing visitors to interact with you through form input. Moreover, you'll ensure that everyone who visits will be interested and entertained by some sophisticated bells and whistles, like video and animation, which are easier to add to your site than you might think.

Finishing Up the Intermediate Web Site

In Chapter 8, you built most of the structure of the intermediate Web site, and progressed well on your way to converting your passion for guitars from a hobby into a business. Through the careful use of tables, frames, and image maps, you made sure that the core content of this Web site would be detailed, well-organized, and easy to navigate.

In the competitive world of online business—or even if striving for an exceptional personal Web site—you may want to do more to make your site stand out from others. For that reason, this chapter concludes Project 2 by incorporating some snazzier possibilities for your Web site, including forms, streaming audio/video, and animation. This chapter discusses the difficulties and risks presented by these intriguing features, and ends with a section on HTML validation and testing.

Creating Forms

Forms are a primary means of maintaining communication between a company and its customers. For that reason, you're almost certain to want to include at least one form in your business site. This part of the chapter tells you how to create a basic, all-purpose form.

Unless you are qualified, do *not* try to create a Web site in which confidential information (such as Social Security or account numbers) will be passed between your site and users, or vice versa. The number one concern of Web-based businesses should be the security of such confidential information. Encryption is a world of study all its own, and you are best advised to hire a professional with extensive knowledge of the computer security field, if your intent is to deal in confidential information.

Determining the Purpose of Your Forms

When you create a form, that form has a purpose. That purpose may be to collect information for a mailing list, for example, or to take online orders from customers, or to take entries for an online contest and respond to the user automatically to indicate that the entry was received. Forms can fulfill many purposes, limited only by your imagination and skill—and the capabilities of your Web server. Figure 9.1 shows part of the basic form you create in this project.

Consider some questions as you think about forms for your site:

- What do you want to accomplish with your forms? Do you want to collect mailing addresses? Do you want to take orders for goods you sell? Do you want to take questions from your site's visitors?
- How many forms do you need, one or several?

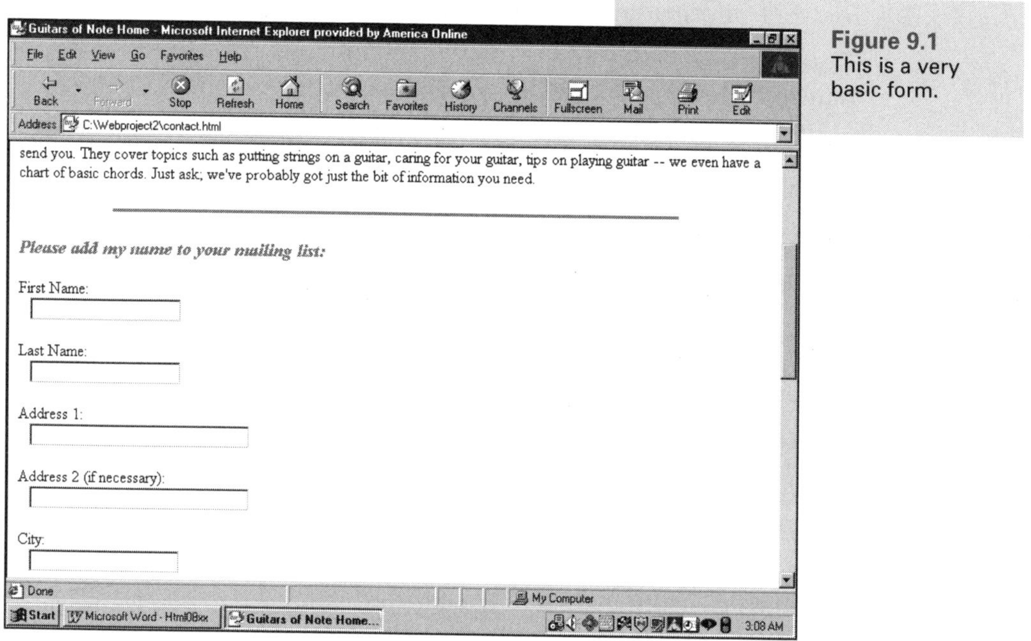

Figure 9.1
This is a very basic form.

- Do you need to be concerned about information security? Almost certainly your answer is yes. Just about the only information you *may* not need to worry about are comments from your site's visitors. Otherwise, encryption is in order. Even if all you're collecting is mailing address information, many people will not want to give out that information if they know someone can intercept it along the way.

Designing Your Forms

Once you've decided that you need one or more forms on your Web site, you need to consider carefully how best to accomplish the goals you have set for your forms. At best, one form that accomplishes everything you could possibly want to do would be unwieldy. At worst, it would be a nightmare.

To avoid information-management problems, design your forms with care. Begin by determining the purpose of each form. If you merely want to collect mailing address information, for example, you need at least the following pieces of information:

- Name
- Street address
- City
- State
- Postal code

You also may want to ask for the following:

- Telephone number
- E-mail address

On the other hand, if you want customers to be able to place orders via your Web site, you will want the preceding information and much more, possibly including the following:

- Customer or account number
- Item number
- Quantity
- Credit card number
- Shipping method
- Shipping address

Do you want your customers or potential customers to be able to ask questions or make suggestions? If so, you'll need to include a box for that input, as well as ask for their e-mail address so you can respond to the question or thank them for their suggestion.

Many times, forms *require* users to fill in certain information boxes. Requiring certain information can be a bit tricky. If you're collecting mailing addresses, of course, you *must* have the pieces of the mailing address. The e-mail address, however, is another matter: You don't *need* a person's e-mail address, and many Web users will not want to give it to you.

Finally, you also need to design your forms so that they are manageable, self-contained units of information. In short, don't try to cram *all* the information you want from a user into one form. In the first place, such a form could be extremely large, depending on how much information you're asking them to supply. In the second place, what you do with the information gathered from different forms may vary. The part of the form that takes orders, for example, will go to an order fulfillment department of some sort. Questions about your products or services, however, will go to the customer service department. By dividing these two types of information into two forms, you can route all information correctly and easily.

Because this book does not cover encryption and security, you build a basic informational form in this project. This form enables site visitors to supply their mailing addresses, and includes a space for them to ask questions or make comments. As simple as this form is, it demonstrates some key things you can do with forms on a Web site.

Starting a Form

You define a form by means of the `<FORM>` and `</FORM>` container tags. The `<FORM>` tag and its attributes are sometimes referred to as a *form header.* Everything else related to the form falls within the container tags.

In a form, users interact with* controls *that you create using the* `<INPUT>` *tag.

Along with the `<INPUT>` tag comes a number of attributes you can set (remember to refer to Appendix A for a list of attributes for any tag). Whether an attribute is useful or not, of course, depends on the control that you're creating. After using the `<INPUT>` tag to create a control, you define the control type by means of the `TYPE` attribute.

Creating the Contact Page

One final page of the Guitars of Note Web site remains to be created. In reality, this page may be one of the most important on the Web site. This is the Contact page, which consists of a form by which users can communicate with the Guitars of Note staff. Users need such a mechanism to get answers to questions about any guitars they may want to buy.

The form you create in this section does *not* involve an automated system of taking orders via credit card. Today, many business Web sites enable customers to place orders via the Web. Business owners interested in such capabilities must concern themselves with an array of issues—secure servers, encryption, firewalls, and so on. Each of these topics easily deserves an entire book of its own. If you're interested in creating a Web site that can handle business transactions, you should at least read a book dealing with Web security issues so you'll know something about the hurdles involved. If you decide to proceed with your plan, you're well advised to hire an expert consultant.

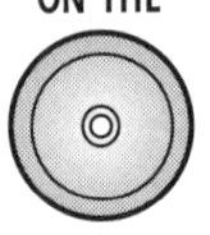

The following page, which involves a great deal of typing, is on the CD. Its name is `contact.html`. If you are game, however, you'll get more out of the exercise by typing the HTML yourself and paying close attention to what the code does.

EXERCISE

To create this last required page, follow these steps:

1. In your text editor, open a new file.
2. Place the following HTML at the top of the file:

```
<!DOCTYPE HTML PUBLIC"-//W3/DTD HTML 4.0 Frameset//EN"
"http://www.w3.org/TR/REC-html40/frameset.dtd">
<HTML>
<HEAD>
   <TITLE>Guitars of Note Contact Page</TITLE>
   <META NAME="keywords" CONTENT="guitar, vintage guitar, guitar
   collecting, solid body, semi-hollow body, hollow body, classical,
   flamenco, steel string, bass, Fender, Gibson, Gretsch, Rickenbacker,
   Martin, National, Epiphone, Guild, Ibanez, Hagstrom, Ovation, Jose
   Oribe, Pimentel, Raimundo, Ramirez, Armstrong, Telecaster, Mustang,
   Les Paul, Jaguar, Country Gentleman, S100 Polara, Val Pro, Artist,
   White Falcon, Anniversary, Hummingbird, Chet Atkins, Nashville,
   Songbird, Precision, Musicmaster, Plexiglas, Thinline, Casino, E360TD
   Riviera, J-160E, J-200, ES-335, ES-150, ES-175, D-28, D-35, 1168-5P,
   EB2, 4001, VI">
```

```
    <META NAME="description" CONTENT="Guitars for sale, specializing in
    vintage collectibles.">
</HEAD>
<BODY>
```

3. Save the document as `contact.html`.
4. Now add the first part of the page, as follows:

```
<DIV ALIGN="center">
<CENTER>
<H1><FONT COLOR="red">Talk to Us!</FONT></H1>
<CENTER>
</DIV>
<P>We're always excited to hear from customers, potential customers, or
Web surfers who have found us by accident. This page is the place to be
if you want to communicate with us. And don't be afraid to do so: We're
actually quite friendly around here. If you want us to add your name to
our mailing list, we'll be happy to do it; all you have to do is let
us know by means of our mailing list request form. You will receive the
Guitars of Note monthly listing of in-stock vintage and used guitars,
as well as learn about our specials and the Guitar of the Month.</P>
<P>On the other hand, maybe you have specific questions or requests in
mind. You can get all kinds of information from us. And if you want to
ask a question – whether about a guitar we have for sale, a guitar you
want to sell, repairs your guitar requires, or just simple advice about
what kind of guitar you should buy – this is the place to do it. We
even have some pamphlets we can send you. They cover topics such as
putting strings on a guitar, caring for your guitar, tips on playing
guitar – we even have a chart of basic chords. Just ask; we've
probably got just the bit of information you need.</P>
```

5. Begin the remainder of the page by typing the following HTML:

```
<HR WIDTH="75%" SIZE="3" COLOR="#009999">
<FORM METHOD="post" ENCTYPE="text/plain" ACTION="mailto:
presgrr@mycompany.com">
   <FONT SIZE="+1" COLOR="red"><EM><STRONG>Please add my name to your
   mailing list:</STRONG></EM></FONT><BR>
   <P>First Name:</P>
      <INPUT TYPE="text" MAXLENGTH="30" NAME="firstname">
   <P>Last Name:</P>
      <INPUT TYPE="text" MAXLENGTH="30" NAME="lastname">
   <P>Address 1:</P>
      <INPUT TYPE="text" SIZE="30" NAME="address1">
```

```
<P>Address 2 (if necessary):</P>
   <INPUT TYPE="text" SIZE="30" NAME="address2">
<P>City:</P>
   <INPUT TYPE="text" MAXLENGTH="40" NAME="city">
```

6. This step involves a long list. Feel free to abbreviate it if you just want to practice, but this is a complete list of the states in the U.S. and the provinces in Canada, which you may want to save for future use. Type the following HTML:

```
<P>State/Province (US/Canada):</P>
   
   <SELECT NAME="states" SIZE="1">
   <OPTION>Alabama</OPTION>
   <OPTION>Alaska</OPTION>
   <OPTION>Arizona</OPTION>
   <OPTION>Arkansas</OPTION>
   <OPTION>California</OPTION>
   <OPTION>Colorado</OPTION>
   <OPTION>Connecticut</OPTION>
   <OPTION>Delaware</OPTION>
   <OPTION>District of Columbia</OPTION>
   <OPTION>Florida</OPTION>
   <OPTION>Georgia</OPTION>
   <OPTION>Hawaii</OPTION>
   <OPTION>Idaho</OPTION>
   <OPTION>Illinois</OPTION>
   <OPTION>Indiana</OPTION>
   <OPTION>Iowa</OPTION>
   <OPTION>Kansas</OPTION>
   <OPTION>Kentucky</OPTION>
   <OPTION>Louisiana</OPTION>
   <OPTION>Maine</OPTION>
   <OPTION>Maryland</OPTION>
   <OPTION>Massachusetts</OPTION>
   <OPTION>Michigan</OPTION>
   <OPTION>Minnesota</OPTION>
   <OPTION>Mississippi</OPTION>
   <OPTION>Missouri</OPTION>
```

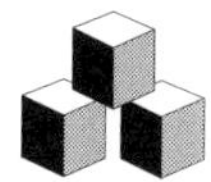


```
<OPTION>Montana</OPTION>
<OPTION>Nebraska</OPTION>
<OPTION>Nevada</OPTION>
<OPTION>New Hampshire</OPTION>
<OPTION>New Jersey</OPTION>
<OPTION>New Mexico</OPTION>
<OPTION>New York</OPTION>
<OPTION>North Carolina</OPTION>
<OPTION>North Dakota</OPTION>
<OPTION>Ohio</OPTION>
<OPTION>Oklahoma</OPTION>
<OPTION>Oregon</OPTION>
<OPTION>Pennsylvania</OPTION>
<OPTION>Rhode Island</OPTION>
<OPTION>South Carolina</OPTION>
<OPTION>South Dakota</OPTION>
<OPTION>Tennessee</OPTION>
<OPTION>Texas</OPTION>
<OPTION>Utah</OPTION>
<OPTION>Vermont</OPTION>
<OPTION>Virginia</OPTION>
<OPTION>Washington</OPTION>
<OPTION>West Virginia</OPTION>
<OPTION>Wisconsin</OPTION>
<OPTION>Wyoming</OPTION>
<OPTION>Alberta</OPTION>
<OPTION>British Columbia</OPTION>
<OPTION>Manitoba</OPTION>
<OPTION>New Brunswick</OPTION>
<OPTION>Newfoundland</OPTION>
<OPTION>Northwest Territories</OPTION>
<OPTION>Nova Scotia</OPTION>
<OPTION>Ontario</OPTION>
<OPTION>Prince Edward Island</OPTION>
<OPTION>Quebec</OPTION>
<OPTION>Saskatchewan</OPTION>
<OPTION>Yukon</OPTION>
</SELECT><BR><BR>
```

7. Now add this HTML:

```
<P>Country (if outside US/Canada):</P>
   <INPUT TYPE="text" MAXLENGTH="40" NAME="country">
<P>Postal Code:</P>
   <INPUT TYPE="text" SIZE="12" MAXLENGTH="15"
NAME="code">
<P><FONT SIZE="+1" COLOR="red"><EM><STRONG>Do you have a question or
comment for us?</STRONG></EM></FONT></P>
   <INPUT TYPE="RADIO" NAME="comments"
VALUE="Yes">Yes, I do.
   <INPUT TYPE="RADIO" NAME="comments" VALUE="No"
CHECKED="CHECKED">No, I don't.
<P>If you have anything you want to ask us, comments you want to pass
on, or requests for information, please type it in the box below. We'll
get back to you as soon as possible. Thank you for visiting Guitars of
Note!</P>
<P>Your E-Mail Address:</P>
   <INPUT TYPE="text" SIZE="30" MAXLENGTH="50"
NAME="email">
<P>Comments/Suggestions/Questions:</P>
   <TEXTAREA NAME="comments" ROWS="5"
COLS="50"></TEXTAREA>
```

8. Finish the page with the following HTML:

```
<TABLE COLS="2">
   <TR>
   <TD><INPUT TYPE="button" VALUE="Submit Form"></TD>
   <TD><INPUT TYPE="button" VALUE="Reset Form"></TD>
   </TR>
</TABLE>
</FORM>
</BODY>
</HTML>
```

9. Save the `contact.html` document.
10. Switch to your browser and open `index.html`.
11. Click on one of the Contact Us links.

Figure 9.2 shows what you should see after scrolling down slightly to view the beginning of the form.

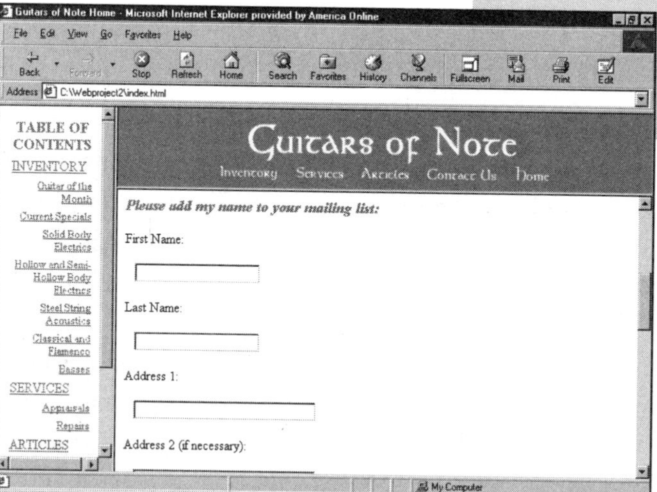

Figure 9.2
Here's the top of the Contact form.

ANALYSIS

As a matter of routine, Step 2 includes the usual HTML that goes at the top of a document. Step 4 is where you entered a red, centered level-1 heading to indicate the purpose of the page. In addition, you entered a couple of paragraphs to give users some ideas of how to use the page to communicate with the company.

In Step 5, you began to get to the meat of the page. After the green rule to divide the page introduction from the form, you inserted the `<FORM>` tag to indicate the beginning of the form itself. The first attribute, `METHOD`, has the value `"post"`, which is one of two possible values, the other being `"get"`. The difference between them is in the way they handle the form's data when someone clicks on the Submit or Send button (or whatever you name it). The post method sends the form's contents to the server as a separate message, whereas the get method adds the data to the end of the URL value you give to the `ACTION` attribute. Which method you use is determined in part by the `ACTION` you choose. If you choose Mailto, as is the case here, you *must* use post, because that's the only one that works with Mailto. If the `ACTION` is a CGI script instead, then either method might work. The one to choose depends on the server that processes the information and the availability of scripts to help with processing. The following section, "Processing Forms," discusses what happens with responses from forms after the user clicks the Submit button.

The next line of HTML tells visitors the default purpose of the form: to add their names to the mailing list. It is in a larger font size and is bold, italic, and red to call attention to itself. The next few lines create the first text-entry box. Note the three instances of ` ` in front of the `<INPUT>` tag. You'll remember from an earlier chapter that this is the HTML means of creating special characters. In this case, the special character is a nonbreaking space. The three spaces specified here will indent the actual text box a little, helping with readability.

After using the `<INPUT>` tag to create a control, you defined the control type by means of the `TYPE` attribute. This `<INPUT>` tag created a text box for the first name of the person filling out the form. A `<P>` and `</P>` container surrounds the text describing the text-entry box (First Name). The `TYPE` attribute declares that this is a text box. The next attribute, `MAXLENGTH`, sets the maximum number of characters that users can type in the box. (For most people in most cultures, 30 characters should be plenty.) Onscreen, the box doesn't seem to have 30 spaces available. In fact, it has only 21—but it will scroll left if the user passes 21 characters. It is possible to make the box bigger onscreen by using the `SIZE` attribute to indicate how long it should be.

Finally, the `NAME` attribute is where you assign a name for the text box. The logical name for this first text box is `firstname`.

HTML 4.0 introduced a new tag, `<LABEL>`, specifically for labeling parts of a form. It is not used in this exercise because it is not yet universally supported.

The next four text boxes are set up in the same way. The fifth one starts out the same way, also, but uses the `<SELECT>` tag right after the three ` ` entries.

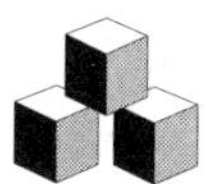

Sometimes, you may want users to choose from a list of items. If they are supplying you with a mailing address, as in this example, you can list the names or abbreviations for all the states, and then they can choose the appropriate one. For lists, you use the `<SELECT>` and `<OPTION>` tags. You can use these tags either to create lists of mutually exclusive choices, or to create lists from which users may select more than one choice at once. Figure 9.3 shows a portion of the drop-down list you created in the exercise.

To create the list, you began with the `<SELECT>` tag. Typically, when constructing a list of this type, you at least want to name the list and set the number of visible lines in the list. By default, users can choose only one item at a time from the list. Because this is a list of U.S. states and Canadian provinces, `"state"` is a logical name for the list. The size of the list box is 1, meaning that only one choice can appear onscreen at once. In practice, what happens is that this becomes a drop-down list box. When a user clicks on the scroll arrow, a portion of the list drops into view. The user then can scroll through the list to find the desired state or province. This information is used for indicating a mailing address, so only one response is permissible.

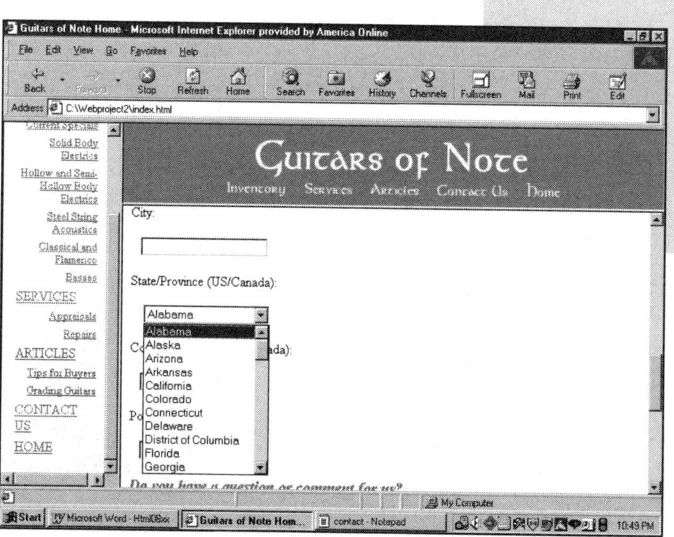

Figure 9.3 Drop-down lists can make input in a form faster and more consistent.

If you want users to be able to choose more than one item at a time from a list, insert the MULTIPLE attribute in the <SELECT> tag.

You use the <OPTION> and </OPTION> container tags to create the items that you want to list under the <SELECT> tag. Scroll bars automatically appear along the right side of the list when you add more items than the list displays (as determined by the <SELECT> tag's SIZE argument you used). For example, if you set SIZE as 4 but the list contains 12 items, a scroll bar appears automatically. The list in the <SELECT> tag in the exercise is very long, because it's a list of all states in the U.S. and all provinces in Canada. Each begins with <OPTION> and ends with </OPTION>. After the </SELECT> end tag are two <BR> tags to create space between the end of the list and the Country text box that follows.

The Country and Postal Code boxes follow the State/Province box. Each is set up like the others, although the MAXLENGTH attribute varies among the text boxes throughout the form.

After the Postal Code text box comes another italicized and boldfaced red heading, which indicates the function of the next portion of the form. In this case, you're asking if the user wants to send any comments or questions to Guitars of Note. Step 7 introduces a new item: the *radio button*. You can identify radio buttons by their round shape. Radio buttons are mutually exclusive—only one button can be turned on at a time. In this case, the only two options are yes and no, and clearly only one or the other needs to be selected at once.

You use the <INPUT> tag and the TYPE attribute to create radio buttons. All you do is set TYPE to "radio". A key to a radio button is the CHECKED attribute. When you want one of the radio buttons to be the default, you set CHECKED to "checked" for that button. In addition, you use the VALUE attribute in the <INPUT> tags for these two buttons. For the Yes button, you set VALUE to "yes". For the No button, you set VALUE to "no". Because most Web site visitors probably won't want to send comments to the company, the default radio button for the answer to this question is No. For that reason, you used the `CHECKED` attribute in the `<INPUT>` tag for the No button.

You also can add text areas to your Web page—places where users enter and edit text—by using the `<TEXTAREA>` and `</TEXTAREA>` tags. You did this in Step 7, where you created the Comments/Suggestions/Questions text box. Creating such boxes is a common use for this tag. You can set the width and height of the `<TEXTAREA>` through attributes. The `ROWS` attribute determines how many rows high the box is onscreen, and the `COLS` attribute determines how wide the box is. In Step 7, you created a box that's five rows high and 50 columns wide.

Note

The user is *not* limited to entering only as much text as fits in the box. The box has a vertical scroll bar, so the user can move around and edit everything she has written.

Finally, the end of the form has two buttons, one labeled Submit Form and the other labeled Reset Form. The first thing to note is that these two buttons are side by side. Creating this arrangement required placing the buttons in a table. The table has two columns and one row. The first cell contains the Submit Form button, and the second one contains the Reset Form button. In each case, you used the `<INPUT>` tag with the `TYPE` attribute set to `"button"`. The difference is in the `VALUE` setting, which determines the label that appears on each button. One is set to `"Submit Form"` and one is set to `"Reset Form"`.

Note

HTML 4.0 introduced the `<BUTTON>` tag. This tag combines the `<INPUT>` tag and its `TYPE="submit"¦"reset"` attribute. You also can place a graphic on the button instead of text. Because not all browsers support `<BUTTON>` yet, Project 2 is using the older, less refined method of creating buttons.

Processing Forms

Web forms filled out by thousands of customers can be very helpful, even profitable, to your company. Unfortunately, things are never quite that simple. In this case, your Web server needs to be able to put the information returned to you into a usable form. This aspect of running a business on the Web is called *forms processing*. Most forms processing takes place on the Web server and involves CGI scripts.

This book does not cover CGI scripting, which is quite commonly used in dealing with information returned from Web site forms. When you create a real site to place on the Web, you may find that the company hosting your site already has a stock of scripts that will do everything you need. In that case, you're in luck and don't need to be so concerned about the information users send you; it will come to you in a usable format.

In the exercise in which you created the form for this project, you used Mailto. If you use Mailto for your form responses—which you should do only for relatively simple responses—you need to be concerned with making sense of those responses. The problem is that the responses don't come to you as simple English words. The words are present, yes, but along with them come loads of other characters that require interpretation. Many programs are available to help with this response interpretation—some are shareware, and others are free. Following is an example of what your Web server receives for a mailing address:

```
First+Name:=Greg&Last+Name:=Robertson&Address+1:=10288+Kilbourne+Road&Address+
2:=&City:=Melkiville&State=IN&Postal+Code=46001
```

Of course, you can read this information—but it requires some effort on your part. If you have appropriate software at the other end to *parse* (identify and read the individual pieces of) this response, you get the following plain-English result:

```
First Name:     Greg
Last Name:      Robertson
Address 1:      10288 Kilbourne Road
Address 2:
```

```
City:           Melkiville
State:          IN

Postal Code:    46001
```

You then can load this information into the proper database, thereby adding a new person to your mailing list.

Many free or inexpensive programs are available that you may want to try for parsing responses to your Mailto responses. URLcook is one, Trans-Form is another, and you should have no difficulty locating other programs that do the same thing.

If you're looking for Mailto programs to deal with form responses, try searching at the following URL:

http://www.download.com/

One way or another, you must run the responses through this type of software and then take the appropriate action. If you receive a response requesting a catalog, for example, that information needs to go to the department that handles catalog requests. If another response is an order for a product, you need to make sure that the information gets to the department that fills those orders.

If you know or employ someone who can write CGI scripts, and the server that hosts your site allows customer-created CGI scripts, then you're in good shape. If the host server is the problem, you may need to find a different one. If lack of a knowledgeable person is the difficulty, you may need to hire someone to help you out in that area.

Hear Ye! Hear Ye!

One feature of many Web sites nowadays is audio. Sometimes this audio loads automatically—maybe without the site visitor even noticing—and then startles the visitor when it begins playing. Other times, the audio is available as a clip that the visitor chooses to download. In either case, if you want to include audio on your Web site, you need to give it some serious thought beforehand.

Considering a Few Technical Concerns

When Edison invented the first phonograph (or talking machine, as it was called) people were excited and amazed—and thought it was some sort of trick. Even his employees didn't quite believe it.

Sound on the Web can be exciting, too. Unfortunately, creating sound files for the Web that are acceptable is much more involved than just pressing the Play and Record buttons on a tape recorder. To produce good results, you need to know a few of the technical aspects of digital recording, as well as have a realistic notion of how long a Web surfer might be willing to hang around to hear what you want them to hear.

At one time or another, you've probably used a tape recorder to record your own or someone else's voice. Perhaps you've recorded someone playing an instrument or singing a song. Although the actual mechanics of how a tape recorder works may be mysterious to you, or at least of no interest, you know that somehow the sounds going into the microphone end up on that brown piece of magnetized tape. You stick that tape in your pocket and off you go.

For most people, entering the world of digital recording simultaneously seems both familiar and slightly odd, especially if what they record never ends up on a tape. Any sounds you want to add to your Web site, of course, sooner or later end up as a file in your computer. And therein lies the strangeness: You can't see a brown magnetized tape, because there isn't one. Yet you easily can send that music or voice to someone around the world in a matter of seconds.

Like any computer file, the sound information consists of binary data. In a text file, you write what you have to write, and that information takes up a given amount of disk space. Unlike with text files, however, you actually have some control over the size of sound files while still delivering the desired information. That control comes in the form of decisions you make when you create the sound file.

The technical term for volume is amplitude.

All sounds that you hear consist of *waves.* These waves are designated by *frequency,* and frequency is measured in *Hertz* (abbreviated *Hz*) and its multiples: kiloHertz, megaHertz, gigaHertz, and so on. Think of frequency as how "frequently" a sound wave passes a given point; the more often a sound wave goes by, the higher the frequency.

The best of human hearing extends from about 16 Hz—16 waves per second—to 20 kHz, or 20,000 Hz—20,000 waves per second. The higher the frequency, the higher the pitch of the sound. Few sounds consist of one frequency. Rather, multiple frequencies are the rule in life. Frequency is only part of the story of sound. Amplitude is also relevant.

Note

All the preceding physical aspects of sound fall within the category of *analog* information. As you probably know, computers deal in *digital* information. For practical purposes, you may want to think of analog and digital as opposites. In order for digital devices—computers—to deal with the analog information of sound, the computer takes *samples* of the analog sound. How often the software takes the samples is the *sampling rate,* and the sampling rate determines how true the resulting sound is to the original.

When the computer software samples the sound, it essentially is cutting the sound into pieces at a rate you choose. This rate, like the frequency of sound, is measured in Hertz. In practice, it's measured in kiloHertz, because the software samples the sound thousands of times per second. The smaller the sample (piece) of sound, the better the resulting sound quality; and the more samples taken, the smaller the pieces of sound. In other words, a higher sampling rate results in better quality sound—but uses up more disk space.

More issues are involved in digitally processing sound, however. So far, the discussion has concerned the frequency (pitch) of sound, but little has been said about amplitude. Both elements are necessary to produce sounds you can use on the Web.

The term for digital slicing involving amplitude is *bit rate.* The two most common bit rates are 8 bit and 16 bit. The higher the bit rate, the more volume the file can handle. And, as you might have guessed, the higher the bit rate, the more disk space the sound file takes up.

The difference in volume between the loudest and quietest parts of the sound is called the **dynamic range.**

Dynamic range is measured in decibels. The more decibels you have, the wider the dynamic range. Not surprisingly, though, more dynamic range comes with the cost of larger file sizes.

The preceding technical details are necessary to help you understand the factors involved in creating audio files for your Web site. You have several decisions to make, and you need to bear those concepts in mind as you decide what to do.

To Stream or Not to Stream?

One of the first decisions you need to make is whether you want to use streaming audio or not. The old—but not necessarily outdated—way of using audio on a Web site is as follows: You record the sound, create a computer file of it, and place a link to the file on your Web page. When a visitor wants to hear it, he or she clicks on the link, and the sound file is then downloaded to the visitor's computer and the sound plays through the computer's speakers.

In most instances, there's probably nothing wrong with this approach. Sometimes, however, it can be a problem.

Handling *large* audio files is a problem if the user has to wait for the files to download. If everyone had high-speed connections dedicated to the Internet, it wouldn't be such a big deal. Many people, however, have slow modems or bad connections, and downloading is slow. More than once I've wanted to hear an audio clip, only to have to wait so long for it to download that I lost interest. You don't want that to happen to your visitors. If the audio file you want to deliver is only 40KB in size, most people will be willing to wait. If it's 900KB, however, most people are likely to give up long before it's downloaded.

In **streaming** *audio, the file is downloaded continuously in small* **packets** *so the user doesn't have to wait for the entire file to download before hearing it.*

The solution for your large audio files may be streaming audio. The streaming packets of data begin playing immediately upon being processed by the user's browser, so the wait time is minimal. Although this technique sounds great, it's not perfect. Not every server can handle streaming audio, because it requires the right software. In addition, many of the streaming systems require the person who wants to listen to the audio clip to have the proper plug-in (a little program) to make it work.

Not everyone will have the plug-in already or will want to make the effort to download it. Audio just isn't that important to many people.

Given that information, you now have to make a decision about which approach to take.

As always, keep your audience in mind when deciding which approach to take. If your Web site is all about selling your band's latest CD, for example, then you'll want to have good quality clips available for visitors to hear. In such cases, streaming audio is probably your best bet. On the other hand, if you only want a clip of your voice saying "Welcome to my Web site," then a low-fidelity recording the user downloads is perfectly adequate.

As you make decisions about the kind of file you want to create, you should remember another fact or two and refresh your memory of the earlier discussion.

It's possible to record in mono *or* stereo for your Web site. Recording in stereo, however, creates files that are twice the size of the equivalent mono file, because you actually have two separate channels of data instead of just one.

A higher sampling rate results in a larger file. Usually, you can set your recording software from just a few kHz to about 44.1 kHz. The standard rates are 11.025 kHz, 22.05 kHz, and 44.1 kHz. To refresh your memory, a 22.05 kHz sampling rate means that the software samples the sound 22,050 times per second. For the sake of comparison, you should know that the sound for music CDs is sampled at twice that rate: 44,100 times per second.

Finally, sampling the amplitude of the sound wave occurs at either an 8-bit or 16-bit rate. Again, twice the rate yields twice the file size for an otherwise-identical signal. Suppose that you record a sound in mono with a sampling rate of 22.05 kHz at a bit rate of 8. As an experiment, you record the same sound again with identical settings, except that the bit rate is 16. The result is a wider dynamic range, as well as a file that is twice the size of the first recording.

The sound files you create do not have to be recorded via a microphone. It is possible to record from a cassette or a CD.

If you record any copyrighted material—from a cassette or CD, for example—without the permission of the copyright holder, be warned that you will be in violation of copyright law. As such, you may find yourself the object of a lawsuit by the copyright holder. If you get written permission from the copyright holder and conform to all of the holder's requirements, then that's a different story.

All sorts of software—commercial, shareware, and free—are available for working with Web audio. Most computers these days come with some sort of audio software installed, so you can try that if it does everything you want it to do. For most people, the preinstalled software is probably adequate. If you want more advanced software, many products are available for purchase or downloading. GoldWave is one example. Among many others are Cakewalk Pro Audio, Anvil Studio, and Cool Edit Pro. Look into RealAudio and Shockwave if you're interested in streaming audio.

Many audio programs are available as shareware or freeware. One great central location for finding that and many other types of software is the following:

http://www.tucows.com/

Adding a Sound Clip to the Web Site

Now that you have some understanding of the issues involved in creating sound files, you can experiment with sound a bit. The CD accompanying this book contains a sound file already, so you don't need to create one. Of course, if you want to create a sound file, have fun! Just keep in mind the issues discussed previously.

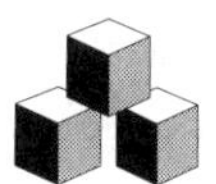

Note

Make sure that you keep the sound file you use in this exercise in the `Webproject2\sounds` folder. Otherwise, it won't work.

EXERCISE

Add a sound file to the Web site by following these instructions:

1. In your text editor, open the `month.html` document.
2. Place the insertion point immediately after the paragraph describing the Fender Mustang, and then press Enter.
3. Type the following HTML:

```
<DIV ALIGN="center">
<CENTER>
<H3><FONT COLOR="#009999">Click <A HREF="sounds/compare1a.wav">here</A>
to listen to the Guitar of the Month!</FONT></H3>
```

4. Save the `month.html` document.
5. Switch to your browser and open `index.html`.
6. Click on the `Guitar of the Month` link in the left frame. Figure 9.4 shows the added line about the audio clip.

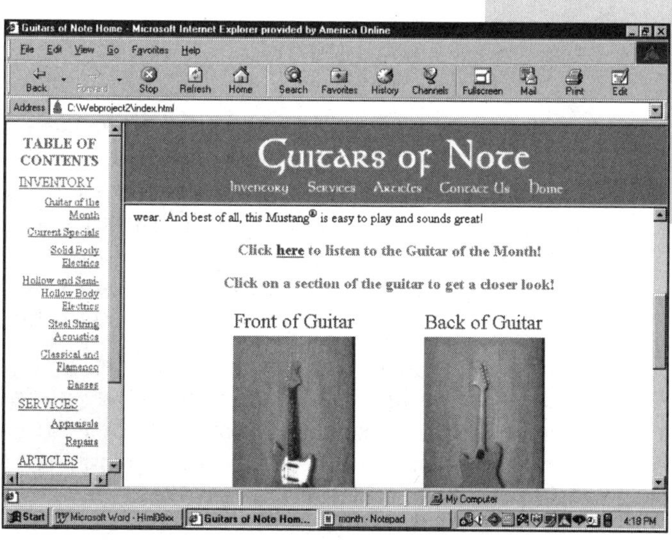

Figure 9.4 Visitors are offered the opportunity to hear the Guitar of the Month.

ANALYSIS

In this exercise, you placed the HTML for the sound file *after* the paragraph that describes the guitar and immediately above the heading that tells users to click on the guitar to see close-ups. Both are <H3> headings in dark green. The difference is that the hyperlink in the newly added HTML links to a sound file, not a graphic. The file format of the sound is .wav, commonly called a *wave file*. Wave files are the most prevalent type of sound file for the PC.

A user clicking on the link shown in Figure 9.4 may see the dialog box shown in Figure 9.5, depending how he has the computer set up. On my computer, proceeding with opening the file "from its current location" results in the little box shown in the middle of the screen in Figure 9.6.

The most common sound file for Macs is the .aif file, and for UNIX machines, it's the .au file. Note, however, that the file for this project on the CD is available only in .wav format. To be able to satisfy users on other platforms, you would add the following HTML to the month.html document as a new line immediately below the sound link you just added:

```
<H4><FONT COLOR="#009999">(Mac users, click <A
HREF="compare1a.aif">here</A> to listen to the Guitar
of the Month; UNIX users, click <A
HREF="compare1a.au">here</A>.)</FONT></H4>
```

Of course, you would need the sound file saved in each of the other two formats for this to work. Taking this approach means that the server that hosts your Web site must store all three files, but even so, users need download only one of them. Note that this heading is reduced slightly in size; you can, of course, create it at the same <H3> level as the others.

How can you decide which audio files to supply? As always, the best approach is to know your audience. If your target audience consists only of PC users, for example, then you don't need to worry about creating the Mac and UNIX audio files.

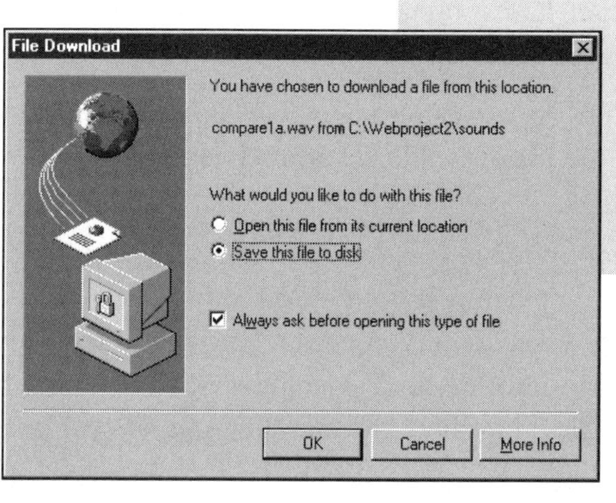

Figure 9.5
A dialog box concerned with file safety may appear on the user's screen.

Figure 9.6
This basic box tracks the playing file.

Seen Any Good Videos Lately?

Among the latest in Web page extras is video. You can find video clips of TV stars on network Web sites, or Web cameras that show the traffic congestion in large cities. The quality of video varies considerably from one Web site to another, depending on the technique and equipment used—and probably also on the amount of money spent by the site's owner.

Downloadable Files versus Streaming Video

The first part of creating video for the Web is the same whether you want to create downloadable files or streaming video: You need to create the video (or already have it on tape). If you tape it on your home video camera, bear in mind a few tips:

- Avoid moving the camera, if possible. If you *have* to move the camera, do it slowly. Please, no rock video style movements or shot angles.
- Don't zoom in and out, which can become irritating. Instead of zooming in when you need a close shot, take a close-up and then edit it in. Likewise, if you need a long shot, take a long shot and then edit it into the final video. Use video editing software to cut between the long shots and the close-ups.
- Don't expect to see great detail in the final version of the video.
- Don't use your camera's capabilities to add titles or other text to your video. Use video software for that purpose after you're done taping.
- Don't rely on your camera's built-in microphone. Instead, invest in an external microphone that you plug into your camera. Even a fairly inexpensive one will improve the sound significantly.

After you have shot your video and are ready to put together your Web pièce de résistance, you have to make a decision. Do you want to create a file that users download? Or do you want to get the action going more quickly with streaming video? To help you make that decision, following is a brief discussion of the good and bad aspects of both, so that you can avoid the ugly consequences.

If you're aiming for the highest quality video—whichever type of video you want to produce—you need a *video capture card.* If you're a Mac user, however, you may be in luck, because many of them come equipped with video capture cards. If you use a PC, chances are good that you *don't* have one of those already. If you're not sure whether you have one, check all the ports, or jacks, on the back of your computer. If you have one that looks like the type you use to hook up your stereo at home, then you may be in luck. These video jacks are usually yellow (around the metal part, that is). If you don't have a video capture card already, be prepared to pay 200 dollars or more for a good one. And if you're going to get into this type of production, you *should* get a good one.

Okay, now that you've got a video capture card, what are you going to do with it? You can't simply capture the video and send it out to your Web site. It isn't that easy. Now you need video editing software. This software is what you use to edit the video, add titles to it, compress it, and generally do all those things that need to be done to create usable Web video. This software can be quite expensive, costing at least twice as much as the video capture card. On the other hand, some programs cost very little or are even free.

Tip

If all this is sounding like more than you want to deal with personally, you always can hire a company to do it for you. If the video you want to produce is critical to your business Web site, for example, hiring professionals will get you the quality you want. The investment in this approach is likely to be more than what you would pay if you bought everything yourself, but in this case, cost is not the issue: The quality of the product is the important thing, and quality goes up with experience.

If your video clips will be short—less than 30 seconds, say—it's probably advisable to stick with downloadable files. Most of the time, downloadable video is of a higher quality than streaming video, so that's a strong argument in favor of short downloadable clips. The most common formats for downloadable video clips are QuickTime (for Macs) and AVI (for PCs).

If your clips are longer than 30 seconds, the decision becomes more complex. The key factor for most Web users is that they don't have the patience or the time to wait for a download that takes several minutes. (And if they do, you need to make sure that the wait was worth their while!)

Suppose that you don't want to make users wait six or seven minutes to download your file, so you decide to go with streaming video. Even though the quality may not be quite as good as a downloadable file, you decide that it's still acceptable. In that case, you need to consider the cost of producing a streaming video.

For the do-it-yourself-Web-site-hobbyist, streaming video may be cost prohibitive, depending on what system you want to use. The reason is that some streaming video systems require the use of a server dedicated to streaming video. And those systems often charge a fee for that capability.

Besides the additional cost of delivering streaming video, you have to make a decision regarding which system you want to use. RealVideo is very popular because the company has been around for quite some time and is well known for its Web audio products. NetShow, a Microsoft product and an exception to the high cost of getting into Web video, is gaining popularity as well, at least in part because it's free. Other options are Videograms, VivoActive, StreamWorks, Vxtreme, and VDOLive. Each one has its advantages, disadvantages, and idiosyncrasies. If you're really interested in pursuing Web video, investigate them and compare features.

If you're interested in streaming video technology, you might want to visit some of the following Web sites:

RealVideo: **http://www.real.com/**

VivoActive: **http://www.vivo.com/**

NetShow: **http://www.microsoft.com/windows/windowsmedia/**

An Overview of the Video Creation Process

In order to clarify how involved video production for the Web can be, this section presents a brief explanation of the process. It's not possible to go into detail for each of the software options available to you. The best this book can do is cover the general process and remind you that details vary from one software package to another.

***Digitizing** is the process of taking analog data, such as video on a videotape or audio on a cassette tape, and changing it into a form usable on a computer.*

After you have shot the video you want to use, you need to *digitize* the video. That's where the capture card and your software come into play. You have numerous options regarding the editing software you use. Adobe Premiere is very popular, but many people like other programs. Ulead has MediaStudio Pro, for example. VivoActive Producer is well regarded, and RealNetworks will *give* you RealEncoder or *sell* you RealPublisher. Emblaze Video is another entry in the field. In short,

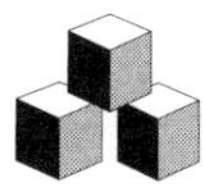

many options are available at widely varying costs. Check them out to see which suits your budget and needs, as well as the methods you want to use.

Following are some Web sites you may want to visit if you're interested in video editing software:

RealVideo: **http://www.real.com/**

Emblaze Video: **http://www.emblaze.com/**

Ulead: **http://www.webutilities.com/**

Macromedia: **http://www.macromedia.com/**

Adobe Premiere: **http://www.adobe.com/**

You have several choices to make when it comes to producing the video. Probably the first choice is what format you're going to use: AVI or QuickTime, for example. While you're at it, also consider the size of the window in which you want the video to appear.

Don't try to create a video that takes up the user's entire screen. Use nothing larger than the standard size of 160 pixels by 120 pixels.

You also need to decide on the window size and the frame rate. I suggest you use a frame rate of somewhere from 10 to 15 frames per second (fps).

Compression is another question, and is a primary reason that Web video fails to match up with a video you might watch on your VCR at home. Without compression, videos would be so huge that no one would have the hardware to handle it. Various compression schemes are available; the one you choose is dependent on what the software makes available to you and your goals for the Web video.

In addition, as you work with the editing software, you need to decide on the target rate that users will be using as they download your video. You may want to create one version for downloading at 28.8Kbps and another for downloading at 56Kbps.

And don't forget the audio portion of your video. Here again, you need to decide on the sampling rate, the bit rate, and whether you want to use mono or stereo. (Of course, using no audio at all saves the most hard disk space and download time.)

After you've made all the required decisions, you set the software's options in accordance with those decisions, then save the file.

Note

If you create more than one version of your video—one AVI and one QuickTime, perhaps—you need to go through the same process for each version. Just remember to save to the correct format at the end.

If you are creating downloadable video files, all you need to do now is make sure that you write the HTML for the link to the video files. Then upload the video files to your Web site.

If you are creating streaming video, however, you now need to encode the file to work with your system of choice. Some methods might emphasize video quality at the expense of audio quality, whereas others emphasize the audio to the detriment of the video. Still others may be suitable for both lots of music and movement. Whichever one you choose, a tradeoff of some sort is involved. Specific instructions vary according to the system you use, so you have to get the details from the software.

Note

Streaming video usually requires the viewer to download a plug-in of some sort. That's another consideration to keep in mind when deciding whether to use downloadable files or streaming video. You may want to decide on a streaming system that doesn't force visitors to download or use a plug-in.

The video you add in the following steps is among the Project 2 files on the CD that accompanies this book. It is in the `\images` subdirectory and is named `month4.avi`.

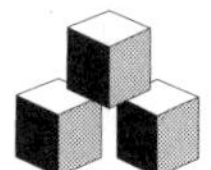

EXERCISE

Add a video to the Project 2 Web site by following these steps:

1. In your text editor, open the `month.html` document.
2. Place the insertion point immediately after the `</H2>` tag near the top of the document (the heading reads `1968 Fender Mustang`). Press Enter twice.
3. Type the following HTML:

```
<H3><FONT COLOR="#009999">Click <A HREF="images/month4.avi">here</A>
first!</FONT></H3>
```

4. Save the `month.html` document.
5. Switch to your browser and open `index.html`.
6. Click on the `Guitar of the Month` link in the left frame. Figure 9.7 shows the new `Click here first!` link on the Guitar of the Month page.

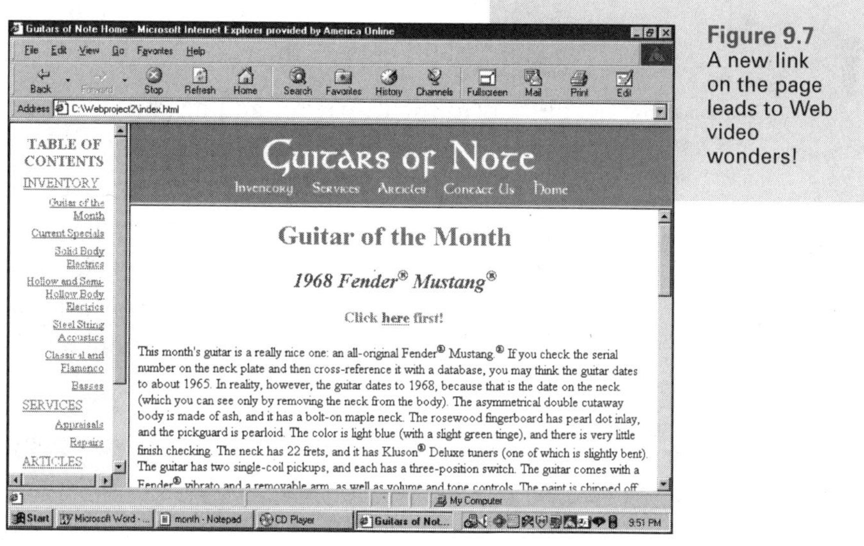

Figure 9.7
A new link on the page leads to Web video wonders!

7. Click on the new link and view the result (see Figure 9.8).

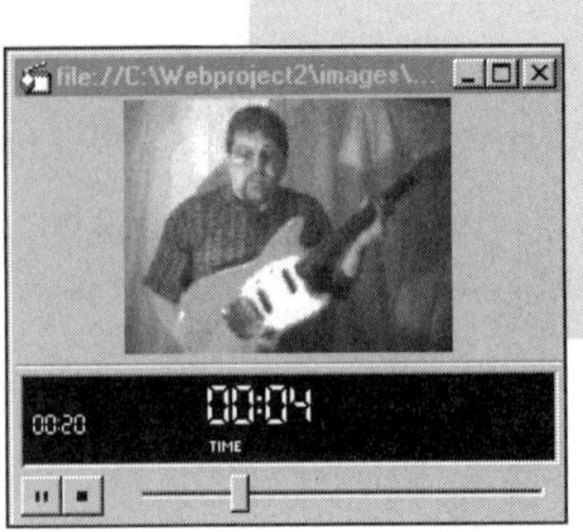

Figure 9.8 This video sales pitch was easy to include on the Web site.

ANALYSIS

As you can see, the *process* of inserting a video in a Web site is not difficult. First, you decide where you want to place it, and then you insert one line of HTML in that location. In this case, the link you typed in Step 3 is a green-colored heading. To establish the link, you use the `<A>` and `</A>` anchor tag pair and the `HREF` attribute with a value indicating the path to the video file. That's all there is to it.

A Webcam is one of a class of digital cameras especially useful for creating content for Web sites.

The most difficult part of adding this video was actually its creation. I used a relatively inexpensive *Webcam* (a Kodak DVC323 digital video camera). Webcams are generally quite small, and you often find them sitting on top of a monitor. These cameras originally were designed for videoconferencing, but you can use them to create Web video also, although the quality is not what you could get from a full-fledged (and expensive) digital video camera.

A codec is a coder-decoder used to go back and forth between compressed and uncompressed formats.

This video is an `.avi` file, which is the very popular Video for Windows format. I shot the video, used the software that came with the camera (Pictureworks Live) to edit out the "ends" of the video, and then used the software to compress the video with the Cinepak codec, which is popular for creating video for the Windows environment and for use on the Web. Many other codecs are also available for use with Web video.

Adding GIF Animation to the Web Site

Each animation program has its own procedures and features, so this chapter cannot delve deeply into them and explain how each one works. Animation on a Web site really is an extra, though, so this section will give an overview of the general process and then show how to incorporate animation into a Web site.

As you know, a cartoon is really a series of images drawn by hand or by computer. Each image is slightly different from the one that comes before it. When the images appear in order, the cartoon creates the illusion of movement or change, or both. The quality of the result depends on a couple of things. One of the determining factors is speed. Changing the images at the rate of one per second will result, at best, in jerky, highly unrealistic movement. Changing images at the rate of, say, fifteen per second is a very different story. You are far more likely to get acceptable results at that speed—acceptable for a cartoon, that is, but probably not for an animation on the Web.

A second quality factor is the amount of change from one image to another. For example, suppose that you're creating an animation in which a man is standing, facing the viewer, and he raises his hand from his side to straight up in the air. That's 180 degrees of movement. If you have one frame with the man's hand at his side, and a second frame with his hand up in the air—and no intermediate frames—the result will not be a sense of motion, but a sense of discontinuity. You'll have two pictures that look like what they are—two separate pictures.

Take that same scenario, but this time create a frame with the arm straight down, a frame with the arm straight up—and a frame with the arm at each intermediate position of 30-degree increments. That adds five more frames, for a total of seven. If you play back the frames at a fast enough speed, the result is more of a feeling of movement.

Of course, you could go on, adding even more intermediate frames. Eventually, you could achieve a really good animation effect. Unfortunately, long before you got to that result, you would have passed the point where the animation would be viable for a Web site.

As with all the more advanced features you can incorporate into a Web site, the chief practical problem with animation is the amount of download time required. Recall that one of the problems with graphics in a Web site in general is the size of the graphics files themselves, which easily can run into the tens of thousands of bytes. If your animation consists of a series of, say, ten 30K graphics, you suddenly have 300K of files to download. And those graphics are only for one animation. Add in other graphics for the Web site, and you'll find yourself asking users to invest a major amount of download time only for graphics. Text—which is probably the most significant part of your site, anyway—takes additional time.

Caution

When creating animation, you need to limit it to as few frames as possible, and make each frame as small (in bytes) as possible.

As far as animation for a Web site is concerned, you need to find that balance between number of frames and quality of result. This balance is likely to require experimentation on your part. Try creating several versions of the animation, and then compare effectiveness with size to arrive at a good compromise.

Don't be too ambitious in your design of an animation. Keeping it simple cuts down on animation size.

Creating an animation essentially involves creating the individual frames and then playing them back at a speed that achieves the effect you desire. Just remember to keep that balance between complexity and file size.

Tip

Many (or even most) animation programs can *optimize* an animation for you, creating the best result with the smallest file size possible. Use that feature to make the process easier on yourself. Check into several animation programs, such as Ulead GIF Animator, Animation Shop, Animagic GIF, GIFmation, and GIF Construction Set. You can certainly find many other programs, so locate one that looks appropriate for what you want to do. Try them out, view demos, and jump in!

Caution

Don't forget that constantly repeating animations can easily raise the viewer's ire. You should limit the number of times any given animation plays to no more than two.

Pizzazz is a good, all-purpose word. It's one of those words that means different things to different people. Some may understand it as a quality that makes something "flashy" or "different." Others may think of it as making something "unique" or "fancy." Any number of other meanings are possible. However you want to think of it, now is the time to add a little more pizzazz to the Guitars of Note Web site.

EXERCISE

Follow these steps to add animation to the Web site:

1. In your text editor, open the `home.html` file.
2. Place the insertion point at the right end of the first `<CENTER>` tag, near the top of the file, and then press Enter twice.
3. Type the following HTML:

```
<BR>
<IMG SRC="images/open.gif" WIDTH="144" HEIGHT="98" ALT="Animation of
Guitars of Note"><BR>
```

4. Save the `home.html` document.
5. Switch to your browser and open `index.html`. Figures 9.9 through 9.11 show the third, sixth, and last frames of the animation as they appear in the main window of `index.html`. (Four other frames of the animation exist but aren't shown in the figures.)

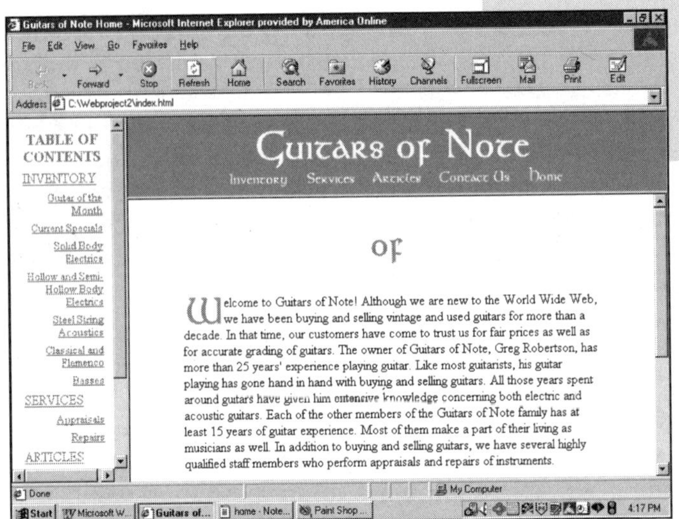

Figure 9.9 The third frame of the animation says "of."

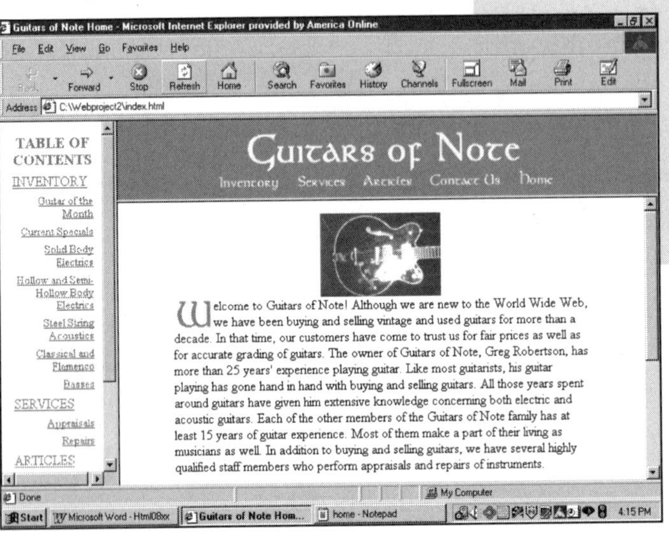

Figure 9.10 The sixth frame of the animation is a photo of a Gretsch Gibson Les Paul Country Gentleman.

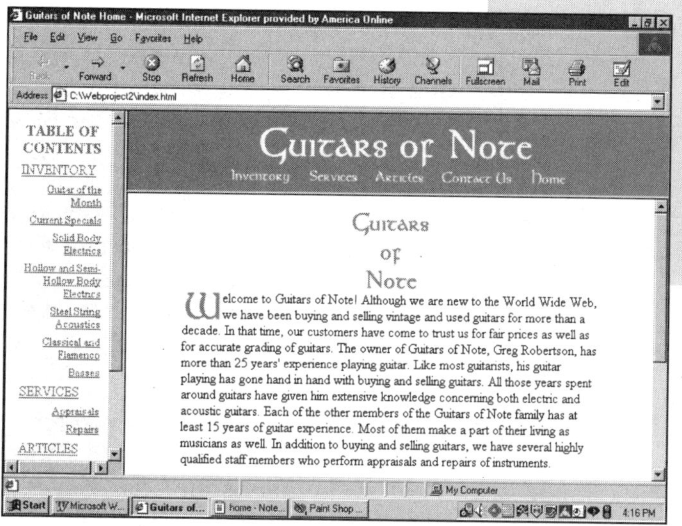

Figure 9.11 The last frame of the animation, "Guitars of Note," remains onscreen as a sort of heading.

ANALYSIS

In Step 2, you placed the insertion point after the `<CENTER>` tag that begins the body of the document. In Step 3, you typed the brief snippet of HTML necessary for the animation to work. The `<IMG>` tag declares the source of the GIF animation as well as its size. You also typed `ALT` text to let users know what goes there. The source of the image is the `/images` subfolder of the `Webproject2` folder. The name of the animation is `open.gif`.

Your safest option is *not* to use the `LOOP` attribute within the tag, because so many browsers don't recognize it. Instead, use your animation program's built-in capability to set the number of times the animation plays.

One of the attributes you can use with `<IMG>` is `LOOP`. The intention behind `LOOP` is to enable the Web builder to define how many times the animation plays before it stops. The software I used to create this simple animation, Ulead GIF Animator, has its own command within the software, however. You can set the looping to a value of `infinite`, which means it will continue to play, or you can specify a certain value. In either case, this value determines how often the animation loops. By using the software's setting, placing a `LOOP` attribute in the HTML doesn't make any difference.

Note also that some browsers may not recognize looping at all, in which case users see either the first or last image of the animation. You may want to consider this when you create the animation, making sure that whichever of those two images appears will make sense within its context.

As you can see, adding animation to a Web site is easy. The most difficult part is likely to be creating the animation, but with all the software available for that purpose, even that may not be difficult.

Testing the Intermediate Web Site

Finishing the Project 2 Web site has been a major undertaking. You've learned many new techniques and skills in the process of creating the site. Now that it's finished, you need to make sure that it works as well as it can. One common reason for creating a Web site is to disseminate information worldwide. In order to achieve that goal, you want your site to be compatible with as many browser versions as possible. At the same time, your primary concern is probably with Internet Explorer and Navigator—these days, when it becomes necessary to make a decision about which browsers to favor, these two top the list.

Recall that upon completion of the personal Web site in Project 1, testing began. That testing (in Chapter 5, "Finishing Up the Basic Web Site") took the form of checking the Web site in several browsers. In addition, the HTML was reviewed by the CSE HTML Validator. This section covers the same testing and validation issues for the Project 2 Web site, which has more pages and greater complexity (due to fancier features) than the Project 1 Web site had.

Viewing the Site through Your Browser

This second project, like the first, was built and tested primarily in Internet Explorer 4. The majority of Web surfers use IE or Navigator, so those are the two primary audiences to keep in mind. Chances are good that one of these is the browser you use regularly on your local machine. The most basic level of checking, of course, is to make sure that you have resolved all problems that were encountered when viewing the Web pages in your own browser as you put together all the pieces of the site.

Using the W3C Validation Service

Even if your site works in Netscape Navigator 3.0 and Internet Explorer 3.0, you certainly want to make it more widely available if possible. Checking the correctness of your HTML is a good first step. As mentioned in a previous chapter, the HTML standards organization (the World Wide Web Consortium) has its own Web site. From there, you can access the W3C validation service. This might be a good place to start:

http://validator.w3.org/

According to the W3C Web site, its validation service uses several programs to do its work. Unfortunately, the W3C validation service can work only with documents that are already on a Web server somewhere. That's a problem, because at this point, your Web site exists only on the computer sitting on your desk. Of course, if you already happen to have a Web site online that you want to check, by all means, try out the W3C validation service.

After you place a site on the Web, whether one based on the projects in this book or one you create entirely on your own, I suggest you go ahead and use the W3C service. You might even want to check your site periodically, especially after changing something major on the site, just to make sure that everything is still in order.

Validating with CSE HTML Validator

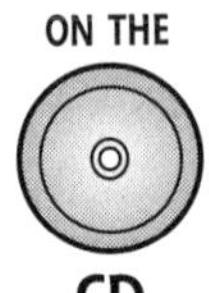

This program is very helpful in finding errors, providing relevant information, and making suggestions. Such suggestions include, for example, recommendations about what to do in cases where a tag has been deprecated.

Project 2 consists of a total of ten HTML documents, namely the following:

- index.html
- links.html
- gnote2.html
- home.html
- month.html
- specials.html
- inventory.html
- articles.html
- services.html
- contact.html

When these files are checked in CSE HTML Validator, the evaluation is the same in each case: "No errors or warnings reported!"

Excellent! This positive evaluation goes a long distance in assuring that browsers compatible with HTML 4.0 will be able to handle the Project 2 Web site. Despite my good results, you should check your own files to make sure that no typos or oversights have led to errors in the HTML that you've created while working on this project.

Note

Don't be dismayed if you find numerous errors showing up in your HTML—at least, not if you do what I do. I often use the cut-and-paste technique to quickly create things like tables or other items that are very similar, and then go in and change details. It's much easier than typing the same words over and over again. If you use cut and paste without first checking the HTML closely, you easily can compound errors and make things come across as worse than they really are.

Comparing Browsers

In testing the Web site for this project, I tried to get as close as I could to the real world by checking the site in the major browsers. I did not test it in Internet Explorer 4.0, because I used that browser as I built the site, and I know it handles the entire site well.

The Project 2 Web site worked without problems in IE 3.02. That was the expected result, because the only tag used that is new to HTML 4.0 (`<DIV ALIGN="center">`) was accompanied by the older `<CENTER>` tag.

The Project 2 Web site worked perfectly in the version of Netscape Navigator included as part of Netscape Communicator 4. The links all worked, and when I clicked on the image maps of the Guitar of the Month page, the pictures appeared by themselves in the content frame. By clicking on the Back button, I returned to the Guitar of the Month page. When I clicked on the audio link, it played immediately. Clicking on the video link made the video window appear by itself in the content frame. I clicked on the picture to make the video play, although nothing indicates this is what the user should do.

Trying the Web site in Navigator Gold 3.01 went without a hitch. The only peculiarities came on the Guitar of the Month page. When I clicked on the video link, the video appeared in the content frame all by itself. The video played when I clicked on the picture itself. When I clicked on the audio link, the clip played right away. When Navigator tried to generate the external viewer to show the close-up pictures, it didn't work because it couldn't find the application. The problem wasn't due to the HTML; it appeared to be due to an installation problem.

Everything worked well in America Online, with one exception: When I clicked on a link to view a picture and then clicked on AOL's Back button, nothing happened.

None of the problems encountered in any browser were major, but they were all things you'd certainly want to investigate and correct before launching an actual site, if there's a reasonable expectation that some of your visitors might use the same browsers that experienced problems.

Avoiding Problems

A few key points to remember can help you avoid problems with your HTML:

- First, make sure that you close all the container tags.
- If you cut and paste your HTML, you need to make sure that what you are pasting is correct. If it's not, you will only cause yourself more trouble, because you will have that many more corrections to make.
- Be on the lookout for missing pound signs in attribute values.
- Finally, here's one other point to remember that can help you minimize problems: If you know your audience and have a good indication of the browsers they are likely to use, then you can take extra care to make sure that your Web site works in those specific browsers. Doing so ensures that the majority of your audience will be able to view and use your Web site without any difficulty.

If you are careful about these items, you are bound to vastly reduce the number of errors in your HTML documents.

When cleaning up errors, begin by supplying the end tags that are missing. That's likely to help with several other types of errors, such as nesting problems and tags that are invalid where they are located.

Summary

This chapter discussed adding forms to your Web site. Forms add a great deal of functionality, but you must be prepared either to create the necessary scripts or to find a host server that already has those scripts available for your use. Your other option—useful when asking for non-critical information—is to use a simple Mailto form. This kind of form sends the user's response to you via e-mail, which would not be safe for confidential information.

This chapter also discussed adding sound to your Web site. Creating the sound file involves several decisions, such as sampling rate, bit rate, and file format. To insert the file into your HTML, you merely create a hyperlink to the file. In addition, the chapter covered adding video to a Web site. If you're striving for a high-impact commercial Web site, this task may best be left to professionals. On the other hand, a hobbyist or a business owner who wants to learn how to create Web video certainly can do so. A video capture card and video editing software are the primary necessities for anyone who wants to create high-quality video for the Web. Streaming video may require other software or expenses. As a rule, downloadable files present the user with better quality, but streaming video doesn't require the user to wait for the entire file to download. Downloadable files are preferable for short videos, whereas longer videos are more practical if presented as streaming video.

Another subject of this chapter was how to add animation to your Web site. Animation essentially consists of individual frames that the user views at a rate you set when you create the animation. Some animations give the impression of movement, but others—such as the one in this chapter—consist of discrete graphics, meaning that change occurs from frame to frame without an attempt to imitate movement. The best way to create animation is to use one of the programs intended specifically for that purpose.

Finally, this chapter discussed testing the Project 2 Web site by running the pages through the CSE HTML Validator and checking the site in various browsers.

Project 2 Summary

This project added greatly to your arsenal of HTML skills. The first project brought you to the point where you could create an attractive, perfectly functional Web site, and this second project built on those skills, giving you the ability to refine your Web site.

You learned techniques for building tables, which are more than just the presentation of information in columnar format. Cells in a table can hold graphics as well as text, so tables are a popular means of placing graphics and text exactly where you want them on a Web page.

You implemented frames to divide a browser window into multiple windows. Each window was linked to certain HTML content, and one of the windows served as the main window, where new items would appear whenever a user clicked on a link. Frames can be very slick, but not all Web browsers are capable of handling frames, so you must consider the audience you anticipate for your Web site before taking the plunge into using frames. You also learned how to provide alternate content for users with browsers that cannot handle frames.

To gather information from your visitors, you created a form for your Web site. Forms are more common on business sites, and less so on personal sites. Companies use forms for activities such as taking orders from customers, accepting addresses from people who want to be on a mailing list, or having site visitors respond to survey questions.

Another useful skill you learned is creating image maps. You defined hot regions within a graphic (GIF or JPEG) to serve as links. Image maps are an effective (and attractive) alternative to text links, as long as you make it clear to visitors that the image contains links. Along with image maps, you incorporated multimedia features such as sound and video into the Web site you built in this project.

HANDS ON PROJECT 3

THE ADVANCED WEB SITE

- Selecting Web site features that are consistent with your chosen tone for the site
- Developing a multiple-stage opening page with a fade effect
- Implementing a scrolling marquee and pulsing text
- Working with JavaScript commands
- Incorporating Java applets into HTML pages
- Validating form input for various field types
- Learning to use cascading style sheets

Project Overview

It's time to take your HTML pages to the next level. This project moves from the simple Web-based business you developed in Project 2 to a more complicated organizational setup, a guitar museum with its virtual doors open to the general public.

This Web site will offer eye candy as well as substance to encourage visitors to stick around and explore the site longer. The pages you'll create for Project 3 are capable of doing much more than just displaying simple text and graphics. Thanks to scripting and applets, there will be items that move, items that disappear, and other surprises to help keep visitors involved and interested in what your site has to offer.

By organizing information about a dozen guitar brands, you'll learn how to present large amounts of content in efficient ways. You'll make revision and maintenance of the Web site easier through the addition of cascading style sheets that allow you to make simple changes in one location to affect a number of pages simultaneously.

Like Project 2, this project includes a form to accept information from visitors. Because people sometimes make mistakes when filling out forms, you'll learn in this project how to stop improper data at the moment of input, before it's submitted to the server. You'll even provide messages to notify users if particular problems are found with their input.

What Is the Advanced Web Site?

In the first two projects, you learned how to create a basic Web site, and how to create an intermediate site with a bit more functionality and dash. There's still another level to explore: the advanced Web site, with flashy features you've probably come to admire in other Web sites. These features take more knowledge and work to create, but the end effect is well worth it. In this project, an online guitar museum, you'll learn how to make HTML pages that are as much applications or programs as they are Web pages.

Web sites today employ a wide variety of tricks to entice users to stay a while. This one will use a fade-in, fade-out effect that's easy to do, using a single JavaScript command. It'll also use a Java marquee that scrolls. Movement always wows the crowds.

Setting the Tone for the Site

Just as the previous projects had their own tones, this project has to establish one too. For the museum, the Webmaster could adopt generally a scholarly tone, a reverential tone, or a playful tone.

A scholarly tone would probably appeal to researchers, and the site could be designed to assist in scholarly research. Pages would be devoted to times, dates, places, and other data. Exhibits would trace guitar types through the decades or centuries. The emphasis would be on the guitars and their histories and uses, with a special emphasis on facts and figures.

On the other hand, the site could be given over to lovers of particular guitar music. The site might then be organized into sections on jazz, blues, flamenco, and so forth. The tone would be that of homage, of striking a visual chord to complement the musical chords.

Yet another possibility would make the site both fun and practical. This would be a site meant to popularize and entertain, with education being more of a happy byproduct.

This project will take a somewhat playful tack. The site will be designed to attract both the working musician and the casual fan. All other decisions will now flow from this one.

The Opening Page

In Figure 10.1, both the singer on the left and the museum's name on the right are interlaced GIFs, which you have already learned about. These GIFs slowly materialize against the black backgrounds of the two side-by-side frames, making the singer look as though he's "beaming in" to the stage.

But what's an opening page without a menu? In Figure 10.2, the singer has vanished, replaced by the menu. This happens about eight seconds after the singer first appears. The museum name stays. The menu is an image map, which you also already know about.

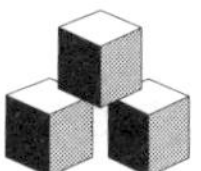

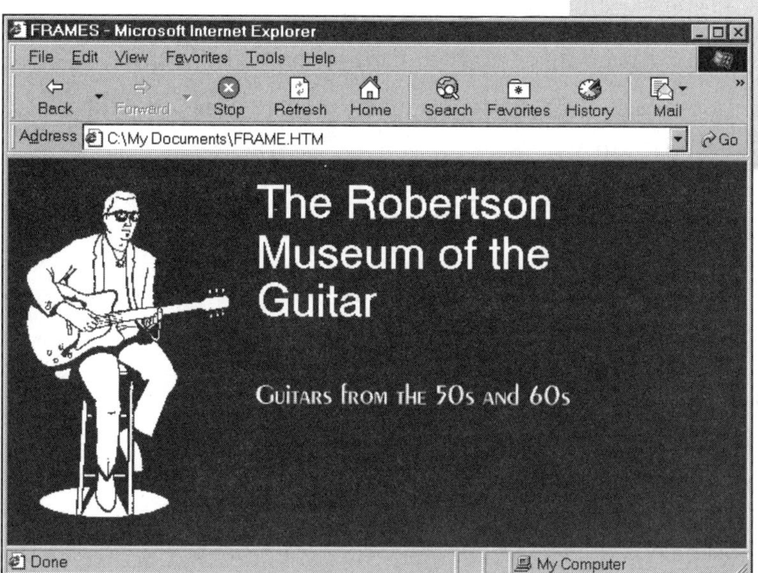

Figure 10.1 This is the first stage of the museum's opening page.

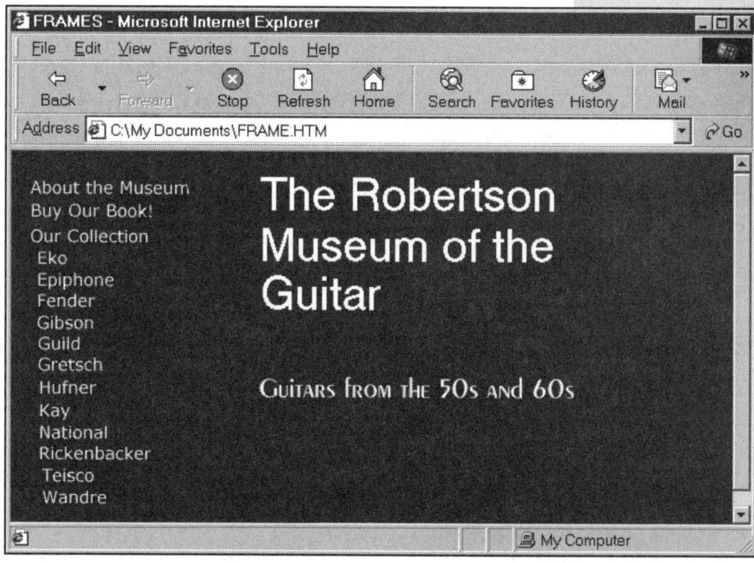

Figure 10.2 This is the second stage of the opening page.

In Project 3, you're going to develop three pages:

- The opening page that you've already seen in this chapter
- The "book page," where the user can leave a name and address to obtain a brochure
- One of the 12 "guitar brand pages," where the museum talks about its collection of each brand of guitar

The Book Page

The book page, `book.html`, is the sort you've doubtless encountered on the Web (see Figure 10.3). The museum uses this page to sell things, of course, but as with most organizations it's using the page to compile mailing lists of possible donors. For this month, the museum is showcasing its world-famous book on guitars of the Fifties and Sixties.

The museum could simply write a basic form, as you've already learned how to do. But computer users are notoriously sloppy when they fill

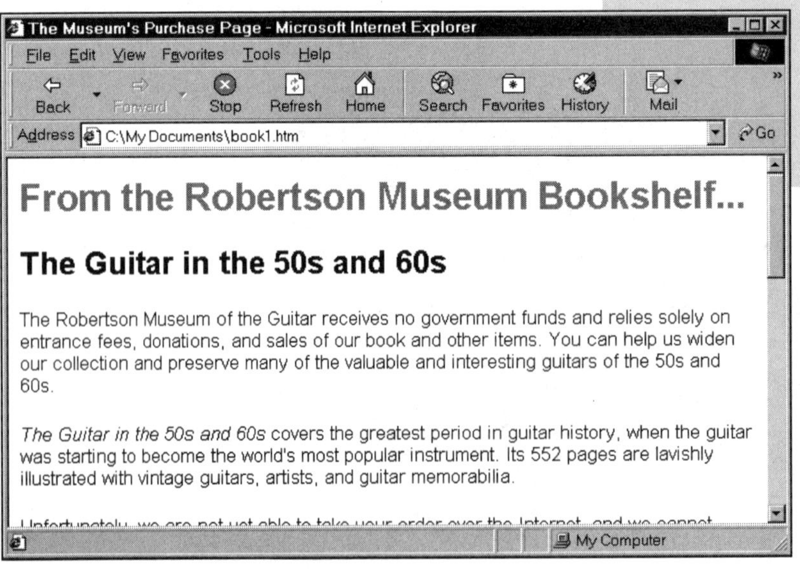

Figure 10.3 The book page is a form that can gather information from the visitor.

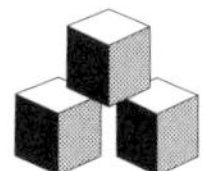

out forms, and you don't want the poor museum Webmaster to spend part of his morning sifting through obviously unusable data. Why not have the visitor's own computer do that checking? This checking, called "validation," makes sure that everything is filled in properly before the form is sent to the museum's server.

There's a JavaScript script on `book.html` that checks these things:

- That the first name is filled in
- That the last name is filled in
- That the address is filled in
- That the ZIP or ZIP+4 is filled out with the proper characters
- Whether the visitor has left comments

Figure 10.4 shows the alert box that the script pops up when the visitor mistakenly types a letter A into the ZIP code field. The script doesn't buy it, and it won't send the data with that A in there.

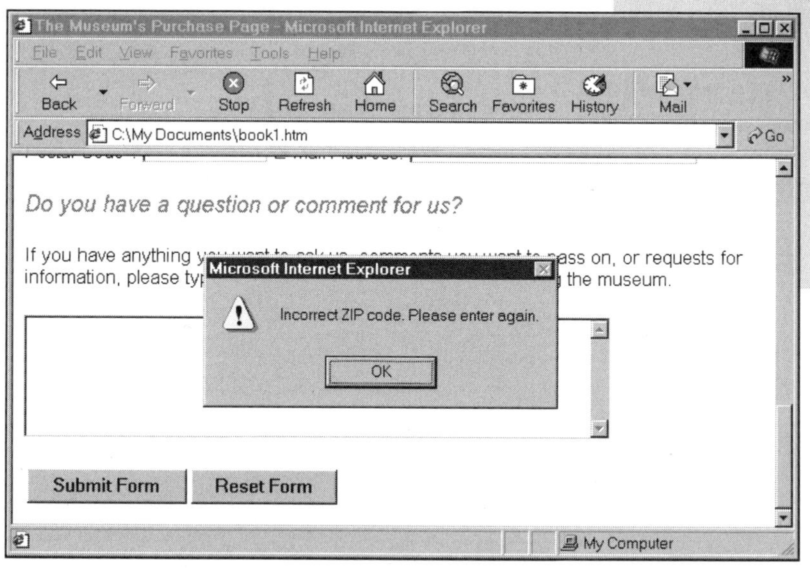

Figure 10.4
The visitor sees this alert box when the ZIP code entry has something invalid, like a letter of the alphabet, typed in it.

The Guitar Brand Page

Because the museum has such a wide variety of guitar brands in its collection, 12 in all, it has to present each brand on its own page (see Figure 10.5).

True to the museum's chosen design for this Web site, the top applet is a fun, eye-catching scrolling marquee and pulsing colored brand name. The marquee and pulsing name are courtesy of a Java applet.

The text in the guitar brand page is under the control of a cascading style sheet. In Figure 10.6, the text about the Fender company is 12 point, maroon, Times New Roman.

In Figure 10.7, with the changing of a single line in the connected style sheet, the text is reloaded as 12 point, red, Arial.

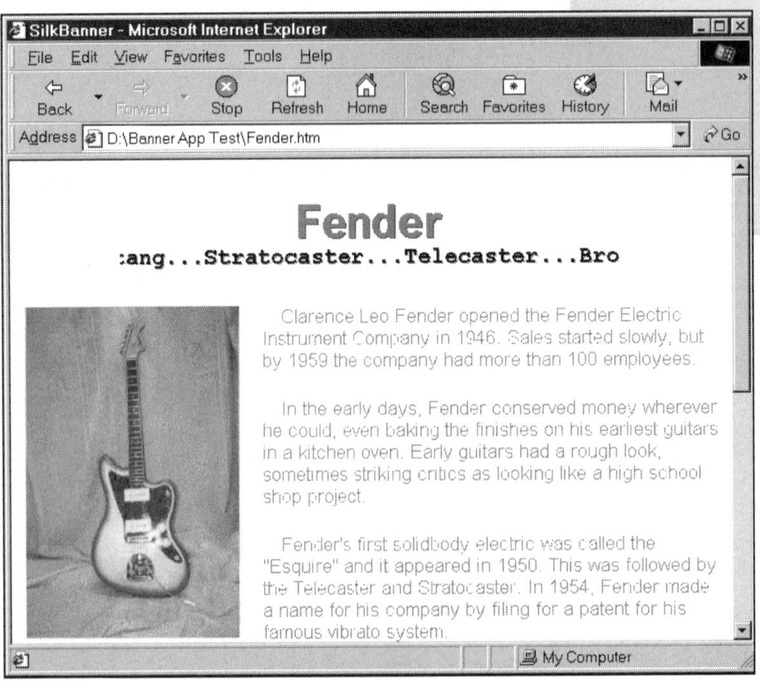

Figure 10.5
The guitar brand page, with its scrolling applet, is replicated for each brand in the museum's collection.

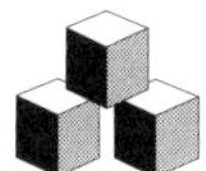

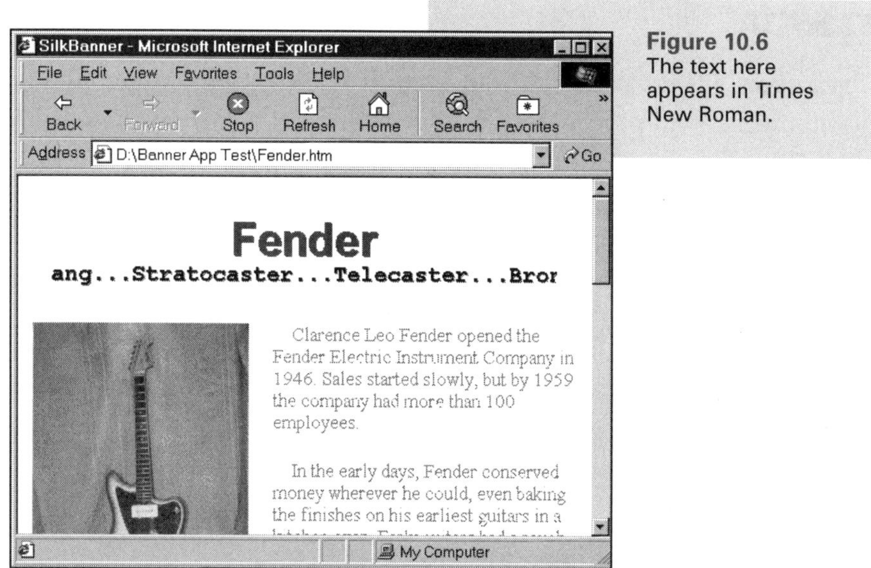

Figure 10.6
The text here appears in Times New Roman.

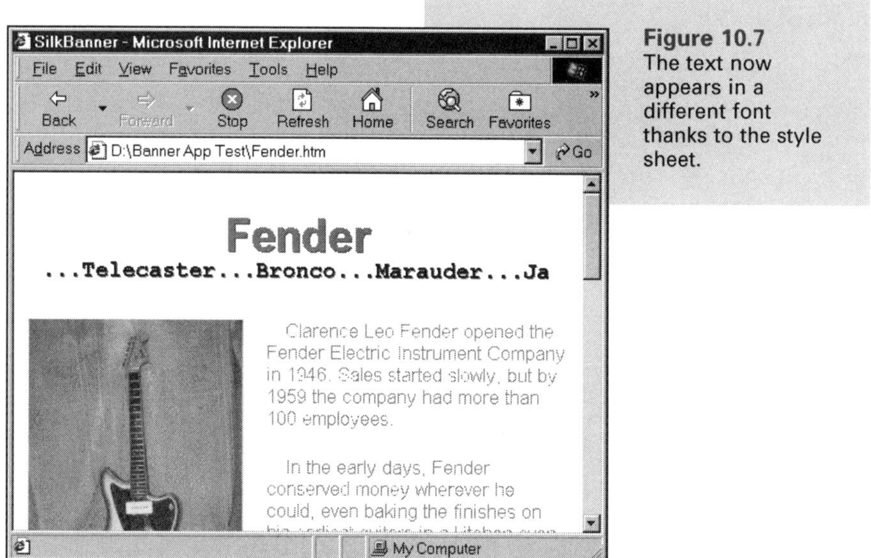

Figure 10.7
The text now appears in a different font thanks to the style sheet.

Once you master simple changes like that, you'll be ready to explore the many more sophisticated possibilities that cascading style sheets offer for your Web pages.

Summary

In the previous projects, you worked with HTML tags and graphics to achieve your Web page effects. This third project builds on those skills while showing you how to incorporate advanced features such as scripting, applets, and cascading style sheets.

CHAPTER 11

Designing the Advanced Web Site

When engineers design buildings or programmers design applications, most don't create a total design in one shot. Instead, most designers of any kind get a general idea of how they want the design to look and feel before they start working on the subunits that they will eventually bolt together. Then they check to see if there are places where one section is crowding out parts of another section.

For this project, the goal of the look and feel is to be interesting and fun, with the hope that education will follow. And with any luck, the site will prompt the user to buy something.

Look and Feel

"Look and feel" is a shorthand way of referring to the site's visual qualities—the impression that's left on the visitor. To check look and feel, you can build a site dummy with visuals that approximate what the visitor will eventually see. In this chapter you'll do exactly that. In the next chapter you'll start adding the engines that make it go.

Operations

What will the site and its pages do? How is it to function? Even though you're not adding much operational code at this point, you need to plan for it.

How Close to the Bleeding Edge?

Technology designers always have a stark question to answer: How close to the bleeding edge do we get? In this case, the bleeding edge consists of daring uses of new technologies and standards. The bleeding edge is a risky place to be, especially in an arena like the Web where competing powerhouses like Microsoft and Netscape can't agree on browser standards.

Although the Cascading Style Sheet standards are controlled by the W3C, not by any specific browser maker, the browser manufacturers can implement the standard quite differently. And even if their current implementation of standards is similar, there's no guarantee that their next versions will be compatible. Write a style sheet that depends too much on a specific browser's interpretation of advanced CSS2 standards, and your shiny new site could be impossible to view in any other browser.

Even using cascading style sheets at all is a bit of a stretch just now, because only browsers that read HTML 4 can use them.

This project takes a conservative approach, keeping well back from the bleeding edge. But it will nevertheless use cascading style sheets, because the newest browsers do implement it, although to different degrees.

Browser Compatibility

Browsers have different strengths and weaknesses. For example, Navigator has layers that are script-accessible, but Internet Explorer doesn't. So given the disparity of browsers, how do you design?

You have three choices here:

- You can design for a given browser and ignore the users of another brand. This can result in some disgruntled users, although it does let you take advantage of a single browser's best features. This is the tactic often taken for intranets, where the company has control over which browsers the employees are using, and thus the browser is known.
- You can design for both by supplying code for both, with an autodetect script that figures out which browser a visitor is using. Supplying dual coding is tricky to do initially, very labor- and time-intensive, and hard to update, but it shows you're really concerned about your users' comfort.
- You can design code that's plain vanilla and runs equally well on both major browsers, giving up the most powerful features of both, but making your life much easier.

This project takes the plain vanilla road. The HTML and scripting used here should run almost anywhere. If you have a huge staff, buckets of money, and your company depends on Web surfers for its daily bread, you might want to go the extra miles and design your site to autodetect and feed the user pages that are tailored specifically for his browser. Few of us have such luxuries of staff, time, or money. Keeping the site vanilla results in a good site for much less of an investment.

Designing the Pages

This site includes:

- An opening page
- A section about the various brands of guitar the museum has
- A place to buy something

You will not create every page in this Web site during Project 3, but after you've created the initial pages, the rest won't be any problem for you.

Designing the Opening Page

For this project, I wanted something snazzy to pull in the visitor. A single page with the museum's name on it would suffice as a basic requirement, but it doesn't have any kind of magnetism about it (see Figure 11.1).

I started with the idea of an artist on stage, all by himself/herself, strumming away. The artist should take up enough screen real estate to be prominent and not be just a little decorative icon in one corner. Could I make that figure appear out of the darkness, as though being picked out by a spotlight? And if I could, then what happens?

Well, the museum's name needs to be in the opening page somewhere, sometime, as does a menu for navigating the site, or at least a control to take the visitor into a navigation page after the opening fun stuff. Here's one of our first big decisions. Do we give the visitor a menu on the first page, or do as some designers are wont to do and make the visitor see an initial "splash" page with a clickable graphic that has to be activated to actually get into the site?

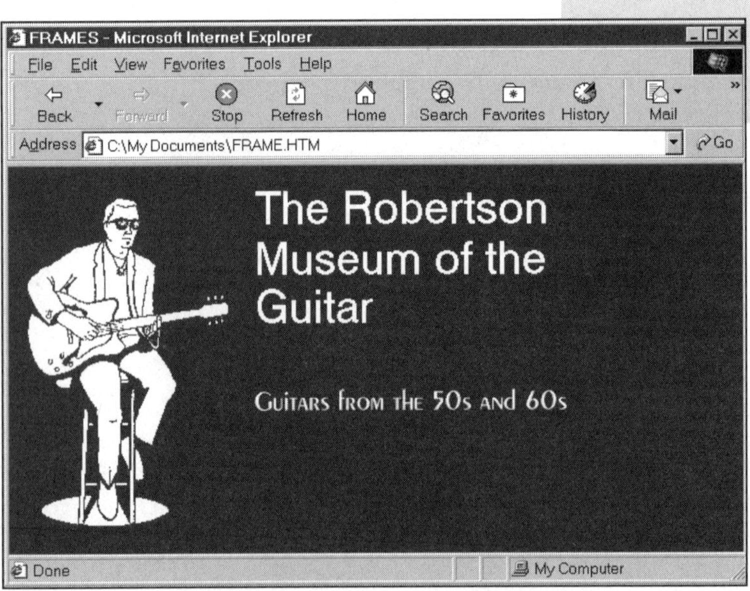

Figure 11.1
Here's the first stage of the opening page.

The evidence I've seen convinces me that most users aren't overly impressed with "splash" pages that force them to click again to actually enter the site. Many users are peevish about wasting their time and don't want to wait and work any more than is necessary to enter a site. So let's put the guitar museum's menu on the opening screen just to be neighborly.

Still, that's a lot of stuff to pack into a single window: a museum name, an appearing artist, and a menu. And it's not a great idea to crowd the opening page with all of them. Something has to become the focal point.

Remember that readers don't see things as totalities. Instead, they scan. That applies to application interfaces, browser windows, or printed pages. If all page elements are equally weighted, the average person's eyes jump to the upper-left corner and then start working sideways and down.

But of course visual designers don't allow that to happen. They use page elements to pull the eye where they want it to go. In general, brighter colors, greater contrast, and movement are all "eye magnets" that pull the viewer's attention. A page with a dancing bear, a day-glow orange headline, and white text on a black box offers the poor user no cue indicating where to look first. This is the "three-ring circus" design that's often the despair of the Web surfer.

So let's not let the user be confounded. This site will be designed to show only one magnetic element at a time. Start with the background. Because the performer appears on a supposedly black stage, the background will be black. And because more than one element will appear, it would be prudent to put them into frames so that they can be easily controlled by a script or HTML code. Frames let you exercise closer positioning of elements by establishing fixed points in the browser window.

Whenever possible, design so as to make things easy on yourself.

Launch Notepad and enter this code. Save it as `index.html`:

```
<HTML>
<HEAD><TITLE>The Robertson Museum of the Guitar</TITLE></HEAD>
<FRAMESET FRAMEBORDERS="no" BORDER="0" COLS="200,*">
<FRAME FRAMEBORDERS="no" SRC="artist.html" NAME="menu" SCROLLING="no">
<FRAME FRAMEBORDERS="no" SRC="name.html" NAME="main">
</FRAMESET>
<NOFRAMES>I'm sorry, but your browser can't render frames.</NOFRAMES>
</HTML>
```

This kind of page is familiar to you by now. This is a frameset page, which splits the browser window into sections that can be separately controlled. You can open this in your browser, but it's frankly not much to look at yet, just a blank window (see Figure 11.2).

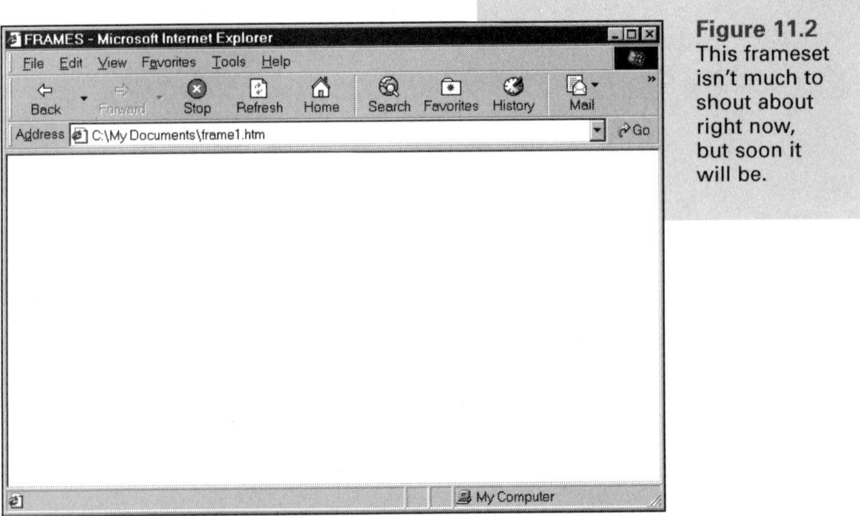

Figure 11.2 This frameset isn't much to shout about right now, but soon it will be.

Now you need `artist.html`, the page that goes into the narrower of the two frames. It has an interlaced GIF that will make the performer appear slowly, as if "beaming in" to the darkened venue. The faster your connection, the less time the beam-in effect lasts. Over an ISDN line, the effect is almost instantaneous, but over the standard 28.8K or 56K line, there'll be a discernible "firm-up" time about it. There are other ways of ensuring that the user sees a beam-in effect no matter what the

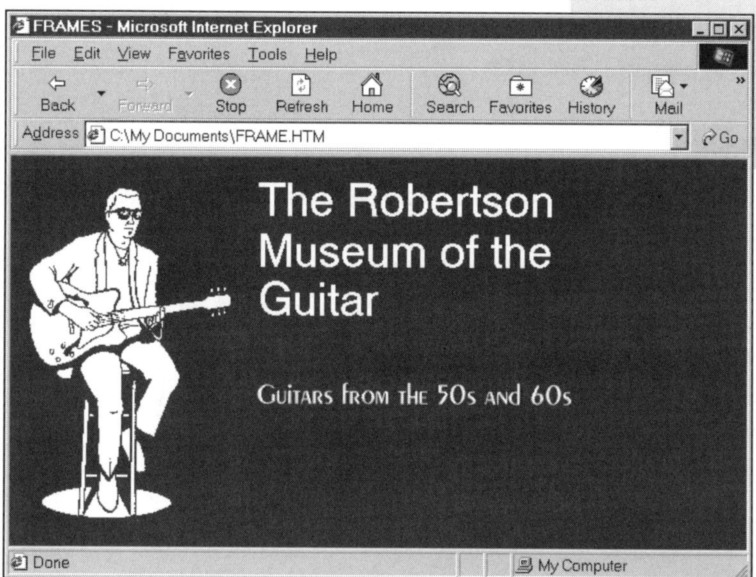

Figure 11.3
The performer here is fully beamed in alongside the museum name.

transmission speed. One such way would be to render the artist as a Java applet, for example. This is much more work, though.

You'll also need `name.html`, which has another interlaced GIF of the name of the museum. The museum name was created in Paint Shop Pro, while the performer was hand-drawn by a local artist and scanned (see Figure 11.3).

ON THE CD

Both of these graphics are available on the accompanying CD.

EXERCISE

1. Type this page into Notepad and save it as `artist.html` (make sure you save it into the same directory as `index.html`):

```
<HTML>
<HEAD>
<TITLE>The Robertson Museum of the Guitar</TITLE>
</HEAD>
<BODY BGCOLOR="#000000">
<SCRIPT>
```

```
setTimeout ("location = 'menuframe.html' ", 8000);
</SCRIPT>
<IMG SRC="images/singer.gif">
</BODY>
</HTML>
```

2. Type this page into Notepad and save it as `name.html` (again, make sure that it's in the same directory):

```
<HTML>
<HEAD><TITLE>Museum of the Guitar</TITLE></HEAD>
<BODY BGCOLOR="#000000">
<IMG SRC="images/name.gif">
</BODY>
</HTML>
```

3. Type this page into Notepad:

```
<HTML>
<HEAD><TITLE>The Robertson Museum of the Guitar</TITLE></HEAD>
<BODY BGCOLOR="#000000">
<IMG SRC="images/menu.gif">
</BODY>
</HTML>
```

4. Save it as `menuframe.html`.

To see a rough approximation of the opening page effect, put `index.html`, `artist.html`, `menuframe.html`, `name.html`, `singer.gif`, `name.gif`, and `menu.gif` into the same directory and point your browser to `index.html`. The effect won't be as dramatic as it will be downloading from a server, because loading from a local drive is many times faster than loading from a server over the Web. The interlaced GIFs in your local environment will almost spring to life, rather than resolving themselves slowly as they do when downloading from a distance (see Figure 11.4).

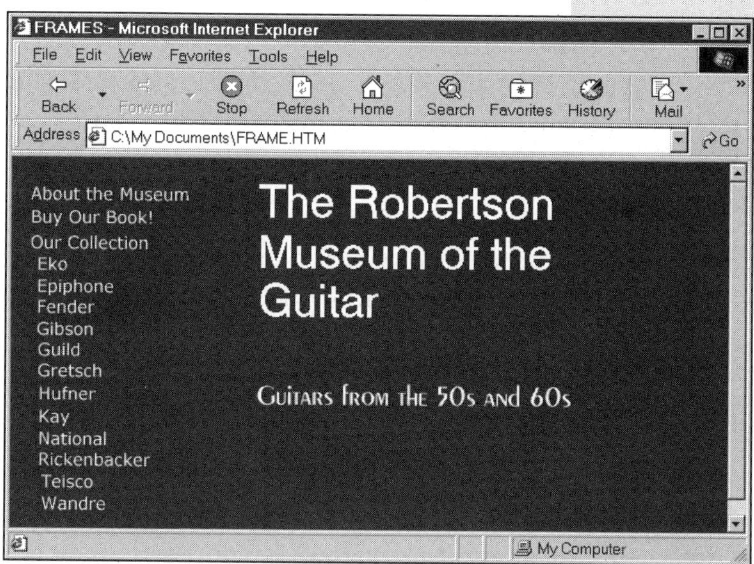

Figure 11.4
This is the opening page after the singer leaves the stage and the menu appears in his place.

ANALYSIS

So far, you have a frameset and three HTML pages.

In `artist.html`, notice the `setTimeout` command inside the `<SCRIPT>` container tag. This single command line is a script in JavaScript, albeit a very short one.

The `setTimeout` function runs a timer that executes another command when it times out. `setTimeout` has two parameters: the thing you want to have happen, followed by the time in milliseconds. The time isn't all that precise, mind you, but it's close. In this case, the value **`8000`** gives you about eight seconds, and then the property `"location = 'menuframe.html'"` kicks in.

A Little about JavaScript

The tiny little script in `artist.html` is a good opportunity to cram in some material about JavaScript that you'll have to know eventually, such as what an "object" and a "property" are.

THE DOCUMENT OBJECT MODEL

The *document object model (DOM)* is the heart of JavaScript's operations. If you've only used languages like Basic, C, or Pascal before, you may be in for a surprise when you cross over into the object-dominated world. If you're familiar with Java or C++, on the other hand, this will be old stuff.

JavaScript looks at its little browser universe as a collection of objects, of discrete things that may be large or small but are always separate from other objects. Objects can communicate with one another. Perhaps the most critical concept is that objects may be "parents" to yet more objects, which are called "children."

We think in object-type terms all the time without realizing it. Look around the house, for example. We know what a "stove" is in general, and what it does, even though there are many different variations on the theme: gas, electric, broiler or no broiler, and so forth. A stove manufacturer usually make several different models to satisfy a range of customers (no pun intended).

A CookRight stove would generically be an object that heats food. It has familiar controls and a familiar function. But when you go to the appliance store to buy a CookRight, you'll be shown the CookRight 2000, the CookRight 3000, and the CookRight Ultima. Each of these models is a child object of the CookRight stove, even though strictly speaking there isn't any generic CookRight stove sitting around somewhere whose knobs you can twiddle.

So does "object technology" seem a little academic, a little unreal? After all, if there's no single, basic, generic "CookRight stove" on the showroom floor, does it make any sense to even call such a hypothetical thing an object?

It does. Just because you can't see an object doesn't mean it has no existence. For the CookRight company, the basic stove is, indeed, a real object. To the stove designers and engineers, the CookRight company has a set of conventions that they stick to when they design all their stoves. The way the knobs are formed and laid out, the lines of the sheet metal, the kind of controls used, the quality standards—all are incorporated into each and every child object, what the CookRight people call a "model." It identifies a CookRight model as uniquely a CookRight. It's the "CookRightness" that makes a CookRight customer pick it out at a glance on the showroom floor. So there is, indeed, a CookRight object. But it's invisible to you and is expressed only by proxy, by its child objects.

Consider the situation in your browser. There's a "document" object, even though you don't see it. Don't believe that? Remember that a document object looks just like a blank browser screen. Visually, there's no way to even know if a blank document is loaded into the browser. The document object is revealed by its children: text, graphics, applets, forms, and other items. But the document object is always there.

The same hierarchical relationship works on more specific levels, too. Think of the CookRight Ultima or any other specific model as having its own children: burners, knobs, hardware, lights, racks, and so on.

This object-oriented way of viewing things in our lives is natural for us. Consider that you care about the specific model of your CookRight only when ordering parts or buying a new stove. After that, you interact with the stove only to cook on it. While cooking, you're concerned only with the controls and the cooking surfaces. You're not concerned with its warranty, its availability, or most of the other factors you weighed when you were buying it. In other words, you're only using the objects and the object level that you need at the moment. When necessary, you can climb up the hierarchy and interact with more general aspects. If you wanted to, you probably could call the CookRight factory directly and talk about the CookRight parent object, although the engineers may think you were strange if you did.

See Figure 11.5 for a chart of the CookRight objects' relationship. The same approach is used for cars, computers, light fixtures, and nearly everything else in human existence. We don't just own things. We own types of things, child objects of other objects. We interact with those objects by driving them, cooking on them, and switching them on or off.

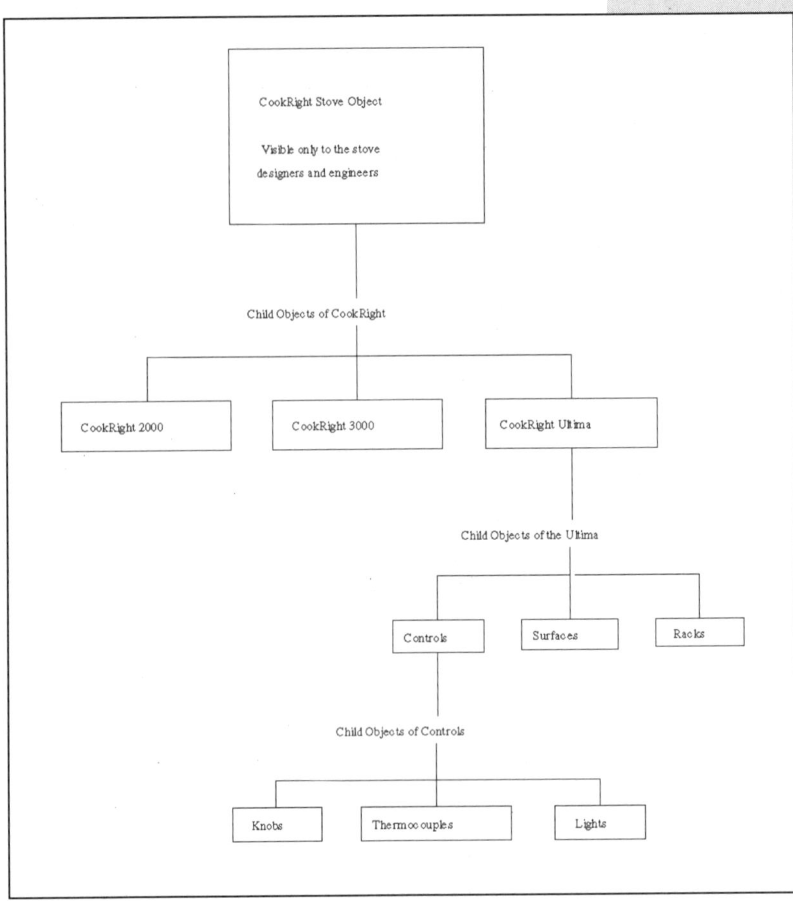

Figure 11.5
This is a "family portrait" of parent and child stove objects.

The document object in its turn has a parent object, the window, which again is an object you don't really see. But when you start writing scripts, you'll find out what the CookRight engineers know to be true, that objects are often visible only to those who have to manipulate them. Later you'll be using JavaScript to directly address objects in the browser universe, and the objects you can manipulate will include `window` and `document`.

An important characteristic of objects is *inheritance*. Just as biological organisms inherit traits from their parents, child objects inherit traits from their parent objects. For example, the CookRight Ultima "inherits" the styling lines of its parent, the factory-visible CookRight general

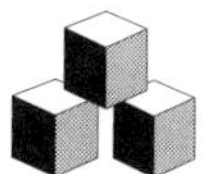

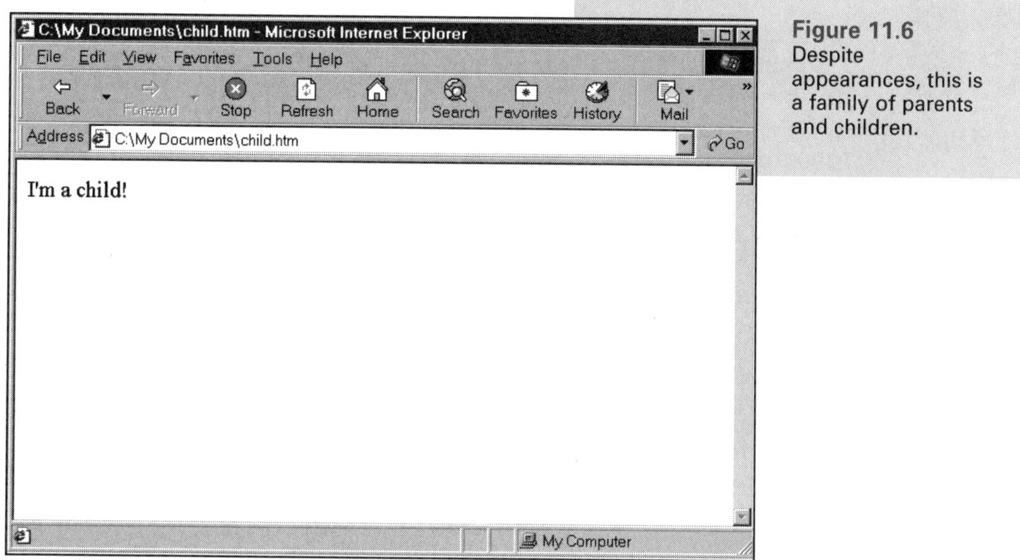

Figure 11.6
Despite appearances, this is a family of parents and children.

stove. In the browser world, the `<P>` tag is a child object of the `<BODY>` tag. If the `<BODY>` tag is defined with green, all of its children will be green, too, including headings and paragraphs, unless you do something to change a particular child object.

In Figure 11.6, for example, the text `I'm a child!` is the `<P>` tag child of the unseen `<BODY>` tag, which itself is a child of the document.

This hierarchy of things may be handy for conceptualizing the whole browser display, but if that were as far as it went nobody would bother with it. The magic lies in how objects talk to one another, in how scripts can get data into and out of objects, and in how objects respond to being contacted. In effect, JavaScript talks to every object, including the document. To do this, JavaScript uses properties, functions, and methods, buzzwords you should learn thoroughly, because most object-type programs use them.

PROPERTIES

A *property* of an object is a part of its "body." An object's property is often a facet of its appearance, although it can be other things, too.

JavaScript calls the object that's loaded into the browser a "document." You probably know it as a "page." This leads to some tanglefooted language. An HTML page with a script on it can self-generate a second page that any user would swear is a new HTML page. It could even be argued that it *is* a new page. But it is still the same document as far as the script is concerned.

For a CookRight stove, properties would include its paint color, trim color, height, depth, and weight, as well as its upper temperature limits and the serial numbers of its various parts.

For example, there is a property `bgColor` for the background color of the document object. For many people, it makes more sense to phrase it the other way around: The document object has a property `bgColor`.

Still wrestling with the concept of properties? Try thinking about it in human terms. Each person (an object) has many properties: skin color, hair color, toe and finger counts, and so on.

You can't ask a stove about its properties. If you want to know its serial number, you have to crawl behind it with a flashlight. Using JavaScript, however, you can query a browser object about any of its properties, and the object will obligingly send back what the current properties are. If, for example, you write a script to query the document's `bgColor` property, the document object will tell you what the document's background color currently is. You then can have your script change that color or take some other action.

As confusing as it sounds, some objects are themselves properties of other objects. The button object, for example, is simultaneously an object itself, a child object of the form object, and a property of the form object. It's sort of like light being both a wave and a particle depending on what you're considering. When scripting, you can use the role of a button that suits your purpose at any given moment.

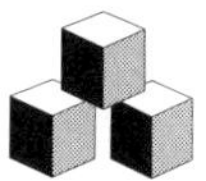

METHODS AND FUNCTIONS

A *method* tells an object to do whatever it is that the object was created to do. Unlike a property, which is a state of existence, a method is an activity.

Each object has its own specific methods. The CookRight Ultima has a "turn on front burner to medium" method. The document object in the browser has an "open" method that opens a document or another window. Humans have methods like "make coffee" and "log on for e-mail."

One of the really clever things about object-oriented programming is that you don't have to know how somebody else made the object do what it does; all you have to know is how to spark it into action. The programmer can act like a general issuing simple orders to the troops, not caring exactly how they execute the orders as long as the coffee gets done and the e-mail is downloaded.

Of course, there comes a time when you want to do something that does not have an object associated with it, such as converting a numeral string to an integer. These kinds of object-independent commands in JavaScript are called *functions*. There aren't very many of them with standard JavaScript, but you can write any number of your own functions. Much of the power of scripting comes from writing special functions. Most of the script you're going to write later in the project involves functions.

How the Location Method Works

Enough lecturing. Back to the code. This is how the itty-bitty script looked:

```
<SCRIPT>

setTimeout ("location = 'menuframe.html' ", 8000);

</SCRIPT>
```

`location` is a child object (and property) of `window`, and determines which URL the browser is pointing to. Remember that to a browser, the whole universe is composed only of places to point to, so `location` refers to where something interesting lives. The whole command line translates to "when eight seconds have elapsed, point the browser to the page menuframe.html in the same directory as the current URL and download it so it can be displayed here."

The setTimeout line waits eight seconds for the visitor to admire the singer, and then it loads the menu into the first frame, replacing the singer. This is how you're going to get the effect of singer, then singer and name, and then menu and name. The trick is done by reloading the first frame. But since the background is black, it looks as if the singer vanishes and the menu appears, rather than a whole page going away and being replaced by a new one.

There's yet another aspect of JavaScript that this one command line teaches. Review the line, paying attention to the several single and double quotation marks. JavaScript isn't terribly particular about using singles or doubles, but you have to be consistent, and you have to alternate when you nest them. In this example, there is an outer set of doubles, with an inner set of singles. If you don't alternate them properly when they're nested, the script won't work because the interpreter won't know what to do.

You could mimic this fade-in effect by using the HTML <META> tag. Rather than use setTimeout, you can experiment by including this code in an opening <META> tag in artist.html:

```
<META HTTP-EQUIV="Refresh" CONTENT="8; menuframe.html">
```

This line also refreshes the page eight seconds after it downloads.

This emphasizes that there are almost always two or three ways to do anything using HTML, JavaScript, and other page elements. I used the setTimeout function to illustrate the principles of JavaScript, and for no other particular reason. Use either method you like; just don't use both the script and the <META> tag refresh technique in the same document.

To Script or Not to Script

Scripts are marvelous creatures, but they're not always appropriate. Use scripts when you need to add some intelligence to your page, or if you need to do a trick that only a script will pull off. If a visitor needs to give your page some kind of input, you'll have to write a script to interpret the visitor's responses.

For example, a visitor might be asked to state a language preference: Spanish, French, or English. The visitor might be asked if she needs enlarged type, or whether she wants to see the graphics that take a long time to download.

Scripts carry their own problems, and one considerable problem is browser differences. Netscape created JavaScript, but when Microsoft put JavaScript into Internet Explorer, it actually used its own version of JavaScript, called JScript. Each browser has a slightly different document object model, too. The upshot is that scripts written for one browser may not work in the other. If you're working totally in IE, you might want to think about using VBScript, an all-Microsoft script language that has a syntax similar to Microsoft Visual Basic.

Another scripting dilemma is maintenance. The more wallop in your Web site, the more often you'll probably have to get in and update your code.

Yet another potential scripting "gotcha" is that browsers don't always handle errors very well. If you make a mistake in your coding, or if the browser isn't fully compatible with the version of JavaScript you've written in, the user can suddenly be face to face with obscure and puzzling message and error boxes, odd page behavior, or the simple inability of your script to run at all.

Some of the effects available in scripting can be duplicated in whole or in part with HTML 4 tags, like the page refresh described previously. Consider whether your page needs a script or if it can get by with HTML. As Thoreau said, "Simplify, simplify."

Designing the Book Page

The museum supports itself partly by the sale of merchandise, and this page is a good example of its enterprising spirit. Here a visitor can leave a name, address, e-mail, and comments, as well as get an order form and brochure sent to him (see Figure 11.7).

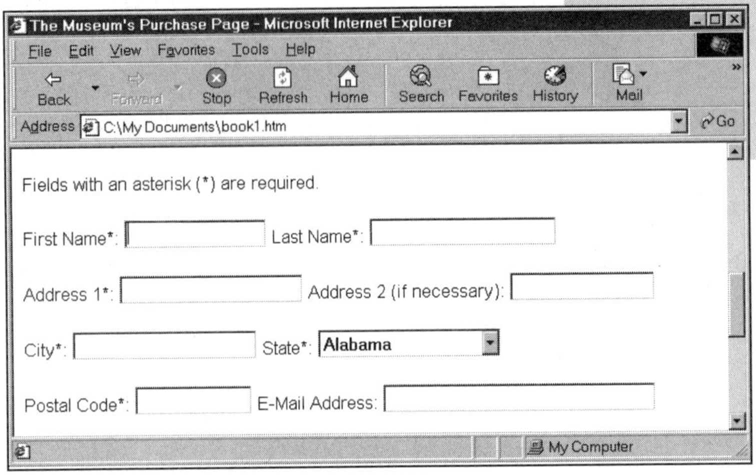

The Museum's Purchase Page - Microsoft Internet Explorer

File Edit View Favorites Tools Help

Back Forward Stop Refresh Home Search Favorites History Mail

Address C:\My Documents\book1.htm Go

Fields with an asterisk (*) are required.

First Name*: Last Name*:

Address 1*: Address 2 (if necessary):

City*: State*: Alabama

Postal Code*: E-Mail Address:

My Computer

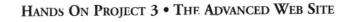

Figure 11.7
This is the book page's form for gathering user input.

Having a place to buy things is almost a regular part of Web site development nowadays. The typical purchase page has an online form for name, address, and so forth, and it includes a field for a credit card number. This process is often termed *e-commerce.* Using e-commerce, a company taking orders on the Web can process your name, address, and other ordering information, put in your order within the company, get it shipped, and send you e-mail confirming your order, all automatically. E-commerce sites are often large ones with sizable investments and big staffs.

The museum isn't set up to sell merchandise via e-commerce, but it can mail out a brochure of its gift shop offerings. The online form therefore takes the user's name, address, e-mail address, and comments. The data is validated locally (in the HTML page) rather than having to be sent back to the server. Validating the data in the browser, rather than on the server, speeds up operations by not requiring constant trips back to the server for data. If your user is on a 28.8K modem, it takes a while to ask the server for something and have it send back the page to the browser.

EXERCISE

Type this code into Notepad and save it as `book.html`. This is a dummy page, a page that you'll use only to see how the finished page will look, not how it will operate.

Although it's a long run of HTML, the typing won't be wasted effort, because the final `book.html` will be built on this foundation. If you typed a similar form into Notepad in an earlier project, you can open it now and modify it to match the following:

```
<HTML>
<HEAD>
<TITLE>The Museum's Purchase Page</TITLE>
<LINK REL=stylesheet HREF="museum.css" TYPE="text/css">
</HEAD>
<BODY>
<FONT SIZE="5" COLOR="red" FACE="arial">From the Robertson Museum
Bookshelf...</FONT>
<P>
<FONT SIZE="4"><B>The Guitar in the 50s and 60s</B></FONT></P>
<P>The Robertson Museum of the Guitar receives no government funds and relies
solely on entrance fees, donations, and sales of our book and other items.
You can help us widen our collection and preserve many of the valuable and
interesting guitars of the 50s and 60s.</P>
<P><I>The Guitar in the 50s and 60s</I> covers the greatest period in guitar
history, when the guitar was starting to become the world's most popular
instrument. Its 552 pages are lavishly illustrated with vintage guitars,
artists, and guitar memorabilia.</P>
<P>Unfortunately, we are not yet able to take your order over the Internet,
and we cannot solicit sales outside of the U.S. But we would like to send
our brochure that lists this book and dozens of other items about guitars
from the Golden Era. Please fill out the form below. You will receive your
brochure by return mail. Please allow four to six weeks for delivery.</P>
<P>Thank you for supporting the museum.</P>
<FORM NAME="visitorData" METHOD="post" ACTION="/htbin/generic">
<P>Fields with an asterisk (*) are required.</P>
<P><LABEL FOR="firstname">
First Name*:
</LABEL>
<INPUT TYPE="text" SIZE="15" MAXLENGTH="30" NAME="firstname">
```

```
<LABEL FOR="lastname">
Last Name*:
</LABEL>
<INPUT TYPE="text" SIZE="20" MAXLENGTH="30" NAME="lastname">
</P>
<P>
<LABEL FOR="address1">
Address 1*:
</LABEL>
<INPUT TYPE="text" SIZE="20" NAME="address1">
<LABEL FOR="address2">
Address 2 (if necessary):
</LABEL>
<INPUT TYPE="text" SIZE="15" NAME="address2">
</P>
<P><LABEL FOR="city">
City*:
</LABEL>
<INPUT TYPE="text" MAXLENGTH="40" NAME="city">
<LABEL FOR="state">
State*:
</LABEL>
<SELECT NAME="states" SIZE="1">
<OPTION>Alabama</OPTION>
<OPTION>Alaska</OPTION>
<OPTION>Arizona</OPTION>
<OPTION>Arkansas</OPTION>
<OPTION>California</OPTION>
<OPTION>Colorado</OPTION>
<OPTION>Connecticut</OPTION>
<OPTION>Delaware</OPTION>
<OPTION>District of Columbia</OPTION>
<OPTION>Florida</OPTION>
<OPTION>Georiga</OPTION>
<OPTION>Hawaii</OPTION>
<OPTION>Idaho</OPTION>
<OPTION>Illinois</OPTION>
<OPTION>Indiana</OPTION>
```

```
<OPTION>Iowa</OPTION>
<OPTION>Kansas</OPTION>
<OPTION>Kentucky</OPTION>
<OPTION>Louisiana</OPTION>
<OPTION>Maine</OPTION>
<OPTION>Maryland</OPTION>
<OPTION>Massachusetts</OPTION>
<OPTION>Michigan</OPTION>
<OPTION>Minnesota</OPTION>
<OPTION>Mississippi</OPTION>
<OPTION>Missouri</OPTION>
<OPTION>Montana</OPTION>
<OPTION>Nebraska</OPTION>
<OPTION>Nevada</OPTION>
<OPTION>New Hampshire</OPTION>
<OPTION>New Jersey</OPTION>
<OPTION>New Mexico</OPTION>
<OPTION>New York</OPTION>
<OPTION>North Carolina</OPTION>
<OPTION>North Dakota</OPTION>
<OPTION>Ohio</OPTION>
<OPTION>Oklahoma</OPTION>
<OPTION>Oregon</OPTION>
<OPTION>Pennsylvania</OPTION>
<OPTION>Rhode Island</OPTION>
<OPTION>South Carolina</OPTION>
<OPTION>South Dakota</OPTION>
<OPTION>Tennessee</OPTION>
<OPTION>Texas</OPTION>
<OPTION>Utah</OPTION>
<OPTION>Vermont</OPTION>
<OPTION>Virginia</OPTION>
<OPTION>Washington</OPTION>
<OPTION>West Virginia</OPTION>
<OPTION>Wisconsin</OPTION>
<OPTION>Wyoming</OPTION>
</SELECT></P>
<P><LABEL FOR="code">
```

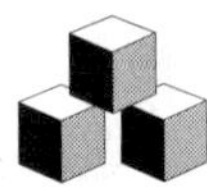


```
Postal Code*:
</LABEL>
<INPUT TYPE="text" SIZE="12" MAXLENGTH="15" NAME="code">
</P>
<P><LABEL FOR="email">
E-Mail Address:
</LABEL>
<INPUT TYPE="text" SIZE="30" MAXLENGTH="50" NAME="email">
</P>
<P><FONT SIZE="+1" COLOR="red"><EM><STRONG>Do you have a question or comment
for us?</STRONG></EM></FONT></P>
<P>If you have anything you want to ask us, comments you want to pass on, or
requests for information, please type it in the box below. And thanks for
visiting the museum.</P>
<P><TEXTAREA NAME="comments" ROWS="5" COLS=50></TEXTAREA></P>
<TABLE COLS="2">
<TR>
<TD><INPUT TYPE="button" VALUE="Submit Form">
</TD>
<TD><INPUT TYPE="button" VALUE="Reset Form">
</TD>
</TR>
</TABLE>
</FORM>
</BODY>
</HTML>
```

ANALYSIS

The page doesn't do anything interesting right now, but it's a good start on an interesting page. This page is a variation on the one you did in Project 2. It has been modified in some ways; for example, it lacks the radio buttons in the earlier version that let the user indicate "Yes, I have comments" or "No, I don't." Those buttons went away in this version because now the page itself will determine if there's a comment in the text box before bundling up the data and shipping it out to the server.

All of the font definitions are set in the tags right now. Later you'll learn how to get them out into a separate style sheet.

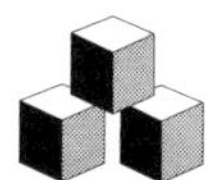

Designing the Guitar Brand Page

Each brand gets at least one page, and I want the pages to be matched in tone and appearance. I could set the various styles for each page on that individual page, but that's a lot of work both creating and maintaining the site. This is a prime place to use cascading style sheets. Then I can design once, write a single style sheet, and use the same styles over and over again on as many pages as necessary (see Figure 11.8).

Each individual brand page should also have at least one magnetic visual element, so each one has a Java applet. And in keeping with the principle of simpler is better, each page can use the same applet, even though its appearance will change from page to page. This particular Java applet will display the guitar brand and scroll several of that brand's models.

Along with the applet, the page needs some text for a short history of the Fender company. It would also be interesting to show an actual Fender guitar as an example.

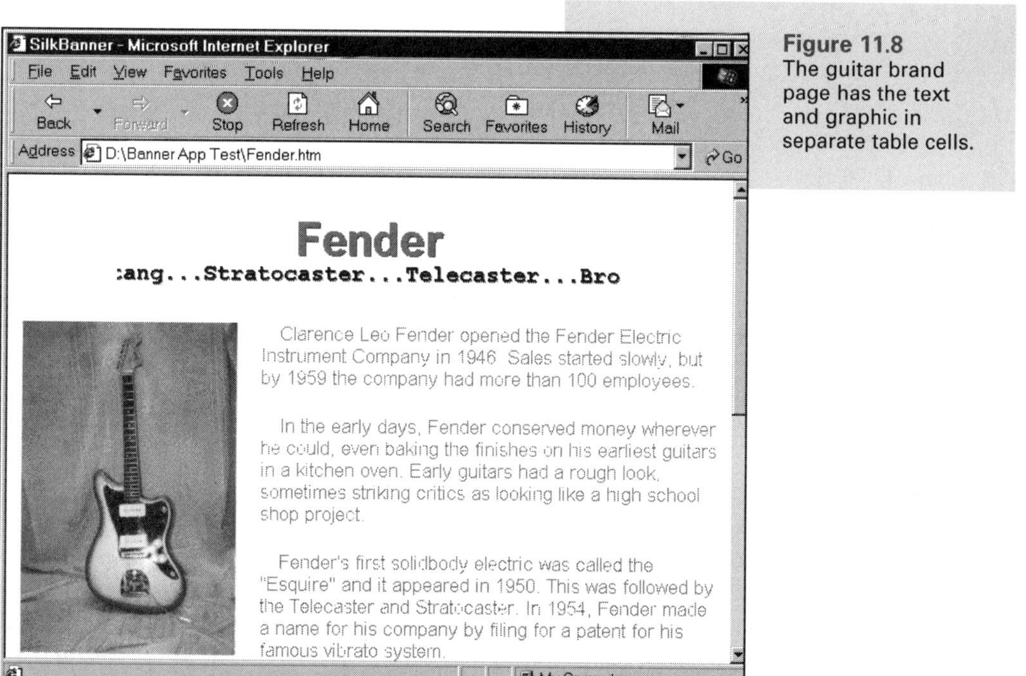

Figure 11.8
The guitar brand page has the text and graphic in separate table cells.

The easy way to do this is with a table without borders. There will have to be cell padding for the tables to get the text a decent distance apart. This cell padding will go away when you use the cascading style sheet later in the project.

EXERCISE

Here's the code for the basic page without the Java applet. Type this code into Notepad and save it as `fender.html`:

```
<!DOCTYPE HTML PUBLIC"-//W3/DTD HTML 4.0
Transitional//EN""http://www.w3.org/TR/REC-html40/loose.dtd">
<HTML>
<HEAD>
<TITLE>Fender</TITLE>
<LINK REL=stylesheet HREF="museum.css" TYPE="text/css">
</HEAD>
<BODY>
<TABLE BORDER="0" CELLPADDING="10">
<TR VALIGN="top">
<TD WIDTH="200"><IMG ALIGN="top" SRC="images/jazz490.jpg"><BR><P>This
Jazzmaster still has its original hang-tags. From the museum
collection.</P></TD>
<TD><P><FONT COLOR="red">Clarence Leo Fender opened the Fender Electric
Instrument Company in 1946. Sales started slowly, but by 1959 the company
had more than 100 employees.</P>
<P>
In the early days, Fender conserved money wherever he could, even baking the
finishes on his earliest guitars in a kitchen oven. Early guitars had a
rough look, sometimes striking critics as looking like a high school shop
project. </P>
<P>
Fender's first solidbody electric was called the "Esquire" and it appeared in
1950. This was followed by the Telecaster and Stratocaster. In 1954, Fender
made a name for his company by filing for a patent for his famous vibrato
system. </P>
<P>
The first truly famous Fender-playing artist was <EM>Buddy Holly</EM>, who
played a Stratocaster. With Holly behind the guitar, sales of the "Strat"
took off. Holly was followed into the Fender fold by <EM>Buck Owens</EM>,
who played a Telecaster.</P>
<P>
In 1965 CBS bought Fender. In the 60s, the company brought out a student
model, the Bronco, and a number of forgettable guitars such as the Musiclan-
der. But they also continued to make the Strat in a multitude of colors and
```

```
special configurations. <EM>Jimi Hendrix</EM> was one star who became a Strat
artist. But the company slid downhill during the latter part of the 60s, as
a prelude to its lackluster performance in the 70s.</P>
<P>
The museum has several fine Fenders, including an original Esquire, several
Stratocasters and Telecasters. We currently own three Stratocasters from the
1950s in original colors.</P></FONT>
</TD>
</TR>
</TABLE>
<CENTER>
<TABLE BORDER=0>
<TR>
<TD><A HREF="index.htm">Home</A></TD>
<TD><A HREF="book.htm">Buy our book</A></TD>
<TD><A HREF="about.htm">About the museum</A></TD>
<TD><A HREF="mailto:somebody@somewhere.net"><P>Contact us</A></TD>
</TR>
</TABLE>
</CENTER>
</BODY>
</HTML>
```

All of this HTML code should be familiar to you from the earlier projects. This page will get some additions in its final form, but this dummy lets you see roughly what you're going to get.

Designing the Style Sheet

The cascading style sheet (CSS) is rapidly turning into a powerful tool for the Web site designer. In its current form, CSS2, you can set up different styles for different media, such as voice, handhelds, print, and desktop monitors. This is an extremely ambitious use of CSS, however, and relies on the browser for reliable display. Most current browsers don't take CSS this far yet.

The style sheet is an example of a page feature that's almost totally for the benefit of the Webmaster. There are some benefits for the visitor, but most of them can be replicated in standard HTML.

You can't define new tags in a CSS but you can define any number of style classes. A *class* is a child object of something. The CookRight Ultima is a class of CookRight, for example. And if the CookRight company comes up with both a gas Ultima and an electric Ultima, then each of them is a class of the CookRight Ultima.

In the style sheet, for example, the <P> tag is standard and can't be deleted or replaced, but you can define classes of <P> in the style sheet, like this:

```
P.maintext {font: times; font-size: 12; line-height: 14pt}
P.caption {font: arial; font-size: 12; line-height: 14pt}
```

These classes are used just like ordinary <P> tags, but with an additional attribute of CLASS, like this:

```
<P CLASS=maintext>When a student picks up a guitar for the first time, there
is an ungovernable urge to strum.</P>
<IMG SRC="images/student.gif">
<P CLASS=caption>This student is having her first lesson.</P>
```

Headings

In the opening page all the wording is done with graphics, so there's no need to worry about the heading appearances. In each guitar brand page, the main heading on the page is the Java applet.

The book page, though, has a prominent heading, "From the Robertson Museum Bookshelf..." And there's a subheading, too: "The Guitar in the 50s and 60s." These headings should be defined in a common place. Generally, headings work best as sans serif fonts. Unfortunately, different computers use different standard fonts. Macs, for example, tend to rely on Helvetica, while PCs usually like Arial. The CSS will have to make allowances for both.

The two headings will be defined with these attributes:

- The first heading will be called `H1.bkpgtitle`. It will be sans serif, 20-point, and in red. This will be the main heading on the book page.
- The second heading will be called `H1.bktitle` and will be used for the book title that the museum is highlighting. It will be sans serif, 16-point, and in black.

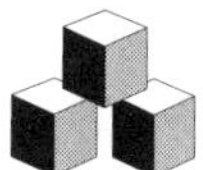

Note

You learned about serif and sans serif fonts while working on Project 1. Fonts actually come in three broad varieties:

- Serif, which includes Times, Times New Roman, Baskerville, Century Schoolbook, and similar typefaces that have "feet"
- Sans serif, which includes Helvetica, Arial, Optima, and similar typefaces that have no "feet"
- Novelty fonts, including just about everything else, such as script fonts, western block style, ransom note types, and so forth (see Figures 11.9 and 11.10).

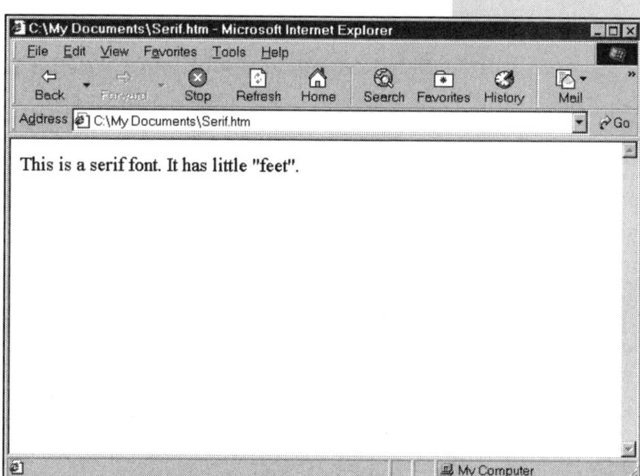

Figure 11.9 This is a serif font. Notice the "feet" on the letters.

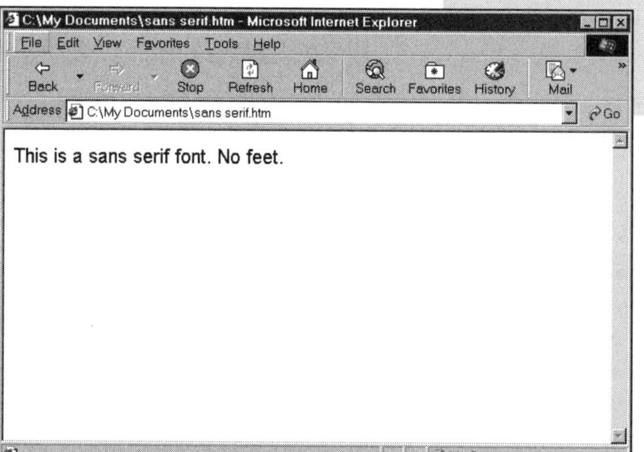

Figure 11.10 This is a sans serif font.

Body Text

Body text in the United States has traditionally been serif, which is often Times New Roman on the PC and Times on the Mac. But the museum's site isn't traditional, so it's been decided that the body text will be sans serif, too.

The two-column effect on the guitar brand page is achieved the time-honored way: with tables. Using a table gives you some convenience in placing text and regulating how it looks.

The text needed for the site as designed so far includes:

- Body text for the book page, including the field labels. This text definition will be a general one, useful anywhere in the site for ordinary use. It will be called `.general` and will be sans serif, 10-point, and black.
- Body text for the guitar brand page. This text is to be called `.brand` and will be sans serif, 10-point, red, with a margin from the left of 10 points, and with a first-line indent of 1 em.
- Body text emphasized for `.brand`. I've emphasized the names of the artists in the text, and I can set `<EM>` for `.brand` separately from `<EM>` for other `<P>` tags. `<EM>` for `.brand` will be black, rather than red, to make it further stand out.
- Body text for the guitar cell caption. This will be `.caption` and will be sans serif, 10-point, italic, and black.
- Text for the comments heading. This is arguably a heading, rather than text, but you can have it either way. I've defined it as `.comment`, and it'll be sans serif, italic, 12-point, and red.

Links

This site uses few links, but more may be included in the future as the amount of text increases. CSS lets you determine how your links look, both visited and unvisited.

Unvisited links will be in the default color of blue. This is so the user isn't confused by finding an unfamiliar color. However, visited links will be a much more subdued teal. Hovering over a link will turn it black.

Tables

Because I'm sticking to tables to display the guitar brand text, some table definitions will have to be in the CSS. These generally will be <TD> definitions. The CSS standard permits a good deal more, but using it is dicey due to browser variability.

You have three kinds of table cells to worry about, as shown in Figure 11.11:

- The left-hand cell of the guitar brand table. This has to be around 160 pixels wide to comfortably hold the graphic. This cell will be `.brand` and will have left-aligned text.
- The right-hand cell of the guitar brand table. This takes up the remaining real estate, with left-aligned text.
- The bottom table of the guitar brand page, which will be named `.bottomlinks`. This has four links in it, which ideally should be widely separated. One way to do this is to specify the pixel width of the cells. Other ways are less demanding, yet all methods have their drawbacks. You can specify measurement as: a percentage, ems, inches, centimeters, points, picas, or exes. Ems and exes are

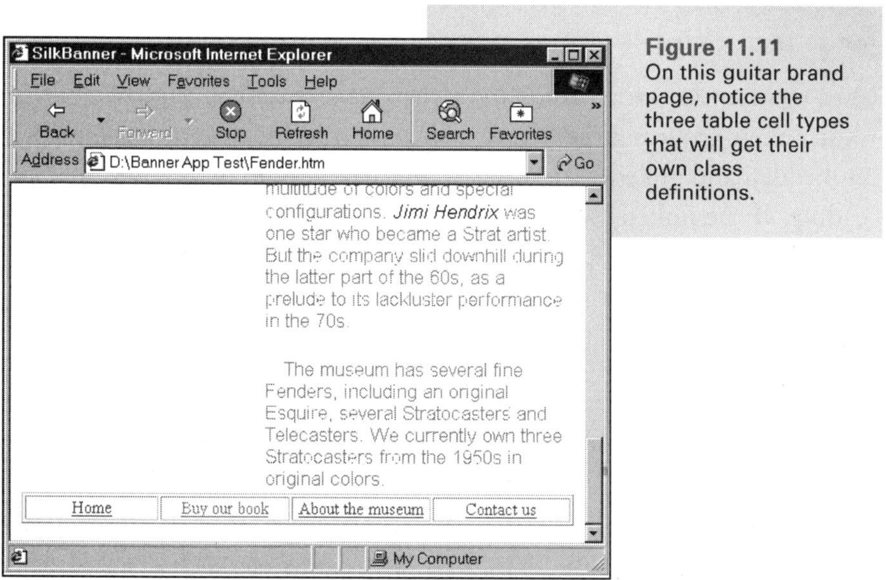

Figure 11.11
On this guitar brand page, notice the three table cell types that will get their own class definitions.

drawn from the font you're using. This makes them highly variable. You'd think that of all the measurements, pixels would be the most universal, but they're not totally reliable either. In this example you'll be using pixels as the measurement, but you can substitute another measurement if you'd like. One hundred pixels gives enough space for all the text to fit into the cell on one line and takes up 400 pixels even on low-resolution monitors.

What Does Cascading Mean?

The "cascading" part of "cascading style sheet" reveals that style definitions have their own hierarchy. The biggest, most comprehensive style definition is in an external style sheet that's linked to an HTML page. This style definition type is called, appropriately enough, a *linked style sheet.* It is "brought into" the HTML page with the `<LINK>` tag. A linked style sheet is particularly handy, because one set of definitions can be used for any number of linked HTML pages.

But you can also have an *embedded style sheet*, which is the same code you would use in the external one, written directly on a page. An embedded style sheet overrides a linked style sheet, meaning that if the two style sheets have a disagreement about a definition, the embedded style sheet wins. This is a principle of cascading, that the definition closest to the affected element is the one that's going to be used.

As a third option, you can define styles one at a time, using *inline styles*, rather than grouping them into a sheet. An inline style overrides both embedded and linked style sheets. The effects aren't cumulative, but cascading. If the linked style sheet for a paragraph style specifies blue, the embedded style sheet specifies green, and the inline style specifies silver, then the rendered text will be silver, not a combination of silver, green, and blue.

Defining the Construction Tasks

If you try to build an entire Web site at one sitting, it probably will overwhelm you. It's smarter to break the site into its various independent units and build each one separately.

Each of the key pages in this project has specific pieces that you can build and then hook together. The following sections specify the pieces, given as tasks, that you'll do step by step as you progress through the next two chapters.

The Opening Page

Make an image map for the menu graphic.

The Book Page

Write a validation function for the first name field.

Write a validation function for the last name field.

Write a validation function for the address1 field.

Write a validation function for the city field.

Write a validation function for the postal code field.

Write a detection function for the comments field.

Write functions to load variables for nonrequired fields.

Write a submission function for sending data to the server.

Write a reset function.

The Guitar Brand Page

Write a call for the Java applet.

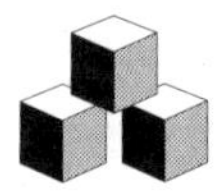

The CSS

Write and debug the cascading style sheet.

Summary

This chapter has presented the basic appearance of the advanced Web site and has defined what tasks you need to perform to make it function as desired. Now you can move on to build the actual Web site.

Beginning to Build the Advanced Web Site

As you may recall from the last chapter, you need to do a number of things for this project.

On the opening page:

- Make an image map for the menu graphic.

On the book page:

- Write a validation function for the first name field.
- Write a validation function for the last name field.
- Write a validation function for the address1 field.
- Write a loading function for the address2 field.
- Write a validation function for the city field.
- Write a validation function for the postal code field.
- Write detection and loading functions for the comments field.

- Write a submission function for sending data to the server.
- Write a reset function.

On the guitar brand page:

- Write a call for the Java applet.

On the cascading style sheet:

- Write and debug the cascading style sheet.

You'll now begin accomplishing each of these tasks.

Testing

When you're using advanced tools like scripting and cascading style sheets, it's often wise to have two or more browsers open at the same time to test the results of your coding. It's much easier to catch something when you've only changed a line or two of code than to track a problem later through dozens or hundreds of lines.

For this project, it's recommended that you have both Navigator 4 and Internet Explorer 4 or 5 so that you can instantly test for compatibility as you type your code.

Navigator and IE act differently when they find bad code. Navigator just refers you to a Web page for clarification, whereas IE will give you some clues about what it found amiss. Be aware, though, that although IE gives you a line number where it found the mistake, and a general idea of what upset the apple cart, that's not always as helpful as it appears. For example, IE may tell you to look at line 287 and give you the error message `object expected`. Although IE doesn't count blank lines in its line totals, 287 lines are a lot to count. The line count starts at the top of the HTML page, and you can wear out your index finger tapping down 287 lines.

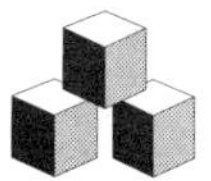

Moreover, the error message `object expected` can mean almost anything, because it merely means "I'm having a problem figuring out what object is meant here." It could mean that you made a mistake typing a function, or that you forgot to define a function and called it anyway . . . or several other things.

Finally, if you give in to temptation and run ahead of me, trying out variations on things covered in this project, you may find that Navigator and IE show your new page features differently. The code you'll be typing in this project is tested for both browsers, so it should work in both of yours. But I can't vouch for that if you start wandering off on your own. Although, to be honest, that's often a wonderful way to learn.

Finishing the Opening Page

The opening page's menu appears on cue, but it doesn't do anything yet. It needs to be made into an image map:

EXERCISE

1. Open menuframe.html in Notepad.
2. Type this map right after the `<BODY>` tag in `menuframe.html`:

```
<MAP NAME="menu">
<AREA SHAPE="rect" COORDS="5,26,113,37" HREF="book.html" TARGET="_top">
<AREA SHAPE="rect" COORDS="8,102,65,117" HREF="fender.html"
TARGET="_top">
</MAP>
```

As you've already learned, this map gives the browser a set of coordinates to use for an image you'll specify in the next coding.

3. Find the `<IMG>` tag for the menu, which looks like this:

```
<IMG SRC="images/menu.gif">
```

4. Add new code to that tag to make it look like this:

```
<IMG SRC="images/menu.gif" BORDER="0" USEMAP="#menu">
```

ANALYSIS

Now the browser will use the menu GIF, which up to this point hasn't done anything interesting, as an image map. You'll link only two hot regions (both rectangles) on the image, because only those pages, `book.html` and `fender.html`, are being developed in this project. The principle for developing and linking more of the hot regions, however, is the same.

The `TARGET="_top"` in the `<AREA>` tag in Step 2 tells the browser to get rid of the frames when you link to one of the other pages. You could, of course, elect to keep the menu frame open and redirect all of the content pages to the right-hand frame.

Save `menuframe.html`. Test by opening `index.html` in your test browsers. As long as all of your work has been kept in the correct directories, this image map should work.

Adding the Scripts for the Book Page

Before starting to write the scripts, do the following:

1. Open the dummy book page `book.html` in Notepad.

   The dummy page needs to be neatened up a bit, to eliminate some old code and to ready the dummy for its metamorphosis.

2. Write the document type declaration above the `<HTML>` tag. It should look like this:

```
<!DOCTYPE HTML PUBLIC"-//W3/DTD HTML 4.0 Transitional//EN"
 "http://www.w3.org/TR/REC-html40/loose.dtd">
```

   The page has no meta information, although you can add some if you choose. Project 1 covered the details of including meta information.

3. Eliminate the font information from the first heading. Right now it looks like this:

```
<FONT SIZE="5" COLOR="red" FACE="arial">From the Robertson Museum
Bookshelf...</FONT>
```

Delete that line and in its place write this one:

```
<H1 CLASS=bkpgtitle> From the Robertson Museum Bookshelf...</H1>
```

4. Do the same thing with its partner heading just below it. Delete that line and write this one:

```
<H1 CLASS=bktitle>The Guitar in the 50s and 60s</H1>
```

ANALYSIS

For the museum, its days of writing Web sites using <FONT> and suchlike are about over, yielding to the cascading style sheet. Later on you'll define an <H1> class of `bkpgtitle` and a class of `bktitle` that will do the work for you.

Writing the Scripts

Directly underneath the form you'll type several functions in one long script, as shown in Figure 12.1.

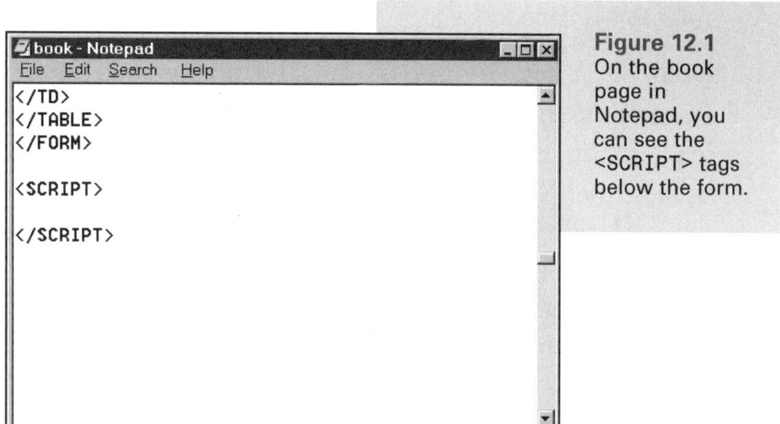

Figure 12.1 On the book page in Notepad, you can see the <SCRIPT> tags below the form.

EXERCISE

1. After the </FORM> tag, write a <SCRIPT> tag.
2. On the next line write a </SCRIPT> tag.
3. Put a few paragraph returns between the new tags added in Steps 1 and 2. All of the JavaScript will go between these tags.

ANALYSIS

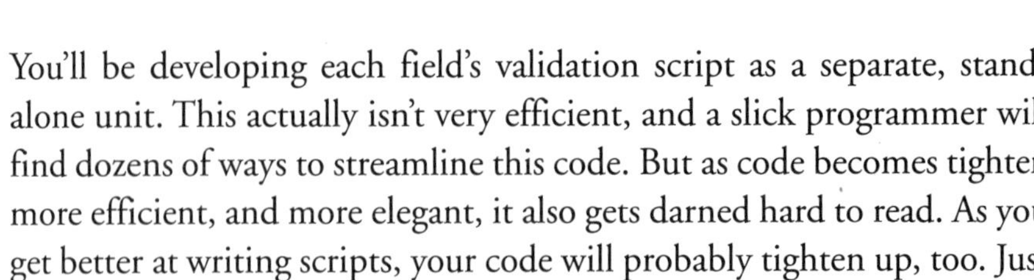

You'll be developing each field's validation script as a separate, standalone unit. This actually isn't very efficient, and a slick programmer will find dozens of ways to streamline this code. But as code becomes tighter, more efficient, and more elegant, it also gets darned hard to read. As you get better at writing scripts, your code will probably tighten up, too. Just be aware that the code here is for illustrative purposes and doesn't represent the highest form of the art.

EXERCISE

Directly under the <SCRIPT> tag, type this code just as shown:

```
<SCRIPT>
<!-
function ValidateMain() {
}
->
```

What you just typed is a *function*. A function is a way of "extending" a language. Every language has commands, but no language has all the commands you'll ever need. By defining a function, you're creating a whole new command that you can call just by using its name. The function has lines of code inside of its braces ({}) that execute when the function is called.

Believe it or not, `ValidateMain()`, the function you just typed, is a valid function, even though it does precisely nothing. If you try to run it by loading this page into a browser, nothing will happen, not merely because there's no code inside the function, but because nothing in your page yet calls this function. Functions don't run by themselves. They're like well-trained dogs that sit quietly until called.

ANALYSIS

For convenience, you're writing a *container* or *main function* that will call the various other functions. This isn't actually necessary, but it's easy to do and ensures that the functions it calls are executed in sequence. Later this main function will be hooked to the Submit button, so when the visitor submits the form, the button fires the main function, which takes care of validation and submission.

Take a long look at the function code, because you'll be seeing it often and it's best to know it intimately. The first line tells the interpreter that this is a function that you're defining, and you're naming it `ValidateMain`.

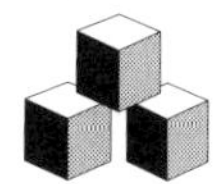

The parentheses after the function name are for variables that pass arguments into the function. In this case we don't need any. Then to complete any function, you'll need a set of braces (which are also called curly brackets): `{}`. Everything between the braces is considered to be part of the function code.

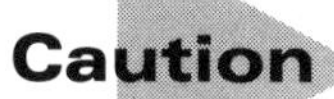

> **Note that the `f` in `function` is lowercase. Keep in mind always that JavaScript is case-sensitive, meaning that it makes a distinction between, say, `MyVariable` and `MYVARIABLE`. It also knows that `Function` isn't a command but `function` is.**

EXERCISE

Functions can call other functions, and often do. Indeed, that's how `ValidateMain()` is going to work.

Add a function name to `ValidateMain()` by typing this:

```
<SCRIPT>
function ValidateMain() {
   validFirstName();
}
```

ANALYSIS

Your first validation function is called `validFirstName()`. For all practical purposes, you're going to add another command to the JavaScript language named `validFirstName()`, one that's used only for one script.

Notice that this new line ends in a semicolon (;). Most JavaScript commands end in a semicolon. Notice, too, that you've just plunked one function down inside of another. This means that `ValidateMain()` is going to call `validFirstName()` from within its braces. This is common in JavaScript, but may take some getting used to.

You won't be writing validation functions for every field in the form, because some of the fields aren't required. Those that are required have an asterisk (*) in their labels. You won't have to validate the state field, for example, because the visitor can only pick from the list you give him, so there's little chance for error. However, you will be writing a function for each field the visitor can fill in, if only to load the results of that field into a variable for later use.

EXERCISE

Validating the First Name

1. Right after the last brace for `ValidateMain()`, on a new line, type this code:

```
function validFirstName()
{
First = document.forms[0].elements[0].value;
if (First == "")
    {
        alert ("Please fill in your first name");
        SubmitOK = false;
        return(SubmitOK);
    }
else
    {
        return(First);
    }
}
```

The indents aren't required; they're only for code clarity as you work through this project. To test this function, do this:

2. Find this HTML line:

```
<TD><INPUT TYPE="button" VALUE="Submit Form">
```

3. Add new code to it so that it looks like this:

```
<TD><INPUT TYPE="button" VALUE="Submit Form" ONCLICK="ValidateMain()">
```

ANALYSIS

Now when the visitor clicks on the Submit Form button, `ValidateMain()` fires instead. Leaving the first name field blank, click on Submit Form and see the alert box pop up, as in Figure 12.2. Reload the page, type your name, and click on Submit Form again. Nothing happens. You've just validated your name.

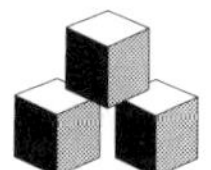

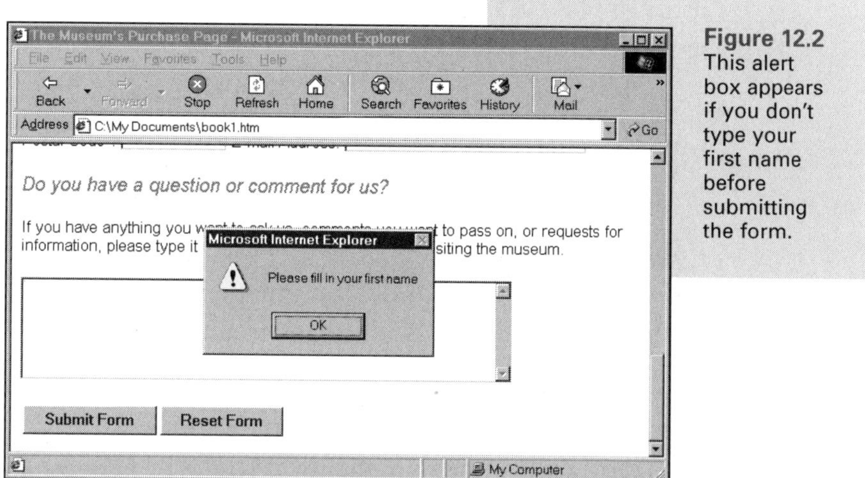

Figure 12.2 This alert box appears if you don't type your first name before submitting the form.

At this point, it's a good idea to test your first script in at least the two most popular browsers. It doesn't take long to do it, and it's helpful to catch any errors or misunderstandings now, while the code is still warm.

Think about what the code is doing. The first line, which names the function, you already know about. The next line is just the opening brace. The third line is where the real code starts.

Variables are containers or placeholders for various kinds of program data.

`First` is a variable. A variable can hold a character string, numerical data, or a Boolean value. These data can be used just like any other data in computations, for writing to the document, reading from a field, and so forth. Programmers often talk about "loading" a variable or "writing to" a variable when talking about putting content into a variable. The verbs they use often depend on what language they learned first.

In JavaScript, unlike some other languages, variables do not need to be explicitly created, meaning that you can just willy-nilly name and create one right in the middle of a line. Such a definition is simple, quick, and convenient, but it can make maintenance much harder, because you'll have to scan the whole program if you need to find the variable definition.

Variables in most languages, including JavaScript, come in two broad varieties: local and global. A *local variable* is available only to the function within which the variable is created. A *global variable* is, as the name implies, available everywhere in the script, and even across other scripts, frames, and other pages.

There is a curious twist to this. "Explicit" variables are formally declared with a `var` statement:

```
var simpleton="I'm a programmer"
```

If this statement occurs outside of a function, the variable is global. If this statement occurs inside of a function, the variable is local to that function. That's easy enough to understand.

If, however, the variable is "implicit" within a function, meaning that you just create it in passing, not with a `var` statement, it's also global. Variables can be created implicitly anytime, and almost anywhere.

Consider this line:

```
simpleton="I'm a programmer";
```

This is an implicit declaration that you might even miss seeing altogether unless it was commented. The line doesn't actually say "`simpleton` is a new variable," but that's what it's doing. Unfortunately, you load existing declared variables with exactly the same syntax that you use to implicitly declare a new variable, so it's easy to confuse declaration/loading with just loading.

Finally, variables in JavaScript are ephemeral creatures. They pop into being when declared in a script and then vanish if the page is refreshed or if the browser points elsewhere. They even vanish if the browser window is resized. This can cause some odd behavior in complex scripts. It's also a bit annoying when you have to reload pages into a frame, because any variables from the old page won't hang around. They just disappear into the bit bucket.

Note

You can get around some of JavaScript's disappearing variables by either writing a cookie to the local drive or keeping your variables in a page and frame that won't likely be reloaded, like a menu bar page. The other pages can then access the variables across the page and the frame.

So what is the variable `First` holding? In this case, it's holding whatever the visitor types into the First Name field. It's hard, however, to see where the variable `First` and the field First Name connect in the code.

Recall that almost everything in JavaScript is an object of some sort. The document is an object, and all the things within it are its child objects. To reference an object, you use dots between the parent and child, as indicated below:

```
parent.child.method
parent.child.property
```

Forms in a document are kept in an array. An *array* can be thought of as a cabinet (the document) with drawers that correspond to the various forms and other objects. Within the drawer for this form, you'll find file folders, one for each of the form's elements. You can always access a particular element in a particular form by asking for "drawer 1, file folder 72."

That's what the script is doing here. Examine this line:

```
First = document.forms[0].elements[0].value;
```

The script is accessing form 0 (array numbering starts with zero, not one), element 0 (the first element in line) and checking the property named `value`. The variable `First` is then loaded with whatever `value` is, even if it's no text at all.

Why are we doing this with `First` anyway? Later you'll define a global variable named `First` that exists outside of this function, and you want to use `First` to store the value of the First Name field.

If you need more information about arrays, there are many good books on JavaScript you can consult.

The line

```
if (First == "")
```

checks to see if the value stored in `First` is blank, which it will be if the visitor tries to submit the form without typing in a first name.

The `if` is a test, and the statement within parentheses is what you're testing. Note the use of the double equal signs (==). One equal sign (=) is used to load a variable with a value, as in `Variable = 1234`. The double equal signs, as in `Variable == 1234`, test the variable for what it's carrying.

That line of script says, "If the first thing is equal to the second, then execute whatever code comes next." The second thing is literally nothing between two quotation marks, signifying that the test quantity is an empty string. If the string is empty, the visitor didn't type anything before she submitted the form. Note also that there's no semicolon after the `if` line; this is one of the few exceptions to the semicolon rule.

After the `if` line is another opening brace, which is indented to show that it's for the `if`, not for the function. You can readily nest braces within braces, as you're doing here, but you might have trouble keeping track of which braces to put where. Indenting them keeps that problem to a minimum.

In this code, everything between the braces is executed when the `if` test is satisfied. In the present case, if there is text in the variable `First`, the rest of the code produces an alert box that pops up (saying `Please fill in your first name`), and `SubmitOK` is loaded with the value `false`. The alert box is just to let you know that the function worked; you'll yank it out later, after it has served its testing purpose. `SubmitOK` will later be created globally and serve as a "flag" to indicate whether the page should or should not be sent to the server. If the variable `First` should prove to have nothing in it, `SubmitOK` is given the value `false`, the function `ValidateMain()` will test `SubmitOK`, `ValidateMain()` will conclude that something is amiss with the data, and the script won't allow the form to be submitted. The line

```
return(SubmitOK);
```

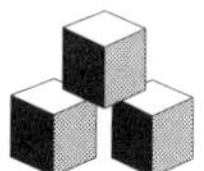

stops the function and sends `SubmitOK` with its value of `false` back to the main function. Later you'll write code that checks `SubmitOK` to see if it has a value of `true` or `false`.

So what if something is in the field, meaning `First` isn't empty? Then the `else` line kicks in. Recall that the `if` line determines if the string is empty, and what to do if it is. The corresponding `else` line is executed if the string is not empty, bypassing the alert box, the `SubmitOK` change, and the return of `SubmitOK`. The `else` condition has its own opening and closing braces. As with `if`, everything between the braces is executed if the condition is `true`. Here there's only a return that stops the function, sends execution back to wherever it was before the function call, and returns the value of `First` so that you can further manipulate it somewhere else in the script.

Of course, numerals are valid characters, so some joker could type `Fr34d` and it would pass muster. You can write routines that validate enough to catch problems of that nature, but they're beyond the scope of this project.

Note

If you like, you can help the visitor a little bit after his mistake by moving the cursor to the field and highlighting it. This is done with a couple of additional methods, `.focus` and `.select`. As with `.value`, you use these methods by specifying a position in an array:

```
document.visitorData.firstname.focus();
document.visitorData.firstname.select();
```

These two lines would be inserted this way:

```
{
    alert ("Please fill in your first name");
    document.visitorData.firstname.focus();
    document.visitorData.firstname.select();
    SubmitOK = false;
    return(SubmitOK);
}
```

The `.focus` method shifts the *focus*, which is the attention given to an object, to the First Name field, while the second method, `.select`, highlights the text in the field. This is all optional, but you can try it if you want.

Validating the Last Name

EXERCISE

1. After the last line of validFirstName(), type these lines:

```
function validLastName()
{
Last = document.visitorData.lastname.value;
if (Last == "")
   {
      alert ("Please fill in your last name");
      SubmitOK = false;
      return(SubmitOK);
   }
else
   {
      return(Last);
   }
}
```

This is the function validLastName(), and its code should look familiar.

2. Return to ValidateMain() and make it look like this:

```
<SCRIPT>
function ValidateMain() {
   validFirstName();
   validLastName();
}
```

Now when ValidateMain() fires, it will execute both functions in order. First validFirstName() operates, and then validLastName() operates. validLastName() won't operate until the return statement in validFirstName() is executed.

3. Save your work, reload the page in the browser, and play with the First Name and Last Name fields, leaving out and filling in your name. Figure 12.3 shows what you get when you don't fill in your last name before submitting.

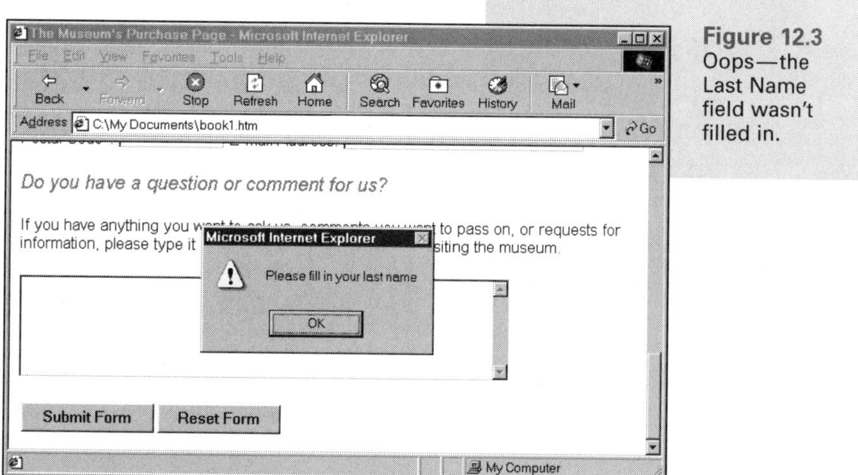

Figure 12.3 Oops—the Last Name field wasn't filled in.

ANALYSIS

The code looks almost exactly like that of `validFirstName()`. There is a difference, however, in how the form element is accessed and read. In the function `validFirstName()`, to access the element you used the array method of `document.forms[].elements[]` to access the element directly. This is simple and straightforward, but harder for you or another programmer to remember.

Fortunately, there's a simpler, more natural way to access the array element you want. `validLastName()` uses the fact that each element and the form itself have been given names as well as array numbers. The form's name is `visitorData`, and the field for the last name is `lastname`. That's much easier to keep track of in code. Now you can substitute them for the array designations:

```
Last = document.visitorData.lastname.value;
```

This line creates another variable, `Last`, and has it loaded with the value of the `lastname` field from the form `visitorData`. The point to this exercise is that you can access the array elements either way. As with just about everything else in JavaScript, there's more than one way to do it. If array numbers seem more natural to you, then by all means stick with that method.

Other than this one change, and of course the return of `Last` rather than `First`, the code is the same as that of `validFirstName()`. If you're still unclear about how some of the code works in either of these two functions, return to the section on `validFirstName()` and read the explanation again.

Validating the Address

EXERCISE

1. After the last line of `validLastName()`, type this code:

```
function validAddress1()
{
Address1 = document.visitorData.address1.value;
if (Address1 == "")
   {
      alert ("Please fill in your street address");
      SubmitOK = false;
      return(SubmitOK);
   }
else
   {
      return (Address1);
   }
}
```

   By this time the function should appear extremely familiar. Except for the obvious differences in variables, it's the same code as `validLastName()`.

2. Go to `ValidateMain()` and type the function name `validAddress1()` into the list, as shown below:

```
<SCRIPT>
function ValidateMain() {
   validFirstName();
   validLastName();
   validAddress1();
}
```

3. Save the page and refresh it in the browser. Experiment with entering and not entering various combinations of first name, last name, and now the address.

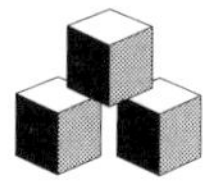

Writing the Address2 Function

You won't have to validate any data from the second address field, because it's optional for the visitor. But if you wanted to, you could use a script function to autodetect text in that field and, if text exists, validate it. You'll learn to do a text autodetect script when we get to the Comments field later.

You do, however, need to at least capture the data from the second address field.

EXERCISE

After the `validAddress1()` code, type this code:

```
function validAddress2()
{
Address2 = document.visitorData.address2.value;
return (Address2);
}
```

Validating the City

EXERCISE

1. After the `validAddress2()` code, type this code:

```
function validCity()
{
City = document.visitorData.city.value;
if (City == "")
   {
      alert ("Please fill in your city");
      SubmitOK = false;
      return(SubmitOK);
   }
else
   {
      return (City);
   }
}
```

2. Go back to `ValidateMain()` and type the function name `validCity()` into the list, like this:

```
<SCRIPT>
function ValidateMain() {
```

```
      validFirstName();
      validLastName();
      validAddress1();
      validCity();
   }
```

3. Save, refresh, and play with the fields.

As you can see by now, you're building a total validation scheme, but doing it one testable unit at a time.

Caution

If you're tempted to type the function calls in `ValidateMain()` out of order, recall that the order of the function calls in `ValidateMain()` determines the order in which the functions will be executed. It's best to put them in order of where the elements appear on the page so that the visitor sees a logical progression of alert boxes.

Note

If your code doesn't work as expected, double-check it against the example. Then start tracking the problem by putting alert boxes here and there to see where the code reaches before it bombs. For example, if you're getting an error while `ValidateMain()` is running, try putting a line for an alert box between the first and second function calls in `ValidateMain()`, as shown below:

```
<SCRIPT>
function ValidateMain() {
   validFirstName();
   alert ("I got here!);
   validLastName();
   validAddress1();
   validCity();
}
```

Then, after the first function runs and before the second one runs, this alert box will appear, telling you that you reached this point. If you get there, move the alert box line to below the second function call, and so on.

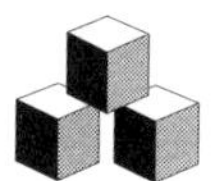

Writing the State Function

The state data doesn't have to be validated, but it still should be captured in a variable, so follow these steps:

EXERCISE

1. After the `validCity()` closing brace, type this code:

```
function validState()
{
State=document.visitorData.state.value;
return(State);
}
```

2. Go back to `ValidateMain()` and type the function `validState()` into the list so that it looks like this:

```
<SCRIPT>
function ValidateMain() {
   validFirstName();
   alert ("I got here!);
   validLastName();
   validAddress1();
   validCity();
   validState();
}
```

3. Save, refresh, and play with the fields again, noting the proper operation of alert boxes.

Validating the ZIP Code

EXERCISE

1. After the `validState()` function code, type this code:

```
function validZIP()
{
Zip = document.visitorData.code.value;
if (Zip == "")
   {
      alert("Please fill in your ZIP code");
       SubmitOK = false;
      return(SubmitOK);
   }
if ((Zip.length!=5) && (Zip.length!=10))
   {
```

```
            alert("Incorrect ZIP code. Please enter again.");
            return;
        }
    ZipString="1234567890-";
    for (Count=0; Count < Zip.length; Count++)
        {
            TempChar= Zip.substring (Count, Count+1);
            if (ZipString.indexOf (TempChar, 0) == -1)
                {
                    alert("Incorrect ZIP code. Please enter again.");
                }
                    return (Zip);
        }
    }
```

2. Once again, add this function to the growing list in `ValidateMain()`.
3. Save the page and reload it into the browser.
4. Try fooling the ZIP code field by putting in too few digits or too many. The script detects a ZIP+4 too, with a hyphen in between.

Validating the ZIP code isn't as easy as just detecting characters, as in the previous fields. The ZIP code must be a string of 5 digits, or of 9 digits and a hyphen. JavaScript doesn't have a built-in function to detect a count of numeric characters, so you have to build one here.

As with the other functions, `validZIP()` starts by loading a variable with the value of a text field. The function then tests for an empty string and shows an alert box if there's nothing in the text box. No surprises here; it's the same code you've come to know.

The next `if`, however, isn't the same. The `if` statement syntax is the same, but the test condition is different. The variable `Zip`, with its loaded string of numerals, is checked for length, which is a property of every variable and can be accessed by `variable.length`.

Look at this line:

```
if ((Zip.length!=5) && (Zip.length!=10))
```

This sets up a double test and performs a Boolean AND, which tests to see if both conditions are true. It's represented in JavaScript by a double ampersand (`&&`). If both conditions are true, then the outcome is also true.

Within each condition is a NOT, represented by an exclamation point (`!`). A NOT inverts a condition. So in almost plain English, the test is, "If the length of the variable `Zip` is not equal to five, AND the length of the variable `Zip` is not equal to ten, then do the code that comes next." In one line of code, you're eliminating all possible conditions except five or ten characters in the variable `Zip`. That's approaching elegant.

Now to validate the existence of numerals and perhaps a hyphen (for a ZIP + 4).

To perform this trick, the function needs to nest an `if` inside of a `for` statement. The `for` statement is equivalent to Pascal's `for-next` loop; it performs an operation a certain number of times, or until something specific happens. It uses this syntax:

for (*initialize counter*; *condition*; *count up or down*)

Review this line from the function:

```
for (Count=0; Count < Zip.length; Count++)
```

It says, "When entering this loop, reset the variable `Count` to zero. Then compare the value of `Count` to the value of `Zip.length` (the length property of `Zip`). If the value of `Count` isn't less than the length of `Zip`, then advance `Count` by one and evaluate again. If the condition is not met, do not execute the code between the braces. When the condition is met, execute the code between the braces."

As you can tell, JavaScript's way of saying it is much shorter.

The `for` statement is testing to see how long `Zip` is. You know from the previous test in the script that it has to be 5 or 10 characters. The `for` statement counts the characters in `Zip`, tallying them one at a time into the variable `Count` until the length of `Zip` is reached. Then counting stops and the line

```
TempChar= Zip.substring (Count, Count+1);
```

creates a new variable `TempChar` and makes it equal to whatever number is in `Count` (either 5 or 10). It does this with the `.substring` method. Remember that methods are how an object is told to do various jobs. The `.substring` method is a string method that uses two arguments, `start` and `stop`:

```
object.substring(start, stop)
```

Say that out of a string of eight characters you want only the first five. Counting starts at zero, so the statement would be:

```
objectstring.substring(0, 4)
```

One other component needs to be set up before checking for the proper characters. The variable `ZipString` is loaded with all the acceptable characters, which are numerals 1 through 0 and the hyphen. This is done with the by-now-familiar practice of writing this simple line:

```
ZipString="1234567890-";
```

At this point you've tested the visitor's input to see if the string is 5 or 10 characters, and you've alerted him if the entered text is not 5 or 10 characters long. You now have a true count of whether the entered text is 5 or 10 characters, and you have a list of acceptable characters to compare them with, loaded into the variable `ZipString`. And you have the entered text itself in `TempChar`, separate from `Zip`.

Now a single line checks the entered text for acceptability:

```
if (ZipString.indexOf (TempChar, 0) == -1)
```

This line elegantly performs the final test. It uses the `.indexOf` method, which is another string method and works much like the `.substring` method. The `.indexOf` method is used to see if a particular character is within a given string. As in this case, it can check against a whole group. It actually tests `ZipString`, which has the acceptable characters, by comparing it to `TempChar`, which has the input characters. If the comparison is acceptable, the `if` statement comes back true, the variable `Zip` is returned, all is well, and the script proceeds. If the test finds a character not in `ZipString`, however, it fires an alert box that tells the visitor in no uncertain terms that he has made a mistake.

This function could have been written in many ways, so you may want to play with this function and see how tight you can get the code.

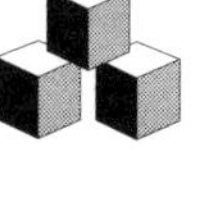

EXERCISE

Writing the E-Mail Function

As with the state function, you don't need to validate the e-mail text, although you should capture the data:

1. After the closing brace for `validZIP()`, type this code:

```
function validEmail()
{
Email = document.visitorData.email.value;
return (Email);
}
```

2. Go back to `ValidateMain()` and add the function `validEmail()` to the list of called functions.
3. Save, refresh, and play with the fields.

ANALYSIS

You could let this code stand, or you could perform validation on it, looking for the two key elements in an e-mail address: the at sign (@) and the period (.). You could do this much the same way that you validated the ZIP code, by using a variable to hold those two characters and checking them against the input string using the `.indexOf` method.

EXERCISE

Handling Comments

1. Below the final closing brace for `validEmail()`, type this code:

```
function validComment()
{
Comments = document.visitorData.comments.value;
if (Comments == "")
   {
      return;
   }
else
   {
      return (Comments);
   }
}
```

▼

2. As before, go back to `ValidateMain()` and add `validComment()` to the list of called functions.
3. Save the page again and refresh it in the browser.
4. Type a few words of commentary and test by clicking on the submit button.

ANALYSIS

Surprise! Nothing happens, whether you type something or you don't. There's nothing to let the visitor know anything, and there doesn't need to be. The visitor already knows if there's text in the field; it's just your script that doesn't know. You're not validating a required field here but merely detecting whether a comment has been typed. That's taken care of with the now-familiar `if` statement. Unlike previously, though, when the `if` statement fired an alert box for invalid entries, all that happens now is that you return quietly. If there is text, you load that text into the variable `Comments` and still return quietly.

Notice that you've neatly replaced the radio buttons in the previous chapter's form with a script line that autodetects text.

It's a good idea to check your code's operation using alert boxes. You can test whether this function is working as advertised like this:

```
function validComment()
{
Comments = document.visitorData.comments.value;
if (Comments == "")
    {
        return;
    }
else
    {
        alert ("You typed" + Comments);
        return (Comments);
    }
}
```

When you're first checking your code, sprinkle alert boxes around so that you can tell what's working. You can always remove them later or comment them out.

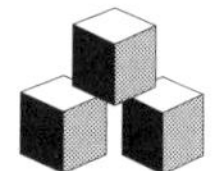

Keeping Code Clear with JavaScript Comments

Most languages let you type comments into the program code. This is a good practice. When reviewing the code later, you may not remember how you structured it, and if someone else has to take over for you, she'll need to know your logic, too. Comments in JavaScript are of the one-line variety or are blocks. One-line comments start with // as follows:

```
//This is a comment
```

This type of comment works only for one line, so when it is used for a lengthy comment, // must preface each line.

Block comments are indicated by putting /* at the beginning and */ at the end. One pair of block comment indicators can apply to any number of lines.

For debugging purposes you can put alert boxes in your scripts and then comment them out as required. The interpreter won't read them, but they're always there when you want to use them temporarily for testing. This is an example of such a debugging alert box:

```
//alert ("I'm here, I'm here!");
```

The alert box won't be displayed unless you delete the two slashes while testing your code.

JavaScript comments are similar to HTML comments in that both contain text that the browser ignores.

Writing the Reset Function

You now have a basic working validation script. However, some further embellishments need to be written. It's customary, for example, to have a reset button to purge the form's data and start over. Different ways are available to do this, as is almost always the case in JavaScript.

The original intent of an HTML form's reset button was to have the server's CGI script reset the form. Nowadays the HTML form reset function reloads the page into the browser. However, doing this is a coding dead end, because it leaves you with no options to take other actions. On the other hand, resetting the form locally with JavaScript isn't hard; you just have to tell the page to reload, leaving your options open. That's what this code does:

```
<INPUT TYPE="button" VALUE="Reset Form" ONCLICK="JavaScript:location =
location;">
```

EXERCISE

1. Find the table cell that holds the reset button. The code looks like this:

   ```
   <TD><INPUT TYPE="button" VALUE="Reset Form">
   ```

2. Add an inline bit of code, so the line looks like this:

   ```
   <TD><INPUT TYPE="button" VALUE="Reset Form" ONCLICK="JavaScript:location
   = location;">
   ```

3. Save the page and reload it into the browser.
4. Click on the Reset Form button.

ANALYSIS

The `ONCLICK` attribute is a snippet of JavaScript. The colon begins the line of code. `location` is the place where the browser is currently pointing. Making `location` equal to `location` makes the page reload. The page should be cached on the local drive when it's first downloaded so that it reloads with minimal wait. Anything in the fields onscreen vanishes, and the visitor is ready to start afresh.

This illustrates the use of inline commands. They have limited usefulness but can come in handy if you need only one quick command.

Finishing the Script

You have some small last-minute things to attend to. First, there's the matter of some global variables that you need to declare.

In JavaScript, you can just create and use variables as you come across the need. This spontaneity seems helpful, but it can be hard to maintain. Good housekeeping suggests that you declare global variables at the top of the script. Besides, that's good discipline and a good way to keep track of your variable list.

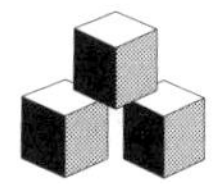

Note

In the past, it was common to place HTML comments around the script code within the <SCRIPT> tags. In other words, your script would look like this:

```
<SCRIPT>
<!–
alert ("This an alert box, isn't it?");
<!–end script–!>
</SCRIPT>
```

The comment container hid the script from browsers that couldn't handle the <SCRIPT> tag. Arguments and fistfights break out today over whether or not to use HTML comments for the <SCRIPT> tags now that The Big Two (the Navigator and IE browsers) both recognize <SCRIPT> tags. Using the comments is a nice concession to owners of older browsers, but when your pages rely on their scripts to operate properly, there's a good argument for leaving the comments off as irrelevant and possibly intrusive. I haven't used them here, but you can insert them if you want.

EXERCISE

At the very top of the script, right under the <SCRIPT> tag, type this:

```
var SubmitOK = true
var First
var Last
var Address1
var Address2
var City
var State
var Zip
var Email
var Comments
```

▼ ANALYSIS

Each var statement declares a separate variable. You could shorten this considerably by declaring all the variables in a single line, like this:

```
Var SubmitOK = true, First, Last, Address1, Address2, City, State, Zip,
Email, Comments
```

The first variable, SubmitOK, is set to true. This is the flag that each test function sets to false if the visitor makes a mistake. Such flags are useful for performing higher-level checks. Global variables are available for common use between scripts on a single page, and even between pages in different windows.

Let's say you had a form in one place and a questionnaire in another, on the same page or even in a different window. The visitor fills out the form with name and address, and fills out the questionnaire separately. You want to submit them both at the same time, even though they exist independently from one another. By declaring global variables and using them as separate flags to indicate correct execution of each form, you can set up a simple routine that says, in essence, "If `SubmitOne` is `true` and `SubmitTwo` is `true`, then submit both forms."

Having all of the other variables listed here as globals can be handy too. If you wanted to show a response to the visitor and ask "Is this correct?" you could write a short routine to open a new window and write the visitor's data into it, via the variables.

Sending Data to the Server

So far you've developed this script as though it were never going to leave the page. And unless you have a server and a CGI script handy, you won't be able to test submitting to the server anyway. But you can experiment with the code that submits the data to the server.

EXERCISE

Right now `ValidateMain()` should look like this:

```
function ValidateMain()
{
   validFirstName();
   validLastName();
   validAddress1();
   validAddress2();
   validCity();
   validState()
   validZIP();
   validEmail();
   validComment();
}
```

If you followed the steps exactly as presented earlier in the chapter, you need to add `validAddress2();` as indicated to make your list complete at this point.

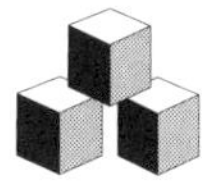

Follow these steps to include code for submitting the page to the server once the input is trouble-free:

1. Before the closing brace, add these lines:

```
if (SubmitOK == true)
   document.visitorData.submit();
```

2. Save the page and refresh it in the browser.
3. Click on the Submit Form button and see what happens.

Note

It's one of JavaScript's strange little quirks that a single line of code to execute after an `if` doesn't require braces, but more than a single line does. To be safe, I've written most of the single-line commands with braces, but you can leave them off, as I've chosen to do after the `if` statement here. Take your pick.

ANALYSIS

You got an error when you tested, right? That's what happens if the page can't find the CGI script you told it to look for (see Figure 12.4). And

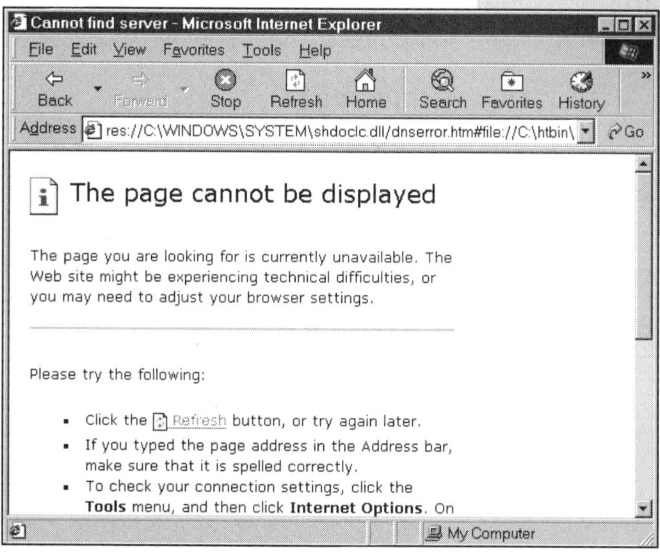

Figure 12.4 This is what you get when the local script can't find your CGI script.

just where did you tell it to look for such a thing? Not in the script, but in the `<FORM>` tag itself. That tag looks like this:

```
<FORM NAME="visitorData" METHOD="post" ACTION="/bin/book.cgi">
```

In order from left to right, you've declared that a form is being built, that its name is `visitorData`, and that when the form is submitted you want it to post to the server to a CGI script named `book.cgi`.

The submission itself is done in the last two lines you've added to `ValidateMain()`. The first line is, of course, an `if` statement. It tests to see if the variable `SubmitOK` is `true` or `false`. If `SubmitOK` is `true` (and it will be only if all of the functions have worked properly), then the next line will be executed:

```
document.visitorData.submit();
```

By now you probably recognize that this is a method—indeed, `.submit` is a form method, and, predictably enough, it submits the form according to the method and action you've called for in the `<FORM>` tag's attributes.

Additional JavaScript Resources

If you're really intrigued by JavaScript and you want to hobnob with some of the world's most enterprising JavaScripters, you can find thousands of scripts and assistance at the following Web site:

http://www.javascript.com

There are scripts here for other, more complex validation routines, for business applications, for games, and even for fouling up the lives of people you don't like. The scripts are free and you can vote for your favorites if so inclined.

There are also loads of JavaScript resources at:

http://www.netscape.com

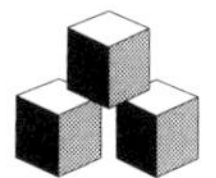

Summary

This chapter has given you a chance to write some JavaScript scripts that bring added functionality to your Web site. You've learned the importance of commenting within scripts, and the benefits of working with alert boxes. In addition, while implementing a variety of validation functions for the book page, you've become comfortable with local and global variables.

You have focused primarily on the construction of the opening page and the book page in this chapter. In the next chapter you'll finish up the project by finalizing one of the individual guitar brand pages, and by creating a linked style sheet that will enable you to easily implement changes in the appearance of all your pages.

Finishing Up the Advanced Web Site

The previous chapter mostly tackled the opening page and the book page for the guitar museum Web site. Now you're ready to complete Project 3 by developing the first of the 12 guitar brand pages, and by creating a linked style sheet that will make your life much easier as you change and maintain your Web pages.

Using the Java Applet on the Guitar Brand Page

Applets are small Java programs that run only in a browser or other limited environment. Unless you get the source code for a particular applet, you won't be able to deduce what arguments need to be passed to the applet—and there are arguments aplenty for some applets.

Using an Applet

The applet you'll incorporate into this page is part of a shareware product from New Zealand called Banner Factory.

You can download it from:

http://www.cafejava.com

You also can get it from the CD accompanying this book.

The applet that comes with Banner Factory is called `afSilkBanner.class`.

Banner Factory can set up the applet for you. That's cheating for this project, but feel free to use Banner Factory's setup software for some other project. For this project you'll write the code the hard way, by hand.

In Chapter 11 you typed a dummy page named `fender.html`. It didn't have an actual applet in it at that time; you'll add the applet now.

EXERCISE

1. Copy all the elements of Banner Factory from the CD to the directory in which you're saving the work files for this project.
2. Open `fender.html` in Notepad. As you did with `book.html` in Chapter 12, you'll have to add some HTML to this dummy page:

   ```
   <!DOCTYPE HTML PUBLIC"-//W3/DTD HTML 4.0 Transitional//EN"
    "http://www.w3.org/TR/REC-html40/loose.dtd">
   ```

   As with `book.html`, this page has no meta information.
3. Add this new code just as you did with `book.html`:

   ```
   <TITLE>Fender</TITLE>
   <LINK REL=stylesheet HREF="museum.css" TYPE="text/css">
   ```

   This code links the style sheet (which you'll complete later) to this page.
4. After the `<BODY>` tag, type this code:

   ```
   <CENTER>
   <PARAM NAME=Goto VALUE="">
   ```

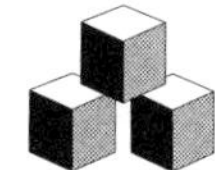


```
<PARAM NAME=Title VALUE="Fender">
<PARAM NAME=TitleFont VALUE="SansSerif">
<PARAM NAME=TitleColor VALUE="FF0000">
<PARAM NAME=TitleGlow VALUE="true">
<PARAM NAME=TitleSize VALUE="40">
<PARAM NAME=TitleTop VALUE="51">
<PARAM NAME=SubTitle VALUE="">
<PARAM NAME=SubTitleColor VALUE="ff0000">
<PARAM NAME=SubTitleFont VALUE="SansSerif">
<PARAM NAME=SubTitleSize VALUE="22">
<PARAM NAME=SubTitleTop VALUE="55">
<PARAM NAME=Message

VALUE="Mustang...Stratocaster...Telecaster...Bronco...Marauder...Jazzmas
ter... ">
<PARAM NAME=MessageColor VALUE="000000">
<PARAM NAME=MessageFont VALUE="Courier">
<PARAM NAME=MessageSize VALUE="20">
<PARAM NAME=MessageTop VALUE="75">
<PARAM NAME=BackColor VALUE="FFFFFF">
<PARAM NAME=Timer VALUE="30">
<PARAM NAME=MessageScroll VALUE="true">
<PARAM NAME=WhiteMask VALUE="false">
<PARAM NAME=Frame VALUE="_self">
<PARAM NAME=OutofScreen VALUE="true">
</APPLET>
</CENTER>
```

5. Save this page (still with the name `fender.html`) and open it in your browser.

The applet should appear in the top center of the page, as in Figure 13.1. The word `Fender` should pulsate in red, and a scrolling marquee should appear under it in black, listing several of the Fender guitar types.

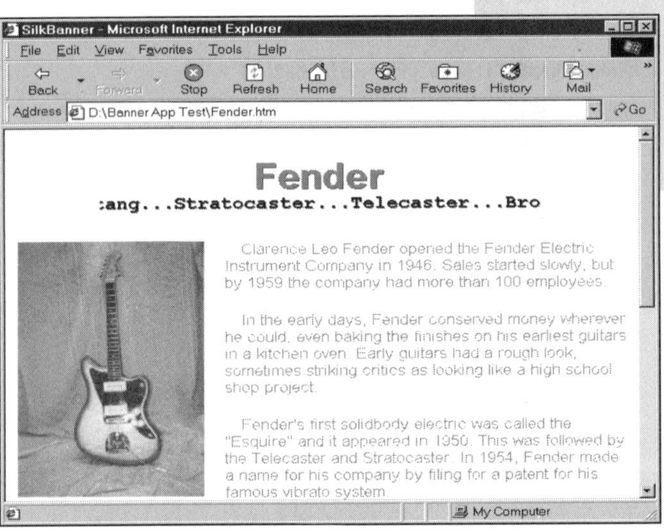

Figure 13.1 This is the guitar brand page with the applet active.

ANALYSIS

One of the virtues of Java applets for this kind of page dressing is that it's infinitely flexible. It's easy to change the characteristics of `afSilkBanner` by just changing the arguments you pass to it. These are held in `<PARAM>` tags. The syntax for the `<PARAM>` tag is:

```
<PARAM NAME=Method/Property VALUE="argument">
```

Nearly every applet requires at least one `<PARAM>` tag. Unless you have some kind of documentation, or the source code for the applet, or some tremendous intuition, you won't be able to pass the correct arguments to the applet via the `<PARAM>` tag. Remember that Java is compiled, not interpreted, so you can't look at its code the way you can scan JavaScript.

Arguments are data that are passed to applets, functions, or other program items. Arguments can be characters or numbers, or even Boolean conditions.

There are 23 methods or properties that `afSilkBanner` can use. Most of them are obvious with a little thought, and the rest can be determined experimentally. For example, consider the first few lines:

```
<PARAM NAME=Goto VALUE="">
<PARAM NAME=Title VALUE="Fender">
<PARAM NAME=TitleFont VALUE="SansSerif">
<PARAM NAME=TitleColor VALUE="FF0000">
```

The `Goto` value sets an URL to point to when the visitor clicks on the banner. You can make this a page of Fender guitar photographs or an appeal for money. Or, as here, you can leave the string empty and send the visitor nowhere. Used with Banner Factory, the `Goto` default is the Banner Factory home page.

The argument `Title` is the string that appears in the main text area of the banner. `TitleFont` is the font family that the browser will use, and it depends on what the default family is on the computer the visitor is using. The text color for this title is red, because FF0000 is an RGB hex code for a particular shade of red. Try changing this value to `00FF00` and see what happens, or get even more daring and play with intermediate color values like `CDAA11`.

The other parameters are set the same way. To change the appearance and behavior of the applet, you just change the arguments you send it.

Some of the parameters you'll probably be most interested in are these:

```
<PARAM NAME=Title VALUE="Fender">
```

This parameter determines the text of the main title.

```
<PARAM NAME=SubTitle VALUE="">
```

You're not using a subtitle for this application, but if you were, this is where you'd type the text for it. You'd type something between the question marks.

```
<PARAM NAME=Message VALUE="Mustang...Stratocaster...Telecaster...
Bronco...Marauder...Jazzmaster... ">
```

This is the text of the scrolling marquee under the title. You could replace the partial list of Fender brands with something even more clever.

```
<APPLET CODE=afSilkBanner.class NAME=afSilkBanner WIDTH=450 HEIGHT=82 >
```

This applet tag lets you set the width and height in pixels. You may want to stretch out the applet a bit more, or shrink it.

Java and JavaScript

The syntax of Java and the syntax of JavaScript are remarkably similar, so much so that you can take your burgeoning knowledge of JavaScript straight to Java if you want to. In fact, with as much JavaScript as you know from the last chapter, you probably can figure out quite a lot of Java coding, too.

Java is much more persnickety about its objects and variables than JavaScript is. Java has its drawbacks, as do all computer languages, but it's rapidly gaining popularity because of its cross-platform capabilities.

One big difference between Java and JavaScript is that Java is compiled, whereas JavaScript is interpreted. *Compiling* is a process of converting the easy-to-read wording you're already familiar with into computer-readable language. The program's more accessible wording is called *source code*. In Java's case, the source code is compiled into *bytecode* that's readable by the browser.

JavaScript never undergoes this transformation. The browser interprets JavaScript just the way you wrote it. That makes JavaScript slower than Java, but it's far easier to develop and maintain.

If you want to get started with Java, you can find the free Java developer kit at:

http://www.sun.com/java/products/platform.jhtml#core

It includes the Java compiler and samples.

Writing and Using the CSS

In general, a cascading style sheet (CSS) is used to set the appearance of fonts, text, links, and tables (plus plenty of other things this book doesn't have time to get into) for every page in the site that uses the style sheet. If you're interested in exploring the outer reaches of what CSS can do, check out the W3C's files on CSS at:

http://www.w3.org

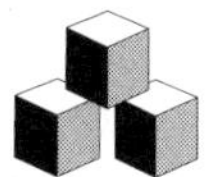

There are two CSS standards: CSS1 and CSS2. CSS1 was, as its name implies, first out of the gate, and its successor, CSS2, has much more capability. This project uses CSS2, because the newest browsers can generally handle most of it, although there are exceptions. CSS1 style sheets are compatible with CSS2, so a style sheet written to CSS1 standards will work fine in a browser designed to CSS2 standards. In Project 3, though, you won't be stretching the limits of CSS2. It's not yet tried-and-true technology.

Although it may seem that CSS is one of those technologies that one or another browser maker came up with and imposed on the others (like JavaScript), CSS is actually a fully-defined set of standards for writing style sheets, promulgated by the W3C. It's a standard for both you, the Web author, and browser makers such as Microsoft and Netscape.

The first step toward writing the CSS is to analyze your site's needs and compile a list of the things you'll need to specify in the CSS. You already did this in Chapter 11, so now it's time to implement those decisions.

Linking the Style Sheet

Even with a style sheet in hand, you won't be able to use it until you link it to the HTML pages it controls. This is accomplished by placing a line like this on each HTML page you want to have affected by the CSS:

```
<LINK REL=stylesheet HREF="cssname.css" TYPE="text/css">
```

The line must be placed somewhere before the </HEAD> end tag.

EXERCISE

1. Open fender.html and book.html and type the following line into the heads of both documents:

   ```
   <LINK REL=stylesheet HREF="museum.css" TYPE="text/css">
   ```

2. Leave book.html open in Notepad.
3. Close fender.html for now.

ANALYSIS

To make life easier while writing and testing a style sheet, you're well advised to open an existing HTML page in Notepad and a separate Notepad session with the style sheet in it. This way you can make changes to both the HTML page and the style sheet. Then you can immediately test the result in your browsers.

Just as with testing scripts, you can write all of the rules and then test them as a complete unit, or you can test each rule as it's written. I advocate testing each rule as it's written. You can test on a dummy HTML page, if you've made one.

In CSS, everything is specified in *rules*. The single line you'll type into the style sheet in the next exercise is an example of a single rule.

Defining Fonts and Text

EXERCISE

1. If `book.html` isn't already open, open it in the browser.
2. Open `book.html` in Notepad.
3. Open another copy of Notepad and start a new document, then save it as `museum.css`. This is the new style sheet for this project.
4. Type the start and end style tags into `museum.css` (on separate lines):

```
<STYLE>
</STYLE>
```

5. Add this line between them:

```
H1.bkpgtitle {font-family: sans-serif; font-size: 20pt; color: red}
```

6. Switch to the Notepad copy with `book.html` open in it.
7. Find the line of code near the top of the body section that displays the top-level heading:

```
<FONT SIZE="5" COLOR="red" FACE="arial">From the Robertson Museum
Bookshelf...</FONT>
```

In this line the text `From the Robertson Museum Bookshelf...` has its size, font, and color set with the `<FONT>` tag.

8. Delete that line and substitute this one:

```
<H1 class=bkpgtitle >From the Robertson Museum Bookshelf...</H1>
```

9. Save both documents and refresh `book.html` in the browser.

Something's wrong after you refresh, isn't it? The heading text isn't Arial, it isn't red, and it's the wrong size. You've already linked to the page with the `<LINK>` tag, haven't you? Take it from me, the style sheet coding is valid. So why doesn't it work?

ANALYSIS

This is a "gotcha" that has to afflict almost every new author of CSSs.

In the document object model, an `<H1>` isn't the same everywhere it appears. Recall that in the browser world, everything except the top object is a child of another object. An `<H1>` can be a child object of `<BODY>`, or it can be a child object of `<DIV>`, or of `<SPAN>`. Each `<H1>` is a different object, which can be separately defined in the CSS.

This particular `<H1>` and its class `.bkpgtitle` is supposed to be a child of `<BODY>`, but you haven't actually said that, and neither IE nor Navigator makes the assumption.

EXERCISE

To make the style rule work, do this:

1. Add this line to `museum.css`, right above the `<H1>` rule:

```
BODY {color: white}
```

2. Save and refresh.

Now the `<H1>` works, as Figure 13.2 shows.

This illustrates the need to always consider the object hierarchy when you're dealing with browsers.

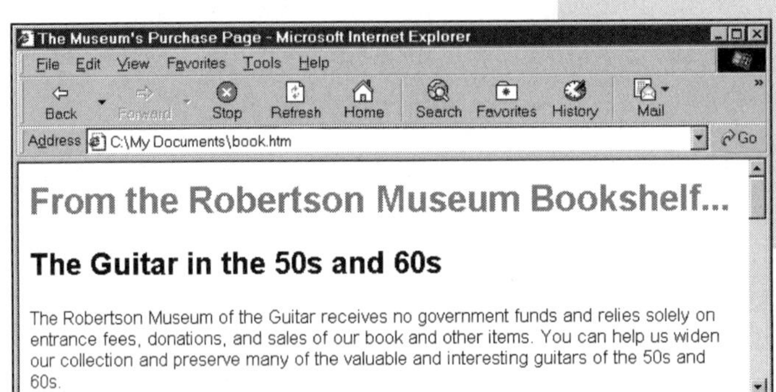

Figure 13.2 The top heading looks fine after you get the hierarchy straight.

EXERCISE

Let's finish up the fonts and text. These two things are combined in the CSS rules. You have another heading to specify, and several different text types:

1. Below the <H1> rule in `museum.css`, add this code:

```
H1.bktitle {font-family: sans-serif; font-size: 16pt; color: black}
P.brand {margin-left: 10pt; text-indent: 1em; font-family: sans-serif;
  font-size: 10pt; color: red; text-align: center}
P.brand EM {font-style: italic}
P.caption {font-family: sans-serif; font-style: italic;
  font-size: 10pt; color: black}
P.general {font-family: sans-serif; font-size: 10pt; color: black}
P.comment {font-family: sans-serif; font-style: italic; font-size:
  12pt; color: red}
```

2. In `book.html`, find the line with the book title in it, which looks like this:

```
<FONT SIZE="4"><B>The Guitar in the 50s and 60s</B></FONT>
```

Again, the dummy version of the page used the <FONT> tag to give a rough idea of how the page should look.

3. Delete that line and substitute this line:

```
<H1 class=bktitle>The Guitar in the 50s and 60s</H1>
```

The first line after this is a <P> paragraph.

4. Revise the <P> tag to make it look like this:

```
<P class=general>
```

   The P.general from the CSS will now be used in this tag.

5. Save and refresh.

After you refresh, the other paragraphs tagged with <P> will look the same, but the one with the .general class is sans serif and 10 point, looking rather sleek on the page.

6. Go to all the other <P> tags on this page and add the .general class to them the same way.
7. Save and refresh.
8. To take care of the single comments text, locate this code:

```
<P><FONT SIZE="+1" COLOR="red"><EM><STRONG>Do you have a question
or comment for us?</STRONG></EM></FONT><P>
```

   Replace it with this:

```
<P class=comment>Do you have a question or comment for us?<P>
```

9. Save and refresh.

You should see by this time how it's all fitting together.

You now have the core of a linked style sheet. The typical CSS rule looks like this, a line from your own style sheet:

```
P.caption {font-family: sans-serif; font-style: italic;
  font-size: 10pt; color: black}
```

To the far left is the selector (P.caption). It's followed by a block that's framed between two braces. Within the block are declarations and values after colons (font-family: sans-serif), separated by semicolons.

The selector is a tag name, optionally followed by a class name. This permits you to define an almost unlimited number of different <P> tags alone. And remember that you now have two <H1> classes, too, to which you can add other heading tags and classes. You can't create your own tags, but that's not much of a barrier when you can create tag classes.

The standard sans serif font for Windows is Arial, whereas the default sans serif font on Macintosh is Helvetica. The CSS rules cover both with `font-family: sans-serif`. The browser picks the most appropriate font for the current platform. You can, if you like, specify a font, but using the more generic `sans-serif` is safer.

Now pay some special attention to this code:

```
P.brand {margin-left: 10pt; text-indent: 1em; font-family: sans-serif;
  font-size: 10pt; color: red; text-align: left}
```

This is where you determine how much space there is between the left-hand and right-hand cell text. In HTML, this is usually done with the `CELLPADDING` attribute of the table cell. When using style sheets, however, it's a better idea to set the margin with `margin-left` (in this case to 10 points). Then the first line is indented one em. An em is somewhat variable from browser to browser, but you don't need precision here, just an attractive indent.

EXERCISE

1. Close `book.html`.
2. Open `fender.html` in Notepad.
3. Open `fender.html` in the browser so that you can see what you're creating.

   In `fender.html`, you need caption text and text for the table. These are defined by the following two style rules:

   ```
   P.brand {font-family: sans-serif; font-size: 10pt; color: red}
   P.caption {font-family: sans-serif; font-style: italic;
     font-size: 10pt; color: black}
   ```

4. In `fender.html`, find the caption under the graphic. It looks like this:

   ```
   <P>This Jazzmaster still has its original hang-tags. From the museum
   collection.
   ```

5. Change the `<P>` tag to read

   ```
   <P class=caption>
   ```

6. Save `fender.html` and refresh it in the browser. The caption under the photograph is now sans serif and italic.
7. In the `fender.html` code, find the first `<P>` tag in the right-hand cell's text.
8. Change it to `<P class=brand>`.

9. Delete the `<FONT>` tag after the `<P>` tag, because you won't need it anymore.
10. Change all the rest of the `<P>` tags to `<P class=brand>`.
11. Save `fender.html` and refresh it in the browser.

Note that the performer's names are now in black.

ANALYSIS

If you've been using both IE 4/5 and Navigator 4, you may notice that some of the effects aren't the same in all browsers. Remember that CSS2 hasn't been fully implemented by every browser maker, so don't make your pages overly dependent on the CSS2 effects. If you want to be really safe, stick with CSS1. The CSS1 standards can be found at:

http://www.w3.org/Style/CSS/

The trick of having the `<EM>` tag make the emphasis text black in addition to italic lies in the placement of the `EM` selector. Recall that in the style sheet, you typed this line:

```
P.brand EM {color: black}
```

As shown in Figure 13.3, this line makes the `<EM>` tag produce black text when it's used within the `.brand` class. An `<EM>` tag used anywhere else behaves as it always has.

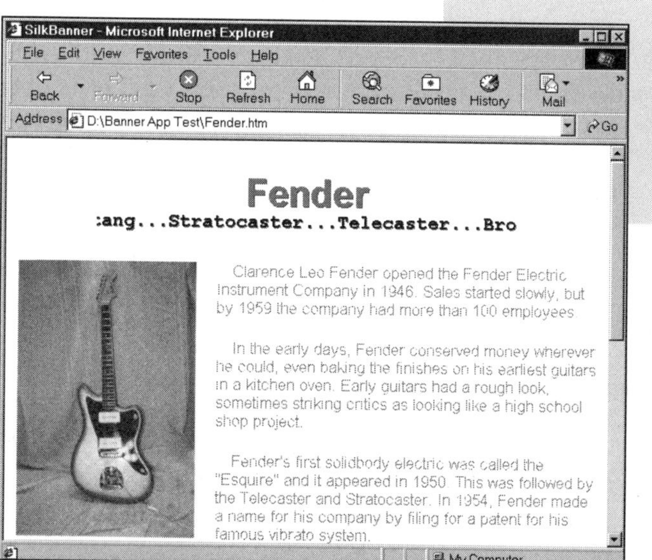

Figure 13.3
Text appears on the guitar brand page as defined by your new CSS.

Defining Links

Now for the links. The unvisited links are to be standard blue, but when visited they should turn teal. And when the visitor hovers over a link, it should turn black.

EXERCISE

1. In the style sheet, add these lines:

```
A.internal {color: blue}
A.internal:visited {color: teal}
A.internal:hover {color: black}
```

2. In `fender.html`, find the four links defined in anchor tags at the bottom of the page.
3. Add the class codes to make the lines look like this:

```
<TD><A class=internal HREF="index.html">Home</A></TD>
<TD><A class=internal HREF="book.html">Buy our book</A></TD>
<TD><A class=internal HREF="about.html">About the museum</A></TD>
<TD><A class=internal HREF="mailto:somebody@somewhere.net">Contact
us</A></TD>
```

4. Save and refresh.
5. Run your cursor over the links. If you're in IE 4 or 5, you'll see them blink to a different color as you pass over.
6. Click on `Home` or `Buy our book`, and then go back to this page after the new page loads. The link has changed color to teal.

IE 4/5 exploits hover, but Netscape 4 doesn't. Still, little is lost for Netscape users, because hover isn't central to the page operation.

Colors in style sheets can be set simply by using a color name, such as `red` or `black`. In fact, you have 16 colors to pick from (a complete list was presented in the "Designating Link Colors" section in Chapter 4).

If you want better control, you can specify colors in RGB (red-green-blue) fashion, like this:

```
P {color: rgb(100, 00, 150)}
```

Note that you have to leave a space between each color component. On my monitor, by the way, this example results in a light violet.

Don't get fanatical about fine-tuning colors with RGB. Many things affect how the visitor sees colors, such as monitor type and brand, video card, operating system, and how he has his computer's settings defined.

Defining Tables

Last, the table definitions need to be done. Most real CSS table definitions are cell definitions of the <TD> tag:

EXERCISE

1. At the bottom of the style sheet, type this:

```
TD.brandtext {text-align: left}
TD.brand {text-align: left; width: 160px;}
TD.bottomlinks {width: 150px; text-align: center}
```

2. Return to fender.html.
3. Find the <TD> tag for the left cell and make it look like this:

```
<TD class=brand>
```

4. Find the right-hand cell's <TD> tag and make it look like this:

```
<TD class=brandtext>
```

5. Find the <TD> tag for the bottom links table and replace it with this one:

```
<TD class=bottomlinks>
```

6. Save and refresh.

ANALYSIS ▼

The cell definitions .brand and .bottomlinks specify widths for their cells (in pixels, designated by px). All three specify text alignment.

This points out an apparent conflict between defined text and its enclosing cells. If a cell specifies left alignment, while the <P> tag specifies center alignment, which wins?

As is usual in cascading style sheets, the specification physically closest to the affected object wins, in this case the <P> tag.

Now that you have your style sheet done, imagine that to fully complete the guitar museum Web site, you would have to create 11 more pages

just like `fender.html`, with information on each one about another brand of guitar. By using the appropriate class-based tags, you can determine how all 11 will look. If you then change your mind and, for example, want to make the brand text maroon instead of red, you need only change one word in one line to make all 12 pages change simultaneously. Score one for the Webmaster.

Summary

Using scripts, Java, and cascading style sheets can add enormously to the flexibility, interest, and maintainability of your site. Earlier in the project you had a taste of JavaScript. In this chapter you have used a ready-made Java applet and have created a linked style sheet that can be used as the basis for an entire Web site.

Although you've successfully completed Project 3 for the purposes of this book, there is much about these topics that you haven't explored yet, so I urge you to play hard with these tools and concoct your own trickery as you think about ways to develop Web sites that will wow the world!

Project 3 Summary

You designed the advanced Web site for this final project with the idea of including some of the flashiest features available for today's Web sites. It took more effort to create these features, but you greatly improved the overall experience for your site's visitors.

Scripting, applets, and cascading style sheets helped you to deliver a fun and involving trip through your site, but you made sure not to go overboard with features that would get in the way of the substantive content that visitors seek.

Your technique for obtaining information from visitors was made more sophisticated in this project, because you verified that input was acceptable prior to submission.

You worked with cascading style sheets to make relatively simple changes to the appearance of your pages, but you can extend that knowledge easily to the many other applications of CSS that are possible within a Web site.

Uploading and Promoting Your Web Site

At this point, you have created at least one Web site of some sort: a personal Web site, a business site, or perhaps a site for a not-for-profit organization. Maybe you've done all three, and maybe you have even ventured out on your own and modified the site (or sites) to suit your own purposes.

Putting Your Site on the Web

Now that you have your own Web site in working order, with all the graphics and frames and sounds and everything else that you wanted to include, you have one more requirement to meet. You have to make it available to the rest of the Web-connected world.

The instructions in this chapter essentially are geared toward placing personal sites on the Web. In most cases, you can create and upload personal Web sites by yourself. In the case of business Web sites, however, procedures aren't necessarily the same. In the first place, businesses typically pay for their sites, and they usually have several possible plans from which to choose. These plans can vary in the amount of space available, the number of features and types of functionality available on the site's servers, and so on. A business owner, then, needs to choose a plan in consultation with the Internet service provider (ISP) or online service such as America Online, CompuServe, or Prodigy.

In addition, ISPs and online services may have optional features, or *add-ons,* for businesses that want them. Custom programming, such as CGI scripts specific to the business's site, is one possibility, as is an FTP server available to the business's customers. Another possibility is the availability of raw statistics (or even statistical analysis) showing how many visitors used your site, how much time they spent (and in which areas), what they downloaded from your site, and so on. Besides scripting, FTP, and statistics, a number of other specific features or services might be available.

In short, a business site is more involved than a personal Web site and thus requires more interaction with and direction from the ISP or online service you choose to service your site.

Most ISPs, online services, corporate networks, and universities are likely to have restrictions on the kind of material that may be put on a Web site residing on their servers. Pornography, for example, and racially/ethnically derogatory material are usually forbidden. And if you're not supposed to conduct any business activities on your page, they will look for that, too. Sometimes, the server owners also watch for copyright infringement.

Information for America Online Subscribers

Once an upstart in the online service arena, America Online (AOL) grew very quickly, surpassing pioneer and prior industry leader

CompuServe. In 1998, AOL bought CompuServe outright. For vast numbers of people, America Online *is* their experience of the World Wide Web.

General Information

AOL account holders are entitled to free space for a personal Web site. The AOL term for this space is My Place. The AOL policy of allowing one account holder to have as many as five screen names (most of which are probably given to family members), however, means that the people with those screen names *also* get free space. In each case, the screen name owner is permitted to have 2MB of storage space. The total amount of storage space allowed per account, then, is 10MB.

If you are the only person who uses your AOL account, you cannot combine those five allotments into one 10MB space. You can, however, create links from one screen name's space to another.

After you have placed your site on the Web, your Web address takes the following form:

```
http://members.aol.com/yourscreenname
```

Of course, your actual screen name replaces *yourscreenname.* Remember not to use spaces. Also, you can keep everything in lowercase, because AOL is not case-sensitive. (Don't assume that is true for the Web as a whole, however. I suggest that you always use mixed case if that's the way an address is written.)

Procedures

When you have created your Web site, and you know it works—you *have* tested it on your home computer, haven't you, for broken links and validation errors?—you need to upload it to your personal My Place space. To do that, you use FTP. America Online has its own FTP pro-

File Transfer Protocol, or FTP, is a way to move files quickly from one Internet location to another.

gram for transferring files, so you don't need to search the Internet for one to use.

Follow these steps to upload your Web site to My Place:

1. Log onto America Online.
2. Go to Keyword: `My Place`.
3. Click on the `My FTPspace` link.

If this is not the first time you've uploaded files to your FTP space, a list of them appears now. If you need to edit one of those existing files, just select it.

4. Click on Upload.
5. AOL now asks for the name of the file you want to upload. Type the name of the file in the Remote FileName text box.

Make sure that you type the exact name of the file you're uploading. When dealing with the Internet, it's not always *necessary* to be concerned about upper- and lowercase. However, it is always *much safer* to get into the habit of typing filenames as written, including upper- and lowercase.

ASCII (or text) files are files that consist of nothing more than simple text.

6. Next you must indicate what kind of file you are uploading. For your HTML pages, the type is text. For graphics files, the type is binary.

No formatting or graphics appear in text files. Files whose extensions are **.txt**, **.asc**, **.html**, or **.htm** are text files. *Binary* files are all other file types.

7. Click on Continue.
8. Next you should see the Upload File window. Click on the Select File option.
9. Browse through your folders, or directories, until you locate the file you want to upload. Select that file.

10. Click on Send File in the Upload File window.
11. Repeat the process for other files you want to upload.

After you have uploaded all of your Web site's files to My Place, you can join Hometown AOL. Hometown AOL is divided into "communities," which are general categories of sites. You place your Web site in the one you think is most appropriate for the type of site you have created.

Follow these steps to join Hometown AOL:

1. Log onto America Online.
2. Go to Keyword: `Hometown` and then click on Add Pages. Alternatively, you can go to Keyword: `My Place` and then click on Join Hometown AOL.
3. Choose the category and community most appropriate to your site.
4. Type a description of your site. This description should give visitors a good idea of what your site is about, so that they can determine whether it's what they're looking for.

That's it. Your Web site is now online.

Later, when you want to change one or more of your files, you can do so by following these steps:

1. Log onto America Online.
2. Go to Keyword: `My Place`.
3. Click on the `My FTPspace` link. The files already present in your FTPspace appear in a list. Now you can edit them and upload the new versions.

Information for CompuServe Subscribers

Once the behemoth of online services, CompuServe now is a part of America Online. CompuServe advertises itself as being for "serious users" of the Internet, and it has a greater proportion of business customers than AOL (and at the time of this writing, slightly higher prices for comparable plans), but that doesn't mean individuals cannot or should not use CompuServe.

General Information

CompuServe offers each member a significant amount of personal space: 5MB. For most people, this probably is all they will ever need.

When you have placed your site on the Web, your Web address takes the following form:

http://ourworld.compuserve.com/homepages/*directoryname*

Your actual directory name replaces *directoryname.*

Procedures

Follow these steps to place your Web site on CompuServe's system:

1. Log onto CompuServe.
2. Go to the `HPWIZ` forum.

   If you use a Mac, go to the `MACPUBWIZ` forum instead.
3. Download the Home Page Wizard software.
4. Start Home Page Wizard.
5. Tell Home Page Wizard that you want to upload files by choosing Upload Files.
6. Click on the Next button.
7. Fill in the information that the software asks you for.
8. Click on the Next button.
9. The batch of information the Home Page Wizard asks for now is optional, but since it's about your site, you should include it. Fill in this information as you see fit.

   This information becomes public and is included in the directory. The wizard asks for this information because other people will use it to find your site. It's important to fill in the information if you want people to locate you through the directory.
10. Click on Next.
11. In the dialog box that appears, select all the files you want to upload. They appear in the lower portion of the dialog box.

12. After selecting all the files to upload, click on Done.
13. Click on Next.
14. Now you tell the Home Page Wizard which page should serve as your home page (the opening page of your Web site). If you have named your files as suggested in this book, the opening page of your Web site is named `index.html` and you designate that file as your home page in this step.
15. Click on Next.
16. In the following window, fill in your account information.
17. Click on Next.

    At this point, the Home Page Wizard takes over and uploads the files.

If you realize that you left out a file that you wanted to upload, you can go back and get it easily. After the Home Page Wizard finishes, click on the Back button, select the forgotten file, and then click on Next.

18. After uploading files, you have the opportunity to delete any files that are already in your server space. Of course, nothing should be there the first time, but whenever you update your site, you may (or may not) want to delete something here.

After completing this process, you see the address of your personal home page. Congratulations! You're now online.

Information for Subscribers to Internet Service Providers

The world is full of companies that offer access to the Internet and World Wide Web without all the special interest areas and proprietary features of online services like AOL and CompuServe. These companies are called *Internet service providers (ISPs).*

If you have a business site, space on your ISP's server is not going to be free. Instead, you will be charged a monthly or annual rate. And probably, as the amount of traffic to your Web site increases, so will your rate. Check with your ISP for specifics regarding the amount of space you can have and the rates charged.

Not all ISPs provide Web hosting services; some only offer Internet access for individuals who want to surf the Net. The quickest way to generate a list of available ISPs is to go to your favorite Internet search engine and enter the search string `Web hosting` or `Web hosting plans`. You may additionally want to limit the search to a specific geographical region or with any other limiting factor that matters to you.

Like AOL and CompuServe, an ISP typically gives each subscriber a certain amount of private space on the ISP's Web server. Policies and procedures regarding Web sites may vary from one ISP to another, so you need to check with a handful of ISPs to find out specifics about their services before you commit to one ISP.

The instructions given here for placing your Web site online via an ISP must be kept general in nature, because ISPs vary from one another regarding specifics. The overall procedure should be similar to that outlined in the following steps, but remember that you must contact your chosen ISP to get precise instructions.

Generally, placing a Web site on an ISP's server works something like the following:

1. You create and test your Web site on a local computer.
2. You use FTP to upload the files to your private space on the Web server. You need to use your name and password to get into this space.

3. You may need to have your own FTP program to upload files. Some, like WS_FTP and CuteFTP, can be downloaded from a number of places on the Internet. If you need specific directions for making an FTP program work, contact your ISP.

If you need to download an FTP program, try one of the following sources:

http://www.tucows.com/
http://www.shareware.com/

4. The ISP may or may not allow you to use subdirectories, such as `\images`. Contact the ISP for details.
5. If your site involves scripts, especially CGI scripts, the ISP may want to check them out before placing them on the server. This is a safety measure to ensure that the scripts will work and do no harm to the server or files. In addition, the ISP wants to make sure that the CGI scripts create no security problems.

Many ISPs already have scripts on their servers that their subscribers can use. This pool of scripts can save you from having to write your own scripts and then submitting them for approval by the ISP. Check with your ISP to see what scripts may be available.

6. The ISP also may have a menu or directory of subscriber Web sites. If so, take advantage of it. It's a good way to begin getting your site noticed.

That should be about it. The ISP you sign up with will give you the specific procedures you need to follow.

All decent ISPs have technical support available online and usually by telephone. Telephone support may not be available 24 hours a day, but ISPs typically have FAQs online to answer the most common questions. Try that first, and then, if necessary, you can submit a question online or by telephone.

Information for Users of Corporate or University Networks or Intranets

All large companies and most smaller ones have departments that deal with the company's computing needs. Likewise, every college and university has a department that handles the school's computing requirements. Many companies have a site on the World Wide Web, and more and more universities and colleges are establishing a presence on the Web, as well. In cases where the company or university has a network—not just individual computers—a network administrator is in charge of what happens with the network. The same is true of intranets, which are basically company- or university-wide systems that take advantage of all the same software, tools, and functionality that work on the Internet, such as e-mail and FTP and Web browsers. The difference is that an intranet is not open to people outside the corporation or university.

An intranet is essentially a closed network that looks and acts like the Internet.

In each of these instances, the company or university has established policies and procedures that govern Web sites or Web pages on the network or intranet. If you are interested in establishing a Web page or Web site for yourself (especially in universities) or for your department (in companies and universities), you need to find out what those policies and procedures are. The best place to start is with the network administrator or someone in the Information Technology (IT) Department. If they allow sites or pages of the kind you're interested in deploying, they can give you details regarding policies, content, and so on.

Publicizing Your Web Site

The point of placing a Web site on the Internet or on a corporate or university network is to make information available to others. Whether this information consists of company product descriptions you want to make available to potential customers or merely your opinion on the resurgence of swing music, you want people to know what you have to say. You don't want to have a Web site that no one visits.

Search engines and Web directories are the keys to helping others find your Web site. A search engine examines your site and indexes it according to the contents of your `<META>` tags and the text of the site. They use

 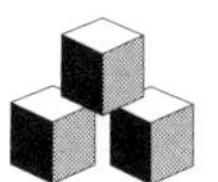

a *spider* (little automated program) to start on one of your site's pages and then follow all the links, indexing as it goes. These spiders occasionally reindex your site, keeping records of your site relatively up to date.

A Web directory is different in a couple of ways. A directory may index your site only once. After indexing the site, the directory places your site in a category. If you change your site's contents later, the index no longer matches up with reality. The second difference is in the way you locate what you're trying to find. Suppose that you want to find information about Martin D-45 guitars. If you're using a search engine such as AltaVista, you enter the search terms you're trying find: "Martin D-45." AltaVista returns all the documents it has indexed that contain those terms. If you want to find sites in a Web directory, you can either search or you can *drill down* to find what you want. When you drill down in this instance—looking for a specific Martin guitar—you might go through the following layers:

Business & Economy
Companies
Music
Instruments and Equipment
Manufacturers
Stringed Instruments
Guitar and Bass
Martin Guitar Company

On the other hand, if you use the advanced search capability of Yahoo! and search for the exact phrase "Martin D-45," Yahoo! locates 464 sites. That's a lot of results—and a lot to wade through in your search for information. Searching is likely to give you more results than drilling down, but drilling down may help you find the exact site you want. It's your choice, so use either or both methods, depending on what you're trying to find.

If someone conducts a search on a given topic, the search engine returns a list of all the sites it finds that have information on that topic. What you need to do is make sure that search engines know your site exists. With the number of search engines in existence (which number in the hundreds), the more you can notify of your site's existence, the more likely it is that someone will find you.

What it all boils down to is that the most important thing you can do is register your site with as many search engines and Web directories as possible. That's where Web promotion services come into play.

Web Promotion Services

Many Web promotion services exist, and their purpose is to help you publicize your site. Some of these services charge a fee, and others are free. They also vary in the number of search engines they notify; many of them can submit your site to hundreds of search engines at once. In all cases, they can save you vast amounts of time.

To begin to get a handle on what Web site promotion services offer, you might want to visit the following URLs, a couple of which *list* services, and the remainder of which *are* services:

http://dir.yahoo.com/Business_and_Economy/Companies/Internet_Services/Web_Services/Promotion/

http://infoseek.go.com/WebDir/Web_site_promotion

http://signpost.merseyworld.com/

http://www.submit-it.com/

http://www.netcreations.com/postmaster/

Adding Your Web Site to Search Engines

If you prefer, you can add the URL of your site to search engines and Web directories by yourself. You may want to do this if you are in no particular hurry, for example, or if you don't care whether your site is

Prima publishes an excellent resource that can help you publicize your site. For more ideas and details on how to make your Web site known, refer to the following book:

William R. Stanek, *Increase Your Web Traffic in a Weekend* (Rocklin, California: Prima Publishing, 1998)

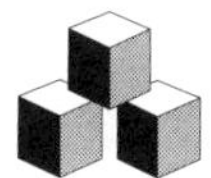

indexed by the hundreds of search engines on the Web. You also may just want to save some money. Besides, there's that feeling of accomplishment that comes with doing something yourself!

The purpose of this section is to help you get a jump start on publicizing your Web site. This jump start involves getting your site indexed by some search engines.

> **Note**
>
> **If you decide to add your URL yourself, start with the major search engines and Web directories. Make sure that you follow their instructions and that your site doesn't violate any of their rules. Their procedures and policies are always subject to change. When you're ready to upload your URL, be sure to follow each search engine's instructions and guidelines scrupulously for the best results.**

Things to Remember When Submitting to Search Engines and Web Directories

For excellent results when submitting your site to search engines and Web directories, keep in mind the following:

- Don't rely on a spider reading your entire Web site and then indexing. Spiders generally read only a portion of the site, namely, the first lines they come across.
- Search engines rely heavily on `<META>` tags when ranking a Web site. If the words in your `<META>` tag's `KEYWORDS` attribute match what the search engine spider finds as it searches your site, your ranking will be higher than it might be if they don't match.
- If you change the content of your Web site, make sure that you also change the `KEYWORDS` attribute to reflect the current content of the site.
- Give your site an accurate title in the `<TITLE>` tag, preferably one that matches at least some of the `KEYWORDS` in your `<META>` tag. Matching words can help raise the ranking of your site.

For a detailed discussion of the `<META>` tag, refer to Chapter 4, "Beginning to Build the Basic Web Site."

AltaVista

A favorite search engine of one of the authors—for Boolean searches—is AltaVista, which has been around for a long time. Follow these steps to add your site to AltaVista:

1. Go online, and then type the following URL in the Address or URL text box:

   www.altavista.com/

2. Press Enter.

   Figure 14.1 shows the AltaVista opening page.

3. Click on the Add a Page link at the bottom of the page.

   Figure 14.2 shows the bottom of the page you use to add your URL to the AltaVista search engine.

4. At the bottom of the page is one text box. Type your URL in that text box.
5. Click on the Submit URL button.

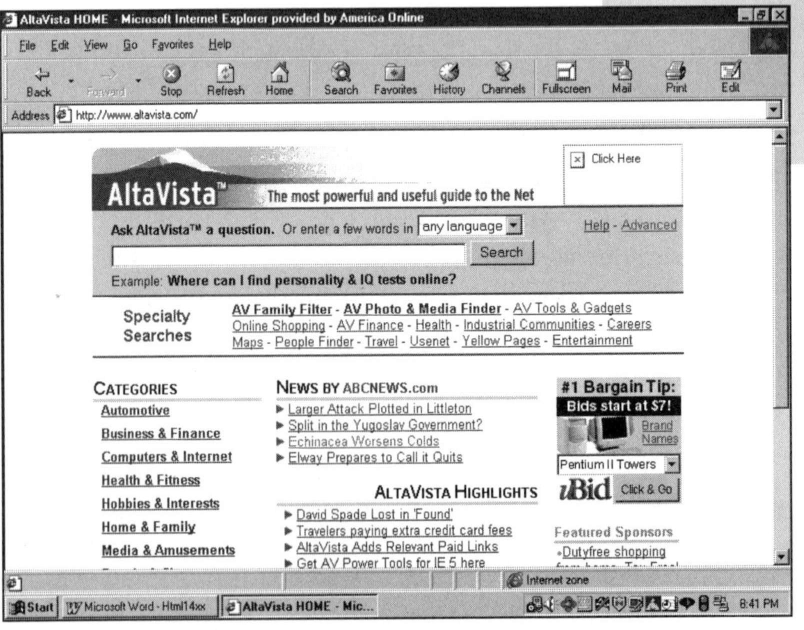

Figure 14.1 This is the AltaVista search engine's interface.

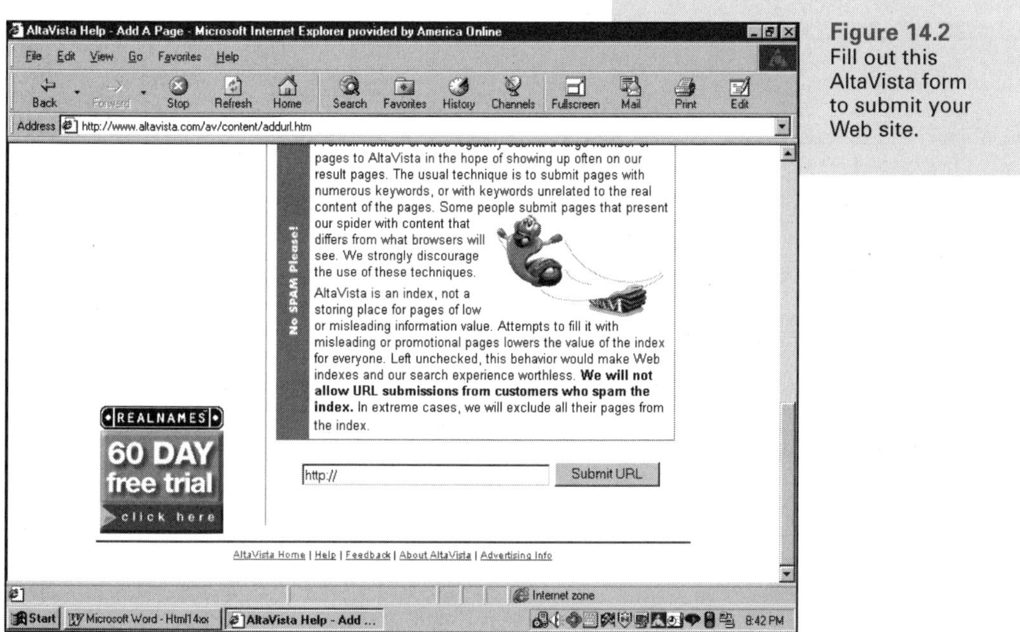

Figure 14.2
Fill out this AltaVista form to submit your Web site.

The URL submission process can't get much simpler than this one. Your page should be available within about 48 hours, if everything went the way it should have gone.

Excite

Excite ia another popular search engine, to which you should be sure to submit your site's URL by following these steps:

1. Go online, and then type the following URL in the Address or URL text box near the top of the screen:

   www.excite.com/

2. Press Enter.

   Figure 14.3 shows the Excite opening page.

3. At the bottom of the opening page, click on the Add URL link.

   Figure 14.4 shows the form that you see.

4. Type your site's URL in the Your URL text box.

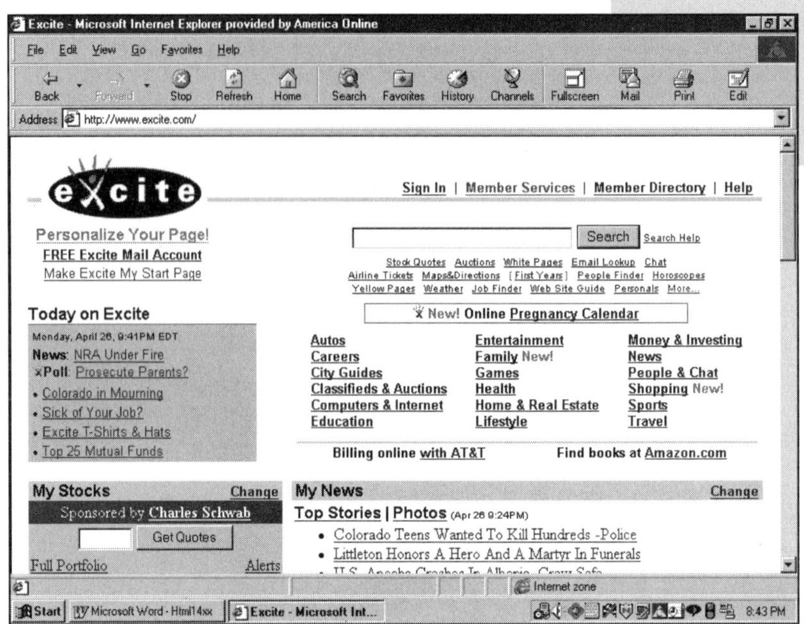

Figure 14.3 This is the Excite search engine's interface.

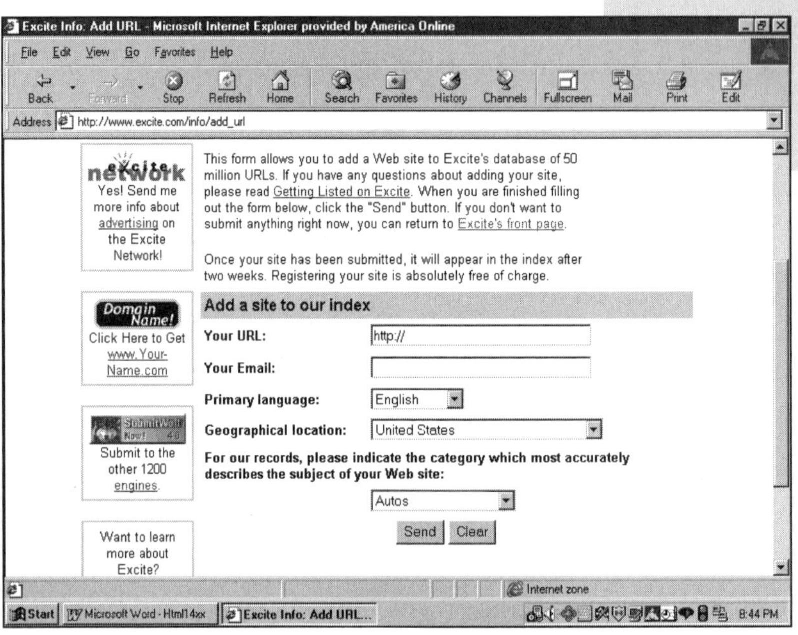

Figure 14.4 Fill out this Excite form to submit your site.

5. Type your e-mail address in the Your Email text box.
6. Select your primary language from the Primary Language drop-down list.
7. Select your geographical location from the Geographical Location drop-down list box.
8. From the drop-down list of categories, select the category that best describes your site's content.
9. Click on the Send button. If you make a mistake, click on the Clear button and repeat Steps 4 through 8.

This one isn't too complex, either.

HotBot

In comparison with some search engines, HotBot is a relative newcomer. It is in widespread use, however, so it behooves you to fill out the form by following these steps:

1. Go online, and then type the following URL in the Address or URL text box near the top of the screen:

   www.hotbot.com/
2. Press Enter.

   Figure 14.5 shows the HotBot opening page.
3. At the bottom of the page, click on the Add URL button.

   Figure 14.6 shows the form you fill out to add your Web site to HotBot.
4. Type the URL of your site in the URL to Add text box.
5. Type your e-mail address in the Your Email Address text box.
6. The next part of the form concerns information HotBot will send you at your request. Some of this information is for Web site builders, and some of it is news. Place check marks in the check boxes as you see fit.
7. Remove check marks from the three check boxes in the last section, if you want.

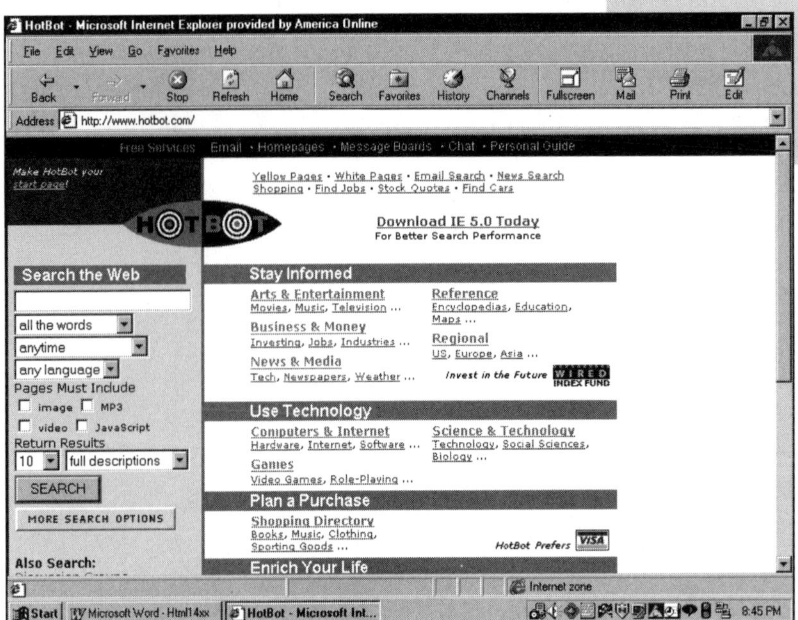

Figure 14.5 This is the HotBot search engine's interface.

HotBot | Add URL - Microsoft Internet Explorer provided by America Online
File Edit View Go Favorites Help
Back Forward Stop Refresh Home Search Favorites History Channels Fullscreen Mail Print
Address http://www.hotbot.com/addurl.asp
Back to Search
Common Questions
Search Tips
Add URL to HotBot
HotBot Tools for Your Page
Advertise on HotBot
HotBot Add URL Form
1. URL to add:
http://
Your email address:
2. Check the boxes below to find out more about these special services for Web site builders:
Get tips, tutorials and insights about Web development from Wired's Webmonkey delivered to your mailbox three days a week.
Subscribe to text-only (ASCII) email
Subscribe to Web-based (HTML) email
Get Wired News' latest news updates delivered to your mailbox every day.
Subscribe to text-only (ASCII) email
Subscribe to Web-based (HTML) email
Done
Internet zone
Start Microsoft Word - Html14xx HotBot | Add URL - M... 8:46 PM

Figure 14.6 Fill out this HotBot form to submit your Web site.

8. Click on the Add My URL button.

That wasn't too difficult, was it?

If you happen to discover one day that your site is no longer listed by HotBot, repeat the preceding series of steps. Your site may have been removed because the HotBot spider couldn't find it the last time it checked. This might have happened if your Web server was down or was busy when the spider checked.

According to HotBot, its Web crawler can take up to 60 days to come back and reindex your site.

Infoseek

Infoseek is an excellent search engine, so be sure to submit your site to it. Follow these steps:

1. Go online, and then type the following URL in the Address or URL text box near the top of the screen:

   www.infoseek.com/

2. Press Enter.

   Figure 14.7 shows the Infoseek opening page.

3. At the bottom of the Web page is a group of links. Click on the one labeled Add URL.

   Figure 14.8 shows the form you fill out to submit your site to Infoseek.

4. Type your site's URL in the Enter the Full URL text box.
5. Click on the Add/Update URL button. If you make a mistake, click on the Clear button and then repeat Steps 4 and 5. If you know of an URL that no longer is present, click on the Report Dead URL button.

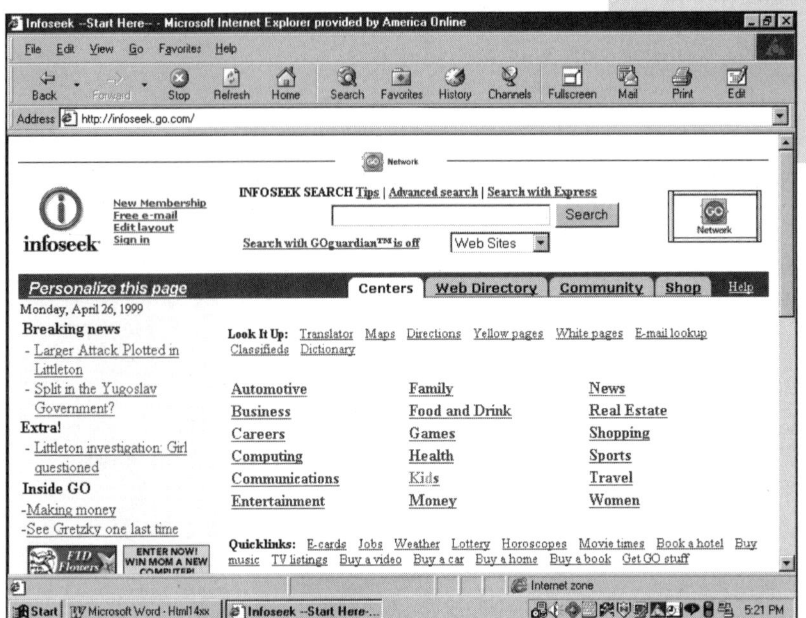

Figure 14.7 This is the Infoseek search engine's interface.

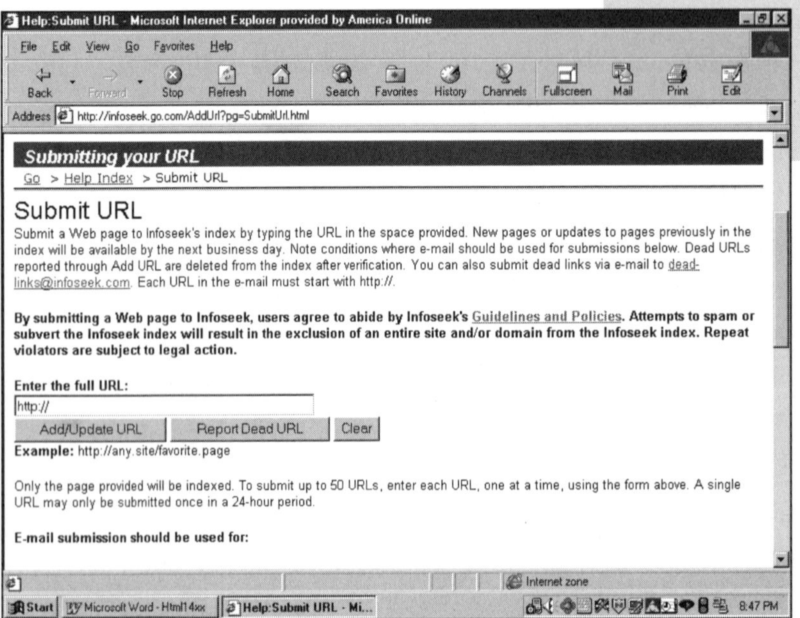

Figure 14.8 Fill out this Infoseek form to submit your site.

Infoseek reports that updates and new sites should be available on the next business day.

Being able to report a dead URL is a great idea, so if you know of any, let Infoseek know. It will help eliminate one more Not Found message.

Lycos

Lycos has been around for quite some time and is one of the major search engines. It is a good search engine to include in the list of search engines to which you submit your URL. Follow these steps:

1. Go online, and then type the following URL in the Address or URL text box near the top of the screen:

   www.lycos.com/

2. Press Enter.

   Figure 14.9 shows the Lycos opening page.

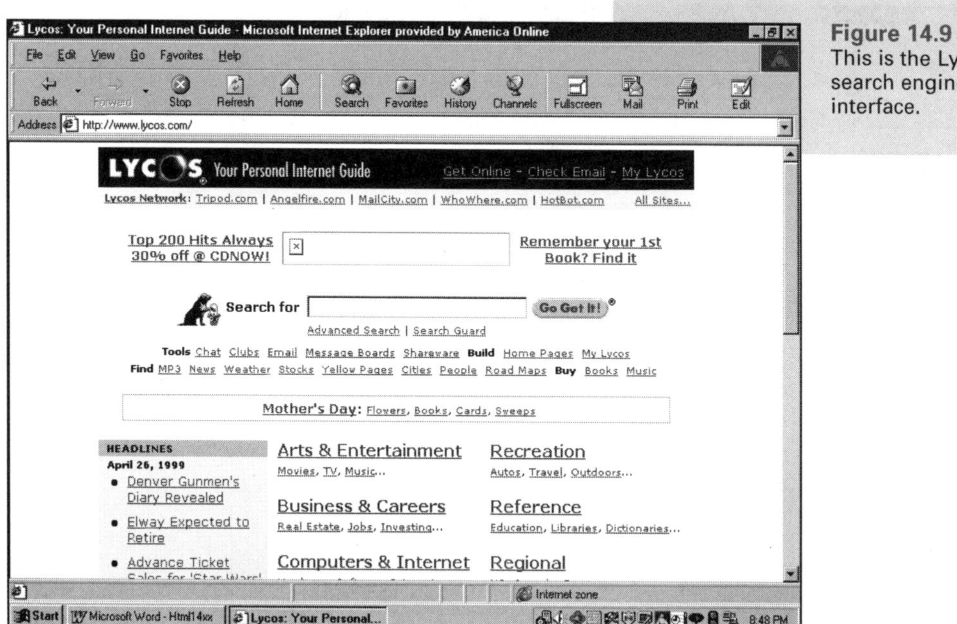

Figure 14.9
This is the Lycos search engine's interface.

3. At the bottom of the Web page is a group of links. Click on the one labeled Add Your Site to Lycos.

   Figure 14.10 shows the form you fill out to add your site to Lycos.
4. If you have delayed submitting your site to Lycos, the Lycos spider may have found it already. Before adding the site, type your site's URL in the Enter Your URL text box to let Lycos check for its presence.
5. Click on the Find URL on Lycos button. If your site is already there, you're in good shape. If your site isn't there, continue to the next section of the form.
6. Type your Web site's URL in the Enter Your URL text box.
7. Type your e-mail address in the Enter Your Email Address box.
8. If you're interested in being notified of Lycos service announcements, leave that check box checked. If not, remove the check mark.

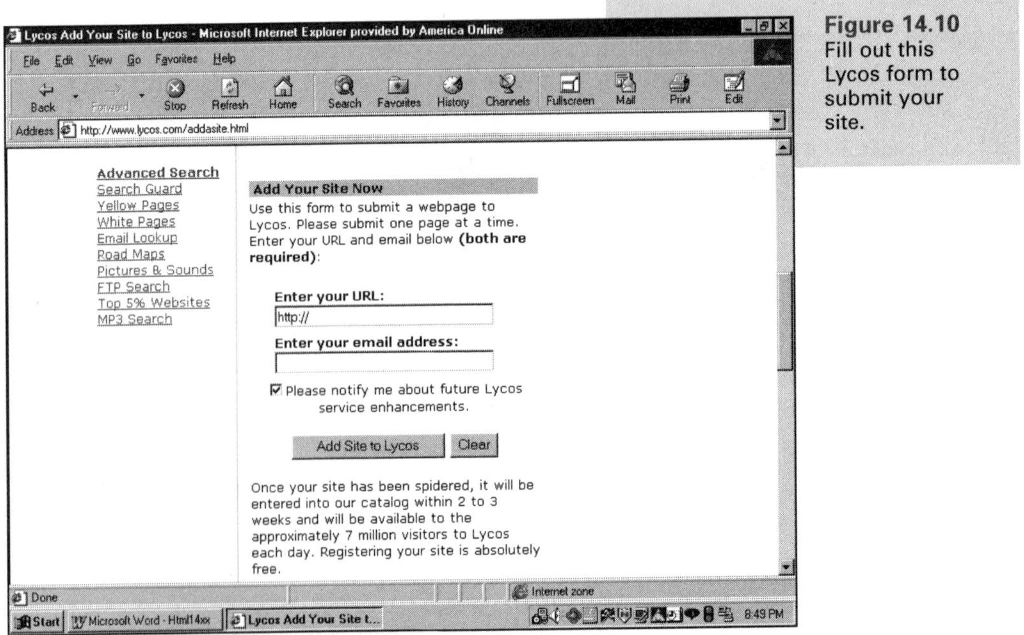

Figure 14.10 Fill out this Lycos form to submit your site.

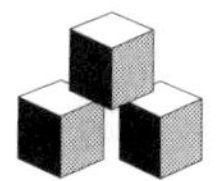

Caution

> **Before clicking on the Add Site to Lycos button in the next step, double-check the accuracy of the information you entered in the preceding steps.**

9. Click on the Add Site to Lycos button. If you make a mistake or change your mind, click on the Clear button, and then repeat Steps 6 through 8.

That's all there is to it! The note from Lycos says that it may take two or three weeks to get your site entered in the catalog, so you may not see results for a little while.

WebCrawler

This perfectly named search engine—they use spiders, remember—is another relative upstart. As you might expect, however, it is very popular. Follow these steps to add your Web site to the WebCrawler search engine:

1. Go online, and then type the following URL in the Address or URL text box near the top of the screen:

   www.webcrawler.com/

2. Press Enter.

   Figure 14.11 shows the WebCrawler opening page.

3. At the bottom of the Web page is a group of links. Click on the one labeled Add Your URL.

   Figure 14.12 shows the form you fill out to add your site.

4. Type your site's URL in the Your URL text box.
5. Type your e-mail address in the Your Email text box.
6. Select your primary language from the Primary Language drop-down list.
7. Select your geographical location from the Geographical location drop-down list.

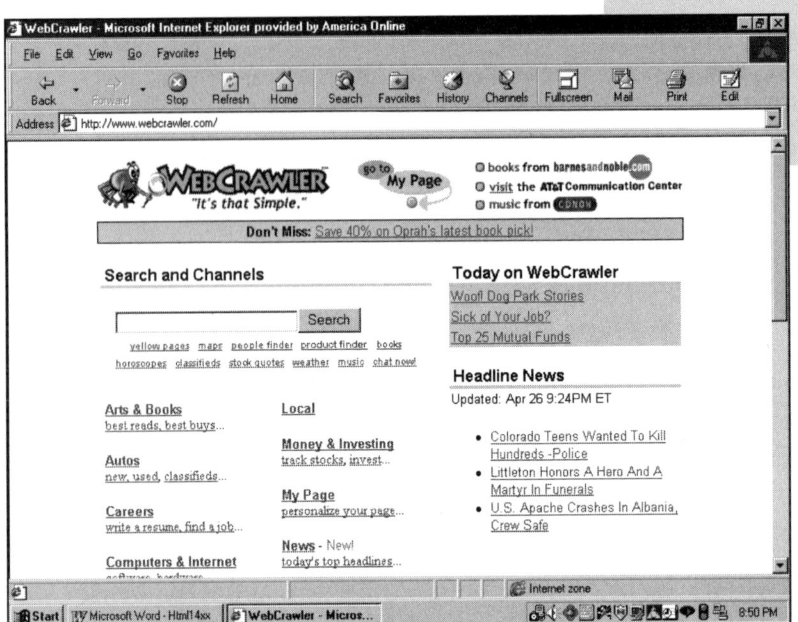

Figure 14.11 This is the WebCrawler search engine's interface.

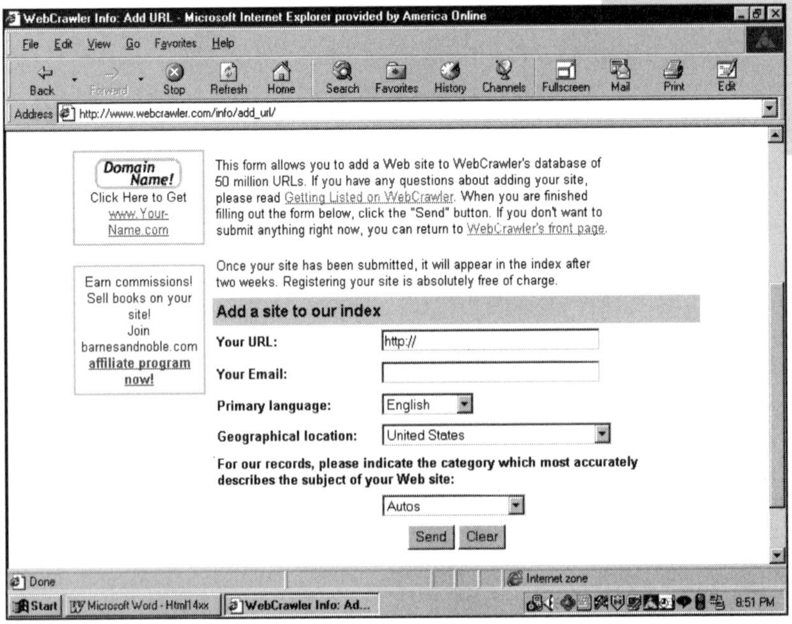

Figure 14.12 Fill out this WebCrawler form to submit your site.

8. From the drop-down list of categories at the bottom of the page, select the category that best describes your site's content.
9. Click on the Send button to submit your site. If you make a mistake, click on the Clear button and repeat Steps 4 through 8.

A little more effort is involved in submitting your site to WebCrawler, but it's still straightforward.

Adding Your Web Site to Web Directories

Now that you've added your Web site's URL to several of the most popular search engines, you can go on to the next type of service and add it there. These Web directories also can help increase your site's traffic.

Adding your site to a Web directory is not quite as straightforward as adding it to a search engine. Sometimes you have to look harder to figure out how to add your site, because the Web directory may not have a link labeled Add URL or Add Your Site.

Infospace

Begin by adding your URL to the Infospace directory by following these directions:

1. Go online, and then type the following URL in the Address or URL text box near the top of the screen:

   http://pic1.infospace.com/info/submit.htm
2. Press Enter.

   Figure 14.13 shows the Infospace registration page for Web sites.
3. Click on the radio button for the Type of Site you are registering, Business or Personal.
4. Type your site's title in the Title of Site text box.
5. Type the URL of your site in the URL text box.

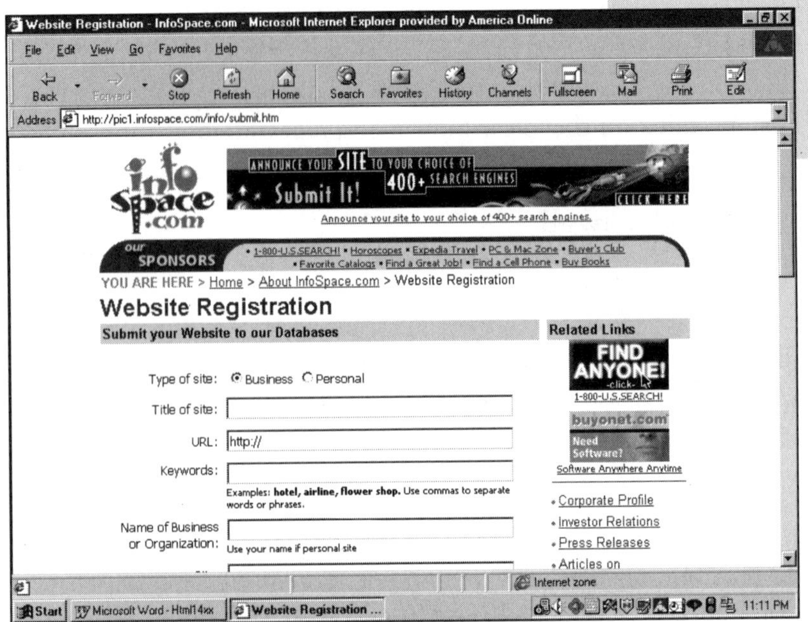

Figure 14.13 This is the Infospace Web site registration page.

6. Type your site's keywords in the Keywords text box, separating them with commas.
7. Type the name of your business (or organization) in the Name of Business or Organization text box.
8. Type your location in the City text box.
9. Select the correct state or province from the State/Province drop-down list.
10. Type the country of your location in the Country text box.
11. If your company or organization has a particular person for site visitors to contact, type his or her last name in the Contact's Last Name box.
12. Type the contact person's first name in the Contact's First Name text box.
13. Type the contact's e-mail address in the Contact's Email Address text box.
14. Type your business telephone number in the Business Phone text box.

15. Type your business fax number in the Business Fax text box.
16. Type a description of your Web site (no more than 25 words) in the Description of Site text box.
17. Click on the Submit to Infospace button to submit your site. If you make a mistake or change your mind, click on the Clear Form button.

You don't need to worry about spending a ton of time filling out this form, because Infospace doesn't index all of this information. In case someone is searching for you as a person, the most important information to include is your name, e-mail address, and geographic location. If someone is searching for your business, be sure to fill out the name of your business and your geographic location.

LookSmart

You can submit your site to LookSmart, but there's no guarantee that it will be included. That's because LookSmart has an editorial board that reviews submitted sites and then decides which ones to include. The decision for or against inclusion depends on the content the editorial board wants.

Follow these steps to submit your site:

1. Go online, and then type the following URL in the Address or URL text box near the top of the screen:

   http://www.looksmart.com/
2. Press Enter.

   Figure 14.14 shows the LookSmart opening page.
3. Look over the 13 categories on the left side of the page. When you find the one that you might be the place where your site will fit, click on it. Another menu of choices pops out to the side.
4. From the new list of menus, click on the one that seems most appropriate for your site's content. Another menu of choices pops out to the side.

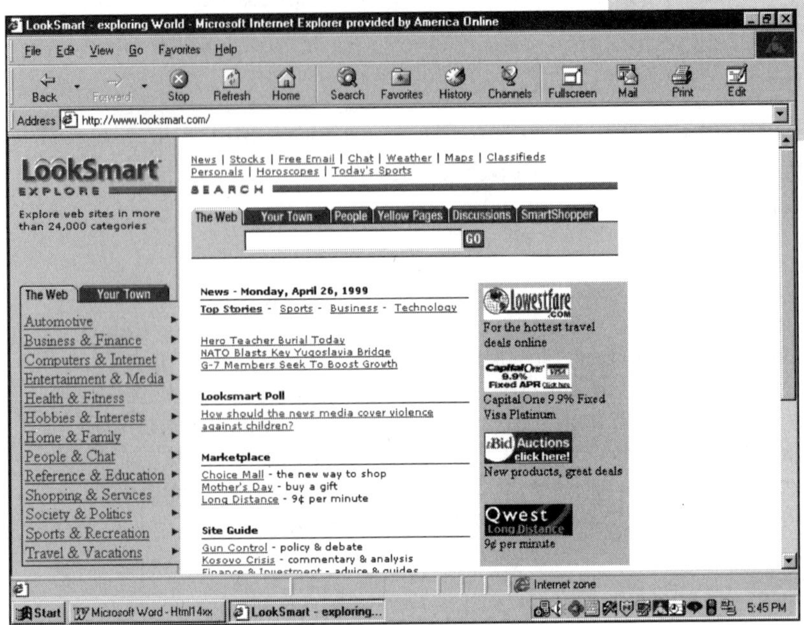

Figure 14.14 This is the LookSmart opening page.

5. Continue choosing the most appropriate options. Menus continue to pop out to the side. When too many menus are present, they begin to be hidden "behind" the original menu of 13 options. Figure 14.15 shows how the page looks in the process of zeroing in on guitars.
6. When you reach the lowest level—that is, no more menus are available—and that is where you want your site to be located, click on the Submit button that now appears on the page. Figure 14.16 shows the Submit button above the list of sites.
7. The page you see next gives you advice on how to review your site. Read those instructions, and then type the title of your Web site in the Title of Web Site text box.
8. Type the URL of your site in the URL of Site text box.
9. Type a review of 145 characters or fewer in the Review box.
10. If you want, type 5 keywords of 15 characters or fewer each in the Keywords text box.

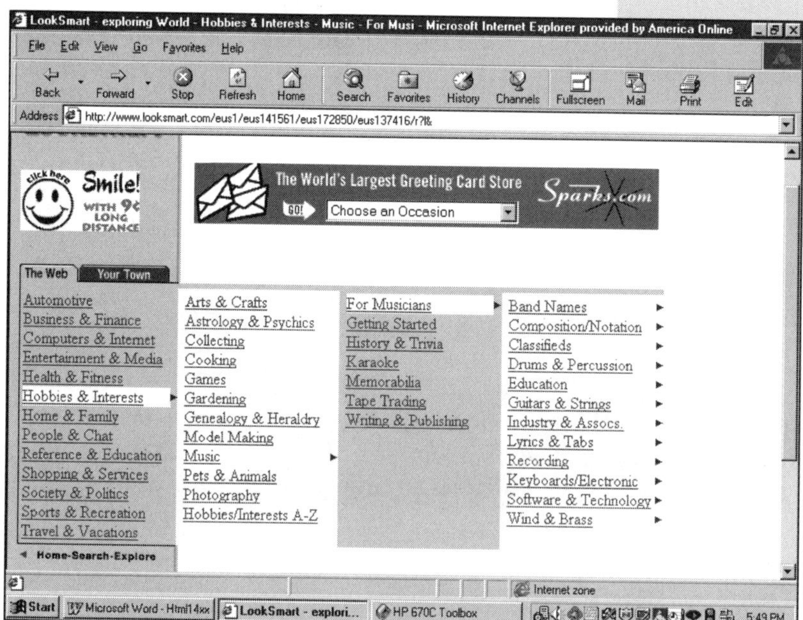

Figure 14.15 Menus grow out to the side as you try to find the best LookSmart category for your site.

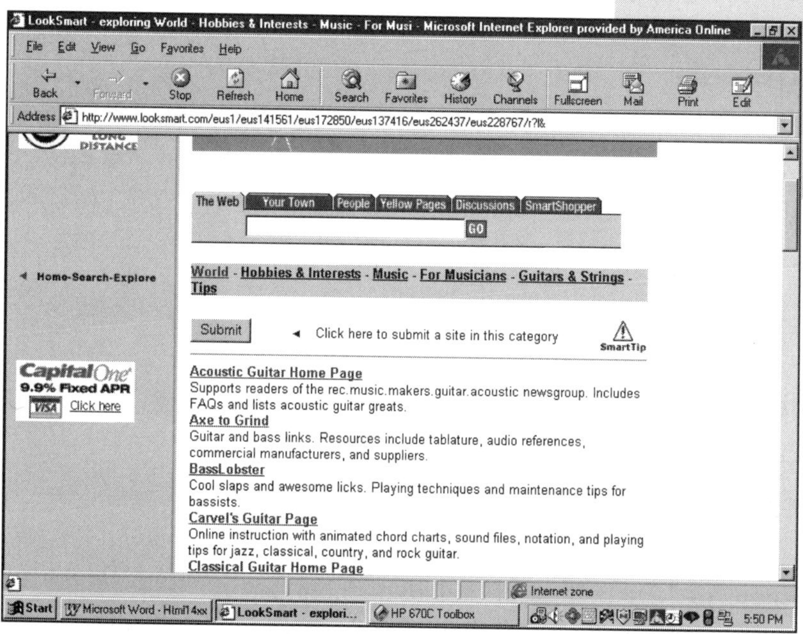

Figure 14.16 Finally! Click on the Submit button to submit your site for review.

11. If you want, type the date you launched your site, using the MM/DD/YY format, in the Date the Site Was Launched text box.
12. Type your first name in the Your First Name text box.
13. Type your last name in the Last Name text box.
14. Type your e-mail address in the Email Address text box.
15. Click on the Submit button. If you make a mistake or change your mind, click on the Reset button and then repeat Steps 7 through 15.

LookSmart offers advice on how best to present your site to its editorial board, as well as examples of reviews so that you can see what they want. Take advantage of this help to give your site its best chance.

Although it isn't a simple matter to get your site listed on LookSmart, it may be worth it. Just make sure that your content is good, or you may not get past the editorial board.

Magellan

Magellan has been around for a number of years, but is gaining prominence of late. Magellan and Excite are working together, as you can see by the URL you type to reach Magellan.

Follow these steps to add your site to Magellan:

1. Go online, and then type the following URL in the Address or URL text box near the top of the screen:

   http://magellan.excite.com/

2. Press Enter.

   Figure 14.17 shows the Magellan opening page.

3. Click on the Add Site button at the bottom of the opening page.

   Figure 14.18 shows the Magellan opening page.

4. Type your site's URL in the Your URL text box.
5. Type your e-mail address in the Your Email text box.

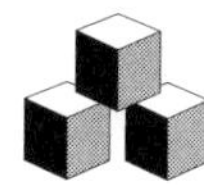

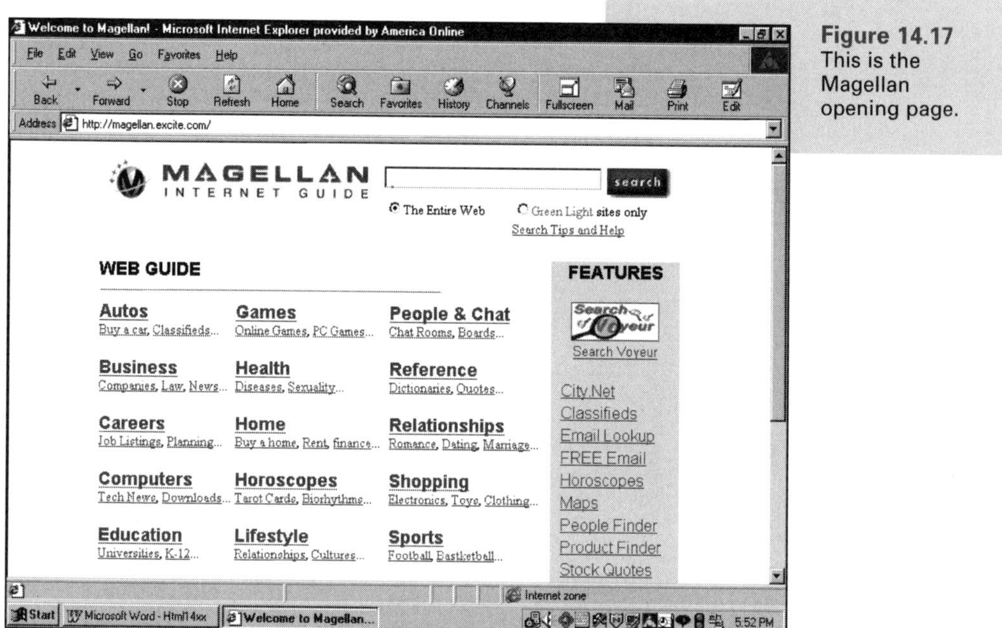

Figure 14.17 This is the Magellan opening page.

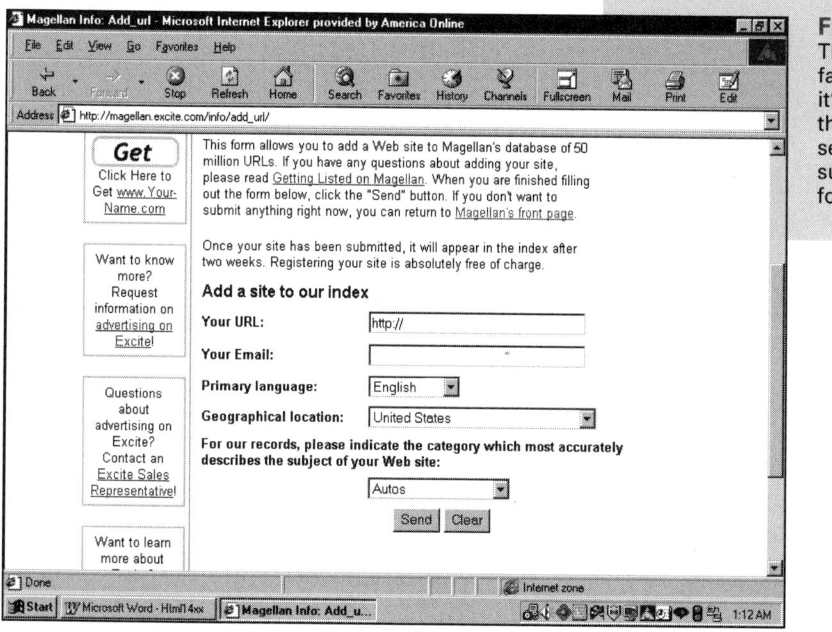

Figure 14.18 This form looks familiar because it's the same as the Excite search engine submission form.

6. Select your primary language from the Primary Language drop-down list.
7. Select your geographical location from the Geographical Location drop-down list box.
8. From the drop-down list of categories, select the category that best describes your site's content.
9. Click on the Send button. If you make a mistake, click on the Clear button and repeat Steps 4 through 8.

You have now finished submitting your Web site to Magellan.

Snap

Snap is a very new and growing service. Take advantage of its growing popularity and submit your site to Snap by following these steps:

1. Go online, and then type the following URL in the Address or URL text box near the top of the screen:

   http://www.snap.com/
2. Press Enter.

   Figure 14.19 shows the Snap opening page.
3. Click on the Submit Your Site's URL Here link at the bottom of the opening page. The page that appears gives you instructions and advice on how best to present your site.
4. Click the Back button on your browser to return to the opening page.
5. Locate the category where you think your Web site will fit best. Click on that category.
6. Another layer of categories appears. Click on the category that seems most appropriate for your site.
7. Continue clicking on categories until you find the one that you think is best.
8. Click on the Submit Your Web Site to the Snap Directory Team link at the bottom of the page.

   Figure 14.20 shows the page where you begin to submit your Web site.

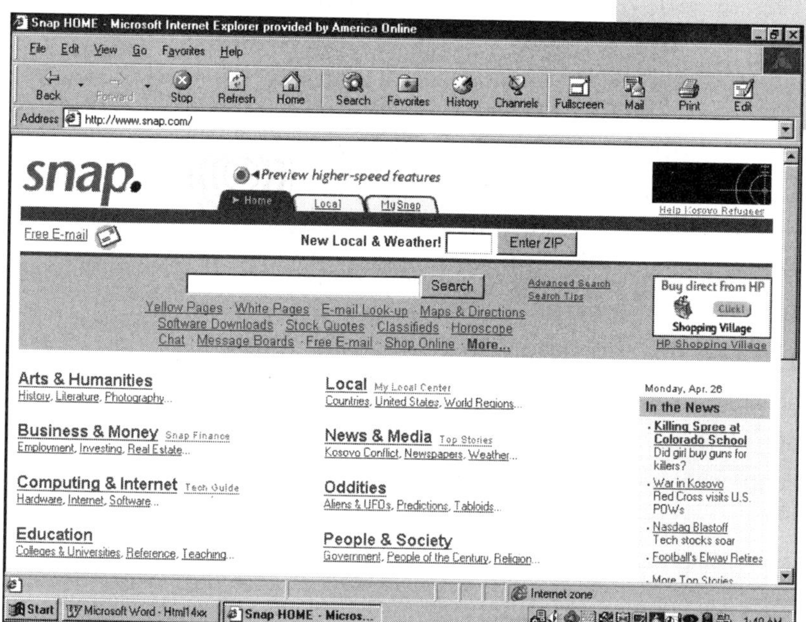

Figure 14.19 This is the Snap opening page.

Snap:Entertainment:Music:Instruments:Guitar:Repair And Maintenance:S - Microsoft Internet Explorer provided by America On...
File Edit View Go Favorites Help
Back Forward Stop Refresh Home Search Favorites History Channels Fullscreen Mail Print Edit
Address http://www.snap.com/directory/submiturl/0,158,-13500,00.html

Site Title Enter the title of your site.

Site URL Enter the full address of your site (for example, http://www.snap.com).

Short Description Enter a 10-15 word description of your site.
No promotional copy please.

Subject / Topic Select the most appropriate topic heading for your Web site from the pull-down menu below.
Entertainment

Navigation Path Enter the specific topic area path for your site.
Entertainment : Music : Instruments : Guitar : Repair And Main

Update old entry Submit new entry
Continue

Home | Search | Help | About Snap | Ad Info | Snap Jobs

Done Internet zone
Start Microsoft Word - Html1... Snap:Entertainmen... Printing page 1... 1:47 AM

Figure 14.20 Here's the first part of the Snap submission page.

9. Type the title of your site in the Site Title text box.
10. Type the URL of your site in the Site URL text box.
11. Type a description of your site in the Short Description text box.
12. The category that best fits your site's content should already be highlighted in the Subject/Topic drop-down list, because you already have drilled down to the level where you want to submit your site. If the category isn't highlighted, select it from the Subject/Topic drop-down list.
13. The next text box, Navigation Path, should be filled in already, because you already have made a series of topic selections. If it's not filled in, you can type it in, but you have to be sure to use Snap's categories in the correct order.
14. Click on the appropriate radio button. If you're submitting your site for the first time, click on the Submit New Entry button.
15. Click on the Continue button.

    The second page of the Snap submission page appears, as shown in Figure 14.21. At the top of this page is a recap of what you

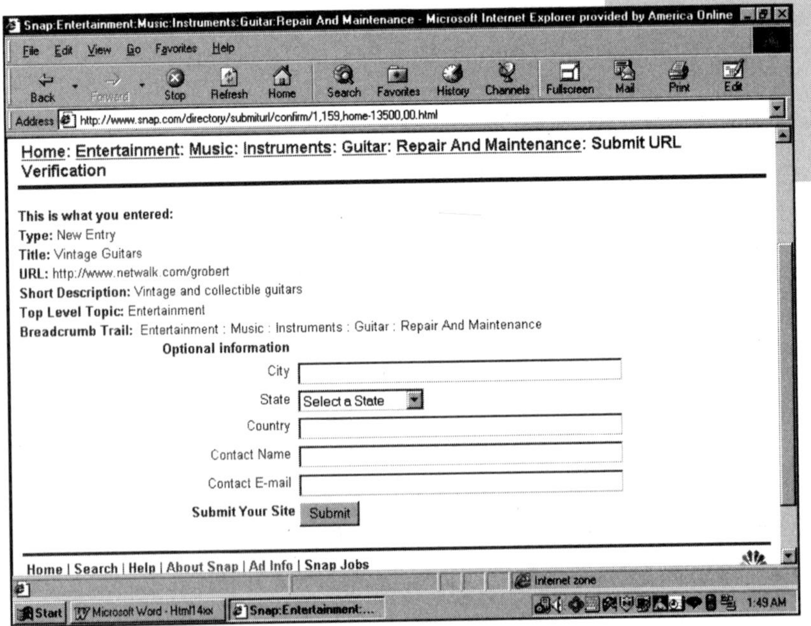

Figure 14.21 Here's the second part of the Snap submission page.

entered on the first page. The information you can enter on the second page is optional.

16. If you want, type the name of your city in the City box.
17. Select the state from the State drop-down list.
18. Type the country in the Country text box.
19. Type the name of a contact person in the Contact Name text box.
20. Type the contact person's e-mail address in the Contact E-mail text box.
21. Click on the Submit Your Site button.

Yahoo!

Yahoo! must have been what the guys who came up with this idea shouted when they realized they might be able to make money with it. Yahoo! has been around forever—as far as Web-related businesses are concerned—and for who-knows-how-many people, this is their way to find the information they want.

Your site may become part of that available knowledge if you follow these steps:

1. Go online, and then type the following URL in the Address or URL text box near the top of the screen:

   http://www.yahoo.com/

   Press Enter.

   Figure 14.22 shows the Yahoo! opening page.
2. As you have done in submitting your site to Web directories, click on the category that fits your site's content best.

   Continue to click on category names until you get to the category where you want to place your Web site.
4. Click on the Suggest a Site link at the bottom of the page. The page that appears, shown in Figure 14.23, gives you instructions on what to do.
5. After you have done everything these instructions say to do, click on the Proceed to Step One button.

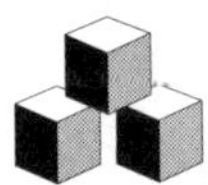

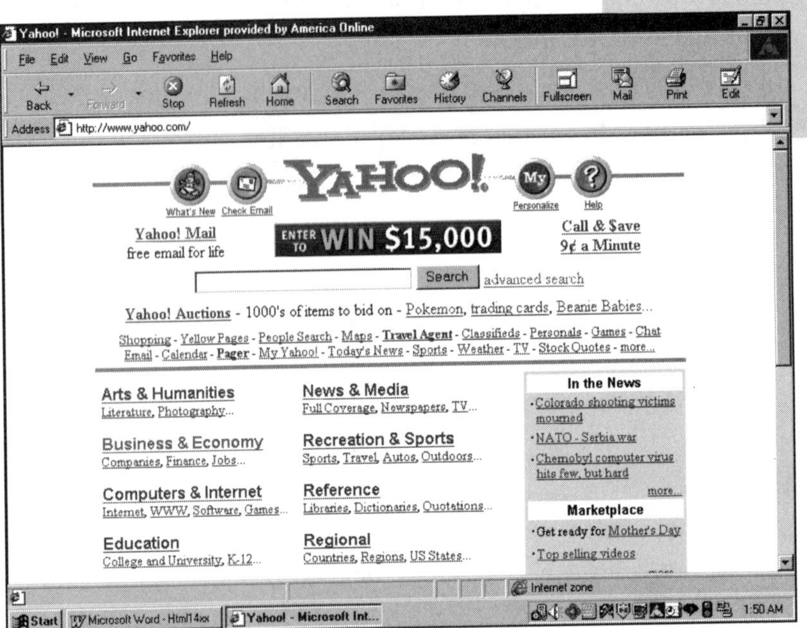

Figure 14.22 This is the Yahoo! opening page.

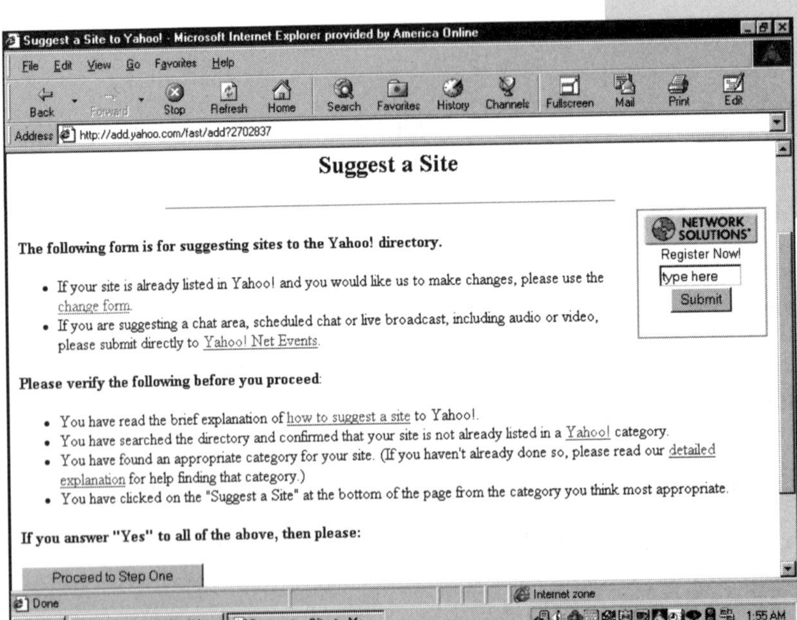

Figure 14.23 This Yahoo! page is where you begin the process of submitting your site.

5. Read the information in the Category section, just in case you have changed your mind about the appropriateness of the category.
6. Type the title of your Web site in the Title text box.
7. Type the URL of your Web site in the URL text box.
8. Type a description of your site (25 or fewer words) in the Description text box.
9. Click on the Proceed to Step Two button at the bottom of the page.
10. This step is optional. If you think your site should be listed in an additional category, type that category name in the top text box. If you think Yahoo! should create a new category for your site, type that in the second text box.
11. Click on the Proceed to Step Three button.
12. Type the name of your site's contact person in the Contact Person text box.
13. Type the contact person's e-mail address in the Contact Email text box.
14. Type the city of your location (if it applies, as in a music store) in the City text box.
15. Type the state or province in the State/Province text box.
16. Type the country in the Country text box.
17. Type the postal code in the Postal Code text box.
18. If you will remove your site after a certain date, type that date in the End Date of Site text box.
19. If your site concerns an upcoming event that will begin and end, type the start date of the event in the Start Date of Event text box.
20. Type the end date in the End Date of Event text box.
21. If you have any other information about your site, type it in the text box in the Final Comments section.
22. Click on the Submit button.

All you have to do now is wait to find out if your site passes muster and makes it into the Yahoo! directory.

Other Means of Making Your Site Known

Other ways of circulating the word about your Web site are possible. You can pursue these other ways yourself, but to some degree, you are also dependent on other people.

Reciprocal Links

For example, you can try *reciprocal links,* in which you locate other people whose sites deal with the same subject as yours and then find out if they are amenable to placing a link to your site on their own site. In return, you agree to add a link to their site on your own page. This reciprocal linking can help others with the same interests as you locate your site. That increases your traffic.

Banner Exchanges

The subject of banner exchanges, on the surface, is not terribly complex. The problem is in the details, because each banner exchange program varies from the others in one or more respects. For that reason, this section discusses banner exchanges in general terms. The URLs of a number of banner exchanges are listed at the end of the section. You can visit those sites to find more details about each service. Using that information, you can begin to make an informed decision about whether you want to pursue this possibility, and if so, which banner exchange best fits your needs.

***A banner exchange** is a means of advertising your site at no cost by swapping banners with other sites.*

In a banner exchange, a banner you've created about your site appears on the Web pages of other members of the banner exchange. In return, you allow other people's banners to appear on your site. Members of the banner exchange pay nothing to have their banners displayed on others' sites. To pay the costs of the banner exchange system, the banner exchange accepts paid advertisements from companies that are not a part of the banner exchange. In return for paying to have their advertisements run in a banner exchange, a company's banner may be seen by millions of people in a very short period of time, depending on the size of the banner exchange.

Banner exchanges vary in the features and capabilities they offer. Sometimes, you can target your banner at certain types of Web sites, mean-

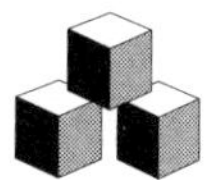

ing that only people with an interest in your site's content will see the banner. This targeting can really help your site's traffic, although there may be a cost involved for this extra feature.

You also have a say in the kinds of banners that can appear on your site. If you don't want banners advertising X-rated Web sites to appear on your site, for example, you can keep them off. Likewise, others can use this rating system to keep your banner off of their site, if they think your site isn't appropriate to their audiences.

Different banner exchanges have different rules, but at least two are common. First, you must agree to insert a bit of code into your site's HTML. This code enables the whole system to work. Second, the banner exchanges limit the size of your banner, both dimensionally and in terms of file size. The reason is that the banners must load quickly.

If you're interested in pursuing the idea of a banner exchange, try the following URLs to gather information:

http://www.1for1.com/

http://www.BannerCAST.com/

http://www.bannerswap.com/

http://www.linkexchange.com/

http://www.linktrader.com/

http://www.smartclicks.com/

Web Rings

A **Web ring** *is a series of Web sites—all dealing with the same general topic—that are linked to each other.*

If you really want to target a certain audience, making sure that people of the same interest will find your site, you may want to look into Web rings.

If you are interested in racing pigeons, for example, a Web ring awaits you. At the time of this writing, that particular ring consists of 82 sites. Chances are good that a Web ring for your particular interest already exists. To find out, follow these steps:

1. Go online, and then type the following URL in the Address or URL text box near the top of the screen:

   http://nav.webring.com/#ringworld

2. Press Enter.

   Figure 14.24 shows the RingWorld page.

3. In the text box, type the topic you want to find.
4. Click on the appropriate radio button based on what you've entered in the text box.
5. Click on the check box or boxes relevant to what you want to search.

   Figure 14.25 shows what happened when I searched for the word *guitar* with both check boxes checked. The result was 512 rings—not 512 *sites*, but 512 separate *rings* each containing multiple sites. This is a good example of why you should be as specific as possible when searching.

6. After you have narrowed down the search results, find one that you want to join. Click on the Home link for that Web ring.
7. After you get to the home site of the Web ring you want to join, just follow the directions given on the site.

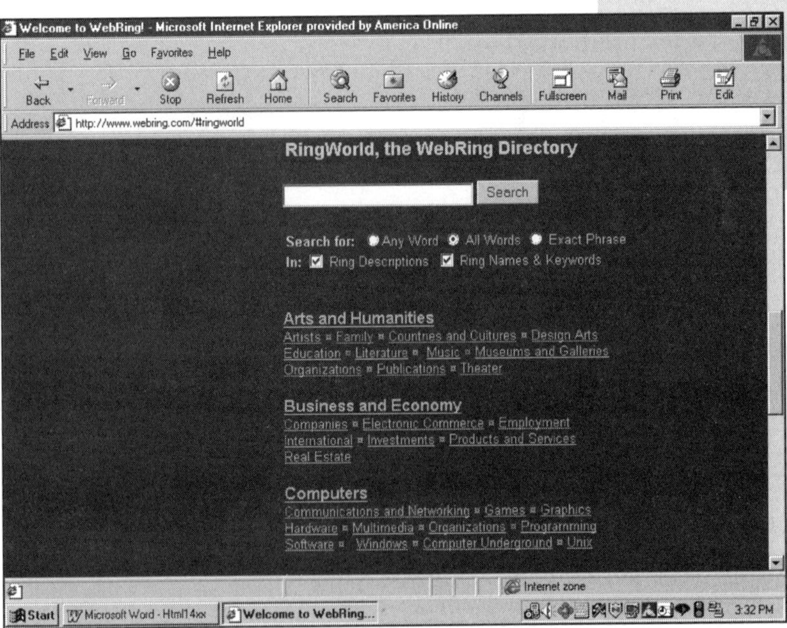

Figure 14.24 Use this RingWorld page to locate a Web ring about a particular topic.

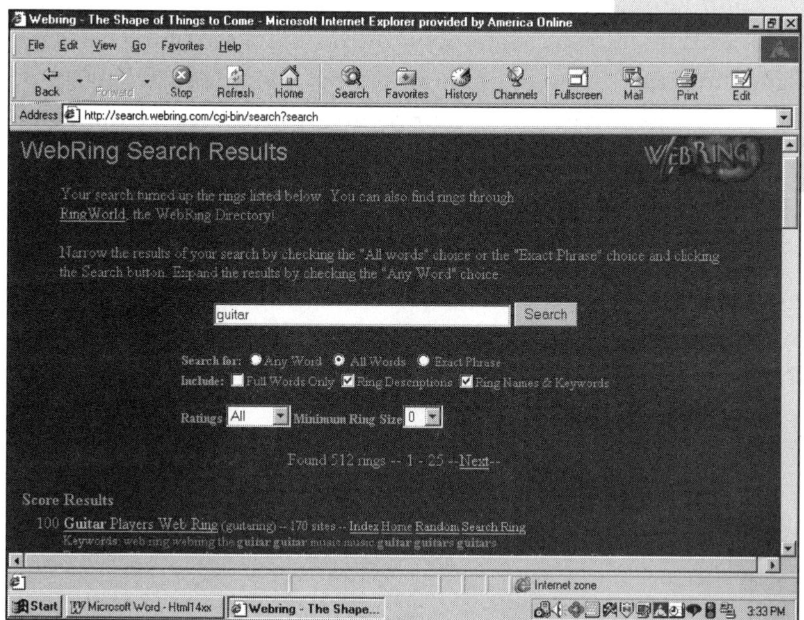

Figure 14.25 This RingWorld search has located 512 Web rings about guitars.

Directions for joining a Web ring vary from ring to ring, so follow the instructions given on the home site of the Web ring.

Tip

You are not required to visit each site on a Web ring in linear fashion, although you can do that if you want. You can jump around, go forward or backward, or even let the ring software pick your next stop randomly.

Now that you have joined a Web ring, you very likely will find that traffic on your Web site will increase. But that's what you wanted in the first place, isn't it?

Promoting Your Web Site Offline

Believe it or not, advertising took place before the invention of the computer and the World Wide Web. In fact, it's still possible to promote your Web site without touching your computer keyboard.

If you are promoting a business Web site, make sure that your business's URL appears on all your stationery (including letterhead, business cards, and notepads). Put it on promotional items also (refrigerator magnets, pens, and anything else your company gives away). And make sure to include your URL in your radio and television commercials, if you run them!

Finally, don't forget that oldest of all forms of communication: your voice. Tell others about your Web site whenever you get the opportunity, but especially if they are interested in the same things that your Web site covers.

For a long list of tips regarding Web site promotion, check out the following URL:

http://builder.com/Business/Promote/ss07.html

Summary

In many ways, this chapter is one of the most important in the book. Even if you don't learn to write HTML by hand, and you use an HTML editor instead, you still need to place your site on the Web.

This chapter has discussed placing sites on the Web under different conditions, focusing especially on doing so through online services or Internet service providers.

Putting your site on the Web, however, is only a part of the process. Promoting your Web site is also extremely important, so this chapter has discussed ways in which you can generate a buzz about your site. You can use Web promotion services, for example, or do it yourself. Doing it yourself may mean submitting your site to search engines and Web directories. Another way to increase your Web traffic is by joining a Web ring or banner exchange program, or simply using reciprocal links. In addition, you can promote your new site using old-fashioned techniques by printing your site address on corporate stationery and including it in advertisements on any and all media.

Quick Reference Guide to HTML 4.0

HTML 4.0 consists of dozens of tags, and most of those tags have one or more attributes. By putting the correct tags, the correct attributes, and the correct attribute values in correct combinations, you can create an outstanding Web site. This book has not covered every tag and every attribute; that isn't possible. In order to give you more complete information, this appendix includes short descriptions of all the HTML 4.0 tags and the attributes most commonly used with them. In addition, deprecated tags are noted, and suggestions for substitutes are given.

This appendix indicates which tags were newly introduced in HTML 4.0 by placing `(4.0)` next to the tag name.

Find it Online

If you want more details on HTML 4.0 tags and attributes, check the following URLs:

For tags:
http://www.w3.org/TR/REC-html40/index/elements.html

For attributes:
http://www.w3.org/TR/REC-html40/index/attributes.html

To make your use of this appendix easier, the tags are arranged in alphabetical order. The tags and attributes are in uppercase, and possible values are in lowercase.

Caution

For readability in this appendix, the primary tag entries are not enclosed within angle brackets (< >) for most of the tags. When you write your HTML, however, make sure that you use the brackets. Likewise, remember to include any necessary quotation marks around values when you write your HTML, even though the values are listed without quotation marks in this appendix.

Note

Virtually every tag has the `CLASS` and `ID` attributes. The inclusion of these attributes across the board is for the purpose of supporting scripting and CSS, which represent the direction that HTML is moving. A number of attributes, such as `BASEFONT` and `FONT`, are now deprecated because of the shift toward CSS.

Note

The entries for many of the tags listed in this appendix indicate that the end tag is optional. If you plan to use CSS, however, make sure that you use both start and end tags. If you don't, you run the risk that your style sheets will not work properly.

<!— enter comment text here —>

Description:	Insert comments
End tag required:	Yes
Deprecated:	No

!DOCTYPE

Description:	Specifies DTD of the HTML document
End tag required:	No
Deprecated:	No

A

Description:	Anchor tag for links
End tag required:	Yes
Deprecated:	No

Attribute	Required	Description
HREF	No	Required when specifying link target
NAME	No	Required when creating target link
TARGET	No	Required when specifying the frame where the linked document should appear

ABBR

Description:	Denotes an abbreviation (`IRS`, `USA`, and so on)
End tag required:	Yes
Deprecated:	No

Attribute	Required	Description
TITLE	No	Specifies spelled-out words of abbreviation
LANG	No	Specifies language of words

ACRONYM (4.0)

Description:	Denotes an acronym
End tag required:	Yes
Deprecated:	No

ADDRESS

Description:	Specifies an address (typically of the Webmaster or another contact person)
End tag required:	Yes
Deprecated:	No

APPLET

Description:	Runs Java applet from within HTML document
End tag required:	Yes
Deprecated:	Yes (use `<OBJECT>` instead)

Attribute	Required	Description
CODE	Yes	Refers to filename for applet's subclass
WIDTH	Yes	Specifies initial width of display area for applet (pixels)
HEIGHT	Yes	Specifies initial height of display area for applet (pixels)
CODEBASE	No	Specifies base URL of applet if it's not the same as the HTML document's URL
ALT	No	Specifies alternative text
NAME	No	Name of applet
ALIGN	No	Aligns element flush left, flush right, top, middle, bottom (values: **left**, **right**, **top**, **middle**, **bottom**)
HSPACE	No	Controls amount of white space on left and right sides (pixels)
VSPACE	No	Controls amount of white space above and below image (pixels)

AREA

Description:	Specifies shape of hot region in image map (client-side)
End tag required:	No (empty)
Deprecated:	No

Attribute	Required	Description
ALT	Yes	Provides text-based alternative to the image-based hot region
COORDS	No	Lists the coordinates defining hot region
HREF	No	Supplies URL associated with hot region
NOHREF	No	Specifies that no action is associated with the hot region
SHAPE	No	Specifies shape of hot region (values: **rect**, **circle**, **poly**, **default**)
TARGET	No	Identifies the frame where the linked document should appear

B

Description:	Boldfaces text
End tag required:	Yes
Deprecated:	No

BASE

Description:	Specifies HTML document's base URL
End tag required:	No (empty)
Deprecated:	No

Attribute	Required	Description
HREF	No	Specifies base URL for HTML document
TARGET	No	Specifies where to load the link

BASEFONT

Description:	Specifies default font for text
End tag required:	No (empty)
Deprecated:	Yes (use style sheets instead)

Attribute	Required	Description
COLOR	No	Specifies color of font
FACE	No	Specifies font
SIZE	Yes	Specifies font size (1 through 7)

BDO (4.0)

Description:	Overrides inherent direction for text presentation (necessary, for example, if Hebrew or Arabic words appear in the middle of English text)
End tag required:	Yes
Deprecated:	No

Attribute	Required	Description
DIR	Yes	Sets direction with the value **ltr** (left to right) or **rtl** (right to left)
LANG	No	Specifies language

BIG

Description:	Displays text in one-size-larger font
End tag required:	Yes
Deprecated:	No

BLOCKQUOTE

Description:	Sets apart a long quotation
End tag required:	Yes
Deprecated:	No

BODY

Description:	Indicates body of document follows
End tag required:	Optional (start tag also optional)
Deprecated:	No

Attribute	Required	Description
ALINK	No	Specifies color of active links
BACKGROUND	No	Specifies background image
BGCOLOR	No	Specifies background color
LINK	No	Specifies color of links
TEXT	No	Specifies color of text
VLINK	No	Specifies color of visited links

BR

Description: Inserts line break

End tag required: No (empty)

Deprecated: No

Attribute	Required	Description
CLEAR	No	Inserts space below text or images (values: **all, left, right, none**)

BUTTON (4.0)

Description: Creates a button labeled with the text between the start and end tags

End tag required: Yes

Deprecated: No

Attribute	Required	Description
NAME	No	Assigns control name to button
TYPE	Yes	Specifies type of button (values: **button, reset, submit**)
VALUE	No	Specifies initial value of button

CAPTION

Description: Specifies caption for a table created with `<TABLE>`

End tag required: Yes

Deprecated: No

Attribute	Required	Description
ALIGN	No	Specifies alignment of table caption (values: **bottom, center, left, right, top**)

CENTER

Description:	Centers element
End tag required:	Yes
Deprecated:	Yes (use `<DIV ALIGN="center">` instead)

CITE

Description:	Denotes a citation (scholarly paper, book, etc.)
End tag required:	Yes
Deprecated:	No

CODE

Description:	Specifies a sample of computer code
End tag required:	Yes
Deprecated:	No

COL

Description:	Specifies column-based defaults for table properties
End tag required:	No (empty)
Deprecated:	No

Attribute	Required	Description
ALIGN	No	Aligns element flush left, flush right, or centered (values: **left**, **right**, **center**)
SPAN	No	Specifies number of columns the COL attributes affect
VALIGN	No	Aligns element vertically (values: **baseline**, **bottom**, **middle**, **top**)
WIDTH	No	Specifies width of column

COLGROUP (4.0)

Description:	Contains a group of columns
End tag required:	Optional
Deprecated:	No

Attribute	Required	Description
ALIGN	No	Aligns element flush left, flush right, or centered (values: **left**, **right**, **center**)
SPAN	No	Specifies number of columns in group
VALIGN	No	Aligns element vertically (values: **baseline**, **bottom**, **middle**, **top**)
WIDTH	No	Specifies width of `COLGROUP`

DD

Description: Definition in a definition list

End tag required: Optional

Deprecated: No

DEL (4.0)

Description: Denotes deleted text

End tag required: Yes

Deprecated: No

Attribute	Required	Description
CITE	No	Refers to source document that explains why a change was made
DATETIME	No	Specifies the date and time a change was made

DFN

Description: First appearance of a term in a document

End tag required: Yes

Deprecated: No

DIR

Description: Denotes directory list

End tag required: Yes

Deprecated: Yes (use `<UL>` instead)

DIV

Description:	Indicates a division within document
End tag required:	Yes
Deprecated:	No

Attribute	Required	Description
ALIGN	No	Aligns elements horizontally (values: **center**, **left**, **right**)

DL

Description:	Denotes definition list
End tag required:	Yes
Deprecated:	Entire tag not deprecated, but `COMPACT` attribute is

Attribute	Required	Description
COMPACT	No	Reduces space between items in list

DT

Description:	Indicates definition term in definition list
End tag required:	Optional
Deprecated:	No

EM

Description:	Emphasizes text
End tag required:	Yes
Deprecated:	No

FIELDSET (4.0)

Description:	Groups related fields
End tag required:	Yes
Deprecated:	No

FONT

Description:	Specifies font characteristics
End tag required:	Yes
Deprecated:	Yes (use style sheets instead)

Attribute	Required	Description
SIZE	No	Specifies size of font
COLOR	No	Specifies color of font
FACE	No	Specifies font

FORM

Description: Indicates a form follows

End tag required: Yes

Deprecated: No

Attribute	Required	Description
ACTION	Yes	Specifies URL pointing to script or program that processes form data
ENCTYPE	No	Expected MIME type of data file submitted by form
METHOD	No	HTTP method used to send form data to server (default **get** appends data to end of processing script URL; **post** sends form data to server in separate HTTP transaction)
TARGET	No	Specifies frame where you want to display the script or program output

FRAME (4.0)

Description: Denotes frame within a frameset

End tag required: No (empty)

Deprecated: No

Attribute	Required	Description
BORDERCOLOR	No	Specifies color of frame border
FRAMEBORDER	No	Specifies whether or not to put border around frame
HEIGHT	No	Specifies height of frame
MARGINHEIGHT	No	Specifies amount of top/bottom margin in frame
MARGINWIDTH	No	Specifies amount of left/right margin in frame

NAME	No	Specifies name of frame for loading linked document
NORESIZE	No	Makes frame not resizable by user
SCROLLING	No	Sets scrolling off/on/automatic (values: **no, yes, auto**)
WIDTH	No	Specifies width of frame

FRAMESET (4.0)

Description: Establishes number of frames and their sizes

End tag required: Yes

Deprecated: No

Attribute	Required	Description
COLS	No	Specifies number and size of columns
ROWS	No	Specifies number and size of rows

H1

Description: Level-1 heading

End tag required: Yes

Deprecated: No

Attribute	Required	Description
ALIGN	No	Aligns heading flush left, flush right, or centered (values: **left, right, center**)

H2

Description: Level-2 heading

End tag required: Yes

Deprecated: No

Attribute	Required	Description
ALIGN	No	Aligns heading flush left, flush right, centered (values: **left, right, center**)

H3

Description: Level-3 heading
End tag required: Yes
Deprecated: No

Attribute	Required	Description
ALIGN	No	Aligns heading flush left, flush right, centered (values: **left**, **right**, **center**)

H4

Description: Level-4 heading
End tag required: Yes
Deprecated: No

Attribute	Required	Description
ALIGN	No	Aligns heading flush left, flush right, centered (values: **left**, **right**, **center**)

H5

Description: Level-5 heading
End tag required: Yes
Deprecated: No

Attribute	Required	Description
ALIGN	No	Aligns heading flush left, flush right, centered (values: **left**, **right**, **center**)

H6

Description: Level-6 heading
End tag required: Yes
Deprecated: No

Attribute	Required	Description
ALIGN	No	Aligns heading flush left, flush right, centered (values: **left**, **right**, **center**)

HEAD

Description:	Denotes information in document heading
End tag required:	Optional (start tag also optional)
Deprecated:	No

HR

Description:	Denotes horizontal rule
End tag required:	No (empty)
Deprecated:	No

Attribute	Required	Description
ALIGN	No	Aligns rule flush left, flush right, centered (values: **left**, **right**, **center**)
NOSHADE	No	Specifies horizontal rule without shading
SIZE	No	Specifies height of rule (pixels)
WIDTH	No	Specifies width of rule (pixels or percentage)

HTML

Description:	Denotes that document is HTML document
End tag required:	Optional (start tag also optional)
Deprecated:	No

I

Description:	Italicizes text
End tag required:	Yes
Deprecated:	No

Although the `<I>` tag is not deprecated, you should use the logical formatting tag `<EM>` instead of `<I>` if you use cascading style sheets.

IFRAME (4.0)

Description: Creates floating frame

End tag required: Yes

Deprecated: No

Attribute	Required	Description
ALIGN	No	Aligns floating frame (values: **absbottom, absmiddle, baseline, bottom, left, middle, right, texttop, top**)
FRAMEBORDER	No	Specifies whether or not to display border
HEIGHT	No	Specifies height of frame (pixels or percentage)
MARGINHEIGHT	No	Specifies amount of top/bottom margin in frame (pixels)
MARGINWIDTH	No	Specifies amount of left/right margin in frame (pixels)
NAME	Yes	Specifies name of frame for loading linked document
SCROLLING	No	Sets scrolling off/on/automatic (values: **no, yes, auto**)
SRC	Yes	Specifies source of file to appear in floating frame
WIDTH	No	Specifies width of frame (pixels or percentage)

IMG

Description: Indicates an image to embed in document

End tag required: No (empty)

Deprecated: No

Attribute	Required	Description
ALIGN	No	Controls text alignment relative to image (values: **absbottom, absmiddle, baseline, bottom, left, middle, right, texttop, top**)
ALT	Yes	Provides text-based description of image

BORDER	No	Controls thickness of border around image (pixels)
HEIGHT	No	Specifies height of image (pixels)
HSPACE	No	Controls amount of white space on left and right sides of image (pixels)
ISMAP	No	Identifies image as server-side image map
SRC	Yes	Specifies source of image file
USEMAP	No	Assigns client-side image map to image
VSPACE	No	Controls amount of white space above and below image
WIDTH	No	Specifies width of image (pixels)

INPUT

Description: Specifies input control for form

End tag required: No

Deprecated: No

Attribute	Required	Description
ALIGN	No	Aligns element flush left, flush right, centered (values: **left**, **right**, **center**) (when `TYPE="image"` only)
ALT	No	Supplies alternative text describing image (`TYPE="image"` only)
DISABLED	No	Disables the button
MAXLENGTH	No	Sets maximum number characters user can enter in control
NAME	Yes	Denotes name of control (not required for `TYPE="reset"` and `TYPE="submit"`)
READONLY	No	Specifies elements contents can only be read
SIZE	No	Specifies size of control
SRC	No	Specifies source of file (`TYPE="image"` only)
TYPE	Yes	Specifies type of control (default is **text**; values: **button**, **checkbox**, **file**, **hidden**, **image**, **password**, **radio**, **reset**, **submit**, **text**)

INS (4.0)

Description:	Indicates inserted text
End tag required:	Yes
Deprecated:	No

Attribute	Required	Description
CITE	No	Refers to source document that explains why a change was made
DATETIME	No	Specifies the date and time a change was made

ISINDEX

Description:	Prompts user for input
End tag required:	No (empty)
Deprecated:	Yes (use `<INPUT>` instead)

Attribute	Required	Description
PROMPT	No	Specifies prompt message for input

KBD

Description:	Indicates text to enter via keyboard
End tag required:	Yes
Deprecated:	No

LABEL (4.0)

Description:	Specifies label for control
End tag required:	Yes
Deprecated:	No

Attribute	Required	Description
FOR	No	Associates label with another control

LEGEND (4.0)

Description: Identifies set of fields in fieldset

End tag required: Yes

Deprecated: No

Attribute	Required	Description
ALIGN	No	Aligns legend text (values: **bottom**, **center**, **left**, **right**, **top**)

LI

Description: Indicates list item

End tag required: Optional

Deprecated: No

Attribute	Required	Description
TYPE	No	Specifies type of numbering/labeling of items
VALUE	No	Specifies sequence number (1 or A, for example)

LINK

Description: Specifies hyperlink between document and another source

End tag required: No (empty)

Deprecated: No

Attribute	Required	Description
DISABLED	No	Disables element
HREF	Yes	Specifies destination address
REL	No	Specifies that the link is to the next document in a series
REV	No	Specifies that the link is to the previous document in a series

MAP

Description: Denotes image map hot regions

End tag required: Yes

Deprecated: No

Attribute	Required	Description
NAME	Yes	Assigns unique name to image map

MENU

Description: Specifies a list created with <LI> follows

End tag required: Yes

Deprecated: Yes (use <UL> instead)

META

Description: Provides browsers with information about document

End tag required: No (empty)

Deprecated: No

Attribute	Required	Description
CONTENT	Yes	Specifies information for certain name
HTTP-EQUIV	No	Causes another document to load after set amount of time
NAME	No	Assigns unique name to control, etc.

NOFRAMES (4.0)

Description: Contains HTML for browsers that don't support frames

End tag required: Yes

Deprecated: No

NOSCRIPT (4.0)

Description: Specifies that text appears in browsers that don't support scripting

End tag required: Yes

Deprecated: No

OBJECT

Description: Inserts object into document
End tag required: Yes
Deprecated: No

Attribute	Required	Description
ALIGN	No	Aligns control-type element (values: **absbottom, absmiddle, baseline, bottom, left, middle, right, texttop, top**)
BORDER	No	Controls thickness of border around object (pixels)
CODE	No	Specifies name of file that contains compiled Java class
CODEBASE	No	Specifies base URL for classid, data, or archive
HEIGHT	No	Specifies height of object (pixels or percentage)
HSPACE	No	Controls amount of white space on left and right sides of object (pixels)
NAME	No	Specifies name of control, etc.
TYPE	No	Specifies type of content for data
VSPACE	No	Controls amount of white space above and below object (pixels)
WIDTH	No	Specifies width of object (pixels or percentage)

OL

Description: Denotes ordered (numbered) list
End tag required: Yes
Deprecated: No

Attribute	Required	Description
START	No	Specifies starting number for list
TYPE	No	Specifies type of numbering/labeling of items

OPTGROUP

Description: Groups choices in a menu
End tag required: Yes
Deprecated: No

Attribute	Required	Description
TITLE	No	Specifies title for option group
DISABLED	No	Disables option group

OPTION

Description: Denotes one choice in list of options
End tag required: Optional
Deprecated: No

Attribute	Required	Description
DISABLED	No	Disables option
SELECTED	No	Indicates item is default
VALUE	No	Specifies default value for text/numeric controls; for Boolean controls, specifies value to return when control is turned on

P

Description: Denotes paragraph
End tag required: Optional
Deprecated: No

Attribute	Required	Description
ALIGN	No	Aligns paragraph flush left, flush right, centered (values: **left**, **right**, **center**)

PARAM

Description: Passes named parameters to applet
End tag required: No (empty)
Deprecated: No

Attribute	Required	Description
NAME	No	Specifies name of property
VALUE	No	Specifies property value

PRE

Description: Displays text in fixed-width font
End tag required: Yes
Deprecated: No

Q (4.0)

Description: Sets short quotation apart
End tag required: Yes
Deprecated: No

Attribute	Required	Description
CITE	No	Specifies URL of source document

S (4.0)

Description: Displays text in strikethrough font
End tag required: Yes
Deprecated: Yes (use `<DEL>` instead)

SAMP

Description: Specifies sample text
End tag required: Yes
Deprecated: No

SCRIPT

Description: Specifies script for page that script engine interprets
End tag required: Yes
Deprecated: No

Attribute	Required	Description
DEFER	No	Parsing script can be deferred until needed
LANGUAGE	No	Specifies script language (deprecated in 4.0)
SRC	No	Specifies URL for external script
TYPE	Yes	Specifies MIME type (replaces `LANGUAGE` attribute)

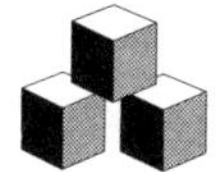

SELECT

Description: Denotes drop-down list or list box

End tag required: Yes

Deprecated: No

Attribute	Required	Description
ALIGN	No	Aligns control-type element (values: **absbottom, absmiddle, baseline, bottom, left, middle, right, texttop, top**)
DISABLED	No	Disables an element
MULTIPLE	No	Indicates multiple items can be selected simultaneously
NAME	No	Specifies name of control
SIZE	No	Specifies size of control

SMALL

Description: Displays text in one-size-smaller font

End tag required: Yes

Deprecated: No

SPAN (4.0)

Description: User-defined element for rendering with style sheets

End tag required: Yes

Deprecated: No

Attribute	Required	Description
TITLE	No	Specifies title for element

STRIKE

Description: Displays text as strikethrough

End tag required: Yes

Deprecated: Yes (use `<DEL>` instead)

STRONG

Description: Displays text with strong emphasis (usually boldface)

End tag required: Yes

Deprecated: No

STYLE

Description: Specifies style sheet for page

End tag required: Yes

Deprecated: No

Attribute	Required	Description
DISABLED	No	Disables element
MEDIA	No	Specifies media for which the style is intended
TITLE	No	Specifies title for element
TYPE	Yes	Specifies type of style sheet

SUB

Description: Displays text as subscript

End tag required: Yes

Deprecated: No

SUP

Description: Displays text as superscript

End tag required: Yes

Deprecated: No

TABLE

Description: Indicates a table (consisting of rows and columns)

End tag required: Yes

Deprecated: No

Attribute	Required	Description
ALIGN	No	Aligns table flush left, flush right, or centered (values: **left**, **right**, **center**)
BACKGROUND	No	Specifies URL for table background image
BGCOLOR	No	Specifies color for background
BORDER	No	Specifies thickness of border (pixels)
BORDERCOLOR	No	Specifies border color
CELLPADDING	No	Specifies amount of space between cell border and contents (pixels)

CELLSPACING	No	Specifies amount of space between table cells (pixels)
COLS	No	Specifies number of columns in table
FRAME	No	Specifies where frame border appears (values: **above**, **below**, **border**, **box**, **insides**, **lhs**, **rhs**, **void**, **vsides**)
HEIGHT	No	Specifies height of table (pixels or percentage)
RULES	No	Specifies visible dividing lines (values: **all**, **cols**, **groups**, **none**, **rows**)
WIDTH	No	Specifies width of table

TBODY

Description: Creates multiple sections in tables

End tag required: Optional

Deprecated: No

Attribute	Required	Description
ALIGN	No	Aligns flush left, flush right, centered (values: **left**, **right**, **center**)
BGCOLOR	No	Specifies background color
VALIGN	No	Aligns element vertically (values: **baseline**, **bottom**, **middle**, **top**)

TD

Description: Specifies table cell

End tag required: Optional

Deprecated: No

Attribute	Required	Description
ALIGN	No	Aligns flush left, flush right, or centered (values: **left**, **right**, **center**)
BACKGROUND	No	Specifies URL for background image
BGCOLOR	No	Specifies color for cell background
BORDERCOLOR	No	Specifies border color
COLSPAN	No	Indicates number of columns cell spans

NOWRAP	No	Keeps browser from wrapping text within cell automatically
ROWSPAN	No	Indicates number of rows cell spans
VALIGN	No	Aligns element vertically (values: **baseline, bottom, middle, top**)

TEXTAREA

Description: Creates multiple-line text-entry area for user input

End tag required: Yes

Deprecated: No

Attribute	Required	Description
ALIGN	No	Aligns control-type element (values: **absbottom, absmiddle, baseline, bottom, left, middle, right, texttop, top**)
COLS	Yes	Specifies width of text area (in characters)
DISABLED	No	Disables element
NAME	No	Specifies name of control, etc.
READONLY	No	Makes element's contents read only
ROWS	Yes	Specifies how many rows tall the text area is
WRAP	No	Specifies handling of word wrapping (values: **off, physical, virtual**)

TFOOT (4.0)

Description: Defines footer for table

End tag required: Optional

Deprecated: No

Attribute	Required	Description
ALIGN	No	Aligns flush left, flush right, or centered (values: **left, right, center**)
BGCOLOR	No	Specifies color for background
VALIGN	No	Aligns element vertically (values: **baseline, bottom, middle, top**)

TH

Description:	Creates row or column heading in table
End tag required:	Optional
Deprecated:	No

Attribute	Required	Description
ALIGN	No	Aligns flush left, flush right, or centered (values: **left**, **right**, **center**)
BACKGROUND	No	Specifies URL for cell background image
BGCOLOR	No	Specifies color for cell background
BORDERCOLOR	No	Specifies border color
COLSPAN	No	Indicates number of columns cell spans
NOWRAP	No	Keeps browser from wrapping automatically
ROWSPAN	No	Indicates number of rows cell spans
VALIGN	No	Aligns element vertically (values: **baseline**, **bottom**, **middle**, **top**)

THEAD (4.0)

Description:	Defines table header
End tag required:	Optional
Deprecated:	No

Attribute	Required	Description
ALIGN	No	Aligns flush left, flush right, or centered (values: **left**, **right**, **center**)
BGCOLOR	No	Specifies color for background
VALIGN	No	Aligns element vertically (values: **baseline**, **bottom**, **middle**, **top**)

TITLE

Description:	Identifies document contents
End tag required:	Yes
Deprecated:	No

TR

Description:	Creates row in table
End tag required:	Optional
Deprecated:	No

Attribute	Required	Description
ALIGN	No	Aligns flush left, flush right, or centered (values: **left**, **right**, **center**)
BGCOLOR	No	Specifies color for row background
BORDERCOLOR	No	Specifies border color
VALIGN	No	Aligns element vertically (values: **baseline**, **bottom**, **middle**, **top**)

TT

Description:	Displays text in fixed-width font
End tag required:	Yes
Deprecated:	No

U

Description:	Displays underlined text
End tag required:	Yes
Deprecated:	Yes (use another tag, such as `<EM>`, as appropriate)

UL

Description:	Denotes unordered (bulleted) list
End tag required:	Yes
Deprecated:	No

Attribute	Required	Description
TYPE	No	Specifies type of numbering/labeling of items

VAR

Description:	Denotes variable
End tag required:	Yes
Deprecated:	No

Overview of Some Popular HTML Editors

This book has taken the approach that the best way to learn HTML is to write the code by hand. Granted, not everyone wants to learn it that way. Most people prefer to let a commercial (or shareware) HTML editor do the work and then live with the result even if it isn't ideal. That doesn't have to be the case, however, if they're willing to use this book to learn how the tags work. For some people, the best of all possible worlds may be to use an HTML editor to create the Web site quickly, and then fix it and fine-tune by getting into the code itself to make desired changes. With that in mind, this appendix summarizes some of the features of several of the more popular HTML editors.

1-4-All

This shareware has numerous useful features, including an interface that enables you to work with several documents at once, a built-in image viewer, internal and external viewers so that you can see what your HTML is producing, a spelling checker and a thesaurus, and support for drag-and-drop techniques. You also can define your own templates, timestamp your documents, and perform search-and-replace operations in one or more documents at a time.

1-4-All also includes eight prewritten JavaScript scripts that you can place in your documents, 16 user buttons that you can configure as you want, a table editor, and a frame wizard. You also can use color coding in your HTML so that you can easily distinguish between your text and your tags. You can see what files are linked in an open file, and you have practically unlimited Undo and Redo capability. The program also offers you project management features, as well as a built-in publishing wizard for uploading your Web site. 1-4-All has many other features in addition to those mentioned here.

Figure B.1 shows the `inventory.html` file from Project 2 as it appears in the 1-4-All internal viewer.

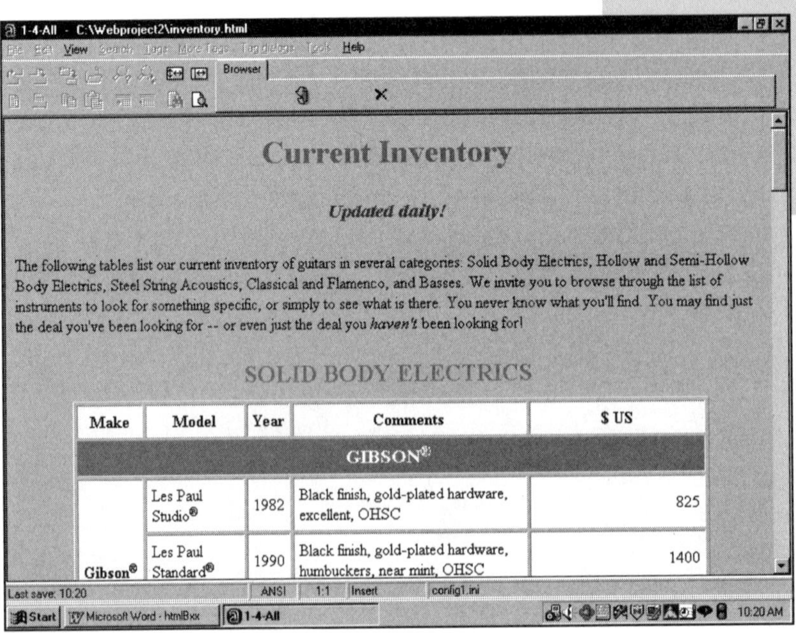

Figure B.1
The 1-4-All internal viewer here displays the `inventory.html` page against a gray background.

As this book went to press, the latest version of 1-4-All was 2.1.

To learn more about 1-4-All, visit the company's Web site:

http://www.mmsoftware.com/14All/

Adobe PageMill

Adobe, long known for its graphics products, also plays a significant role in the world of Web Page creation. Adobe PageMill enables you to use drag-and-drop techniques to build your Web pages, and it can create frames and tables for you. One attractive feature of PageMill is the inclusion of a very large number of elements that are already optimized for use on the Web: Java applets, animation, images, and templates (which you can customize). PageMill also includes a trimmed-down version of Adobe Photoshop, called Photoshop LE, that you can use to work with images. You can use this version of Photoshop to create graphics for various purposes (backgrounds and logos, for example), as well as to fix and alter images.

As far as site management is concerned, you can view a graphical representation of the links within your site. Also, the hierarchical structure of your Web site is visible in Site Overview, as shown in Figure B.2. PageMill also can check the spelling of all the documents in your site, as well as search and replace text, links, and images. If errors occur in your site, PageMill notes what they are and enables you to correct them. In addition, the program supports Java applets and ActiveX controls. PageMill also includes Matt's Script Archive, which supplies you with more than 20 CGI scripts that you can use on your site. More than 100 JavaScript scripts are available to you from The JavaScript Source.

If you want, you can write and edit your HTML directly, and then preview your page. When you're ready to upload your site, you use PageMill's built-in FTP Uploader. And if you're building a commercial

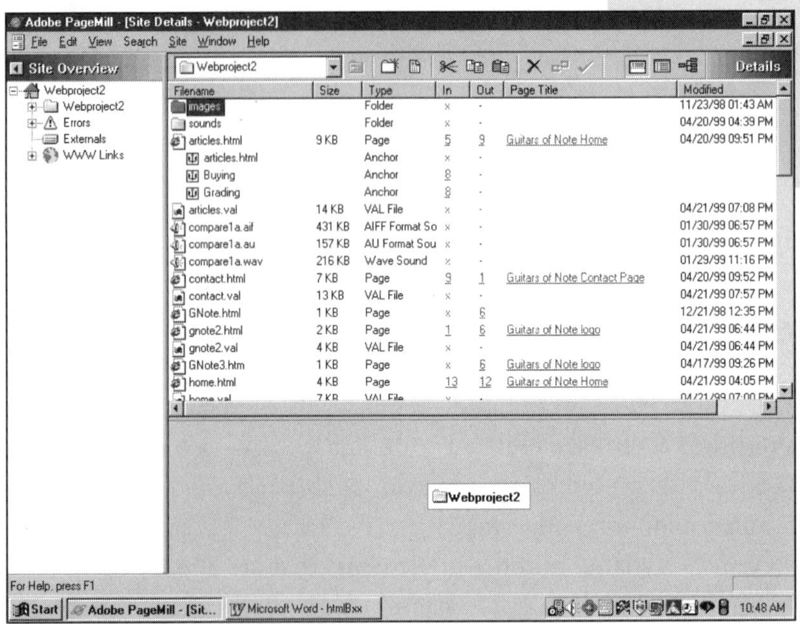

Figure B.2
PageMill's Site Overview shows the hierarchical structure of a Web site.

Web site, you may be interested in PageMill's link to Open Market ShopSite Express software, which can help you with critical, business-related issues, including security.

As this book went to press, the latest version of Adobe PageMill was 3.0.

For more information, check out the following URL:

http://www.adobe.com/prodindex/pagemill/

Agile HTML Editor

Agile, a highly regarded HTML editor, offers a wide variety of features to help you create sites. Some of its features include user-defined templates, the automatic inclusion of `WIDTH` and `HEIGHT` attributes in `<IMG>` tags, and easy configuring of tags by right-clicking. You also can save

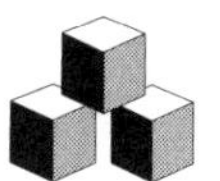

parts of your HTML that you use often or that are quite involved, and then insert those sections of HTML again via menus.

Agile has built-in information about any HTML tag, which you can access merely by pressing a key. You also can see which tags and attributes conform to the HTML standard you chose to use, and Agile even tells you what each item does.

As this book went to press, the latest version of Agile HTML Editor was 1.2.

Visit the following Web site for more information or to get the program:

http://www.compware.co.uk/

Arachnophilia

This absolutely free HTML editor is another extremely popular means of creating Web sites. One of its features is a set of built-in tutorials. These tutorials can help you with JavaScript, frames, your HTML, and the Internet generally, all in step-by-step fashion. Arachnophilia supports CGI, Perl, C++, Java, and JavaScript scripts. You also can define your own toolbars for tags or content, and keyboard macros can include commands as well as other macros.

Arachnophilia also enables you to define your own Web page templates, saving time when you want to use the same format later. You can perform search-and-replace operations on all documents that are open. As you make changes in the HTML, you can see the effect of each change by viewing the document in the built-in internal browser. In addition, you can use as many as six other Web browsers to see how your work looks. One of the best features of all may be the program's capability to create HTML pages automatically out of formatted text, tables, and outlines from any application that is compliant with Windows 95. Finally, Arachnophilia has built-in FTP capability, so you can upload your completed Web pages easily.

As this book went to press, the latest version of Arachnophilia was 3.9.

The Arachnophilia Web site can tell you more about the program. It also offers many interesting, noncomputer-related articles and quotations. You can find the Web site at the following URL:

http://www.arachnoid.com/

CoffeeCup HTML Editor++ Pro

Here is an advanced—and very popular—shareware product that you can use to do just about anything you need to do when building or working with a Web site. HTML Editor++ Pro has features all over the place. Designers help you with frames, forms, and tables. Figure B.3 shows the Frame Designer. Wizards are available to take you through the process of creating and using tables, e-mail links, and colors. The program can save you the time and effort required to create many elements of Web pages, because it comes with built-in sounds (`.wav` files), more than 175 animated GIFs, more than 240 icons and graphics, 30 backgrounds, and 10 Web page graphic consoles. The software can insert the `HEIGHT` and `WIDTH` attributes of your images automatically.

You also can view and convert images, customize floating toolbars, customize the colors assigned to tags, and customize the built-in spelling checker. You can "stamp" the date and time on your work, if you want. If you make a mistake, you can use Undo (and Redo) to your heart's content—the program doesn't limit you to, say, the last 10 changes. When testing your HTML, you can test it in any browser you have. And if your HTML doesn't work correctly, a line reader tells you where the problems are so that you can fix them.

CoffeeCup HTML Editor++ Pro doesn't desert you when it's time to work with scripts, either. To help you in that arena, the program comes with 10 JavaScript scripts, and you get 40 more when you register your

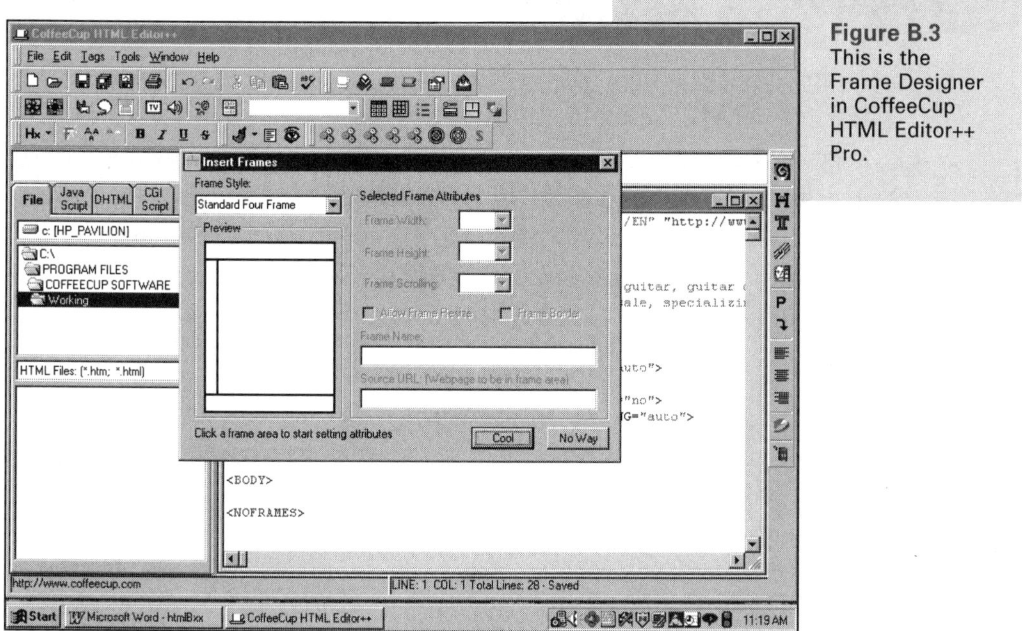

Figure B.3
This is the Frame Designer in CoffeeCup HTML Editor++ Pro.

copy of the software. To help keep you up to speed, you also get 12 DHTML scripts for your Web site, plus 5 CGI scripts. When you have your Web site put together and working, you can use the built-in FTP capability to upload and download files as necessary. CoffeeCup HTML Editor++ Pro has many other features besides those mentioned here, but as you can see, it is a very capable program.

As this book went to press, the latest version of CoffeeCup HTML Editor++ Pro was 6.2.

Check out the company Web site at the following URL:

http://www.coffeecup.com/

CoffeeCup HTML Express

From the same people who produce the popular shareware product CoffeeCup HTML Editor++ Pro, the Express version is intended to help beginners create a Web page with little investment of time and effort. This software is simple and holds your virtual hand as it takes you through each step toward creating a Web page. If you're an experienced Web site builder, you can build the basic Web page quickly, and then use your knowledge of HTML to go in and modify it to what you want.

CoffeeCup HTML Express has a number of built-in attractions, including more than 35 background images, more than 55 graphics (in the form of buttons, bullets, and arrows), and six Web page templates. CoffeeCup HTML Express features wizards for Web pages, links, colors and fonts, and `<META>` tags. This program also gives you shortcuts for entering text, as well as a list designer. In addition, the software contains a built-in browser, and allows drag-and-drop insertion of images. CoffeeCup HTML Express also enables you to create your own Web page templates. Finally—and significantly—you can upload Web pages or revised elements with a one-button FTP upload feature.

Figure B.4 shows the Page Themes dialog box, where you can choose from nearly 60 themes for the look of your Web page.

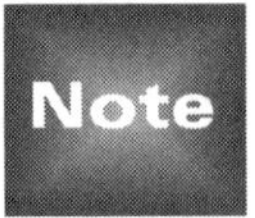

As this book went to press, the latest version of CoffeeCup HTML Express was 3.0.

Check out the company Web site at the following URL:

http://www.coffeecup.com/

Dreamweaver

Macromedia—known for Director, FreeHand, and Shockwave, among other products—touts Dreamweaver as a WYSIWYG program for professional site developers. One of Dreamweaver's more interesting features is its integration with HomeSite 4.0 or BBEdit (depending on the

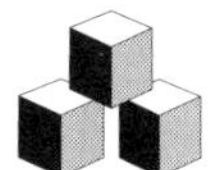

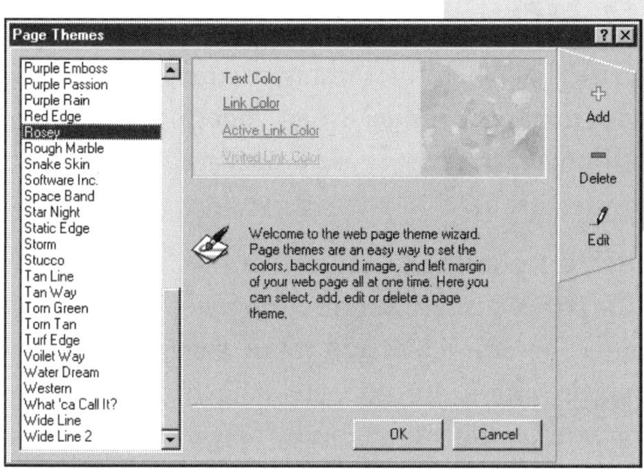

Figure B.4 You can select from a number of preset Web page themes in CoffeeCup HTML Express.

operating environment). This integration gives you quite advanced HTML editing capability. To assist you in writing clean HTML, Dreamweaver has a Cleanup HTML command, which does just that: It cleans up the HTML by removing things like empty tags and comments. In addition, you can define third-party tags in Dreamweaver.

You can use Dreamweaver's visual site map to organize and manage your Web site, including operations such as moving, renaming, and linking pages. Dreamweaver automatically keeps track of changes you make to links within your pages. You can create and use templates to maintain a consistent look within your Web site, even if several people are contributing content to the site.

Among the other features, one is of particular note. Dreamweaver goes beyond HTML to also support XML (Extensible Markup Language).

As this book went to press, the latest version of Dreamweaver was 2.01.

To learn more about Dreamweaver, visit Macromedia at the following URL:

http://www.macromedia.com/software/dreamweaver/

FrontPage 98

If only by virtue of Microsoft's industry strength, FrontPage 98 is ubiquitous and a force to consider when choosing a program for building Web sites. Many, many people use FrontPage to build Web sites and are happy with the results.

One interesting FrontPage feature is its wizard that enables users to import Web pages created in other programs. You can use the WYSIWYG interface to edit tables and frame pages in FrontPage 98. FrontPage offers help with forms, too, enabling you to create and save forms that will have responses automatically sent to your e-mail address.

FrontPage makes use of what Microsoft calls *themes,* which are built-in designs that make it easier to create a Web site while maintaining a consistent look. The program has tools for editing images, as well as a GIF animator, and the FrontPage 98 version supports CSS and DHMTL.

You can switch between three different views of the document you're creating: WYSIWYG editing, HTML editing, and Preview. Like many other programs, FrontPage 98 has the built-in capability to publish your site to the Web (or update the entire site) with one button—only files that have changed are uploaded. FrontPage's Navigation View enables you to see and alter the structure of the site.

Among the other interesting features are what Microsoft calls *hover buttons.* These buttons use Java applets to create special effects that occur when a user leaves the mouse "hovering" over one of your site's buttons. Finally, FrontPage also has Banner Ad Manager, which you can use to create banner ads that rotate.

If you want to know more, check out the FrontPage area of the Microsoft Web site:

http://www.microsoft.com/frontpage/

HomeSite

Many people consider Allaire's HomeSite the best HTML editor available. Rather than referring to it as WYSIWYG ("What You See Is What

You Get"), Allaire claims that HomeSite is WYSIWYN ("What You See Is What You Need"). One emphasis in HomeSite is clean HTML, something that not all HTML authoring programs can deliver. Often, HTML editors use proprietary tags or create code that is not as streamlined as it could be.

HomeSite has a large number of features to help you produce the result you want. Among those features are support for various programming languages, including JavaScript, ASP, and Perl, as well as support for DHTML. If you don't know JavaScript, HomeSite has a wizard to help you write the JavaScript you need, as shown in Figure B.5. Another asset of HomeSite is ActionScripts, which are scripts you can create to automate tasks you perform repeatedly in HomeSite.

To simplify creating and editing style sheets, HomeSite includes a new Style Editor. You also can use HomeSite to validate your HTML, verify links, check spelling, and maintain unchanged the HTML of any documents you created in another program and then imported into HomeSite. In addition, you can customize a number of aspects of HomeSite, including hot keys. Site View mode allows you to see the hierarchical structure of your entire Web site, and Design View lets you quickly start building a page.

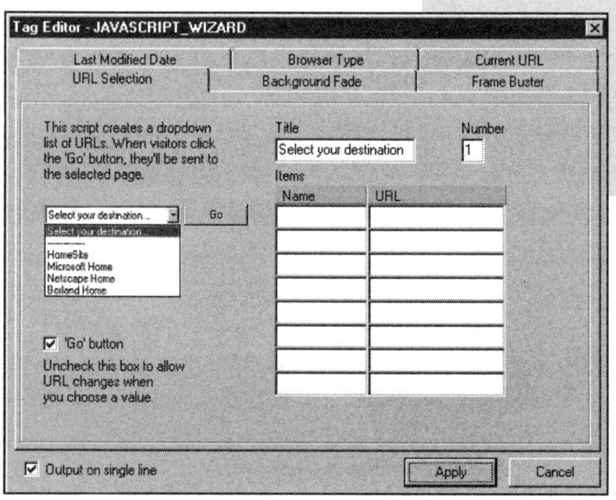

Figure B.5
The HomeSite JavaScript Wizard can help your scripting efforts.

As this book went to press, the latest version of HomeSite was 4.01.

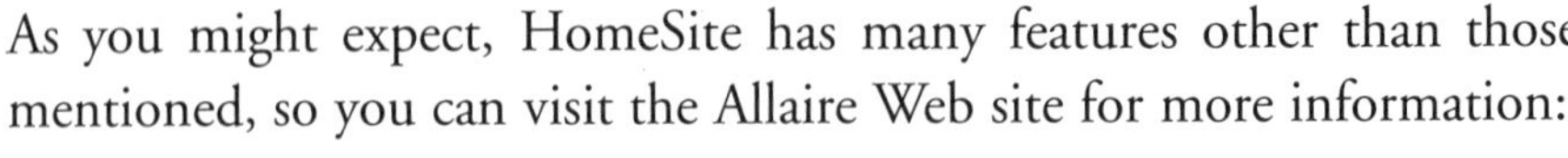

As you might expect, HomeSite has many features other than those mentioned, so you can visit the Allaire Web site for more information:

http://www.allaire.com/products/homesite/

HotDog Professional

One of the most intriguingly named HTML editors, HotDog Professional 5.5 is very capable and is popular with many Web site builders. The program highlights syntax and tags in ways that you can customize, and highlights errors as well. The latest version of the program includes ToolTips for tags, colors, images, and syntax errors.

The ROVER view lets you see changes as you make them. Wizards are available for tasks that require a lot of effort, and you can customize toolbars and shortcut keys (among other things) to make the program comfortable for you to work with. To overcome the most boring aspects of creating a Web site, the latest version of Hot Dog Professional comes with SuperToolz, Web-related applications created for the purpose of easing the wearisome parts of creating a Web site.

In the interest of ultimate accessibility, you can save your files in Windows, Macintosh, and UNIX formats.

As this book went to press, the latest version of HotDog Professional was 5.5.

Check out the following URL if you want to know more about this product:

http://www.sausage.com/hotdog5/

What's on the CD-ROM?

The CD that accompanies this book contains shareware that will help you write more effective HTML code, as well as all the example files related to the book projects.

Running the CD

To make the CD more user friendly and take up less of your disk space, no installation is required. This means that the only files transferred to your hard disk are the ones you choose to copy or install.

Caution

This CD has been designed to run under Windows 95/98 and Windows NT 4. Neither the CD itself nor the programs on the CD will run under earlier versions of Windows.

Windows 95/98/NT 4

Since there is no install routine, running the CD in Windows 95/98/NT4 is a breeze, especially if you have autorun enabled. Simply insert the CD in the CD-ROM drive, close the tray, and wait for the CD to load.

If you have disabled autorun, place the CD in the CD-ROM drive and follow these steps:

1. From the Start menu, select Run.
2. Type **D:\CDInstaller.exe** (where D:\ is the CD-ROM drive).
3. Select OK.

The Prima License

The first window you will see is the Prima License Agreement. Take a moment to read the agreement, and click the "I Agree" button to accept the license and proceed to the user interface. If you do not agree with the license, click the "I Decline" button to close the user interface and end the session.

The Prima User Interface

Prima's user interface is designed to make viewing and using the CD contents quick and easy. The opening screen contains a two-panel window with three buttons across the bottom. The left panel contains the structure of the programs on the disc. The right panel displays a description page for the selected entry in the left panel. The three buttons across the bottom of the user interface make it possible to install programs, view the contents of the disc using Windows Explorer, and view the contents of a help file for the selected entry. If any of the buttons are "grayed out" it means that button is unavailable. For example, if the Help button is grayed out, it means that no Help file is available.

Resizing and Closing the User Interface

As with any window, you can resize the user interface. To do so, position the mouse over any edge or corner, hold down the left mouse button, and drag the edge or corner to a new position.

To close and exit the user interface, either double-click on the small button in upper left corner of the window, or click on the exit button (marked with a small "x") in the upper right corner of the window.

Using the Left Panel

The left panel of the Prima user interface works very much like Windows Explorer. To view the description of an entry in the left panel, simply click on the entry. For example, to view the general information about Prima Publishing, Inc., click on the entry "Prima Publishing Presents".

Some items have subitems that are nested below them. Such parent items have a small plus (+) sign next to them. To view the nested subitems, simply click on the plus sign. When you do, the list expands and the subitems are listed below the parent item. In addition, the plus (+) sign becomes a minus (-) sign. To hide the subitems, click on the minus sign to collapse the listing.

You can control the position of the line between the left and right panels. To change the position of the dividing line, move the mouse over the line, hold down the left mouse button (the mouse becomes a two-headed arrow) and drag the line to a new position.

Using the Right Panel

The right panel displays a page that describes what functionality an installable program you chose in the left panel provides.

In addition to a general description, the page may provide the following information:

- **World Wide Web Site.** Many program providers have a Web site. If one is available, the description page provides the Web address. To navigate to the Web site using your browser, simply click on the Web address (you must be connected to the Internet). Alternately, you can copy the Web address to the clipboard, and paste it into the URL line at the top of your browser window.
- **Email Address.** Many program providers can be contacted via e-mail. If available, the description page provides the e-mail address. To use the e-mail address, click on it to open your e-mail program (to send e-mail, you must be connected to the Internet). Alternately, copy the address to the clipboard, and paste it into the address line of your e-mail program.
- **Readme, License, and other text files.** Many programs have additional information available in files with such names as Readme, License, Order, etc. If such files exist, you can view the contents of the file in the right panel by clicking on the indicated hyperlink (such as the word "here" displayed in blue). When you are done viewing the text file, you can return to the description page by reclicking on the entry in the left panel.

Command Buttons

Install. Use this button to install the program corresponding to your selection onto your hard drive.

Explore. Use this button to view the contents of the CD using Windows Explorer.

Help. Click on this button to display the contents of the Help file provided with the program.

Read File. The Install button turns into the Read File button when you make a selection that has an Adobe Acrobat file attached. Clicking on the Read File button launches Adobe Acrobat Reader and opens the selected file. You must have previously installed Adobe Acrobat Reader, either on your own or from the disc included with the book.

Pop-Up Menu Options

Install. If the selected title contains an install routine, choosing this option begins the installation process.

Explore. Selecting this option allows you to view the folder containing the program files using Windows Explorer.

View Help. Use this menu item to display the contents of the Help file provided with the program.

The Software

This section gives you a brief description of the shareware and evaluation software you'll find on the CD.

The software included with this publication is provided for your evaluation. If you try this software and find it useful, you must register the software as discussed in its documentation. Prima Publishing has not paid the registration fee for any shareware included on the disc.

1 Cool Button Tool. The program will let you create any number of button styles and behaviors. Button attributes include color, depth, transparency, text color, border color, AU and WAV sound, GIF and JPEG bitmaps, and even drag-and-drop buttons. The applet generator requires Internet Explorer 3.0 or later, but the generated applets will run on any Java-enabled browser. You can add animation to your buttons that can play in response to events such as mouse clicks, or when the applet starts up. You can also incorporate start-up transitions that, for example, slide buttons onto the applet area when the applet starts.

1-4 All HTML Editor. 1-4-All is a tag-based, shareware HTML editor for 32-bit Windows. It will run on Windows 95 and Windows NT 4. It provides a window with access to files, an editing area, and a message area. You can even preview all the different types of files that 1-4 can handle. You can drag and drop HTML files and images, and, of course, write your own code and add HTML tags.

1st Java Navigator. This is a powerful tool for managing the navigation of Web-based intranet and Internet systems. It assists you in the design, creation, and implementation of Java navigation applets. The Commander, which is an integral part of the package, is a powerful yet easy Wysiwyg management tool, which assists you in the creation of the HTML code needed to apply the Java applets to an HTML page. No knowledge of HTML is required for the process, and full explanations are included for every step. The fourth generation release includes a host of new options for helping you customize the applets to suit the theme of your system. There is a choice of overall style, including a Tree, which looks and feels similar to Windows Explorer, a Tab applet, which is like a traditional card system, and a TabTree, which is a combination of the two.

3D Color Text Applet. This Java applet allows you to display text with a 3D running color special effect and a sound effect. Features include a few configurable parameters; you can define the font, style, and size of text, as well as specify the 3D shadow depth. This version of 3D ColorText Java Applet can be used offline for an unlimited time period. A sound card is required in order to incorporate sound effects

ACDSee. ACDSee 32 is a fast and easy-to-use image viewer for Windows 95/98 and Windows NT. A full-featured image viewer quickly displays your images in high quality, while the image browser lets you efficiently find and organize your images. The program supports most popular image formats — BMP, DCX, GIF (including animation), IFF, JPEG, PCD, PCX, PIC, PNG, PSD, TGA, TIFF (including multipage) and WMF. You can print your images with their names and descriptions, as well as use the images in a slideshow.

AceExpert3. In addition to being an HTML editor, AceExpert also assists you with predefined Java applets and JavaScripts. AceExpert is a good tool for Web page creation and HTML editing. Features include CSS support, 30 predefined JavaScripts, a JavaScript assistant, ActiveX support, table/frame wizards, support for HTML 3.2, 300 images, and 150 animated GIFs. The latest version of AceExpert offers HTML syntax checking, an image browser, wizards and 20 templates for creating Web pages, the ability to search and replace in multiple files, a new visual table tool, a Code Explorer, a spelling checker, 50 predefined Java applets, 12 predefined JavaScripts, five predefined DHTML scripts, HTMLcat reference, easy integration of style sheets, and an FTP manager.

ActiveLink. With ActiveLink, you can create dynamic "rollover" links for your Web page without writing any scripts. Simply select the links you would like to turn into dynamic rollovers, and ActiveLink will do the rest.

Advanced Imagemap Designer. Advanced Imagemap Designer is a tool that helps you create dynamic, Java-based image maps for your Web pages. All you have to do is design an image map visually by defining the hot spots on an image. The image maps you create can display pop-up images and play sounds when the user passes the mouse over a hot spot, clicks on the image, or selects it. Since Advanced Imagemap Designer is a visual tool, you do not need any Java or HTML programming knowledge to use it.

Agile HTML Editor. Agile HTML Editor is an HTML editor that has been updated for the latest standards. It enables you to write HTML code with full help on every aspect of HTML—it even has the HTML 3.2 standards built right in. The full-featured editor allows for unlimited file size, unlimited multi-level undo/redo, drag and drop file opening and editing, and search and replace.

Applet Button Factory. Applet Button Factory lets you create custom Java applet buttons, even if you don't know anything about Java or the HTML code. Fill in various options that define the number of buttons, size, border thickness and color, text, optional image files, and other characteristics. Various button options can cause the button text color to change during a mouse-over event or even cause the button to be pressed automatically. A separate window opens to instantly show you the results of your settings and modifications. When you're satisfied with your work, Applet Button Factory creates code to be copied to your Web page or builds a page from scratch for you to modify. Several samples and online help are included.

Applet Headline Factory. Create Java applet headlines easily, without any Java or HTML programming knowledge. Use headlines to announce news and link to other pages, thereby saving space while improving the look and feel of your site. Applet Headline Factory gives you full control over size, style, color, borders, scroll settings, and much more. These headlines work well in frames and tables, allow the use of images in the headlines, and offer adjustable scroll buttons and "grab control" for your visitors. With Applet Headline Factory you can even put a message in the browser status bar that displays when the user slides the mouse over the headline. An applet previewer is included, so you can view your work as you create your headlines.

Applet Marquee Wizard. With the Applet Marquee Wizard anyone can easily create smooth-scrolling Java banners. Each banner is customizable in such areas as scrolling direction, font properties, colors, and links—all of which can be altered easily using the Wizard's intuitive interface.

Applet Navigation Factory. Applet Navigation Factory is designed to help you make navigation menus for your Web site without any Java or HTML experience. You can customize the loading message before the applet appears; use gradient backgrounds; put images in your applets; make pop-up hints and outline boxes for your menu items; use any color for text, borders, or backgrounds; make mouseover effects; control border styles and widths; and view the HTML code as you are creating applets. The applets work in frames and tables easily. The previewer allows you to see the applet as you create. You can easily test your applets in a browser while you are creating them.

Applet Password Wizard. Applet Password Wizard allows you to create user names and passwords to protect your Web pages. Without knowing Java or HTML you can create an unlimited number of user name/password entries. You can set up the applet to send the user to another URL of your choice should they fail to supply a proper user name and password. This allows you to secure sensitive content on your Web site. It works in frames and tables easily, and allows you to control border styles, widths, and background colors. The applet previewer displays your work as you create. You can also view the HTML code as you are creating banners. A shortcut helps you browser-test your work while you create.

Arachnophilia. This robust application can import and automatically convert RTF documents, tables, and outlines from any Windows 95-compliant application to HTML. It also supports up to six Web browsers, CGI, frames, Perl, C++, Java, and JavaScript development. Other features include a built-in intelligent FTP client, automatic uploading of changed files, user-defined templates, user-customizable toolbars for quick access to frequently used tags, global search and replace, and a multiple-document interface with full drag-and-drop capability. In addition, Arachnophilia includes built-in tutorials on HTML development, JavaScript, frames, and the Internet.

Au2HTML. Au2HTML is a program that creates thumbnails and HTML index pages of your images. Simply point this program to a directory that contains the files, and it automatically generates the index files and/or thumbnails of that directory. It will even index your non-graphics files. It also has a built-in HTML editor, HTML code generator, thumbnail generator, browser path, and external FTP for easy transferring of HTML pages and files.

Banner Factory. Applet Banner Factory is a Java banner development tool. You can create professional 3D banners without any knowledge of Java programming or HTML. Include metallic/glowing titles, scrolling messages, background images, and 3D effects. After you have created a banner to suit your needs, Applet Banner Factory will generate all the necessary HTML code required to include it on your Web page.

Cheap Date. Cheap Date is designed for the creation of HTML calendars divided into days, months, quarters, years, and fiscal years. Users can add events on daily and monthly calendars, add color to text and backgrounds, add a title, and add their own graphics. This version adds the ability to create, save, and apply recurring events.

CoffeeCup HTML Editor ++ 98. This application includes a spell-checker, meta data, a horizontal rule dialog, web TV, sound gallery, special character, and four very robust HTML designers (wizards) to help make tables, lists, forms and frames a snap. You'll also find the usual host of font tools, including a header size drop-down menu, font color and font tag designer. Lists of Java and CGI scripts have been added, including a dozen DHTML snippets (40 more JavaScripts with registration). There's also an Image Companion that shows you a preview thumbnail of any image file in any folder. Tag highlights can be quickly toggled on and off. There's also a handy tag stripper. If you're a serious Web author, you need to take a serious look at the powerful and immensely functional CoffeeCup++ 98. The complete help file includes an HTML reference.

CoffeeCup HTMLEditor Express. CoffeeCup HTML Editor Express is a "quick start" Web page creation utility that is designed to guide the beginner step-by-step through the creation of a Web site. The neat, attractive interface is divided into two sections, with a row of large icons at the top and a tabbed dialog box on the bottom. The eight icons represent the eight steps in the page-building process: Start, Colors, Images, Links, Text, Bullets, Save, and Upload. The Start dialog box offers the user a list of templates to begin a page, from Basic Image Left to Fancy Table. You can also add meta tag data at this point. In Colors, set the colors for background, text, and links. You can also insert an image file to use as a background. The Bullets step lets you choose from a list of seven different bullet styles—from discs to letters. As you work, CoffeeCup HTML Editor Express displays context-sensitive tips to remind you of details—such as where to save your files once you're done.

CoffeeCup ImageMapper++. CoffeeCup Image Mapper++ transforms the tedious task of creating image maps into a simple click-and-drag operation. Image maps—those clickable pictures on Websites that contain multiple hotspots linked to different destinations—are a bear to hand-code. With Image Mapper++, though, creating a hotspot couldn't be easier: Choose an image, then use one of three drawing tools (a rectangle, circle, or freehand tool) to draw the outline of the hotspot. You're then prompted to enter a destination URL, status bar text, and a pop-up caption that will appear when the visitor moves the mouse pointer over the hotspot. Create as many hotspots as you need, then save and test the resulting HTML code. As you create your hotspots, the HTML code is displayed in a window at the bottom of the screen—a neat way to learn how to code an image map yourself.

CoffeeCup StyleSheet Maker++. CoffeeCup StyleSheet Maker++ makes it easy to create fancy, professional-looking cascading style sheet Web pages. You customize your style sheet by selecting from more than 50 tags in a pull-down menu, or define your own custom classes and IDs. The program creates style tags on the fly in a detachable and sur-

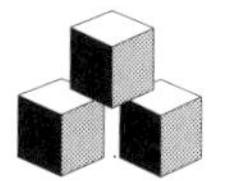

prisingly capable source code editor. A tabbed menu system provides formatting options for font and background colors, font sizing and qualifying, borders, margins, and alignment. Testing is simple: Try out the style sheet changes on an existing HTML document, or use the included samples.

Color Match. This small, free program allows you to create colors and color codes to use in your HTML code. Simply move the scroll bar sliders back and forth. Watch the Sample Color Box until you've blended just the shade you want for your web page backgrounds, text or links. Then, press the button that says "Paste HTML Code to the Clipboard." From there, simply paste it into your code.

CoolMap. CoolMap not only works as an image map but also comes with a built-in design center that makes image map design and maintenance visible: CoolMap can generate an HTML script which calls itself. A sound will also be played when the mouse is moved over a particular hot area. The corresponding URL will be opened when the user clicks that hot area.

CSE HTML Validator. CSE HTML Validator is a user-configurable HTML development tool that assists in the creation of syntactically correct HTML documents. Just give CSE HTML Validator an HTML document, and it will produce a list of syntax errors in your document. You can use the syntax error list to help correct your document before publishing it. HTML Validator also includes tools that change HTML tags and attributes to uppercase or lowercase, strip HTML tags, convert different text file formats into other text file formats, and let you use templates in your documents.

Frame-It! is a feature-packed HTML frame generator, which allows you to generate complex and impressive HTML frames, using only your mouse. With this program you can define complex frames within a few minutes, including specifying the height and width of each frame. You can create and delete framesets, and save a frameset to the clipboard or a file.

GIF Construction Set. GIF Construction Set for Windows is a powerful collection of tools to work with multiple-block GIF files. It includes facilities to manage palettes and merge multiple GIF files together. It can create animations, transparent GIF files, interlaced GIF files, and add non-destructive text to images.

HTML Calendar. HTML Calendar is a Windows-based program which automatically generates HTML code for a web calendar for any month from 1998–2002. This program isn't very feature heavy, but it's simple to use, and the resulting code can be modified easily.

HTML Media Page Writer. HTML Media Page Writer helps you easily create Web pages showing all of your GIF and JPEG pictures in a table. You can also create a "picks" list and list WAV and MIDI sound files in the registered version. Pictures are marked with alternate text and can be viewed in actual size when clicked. You can choose pictures or text to represent your sound files, which automatically play when clicked.

HTML Power Tools. Eight separate tools comprise HTML PowerTools for Windows. These are powerful HTML development tools for Windows, for use alongside your HTML or text editor. They include customizable offline HTML validation and link checking, HTML-specific spell-checking, HTML-aware search and replace, site-wide META tag management, automatic HTML file "last modified date" stamping, IMG tag automatic width, height, and ALT insertion, HTML to text batch conversion, and more.

HTML Table Designer. This utility aids in building HTML tables filled with formatted data. HTML Table Designer lets you adjust cell padding, cell spacing, and border width, turn the border on or off, adjust the number of columns and rows, add captions, and center the table. You can even use data from a text file, with spaces as a delineators.

HtmlBuild. HtmlBuild is a powerful program that converts Microsoft Excel 95 (version 7.0) spreadsheets to HTML tables and pages. It offers many options that allow you to customize virtually every feature of the tables allowed in HTML 3.2. HtmlBuild even converts all links and e-mail addresses to hyperlinks, and supports adding JavaScript to the page. This program has an easy-to-use interface that allows beginners and advanced Web designers alike to create great-looking tables.

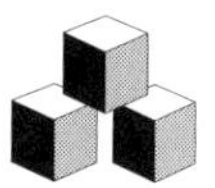

HTMLEd/HTMLEd Pro. HTMLed and HTMLed Pro are authoring tools used to create HTML documents for the World Wide Web. HTMLEd contains a Form Designer (for designing HTML forms and collecting information on the Web) and a Table Designer (for creating tables to use in your web pages). HTMLEdPro adds a Frame Designer (for creating frame-based pages) and an ImageMap designer. It also includes the ability to import RTF (rich text format) files and to upload your Web site to a server.

LiveImage. LiveImage helps you create and edit clickable image maps that are used on the World Wide Web. These image maps are used just like regular hyperlinks—but instead of just having one image having a single response, you can put together a larger image that has specific areas that perform different actions. LiveImage is designed to help you get image maps working for you, right now. LiveImage takes care of all the messy details of reading and writing the data that defines the areas of the image map. LiveImage will walk you through the hardest part of the process, and can even let you generate some common types of graphics. The application supports Zooming, Area Creation, Grids, Image Creation, Image Conversion, and more!

LViewPro. LView Pro is a powerful but easy-to-use image-file editor with handy toolbar icons and extensive options. Files can be opened in a number of formats, such as .jpg, .gif, .bmp, .tiff, and .tga. Objects can be viewed, flipped, rotated clockwise or counterclockwise, and lightened or darkened. LView Pro includes a special macro-editing mode that can accomplish several image enhancements at once from a common menu. File groups can be displayed as slideshows or inserted into a single-file contact sheet. LView Pro is designed for Internet usage, capable of producing transparent-background images and interlaced GIF files.

MaduraPage. MaduraPage is a Java authoring tool for the Web that allows animation, image filtering, audio effects, overlapping objects, and text editing, so no separate HTML editor is needed. The resulting pages can be viewed by any browser that supports JDK 1.0 (Navigator 3.0 and IE 3.0 and later versions). Because the output is a Java applet, no plug-ins are required.

MapMaker32. This small program lets you create client-side image maps by dragging a BMP, JPEG, or GIF file onto the MapMaker window. You map rectangles using the mouse and simply enter the link you want that part of the image to point to. The resulting HTML can then be saved to a file or to the clipboard.

Menu Wizard. Menu Wizard creates graphics and integrates JavaScript code into HTML pages to create a frame-embedded menu system. Features include three-state buttons with different effects of color, font, shading, blur, bevel, background transparency, or background images. Scripting includes different JavaScript versions and backup for non-scripting browsers. The program transfers the pages to the user server using WebPost or FTP.

MenuMaster. MenuMaster is a collection of 20 applet menus. The package is delivered with Visual Applet Configurator (VAC), a configuration tool that makes it possible to customize the applets without any knowledge of Java programming. In this demo, 5 of 20 applets can be used for free. The 15 other applets can be evaluated and tested locally on your hard disk.

NetObjects Fusion. The latest version of NetObjects Fusion delivers an open Web site building environment that provides enhanced flexibility and layout control along with robust site management and cross-browser support. Choose from graphical page layout mode for pixel-perfect positioning of elements or text editor mode when ultralean HTML is a top priority, or work with an external HTML editor. Allaire HomeSite is included free to create part or all of a page. Take advantage of Dynamic Actions, the visual, message-based environment for creating DHTML-based animation and interactivity. This trial version of NetObjects Fusion contains all of the features and functionality of the full version, except you cannot stage or publish the sites you create with it. Version 4.0 features an expanded Java application programming interface supporting Java Development Kit 1.1 and Swing 1.0; wizards to design applications that connect to databases or application servers without programming; e-commerce components; new SiteStyles, including sample sites complete with content you can adapt for your own uses; an improved layout editor; and better control over HTML publishing.

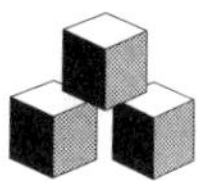

Pretty HTML. Pretty HTML is an easy-to-use program that formats your HTML Web pages. After processing, your HTML code is neatly arranged, commented, spaced, and indented, making it much easier to read and maintain. You can also use Pretty HTML to compress your Web pages by eliminating unnecessary spaces and carriage returns. Process your Web pages one at a time or batch-format entire folders in a single operation. Pretty HTML offers a number of options to ensure that the HTML formatting is done to your liking. To play it extra safe, you can have the program make backup copies of your originals. You can also use Pretty HTML as a capable HTML editor. Editing features include syntax highlighting, search and replace, custom formatting of selected text-only, and easy preview in your default browser.

Scribbler 98. Scribbler is a JavaScript, VBScript, and DHTML editor for amateur and professional Web writers. It offers sidebars with all the standard elements of each supported language. Just double-click or drag and drop these elements into your code. The sidebars list all the instructions, objects with their methods, events, and library functions in each language for your easy reference and insertion, so there's no need to browse separate language manuals. If you want more extensive samples for the language features, there is a build-in library of more than 30 scripts right at your fingertips. Other features include syntax highlighting and integrated preview and debugging.

Spider Writer HTML Editor. The Spider Writer Web development suite takes the hassle out of writing and maintaining Web pages. It consists of a feature-rich HTML editor, a full FTP client, and an image map editor. Dialog boxes help you create and edit all HTML tags and display Wysiwyg previews of tags before you insert them. Included wizards visually create frames, tables, and text color gradients. A scripting wizard automatically inserts free JavaScripts into documents. The Item Browser, among other functions, allows you to browse the files on your hard drive and open or insert them into your documents. Document Weight calculates download times, while Link Verification looks for broken links. The editor also features tag coloring, spell and syntax checking, global find and replace functions, automatic indenting, and an integrated Web browser.

Style One. Style One is a cascading style sheet editor with 100 percent compliance to the W3C recommendation for CSS level 1, including the proposal for HTML content positioning. You simply choose the properties and values you want, and the program will automatically generate the corresponding style sheet statements. Features include tabs to find and edit all the properties, an intuitive interface for editing properties with select boxes, special edit dialogs and quick-reset buttons, and an integrated viewer to preview the resulting style sheet.

Web Forms. WebForms is a WWW forms generator which automatically creates HTML forms and reads their responses. Responses are sent to your e-mail address. No HTML knowledge, and CGI is optional. It also generates Perl scripts. Comes with online help system and tutorial. WebForms is great for taking customer orders, doing surveys, or anything you can think of that requires user input on the WWW.

Web Painter. WebPainter is a cel-based paint and animation software program for the World Wide Web. WebPainter's intuitive interface and unique animation tools makes it easy to add attention grabbing animation and graphics to your Web pages or corporate Intranets. WebPainter includes all the tools needed to create professional Web animation and graphics. Its ease of use and unique cel animation interface help you create small-sized, high-quality GIF animations, QuickTime movies, and JPEG and GIF files with the fewest possible steps. By combining bitmap and vector graphic tools, image layering features, SMPTE special effects, automatic transitions, image filters, and powerful export features, users can quickly create professional animation and graphics for their corporate, educational, or personal Web sites. It also includes more than 1,000 professionally designed, royalty-free GIF animations to get you started.

Web Thumbnailer. With Web Thumbnailer you can easily make thumbnails of images for your Web pages. No more nonproportional thumbnails that stretch your pictures into strange-looking mosaics. No more agonizing over making each and every thumbnail separately. Simply select the desired images from your directory and set your HTML parameters and options. Web Thumbnailer generates the code, which you can then paste into your Web page.

Glossary

absolute URL. An absolute URL is the full path of the item to which you are linking. See *URL*, and contrast with *relative URL*.

accessibility. The capability of many different browsers and versions of browsers to display your Web site. Accessibility varies according to how compliant a browser is with HTML standards. If your site uses Strict HTML 4.0 standards, for example, some older browsers may not be able to display everything your site offers, such as effects that rely on *Dynamic HTML* or a *Cascading Style Sheet*. You increase accessibility by using older HTML standards.

amplitude. The technical term for the volume of a sound wave.

analog. In terms of sound, analog refers to the physical aspects of sound. The sounds stored on a cassette tape, for example, are in analog format. See *digital*.

anchor tag. One part of a link to a location on your Web site is the anchor tag, which is the tag pair `<A>` and `</A>`. See *HREF*.

animation frame. In animation, a frame is one of a series of images that, when viewed sequentially and at a fast enough rate, create the impression of movement or change. Do not confuse with *frame*.

ASCII file. Same as *text file*. ASCII files are files that consist of nothing more than simple text. No formatting or graphics appear in text files. Files whose extensions are `.txt`, `.asc`, `.html`, or `.htm` are text files. See *binary file*.

attribute. Attributes go hand in hand with *tags*. You use attributes to make the text, graphic, or sound within a tag do a certain thing or appear a certain way. An example of a tag with an attribute is `<BODY BGCOLOR="blue">`, which gives a Web page a blue background. The tag is `<BODY>`, the attribute is `BGCOLOR` (background color), and the attribute's value is `"blue"`. See *tag* and *value*.

banner. A graphic somewhere on a Web page that may consist of text, art, or some combination of the two. Common uses for banners include advertisements, company logos, designs that jazz up the Web page, and welcome messages.

banner exchange. A means of advertising your site at no cost. A banner you create to advertise your site appears on the Web pages of other members of the banner exchange. In return, you allow other people's banners to appear on your site.

binary file. Files other than ASCII (or text) files. Contrast with *ASCII file*.

bit rate. This rate determines the dynamic range of your Web audio files. The two commonly used bit rates are 8 and 16. A 16-bit audio file is much larger and louder (because the difference between the quietest spots and the loudest spots is wider) than an 8-bit audio file. See *dynamic range*.

broken link. A link that no longer works. Breaks occur when the page or section to which you linked is no longer at the URL your HTML specifies.

browser. Software that interprets HTML and provides an interface for displaying Web pages on your monitor. Internet Explorer and Navigator are the most widely used browsers.

bulleted list. See *unordered list.*

Cascading Style Sheet. Same as *CSS.* Web builders now can create style sheets, called Cascading Style Sheets, to make better use of HTML 4.0. Using style sheets and scripts, it's possible to make all kinds of things happen as a user moves a mouse across a Web page or clicks on a link. Cascading Style Sheets are a key to the dramatically different appearance of Web sites that use *DHTML.* For more information about CSS, refer to the following URL:

http://www.w3.org/Style/CSS/

cell. The intersection of a row and column in a table. A cell can contain a data element, a heading, or some other portion of a Web page's content, such as a paragraph or an image. See *row, column,* and *table.*

clickable image map. See *image map.*

client-side. Client-side processing takes place on the user's computer, saving the Web server's power for other things. Usually, client-side processing is preferable to server-side processing. Contrast with *server-side.*

codec. A coder-decoder necessary to go back and forth between the compressed and uncompressed formats of a Web video. Many codecs are available for use with Web video. The Cinepak codec is popular for creating video for the Windows environment and for use on the Web.

column. Used in relation to tables, a column is a set of vertically grouped cells. See *row, cell,* and *table.*

container tag. The most common type of tag, having both *start* and *end tags.* Everything within the container tag is affected by it. An example of a container tag is the combination of start tag `<FONT>` and end tag `</FONT>`. See *start tag* and *end tag.*

controls. Objects that users interact with in a form. Drop-down lists, input forms, and buttons are some examples of controls. You use the `<INPUT>` tag to create user input controls.

coordinates. You use coordinates in defining the hot region of an image map. You need to use an image-mapping program or a graphics program to determine the coordinates of the *hot region.*

CSS. See *Cascading Style Sheet.*

data cells. These cells are the cells in an HTML table that are not header cells. Typically, they hold the table's data.

decibel. The unit of measurement for dynamic range. The more decibels you have, the wider the dynamic range. More dynamic range comes at the cost of larger file sizes.

deprecated. In the world of HTML, an element that has been deprecated has been declared on the way to obsolescence. You can still use a deprecated element, but a new tag has been standardized to take its place. If you want to know the specifications for the latest version of HTML (4.0), visit the following URL:

http://www.w3.org/TR/REC-html40/

DHTML. See *Dynamic HTML.*

digital. Computers deal in digital information. The sounds stored on a computer, for example, are in digital format. Contrast with *analog.*

digitize. This is the process of taking analog data, such as the video on a videotape or the music on a cassette tape, and changing it into a form usable on a computer.

directory service. A directory service is one means of researching or searching the Internet for information or a Web site. Directory services categorize Web sites and information, but do not attempt to list *all* Web sites. Yahoo! and Magellan are examples of directory services. See *search engine* and *Web directory.*

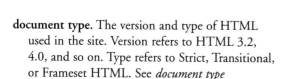

document type. The version and type of HTML used in the site. Version refers to HTML 3.2, 4.0, and so on. Type refers to Strict, Transitional, or Frameset HTML. See *document type declaration.*

document type declaration (DTD). A means of indicating directly in your HTML what version (such as 3.2 or 4.0) and type of HTML (Strict, Transitional, or Frameset) you used to write the document.

domain name. A domain name specifies a site on the Internet. In **http://www.yourcompany.com**, the domain name is **yourcompany.com**. The **com** portion is called the top-level domain. Other top-level domains include **gov**, **edu**, **net**, and **mil**.

drill down. Work your way through layers of categories in a Web directory. If you want to find specific sites listed in a Web directory such as Yahoo!, you can drill down to locate what you want.

DTD. See *document type declaration.*

Dynamic HTML. Dynamic HTML makes use of Cascading Style Sheets, new tags, and scripts to enable Web builders to create very attractive and custom Web sites that have new capabilities. See *Cascading Style Sheet.*

dynamic range. The difference in volume between the loudest part of a sound and the quietest part. See *bit rate.*

empty tag. An HTML tag (for example, `<BASEFONT>`) that does not require an *end tag.* Contrast with *container tag.*

end tag. One of the two required parts of a container tag. The end tag comes last, and takes the same form as the start tag, but with a slash (`/`) after the <. An example of an end tag is `</STRONG>`, which is paired with the start tag `<STRONG>`. See *start tag.*

external links. Links to locations outside the Web site that contains the current Web page.

extranet. An *intranet* variation that allows some people outside the company or organization to access the company intranet. Company clients, for example, may be allowed to access the company's intranet for certain purposes.

FAQ. Abbreviation for **Frequently Asked Questions.** The use of a FAQ file is common on the Web to help answer common questions about a given topic. Technical support departments of hardware and software companies, as well as ISPs, often use FAQs to answer many of the questions they otherwise would have to answer on an individual basis.

File Transfer Protocol. This protocol (set of conventions) is what you use to upload files to your Web site. You also may find yourself using FTP to download files from a site.

fixed-width font. A fixed-width font is one in which each letter takes up the same amount of horizontal space as every other letter. An example of a fixed-width font is Courier. Same as *monospace font.*

form header. The `<FORM>` tag and its attributes.

forms processing. Putting the information returned to you from a filled-out form into a usable format. Most forms processing takes place on the Web server and involves CGI scripts.

fragment identifier. Same as *target name.* Indicated by the `#` in an anchor tag. The browser needs this identifier to know where to send a visitor who clicks on that link.

frame. A window inside the large browser window. A site with frames can show two or more Web pages at once. Do not confuse with *animation frame.*

frequency. A characteristic of sound waves. Frequency is how "frequently" a sound wave passes by a given point; the more often a sound wave goes by, the higher the frequency. See *hertz* and *wave.*

FTP. See *File Transfer Protocol.*

hand coding. Typing HTML directly in a text editor such as Notepad, instead of telling a wizard or other front-end tool what you want to do and then having the HTML produced for you. This term also applies to producing code "from scratch" in any other programming language.

header cells. A term that refers to HTML tables. Header cells are those cells that appear at the top of a column of cells or at the far-left end of a row of cells.

heading. Essentially the title for a section of a Web site, book, or article. Besides telling readers what that section contains, a heading also adds white space to a Web site.

hertz. A unit of measurement for a sound wave's frequency. Frequency is measured in *hertz* (abbreviated *Hz*) and its multiples: kilohertz, megahertz, gigahertz, and so on. See *frequency* and *wave.*

hex code. See *hexadecimal code.*

hexadecimal code. A value in the base-16 mathematical system consisting of combinations of the following characters:

0 1 2 3 4 5 6 7 8 9 A B C D E F

hit. A hit is when something happens on a Web server. For example, when someone clicks on a link somewhere and lands on your Web site, it's a hit. If that person then clicks on an internal link to view the second page of your Web site, that's another hit. Your site may receive several hits from one person. Each hit, in other words, does not represent a different visitor to your site. See *user session.*

hit counter. This type of software tracks how many times an action occurs on your Web server.

horizontal rule. A straight line that runs across a Web page. You can use it to separate the contents of a page into sections.

hot area. See *hot region.*

hot region. An area within an image map that can be clicked to activate a link.

hot spot. See *hot region.*

HREF. Short for *hypertext reference,* which is one of the attributes of the `<A>` tag. The value you assign to the `HREF` attribute in an internal link is the name of the file to which you are linking. See *anchor tag.*

HTML. See *HyperText Markup Language.*

http. See *HyperText Transfer Protocol.*

hyperlink. Same as *link.* A link is a connection between two Web sites, or between pages of a single Web site, or even between two locations on a specific Web page. In text, links usually show up as underlined blue words, although the color can vary according to the site builder's preferences. A graphic, or portion of a graphic, also can be a link (see *image map*).

HyperText Markup Language. The programming "language" that makes the Web work, HTML consists of tags, attributes, and values. A browser reads the HTML, and interprets it to create the images you see onscreen.

HyperText Transfer Protocol. These conventions make it possible to transfer information between a Web server and a Web browser. See *FTP.*

image map. An image with links built into it. If a user passes the mouse over a *hot region* of the image, the arrow turns into a hand, indicating that a hyperlink is present in that spot. Clicking on different links within the same image map usually takes the user to different locations. Image maps often have text in each hot region to indicate the purpose of each particular link.

inline graphic. A graphic that falls in the flow of the document. In other words, you indicate in the HTML where the graphic goes, what its filename is, and where the browser can find it to load.

internal link. A link to another location within the same Web site.

Internet service provider (ISP). A company that offers access to the Internet to individuals and businesses, and that usually provides its customers a set of selected tools for taking advantage of the World Wide Web, e-mail, and other Internet offerings. Contrast with *online service provider.*

Internet. A worldwide series of computer networks connected via telephone lines, fiber optic cables, satellites, and so on. Each computer on the Internet has a unique address (see *URL*), which makes things such as Web sites and e-mail possible. The Internet has several constituent parts and protocols, including the World Wide Web, FTP, and telnet.

Internet Protocol address. See *IP address.*

intranet. An intranet is essentially an organization-wide Web. It makes use of the same features and tools as the Internet, including Web pages and e-mail, but is created for internal use in a company.

IP address. Identifies a specific computer on the Internet.

justified. Justified text is text that extends from margin to margin on every line. In other words, neither the left nor the right side of the paragraph is ragged; each side is nice and even. The extra space on a line is divided between the words, so that (usually) no big gaps are apparent. Justified text normally has a very neat appearance.

Kbps. Short for "kilobits per second," it's a designation for download speed.

leading. The amount of space between lines of text within a paragraph (pronounced "ledding").

link. See *hyperlink.*

link target. In constructing a link, the entire tag (as in `<A HREF="fender.html">`) is the *link target.*

logical formatting. Refers to using the `<EM>` and `<STRONG>` container tags. These tags tell the browser to place emphasis (`<EM>`) or strong emphasis (`<STRONG>`) on the text. See *physical formatting.*

Mbps. Short for "megabits per second," it's a designation for download speed.

media server. Servers dedicated to delivering live video over the Web are media servers. Some streaming video systems require a media server.

monospace font. See *fixed-width font.*

My Place. The America Online name for the free space all AOL account holders are entitled to use for a personal Web site.

online service provider. Companies like America Online, CompuServe, and Prodigy are online service providers. They do more than just give subscribers access to the Internet; they each include their own special features, and work hard at fostering a sense of community among their millions of members.

optimize. The process of reducing file size while maintaining the highest quality possible. Optimization is especially relevant with graphics files, because download times are too long if graphics files are left unoptimized.

ordered list. A list in which the items are numbered or otherwise explicitly sequenced. See *unordered list.*

packet. A small package of video or audio data, packets make streaming audio and video work. With streaming, users don't need to wait until the entire audio or video file has been downloaded before listening to it or viewing it. As soon as the packets arrive, the browser starts playing the file.

parse. What software does when it "reads" the information returned after a user fills out a form.

personal Web site. A normal Web site, but one that is devoted to an individual's interests, not to a business.

physical formatting. Telling a browser exactly what to do with the text, such as italicize it or put it in boldface. See *logical formatting.*

pixel. Basically, a pixel is a dot of light. In reference to monitors, for example, you hear about *screen resolution,* which is given as a measurement of the form "1024×768." Those numbers refer to the number of pixels across the screen (1024) and the number of pixels down the screen (768). See *screen resolution.*

plug-in. A small program that some software packages require a user's computer to have loaded in order for the software to work.

promotion. Spreading the word about your Web site. Registering your Web site with search engines and directory services, joining banner exchanges, and joining Web rings are some of the ways you can promote your Web site.

proportional spacing. A proportionally spaced font is one in which the letters take up varying amounts of horizontal space, depending on the width of the letter. A lowercase `i`, for example, is narrower than an uppercase `W`. An example of a proportionally spaced font is Times New Roman.

reciprocal links. When two Web site owners place links to each other's sites, it's called reciprocal linking, and it usually happens when the owners have the same or similar interests and Web content. Reciprocal linking is likely to increase your Web traffic because people interested in your site's contents can find it from another, similar site.

relative URL. If you are linking to a part of your own Web site, the page *from* which you are linking and the page *to* which you are linking share part of that address in common. If you are creating a link from the `/inventory/newstock` folder to the `/inventory/sales.html` folder, for example, you need to list only `sales.html` as the link target. That's because everything else is common to both HTML documents. The part you enter is the relative URL. See *absolute URL.*

row. In HTML tables, a row is a set of horizontally grouped cells. See *column, cell,* and *table.*

sample. In order for computers to deal with analog sound, the computer takes samples of the analog sound. The samples are taken at set intervals. See *sampling rate.*

sampling rate. When creating Web audio, you have to choose how often the software samples the original audio. How often the software takes the samples is the sampling rate, and this determines how true the resulting sound is to the original. 11.025 kHz is typically as low as people go for decent quality, and 44.1 kHz is CD-quality audio.

sans serif. A sans serif (literally, "without serif") font is one that doesn't have serifs on the letters. Contrast with *serif.*

screen resolution. A measurement of the number of pixels a monitor displays. The more pixels your monitor has, the better the resolution, and the better the image quality. If an artist draws your face, using only 100 dots to do so, and then draws it again, this time using 1000 dots, which one will look better? Obviously, the latter will, because it's a "higher resolution." Usually, you can change the resolution setting of a monitor, but they always have a maximum resolution. See *pixel.*

script. A short program that performs a certain function within a Web site. Usually written in JavaScript or Visual Basic, although other programming languages may be used. Including scripts in your Web site greatly increases what you can do with your site—but it also increases the amount of effort required to create the site.

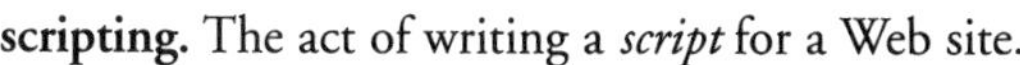

scripting. The act of writing a *script* for a Web site.

search engine. Does wide-ranging searches of the Web. Upon finding a site, a *spider* examines the site and indexes it according to the contents of the site's <META> tags and text. See *directory service* and *Web directory.*

serif. A short line that extends from the strokes used to make the shape of a letter. A serif font is one that has serifs on its letters. Contrast with *sans serif.*

server. A computer that "serves up" information to computers that request it; the hub of a network, functioning as both a repository of information and as a processing center. Some of the information in a server is available to the public. Servers also store Web sites that individuals or companies create. Few people own their own servers.

server-side. Server-side processing takes place on the Web server, using the server's processing power. Contrast with *client-side.*

site promotion. See *promotion.*

spider. Automated program that indexes the <META> tags and text of Web sites. Usually, it starts on one of the site's pages and then follows all the links, indexing as it goes. Spiders occasionally index sites again, keeping their records of your site relatively up to date. A *search engine* usually relies on a spider to locate and index sites so that users can find what they want.

start tag. One of the two required parts of a container tag. The start tag comes first, and takes the same form as the *end tag,* but without the slash (/). An example of a start tag is <TR>. Its corresponding end tag is </TR>.

streaming. In streaming, the user doesn't have to wait for an entire audio or video file to download before hearing or seeing it. Instead, the file is downloaded continuously and begins to play as much as possible, as soon as possible.

table. In HTML, a table consists of one or more columns of cells. A table may be just a table of information, as you might find in a book. Web site builders, however, often use tables to position graphics on the Web page. See *row, column,* and *cell.*

tag. Tags are the building blocks of HTML; browsers rely on the tags for information about how to create and display particular Web content. Without tags, the Web would not exist.

target name. Same as *fragment identifier.* Indicated by the # in an anchor tag. The browser needs this identifier to know where to send a visitor who clicks on that link.

thumbnail. A small version of a graphic. Links are usually established so that clicking on a thumbnail leads to a full-size version of the same image.

tiling. The arranging of open windows so that they all appear onscreen simultaneously. No window is minimized or hidden behind another window.

Uniform Resource Locator. Same as *URL.* Contains information critical for software to pinpoint and work with resources on the Internet. For example, the URL **http://www.primapublishing.com/** specifies the protocol to be used (**http**) as well as a domain name (**primapublishing.com**) to be converted to an IP address so that the browser can access the desired Web site.

unordered list. Same as *bulleted list.* An unordered list does not have explicit sequencing; each item simply has a bullet of some kind. Contrast with *ordered list.*

URL. See *Uniform Resource Locator.*

value. When you use an attribute with a tag, you may assign that attribute a value. See *tag* and *attribute.*

video capture card. Your computer needs one of these in order for you to create videos to place on your Web site. Newer Macs typically come with one installed.

W3C. See *World Wide Web Consortium.*

wave. All sounds consist of waves. See *frequency* and *hertz.*

wave file. One file format for sound is `.wav`, and any file in this format is commonly called a wave file. These are currently the most common type of sound files for the PC.

Web. See *World Wide Web.*

Webcam. A desktop video camera that is relatively inexpensive.

Web directory. One of the means of locating information on the Web, a Web directory differs from a search engine. A Web directory indexes a site and then categorizes the site for listing on the directory, so changing the site's content later may render the indexing obsolete. Same as *directory service;* contrast with *search engine.*

Web ring. A series of Web sites, all dealing with the same general topic, that are linked to each other.

Web site promotion. See *promotion.*

World Wide Web. Same as *Web.* The part of the Internet most familiar to the average person. When you visit or create a Web site, you're using the WWW. Its graphical nature is what has made it so popular.

World Wide Web Consortium. Same as *W3C.* This organization sets the standards for each version of HTML, after receiving input from member organizations. The W3C has a very useful Web site of its own, where you can find out just about anything you want to know about HTML and topics related to it:

http://www.w3.org/

WWW. See *World Wide Web.*

Index

A

<A> tag, 143
different elements with, 145
NAME attribute with, 148
absolute URLs, 144
accessibility of site, 23
ACTION attribute with <FORM> tag, 294-295
ActiveX controls, 4, 5
address, validating, 388
ADDRESS2 function, 389
<ADDRESS> tag, 156
<A> tag with, 145
Adobe
PageMill, 2
Premiere, 312
advanced Web site, 333. *See also* cascading style sheets; scripts
book page, 336-337
construction tasks for, 371
designing, 357-363
scripts, adding, 376-402
Guitar Brand page, 338-339
construction tasks for, 371
designing, 363-365
Java applets on, 405-410
opening page, 334-336
construction tasks for, 371
designing, 344-357
finishing, 375-376
operations of, 342-343
tone for, 334
aesthetics of site, 39
afSilkBanner.class, 406-409
<A HREF> tag, 243
.aif files, 308
alert boxes, 396
comments on, 397
ALIGN attribute
with <DIV> tag, 105
with <H1> tag, 103-104
with <IMG> tag, 162-163
ALIGN=”center”
for banners, 162
for divisions, 106
with <HR> tag, 109
ALIGN=“justify,” 86-87
ALIGN=“left,” 162-163
flowing text with, 173
ALIGN=“right,” 162-163
aligning text, 86-89
<ALIGN> tag, 86
ALINK attribute, 82-83
ALINK=“lime,” 82, 83
Allaire’s HomeSite, 193
ALT attribute, 163
<AREA> tag needing, 276
for GIF animation, 321
with graphics, 164-165
for hot regions, 277
supplying, 209
AltaVista, 433, 436-437
ALT=“graphic,” 165
alternate content, providing, 264-268
America Online, 424
FTP (file transfer protocol) on, 425-426
My Place, 425
procedures, 425-427
subscriber information, 424-427
version 4.0, 186
ampersand (&), 116-117
amplitude, 302, 303
sampling the, 305
analog information, 303
anchor tag, 143

AND condition, 393
angle brackets, 116
Animagic GIF, 319
animated GIFs, 37-38, 204
  adding, 317-322
  download time for, 318
  software programs for, 319
animation, 204
  adding, 317-322
  on banner graphics, 47
  designing, 318
  software programs for, 319
Animation Shop, 319
Anthill Scripter, 12
Anvil Studio, 306
applets. *See* Java applets
<AREA> tag, 276
  TARGET="_top" in, 376
arguments with applets, 408
Arial font, 94-95, 367
  for Windows, 415
arrays, 383
Articles page, 215
Artswork, Form Validation Tools, 12
ASCII files, 426
asterisk (*), 379
attributes, 7
  of <BODY> tag, 76
  equal sign (+) with, 14
  quotation marks with, 14
  rules for designing, 14
  uppercase letters for, 15
  values with, 7
audience
  for basic Web site, 22-24
  colors and, 113
  graphics and, 33-34
audio
  bit rate, 303
  dynamic range, 304
  on feature page, 212
  mono, recording in, 305
  page, adding to, 301-309
  sampling sound, 303
  sources for, 306
  steps in adding, 306-309
  stereo, recording in, 305
  streaming audio, 202, 304-306
    sources for, 306
  technical issues, 302-304
  turning off, 201
  using sound, 201-202
  video with, 314
  wave files, 308
.au files, 308
author of document, listing, 72
automatically loading document, 72
AVI, 311, 314

B

<B> tag, 101
  in table data cells, 219
Back button, 149
background colors
  assigning, 76-78
  bgColor property, 354
  of graphics, 269
  hexadecimal codes and, 112-113
  on opening page, 345-346
  to tables, 255
background images, **78-81**
  blending adjacent images, 79
  CD, images on, 79
  tiling, 78
BACKGROUND="Images/sunback.gif," 80-81
balancing page, 40-41, 58
Banner Factory, 406-409
banner graphics, 46
  contents of, 47
  exchanges, 460-461
  on individual pages, 57
  inserting, 161-164
  on second page, 166-167
base fonts, establishing, 91-92
<BASEFONT> tag, 91-92
Basic, 350
basic Web site
  audience, 22-24
  defined, 20
  goals for, 20-22

intermediate Web site, comparing, 194
testing, 180-187
Baskerville font, 367
beam-in effect, 346-347
BGCOLOR attribute
to <BODY> tag, 76-77
hex codes with, 112-113
for tables, 229-230, 261
to <TR> tag, 254-255
BGCOLOR-"black," 79, 81
bgColor property, 354
<BIG> tag
enlarging text, 95-96
overusing, 96
binary files, 426
bit rate, 303
black
backgrounds, 87
hex color code for, 112
bleeding edge, 342
block comments, 397
<BLOCKQUOTE> tag, 88-89
<BODY> tag, 76-83
<BASEFONT> tag in, 92
BGCOLOR attribute, 76-77
<FRAMESET> tags and, 265
of home page, 259
object of, 353
returns between, 69
for tables, 221
boldfacing, 41
with <STRONG> tag, 98, 99-102
in table data cells, 219
bookmarks, frames and, 9
book page. *See* advanced Web site
Boolean searches
with AltaVista, 436-437
AND condition, 393
in variables, 381
BORDER attribute, 254
with tables, 225
borders. *See also* tables
FRAMEBORDER attribute, 237
image maps and, 271-272
broken hyperlinks, 184-185
browsers
ALT attribute and, 165
client-side image maps, support for, 197
colors and, 113
comparing browsers, 186-187, 325-326
compatibility issues, 12-13, 342-343
designing for, 343
<DIV> tag support, 106
downloading, 186
font settings and, 102
frames and, 9, 13, 196
graphics, dimensions for, 163
intermediate Web site, viewing, 323
looping, support for, 322
returns between HTML lines, 68
scripts and, 357
<SUP> tag support, 101
table colors, 261
two browsers, testing on, 374-375
viewing site through, 181
WIDTH attribute support, 109
**
 tag,** 85
with hyperlinks, 267
wrapping text with, 176
bulleted lists, 114
clarifying purpose of, 118
completing, 118-119
creating, 114-123
finalizing, 120-121
indents and, 122
nested lists, 121
ordered lists, combining, 126-127
types of bullets, 121
on Welcome page, 55-56
<BUTTON> tag, 299
bytecode in Java, 410

C

C, 350
C++, 350
Cakewalk Pro Audio, 306
capitalization
in site, 41
for tags, 15
captions for graphics, 176

cascading style sheets, 342
  body text, 368
  colors in, 418-419
  construction tasks for, 371
  definition of cascading, 370
  designing, 365-370
  <EM> tag in, 417
  fonts, defining, 412-417
  headings, 366-367
  hyperlinks
    defining, 418-419
    in headings, 368
  linking style sheets, 411-412
  margins, setting, 416-417
  <P> tag in, 419-420
  rules in, 412
  selectors, 415
  standards, 411
  tables, defining, 419-420
  tables in, 369-370
  text, defining, 412-417
  writing, 410-420
case-sensitivity of JavaScript, 379
CD sound files, recording, 306
cell padding, 364
CELLPADDING attribute, 364, 416
  with <TABLE> tag, 225-227, 254
CELLSPACING attribute, 282
  colors with, 261
  with <TABLE> tag, 225, 226-227, 254
center alignment, 87
  with divisions, 106
  with headings, 104
  table cell contents, 260-261
<CENTER> tag
  for banners, 162
  with <DIV ALIGN="center"> tag, 271
  <DIV> tag with, 106-107
  for GIF animation, 3121
  for table of contents, 243
  for tables, 226-227
Century Gothic font, 94-95
Century Schoolbook font, 367
CGI scripts, 424
  forms processing and, 300-301
  in <FORM> tag, 401-402
character formatting, 41
CHECKED attribute, radio buttons and, 298-299
Cinepak codec, 316
circles
  bullets, circle, 121
  for hot regions, 275
city, validating, 389-390
CLASS attribute, 366
classes, defining, 366
CLEAR attribute, wrapping text with, 176
client-side image maps, 196-197, 268-283
codecs, 316
<CODE> tag, 102
ColdFusion, 2, 5
COLOR attribute
  with definition lists, 130
  <FONT> tag, 95
  for horizontal rule, 109
  to <TABLE> tag, 261
colors. *See also* hexadecimal codes; RGB components; tables
  browser-safe palette, 113
  in cascading style sheets, 418-419
  choosing color scheme, 76-78
  GIF files and, 158
  for horizontal rules, 109
  in HTML, 81-82
  for hyperlinks, 81
  pound sign (#), 14
  red-and-yellow sunburst effect, 167
  in style sheets, 418-419
  text colors, 95
  for underlining in site, 101
COLS attribute with <FRAMESET> tag, 233
COLSPAN attribute with <TABLE> tag, 255
columns. *See also* tables
  newspaper-style columns, 42
comments
  block comments, 397
  CSE 3310 and, 182
  functions handling, 395-396
  JavaScript comments, 397
  in <SCRIPT> tag, 399
  writing notes, 72-75

Comments variable, 396
comment tags
  adding to HTML, 73
  on borrowed code, 11
communicating with visitors, 155-157
company name graphic fo, 270-272
compatibility of browsers, 342-343
compiling Java, 410
compression. *See* file compression
CompuServe, 424
  Home Page Wizard, 428-429
  procedures on, 428-429
  subscriber information, 427-429
confidential information in forms, 286
contact information on Welcome page, 49
contact page, 215-216, 289-299
  creating, 289-299
  finishing, 294
  first part of page, creating, 292-293
  <INPUT> tag, using, 296
  lists, adding, 292-293
  <P> tag in, 296
container functions, 378
container tags, 7
CONTENT attribute, 8
  with <META> tag, 70-71
content of site, 43
continuity of design, 61
cookies, variables and, 382
Cool Edit Pro, 306
COORDS attribute for hot regions, 277
copy and paste. *See* cut and paste
copyrights, 3, 11, 27
  layout and design and, 39
  placement of information, 49
  SIZE attribute with, 95
  for sound files, 306
  symbol for, 117
corporate networks, subscribers to, 432
Courier font, 102
credit account numbers in forms, 286
cropping JPEG graphics, 159-160
CSE validation, 182-184
  for intermediate Web site, 324-325
Current Inventory page, 213-214
Current Specials link, 213
cut and paste, 184
  avoiding problems with, 326
  errors, correcting, 325

D

<DD> tag, 130
  <A> tag with, 145
DeBabelizer, 36, 160
decibels, 304
decorations, 161
default.htm, 68
definition lists, 127-130
***The Deluxe Transitive Vampire* (Gordon),** 25
<DEL> tag, 101
deprecated elements, 66, 183
description of site, 72
designing pages
  balancing page, 40-41
  considerations in, 40-42
  continuity of design, 61
  ideas for, 38-39
  individual pages, 57-62
  possibilities, considering, 45-46
  reviewing design, 60-61
  white space and, 40
digital cameras, 316
digital recording, 302
digital slicing, 303
digitizing video, 312-313
directories. *See* Web directories
disc bullets, 121
divisions, creating, 104-107
<DIV ALIGN="center"> tag, 243, 271
<DIV> tag, 104-107
  for banners, 162
  <CENTER> tag with, 106-107
<DL> tag, 127-130
.doc files, 64
<!DOCTYPE> tag, 65-66
document declaration, 68
document object model (DOM), 350-353
document type, 66
domain name, 9
double quotations marks (" "), 233

downloading
audio, sources for, 306
browsers, 186
GIF animation and, 37-38
graphics, 33
MapEdit, 268
streaming audio, 304-305
thumbnails, 171
drop-caps, creating, 259
<DT> tag, 130
<A> tag with, 145
dynamic HTML (DHTML), 5-6
basic Web site excluding, 20
dynamic range, 304

E

e-commerce, 358
editing videos, 310
***The Elements of Styles* (Strunk & White),** 25
ellipsis (...), 86
else condition, 385
e-mail
forms, addresses in, 288
forms and, 200
function, writing, 395
Mailto link, 156
embedded style sheets, 370
Emblaze Video, 312
emphasizing text, 98-102
empty tags, 7-8
<EM> tag, 98-99, 368
in cascading style sheets, 417
in table data cells, 219
encryption, 286, 480
orders on Web, 290
end tags, 7, 76
with <A> tag, 143
errors with, 327
EN identifier, 66
enlarging text, 95-96
<ENTER> tag, 183
equal sign (+), 14
Equilibrium DeBabelizer, 160
error messages, 374-375
errors
with copy-and-paste technique, 184
in HTML, 325
Excite, 437-439
explicit variables, 382
external links, 153-154

F

FACE attribute
<FONT> tag, 95-96
sans serif typeface, ensuring, 95
fade-in effect, 356
feature page, 211
file compression
JPEG files, 158-159
photographs, 158
rates for, 159
of video, 313
File Download dialog box, 308, 309
firewalls, 290
firm-up time, 346-347
first name, validating, 380-385
first page of site, 68
fixed-width fonts, 102
flowchart for site, 41-43
flowing text
around graphics, 171-180, 176
in table cells, 260
two graphics, flowing text between, 175
.focus method, 385
folders, 9
for HTML document, 64
for table documents, 220
font-family: sans-serif, 415-416
fonts
base fonts, establishing, 91-92
for book page, 362
browsers and, 102
cascading style sheets, defining in, 412-417
changing sizes of, 89-91
colors, 95
enlarging text, 95-96
fixed-width fonts, 102
for graphics, 269

in introductory paragraph, 136
for large-size print, 92
novelty fonts, 367
proportionally spaced fonts, 102
relative font sizes, 90-91
sans serif fonts, 94-95, 367
in cascading style sheets, 415-416
serif fonts, 94-95, 367
shrinking text, 96-97
sketching out, 47
variety for, 164
varying sizes in site, 41
<FONT> tag, 89-91
in cascading style sheets, 413, 414
COLOR attribute, 95
with definition lists, 130
FACE attribute, 95-96
headings with, 103
messages, 183
SIZE attribute, 89-91
in <SMALL> tag, 97
for superscripts/subscripts, 102
formatting text, 89-102
logical formatting, 98
in table data cells, 219
form headers, 289
forms. *See also* contact page
accepting feedback with, 199-200
in arrays, 383
basic Web site excluding, 20
confidential information in, 286
designing forms, 288
encryption issues, 286, 480
<LABEL> tag, 296
Mailto responses, 300-301
management of, 289
parsing responses, 300-301
processing forms, 300-301
purpose of, 286-288
radio buttons in, 298-299
Reset Form button, 299
starting forms, 289
Submit Form button, 299
forms processing, 300-301
Form Validation Tools, Artswork, 12
<FORM> tag, 289
ACTION attribute with, 294-295
CGI script in, 401-402
METHOD attribute with, 294
for-next loop, 393
for statement, 393
fourth page, adding, 138-141
fragment identifier, 146
frames, 196-197
adding link-related HTML, 262-263
advantages of, 10
alternate content in, 264-268
animation frames, 204
basic Web site excluding, 20
browsers and, 9, 13
contents of frames, creating, 238
creating frames, 231-238
hand, coding by, 231
hyperlinks and, 10
layout with, 9-11, 208-217
linking pages and, 244-248
links.html page, creating, 238-243
loading pages for Web site, 263-264
main links and, 210
as menu holder, 10
naming frames, 237-238
SCROLLING="auto" attribute, 245
space between, 236
tiled areas, creating, 230-231
for video, 313
frameset page, 346
<FRAMESET> tag, 67, 231-238
<BODY> tag and, 265
COLS attribute with, 233
FRAMEBORDER attribute, 237
FRAMESPACING attribute, 236
ROWS attribute with, 235
FRAMESPACING attribute, 236
<FRAME> tag, 233-238
frequency, 302
FrontPage 98, 2
FTP (file transfer protocol), 8, 424
America Online gram, 425-426
intranets and, 432
ISP (Internet service provider) and, 430-431

functions, 355
ADDRESS2 function, 389
city, validating, 389-390
comments, handling, 395-396
defining functions, 378
e-mail function, writing, 395
first name, validating, 380-385
last name, validating, 386-388
order of function calls, 390
Reset function, writing, 397-398
in scripts, 377
state function, writing, 391
ZIP codes, validating, 391-394

G

GIF Animator, Ulead, 319
LOOP command, 322
GIF Construction Set, 319
GIF files, 3. *See also* animated GIFs
advantages of, 35-37
ALT attribute with, 165
few colors, using for, 158
fonts and, 164
image maps as, 197
interlaced GIFs, 334
overview of, 268-269
pixels and, 160
transparent GIFs, 78
GIFmation, 319
gigaHertz, 302
global variables, 381-382
glossary, definition lists, 127-130
GoldWave, 306
Gordon, Karen Elizabeth, 25
Goto value, 409
grammar, 25
***Grammatically Correct* (Stilman),** 25
graphics. *See also* GIF files; JEPG files; photographs
adding graphics, 157-169
additional graphics, 165-169
aligning graphics, 162-163
ALT attribute with, 164-165
browsers displaying, 23
captions for, 176
company name graphic, creating, 270-272
copyright permissions, 11, 27-28
dimensions for, 163
drop-caps, creating, 259
on feature page, 211-212
flowing text around, 171-180
guidelines for using, 34
inline graphics, 157
intermingling text and, 40-41
larger images, 37
<META> tag for, 271
optimizing software, 36
purpose of graphics, 33-35
red-and-yellow sunburst effect, 167
scanned graphics, 347
screen resolution and, 160
software programs, 3-4
thumbnails, 171
tips for creating, 158-160
two graphics, flowing text between, 175
using graphics, 32-39
vector-based images, 160
on Welcome page, 46
white space and, 40
greater than (>), 117
Guitar Brand page. *See* advanced Web site
Guitar of the Month page
creating, 278-283
second table, adding, 280-281
sections, creating, 280-281

H

hardware for audio, 202
headings
alignment of, 104
with cascading style sheets, 366-367
creating, 103-104
for tables, 219
use of, 41
<HEAD> tag, 70
<BASEFONT> tag in, 92
returns between, 69
title nested in, 70

HEIGHT attribute
flowing text with, 173
for graphics, 163
for hot regions, 277
Helios Software's TextPad, 193
Helvetica font, 94, 367
for Macintosh, 415
Hertz (Hz), 302
hexadecimal codes, 14, 82, 111-113
defined, 111
<Hn> tag, 103
<A> tag with, 145
Home link, adding, 149-153
home page, 211
creating, 256-260
Home Page Wizard, CompuServe, 428-429
HomeSite, 193
<H1> tags, 251
horizontal rules, 107-110
color, assigning, 109
length, changing, 109
HotBot, 439-441
HotDog Pro, 2
HoTMetaL, 2
hot regions, 197, 268
defining, 272
linking, 376
in photographs, 283
shapes for, 275
hovering over link, 418
HREF attribute
with <A> tag, 143
for hot regions, 277
value assigned to, 146-147
<HR> tag, 107-110
ALIGN="center" attribute for, 109
HSPACE attribute, 173
HTML 4.0 Frameset, 67
HTML 4.0 Strict, 66-67
HTML 4.0 Transitional, 66, 67
HTML editors, 1, 2
types of, 183
HTML (Hypertext Markup Language). *See also* dynamic HTML (DHTML)
avoiding problems with, 326-327
<BUTTON> tag in, 299
colors in, 81-82
copying code, 11
defined, 4-5
depreciated HTML element, 66
errors in, 325
rules for writing, 14-16
uses of, 5
version, 66
HTML tables. *See* tables
<HTML> tag, 7, 14, 69
HTTP (Hypertext Transfer Protocol), 8
<H2> tags, 254
hyperlinks. *See also* cascading style sheets
absolute URLs, using, 144
adding link-related HTML, 262-263
alternate content with, 266-267
checking links, 184-185
colors, designing, 81-83
Current Specials page, 213
defined, 141
external links, 153-154
checking, 184
frames and, 10, 244-248
graphics as, 161
Home link, adding, 149-153
hovering over link, 418
on individual pages, 59-60
internal links
another page on site, linking to, 142-145
creating, 141-146
finishing all links, 148-149
to specific locations, 145-149
links.html page, creating, 238-243
list of, 50
main links and frames, 210
navigational links, 149-153
reciprocal links, 460
to sound files, 308
specific location on page, linking to, 145
suggestions for, 43
top-level links, limiting, 211
unactivated links, colors for, 82
to video clips, 203
on Welcome page, 47

I

<I> tag, 101
  in table data cells, 219
if line in script, 384
if statement
  alert boxes with, 396
  single-line commands, 401
illustration copyrights, 28
image maps, 197-199
  client-side image maps, 196-197, 268-283
  hot regions, 197
  photographs as, 283
  server-side image maps, 196
  specifications, file for, 277
  steps in creating, 272-275
image optimization software, 37
  video, 204
ImageReady, 36
<IMG> tag
  for banners, 162
  for GIF animation, 321
  information in, 271-272
  LOOP attribute with, 321-322
  USEMAP attribute in, 275-276, 277
***Increase Your Web Traffic in a Weekend* (Stanek),** 434
indenting paragraphs, 87-89
indents in bulleted lists, 122
index.htm, 68
index.html, 68
  external links, checking on, 154
  opening file, 74-75
.indexOf method, 394
information
  overdoing, 44
  planning for, 32
  presentation of, 24
  writing your material, 24-26
Information Technology (IT) Department, 432
Infoseek, 441-443
Infospace, 447-449
inheritance, objects and, 352-353
inline graphics, 157
inline styles, 370
<INPUT> tag, 289
  for contact page, 296
  for radio buttons, 298-299
interlaced GIFs, 334
  beam-in effect, 346-347
intermediate Web site. *See also* frames
  Articles page, 215
  basic Web site, comparing, 194
  Contact page, 215-216
  Current Inventory page, 213-214
  Current Specials page, 213
  defined, 193
  feature page, 211-212
  forms, 199-200
  goals for, 193-195
  Home page, 211
  image maps, 197-199
  layout for, 208-217
  Services page, 214-215
  tables, 195-196
  testing, 322-327
internal links. *See* hyperlinks
international audience, 26
Internet Explorer, 6, 12-13, 186
  bad code on, 374-375
  <DEL> tag support, 101
  HTML tags, 68
  index.html file, opening, 74
  intermediate Web site on, 325
  justified text, 86
  Refresh button, 84
  scripts and, 357
  viewing site through, 181
interpreting JavaScript, 410
intranets, subscribers to, 432
introductory paragraphs, 136
inventory.html page, 243
ISP (Internet service provider), 424
  FTP programs, 430-431
  hosting services, 430
  subscriber information, 429-431
  technical support, 431
italicizing, 41
  creating italic text, 98-99
  with <EM> tag, 98-99
  in table data cells, 219

J

Java, 5, 350
developer kit resource, 410
JavaScript and, 410
Java applets, 4, 405-410
with Banner Factory, 406-409
flexibility of, 408
on Guitar Brand page, 363-365
parameters, setting, 409
<PARAM> tag with, 408
using, 406-409
JavaScript, 5, 12, 73. *See also* objects
arrays, 383
book.html script, 337
case-sensitivity of, 379
comments, 397
AND condition, 393
document, defined, 354
document object model (DOM), 350-353
finishing script, 398-400
Java and, 410
ONCLICK attribute, 398
resources for, 402
servers, sending data to, 400-402
single-line commands, 401
variables in, 381
JavaScript It, 12
JPEG files, 3
advantages of, 35-37
cropping before saving, 159-160
finishing addition of, 177-179
image maps as, 197
photograph, saving, 169-170
for photographs, 158
pixels and, 160
size of, 158-159
on Welcome page, 54-55
justifying text, 48, 86-87

K

keywords
search engines and, 72
for site, 71
KEYWORDS attribute, 435
kiloHertz, 302
Kodak DVC323 digital video camera, 316

L

<LABEL> tag, 296
last name, validating, 386-388
layout
with frames, 208-217
for individual pages, 57-62
for intermediate Web page, 208-217
layout ideas, 38-39
leading, 96
superscripts/subscripts affecting, 102
left alignment, 87
with headings, 104
less than (<), 117
letterhead, URLs on, 464
line breaks, inserting, 86
LINK attribute, 82-83
LINK="yellow," 82
linked style sheets, 370
links. *See* hyperlinks
links.html page, 238-243, 244-248
link targets, 143-144
link text, 143-144
<LINK> tag in cascading style sheets, 413
lists. *See also* bulleted lists; ordered lists
contact page, adding to, 292-293
definition lists, 127-130
mixing types of, 126-127
<OPTION> tag for, 297-298
<SELECT> tag for, 297-298
types of lists, 114
on Welcome page, 50
literal maps, 197
<LI> tag, 114-123
<A> tag with, 145
manufacturers' names, adding, 144
with <OL> tag, 126
loading pages for Web site, 263-264
local variables, 381-382
location method, 355-356
logical formatting, 98
logos, 161
third page, adding to, 167-168
on Welcome page, 46
look and feels of site, 341-342

LookSmart, 449-452
LOOP attribute, 321-322
looping, browsers supporting, 322
Lycos, 443-445
Lynx, 12
  graphics, 23

M

Macromedia Fireworks, 36
Mac users
  sound files, 308
  video capture cards for, 310
Magellan, 452-454
Mailto link, 156, 300-301
  parsing responses, 300-301
  programs, searching for, 301
main functions, 378
MapEdit, 268
  advantages of, 275
maps. *See also* image maps
  literal maps, 197
<MAP> tag, 275
margin-left, 416-417
margins in cascading style sheets, 416-417
marquees, Java applet for, 409
MAXLENGTH attribute
  in contact page, 296
  variances in, 298
MediaStudio Pro, Ulead, 312-313
megaHertz, 302
menuframe.html, 356
messages, CSE 3310 and, 182
meta-information, 70-72
<META> tag, 8, 70-72
  fade-in effect with, 356
  graphics and, 271
  search engine and, 435
  search engines using, 432-433
METHOD attribute with <FORM tag>, 294
methods, 355
  .indexOf method, 394
  location method, 355-356
  methods.focus method, 385
  .select method, 385
methods.focus method, 385
Microsoft DHTML, 6
Microsoft Internet Explorer. *See* Internet Explorer
Microsoft Paint, 3
Microsoft Visual Basic, 357
Microsoft Word, 64
mistakes. *See* errors
monitors, 4-5
mono, recording in, 305
movies, copyrights for, 28
MULTIPLE attribute in <SELECT> tag, 298
music. *See* audio

N

NAME attribute, 8
  <A> tag and, 147, 148
  for contact page, 296
  for frames, 237-238
  with <META> tag, 70-71
naming frames, 237-238
navigational links, 149-153
navigation buttons, 9
NCSA Mosaic, 12
nesting tags, 15
NetObjects ScriptBuilder, 12
Netscape Communicator, 186
Netscape DHTML, 6
Netscape Navigator, 12-13
  bad code on, 374-375
  <DEL> tag support, 101
  HTML tags, 68
  index.html file, opening, 74-75
  intermediate Web site on, 325
  justified text, 86
  Reload button, 84
  scripts and, 357
  viewing site through, 181
Netscape Navigator Gold, 186, 325-326
Netscape Visual JavaScript, 12
NetShow, 312
newspaper-style columns, 42
***The New Well-Tempered Sentence: A Punctuation Handbook for the Innocent, the Eager, and the Doomed* (Gordon),** 25
<NOFRAMES> tag, 264-268
NOSHADE attribute with horizontal rules, 108
NOT condition, 393

notes. *See* comments
novelty fonts, 367
numbered lists. *See* ordered lists
number of pages in site, 45

O

objects
  classes, 366
  document object model (DOM), 350-353
  functions, 355
  methods, 355
  properties of, 353-354
Object URL dialog box, 275
offline, promoting site, 463-464
<OL> tag, 123-126
ONCLICK attribute, 398
Opera version 2 Reload button, 84
Optima font, 367
<OPTION> tag for lists, 297-298
ordered lists
  bulleted lists, combining, 126-127
  creating, 123-126
orders on Web, 290
overlapping tags, 15

P

<P> tag, 8, 83-85
  <A> tag with, 145
  in cascading style sheets, 366, 415, 419-420
  in contact page form, 296
  object of, 353
  with ordered lists, 125
  <SMALL> tag nested in, 97
pages. *See also* designing pages; home page; Welcome page
  additional pages, adding, 132-141
  Articles page, 215
  Contact page, 215-216
  Current Inventory page, 213-214
  Current Specials page, 213
  feature page, 211-212
  first page of site, 68
  fourth page, adding, 138-141
  individual pages, designing, 57-62
  links.html page, creating, 238-243
  second page, adding, 132-136
  Services page, 214-215
  text areas, adding, 299
  third page, adding, 136-138
Paint Shop Pro, 111, 347
  PSP files, 158
<P ALIGN="center"> tag, 267
paragraphs
  alignment in, 86-87
  breaking up, 41
  creating, 83-85
  indenting both sides of, 87-89
  introductory paragraph, placing, 58
  justified text in, 48
  leading, 96
  white space and, 40
  wrapping text, 176
<PARAM> tag in Java applets, 408
parsing forms responses, 300-301
Pascal, 350
  for-next loop, 393
patterned backgrounds, 78-81
PC users
  sound files, 308
  video capture cards for, 310
percentage values in tables, 261
Perl, 5
photo CDs, 36
photographs
  adding, 169-171
  copyright law and, 28
  flowing text around, 171-180
  hot regions in, 283
  as image map, 283
  JPEG files, saving to, 169-170
  originals, working with, 158
  thumbnails, 171
  uncompressed images, 158
  on Welcome page, 46
physical placement of site, 39
Pictureworks Live, 316
pitch of sound, 302-303
pixels, 160
placeholder text, 21
placing orders on Web, 290
plug-ins

streaming systems requiring, 304-305
for streaming video, 314
PNG files, 3, 35. *See also* GIF filesSee also JEPG files
image maps as, 197
Poe, Edgar Allen, 28
polygons for hot regions, 275
pornography, 424
pound sign (#), 14, 146-147
problems with, 326
with USEMAP attribute, 276
<PRE> tag, <A> tag with, 145
primary sources, 27
Prodigy, 424
Project1TIPS.html file, 123
proofreading, 26
properties of object, 353-354
proportionally spaced fonts, 102
public domain, works in, 28
PUBLIC identifier, 66
publicizing Web site. *See* search engines; Web directories
punctuation, 25

Q

QuickTime, 311, 314
quotation marks ("), 116
with attributes, 14

R

radio button in forms, 298-299
ransom note type fonts, 367
"The Raven" (Poe), 28
readability of code, 15-16
RealAudio, 306
RealEncoder, 312
RealNetworks, 312-313
RealPublisher, 312
reciprocal links, 460
red-and-yellow sunburst effect, 167
Refresh button, 84
registered trademark, 116, 117
relative font sizes, 90-91
Reload button, 84
repetitive music, 201
Reset Form button, 299
Reset function, writing, 397-398
returns between HTML lines, 68
RGB components, 111-113
in style sheets, 418-419
right alignment, 87
flowing text with, 174-175
with headings, 104
RingWorld, 462
rows. *See* tables
ROWS attribute with <FRAMESET> tag, 235
ROWSPAN attribute with tables, 256

S

<S> tag, 101
sampling rates, 305
<SAMP> tag, 102
sans serif fonts, 94-95, 367
in cascading style sheets, 415-416
Save As for photographs, 158
saving
second page, 135
versions of HTML file, 115
scanned graphics, 347
scanning, 3
screen resolution, 160
script fonts, 367
scripts, 376-402. *See also* functions
decision to use, 356-357
finishing script, 398-400
if line, 384
ISP scripts, 431
servers, sending data to, 400-402
software, 12
variables in, 381-382
writing scripts, 377—379
<SCRIPT> tag, 355, 377
comments within, 399
SCROLLING attributes, 247
SCROLLING="auto" attribute, 245
search engines, 22
adding site to, 434-435
AltaVista, 436-437
Excite, 437-439
HotBot, 439-441
Infoseek, 441-443
keywords with, 72

Lycos, 443-445
<META> tag and, 432-433, 435
tips for using, 435
<TITLE> tag and, 435
URLs, adding, 435
WebCrawler, 445-447
secondary sources on site, 26-28
second page
adding, 132-136
banner graphics on, 166-167
security. *See also* encryption
forms, information in, 286
servers, secure, 290
.select method, 385
selectors, 415
<SELECT> tag
in contact page, 296-297
for lists, 297-298
MULTIPLE attribute in, 298
semicolon (;), 116
serif fonts, 94-95, 367
servers
forms processing, 300-301
secure servers, 290
sending data to, 400-402
server-side image maps, 196
service marks, 114
Services page, 214-215
setTimeout line, 356
shading in horizontal rules, 108
SHAPE attribute, 277
shareware HTML editors, 2
Shockwave, 306
shrinking text, 96-97
SIZE attribute
copyright statement, font for, 95
<FONT> tag, 89-91
with horizontal rules, 108
for superscripts/subscripts, 102
size of graphics, 268-269
sketching out site, 38-39
<SMALL> tag, 96-97
Snap, 454-457
Social Security number in forms, 286
songs, copyrights for, 28
sound. *See* audio
sound waves, 302
source code in JavaScript, 410
space between frames, 236
spell-checking site, 26
spiders, 433
HotBot spider, 441
relying on, 435
square bullets, 121
SRC attribute, 244-245
for graphics, 162
Stanek, William R., 434
start tags, 7, 76
state function, writing, 391
stereo, recording in, 305
Stilman, Anne, 25
streaming audio. *See* audio
streaming video. *See* videos
StreamWorks, 312
strikethrough text, 101
<STRIKE> tag, 101
<STRONG> tag, 98, 99-102
with definition lists, 130
in table data cells, 219
with tables, 255
Strunk, William, Jr., 25
styles
embedded style sheets, 370
inline styles, 370
linked style sheets, 370
style sheets. *See also* cascading style sheets
basic Web site excluding, 20
colors in, 418-419
Submit button, 378
Submit Form button, 299
subscript text, 101-102
subtitle
on Welcome page, 48
on white space, 48
<SUB> tag, 101-102
superscript text, 101-102
leading and, 117
<SUP> tag, 101-102
trademark symbols and, 116

T

table of contents, 44
centering, 242-243
tables, 195-196
aligning cell contents, 260-261
background colors to, 255
basic Web site excluding, 20
blank cells in, 282
borders
adding borders, 225
coloring borders, 230
in cascading style sheets, 369-370, 419-420
centering, 226-227
colors
adding colors, 228-230
one color for entire table, 261
columns, defining, 218-219
complex tables, defining, 250-256
data cells in, 219
exercise for building, 220-224
flowing text in, 260
Guitar of the Month page, creating in, 280-281
headings in, 219
<H2> tags with, 254
modifying tables, 224-225
percentage values in, 261
rows, defining, 218
ROWSPAN attribute, 256
simple table, defining, 217-224
structure for, 218
subheadings in, 255
white space in, 224
<TABLE> tag, 254
CELLPADDING attribute, 225-227
CELLSPACING attribute, 225, 226-227
<CENTER> tag and, 226-227
colors with, 261
COLSPAN attribute with, 255
ROWSPAN attribute, 256
for simple tables, 217-224
width of table, 259
tags, 7-8. *See also* attributes
for background images, 79-80
fundamental tags, order for using, 65
nesting tags, 15
order for using, 65
overlapping tags, 15
rules for using, 14
uppercase letters for, 15
tape recorders, 302
TARGET attribute in links, 245
TARGET="_top," 376
target names, 146
<TD> tag, 218-219
in cascading style sheets, 419-420
centering with, 260
telephone numbers in forms, 288
templates for frames, 10-11
text. *See also* flowing text; paragraphs
cascading style sheets, defining in, 412-417
colors, 95
emphasizing text, 98-102
enlarging text, 95-96
formatting text, 89-102
graphics, flowing text around, 171-180
groundwork for, 64-75
HSPACE attribute with, 173
line breaks, inserting, 86
shrinking text, 96-97
on Welcome page, 46
text areas, adding, 299
<TEXTAREA> tag, 299
TEXT attribute, 76, 77
TextPad, 193
TEXT="white," 82
third page
adding, 136-138
logos, adding, 167-168
thumbnails, 171
<TH> tag, 219
centering with, 260
TIFF files, 158
tile areas, creating, 230-231
tiled backgrounds, 78, 80
Times font, 367
Times New Roman font, 102, 367
tips
absolute URLs, using, 144
alert boxes, 396
ALIGN attribute, values in, 87

ALT attribute, 165
America Online, 425
animation
- frames and, 38
- software programs for, 319

arrays, 383
audio
- repetitive music, 201
- streaming audio, 305

background colors
- design and, 78
- in tables, 260

browsers, downloading, 186
captions for graphics, 176
character codes, 117
colors for tables, 230
complaints about site, 42
compression rates, 159
CompuServe, adding files on, 429
copyright issues, 28
cut-and-paste technique, 184
designing pages, 38-39
- continuity of design, 61
- ease, designing for, 345
- suggestions for, 43

errors, correcting, 327
file compression rates, 159
fonts
- sketching out, 47
- variety, adding, 164

FRAMEBORDER attribute, 237
frames
- animation and, 38
- examples of, 11

grammar suggestions, 26
graphics
- captions for, 176
- CDs with images, 36
- creating graphics, 158-160
- DeBabelizer for, 160
- guidelines for using, 34
- programs, 4

headings
- table headers, 219
- use of, 41

hexadecimal codes, 112
horizontal rules, display of, 109
HotBot, listing sites on, 441
HTML editors, types of, 183
hyperlinks
- checking, 184
- suggestions for, 43
- top-level links, limiting, 211

image map specifications, file for, 277
Infospace information forms, 449
ISP (Internet service provider)
- hosing services, 430
- scripts from, 431
- technical support, 431

JPEG files for photographs, 170
keywords, entering, 71
larger size print, using, 92
layout ideas, 38-39
list writing, 117
LookSmart, 452
Mailto programs, 301
MULTIPLE attribute in <SELECT> tag, 298
photo CDs, 36
photographs to JPEG files, saving, 170
programs, switching between, 84
Project1TIPS.html file, 123
properties, 354
public domain, works in, 28
publicizing Web site, 434
rectangles, creating, 275
sketching out stage, 47
starting HTML document, 69
streaming audio, 305
switching between programs, 84
table of contents, 44
tables
- background colors in, 260
- colors to, 230
- headers, 219
- white space and, 224

titles for documents, 70
<TR> tag attributes, 219
two graphics, flowing text between, 175
underlining in site, 101
unshaded horizontal rules, display of, 109

tips *(continued)*
URLs (Uniform Resource Locators), pronouncing, 8
videos
professionals, hiring, 311
size of video, 313
W3C validation service, 324
Web rings, visiting, 463
Windows Notepad, starting, 64
Title argument, 409
TitleFont argument, 409
titles for documents, 70
<TITLE> tag, 70
search engines and, 435
topics of site, 32
trademark symbols, 114, 116-117
Trans-Form, 301
transparent background colors, 269
transparent GIFs, 78
<TR> tag, 218
BGCOLOR attribute with, 254-255
one cell, row with, 259
<TT> tag, 102
TYPE attribute
in contact page, 296
in forms, 289
for radio buttons, 298-299
typefaces. *See* fonts

U

<U> tag, 101
Ulead
GIF Animator, 319, 322
MediaStudio Pro, 312-313
SmartSaver, 36
<UL> tag, 114-123, 126-127
UmberSSK font, 269
underlining text, 41, 101
Uniform Resource Locators (URLs). *See* URLs (Uniform Resource Locators)
university networks, subscribers to, 432
UNIX machines, sound files on, 308
unordered lists. *See* bulleted lists
uppercase letters. *See* capitalization
URLcook, 301
URLs (Uniform Resource Locators), s8-9
absolute URLs, 144
for banner exchanges, 461
Goto value setting, 409
on letterhead, 464
search engines, adding to, 435
Web directories, adding to, 435
Web promotion services, 434
USEMAP attribute, 275-276
in <IMG> tag, 277
pound sign (#) with, 287

V

VALIDATEMAIN() function, 378-379
validation
book page, 337
with CSE 3310, 182-184
W3C validation service, 182
VALUE attribute for radio buttons, 298-299
variables, 381-382
Comments variable, 396
explicit variables, 382
global variables, 381-382
holding in, 383
local variables, 381-382
ZIP codes, validating, 391-394
ZipString variable, 394
VBScript, 12, 357
VDOLive, 312
vector-based images, 160
video capture cards, 310-311
Videograms, 312
videos
audio with, 314
codecs, 316
copyright law and, 28
digitizing video, 312-313
downloadable files, 309-312
on feature page, 212
links to clips, 203
overview of process, 312-316
size of, 313
steps for adding, 315-316
streaming video, 203, 309-312
plug-ins for, 314

using video, 202-203
Webcams, 316
viewing
browsers, viewing site in, 181
intermediate Web site, 323
vision-impaired people, 23
visitors to site, 155-157
VivoActive, 312
VLINK attribute, 82-83
VLINK="red," 82
Vxtreme, 312

W

W3C validation service, 182
for intermediate Web site, 323-324
wave files, 308
Webcams, 316
WebCrawler, 445-447
Web directories
adding site to, 447-459
Infospace, 447-449
LookSmart, 449-452
Magellan, 452-454
process of, 433
Snap, 454-457
tips for using, 435
URLs, adding, 435
Web rings, 461-463
Yahoo!, 457-459
Webmaster, Mailto link and, 156
Web promotion services, 434
Web rings, 461-463
Website Abstraction, 12
Welcome page, 43
articles, placement of, 51-52
designing, 46-56
elements of, 46-47, 48-49
graphic, adding, 179-180
hyperlinks on, 50, 142-145
initial design of, 53-54
layout of, 47-56
photographs on, 46
video greeting on, 203
western block style fonts, 367
White, E. B., 25
white, hex color code for, 112
white space, 40
headings and, 103
in tables, 224
on Welcome page, 48
WIDTH attribute
flowing text with, 173
for graphics, 163
with horizontal rules, 109
for hot regions, 277
with <TABLE> tag, 254-255
Windows Notepad, 1, 2-3
starting, 64
WordPerfect, 64
World Wide Web, 9
World Wide Web Consortium (W3C), 66. *See also* W3C validation service
cascading style sheets information, 410
character symbols, 66
.wpd files, 64
wrapping text. *See* flowing text

X

X-rated Web sites, 461

Y

Yahoo!, 433, 457-459

Z

ZIP codes, validating, 391-394
ZipString variable, 394
zooming in videos, 310

License Agreement/Notice of Limited Warranty

By opening the sealed disk container in this book, you agree to the following terms and conditions. If, upon reading the following license agreement and notice of limited warranty, you cannot agree to the terms and conditions set forth, return the unused book with unopened disk to the place where you purchased it for a refund.

License:
The enclosed software is copyrighted by the copyright holder(s) indicated on the software disk. You are licensed to copy the software onto a single computer for use by a single concurrent user and to a backup disk. You may not reproduce, make copies, or distribute copies or rent or lease the software in whole or in part, except with written permission of the copyright holder(s). You may transfer the enclosed disk only together with this license, and only if you destroy all other copies of the software and the transferee agrees to the terms of the license. You may not decompile, reverse assemble, or reverse engineer the software.

Notice of Limited Warranty:
The enclosed disk is warranted by Prima Publishing to be free of physical defects in materials and workmanship for a period of sixty (60) days from end user's purchase of the book/disk combination. During the sixty-day term of the limited warranty, Prima will provide a replacement disk upon the return of a defective disk.

Limited Liability:
THE SOLE REMEDY FOR BREACH OF THIS LIMITED WARRANTY SHALL CONSIST ENTIRELY OF REPLACEMENT OF THE DEFECTIVE DISK. IN NO EVENT SHALL PRIMA OR THE AUTHORS BE LIABLE FOR ANY OTHER DAMAGES, INCLUDING LOSS OR CORRUPTION OF DATA, CHANGES IN THE FUNCTIONAL CHARACTERISTICS OF THE HARDWARE OR OPERATING SYSTEM, DELETERIOUS INTERACTION WITH OTHER SOFTWARE, OR ANY OTHER SPECIAL, INCIDENTAL, OR CONSEQUENTIAL DAMAGES THAT MAY ARISE, EVEN IF PRIMA AND/OR THE AUTHOR HAVE PREVIOUSLY BEEN NOTIFIED THAT THE POSSIBILITY OF SUCH DAMAGES EXISTS.

Disclaimer of Warranties:
PRIMA AND THE AUTHORS SPECIFICALLY DISCLAIM ANY AND ALL OTHER WARRANTIES, EITHER EXPRESS OR IMPLIED, INCLUDING WARRANTIES OF MERCHANTABILITY, SUITABILITY TO A PARTICULAR TASK OR PURPOSE, OR FREEDOM FROM ERRORS. SOME STATES DO NOT ALLOW FOR EXCLUSION OF IMPLIED WARRANTIES OR LIMITATION OF INCIDENTAL OR CONSEQUENTIAL DAMAGES, SO THESE LIMITATIONS MAY NOT APPLY TO YOU.

Other:
This Agreement is governed by the laws of the State of California without regard to choice of law principles. The United Convention of Contracts for the International Sale of Goods is specifically disclaimed. This Agreement constitutes the entire agreement between you and Prima Publishing regarding use of the software.